THE POWER OF REL

The Power of Religion in Late Antiquity

Edited by
ANDREW CAIN

and

NOEL LENSKI
University of Colorado at Boulder, USA

LONDON AND NEW YORK

First published 2009 by Ashgate Publishing

2 Park Square, Milton Park, Abingdon, Oxfordshire OX14 4RN
711 Third Avenue, New York, NY 10017

Routledge is an imprint of the Taylor & Francis Group, an informa business

First issued in paperback 2018

British Library Cataloguing in Publication Data
Biennial Conference on Shifting Frontiers in Late Antiquity (7th : 2009 : Indiana University)
The power of religion in late authority : selected papers from the Seventh Biennial Shifting Frontiers in Late Antiquity Conference.
1. Church history–Primitive and early church, ca. 30–600–Congresses. 2. Rome–Religion–Congresses. 3. Christian literature, Early–History and criticism–Congresses. 4. Religion and politics–History–To 1500–Congresses.
I. Title II. Cain, Andrew. III. Lenski, Noel Emmanuel, 1965–
270.2–dc22

Library of Congress Cataloging-in-Publication Data
Biennial Conference on Shifting Frontiers in Late Antiquity (7th : 2007 : Boulder, Colo.)
The power of religion in late antiquity : selected papers from the Seventh Biennial Shifting Frontiers in Late Antiquity Conference / edited by Andrew Cain and Noel Lenski.
p. cm.
Includes bibliographical references and index.
ISBN 978-0-7546-6725-4 (hardcover : alk. paper)
1. Church history–Primitive and early church, ca. 30–600–Congresses. 2. Power (Christian theology)–Congresses. I. Cain, Andrew. II. Lenski, Noel Emmanuel, 1965– III. Title.

BR162.3.B54 2007
270.2–dc22

2009010005

ISBN 978-0-7546-6725-4 (hbk)
ISBN 978-1-138-38275-6 (pbk)

Contents

PART III Emperors and the Deployment of Religious Power

PART IV Ecclesiastical Hierarchies and the Limits of Religious Power

PART V Constantine and the Power of the Cross

PART VI Rome: The Center of Power

PART VII The Power of Religion in the Barbarian West

PART VIII The Power of Religion in the Communities of the East

List of Figures

Notes on Contributors

Emily Albu, Associate Professor of Classics at the University of California, Davis, studies classical receptions (late antique, medieval, and modern). She has written *The Normans in Their Histories* (2001) and is currently working on the Peutinger map.

Lisa Bailey is a Lecturer in History and in Classics and Ancient History at the University of Auckland. She works on late antique religion, especially preaching and pastoral care, and is the author of the forthcoming *Christianity's Quiet Success: The Eusebius Gallicanus Sermon Collection and the Power of the Church in Late Antique Gaul.*

Gillian Clark is Professor of Ancient History at the University of Bristol. She works on the intellectual and cultural history of Late Antiquity, especially Augustine. Recent publications include *Christianity and Roman Society* (2004).

Elizabeth DePalma Digeser is Associate Professor of History at the University of California, Santa Barbara. Her research focuses on late Roman thought, religion, and politics, and she is the author of *The Making of a Christian Empire: Lactantius and Rome* (2000).

H.A. Drake is Research Professor of History at the University of California, Santa Barbara. He specializes in the interaction of religion and politics in Late Antiquity and is the author of *Constantine and the Bishops: The Politics of Intolerance* (2000).

Jan Willem Drijvers is Lecturer in Ancient History at the University of Groningen. He works on late Roman historiography, late ancient Christianity, and the relations between the Roman and Sassanid Empires. He is co-author of the *Philological and Historical Commentaries on Ammianus Marcellinus.*

Hugh Elton is Associate Professor in the Department of Ancient History and Classics at Trent University, Canada. He studies late Roman political and military history and late Roman Anatolia, and is the author of *Warfare in Roman Europe, AD 350–425* (1996).

Judith Evans Grubbs is Professor of Classics at Washington University in St. Louis. She works on Roman imperial law and the family and is the author of *Law and Family in Late Antiquity: The Emperor Constantine's Marriage Legislation*

(1995) and *Women and the Law in the Roman Empire: A Sourcebook on Marriage, Divorce, and Widowhood* (2002).

Sabine R. Huebner is Adjunct Assistant Professor of Ancient History at Columbia University and a designated member of the Institute of Advanced Study in Princeton. She is the author of *Der Klerus in der Gesellschaft des spaetantiken Kleinasiens* (2005), the co-editor of *Growing up Fatherless in Antiquity* (2009), and has just submitted a monograph on "Family Strategies and Household Structures—The Graeco-Roman East in Cross-Cultural Perspective."

Lucy Grig is Lecturer in Classics at the University of Edinburgh. She studies late antique cultural history and is the author of *Making Martyrs in Late Antiquity* (2004).

Edward James holds the Chair in Medieval History at University College Dublin. His most recent book is *Europe's Barbarians, AD 200–600* (2009).

Aaron P. Johnson is a Harper Fellow in the Society of Fellows, University of Chicago. He works on Greek literature in Late Antiquity and early Christianity, and is the author of *Ethnicity and Argument in Eusebius' Praeparatio Evangelica* (2006).

Sergio Knipe is completing a PhD at Cambridge University. His research interests include sacrifice, Neoplatonist theurgy, and pagan religious thought in Late Antiquity.

Jacob A. Latham is a Senior Fellow, Interdisciplinary Humanities Center, University of California, Santa Barbara. His research interests include religious, urban, and cultural history in the Roman Empire and Late Antiquity and he is preparing a monograph on public ceremonies in late ancient Rome, ca. 300–700

Hartmut Leppin is Ordentlicher Professor für Alte Geschichte at the Johann Wolfgang Goethe-Universität Frankfurt am Main. He studies late Roman political and religious history and is the author of *Theodosius der Große. Auf dem Weg zu einem christlichen Imperium* (2003).

Rita Lizzi Testa is Professor of Roman History at the University of Perugia. The main subject of her research activity is institutional and religious change in the fourth and fifth centuries. She is the author of *Il potere episcopale nell'Oriente romano. Rappresentazione ideologica e realtà politica (IV–V secolo d.C.)* (1987), *Vescovi e strutture ecclesiastiche nella città tardoantica (l'Italia Annonaria nel IV–V secolo d.C.)* (1989), and *Senatori, popolo, papi. Il governo di Roma al tempo dei Valentiniani* (2004).

Jacqueline Long is Associate Professor in the Department of Classical Studies at Loyola University Chicago. Her research focuses on late Roman literature and history. Publications include *Claudian's In Eutropium, or, How, When, and Why to Slander a Eunuch* (1996) and, with Alan Cameron and Lee Sherry, *Barbarians and Politics at the Court of Arcadius* (1993).

Josef Lössl is a Reader in Patristics and Late Antiquity at the Cardiff University School of Religious and Theological Studies. He studies the history, literature, and thought of early Christianity. His latest book, *The Early Church. History and Memory*, is to be published in 2010.

Ralph W. Mathisen has appointments in History, Classics, and Medieval Studies at the University of Illinois at Urbana-Champaign. He is specialist in the society, culture, and religion of Late Antiquity.

Wendy Mayer is Visiting Research Fellow in the Centre for the Advancement of Research and Centre for Early Christian Studies, Australian Catholic University. She studies the social history of late antique Antioch and Constantinople and is the author of *The Homilies of St John Chrysostom—Provenance. Reshaping the Foundations* (2005).

Richard E. Payne is a Junior Research Fellow at Trinity College, Cambridge, and an Assistant Professor at Mount Holyoke College. His research focuses on the social history of the Iranian world in Late Antiquity.

Charles Pazdernik is Associate Professor of Classics at Grand Valley State University in Allendale, Michigan. His work focuses on the political and legal history of the age of Justinian and on classical and classicizing historiography.

Giacomo Raspanti is Professore a contratto di Letteratura Cristiana Antica at the Università di Palermo. He works on biblical exegesis in the patristic period and pagan and Christian oratory in Late Antiquity. He is the author of *S. Hieronymus, Commentarii in epistulam Pauli Apostoli ad Galatas, Corpus Christianorum Series Latina 77A* (2006).

Danuta Shanzer is Professor of Classics and Medieval Studies at the University of Illinois at Urbana-Champaign. She works on late antique and early medieval philology, literature, literary history, and history.

Hagith Sivan teaches at the University of Kansas (Lawrence). Her most recent publication is *Palestine in Late Antiquity* (2008). She is currently working on a new biography of Galla Placidia.

Justin Stephens is Assistant Professor of History at the Metropolitan State College of Denver. His area of interest is late Roman political, religious, and intellectual history.

John Weisweiler is a research student at St. John's College, Cambridge. He studies late Roman social and cultural history and is writing a doctoral thesis on aristocratic competition in late antique Rome.

Bailey K. Young is Professor of History at Eastern Illinois University. His research interests range from Merovingian archaeology to castles and landscape, and he is currently co-director of the Walhain castle excavations in Brabant, Belgium.

Acknowledgements

This volume grew out of the seventh biennial Shifting Frontiers in Late Antiquity Conference, held on the campus of the University of Colorado at Boulder, 22–25 March 2007. Forty-four outstanding papers were presented by speakers from nine different countries during those four days. Most of these were then submitted for review and twenty-eight were selected for publication based on their quality and adherence to the theme of power and religion. Every paper was carefully edited and underwent extensive rewriting in order to shape them all into eight coherent and interrelated sections, each focused on key subfields of inquiry.

The conference was made possible through the support of the Society for Late Antiquity with financial assistance from the President's Fund for the Humanities, the Graduate Committee on Arts and Humanities, the Council for Research and Creative Work, the Dean's Fund for Excellence, the Center for British and Irish Studies, and the Departments of Classics, History, Philosophy, Art and Art History, and Religious Studies. It was co-organized by the editors of this volume as well as by Professor Scott Bruce of the Department of History. A number of students played a crucial role in organization and logistics, especially Fred Abrams, Andrew Clay, Grant Colvin, Charles Crabtree, Andrew Detch, Kevin Funderburk, Briana Gustafson, Chelsea Jewell, Mary Junkersfeld, Jason Linn, Matthew Raica, Brent Schmidt, Amanda Sherpe, Troy Tice, Barbara Werner, and Peter Yost. The editors owe a tremendous debt to all of these organizations and individuals, without whom their own labors would have been Herculean, or rather Sisyphean. We should also like to thank our contributors for their formidable virtues as scholars, which are so evident here, and for their magnanimous tolerance of our meddling editorial hands. Our gratitude goes out to John Smedley for his encouragement of our efforts and his ongoing help with the collective and ever-evolving project that is Shifting Frontiers. Above all, we express our thanks to our families for their unflagging support of our endeavors.

Abbreviations

Abbreviations of journal titles follow the list provided by *L'Année Philologique* (Paris, 1924–). Abbreviations of the names of late antique sources follow A.H.M. Jones, J.R. Martindale, and J. Morris (eds.), *The Prosopography of the Later Roman Empire*, 3 vols. (Cambridge, 1971–92). Abbreviations for Classical sources follow S. Hornblower and A. Spawforth (eds.), *The Oxford Classical Dictionary*, 3rd ed. (Oxford, 1996). Additional abbreviations include:

AASS	*Acta Sanctorum*
CCSL	*Corpus Christianorum, Series Latina*
CIL	*Corpus Inscriptionum Latinarum*
CSCO	*Corpus Scriptorum Christianorum Orientalium*
CSEL	*Corpus Scriptorum Ecclesiasticorum Latinorum*
ILCV	*Inscriptiones Latinae Christianae Veteres*
ILS	*Inscriptiones Latinae Selectae*
MGH.AA	*Monumenta Germaniae Historica. Auctores Antiquissimi*
MGH.Leg.	*Monumenta Germaniae Historica. Leges*
MGH.SRM	*Monumenta Germaniae Historica. Scriptores Rerum Merovingicarum*
NPNF	*The Nicene and Post-Nicene Fathers of the Christian Church*
PG	J.-P. Migne (ed.), *Patrologia Graeca*
PL	J.-P. Migne (ed.), *Patrologia Latina*
PO	*Patrologia Orientalis*
PLRE 1	A.H.M. Jones, J.R. Martindale, J. Morris (eds.), *The Prosopography of the Later Roman Empire, Volume I. AD 260–395* (Cambridge, 1971).
PLRE 2	J.R. Martindale (ed.), *The Prosopography of the Later Roman Empire, Volume II. AD 395–527* (Cambridge, 1980).
PLRE 3	J.R. Martindale (ed.), *The Prosopography of the Later Roman Empire, Volume III. AD 527–640* (Cambridge, 1992).
PLS	*Patrologiae Latinae Supplementa*
SCh	*Sources chrétiennes*
SEG	*Supplementum Epigraphicum Graecum*
V	*Vita*

Introduction: Power and Religion on the Frontier of Late Antiquity

Noel Lenski
University of Colorado, Boulder

Readers of this volume could have learned much about the relationship between power and religion had Augustine contributed an article. His discussions of the subject are remarkably sophisticated and share many of the insights of modern theorists. Like us, he understood that power was not simply physical force but rather some external agent that we can feel without seeing. Like us, he accepted the freedom of the individual will and its ability to accept or reject the power of religion. Also like us, he was convinced that the options to do either were very much more circumscribed than most would like to admit. Our free will is enmeshed in systems of signification that we can only begin to comprehend and from which we can never extricate ourselves; its acceptance of religious truth is perpetually shaped by constant pressure from the power exerted by religion. At times that power merely nudges us toward certain attitudes and behaviors; at others, however, it veritably shoves us, even beats us, into compliance.

It goes without saying that Augustine's notions of religious power also differed in fundamental ways from our own. Above all, of course, Augustine conceived of religious power and truth as being rooted in an immanent and transcendent god for whom modern and post-modern thinkers have little room in their critical toolkit. This meant that, in contrast with moderns, he understood truth as an essential rather than contingent category. Yet, for all that he inhabited a world separated by centuries from the disenchantment of us moderns, he was aware that human understanding perceived multiple "truths." He simply assumed that most such truths were, in truth, falsehood.

Augustine's example proves that, at a minimum, the groundwork for the ideas explored in this volume was already well laid in Late Antiquity. The essays presented here—including a much richer study of Augustine—approach the question of power and religion in the period of Late Antiquity, that is, the period from the late third through the early seventh centuries. They explore issues such as: What is the power of religion? How did the people of Late Antiquity conceive of it? Were their understandings of the interrelation of power and religion related to those of Augustine? Were they related to our own? How did the power of religion affect their lives? How did it shape their social, political, cultural, and familial relations? How did it inform their conception of their own world?

Power, Religion, and Late Antiquity as Frontier

To investigate these questions, we must begin by asking what power and religion mean in the broadest sense and how the two interrelate. We can start with the notion of power. Here the most pertinent insights are those of Foucault, who developed the ideas of Marxist and Structuralist thinkers in his lifelong quest for a universal definition of power. In his early work and particularly in his *Discipline and Punish* he elaborated the theorem that power is directly linked to economy.[1] It is a sort of capital whose value can be realized only in transactions between parties. This means that it is shared by all; no one individual has absolute power or even control over the essence of power. It is a dynamic that enmeshes ruler and ruled, sovereign and subject, and organizes behavior in ways unbeknownst to most and fully comprehensible to none. At least originally, Foucault insisted that power can and does operate independently of human agents. He came to acknowledge, however, that power does ultimately inhere in individuals. This does not deny that its essence is in shared relationships, but rather it takes account of the fact that, as with capital, it can be amassed or hoarded by certain social and political groups.

Power trades in discourses of truth or knowledge and operates by associating actions and relations with these truths, which it simultaneously formulates and enforces.[2] In Foucault's eyes, therefore, power is to be distinguished from violence, which does not entail a dynamic exchange between active agents but a static relationship of physical domination over passive individuals. As his thought developed, Foucault came to regard power as a link between individuals on the basis of what he called "government."[3] This word must be understood in the broadest sense of "guiding" or "directing" not just of the state but also of behaviors, family relations, and communities. To govern, in this sense, is to structure the possible field of action of others. Foucault's power is thus necessarily exercised over free subjects: it is not physical domination but the persuasion of a group of individuals to bend to the authority that all recognize as collectively valid. By purveying the knowledge generated by the collectivity as truth, power convinces its subjects—largely subconciously—to govern their actions and relations according to those truths.

If power governs the collectivity, religion in some sense defines it. This was certainly the conception of Émile Durkheim, who argued that religion is "a projection of the social values of society" or even "society worshipping itself." Fundamental to his definition is the dualist dichotomy between the "sacred" and

---

1 M. Foucault, *Discipline and Punish: The Birth of the Prison*, trans. A. Sheridan (New York, 1977).

2 M. Foucault, "Power, Right, Truth," in C. Gordon (ed.), *Power/Knowledge* (New York, 1980) 92–108.

3 Summarized at M. Foucault, "The Subject and Power," in H.L. Dreyfus and P. Rabinow (eds.), *Michel Foucault: Beyond Structuralism and Hermeneutics*, 2nd ed. (Chicago, 1982) 145–62.

the "profane": "religion is a unified system of beliefs and practices relative to sacred things, that is to say, things set apart and forbidden."[4] Insofar as religion is a reflection of society, the sacred represents society's interests as embodied in communally recognized symbols; the profane, on the other hand, involves mundane individual concerns.

Roughly contemporary with Durkheim, Max Weber argued not so much that religion reflects social realities as that it shapes them.[5] Rather than attempt to arrive at an essential definition of religion, Weber attended to the effects of religion on social structures and collective behavior. In so doing, he demonstrated the dynamic between belief and practice in a way that folds religion more thoroughly into the varied mix of collective behavior. Religion—which for Weber meant first and foremost systems of belief—has the power to alter social practice in fundamental ways.

Clifford Geertz made further progress in conceptualizing the category of religion as, "a system of symbols which act to establish powerful, pervasive, and long-lasting moods and motivations in men by formulating conceptions of a general order of existence and clothing these conceptions with such an aura of factuality that the moods and motivations seem uniquely realistic."[6] Geertz thus combines Durkheim's religious anthropology with Weber's functionalist sociology and adds the insights of post-structuralism by attaching greater weight to the value and manipulation of symbols. For Geertz, such symbols constitute culture patterns that provide not only "models *of* reality" but also "models *for* reality," that is, they construct reality even as they reflect it. Religion creates an understanding of the cosmos through the deployment and redeployment of signs to which society attaches a unique kind of meaning that governs individual and collective action.

Useful critique of Geertz as well as Foucault has arisen from the quarters of post-colonial theory, which has shown three things of relevance to the studies that follow. First, contrary to Foucault, violence and physical force cannot and should not be left out of explorations of the relations of power. The use of violence is not antithetical to power but one extreme on the continuum of social relations delimited by power; violence carries power to its utmost and thus fully discharges its capacity, with the consequence that it exhausts the effects of power, but only temporarily. The use of violence and above all the threat of violence thus remain crucial to the maintenance and development of relations of power. Moreover, coercion—both physical force and the domination of relations of production and

[4] E. Durkheim, *The Elementary Forms of Religious Life*, trans. K.E. Fields (1915; reprint. New York, 1995) 44.

[5] M. Weber, *The Protestant Ethic and the Spirit of Capitalism*, trans. S. Kalberg (1904–05; reprint. Chicago, 2001).

[6] C. Geertz, "Religion as a Cultural System," originally published in M.P. Banton (ed.), *Anthropological Approaches to the Study of Religion* (London and New York, 1966) 1–46, then reprinted in Geertz, *The Interpretation of Cultures: Selected Essays* (New York, 1973) 87–125 at 90.

property-holding—are also crucial in governing religious activity and above all in delimiting the options for generating and transmitting religious knowledge.

Secondly, universalizing definitions of religion and indeed of power are fraught with difficulty precisely because the very urge to universalize strips such definitions of contextual meaning. Geertz's emphasis on symbols and belief underplays the importance of lived practice in generating religious truths, which cannot so easily be divorced from their historical situations. As subsets of cultural systems, religions are one of many contingent practices that can only be understood in their temporal, spatial, and historical contexts. Thus, while Geertz's definition remains foundational, it can only be made useful when applied to historically grounded narratives like those offered here.[7]

Finally, robust investigations of religious power must take into account "all players in the game," not just those who dominate power relations but also those subject to domination. All participants in the social and religious collective are agents, and even those subjected to hierarchical or coercive authority exert surprisingly profound influence on the construction of religious symbols, truths, and ideologies.[8]

In their seminal work *Of Revelation and Revolution*, the Comaroffs argued that relations of religion and power are readily brought into focus on the colonial frontier:

> Because frontiers are uncharted spaces of confrontation—spaces in which people fashion new worlds by negotiating hitherto uncommunicated signs—they are a prime context for exploring the relations among culture and power, hegemony and ideology, social order and human agency.[9]

The cultural confrontation generated by frontier situations requires societies to confront the taken-for-granted fabric of religious knowledge and rethink it in creative and revealing ways. In the effort to limit ambiguities of meaning and proliferations of power, frontier societies, and particularly ruling regimes faced with frontier situations, are pushed to define the nature of their power more openly and actively and, at the same time, to transform the basis of that power—the knowledge that underpins it—more freely and rapidly.

As "Shifting Frontiers" (the name of our conference series) implies, Late Antiquity is aptly viewed as a historical frontier. It was a period of cultural and social shift during which the pace of historical transformation was accelerated.

---

7 See T. Asad, *Genealogies of Religion: Discipline and Reasons of Power in Christianity and Islam* (Baltimore, 1993) with further bibliography. See also W. Keane, *Christian Moderns: Freedom and Fetish in the Mission Encounter* (Berkeley, 2007), for a strong defense of the semiotic model of power relations even in the colonial situation.

8 J. Comaroff and J. Comaroff, *Of Revelation and Revolution: Christianity, Colonialism, and Consciousness in South Africa, Volume One* (Chicago, 1991).

9 See Comaroff and Comaroff, *Of Revelation and Revolution*, 313.

Barbarian invasions, Christianization, political upheaval, multi-cultural interchange, imperial fragmentation, and theological crystallization all characterize this tumultuous period, rich in sources and problems, during which antiquity gave way to the Middle Ages. As the power of Rome exploded in the wake of external threats scattering its fragments across the Mediterranean basin and well beyond, religion in many ways filled the vacuum that Rome's political hegemony had once occupied. The kaleidoscopic plurality of religious cults once scattered across the ancient landscape gave way to a homogenization of religious power around the three interrelated Abrahamic traditions of Judaism, Christianity, and Islam. These squeezed out competing religious traditions by successfully redefining religious truth along monotheistic and theologizing lines and—in the instance of Christianity and later Islam—by deploying the coercive force of the state as a way to valorize and enforce the truths they purveyed.

The frontier nature of late antique religion has of course been studied before, though perhaps not in these express terms. To take just three examples, Brown's famous article on "The Rise and Function of the Holy Man" has shown how the redefinition of religious truth along Christian lines created a need for the relocation of power away from the holy "places" of antiquity—its temples and shrines—and into the person of the holy man.[10] This refocalization of power hastened and abetted the process of religious transformation by putting the collective religious understanding of the community under the control of the individual rather than vice versa. Secondly, Shaw's work on "Body/Power/ Identity: Passions of the Martyrs" has shown how Late Antiquity witnessed a transformation in the definition of power and thus also the locus of power.[11] Building upon the Stoic valorization of self-control and endurance, Christians and Jews transformed martyrs, and in turn ascetics, from symbols of powerlessness into the standardbearers of power. The symbolic valence of suffering shifted from negative to positive, allowing Christianity, Judaism, and Islam to redefine the nature of power and power relations. Finally, Fowden's *Empire to Commonwealth* showed how the fragmentation of ancient political hegemonies in Late Antiquity coincided with the rise of monotheisms that were able to replace the power of the

---

[10] P. Brown, "The Rise and Function of the Holy Man in Late Antiquity," *JRS* 61 (1971) 80–101 = Idem (ed.) *Society and the Holy in Late Antiquity* (Berkeley, 1989) 103–52. See also Brown's retrospective on this article in Idem, "The Rise and Function of the Holy Man in Late Antiquity, 1971–1997," *JECS* 6 (1998) 353–76. Much of Brown's work focuses on relations of power, most overtly *Power and Persuasion in Late Antiquity: Towards a Christian Empire* (Madison, WI, 1992) and *Authority and the Sacred: Aspects of the Christianisation of the Roman World* (Cambridge, 1995).

[11] B.D. Shaw, "Body/Power/Identity: Passions of the Martyrs," *JECS* 4 (1996) 269–312.

state—particularly on the eastern frontier—but eventually also to supplement and redefine state power.[12]

Such examples of Late Antiquity as a frontier space in which power and religion were renegotiated could of course be multiplied and indeed are in the studies contained in this volume. These offer a rich and varied series of investigations that sketch out the boundaries of the power-religion dynamic and demonstrate how well these can be articulated using the abundant evidence that survives from the period.

Part I Religion and the Power of the Word

The volume is divided into eight sections. The first, on "Religion and the Power of the Word," explores the intersection of religion, power, and text. In four case studies, it demonstrates the axiom that language is power and its corollary, religious language is religious power. The first chapter, by Emily Albu, examines how Fulgentius applied the tools of the allegorist to violently reshape ancient mythographic traditions. By first dismantling the heroic in his *Mitologiae* and then, in his *Expositio Virgilianae continentiae*, rehabilitating Vergil's *Aeneid* as a *roman à clef* about the role of virtue in the life journey, Fulgentius reappropriated the power of the pagan literary past to suit a Christian west even as this territory ceased to fall under the political sway of Rome. This mode of inquiry not only relocated the power of the Classical myths and literature into a safe-zone for reuse in a sixth-century Christian context, it exerted tremendous influence over subsequent medieval approaches to literary interpretation.

In the second chapter, Josef Lössl shows us a world in which Christian exegetes struggled to gain control of the apocalyptic tradition by imposing their own readings on the book of Revelation. Two primary camps, historicist and allegorist, had emerged by the late third century. Lössl's examination shows that an often neglected writer from the Latin west, Victorinus of Poetovium, played an important role in transplanting these debates into Latin Christendom. In his *Commentary on the Apocalypse*, the first biblical commentary to survive in Latin, Victorinus takes a middle path between the two extremes. He was unwilling to part with the notion of a historical millennium, which indeed seemed to be playing itself out in the persecutions of his third-century world. Nevertheless, he imported much from the allegorist tradition, and particularly the notion of a "recapitulation" of creation's paradisal past in the last days. This would have lasting effects on later commentators like Tyconius and, above all, Augustine.

Giacomo Raspanti offers the third chapter, where he investigates the power discourse in Ambrose's oration *On the Death of Theodosius*. After demonstrating that *clementia* and its various cognates like *indulgentia*, and *misericordia* appear

[12] G. Fowden, *Empire to Commonwealth: Consequences of Monotheism in Late Antiquity* (Princeton, 1993).

throughout the speech as a sort of leitmotif, he goes on to show that this theme can be linked to a Classical intertext, Seneca's *De clementia*, at the lexical and thematic level. Ambrose's goal in referencing Seneca was to connect a pagan text and Roman historical tradition with his own Christian discourse and circumstances in order to prepare the Empire for a peaceful transition of power in the aftermath of the pagan–Christian conflict of 394.

The section culminates in the essay of Danuta Shanzer who investigates the one certain allusion to the Bible found in Boethius' *Consolatio Philosophiae*, 3.12.22, whose intertext is Wis. 8:1. Having laid out a typology of allusions and applied this critical tool to all previously alleged biblical allusions in Boethius' work, she is able to show how shadowy are any hints of scripture, let alone New Testament scripture or Christian *Sondersprache*. Shanzer then goes on to posit that Boethius' careful avoidance of Christian discourse may represent a deliberate effort to create a double transparency that would have allowed various sorts of readers to see what they chose in his text. This approach resulted, she argues, from an Ostrogothic cultural microclimate that favored religious tolerance and avoided explicit theological discourse in order to facilitate the exercise of power in a multicultural and religiously divided world.

The discussion thus shows how language and power are inextricably linked and how language's ability to replicate and transform itself is tapped to revise and redeploy the power of the word in new contexts. From Fulgentius' use of Virgil, to Victorinus' use of Revelation to Ambrose's use of Seneca, to Boethius' use—and avoidance—of the Bible, text is brought into synergy with intertext to augment the power of both. The ability of all these late antique authors to control the reading of past texts enabled them to revive and redirect the power of others' language to add new meaning and power to their own contemporary texts and contexts.

Part II Power Over the Divine: Porphyry, Iamblichus, and the Struggle for the Philosophical Tradition

Neoplatonism and the debate over theurgy are the focus of the second section. The Neoplatonists of the third and fourth centuries understood well that religion, which they conceived of as *philosophia*, offers the means to tap into the power of the sacred. They were, moreover, in agreement about the source of that power, the One. Nevertheless, disputes arose over *how* to channel the power of the One and *who* could be granted access to it.

Elizabeth Digeser opens the section by exploring the conflict between Porphyry and his one-time pupil Iamblichus over the return of the soul to the divine. Though both accepted the notion that there were three kinds of souls, each variously enabled to encounter the divine, Iamblichus' notion that ritual acts (theurgy) could provide a *via universalis* for all souls toward a higher ontological state met with serious objections from Porphyry. In his *On the Return of the Soul* and *Philosophy from Oracles* Porphyry contended that ritual was not only useless but also potentially deleterious to the philosophical soul in its journey. Digeser goes on to argue that this flash point within pagan philosophical circles ignited a concomitant controversy with the Christians, whose own ritualized and materialist approach to salvation Porphyry criticized. Thus an esoteric doctrinal debate among Neoplatonist philosophers spawned as its byproduct anti-Christian feelings that helped foment the Great Persecution.

Investigating the same community of texts, Sergio Knipe argues in the sixth chapter that Iamblichus' *De mysteriis* was written as a theoretical justification of "the supernatural, coercive power of theurgy" against the objections of Porphyry. For this reason, Iamblichus is keen to demarcate the difference between legitimate and illegitimate ritual, for in the site of contestation that is spiritual discourse, it was crucial to stake out the high ground against attacks that might portray theurgy as a form of sorcery. Thus, while Iamblichus claimed access to the sacred via ritual, he carefully avoided any implication that he could manipulate the divine: theurgy could channel divine power but not control it. In this sense, Iamblichus' debate with Porphyry turned on the question of "*who* exercised … supernatural power and *in what way.*"

In the book's seventh chapter, Aaron Johnson moves to another Porphyrean text, the *Philosophy from Oracles*, and shows how it constituted a master reading of oracular texts qua esoteric philosophical pronouncements. Through a careful explication of this enigmatic work's fragmentary preface, Johnson reveals that Porphyry's collection (*sunagōgē*) of oracles is really an introduction (*eisagōgē*) for students designed to lead them to the deeper truths lurking behind these pronouncements. By asserting power over the texts in this way, Porphyry also assumed control over late pagan religious and philosophical interpretation. In so doing, he quite unintentionally steered it in new directions that would allow it to compete with Christianity and even to survive the coming assault that ultimately led both to the cessation of oracular consultation and the destruction of Porphyry's original works.

Taken together, this triptych of chapters shows a dialogue in which Porphyry and Iamblichus vied for authority over the Platonic tradition and over the very question of religious truth. Because both were trained in the same tradition, both shared a common framework for understanding the ontology of the sacred. They nevertheless fought bitterly for control over the practical means for accessing this shared truth and thus for control over the membership of their shared community. The consequence of their debate was a problematization of ritual and its proper role in religion that influenced the course of both paganism and Christianity in Late Antiquity.

Part III Emperors and the Deployment of Religious Power

The third section examines how religious, and specifically Christian, authority was inextricably linked with imperial power. Every emperor sought to amass capital from the religious sphere even as every emperor also struggled to circumscribe the power of religion over his field of action. Judith Evans-Grubbs opens with a study of laws on infant exposure and how the attitudes of the Christian church affected imperial policy on this vexed question. She marshals a series of constitutions that show how Constantine took measures to prevent exposure, in part by equating it with parricide, in part by dissolving the parental rights (*patriapotestas*) of those parents who abandoned their children. While Constantine seems to have been directly influenced by Christian principles, his legal action had the unintended and arguably less than charitable consequence of making the enslavement of children easier. Indeed, by tracing church and state regulations on exposure through the reign of Justinian, Evans-Grubbs shows that the state continued to use its power to enforce Christian ideals, but always with similar unintended consequences that likely increased the incidence of exposure.

In the ninth chapter, Hugh Elton shows how complex was the process of imperial decision-making on religious matters. He focuses on the events between the Council of Ephesus in 431 and the Formula of Reunion used by Theodosius II to draw recalcitrant bishops in Cilicia back into the church in 433. Elton outlines a complex network of players including bishops, civilian bureaucrats, and military officials that leaves much less room for influence to the traditional bugbears of the late antique sources: empresses, eunuchs, and barbarians. By adducing examples from across the reign of Theodosius, Elton shows that this emperor—normally thought to be a cipher—played an active role as the final arbiter and enforcer of major ecclesiastical decisions.

Charles Pazdernik then explores the loyalty oath imposed on governors by Justinian in 535 with his *Novel* 8. He shows how this law inscribes religious language and power into a text designed to enforce cooperation and limit corruption among a group of officials whose authority and autonomy every emperor struggled to control. Justinian ostentatiously stored this law among sacred vessels in the cathedral like some relic, and he demanded that officials invoke the dire curse of Cain upon their own heads for non-compliance with it. This strategy allowed him to borrow power capital from the religious sphere which he then invested in his secular authority in order to purchase the compliance of bureaucrats.

The section closes with Hartmut Leppin, who focuses on Justinian's encounters with four holy men. He shows how Justinian studiously avoided attacking each of them even when they behaved with pronounced effrontery toward him. On the contrary, Justinian regularly humbled himself before holy men both as a means to avoid any implications that he was persecuting those with spiritual gifts and to gain access to the religious power they possessed. Knowing that the essence of Christian spiritual authority lay in the conspicuous display of humility, Justinian humbled his imperial persona in order to tap into a source of power that won acceptance for him among subjects, soldiers, administrators, and ultimately also the clergy.

The post-colonial critique of Foucault's conception of power and of Geertz's definition of religion is crucial to the readings presented here. Power cannot be described without due attention to the "power structure," and religion cannot be divorced from politics. Modernist notions of a separation of "church and state," a parceling out of the cosmos into neatly demarcated political and religious categories, seem implausible in the post-modern world and downright impossible in the ancient. What separates Late Antiquity from earlier periods of ancient history, however, is that the ruler downshifted from the embodiment of the sacred to the conduit to it. No longer did the emperor claim to *be* the divinity but to *represent* it and thus to offer access to the power of the sacred through the passage of laws, the definition of religious doctrine, the deployment of religious language, and the adaptation of a religious demeanor.

Part IV Ecclesiastical Hierarchies and the Limits of Religious Power

This series of studies contextualizes the power of the clergy within the limits of the social and political world. In every instance, the clerics are shown to be thirsty for power and to struggle to comprehend its manifestations. In every instance, their search for power is also shown to be limited by competing interests and their understanding of power to be shaped by these limitations.

In the twelfth chapter Sabine Huebner investigates the interplay between power and religion in the appointment and maintenance of the eastern clergy. Just as the late Roman imperial bureaucracy became increasingly comfortable with the notion that money would be exchanged as part of the process of conferring offices or conducting official business, the eastern clergy began expecting to pay to obtain posts. A sort of hierarchy of place and position developed that encouraged venality among the clergy, at the bottom because clerics made too little from their churches to support themselves without undertaking secular professions and collecting fees, and at the top because the desirability of key offices and prized locales created market demands that were ultimately arbitrated through cash payments.

Justin Stephens delves into the nascent political philosophy evident in John Chrysostom's early writings and particularly the *Discourse on Saint Babylas*. He argues that Chrysostom presents a clear notion of what he regarded as the proper relationship between emperor and bishop already in the earliest years of his priesthood. For Chrysostom the bishop, as arbiter of divine law, had a superior claim to power over the emperor. Stephens uses this understanding to reassert the imperative that the line between secular and sacred can only be drawn provisionally. He goes on to show how Chrysostom later implemented his notion of episcopal power during the confrontations he experienced—and provoked—while serving as bishop of Constantinople.

In the fourteenth chapter, Gillian Clark offers a sweeping perspective on Augustine's conception of power. She shows how little power Augustine possessed and how much of it was what might be termed "soft power," *auctoritas*, the ability to persuade by his reputation or his words. In many ways his acute awareness of the limitations on his power induced Augustine to think more carefully and extensively about the question of power. In the *City of God* he focuses on it quite squarely. Ultimately, Clark argues, Augustine's concept of power is founded in his experience of the world, for true power is based on the order (*ordo*) established for the universe by god—a notion not so far removed from that arrived at by modern sociologists, provided one substitutes "society" for "god." Yet Augustine was in no way willing to concede that worldy power and religious power were synonymous. On the contrary, only true religion whose object was the glorification of god, could offer true freedom, while worldly power was little more than a pale reflection of the city of god and thus a distraction from the truth.

The power of penance in the *Eusebius Gallicanus Sermons* is then explored by Lisa Bailey. This collection of fifth-century homilies figures active penance as a necessity for the forgiveness of sins. In contrast with Augustine, whose preaching of unmerited grace encouraged a sort of active passivity, the *Eusebius Gallicanus* calls on congregants to become "their own most severe judges" in an effort to coerce a more engaged approach to forgiveness through fasting, almsgiving, and lamentation. In an environment where preachers had limited power over their congregants and more circumscribed rhetorical skills than Augustine, this approach allowed them to co-opt their flock into active participation in the project of salvation. It was, in other words, a subconscious but very real admission to the communal nature of religious power.

We are left with the conclusion that religious power is a site of negotiation between active agents: those designated as holders of religious authority are uniformly aware of the limitations on their power, and those they attempt to "govern" share control with them over their fate in the cosmos. The dialogue over the meaning of the sacred that is religious discourse has no truly dominant and submissive polarity but represents a collectivity of power shared between clergy and lay. Recognizing these limitations, religious authorities struggled mightily to induce their followers into compliance with the paradigms of religious truth they purveyed. They understood that, without the conscious and unconscious complicity of the masses in the shared project of religious self-definition, they were powerless.

Part V Constantine and the Power of the Cross

The three papers in this section turn attention to the famous vision of Constantine, a subject of considerable debate in the past decade. In one way or another all take as their starting point the groundbreaking article of Weiss, who has argued that Constantine's vision was actually a celestial phenomenon known as a solar halo witnessed by the emperor in 310.[13] Nevertheless, each paper carries the argument

13 P. Weiss, "Die Vision Constantins, " in J. Bleicken (ed.), *Colloquium aus Anlass des 80. Geburtstages von Alfred Heuss*, Frankfurter althistorische Studien 13 (Kalmunz, 1993) 143–69,

in different directions, adding complication to Weiss's linearity and questioning the finality of his conclusions.

H.A. Drake approaches Weiss's argument with a simple but revealing contrafactual: suppose Constantine had never seen this halo phenomenon? Without denying Weiss's intriguing conclusions, he shows how the public propagation of Constantine's vision—or visions—fit into a broader context of the emperor's religious expression, which in turn fit into a broader context of imperial religious expression in Late Antiquity. By examining continuities in Constantine's behavior and self-representation and above all by showing the consistency of solar imagery, Drake reveals that the halo phenomenon could only ever have served to confirm Constantine's belief in his mission, not to create it.

Our sources for Constantine's vision are of course anything but uniform. Starting from an awareness of their differences, Jacqueline Long shows how the three portrayals of visions reported in contemporary sources are all rooted in quite specific historical and literary circumstances. Looking to allay fears of foreign invasion in the wake of the overthrow of Maximian, the panegyrist of 310 grafted Constantine into an artificially long lineage of imperial defenders and used the solar vision to shed the warm glow of divine light on the empire's new champion. In his *On the Death of Persecutors* Lactantius located Constantine at the endpoint on a continuum of divine justice against persecutors of the Church; for him the vision served as confirmation of the agency of god in Constantine's defeat of the persecutor Maxentius. Writing as much for Constantine's successors as the emperor himself, Eusebius of Caesarea made Constantine the subject of a quest for divine rulership who found god's approval manifested in the dual vision he attributes to him, halo and dream.

Jan Willem Drijvers also starts with the staurophany of Constantine and reinforces the argument that it allowed the emperor to transform what had formerly been a symbol of defeat into one of victory. He then goes on to examine two other celestial appearances of the cross, beginning with that in 351 reported by Cyril of Jerusalem. Once again, the bishop interprets the cross as a symbol of victory, specifically the anticipated victory of Constantius II over the usurper Magnentius, but also of power more generally and especially the power of Christianity over Judaism and of Jerusalem over its rival see of Caesarea. Finally, the appearance of a cross in the sky shortly after the earthquake which put a stop to Julian's rebuilding of the temple in Jerusalem in 363 was also interpreted as a sign of the power of Christ over the Jews.

The reign of Constantine thus ushered in a new symbol of religious power, the representation par excellence of Christian triumphalism, the cross. By focusing on this sign, this section offers a case study of how Durkheim and Geertz are correct to assert that religion is at its core a system of symbols. The papers demonstrate how dynamic this system can be, for Christianity not only caused a shift in the meaning

---

translated and expanded at "The Vision of Constantine," trans. A. Birley, *JRA* 16 (2003) 237–259.

of the cross from a token of disgrace to a talisman of power, it also cast this talisman into a field of competing interests that attached their own varying nuances to its significance. In other words, the moment Christianity valorized the cross as a generic symbol of power, it brought this symbol into the field of competition for power with the result that its meaning instantly became destabilized once again.

Part VI Rome: The Center of Power

The sixth section examines the remaking of Rome from the imperial capital and bastion of traditional pagan religion into a Christian city and center of power. The abandonment of Rome by the imperial court and its gradual shift from pagan to Christian domination is described as a complex and dynamic transformation where Rome as space and symbol became a site of intense negotiation over power and religion.

Rita Lizzi Testa opens the section by questioning the notion that the Roman priesthoods of Late Antiquity were all but moribund. She shows how the amassing of multiple priesthoods by Roman aristocrats in no way indicated the undervaluation of these offices; she demonstrates that senatorials continued to seek such offices even past Theodosius' sanctions of 391; she shows that the famous "altar of victory" controversy involved fewer impediments to the practice and funding of the state cults than have previously been assumed. She then turns to the question of what precisely late antique priests—particularly *pontifices* and *augures*—did. A vast array of sources are adduced to demonstrate that, even in the absence of sacrificial rites, these continued to perform a wide variety of duties, including the inauguration of fellow priests, the consecration of public structures and spaces, and the regulation of much official activity. Far from witnessing a diminution in their power, late pagan priests saw a removal of imperial oversight and involvement in the state cults that left open the possibility to reinvent their functions and public roles.

Lucy Grig explores the semantic value of the Capitoline as a metaphor and metonym for the power of Rome, its empire, and its religion. Beginning with pagan texts of the fourth century, she demonstrates how the Capitoline retained its role as the quintessential signifier of city and empire deep into Late Antiquity. She then turns to a series of late fourth- and early fifth-century Christian texts that begin to destabilize this linkage and remake the Capitoline into a site infamous for its reputed associations with illicit pagan activity. Over time the martyrologies of the fifth century and later pick up on this idea and dramatize the Capitoline as a "heart of darkness" well suited to the bloody enactment of violence against the legendary believers of the past. The Capitoline was thus a powerful rhetorical locus for the debate over the nature of power and religion throughout the period of Late Antiquity.

Moving to late sixth- and early seventh-century Rome, Jacob Latham offers an investigation of the two seven-formed processions (*letaniae septiformes*) performed under Gregory the Great in 590 and 603. He shows how these ceremonies were used to articulate the city's population along new social and religious lines dictated by the papacy. Gregory's success at "interpellating" the Christian subject into an ecclesially defined order eventually had broader repercussions when pilgrim itineraries appropriated the same routes and codified them as the spatial outlines of a Christian Rome. The *letaniae septiformes* thus augmented the power of the papacy to transform Rome from a classical into a Christian city, both socially and geographically.

Post-Marxist critique has shown how the control of space, both as a symbolic marker and as a physical entity, is crucial to the understanding of power.[14] In classical antiquity Rome had always been the physical capital of the world, the *caput mundi*. By Late Antiquity, however, it had become a political and cultural isolate, an island of atavism. In response to this loss of power, it sought to perpetuate its status by restructuring the basis of its claims to authority along religious—and specifically Christian—lines. In this sense, this section may seem to be titled ironically, for late antique Rome lost its status as the world's political capital. But these papers show how it succeeding in refashioning itself into a symbolic capital through the reinvention of a new religious present that secured its place as a center of power into the future.

Part VII The Power of Religion in the Barbarian West

Rome's cession of power in the west to the barbarian successor kingdoms resulted in a renegotiation of religious meaning and a new sharing out of religious capital between the various ethnic and cultural groups that competed with one another in a less stable political world. Ralph Mathisen explores this problem by examining the religious expression—in the form of a church endowment—of a major fifth-century power holder. As we know from early modern drawings of a now lost mosaic, the barbarian general and patrician Ricimer dedicated a church to S. Agata in Rome. A closer look at the iconography and inscription revealed in these drawings demonstrates that in the process Ricimer made no effort to draw attention to his barbarian origins or his Arianism. On the contrary, he used the church and its dedication as a way to assimilate himself to Roman traditions of religious expression and to insinuate himself into the senatorial and imperial power structure. Indeed, by using the phrase *salus totius humani generis* in close connection with his own name in the inscription, Ricimer strongly implied that he stood in an analogous position to the emperor as the legitimate representative of heavenly power on earth.

Edward James delves into the question of why Gregory of Tours, who professed in his *History of the Franks* to be interested in describing the fate of heresy, devoted so little attention to the question of Arianism. Even the momentous conversion

---

14 H. LeFebvre, *The Production of Space*, trans. D. Nicholson-Smith (Oxford, 1991).

of the Visigoths of Spain from Arianism to Catholicism in 589 is distinctly underplayed. By isolating Gregory's discussions of Arianism, James is able to show how little theological argument most involve and how those few which do include debate implicate Gregory himself. The fact that Gregory felt compelled to style himself as a defender of orthodoxy in his *History* is attributed to Gregory's precarious position within his own diocese. This fragile situation compelled him to play up his achievements against Arians in his efforts to retain power.

A Merovingian plate buckle fashioned by an artisan named Landelinus forms the basis of the twenty-fourth chapter by Bailey Young. The iconography, a horseman atop an ithyphallic mount surrounded by religious symbols like the chi-rho, collects up artistic vocabulary from pagan as well as Christian contexts into a bricolage of effective signifiers designed to protect the owner from physical and spiritual harm. Young shows how the buckle fits into a type common across post-Roman Gaul in the period that displays a sort of "do-it-yourself" Christianity whose symbols and theology were driven from the bottom up. Frankish and Burgundian artists and patrons exercised their own power over the forms of Christian expression in their region—still very much a matter of negotiation—and in so doing tapped into Christianity's power by reassigning valences to religious symbols old and new.

Power and religion thus meet in productive ways on the barbarian frontier, much as the Comaroffs predict. The instability created by the collapse of Roman hegemony and the rise of competing successor states demanded a renegotiation of religious truth in the west. Where some, like Ricimer, sought to gloss over religious difference and graft themselves into pre-existing Roman modes of expression, others, like Landelinus, felt the need to interleave traditional pagan symbols with the new vocabulary of Christian art. Somewhere in the middle, Gregory of Tours found himself isolated on the barbarian frontier and turned for validation to a tenuous but vociferously asserted claim to "orthodoxy," the touchstone of religious truth and thus power.

Part VIII The Power of Religion in the Communities of the East

The final section continues to examine the power of religion on the frontier, this time in the eastern Mediterranean. The abundance of source traditions, and particularly sources in languages other than the Latin and Greek of the Roman metropolis, allow for an even deeper connection with post-colonial explorations.

In her essay on religious factionalism and space in late antique Antioch, Wendy Mayer offers two case studies, the cult of Babylas and the construction of churches under Justinian. In the first instance, she shows how the Babylas cult was exploited by Christians against pagans, by neo-Nicenes against their opponents, and ultimately by religious authorities against the emperor in a series of power plays for control of religious and political authority in the fourth century. Turning to the sixth century, she then demonstrates that Justianian and Theodora carefully selected the saints' cults they chose to promote in Antioch—particularly those of Michael, Cosmas and Damian, and the Theotokos—in order to promote their own imperial authority in this important capital. In every instance power resulted from the control of space, by which one can understand both the control of physical places and the control of the discourse that gives places social meaning.

In the twenty-sixth chapter, Hagith Sivan portrays the creation of the Jerusalem feast of Mary's maternity on 15 August as a move by John of Jerusalem to promote his own power and the power of his see over against both the Jews of Palestine and the monastic Christians of Bethlehem. By placing this feast temporally on the same date as the commemoration of the destruction of the Temple, the ninth of Av, John challenged the Jews for control of this solemn feast day. Similarly, by placing it spatially on the road midway between Jersualem and Bethlehem, he also challenged the claim of that town and its monasteries—under the authority of his nemesis Jerome—for control of the title to Christ's birthplace. In the process, John introduced a new and more earthly Mary whose embodiment as birthing-mother anticipated the Theotokos controversy that would erupt in the decades to come.

John Weisweiler joins longstanding debates on Ammianus' attitude toward Christian religion but brings fresh insights to the problem using new observations and texts. He shows how Ammianus played upon the conventions of Latin literature and above all contemporary Greek and Syriac hagiography to deflate the claims of Christianity to have constituted a new source of power for the state. From his portrayal of the general Sabinianus frolicking among martyr shrines in Edessa while Shapur invaded upper Mesopotamia, to his innuendo that the bishop of Bezabde was complicit in that city's downfall, to his portrait of female ascetics as targets of Shapur's cozening concessions to Roman captives, Ammianus consistently undermines Christianity's pretence to being a bulwark in defence of the power of the empire.

Finally, Richard Payne closes this collection of studies with an examination of the letters of the seventh-century bishop of Arbela, Ishoyahb III, to the people of Nisibis. Standing as catholicos of the Church of the East in a period when eastern Christianity had lost its political center of gravity with the disappearance of the Sasanian state, Ishoyahb had to reconstruct his authority along new lines. He did so by deploying orthodoxy, and particularly the enforcement of the two *qnome* formally sanctioned by Babai the Great, as the rallying point for adherence to the faith and thus the touchstone of obedience to his sway. In his letters to the Nisibenes, Ishoyahb promoted his own relationship with the new Muslim power structure as a way to encourage adherence from the Nisibenes, and he courted the allegiance not just of Nisibis' clergy but of its venerable aristocracy. In so doing, he was able to mobilize a purge of "heretics" that simultaneously channeled power in his favor and redefined allegiance to the church on terms he could control.

As sites of military and political confrontation, frontiers are inherently a locus of cultural contestation. At the edges of its eastern empire Rome had always struggled to assert its power and identity against the cultural and political "other" even as it sought to control and co-opt that other. These papers show that in Late Antiquity, as frontiers were further destabilized, the other became all the more difficult to define. The pagan power structure of the high empire had given way to Christian dominance in Antioch, scrambling the definition of religious truth and forcing pagans into subjection to what had once been the subject other. So too Jerusalem had shifted from Jewish to Christian capital, a destabilization of the city that created a space where Christians not only competed with Jews but also with one another for control of this sacred space and its meaning. The traditionalist Ammianus fought to hang onto his definition of pagan Roman power by subtly critiquing those—largely Syrian—Christians who were in the process of reappropriating religious power from pagans, and imperial power from Rome. And in the seventh century Syrian Christians in former Sasanian territory were challenged to redefine religious power in a world where the Muslim invasions had rocked traditional power structures and left the question of religious authority up for grabs.

PART I
Religion and the Power of the Word

Chapter 1
Disarming Aeneas: Fulgentius on *Arms and the Man*

Emily Albu
University of California, Davis

Just two weeks before the 2007 Shifting Frontiers VII conference in Boulder, the action epic *300* opened in theaters. Screenwriter and director Zack Snyder had ample heroic material with which to work in the three hundred Spartans who fought to the death against a throng of invading Persians at Thermopylae. But Snyder had no interest in allowing the ancient sources to retell their story. Rather, he faithfully animated the images in Frank Miller's graphic novel *300*, itself inspired by the 1962 film, *The 300 Spartans*.[1] As one reviewer of Snyder's film wrote, the result is "an over-the-top take on ancient Greek history."[2] Another critic summarized the movie more concisely: "The Chippendales wage war."[3] Some admirers of the film thought it a spectacular reworking of the heroic genre for the computer-gaming generation. Other viewers considered its intentions less benign and noted that the film displays beautiful Greeks fighting bravely for western freedom and democracy against evil hordes of grotesque slaves, and oddly orientalized Africans. The fearless Spartans do not die in vain, and their sacrifice inspires all Greeks to mobilize against the Persians bent on annihilating Athenian democracy. Judging this to be thinly veiled propaganda in favor of an American assault on his country, a spokesman for the Iranian government condemned *300* for glorifying "hostile behaviour which is the result of cultural and psychological warfare" and for offering "an insult to Iran."[4]

The new millennium has seen a resurgence of films set in antiquity, featuring ancient heroes recast for our own age and often harboring a latent political agenda. *Gladiator* began this revival with a hero remarkably attuned to the George W. Bush

---

[1] F. Miller, with L. Varley (colorist), *300* (Milwaukie, OR, 1999). The work first appeared as a five-volume series issued May–September 1998.

[2] C. Puig, "300? It's Quite a Number: An Over-the-Top Take on Ancient Greek History," *USA Today* (8 March 2007).

[3] M.A. Perigard, "'300': Far from a Perfect 10," *Boston Sunday Herald* (29 July 2007) 34.

[4] Reported by R. Tait in *The Guardian* (15 March 2007).

campaign rhetoric of the 2000 election.[5] Maximus is a strong and simple man, a devoted husband, father, and patriot, and an outsider determined to restore decency and honor to a corrupt and cynical empire. The Achilles of the film *Troy* reveals how the national mood had shifted by 2004, as he scorns the bellicose yet cowardly Agamemnon in words widely interpreted as a critique of Bush.[6]

Much like today's film-makers, Christian mythographers in Late Antiquity appropriated ancient heroes for their own purposes.[7] But they worked with a greater sense of urgency. Their mission was to discredit the core meaning of the stories that had long defined their own civilization and the place of human beings in the cosmos. Variously using philosophical arguments or flights of mystical imagination, they deployed creative etymologies, allegory, or other rhetorical devices in order to dismantle the received notions of these pagan texts and to replace them with radically different Christian ways of thinking.

Fulgentius the Mythoclast

A late antique master of this art was Fulgentius the mythographer.[8] Modern scholars have been highly critical of his works. Thus, for example, this well-known assessment by Laistner: "Among the remnants of an effete and expiring classicism none are more pretentious, yet essentially trivial, than the three treatises which bear the name of Fabius Planciades Fulgentius."[9] Yet Fulgentius mesmerized

---

[5] E. Albu, "*Gladiator* at the Millennium," in K. Day (ed.), *Celluloid Classics: New Perspectives on Classical Antiquity in Modern Cinema,* special issue of *Arethusa* 41 (2008) 185–204.

[6] "Imagine a king who fights his own battles. Wouldn't that be a sight?" Cf. Hector, on viewing Agamemnon's army: "I see 50,000 men brought here to fight for one man's greed."

[7] For a list of late antique mythographers and their works, see J. Chance, *Medieval Mythography: From Roman North Africa to the School of Chartres,* A.D. *433–1177* (Gainesville, 1994) xxxii.

[8] Fulgentius, *Fulgentii Opera*, ed. R. Helm (Leipzig, 1898; reprint. Stuttgart, 1970). All references to the texts are to this volume: book and chapter for the body of the *Mitologiae*; page and line for *Continentia* and for the prologue to the *Mitologiae*. Gregory Hays is completing a new edition for Oxford University Press and maintains an invaluable bibliography on Fulgentius at http://people.virginia.edu/~bgh2n/fulgbib.html. I am grateful to him for reading a draft of this article and for offering sage corrections (though any errors that remain are of course my own). As for the English translation by L.G. Whitbread (Columbus, OH, 1971), it is frequently misleading: see, for example, the review by R.T. Bruère in *CP* 68 (1973) 143–5. On the problems raised by calling this Fulgentius "the mythographer," see G. Hays, "The Date and Identity of the Mythographer Fulgentius," *JML* 13 (2003) 163–252 at 164 n.3.

[9] "... namely, the *Mythologiae* in three books, the *Expositio Virgilianae Continentiae* and the *Expositio Sermonum Antiquorum*." M.L.W. Laistner, "Fulgentius in the Carolingian Age," in C.G. Starr (ed.), *The Intellectual Heritage of the Early Middle Ages: Selected*

medieval writers and readers and transformed the reading of ancient myths for more than a thousand years.

We do not know precisely who he was or when he lived. He has often been identified as the anti-Arian bishop Fulgentius of Ruspe (468–533). Hays, however, has recently demonstrated that they were almost certainly not one and the same person.[10] Although both Fulgentii lived in North Africa, the mythographer seems to have written his *Mitologiae* after the bishop's death, most likely in the 540s or 550s but perhaps near the very end of the sixth century. Clues to the mythographer's identity are extracted mainly from his own texts: *Mitologiae* (*The Mythologies*) in three books, *Expositio Virgilianae continentiae* (*An Explanation of Vergilian Continence / Contents*), *Expositio sermonum antiquorum* (*The Explanation of Obsolete Words*), and *De aetatibus mundi et hominis* (*On the Ages of the World and of Man*). The first two of these, the *Mitologiae* and *Continentia*, conspire to demolish the network of tales and beliefs that supported Greco-Roman paganism.

Both the *Mitologiae* and *Continentia* expose their author as a late antique deconstructionist who fired an assault on the conventional ways of understanding the ancient myths. They also present a rigid moralist who aimed literary criticism as his weapon of choice against pagan lust in protection of Christian values, combining the eclectic pedantry of a late antique schoolman with the prudish sensibilities of the new moral majority toward the ancient heroic ideals. He proved unusually adept at this and singularly persuasive, seducing readers with his distinctive blend of erudition, wit, sarcasm, and rhetorical razzle-dazzle. His attack was relentless. The *Mitologiae* reduced gods and heroes, one after another, to etymological or allegorized constructs, in the process repeatedly ridiculing the lies and depravities contained in the ancient tales.

Modern critics have sometimes tried to defend allegory as an honest attempt at reconciling the irreconcilable. Here, for instance, is what Comparetti says about Fulgentius and allegory:

> [Allegory] is the instructive and honest resource of men, whose minds are dominated at one and the same time by two contradictory influences of equal power, from neither of which are they able to free themselves. Allegory is a species of dialectical hallucination, which owes its origin to those earnest convictions which are natural to a vigorous and impulsive temperament.[11]

Essays by M.L.W. Laistner (Ithaca, NY, 1957) 205–15 at 204 = *Mélanges Hrouchevsky* (Kiev, 1927) 445–56. Nearly two-thirds of a fourth work, *De aetatibus mundi et hominis*, also survives. Some writers still include *Super Thebaiden* in the Fulgentian corpus, but for the counter-argument see G. Hays, "Pseudo-Fulgentian *Super Thebaiden*," in J.F. Miller, C. Damon, and K.S. Myers (eds.), *Vertis in Usum: Studies in Honor of Edward Courtney* (Munich and Leipzig, 2002) 200–218.

10 Hays, "Date and Identity."

11 D. Comparetti, *Vergil in the Middle Ages*, trans. E.F.M. Benecke (1895; reprint, with an introduction by J.M. Ziolkowski, Princeton, 1997) 106.

Fulgentius' motives for his own hallucinations may have been more calculated. He seems obsessed with exposing the sexual decadence of pagan culture and with revealing the old gods as lechers and perverts and the old literature as pornography. So his prologue to the *Mitologiae* (10.19–11.18) disabuses the muse Calliope of her expectation that this is a standard work on Greco-Roman myth:

> The title of my little work has misled you, Your Noble Garrulousness. I do not sing about the horned adulterer being smitten, or the maiden deceived by a false shower, as the god (in that first instance) by his own judgment preferred a beast to himself and (in the second) seduced with gold the woman he could not get with his political clout [*potestate*]. I do not write about the thigh of a young lover fed to a swine's jaw, nor in my little work has juvenile licentiousness dangled beneath a falsely assumed wing. I do not explore the adulterer slinking around in swan's plumage, foisting his chick-bearing eggs on maidens instead of pouring child-bearing seed into their innards ... What I wish to do is to expose those altered vanities ...; and so I look for the faithful performance of reality, so that once the fictional invention of lying Greece has been destroyed, we may grasp what allegorical understanding one ought to discern in these stories.[12]

In other words, Fulgentius would both demolish the obscene pagan tales and rescue from them some edifying meaning, to which people were finally receptive, now that their world was Christian.

In this process he showed considerable prurient interest in highlighting the obscenity that he found lurking within the story, as in the Danaë interpretation above (and repeated at 1.19), where the golden shower is simply a metaphor for Jupiter's sex-for-gold scandal. Time and again Fulgentius zeroed in on the aetiological/allegorical core of pagan myth, which he repeatedly explained as lust-driven. So the pagans depicted Venus "floating in the sea, because all lust suffers shipwreck" (2.1);[13] Hercules' love for Omphale symbolized the battle against lust (2.2); and "Antaeus stands for lust, so also in Greek we say *antion*, contrary; and likewise he was born from the earth because lust alone is conceived from

[12] *Index te libelli fefellit, generosa loquacitas; non mihi cornutus adulter arripitur nec imbre mendaci lusa* [*Danaë*] *uirgo cantatur, dum suo iudicio deus sibi pecudem praetulit et hanc auro decepit quam potestate nequiuit; non suillo canimus morsu depastum amantis iuuenis femur nec in meis libellulis sub falsa alite puerilis pependit lasciuia; non olorinis reptantem adulterum plumis, oua pulligera uirginibus inculcantem quam semina puerigena uisceribus infundentem ...; certos itaque nos rerum praestolamur effectus, quo sepulto mendacis Greciae fabuloso commento quid misticum in his sapere debeat cerebrum agnoscamus*. All translations are my own, though for this one especially I gratefully received correction and advice from Greg Hays.

[13] *Hanc etiam in mari natantem pingunt, quod omnis libido rerum patiatur naufragia...*

the flesh" (2.4).[14] In the same vein, when he interpreted Scylla to mean "disorder" (*confusio*; 2.9), he asked, "And what is *confusio* if not lust (*libido*)?"[15]

Fulgentius thus ripped the ancestral gods and heroes from their venerable positions as cultural icons. Some he made thoroughly unpalatable by exposing them as serial sex-offenders. Others he turned into shadowy figures, symbols of pagan decadence. Everywhere he discovered erotic signs encoded in pagan myths that were unfit for Christian ears. After deconstructing the heroic in the *Mitologiae*, Fulgentius then constructed a new Christian path for *virtus* in his *Expositio Virgilianae continentiae*, which reinterpreted the *Aeneid* book by book to show how Vergil really meant to create a kind of "pilgrim's progress" revealing the stages of maturation of the human soul.

The pun in the title cleverly emphasizes Fulgentius' point. Classical authors such as Cicero and Sallust used *continentia* to mean "the restraining of one's passions and desires." Lewis and Short give another meaning for late Latin only: "the contents of a work."[16] Souter's *Glossary of Later Latin to 600 A.D.* confirms the range of meaning that the word had come to embrace by Fulgentius' day: "chastity; context; contents; support" and even, for the fifth-century Caelius Aurelianus, "touch."[17] Surely Fulgentius meant the title to play on the possibilities offered by *continentia*: *An Explanation of Vergilian Continence / Contents*. Virtue and restraint *were*, for Fulgentius, the true contents of Vergil's *Aeneid*.

Fulgentius and Vergil

Fulgentius was by no means the first interpreter to put Vergil under a microscope, scanning his pages word by word for secret messages that supported his own world view. Nearly every educated person, it seems, summoned Vergil as an expert witness on points ranging from grammar to spirituality, and Fulgentius pilfered a great deal from his predecessors.[18]

In the *Continentia*, Fulgentius brings on the ancient poet himself, here a knuckle-rapping schoolmaster (much like Fulgentius, one suspects), who materializes for the purpose of expounding the *virtus* his work embodied.[19] The appropriation of Vergil's authoritative voice was a brilliant stroke. Fulgentius

---

14 *Anteus enim in modum libidinis ponitur, unde et Grece antion contrarium dicimus; ideo et de terra natus, quia sola libido de carne concipitur*. The giant Antaeus was the son of Gaia (Earth).

15 *Et quid confusio nisi libido est.*

16 C.T. Lewis and C. Short, *A Latin Dictionary* (1879; reprint, Oxford, 1975) 448.

17 A. Souter, *A Glossary of Later Latin to 600 A.D.* (1949; reprint, Oxford, 1996) 76.

18 On the meticulous scrutiny of Vergil's texts, see F. Debordes, "Virgile s'explique," *Europe* 71 (1993) 81–92, at 83–5.

19 On Fulgentius' Vergil as medieval schoolmaster, see J.W. Jones, Jr., "Vergil as *Magister* in Fulgentius," in C. Henderson, Jr. (ed.), *Classical, Mediaeval, and Renaissance Studies in Honor of Berthold Louis Ullman* (Rome, 1964) 1.273–5.

went one step further by repeatedly blurring the line between his own voice and Vergil's. In the *Continentia* (98.23–99.1), for instance, Vergil introduces Cerberus, the three-headed dog of the underworld, by reminding the reader, "I have already explained the story previously as standing for a legal dispute and public litigation." Vergil is not of course referring to his own corpus but is citing *Mitologiae* 1.6. The *Continentia*'s conclusion betrays a slightly different sort of authorial confusion when Vergil's monologue ends abruptly. As the ancient poet briefly accounts for the final book of his *Aeneid*, equating the nymph Juturna with destruction and her mortal brother Turnus with drunken rage, another voice seems to interrupt with *finit*—"the end"—before Fulgentius inserts a single-sentence farewell to a *dominus*, presumably the unnamed "lord" of the prologue, with Vergil unceremoniously dispatched.[20] These apparent lapses have exasperated modern readers, who considered them signs that Fulgentius was careless, confused, or inept.[21] On the contrary, it seems likely that he knew exactly what he was doing here in gradually conflating his voice with that of the venerated master.

In the beginning, though, Fulgentius' Vergil distances himself from the lowly grammarian who has summoned him. When Vergil appears (85.12–16), "drenched in the glittering eloquence of the Ascraean fountain," he must first quiz Fulgentius, whom he persistently addresses as *(h)omuncule*, to assure himself that he is not wasting his time explaining the book to an imbecile.[22] Has this insignificant fellow even read the *Aeneid*? Only when Fulgentius dutifully summarizes the first book of the *Aeneid* (90.21–91.5) does Vergil deign to unlock its secrets of moral philosophy, starting with the opening words of his epic, which he is at pains to defend. How could he have begun an ethical treatise with the inauspicious *arma*? In a rhetorical defense, Vergil performs sleight of mind to argue that *arma* stands for *virtus* and that *vir* means *sapientia*, "for all perfection lies in manliness of body and wisdom of temperament" (87.5–6).[23]

> In a person's life there are three stages; the first is *possessing*, the second, *training what you possess*, and the third, *adorning what you train*. So reflect on those three stages placed in a single line of mine, that is, *arma*, *virum*, and *primus*: *arma*, i.e. manliness (*virtus*) refers to the physical component; *virum*, *i.e.* wisdom, refers to the intellectual component (*ad substantiam sensualem*); *primus*, *i.e.* "foremost," refers to the (final) element of discernment (*ad*

[20] *Cont.* 106.9–107.5. See Whitbread, 153 n.30.

[21] See, e.g., Comparetti, *Vergil*, 112: "So far, indeed, is the author from being bound by any rule, that he does not even respect the machinery of his own imagination, and makes Vergil speak at times as if he were Fulgentius. And to his carelessness is added ignorance in proportion, as when he makes Vergil quote from Petronius and even from Tiberianus! The book has not even any proper conclusion, for the author quite forgets that, as Vergil has been speaking hitherto, he himself ought to appear and say farewell to the reader."

[22] *Cont.* 90.19–21.

[23] *Omnis enim perfectio in uirtute constat corporis et sapientia ingenii.*

> *substantiam censualem*), resulting in this order: possessing, training, adorning. And thus I have demonstrated, through the symbolic representation of a story, the full human condition; that it is first nature, then learning, then happiness. (89.18–90.3)[24]

What is going on here? Have we fallen down a rabbit hole into a world where nothing is as it had seemed? In a word—yes. The *Aeneid*, it turns out, is not the epic tale of a hero and the obstacles he must overcome in order to assure an empire for his descendants. It in fact has nothing at all to do with Rome. Nor is it about a unique individual but about a generic Everyman, whose pilgrim's progress Fulgentius identifies with milestones in Aeneas' wanderings and battles.

The shipwreck in book 1 is thus an allegory for the hazards of birth. To make this perfectly obvious, says Vergil, he made Juno (goddess of childbirth) the architect of this storm.[25] She gets help from Aeolus, that is, "world-annihilation," by offering him as his bride the nymph Deiopea. "Now *demos* means 'public' in Greek, while *iopa* means 'eyes' or 'a vision.' Therefore, those born in the world experience worldly peril, while to the goddess-born is promised a public vision of perfection."[26] Just as Aeneas escapes burning Troy with seven ships, so seven is the lucky number for birth (91.18–20). And so on—with Achates symbolizing the difficulties of infancy (92.13–93.5), Iopas' song as the nurses' lullabies (93.11–16), and Polyphemus as the "terrible twos" or childish abandon, whose single eye (vainglory) is blinded by the trickster's fire (93.21–94.8). Often the etymologies require little stretching to support the argument, as when our pilgrim allies himself with the good man Euander (104.18–105.3), who describes the victory of virtue over evil (Cacus). But more outrageous and creative interpretations abound, educed willy-nilly from Greek and Latin. So the man chooses his mate Lavinia, the road of hardships (Laviniam = *laborum viam*; 104.7-8), and struggles against anger (Turnus = θοῦρος νοῦς = *furibundus sensus*; 105.12–16).

These etymologies expose Fulgentius as an ideologue intent on extracting from his text the meaning that he had set out to find. For him the *Aeneid* must be a work detailing the stages of human development and a guidebook to proper moral development. Thus Fulgentius the mythographer and his Vergil the moral

---

24 *... trifarius in uita humana gradus est, primum habere, deinde regere quod habeas, tertium uero ornare quod regis. Ergo tres gradus istos in uno uersu nostro considera positos, id est: "arma", "uirum" et "primus":"arma", id est uirtus, pertinet ad substantiam corporalem, "uirum", id est sapientia, pertinet ad substantiam sensualem, "primus" uero, id est princeps, pertinet ad substantiam censualem, quo sit ordo hiuusmodi: habere, regere, ornare. Ergo sub figuralitatem historiae plenum hominis monstrauimus statum, ut sit prima natura, secunda doctrina, tertia felicitas.*

25 *Cont.* 91.9–11.

26 *Demos enim Grece puplicum dicitur, iopa uero oculi uel uisio; ergo nascentibus in mundo seculare est periculum; cui quidem perfectionis puplica a dea partus promittitur uisio.*

philosopher redefine *virtus* by disparaging or allegorizing the warrior's passion for battle while betraying considerable interest in the passion of lust, the greatest impediment to the soul's attainment of wisdom. The *Aeneid*'s last six books (superficially on the wars in Italy) interested Fulgentius' Vergil so little that he disposes of them in short order (103.13–107.4). Book 11 earns only a sentence, on the armor and weapons of Turnus' fierce ally Mezentius, displayed by Aeneas as a trophy of war.[27] It is tempting to think that Vergil's suspicions of Fulgentius were close to the mark (90.19–21). Fulgentius' reading of the *Aeneid* might have been limited to the early books, the ones most commonly read as school texts in his day as in our own.[28] As for book 11, perhaps he read closely only the opening lines (1–11), skimming over the celebrated passages that frame this book, the lament for Pallas (11.24-98) and the death of Camilla (11.497–835).

If Fulgentius had truly tired of the *Aeneid*'s carnage, he was surely reflecting the battle-weariness of his own age. It was no coincidence that he dismissed *arma* and advanced to the ethical plane at a time when the Romans (whose foundation myth celebrated a civilization forged with great sacrifice and destined for world domination) had succumbed to Germanic incursions. In denying the Roman myth Fulgentius was mounting an attack on the center of pagan culture and its heroic ideals. Was he also implicitly holding paganism responsible for the demise of Roman civilization, whose culture he thought rotten at its mythic core? At the very least he estranged himself from traditional Roman religion while endorsing a new world view, a new concept of the heroic.

Some postmodern commentators on Fulgentius have pronounced him an avant-garde literary critic. In the judgment of that sympathetic audience, the mythographer had anticipated the work of the most daring semioticians, showing them how to separate words (*verba*) from things (*res*), "the linguistic sign from the thing signified," in Latin sufficiently obscure to confuse or even awe many a reader.[29] In the mysterious spaces between *res* and *verba*, Fulgentius and his admirers insist, the enlightened reader can construct truths that both confound and transcend the literal meaning of the stories that these words appear to tell. These

27 *Cont.* 106.7–9. The manuscripts read "Messapus" (in various spellings), and Whitbread repeats the error at 135 and 153 n.28.1. But the text here cannot refer to the Latin leader, son of Neptune "whom no man may kill by fire or sword" (*Aen.* 7.691–2).

28 On the abiding preference for the first six books—especially for books 2, 3, and 4—see K.W. Gransden, *Virgil's Iliad: An Essay on Epic Narrative* (Cambridge, 1984) 1. Even medieval glosses illustrate this tendency, appearing with diminishing frequency in the later books. See, for instance, C. Baswell, *Virgil in Medieval England* (Cambridge, 1995) 54.

29 This language comes from R. Edwards, "The Heritage of Fulgentius," in A.S. Bernardo and S. Levin (eds.), *The Classics in the Middle Ages: Papers of the Twentieth Annual Conference of the Center for Medieval and Early Renaissance Studies* (Binghamton, NY, 1990) 141–51 at 142. Edwards here sums up the argument he had made in "Fulgentius and the Collapse of Meaning," *Helios* n.s. 3 (1976) 17–35.

truths come with their own cultural agenda, as they obliterate an old way of seeing and believing.

Readers who question Fulgentius' methods may appreciate an observation from Dickens' novel *Bleak House*: "Allegory makes the head ache—as would seem to be Allegory's object always, more or less."[30] Applying Dickens' statement to the *Expositio Vergilianae continentiae*, Huppé concluded: "The *Exposition* is, indeed, so glaringly, gratuitously allegorical as to be an affront to any common-sensical reader of the *Aeneid*, for whom its absurdity could only be explained by its having been written in the benighted darkness of the Augustinian twilight."[31] In a frequently cited assessment, Comparetti had already expressed this critique even more boldly:

> the process of Fulgentius is so violent and incoherent, it disregards every law of common sense in such a patent and well-nigh brutal manner, that it is hard to conceive how any sane man can seriously have undertaken such a work, and harder still to believe that other sane men should have accepted it as an object for serious consideration.[32]

Were Fulgentius and his medieval audience all mad? His disorienting imagery did alter the minds of his readers, who absorbed his techniques and learned to think like him, dismantling heroic characters and action, and then picking through the wreckage to find moral truths that lay beneath the rubble. For the generations of students trained by his texts, the foundational stories of Greek religion and Roman civilization could never again be received as they used to be heard.

Fulgentius and his Influence

Fulgentius exercised an enormous influence during the Carolingian period, when his works seem to have served as school textbooks. A tenth-century catalog of manuscripts at Bobbio reveals that this library alone had three copies of his most popular work, the *Mitologiae*, known to John Scotus, Sedulius Scotus, Ermenrich of Ellwangen, and many of their distinguished contemporaries.[33] One of them, Walahfrid Strabo (ca. 810–49), even gave his friend Gottschalk the nickname Fulgentius.[34]

---

30 Quoted in B.F. Huppé, "Aeneas' Journey to the New Troy," in Bernardo and Levin, *Classics in the Middle Ages*, 175–87 at 178.

31 Ibid., 179.

32 Comparetti, *Vergil*, 112. Cf. Edwards, "Fulgentius and the Collapse," 17.

33 Laistner, "Fulgentius in the Carolingian Age," 204–11.

34 In personal correspondence Greg Hays has pointed out to me that Walahfrid might be referring to the bishop of the same name, "or to the hybrid Fulgentius, if [he] thought they were the same person."

Later writers, too, found him to be a valuable link between the Christian and pagan worlds. Consider, for instance, Dudo of Saint-Quentin, the first Norman historian. He wrote ca. 994–1015 for the Norman dukes, who wanted to celebrate their past and to legitimize their fledgling dynasty. Dudo produced a massive travesty of Vergil, a mock-heroic parody of the *Aeneid* characterized by flamboyant language, sarcasm, and layered meanings. In an elaborate and self-conscious prefatory poem to his book, he pretended to fret that he could not protect his book from public ridicule. What, then, would be the consequences for himself? After all, he wrote, "a tower of bronze scarcely protected Danaë once from a shower of golden rain, as Fulgentius the Mythographer discloses."[35] It is a witty allusion, even hinting to the sophisticated Frankish clerics in his audience, who knew the mythographer's interpretation of this story, that Dudo was prostituting himself by accepting Norman benefices in exchange for doing the dukes' bidding. If Dudo was influenced directly by Fulgentius, we can understand how he acquired his distinctive attitude, his skepticism and ironic distancing. He learned to take nothing at face value. In his pages the Normans of their own heroic age are treacherous schemers, dangerous to friend and foe alike—certainly an accurate assessment. And thanks to Fulgentius, who read the *Aeneid* as an epic of human moral development, Dudo could easily strip the *Aeneid* of its heroic surface and mine its plot and language in highlighting the progressive Christianization of Norman dukes, even while making covert jokes at the Normans' expense. Dudo's irreverent sense of humor must owe something to Fulgentius. When Dudo takes aim at Norman warriors and the princes of *their* heroic age, mocking the very people he was hired to celebrate, the tone often matches Fulgentius' peculiar levity.[36]

Fulgentius' aggressively subversive texts settled into the consciousness of generation after generation of medieval writers and influenced a worldview that impugned the old heroic values by associating them with perversion and then replacing them with a new heroic ideal of Christian morality. This was no simple task, but Fulgentius undertook it with gusto, as in this passage following his discussion of the myths of Teiresias (*Mitologiae* 2.5): "However stupendous the Greek lie, it becomes that stupendously admirable when it is explained."

Fulgentius' explanations take us deep into an alternative reality, one without sex or sexuality, without Spartan or Roman manliness, without even a corporeal Aeneas. Like the boldest twenty-first century films, his remakes of pagan classics twisted the ancient material in order to wring out an altogether new message while also disfiguring the old stories. By grappling with that message embedded in bizarre and contorted allegories, we can enter his brave new world of *Virgile moralisé* and experience Fulgentius' own brand of cultural and psychological warfare against Greco-Roman paganism.

---

[35] J. Lair (ed.), *De moribus et actis primorum Normanniae ducum, auctore Dudone Sancti Quintini decano* (Caen, 1865).

[36] See E. Albu, *The Normans in Their Histories* (Woodbridge, 2001) 7–46; Eadem, "Dudo of Saint-Quentin: The Heroic Past Imagined," *HSJ* 6 (1994) 111–18.

Chapter 2
"Apocalypse? No."—
The Power of Millennialism and its Transformation in Late Antique Christianity

Josef Lössl
Cardiff University

"This is gloomy stuff; and I apologise for it."[1] Thus the narrator of Anthony Burgess's novel *The Kingdom of the Wicked* refers to the beliefs of the earliest Christians. Here one feels similarly inclined to apologize, though the gloom in this case is caused less by the social and political fallout of the early Roman Empire than by a particular kind of early Christian response to it. Millennialism is the belief in a messianic rule lasting for a thousand years.[2] According to the main early Christian source, the New Testament book of Revelation (Rev. 20), an apocalyptic event is followed by the rule of Christ and his followers on earth, at the end of which a final judgment will take place and the blessed will be rewarded with eternal life while the wicked are punished with eternal damnation. The history of this belief in early Christianity is well documented.[3] The aim of this paper is not to retrace this history but to explore the dimension of religious power that early Christian millennialism exerted, particularly by its presence in sacred texts, the interpretation of which posed some fundamental hermeneutical challenges for early Christian biblical exegetes.

As they gradually learned to master these challenges, millennialism was transformed into a more universal kind of historical-eschatological thought, a prime example of which can be found in Augustine's *City of God.* The roots of Augustine's eschatological thought have been traced to the work of Tyconius, a

---

[1] A. Burgess, *The Kingdom of the Wicked* (London, 1986) 89.

[2] Some types of millennialism consider other time frames as well. For example, 4 Esra 7:26–30 states that the Messiah and the just will reign for 400 years before entering eternity. Note that for the earliest forms of Christian millennialism, no clear-cut distinction can be made between Jewish and Christian sources; see D. Frankfurter, "The Legacy of Jewish Apocalypses in Early Christianity," in J.C. VanderKam and W. Adler (eds.), *The Jewish Apocalyptic Heritage in Early Christianity* (Assen, 1996) 129–200.

[3] For a seminal account, see H. Bietenhard, "The Millennial Hope in the Early Church," in *SJT* 6 (1953) 12–30; see also B.E. Daley, *The Hope of the Early Church: A Handbook of Patristic Eschatology* (Cambridge, 1991) passim.

North African Donatist theologian who lived a generation before the bishop of Hippo (ca. 330–ca. 390).[4] By contrast, the mediating role of another significant early Christian writer in this development is rather less recognized.[5] The Pannonian bishop and martyr Victorinus of Poetovium (modern Ptuj in Slovenia) lived a century before Tyconius. He was born around 230. The date of his death is less certain. The conventional view is that he died a martyr in 304 at the outset of the Great Persecution,[6] but he could also have died in an earlier persecution.[7] His commentary on Revelation (*Commentarius in Apocalypsin* [*Apoc.*]) dates from the persecution of Valerian (ca. 260). His method of appropriating earlier Greek and Latin sources and of working them into his commentary with an eye to synthesizing millennialist and anti-millennialist exegesis deserves close analysis because it is a pioneering contribution to the development of western eschatological thought.

Victorinus' commentary on Revelation is significant for another reason too: it is the earliest extant biblical commentary in Latin. Victorinus pre-dates the next wave of Latin commentators, Marius Victorinus, Ambrosiaster, Jerome, and others, by a century. He wrote other commentaries as well,[8] but *Apoc.* is the only one extant. And Latin was not even Victorinus' first language.[9] His *oeuvre* emerges at least in part from translation from Greek.[10] More importantly, Victorinus transformed his sources, Greek and Latin, into what is now the earliest extant consciously methodical and hermeneutical Latin biblical commentary. Finally, it is not entirely accidental that this commentary is on the book of Revelation and that one of the

---

4 See K. Pollmann, "Apocalypse Now?! – Der Kommentar des Tyconius zur Johannesoffenbarung," in W. Geerlings and C. Schulze (eds.), *Der Kommentar in Antike und Mittelalter: Beiträge zu seiner Erforschung* (Leiden, 2002) 33–54.

5 Pollmann, "Apocalypse Now?!," 42 n.30, recognizes Victorinus' importance and refers to the pioneering study by M. Dulaey, *Victorin de Poetovio: Premier exégète latin*, 2 vols. (Paris, 1993). Dulaey focuses less on Victorinus' transformation of millennialist thought than on his dependence on earlier thinkers.

6 This view is based on a remark of Jerome's (*Vir. ill.* 74) that Victorinus *ad extremum martyrio coronatus est*; see M. Dulaey, *Victorin de Poetovio: Sur l'Apocalypse et autres écrits* (Paris, 1997) 15–16.

7 An earlier persecution under Numerian (283–84) has been raised as a possibility, though historical evidence for such a persecution remains (at best) scanty; see R. Bratož, *Krščanstvo v Ogleju in na vzhodnem vplivnem območju oglejske cerkve od začetkov do nastopa verske svobode* (Ljubljana, 1986) 361–3; Dulaey, *Victorin de Poetovio sur l'Apocalypse*, 16.

8 See Jer. *Vir. ill.* 74: *Compositione verborum sunt autem haec: commentarii in Genesim, in Exodum, in Leviticum, in Esaiam, in Ezechiel, in Abacuc, in Ecclesiasten, in Canticum canticorum, in Apocalypsin Iohannis, Adversum omnes haereses et multa alia.*

9 As Jer. *Vir. ill.* 74, writes: "He did not know Latin as well as he knew Greek" (*non aeque latine et graece*).

10 One of these concerns the main problem of Revelation, the fact that it reveals something by concealing it behind impenetrable metaphors. These are held to be fruits of prophetic gnosis, issued from a divine source. The question was also, were they related to an end within or beyond history? See Pollmann, "Apocalypse Now?!," 42 n.30.

most challenging problems with which it grapples is understanding the story of the millennial rule of Christ and his followers (Rev. 20).

To be sure, early Christian millennialism goes back a long way. The oldest known Christian witness, Papias, writing in the early second century, quotes a saying attributed to Jesus which applies the number 10,000 to the notion of plenty.[11] Irenaeus, who quotes Papias, sees in him a witness to the authenticity of the millennial hope. The Papias reference also bears resemblance to a passage in the Syriac version of Baruch 29:5, a Jewish apocalyptic writing.[12] Both Jewish and Christian traditions saw the number 1,000 as an allusion to a millennial rule of the Messiah at the end of time, the only difference being that the Christians tended to identify this Messiah with Jesus of Nazareth returning as Christ. The *Epistle of Barnabas* 15.1–9 links the creation story with the story of the end. God created the world in six days and will bring it to an end in the course of 6,000 years, for one day is with the Lord as 1,000 years (Ps. 90:4; *Barn.* 15.4). God rested on the seventh day. This will be the 1,000 years of Christ's rule, a time of bliss.

The *Epistle of Barnabas* dates from around 130. It distances itself from Judaism while at the same time being strongly influenced by it. Later writers identified the millennial hope as a characteristic of Jewish faith and argued polemically that behind it lies a Jewish hope for earthly pleasures. In this early stage there was still a recognition that the millennial hope is less motivated by a desire for earthly pleasures than by a desire to come to terms with the questions posed by a hope for an event that is expected to take place within history, but in such a way that it is not subject to the contingencies of history, such as mortality, illness, and moral corruption. It is likely that later polemics against the materialist hopes of early millennialism, whether such crass materialism was actually ever professed or not, were rather motivated by the attempt to gain control over the apocalyptic genre, empty it of its dangerous historical and political content, and integrate it into an eschatology that largely focused on an afterlife.

Whatever later polemics suggested, in the most sophisticated and reflective early Christian millennialist writings the description of earthly bliss in connection with the millennial rule was not motivated by a perverse desire to describe earthly pleasures but by the exegetical discovery that the millennial period was basically a return to paradise as described in Genesis 1. We find this already in Justin Martyr (ca. 150) and in Irenaeus (ca. 180).[13] A passage from a lost work by Justin against Marcion, quoted by Irenaeus, reads as follows:

---

[11] Papias, *De interpretatione dominicorum oraculorum*, cited in Iren. *Haer*. 5.33.3–4.

[12] 2 Baruch 29:5–6: "…on each vine there shall be a thousand grapes, and each grape shall produce a cot of wine;" compare Papias *apud* Iren. *Haer*. 5.33.3: "on every cluster ten thousand grapes, and every grape … will give twenty five metretes of wine." It is Irenaeus who understands the Papias text as an explicit reference to the millennial rule of Christ.

[13] Iustin. *Dial.* 81; Iren. *Haer*. 5.28.3; see P. Bobichon, *Justin Martyr: Dialogue avec Tryphon* II (Fribourg, 2003) 965–8.

> I would not have believed the Lord himself, if he had proclaimed another god alongside our demiurge, maker and provider. But since the only son of the only God … came to us, recapitulating (*recapitulans*) that which he formed with regard to himself, my faith in him is firm …[14]

Recapitulation (*anakephalaíōsis* in Greek) as a theological concept is usually attributed to Irenaeus. Now the reference just cited suggests that in some form or other the idea was already present in Justin. This should not come entirely as a surprise. Educated authors such as Justin and Irenaeus would have known *recapitulatio* as a rhetorical device. It was an element of *peroratio*, the winding down of a speech. It usually echoed the *prooemium*, the opening passage, and simply listed again the speech's main points.

For traditionalist rhetoricians it was very important, in view of the intended impact of a speech, that no new material be introduced at the end. Only points mentioned in the main parts of the speech were allowed to be repeated in the *recapitulatio*. Otherwise, it was thought, the message might be blurred. It is conceivable that Justin and Irenaeus applied this concept to biblical exegesis. In that case the creation narrative in Genesis 1 would have constituted the *prooemium*, while the New Testament, culminating in Revelation, would have represented the *recapitulatio*. Both ends (promise and fulfilment) would have to have matched. In particular, the *recapitulatio* should not exceed any expectations raised by the *prooemium*. In fact, both beginning and end should be like condensed versions of the main parts in the middle. Again, in particular, the *recapitulatio* should clarify the content, meaning, and purpose of the whole of the Bible.

One way of understanding the *recapitulatio* was that it represented an epitomated version of the whole speech. This rhetorical device was called *synecdoche*. There is a passage that shows that Irenaeus used the word *recapitulatio* in exactly this sense:

> The son of God … became incarnate and was made a human being in order that he would recapitulate in himself the long term development of humanity by offering us salvation in brief, in order that we would receive in Christ Jesus that which we lost in Adam, namely existing in the manner of God's image and likeness (Gen. 1:26).[15]

All key concepts in this passage are based in the art of rhetoric. *Longa expositio* is the full version of a text, in fact a full exegetical commentary; *compendium*

---

[14] Iustin. *Adv. Marc.* (frg.) *apud* Iren. *Haer.* 4.6.2: *Ipsi quoque domino non credidissem alterum deum annuntiavit praeter fabricatorem et factorem et nutritorem nostrum; sed quoniam ab uno deo, qui et hunc mundum fecit et nos plasmavit et omnia continet et administrat, unigenitus filius venit ad nos, suum plasma in semetipsum recapitulans, firma est mea ad eum fides …*

[15] Iren. *Haer.* 3.18.1.

is its summary. We also see repeated the link between *prooemium* (Gen. 1) and *peroratio*, or *recapitulatio* (the message of the New Testament). Interestingly, the expression *in compendio* (in Greek *suntómōs*, "briefly") has puzzled some scholars,[16] for it creates an impression of the salvific action of Christ as proclaimed in the New Testament as being somewhat diminished by being referred to as "brief." To the extent that this impression is justified, we may be dealing here with a literary-rhetorical device called *abusio*. This is a sub-type of a metonymical-synecdochic catachresis, when a word (*compendium*) close in meaning to the word that would be properly used (namely, *recapitulatio*) is "ab-used" or used in an "improper" way in order to create a certain impression.[17] Therefore, although Irenaeus does replace the expression *recapitulatio* (*anakephalaíōsis*) with the synonym "abridgment," "epitome," "brief summary" (*compendium*, *súntomos*), he does not seem to intend thereby to belittle it. He merely explains the biblical text in literary-rhetorical terms.

As Brox has shown in a seminal article,[18] what underlies the development of Irenaeus' theological concepts is a complex biblical hermeneutic. This may also explain to some extent why Irenaeus was so intent on closing the biblical canon. An area not covered by Brox in his study is Irenaeus' exegesis specifically of eschatological and apocalyptic texts. But it is in this area that the exegetical dimension of Irenaeus' millennialism could best be understood. When, for example, in book 5 of *Adversus Haereses* Irenaeus describes in detail the pleasures of the earthly millennium, his primary intention is not to arouse in his audience a desire for physical pleasure or power, nor to stir hopes that the Jewish temple is going to be rebuilt in Jerusalem, but to match the biblical accounts that anticipate the end of the world with those which recall its beginnings, and thereby to keep the eschatological scope within an historical framework.

Irenaeus' work seems to reflect a particular transitional stage of early Christian literature. Throughout the second century apocalyptic and other prophetic literature was still produced as a means of interpreting existing scriptures. At the same time a more rationalist exegetical literature was also being produced. Irenaeus was involved in the latter project and rejected the former even as he worked to define a biblical canon that excluded any new additions of "prophetically inspired" literature. Nevertheless, in his time prophetic and exegetical literature seems to have been produced alongside one another. An independent witness for this process might be Lucian of Samosata's *De morte Peregrini* 11. Lucian reports that Peregrinus was simultaneously a prophet, an exegete, and an author of sacred books. Frankfurter has written recently about the continuing legacy of

---

16 See N. Brox, *Irenäus von Lyon Adversus Haereses: Gegen die Häresien* (Freiburg, 1995) 3.220 n.42.

17 See H. Lausberg, *Handbook of Literary Rhetoric* (Leiden, 1998) 204–7, 260–63; *Rhet. Her.* 4.45: *abusio est quae verbo simili et propinquo pro certo et proprio abutitur ...*

18 N. Brox, "Die biblische Hermeneutik des Irenäus," in Idem, *Das Frühchristentum: Schriften zur historischen Theologie* (Freiburg, 2000) 233–54.

Jewish apocalyptic writing in early Christianity and the connection in that context between prophetic leadership, apocalyptic and gnostic symbolism, and the use of exegetical techniques to make the new productions, which were after all treated as the outflow of "revelations," fit with the existing traditions. Philo of Alexandria has also been studied in this context.[19] Though he and later followers of his exegetical approach rejected apocalyptic and millennialism, it was this increasing pressure to rationalize prophetic claims exegetically that made it possible to transform millennialist assertions into more coherent statements about history and the end of time. Victorinus of Poetovium's commentary on Revelation was to be, as it were, a prime witness for this process in the Latin west.

More generally, Clement of Alexandria and Origen are considered Philo's early Christian heirs. Both rejected millennialism outright, without even trying to mitigate the consequences this had for their concept of history. In *De principiis* 2.11.2, dating from around 220, Origen attacked attempts at historical exegeses of the millennium as superficial, crudely physical, and ultimately motivated by the desire for sensual pleasures. He singled out the sensual delights of the aesthetics of jewellery as described in Rev. 21:18–20 (the walls of the new Jerusalem made of precious stones). Origen does not call into question the Christianity of the millennialists. He concedes that they believe in Christ, yet they do so in a Jewish manner that fails properly to respond to the divine promises.[20]

As with Irenaeus, Origen's concern is how to interpret Scripture "properly." His rejection of millennialism is based on an understanding of the scriptural message that is fundamentally different to that of Irenaeus, one that is spiritual-intellectual, and not historical-literal. But what is also interesting is that Origen identifies the historical and literal understanding of scripture as "Jewish." His intention in doing so is not to inform his audience about Jewish exegesis. Rather, he highlights this particular characteristic of Jewish exegesis, whether authentic or not, in a purely polemical fashion. He seems to imply that any exegete, whether Jewish or Christian, who attributes historical significance to apocalyptic and millennial hopes, believes in the re-establishment of a Jewish state in Palestine with Jerusalem as capital. At the time, such would have been an utterly unrealistic and essentially utopian, indeed subversive and politically dangerous, idea.

There were authors who showed far less concern for these implications than Origen. In *Adversus Marcionem* 3.24 Tertullian argues, most firmly from scripture and its prophetic character, that the new Jerusalem must be understood as a real city descending from heaven, and uniquely he backs this claim with a report, confirmed apparently by an independent ("pagan") eyewitness account, of a vision of an image of the heavenly city hovering over Judaea like an ethereal spaceship, appearing and disappearing every morning for 40 days. Yet again, what was important for Tertullian was not just that this apparition was real but that it

[19] Frankfurter, "The Legacy," 129–30 and 144–5 (on Philo).

[20] Orig. *Princ.* 2.11.2: ... *Christo quidem credunt, Iudaico autem quodam sensu scripturas divinas intellegentes nihil ex his dignum divinis pollicitationibus praesumpserunt.*

confirmed a Montanist prophecy according to which such an image would appear in the sky as confirmation that the real Jerusalem would come down soon. Sure enough, around that time the claim was made that it had indeed arrived, although not in Judaea but in Asia Minor, in Pepouza.[21] But Tertullian was not only keen to demonstrate that specific events were fulfilments of Montanist prophecies, he was also interested in the wider link between Old Testament prophecies and their fulfilment in the New Testament, including events that still lay in the future, like those predicted in Revelation; and against Marcion in particular he emphasized what we already mentioned in connection with Irenaeus, and what we recognized as a fundamental principle in literary rhetoric concerning *peroratio* and *recapitulatio*, namely that the end of the story must match its beginning, that is that the end time will usher in another paradise. In fact, Tertullian's anti-Marcionite agenda drives the argument even further: The end is in some respect identical with the beginning, since in theological terms we are speaking of one and the same God: the creator is also the redeemer.[22]

Tertullian's example also demonstrates that the belief in the millennium is not inherently "Jewish," as Origen suggests, but that it came to be defined as Jewish in the process of being increasingly interpreted in spiritual terms. For Tertullian, it is still possible to apply the millennium spiritually to Christ and the church, and then understand the coming down of this "new Jerusalem" "literally," in the context of the 1,000-year scheme indicated in Revelation and handed down by Papias and others.

By contrast, Origen in his passage confirms the impression that the millennial rhetoric and literary imagery and the panorama it projects emerges from a particular exegetical approach. He writes that the millennialists develop their imagery logically, while Irenaeus had spoken of exegetical necessity. Origen of course follows the *consequentia* (*akolouthía*) of his own exegetical paradigm. He knows that millennialist exegesis has a rationale, but he rejects this rationale as sensual, whereas in his view the ultimate meaning of Scripture is spiritual.

Origen (*De principiis* 2.11.2) did not say against whom his refutation of millennialist sensuality was aimed. But his pupil Eusebius levels the charge against

---

[21] For the location see now W. Tabbernee, "Portals of the Montanist New Jerusalem: The Discovery of Pepouza and Thymion," *JECS* 11 (2003) 87–93; P. Lampe, "Die montanistischen Tymion und Pepouza im Lichte der neuen Tymioninschrift," *ZAC* 8 (2004) 498–512.

[22] Tert. *Adv. Marc.* 3.24: *De restitutione uero Iudaeae, quam et ipsi Iudaei ita ut describitur sperant, locorum et regionum nominibus inducti, quomodo allegorica interpretatio in Christum et in ecclesiam et habitum et fructum eius spiritaliter competat ... quia non de terrena, sed de caelesti promissione sit quaestio ... sed alio statu, utpote post resurrectionem in mille annos in ciuitate diuini operis Hierusalem caelo delatum ... constat enim ethnicis quoque testibus in Iudaea per dies quadraginta matutinis momentis ciuitatem de caelo pependisse ... haec ratio regni ...*

a certain Cerinthus, whom he dates to the time of Trajan (98–117).[23] He cites Gaius of Rome and Dionysius of Alexandria as witnesses and adds that already Irenaeus had condemned Cerinthus as a heretic. What he does not state, let alone attempt to explain, is that Irenaeus was himself a millennialist.[24] The situation was more complex than Eusebius would admit. Gaius seems to have suggested that Revelation was a fabrication of Cerinthus' and was falsely attributed by him to an apostle. This would have been John, the son of Zebedee, also the assumed author of the Fourth Gospel, though already Papias apparently suggested the existence of two Johns to disassociate the Fourth Gospel from Revelation; and on this point Dionysius, who agreed with Gaius in his condemnation of millennialism, followed Papias rather than Gaius, whom he considered a heretic.[25] But even Gaius, who rejected the canonicity of Revelation, found it worth a commentary, as reported by Hippolytus of Rome, who himself wrote a commentary on Revelation against Gaius that developed a detailed argument from chronology and built on the reckoning which we first encountered in the *Epistle of Barnabas*.[26] Far from being a playground for irrationalists, therefore, the book of Revelation and its millennialist message was a key text for defining the relationship between history and eschatology in early Christian biblical exegesis. Origen's rejection of millennialism stated clearly the alternatives: history or allegory. Gaius suggested a third possibility: excluding the book of Revelation from the canon. But in the end even he had to write a commentary on Revelation, or a work to that effect, in order to sustain his argument, thus paradoxically providing the book with renewed prominence.

Origen's position drew more fire than Eusebius' report suggests, notably from an Egyptian contemporary of Origen, Nepos of Arsinoe, who wrote a tract *Against the Allegorists*;[27] so too Methodius of Olympus, who died probably in 311, penned a "dialogue *On the Resurrection* [that] is clearly intended to be an apology for a more 'realistic' view of the risen body and its rewards than he understood Origen to have taken."[28] Later Apollinaris of Laodicea (ca. 310–ca. 390) is said to have continued along similar lines: the Old Testament prophecies must not be spiritualized, while the millennial passages of Rev. 20 must be taken into account.

---

23 See Eus. *HE* 3.28; for a recent appraisal, see M. Myllykoski, "Cerinthus," in A. Marjanen and P. Luomanen (eds.), *A Companion to Second-Century Christian "Heretics"* (Leiden, 2005) 213–46.

24 Iren. *Haer*. 1.26.1–3 "reports" that Cerinthus taught of a separation between God and the force that made the world, and between Jesus and Christ. But no mention is made of his millennialism.

25 For more detail on Gaius' position, see Myllykoski, "Cerinthus," 215–18, 237–42.

26 Compare Bietenhard, "The Millennial Hope," 18–20.

27 Daley, *The Hope of the Early Church*, 60–61.

28 Ibid., 62.

Jerome (*Vir. ill.* 18), who claims to have attended some of Apollinaris' lessons,[29] sees him belonging to the same tradition as Papias, Irenaeus, Tertullian, Victorinus of Poetovium, and Lactantius, and writes in his own commentary on Daniel that he took his calculations on the 70-week scheme from the works of the third-century chronicler Sextus Julius Africanus.[30] Indeed, in Tertullian we find a very similar line of thought: if the first resurrection was supposed to be the one from sin in baptism, and the second the one at the end, why would Revelation dwell on the number 1,000 years? Clearly, these 1,000 years had to be taken seriously, with the first rising at the start and the second at the end.[31] Interestingly, another anti-Origenist literalist and teacher of Jerome's, Epiphanius of Salamis, does not consider Apollinaris an outright millennialist,[32] but he nevertheless refutes his position by pointing to New Testament verses highlighting on the one hand the presence of the eschaton, and on the other the discontinuity between the present and the eschaton, for example Matt. 22:30 (after the resurrection people will no longer marry). He rejects in particular Apollinaris' apparent suggestion that there would have to be a revival of the Jewish law during the millennium because of Jesus' physical presence.[33]

The link between the perpetuation of the millennialist tradition and at the same time its "taming" through biblical exegesis continues to be important, but from the late third century onwards, there is an increasing "dialectical" convergence of the Origenian and the non-Origenian approaches. Jerome typifies this development. He was originally strongly influenced by Origen and, in his commentary on Ezekiel (11.36), considers the details of the new Jerusalem in Rev. 21 as allegorical references to the historical church, though, as we have seen, Tertullian did so as well, only to go on to say that it was this new Jerusalem, redefined as a Christian rather than a Jewish *políteuma*, that would descend from heaven. In his commentaries on Daniel and Isaiah, Jerome rejects millennial literalism as *fabula*, myth.[34] But at the same time he reports the millennial interpretations of Tertullian, Victorinus, Irenaeus, and Apollinaris as Christian tradition, not to be identified with the "earthly," "materialistic," "Jewish," hopes condemned by Origen.[35]

---

[29] Compare P. Jay, "Jérôme auditeur d'Apollinaire de Laodicée à Antioche," *REAug* 20 (1974) 36–41.

[30] Jer. *Comm. in Dan.* 9.24.

[31] Tert. *Res. carn.* 25: *Etiam in Apocalypsi Iohannis ordo temporum sternitur ... Cum igitur et status temporum ultimorum scripturae notent ... illa corporalis praeiudicetur ... cum vero et in ultimum tempus edicitur corporalis agnoscitur ... Cur enim iterum adnuntiaretur resurrectio eiusdem condicionis, id est spiritalis, cum aut nunc eam deceret expungi sine ulla differentia temporum aut tunc sub omni clausula temporum?*

[32] Epiph. *Adv. Haer.* 77.36.5; see Daley, *The Hope of the Early Church*, 80.

[33] Epiph. *Adv. Haer.* 77.36–8; compare Bietenhard, "The Millennial Hope," 23.

[34] Jer. *Comm. in Dan* 2.7.17: *Cessat ergo mille annorum fabula*: "the tale of the millennium is therefore null and void"; compare Jer. *Comm. in Is.* 16.59.14.

[35] For numerous references see Daley, *The Hope of the Early Church*, 102.

This is where the importance and key position of Victorinus of Poetovium's commentary on Revelation becomes readily apparent. Before Victorinus no Latin exegete wrote commentaries. Even in Greek the commentary was a very new genre. Hippolytus' commentary on Daniel is arguably the oldest extant biblical commentary in Greek. Significantly, it too was written in the context of the millennialist debate. Victorinus himself was originally a Greek speaker but had to adapt to a Latin environment. A lively millennial tradition already existed in both east and west, closely related to the development of biblical exegesis and hermeneutics. Some earlier works, such as Irenaeus', were originally written in Greek and later translated into Latin; others, such as Tertullian's, were written in Latin but were strongly influenced by Greek literature. But no Latin commentary had yet been written, not even a translation, not even of one of Origen's works.

Revelation was not the only biblical book on which Victorinus wrote a commentary, but it is the only one extant, albeit not in its entirety. The single fifteenth-century manuscript on which we ultimately rely for the text contains a version that is almost certainly abridged.[36] Of the other commentaries a single fragment on Matthew remains. Still, whatever the state of its preservation, Victorinus' *Apoc.* is the first methodical and intentional biblical commentary in Latin, and Victorinus's choice to explicate the book of Revelation is significant given the importance of the millennialist debate which we have just outlined.

Jerome makes much of Victorinus' dependence on Origen[37] and belittles him on this score as showing "*simplicitas*."[38] How does this square with Victorinus' millennialism? Is it possible for Victorinus to depend on Origen while remaining a millennialist through and through? For Rev. 20 and 21 he clearly takes literally the promise of the "first resurrection," in which the just will rise and rule with Christ, and then a "second resurrection" a thousand years later, when all the dead will rise to be judged. Then, he continues, following that judgment, there will be a "second death" for all the condemned sinners. This will be eternal punishment in hell.[39] The outlines of Victorinus' millennialism are somewhat less distinct than those of Papias or Irenaeus. First of all, Victorinus interprets allegorically several of the details of the New Jerusalem.[40] More importantly, however, Victorinus adapts from Irenaeus the technique of reading the book of Revelation with the recapitulation theme in mind. Victorinus was the first to apply it systematically to an exegesis of the book of Revelation, and the fact that he does so in the context of composing a commentary is crucial for the influence which he would have. Tyconius was to draw far-reaching conclusions from this. He used the *recapitulatio*

---

36 Rome, BAV, *Ottobon. Lat.* 3288 A (15th century); Rome, BAV, *Ottobon. Lat.* 3288 B (a 16th-century copy of A); Rome, BAV, *Lat.* 3586 (a 16th-century copy of B); compare Dulaey, *Victorin de Poetovio sur l'Apocalypse*, 44.

37 Jer. *Epp.* 61.2, 84.7; *Apol. adv. Ruf.* 3.14.

38 Jer. *Apol. adv. Ruf.* 1.2.

39 Victorin. *Apoc.* 20.2; compare Daley, *The Hope of the Early Church*, 66.

40 Victorin. *Apoc.* 21.6.

concept in his commentary on Revelation, but also, even more significantly, included it in his *Book of Rules*, where Augustine picked up on it when writing his *De doctrina christiana* and developing his philosophy of history in *De civitate dei*.[41] Interestingly, Jerome also tries to make Victorinus' millennialism work in a context in which it increasingly goes out of fashion in favour of an eschatology that still assumes there will be an apocalypse, but not one predictable through a detailed deciphering of Old Testament prophecies in combination with detailed studies of ancient chronology. Nevertheless, the history of the chronicle through the Middle Ages shows us that this approach too was modified for a new purpose, with Eusebius and Jerome as patrons.

In what follows a few examples will illustrate how Victorinus' approach remains similar to that of earlier millennialists, but also how it begins to differ. In *Apoc.* 4 Victorinus discusses Rev. 4:1, the theme of the "open door" and the voice that tells the narrator to "come up." The fact that the opening of the door is made an issue, Victorinus writes, indicates that it is thought of as having been closed. Something was hidden and is now revealed. The process of revelation has something to do with "going up," with "ascension." The ascension is Christ's ascension to the Father "with his body."[42] The voice, Victorinus stresses, that comes down is identical with the one going up. There are not two gods. Jesus is the Christ, and the Christ and the Father are one. This could be, as in the Tertullian passage, an allusion to a Marcionite position. But Victorinus pushes his message also in another direction. He indicates that as a Jew the narrator would have recognized the voice as that of Yahweh and would have identified him with Christ. The reference to the son of man and the candelabra is to Rev. 1:13. The candelabra refers to the temple, God's dwelling place on earth. Now, Victorinus concludes this passage, "he" (the narrator) "reworks" (*recolit*) the Old Testament, which is God's word in the form of "similes" or "similitudes," "likenesses," "imitations," and through the book of Revelation, he "summarizes" (*coniungit*) all the earlier prophets and thus makes the scriptures accessible (*adaperit*). The proper meaning of *coniungit* here is "to link up" or "join," but the technique to which Victorinus is referring is more than just that. It is also Irenaean *recapitulatio*, the idea that the summary renders the same content as the main body of the work, only in a more accessible, concise, and concentrated form. There are several passages in Irenaeus that link *coniungere* with *recapitulatio* in this way.[43]

While Victorinus took this latter idea from Irenaeus, and while he is influenced in other ways by Irenaeus, not least in his continued adherence to millennial views, the notion that the book of Revelation in particular constitutes a *recapitulatio* of

---

41 Pollmann, "Apocalypse Now!?," 42 n.30.

42 Compare Iren. *Haer.* 3.16.18. Victorinus perhaps takes the image from Acts 1:9.

43 E.g. Iren. *Haer.* 3.22.3: *Propter hoc Lucas genealogiam ... ostendit, finem coniungens initio et significans quoniam ipse est qui omnes gentes exinde ab Adam dispersas et universas linguas et generationes hominum cum ipso Adam in semetipso recapitulatus est.*

the entirety of Scripture seems to be his. It is with this idea that he points beyond earlier millennialist positions and that he influenced not only Jerome, but, more momentously, Tyconius and, through Tyconius, Augustine.

Victorinus' millennialism, his interpretation of the book of Revelation in a very concrete, historical, literal sense, relevant to the situation in which he and his church found themselves, is at least in part influenced by this situation, namely the persecution under Valerian (most probably). This is clear from *Apoc.* 7 on Rev. 7:2, "'an angel descending from the east,' which means the prophet Elijah, who will anticipate (*anticipaturus est*) the times of the Antichrist to restore the churches and to shield them from the intolerable persecution. We read about this in the unfolding (*in apertione*) of the preaching of both the Old and the New Testament." Examples from Malachi and Matthew follow. Thus Victorinus contrasts not only the Old Testament with the New but also Revelation with the rest of the Bible.

An example reminiscent of the earlier passage from Irenaeus, where Victorinus relates a fuller to a less full explanation, is found in *Apoc.* 8.2:

> The trumpet signifies the word of power, and it is fitting that what is expressed by the word "trumpet" is repeated by the expression "phials"; but not because something has happened twice but because what was going to happen in the future was first being decreed by God in order that it may happen. It is for that reason that it was said twice. Therefore, what is expressed in the word "trumpet" in a lesser sense (*minus*) is expressed in the word "phials" in a fuller sense (*propensius*). And we need not be concerned about the order in which the events are presented; for the sevenfold holy spirit, after having gone through all the events till the most recent times and even to the end, recapitulates (*redit rursus*) the same times again and supplements (*supplet*) what he has previously presented in an insufficient (*minus*) way.

As mentioned earlier, in the view of traditionalist rhetoricians it was important that no additional content be added to the *recapitulatio*. The summing up should merely repeat the themes of the speech as announced in the *prooemium*, nothing more, nothing less. But here, it seems, something is revealed in the end which is not contained in the earlier parts of the biblical narrative. There seems to be here a glimpse of a new and more open approach, one that relativizes the belief in the millennium.

Crucial here is that, although Victorinus takes history, that is to say the order of events in time, very seriously, he does so with the mind of a rhetorician. The order of time is subject to a higher order. This idea comes out emphatically in *Apoc.* 11.5:

> Thus it is necessary to study the prophetic text attentively and with the greatest care and understand that the holy spirit presents his material at first with rough brush strokes (*sparse*) and reverses the order of events progressing to the most

> recent times only to return again to that which went before [in order to fill in the gaps], presenting an event twice, even though it only happened once ... Thus to interpret the sequence of events which the book of Revelation relates is not so much to explain their chronological sequence but the logic (*ratio*) of their order of presentation.

This line of argument could seriously undermine the millennialist cause. While Victorinus, as can be seen from *Apoc.* 8.2, was still wedded to a literalist understanding of the millennium as spelled out in Rev. 20, Jerome in his revised edition of *Apoc.* tried to purge it by saying that the number 1,000 just means "many" in the sense in which it is used in Ps. 104/105:8: "The word which he issued to a thousand generations."[44] But unlike Victorinus, Jerome disregarded the other elements of the prophecy of Rev. 20, namely that the 1,000 years are set between the two resurrections, and that the first resurrection is a reward for martyrdom. Considering that Victorinus wrote his commentary in a time of persecution, it is conceivable that he was far more reluctant to play fast and loose with the millennialist content of Rev. 20 than later commentators, or commentators with a more allegorist agenda.

One author who did develop the *recapitulatio* idea further was Tyconius. His commentary on Revelation is not extant,[45] but what we have of him is a *Book of Rules*, a methodology for biblical exegesis, rule six of which deals with the figure of *recapitulatio.*[46] It summarizes much of what can be found already in Irenaeus and Victorinus: that the Bible repeats itself in saying the same things in different ways and in different degrees of completeness and intensity; that chronology is not the final criterion for understanding events narrated in the Bible; that certain events which are told as having occurred only once, could in fact happen repeatedly until the end time; and therefore that even though we must still take Revelation seriously in terms of its eschatological message, we cannot with certainty apply its numbers and chronological elements to real history. Thus Tyconius does not allegorize or completely spiritualize the message of Revelation in the way Origen suggested, but he does say that we cannot apply its prophecies to specific events in history, for example to a specific persecution, as Victorinus seems to have been inclined to do.

The aim of this paper has been to draw some links between the phenomenon of early Christian millennialism and exegetical strategies aimed at retaining the literal meaning of Scripture while providing believers with an eschatological perspective that satisfied their hopes even as it remains rational and realistic. One group, including Justin, Irenaeus, and others, adapted the literary-rhetorical concept of

---

44 Jer. *Victorin. Apoc.* 20 (*PLS* 1.165).

45 For its history and reception, see K. Steinhauser, *The Apocalypse Commentary of Tyconius: A History of Its Reception and Influence* (Frankfurt, 1989).

46 See F.C. Burkitt, *The Book of Rules of Tyconius* (Cambridge, 1894) 66–70; W.S. Babcock, *Tyconius: The Book of Rules* (Atlanta, 1989) 108–14.

recapitulatio for this purpose; another, among them Origen and later Eusebius, rejected millennialism outright. Against this background the third-century Latin author Victorinus of Poetovium shows himself as an important mediator between the two extreme positions. Having been influenced by both Origen and Irenaeus, and also having been the first Latin author to write a commentary on Revelation, indeed the author of the first Latin biblical commentary extant, he occupies a key position in the development of Christian historical thinking, as his influence on Jerome and Tyconius (and through Tyconius on Augustine) shows. Significantly, he pre-dates Eusebius and thus marks the beginning of a distinctly western eschatological tradition that attempted to harness religious power with the force of reason.

Chapter 3

Clementissimus Imperator: Power, Religion, and Philosophy in Ambrose's *De obitu Theodosii* and Seneca's *De clementia*

Giacomo Raspanti
Università degli Studi di Palermo

Duval's observation from 30 years ago that Ambrose's *De obitu Theodosii* (*Obit. Theod.*) is a political discourse in the context of funerary liturgy remains valid today.[1] In February 395,[2] on the fortieth day (*quadragesima*) after Theodosius' death, the bishop delivered this oration. In this paper I shall examine how Ambrose used this speech, which I shall argue he modelled on Seneca's *De clementia*, to highlight how the deceased emperor's political policies arose from his virtue of clemency and why this made him, both in theory and in practice, an excellent ruler.[3]

---

1 Y.-M. Duval, "Formes profanes et formes bibliques dans les oraisons funèbres de saint Ambroise," in M. Fuhrmann (ed.), *Christianisme et formes littéraires de l'antiquité tardive en Occident* (Geneva, 1977) 235–301 at 274.

2 A.V. Nazzaro, "Ambrogio vescovo di Milano e l'imperatore Teodosio I il Grande," in R. Uglione (ed.), *Atti del Convegno nazionale di studi: Intellettuali e potere nel mondo antico, Torino, 22–23–24 aprile 2002* (Alessandria, 2003) 259–301 at 267.

3 According to G. Bonamente, "Potere politico ed autorità religiosa nel *De obitu Theodosii* di Ambrogio," in *Chiesa e società dal secolo IV ai nostri giorni: Studi storici in onore di P. Ilarino da Milano* 1 (Rome, 1979) 83–133 at 86–7, *Obit.Theod.* cannot be considered a political discourse reworked into the typical form of the sacerdotal homily; if anything it is a brief treatise on political theology. Like Duval, M. Biermann, *Die Leichenreden des Ambrosius von Mailand: Rhetorik Predigt Politik* (Stuttgart, 1995) 143–50, emphasizes the close connection between the exegesis of biblical texts read during funerals and the political and religious themes of Ambrose's discourse.

Clemency in *De obitu Theodosii*

Scholars appear to have overlooked a motif that pervades *Obit.Theod.*, Ambrose's insistence on the *clementia* of the deceased emperor.[4] The opening chapters centre on the many instances of clemency or, more precisely of indulgence (*indulgentia)*,[5] that marked Theodosius' policies in his final months so emphatically that they became the very emblem of his reign and the noblest inheritance he bequeathed to his children.[6] In the preamble the bishop addresses the dead man as *clementissimus imperator* and recalls his ability to temper the hardships of the world with indulgence, even to the extent of preventing some crimes from being punished.[7] The emperor's indulgence first showed itself in the political and legal fields: after the victory at the River Frigidus Theodosius granted amnesty to his rivals who, led by Eugenius, had taken up arms against him,[8] and according to Ambrose he was distressed by the fact that these acts of clemency had been unsuccessful.[9] Then the bishop recounts a deed that gives further evidence of the deceased's clemency,

---

4 See F.E. Consolino, "L'*optimus princeps* secondo Ambrogio: virtù imperatorie e cristiane nelle orazioni funebri per Valentiniano e Teodosio," *RSI* 96 (1984) 1025–45 at 1041; M. Sordi, "La concezione politica di Ambrogio," in G. Bonamente and A. Nestori (eds.), *I Cristiani e l'Impero nel IV secolo: Colloquio sul Cristianesimo nel mondo antico (1987)* (Macerata, 1988) 143–54 at 150; Biermann, *Die Leichenreden*, 104–10; J. Ernesti, *Princeps christianus und Kaiser aller Römer: Theodosius der Große im Lichte zeitgenössicher Quellen* (Paderborn, 1998) 205–7.

5 F.E. Consolino, "Teodosio e il ruolo del principe cristiano dal *De obitu* di Ambrogio alle storie ecclesiastiche," *CrSt* 15 (1994) 257–77 at 259: "Questa *indulgentia*, che Ambrogio considera di ispirazione cristiana, non differisce negli effetti pratici dalla *clementia* degli imperatori pagani, poiché sul piano politico si è concretizzata nel perdono agli avversari."

6 See the *indulgentiarum hereditas* of *Obit.Theod.* 5 (*CSEL* 73.374). The text referred to for quotations (including page number) is: O. Faller (ed.), *Sancti Ambrosii opera: De Obitu Theodosii, CSEL* 73.7 (Wien, 1955). M. Zelzer, "Überlieferung und Rezeption der Kaiserreden des Ambrosius," in B. Gain, P. Jay, and G. Nauroy (eds.), *Chartae caritatis: Études de patristique et d'antiquité tardive en hommage à Yves-Marie Duval* (Paris, 2004) 113–25, demonstrates that Faller's reconstruction of the complex manuscript tradition of *Obit.Theod.* is erroneous. Faller supposes that the oration was published separately, together with the two other funeral orations, and not, as Zelzer writes, in the tenth book of Ambrose's letters. Whatever the case, until a new *stemma codicum* is devised, we must rely on Faller's text.

7 *Obit.Theod.* 1 (*CSEL* 73.371).

8 A. Borgo, "*Clementia*: studio di un campo semantico," *Vichiana* 14 (1985) 25–73 at 38 and 58, observes not only that there is a close connexion between clemency and the victorious outcome of a conflict, but also that the concept of clemency "è sempre stato legato per i Romani al potere, ed in particolare ad un potere acquisito con le armi … Dunque, non poteva essere clemente se non chi detenesse il potere, ed il potere nasceva solo dalla vittoria in guerra: la clemenza, dunque, era soprattutto clemenza del vincitore."

9 *Obit.Theod.* 4 (*CSEL* 73.373).

this time in his fiscal policy:[10] he promised to revive the provision made on 12 June 393 to reduce the grain tax.[11] Analysing the first five chapters of *Obit.Theod.* we note that the term *indulgentia* occurs four times and that these instances are grouped around the opening, that is, the most striking part of the speech. They serve as advertising slogans for the policy of the emperor that has just died, but also as a cue to his successor to continue these policies.

Starting at chapter 12 Ambrose describes *misericordia* (mercy), a virtue similar to *clementia*, as the most important feature of Theodosius' politics. He reflects on the arrogant nature of power and on the exceptionality of an emperor who does not yield to it. Evidently for Ambrose and his audience it seemed normal for the imperial authority to resort to revenge and the use of terror.[12] The antidote for this tendency is mercy, a natural feeling of compassion that becomes simultaneously a political virtue. Indeed Ambrose clarifies that Theodosius paradoxically transformed his ire and indignation into an opportunity for mercy and a remedy for the guilty in that the request for clemency, not separated from an admission of guilt, offered him a justification for rational political action motivated by clemency. This virtue made it possible for the emperor to bind his subjects to himself by a feeling of devotion instead of terror.[13] Moreover, Ambrose points out that only the correction of his subjects and not the cruel infliction of punishment was of concern to Theodosius, who preferred paternalistic reproach as a means to achieve his goal of pacifying the Empire.[14]

Ambrose claims that Theodosius' clemency stemmed from his recognition of the precariousness of the human condition: as a Christian, he knew that he, like his subjects, was dependent on God and thus that he had to feel pity for human weakness, from which he was not himself immune.[15] The importance that this theme assumes in the Ambrosian reflection on power and political clemency is directly related to the prominence that Psalm 114, read during the ceremony in honour of Theodosius, has in *Obit.Theod.*[16] The character of Theodosius is made to

10 See J. Gaudement, "*Indulgentia principis,*" *Conferenze Romanistiche* (Milano, 1967) 2.21–2.

11 *Obit.Theod.* 5 (*CSEL* 73.373–4): See Biermann, *Die Leichenreden*, 181.

12 *Obit.Theod.* 12 (*CSEL* 73.377).

13 *Obit.Theod.* 13–14 (*CSEL* 73.377–8).

14 *Obit.Theod.* 13–14 (*CSEL* 73.378): *Hanc vocem eius homines amplius quam poenam timebant, quod tanta imperator ageret verecundia, ut mallet sibi homines religione quam timore adstringere. ... Satis est in indignatione laudem clementiae repperire quam ira in ultionem excitari.*

15 *Obit.Theod.* 16 (*CSEL* 73.379): *Bonum est misericors homo, qui, dum aliis subvenit, sibi consulit et in alieno remedio vulnera sua curat. Agnoscit enim se esse hominem, qui novit ignoscere.* See also *Obit.Theod.* 24–6 (*CSEL* 73.383–4). See B. Gerbenne, "Modèles bibliques pour un empereur: le De obitu Theodosii d'Ambrose de Milan," in *Rois et reines de la Bible au miroir de Pères* (Strasbourg, 1999) 161–76 at 167–9.

16 See Duval, "Formes profanes," 274–6, and Consolino, "L'*optimus princeps*," 1039.

comment on the incipit of Ps. 114 and to explain that he manifested the Scriptural verse in his own person: the motif of charity, emerging from the exordium of Ps. 114, is therefore related by the orator to the central theme of clemency toward enemies.[17]

In the third part of *Obit.Theod.*[18] Ambrose outlines a genealogy of rulers who resemble Theodosius in maintaining the sort of good government characteristic of recent history. Gratian figures alongside him as another example of an ideal emperor. Among the virtues that enabled these two men to be competent and praiseworthy rulers, pride of place is given to mercy: Ambrose speaks of a *misericordiae consortium*, a sort of tacit dynastic pact formed around a common mode of political action based on moderation and compassion.[19] Contrasted with these two rulers are the usurpers Maximus and Eugenius, whom Ambrose deems worthy of eternal condemnation because they blatantly disregarded the cardinal virtues of Roman culture and society, *fides*, *pietas*, and *clementia*.[20] But in this genealogy of ideal *principes* the forerunner, according to Ambrose, is Constantine.[21] After he had died, Theodosius joined Constantine in the celestial kingdom and thus received his reward for fidelity to the heritage—that is to say, the Christian faith—that Constantine had handed down to his successors.[22] Moreover, in keeping with the main themes of *Obit.Theod.*, the line of continuity connecting Constantine, Gratian and Theodosius is apparent in the political and moral qualities the Christian faith instilled in them.

At this point comes the famous excursus on the "finding of the cross."[23] Here the story is told about how Constantine's mother Helena, guided by the Holy Spirit, travels to Golgotha, finds the nails of the True Cross, and sends them to Constantine, one for his crown and the other for his horse's bridle.[24]

---

17 *Obit.Theod.* 17 (*CSEL* 73.380).

18 On the subdivision of the oration into parts see Ernesti, *Princeps christianus*, 202–27.

19 *Obit.Theod.* 39 (*CSEL* 73.391–2).

20 *Obit.Theod.* 39 (*CSEL* 73.392).

21 See G. Bonamente, "Costantino santo," *CrSt* 27 (2006) 735–68 at 765–8.

22 *Obit.Theod.* 40 (*CSEL* 73.392). See Bonamente, "Potere politico," 124; M. Stoppini, "Da Ambrogio a Giovanni Crisostomo: una reinterpretazione di Teodosio il Grande," *AFLPer(class)* n.s. 19 (1997–2000) 271–84 at 278; V. Aiello, "Il tempo del potere negli auspici di Ambrogio vescovo di Milano," in L. De Salvo and A. Sindoni (eds.), *Tempo sacro e tempo profano: Visione laica e visione cristiana del tempo e della storia* (Soveria Mannelli, 2002) 117–30 at 126–9.

23 *Obit.Theod.* 41–51 (*CSEL* 73.393–8).

24 *Obit.Theod.* 47 (*CSEL* 73.396). On Helena in the excursus see A.V. Nazzaro, "Incidenza biblico-cristiana e classica nella coerenza delle immagini ambrosiane," in L.F. Pizzolato and M. Rizzi (eds.), *Nec timeo mori: Atti del Congresso internazionale di studi ambrosiani nel XVI centenario della morte di sant'Ambrogio (1997)* (Milan, 1998) 313–39 at 325–7.

For Ambrose this episode does not represent the redemption of the Roman Empire as an institution and the celebration of the beginning of the Christian Empire[25] as much as it does the setting of a new political course inside the Empire once a Christian was able to be emperor and to renew, by virtue of his faith in God, the ideals of the Roman political tradition. The bishop's reflections in the excursus focus on Constantine's profound interior "*metanoia*" and the changes that his faith brought about in society.[26] These changes concerning Christians and non-Christians manifested themselves not only in the religious sphere, with the cessation of the persecutions, but also in the political sphere, in the management of imperial power. That is to say, the emperor, who models himself on Christ, exercises moderation in his judgment and does not rule harshly or unjustly.[27] The moderation always hoped for in Augustus' successors represents the new contribution of Christianity to the Empire in the political vision of the *Obit.Theod.*, for faith in Christ (ideally) is a guarantee that moderation marks every measure taken by emperors toward their subjects.

In chapters 50 and 51, two of the most important chapters in the entire funeral oration, Ambrose contrasts the vices of bad emperors of the past and the moral excellence of Christian emperors. For instance, he cites examples of pagan emperors (Caligula and Nero) who in the audience's imagination evoked tyrannical misgovernment and were symbols of the failure of pagan culture and philosophy to manage power morally.[28] In contradistinction to them Ambrose cites the Christian emperors Gratian and Theodosius, who were heirs to Constantine's personal and public *metanoia*.[29] Whereas formerly emperors were known for insolence, dissoluteness, and wicked tyranny, now they conduct themselves in a

---

25 This is the opinion of Sordi, "La concezione politica," 146; see also Eadem, "La morte di Teodosio e il *De Obitu Theodosii* di Ambrogio," *ACD* 36 (2000) 131–6 at 132. Very close to Sordi's are the arguments of Ernesti, *Princeps christianus*, 226–7.

26 M. Rizzi, "Le teologie politiche," in G. Alberigo, G. Ruggiero, and R. Rusconi (eds.), *Il Cristianesimo: Grande atlante* (Turin, 2005) 1057, must be correct when he speaks not of Ambrose extolling the Christian sovereign, a representative of Christ like the Constantine of Eusebius, but of Theodosius as a Christian that has become sovereign or of a Constantine as a sovereign that has become a Christian.

27 *Obit.Theod.* 48 (*CSEL* 73.396): *Recte in capite clavus, ut ubi sensus est, ibi praesidium. In vertice corona, in manibus habena: corona de cruce, ut fides luceat, habena quoque de cruce, ut potestas regat sitque iusta moderatio, non iniusta praeceptio.*

28 *Obit.Theod.* 50–51 (*CSEL* 73.398): *Sed quaero: Quare sanctum super frenum (Zach. 14:20), nisi ut imperatorum insolentiam refrenaret, comprimeret licentiam tyrannorum, qui quasi equi in libidines adhinnirent, quod liceret illis adulteria inpune committere? Quae Neronum, quae Caligularum ceterorumque probra conperimus, quibus non fuit sanctum super frenum!*

29 *Obit.Theod.* 51 (*CSEL* 73.398): *Exuerunt se camo perfidiae, susceperunt frena deuotionis et fidei ... Inde reliqui principes Christiani—praeter unum Iulianum, qui salutis suae reliquit auctorem, dum philosophiae se dedit errori—inde Gratianus et Theodosius.*

morally upright fashion and submit to God's mandate to love one's neighbour.[30] The polarity between tyrannical and Christian rulers that emerges at the end of the excursus on the "finding of the cross" dominates the last five chapters of *Obit. Theod.*, and in particular chapters 52, 53, and 56. The model emperors, Gratian and Theodosius, are not covered with a purple mantle, a garment typical of kings but also a symbol of lust and tyrannical arrogance, but with glory obtained through the merits of virtues, namely indulgence and clemency.[31] Significantly, at the end of chapter 53 the virtues of temperance, tolerance, and mercy, expressed through the application to Theodosius of the biblical verset, "He bore the heavy yoke," achieve the highest political outcome possible for an emperor, that is to say keeping tyranny at bay.[32] In the peroration the political rhetoric summarizes Theodosius' earthly achievements and thereby suggests a proper course for his successors: Theodosius is the victorious emperor who has freed Italy of tyrants, and consequently he deserves one of the most traditional and solemn titles of ancient Rome, that of *libertatis auctor*.[33]

Reminiscences of Seneca's *De clementia* in *De obitu Theodosii*

There is no doubt but that the primary intertext of *Obit.Theod.* is Scripture[34] and that Ambrose, convinced that this book is the fundamental source of all knowledge and virtue, would never have wanted to give the impression that his funeral oration for Theodosius was inspired by pagan sources. Yet his insistent evocation of Theodosius' acts of clemency does not seem to be a simple regurgitation of official imperial ideology.[35] Rather Ambrose appears to have desired to connect his oration

---

30 See Biermann, *Die Leichenreden*, 187–8.

31 *Obit.Theod.* 52 (*CSEL* 73.398–9): *Ambulabunt plane ac maxime Gratianus et Theodosius, prae ceteris "principes," non iam armis militum, sed meritis suis tecti, non purpureum habitum, sed amictum induti gloriae. Qui cum hic delectarentur absolutione multorum, quanto magis illic pepercisse se pluribus recensendo pietatis suae recordatione mulcentur.*

32 *Obit.Theod.* 53 (*CSEL* 73.399).

33 *Obit.Theod.* 56 (*CSEL* 73.401).

34 See especially Gerbenne, "Modèles bibliques," 161–71; see also Biermann, *Die Leichenreden*, 143–50.

35 One certainly cannot rule out the relationship between *Obit.Theod.* and Latin panegyrics, which is demonstrated by A. Lovino, "Su alcune affinità tra il Panegirico per Teodosio di Pacato Drepanio e il *De obitu Theodosii* di Sant'Ambrogio," *VetChr* 26 (1989) 371–6 at 376. Also useful are the considerations by F.E. Consolino, "Il discorso funebre tra Oriente e Occidente: Gregorio di Nazianzo, Gregorio di Nissa, Ambrogio," in F. Conca, I. Gualandri, and G. Lozza (eds.), *Politica cultura e religione nell'impero romano (secoli IV–VI) tra Oriente e Occidente: Atti del II Convegno dell'Associazione di Studi Tardoantichi (1990)* (Napoli, 1993) 171–84 at 182–3, who emphasizes two primary differences between the *Obit. Theod.* and a panegyric: first, Ambrose was addressing the young Honorius and his oration

with a specific text from the early imperial period, Seneca's *De clementia*, which must have represented a theoretical and literary point of reference for his main theme.[36] Let us consider, then, the possible genetic relationship between these two works.

The pervasiveness of the theme of clemency in *Obit.Theod.* is the first generic clue that would seem to support the hypothesis that Ambrose used Seneca's writing as a point of reference. Seneca states: "Clemency is proper to no one more than to the king and the prince."[37] He says further:

> Does not he who behaves according to the divine nature, being beneficent, generous and powerful for good aims, have a place close to the gods? It is right to aspire to that, to imitate that, to be considered *Maximus* in such a way as to be considered at the same time *Optimus*.[38]

It is at least plausible to imagine that Ambrose did not want simply to praise Theodosius according to the conventions of panegyric, but also that he hoped to evoke the authority of the *De clementia*, thus sustaining a political debate rooted in a past that was remote but still fundamental for the Empire.

Secondly, there emerges a more precise correspondence between the goals of clemency as envisaged by the two authors. Ambrose's statement at the beginning of *Obit.Theod.* that Theodosius' clemency softens the hardships of the world finds a possible parallel in Seneca's discussion of the effects that appeasement and pacification by an emperor's clemency produce in those that surround him.[39] In short, for Seneca, as for Ambrose, a tranquil empire is an empire in which the emperor is clement and inclined to forgiveness.[40]

From a strictly political point of view, a common vision of the aims of an emperor's power and even certain similarities in the historical circumstances unite

---

is much more authoritative, for he proposes to relate what God and his church expect of a *pius princeps*; second, Ambrose was speaking as bishop from his pulpit and thus for a much wider audience than most panegyrists.

36 The question of the presence of Seneca in Ambrose's works is still open. M.-P. Labrique, "Ambroise de Milan et Sénèque: à propos du *De excessu fratris II*," *Latomus* 50 (1991) 409–18 at 409–10, holds that, while it is certain that Ambrose knew Cicero's works, the same does not apply to Seneca, whose influence on the bishop of Milan is far from being recognized by everyone. Labrique defines as "unquestionable" the presence of Senecan reminiscences in *De excessu fratris II* (418).

37 *Clem.* 1.3.3 (Malaspina, 154–5). References are to the chapter, paragraph and page in E. Malaspina (ed.), *L. Annaei Senecae De clementia libri duo: Prolegomeni, testo critico e commento* (Alessandria, 2002).

38 *Clem.* 1.19.9 (Malaspina,174).

39 *Clem.* 1.16.1 (Malaspina, 170): *Haec clementia principem decet; quocumque venerit, mansuetiora omnia faciat.*

40 Cf. *Clem.* 1.13.1–2 (Malaspina, 167), and *Obit.Theod.* 4 (*CSEL* 73.373), 10–11 (*CSEL* 73.376–7), 56 (*CSEL* 73.400–401).

these two works: both authors address a very young prince—Nero and Honorius, respectively—who faced major risks from negative influences at court and even from possible uprisings. Another theme shared by *De clementia* and *Obit.Theod.* is also of relevance in that Seneca declares that clemency not only ensures peace and security for empires but also permits kings to possess an inheritance to hand down to their sons and grandsons (the kingdom); the power of tyrants, by contrast, is brief and does not have the privilege of heirs.[41] Seneca therefore establishes a close connection between the political virtue of *clementia* and the *haereditas regni.* This theme would also have struck Ambrose, who was interested in the succession of the Theodosian line. In other words, his insistence on Theodosius' clemency arises from his awareness that this virtue permitted Honorius and Arcadius the possibility of being heirs and, moreover, only the same virtue would permit them to maintain their power.

In *Clem.* 1.11.4 Seneca points out the difference between the tyrant's cruelty and the king's need to punish, and he condemns the tyrant's lack of self-control in the management of politics and his total subservience to the desire for pleasure (*voluptas*). Just as Ambrose portrays terror as the common face of power,[42] Seneca's Nero is made to admit that *potentia per terrores* is the usual habit of great empires.[43] Therefore, the virtue of self-control and the ability to refrain from ire is unusual. In short, the desire expressed to see moderation as a means to a proper use of power[44] is directly connected to the awareness, in both Seneca and Ambrose, that unrestrained ire is the most natural feeling for anyone who holds absolute power. It deprives the exercise of power of its rationality and fosters the desire for revenge, which is detrimental to the social order. Just as the ideal Senecan emperor does not transform indignation at seeing injustices into ire but rather overcomes it with the generosity of indulgence,[45] so also Ambrose's Theodosius was able

---

41 *Clem.* 1.11.4 (Malaspina, 165): *Clementia ergo non tantum honestiores sed tutiores praestat ornamentumque imperiorum est simul et certissima salus. Quid enim est, cur reges consenuerint liberisque ac nepotibus tradiderint regna, tyrannorum exsecrabilis ac brevis potestas sit? Quid interest inter tyrannum ac regem ..., nisi quod tyranni in voluptatem saeviunt, reges non nisi ex causa ac necessitate?* Cf. *Obit.Theod.* 5–6 (*CSEL* 73.373–4).

42 See *Obit.Theod.* 12 (*CSEL* 73.377).

43 *Clem.* 1.1.3 (Malaspina, 151–2); see also *Clem.* 1.7.3 (Malaspina, 159). Biermann, *Die Leichenreden*, 115, observes that the formal choice made by Seneca at the beginning of the treatise to have Nero himself speak of clemency might be compared to Ambrose's decision to have Theodosius comment on Psalm 114 on love and mercy. For Biermann, however, this does not necessarily imply Ambrose's dependence on Seneca.

44 Compare *Obit.Theod.* 12 and the definitions of *clementia* in *Clem.* 2.3.1–2 (Malaspina, 182–3).

45 *Clem.* 1.5.5–6 (Malaspina, 157–8): *Magni autem animi proprium est placidum esse tranquillumque et iniurias atque offensiones superne despicere. Muliebre est furere in ira, ferarum vero et <ne> generosarum quidem praemordere et urguere proiectos ... Non decet regem saeva nec inexorabilis ira (non multum enim supra eum eminet, cui se irascendo exaequat).*

to restrain the impulses of ire with indulgence and to seek after *laus clementiae* instead of being induced to vengeance by wrath.[46]

But if in *De clementia* and *Obit.Theod.* there is a common call for moderation, self-control and a political use of clemency, the philosophical and cultural distance between the two authors is nevertheless evident. The Senecan emperor looks on offences with arrogant superiority when he refrains from ire. He exercises indulgence in order to rise above the masses and presumes to become like the gods in that the *sapiens*, like the gods, looks on the precariousness of human society with absolute emotional detachment.[47] The Ambrosian *homo*, by contrast, is aware of the fragility of the human condition, and without aspiring to divinity he takes pity on other men just as he does on himself and does not regard foolish men with contempt.[48] If by Seneca's reckoning *clementia* is a rational virtue of the good emperor who follows the model of the Stoic *sapiens,* the *misericordia/indulgentia* that Ambrose advocates has a significant emotional component that Seneca explicitly condemns in the second book of *De clementia* because passions must not in any way disturb the sage.

Clemency, according to Seneca, cannot be compared with *misericordia,* which is a vice of the soul and deviates from the truth.[49] For virtuous men appreciate clemency but avoid mercy, a feeling of pity that is typical of silly old women who are affected by the worst criminals' tears.[50] Removing from himself this irrational and emotional component, the sage will make sure he does willingly and with noble-mindedness everything that those who feel pity do.[51]

Unlike Seneca, Ambrose emphasizes that clemency is the necessary pity felt by the emperor for human misery. It is the awareness of his own and other men's precariousness that must lead him to trust in God and not to be presumptuous about his own virtue, as if he aimed to achieve the detached condition of the gods. Moreover, this does not involve a rejection of justice in the name of *miseratio,* compassionate charity and forgiveness.[52] In Ambrose's thought, mercy and justice are indissolubly connected: or rather, mercy is justice itself because it restores the

46 *Obit.Theod.* 13–14 (*CSEL* 73.377–8).

47 See *Clem.* 1.5.7 (Malaspina, 158).

48 See *Obit.Theod.* 16 at n.15

49 *Clem.* 2.4.4 (Malaspina, 184).

50 *Clem.* 2.5.1 (Malaspina, 184): *Ergo quemadmodum religio deos colit, superstitio violat, ita clementiam mansuetudinemque omnes boni viri praestabunt, misericordiam autem vitabunt: est enim vitium pusilli animi ad speciem alienorum malorum succidentis. Itaque pessimo cuique familiarissima est, anus et mulierculae sunt, quae lacrimis nocentissimorum mouentur, quae, si liceret, carcerem effringerent. Misericordia non causam, sed fortunam spectat; clementia rationi accedit.*

51 At *Clem.* 2.6.2–3 his great generosity and humanity toward all kinds of needs and social problems is delineated.

52 *Obit.Theod.* 25–6 (Malaspina, 383–4).

poor and guilty to that right to goods (including material ones) that God puts at everyone's disposal equally.[53]

Conclusions

Let us now consider why Ambrose emphasized Theodosius' clemency and why he chose to echo the *De clementia* in his *Obit.Theod.* The historical and political circumstances surrounding this funeral oration must be borne in mind. Ambrose's text was addressed to the young Honorius[54] and more broadly to the court that, together with Stilicho, surrounded him.[55] He took the opportunity provided by Theodosius' funeral to exhort Honorius, and those who were going to counsel him, to continue the political legacy of his father. To this end, Ambrose found the Senecan theme of the interdependence between *clementia principis* and *haereditas regni*[56] to be useful for his purposes. Additionally, we must consider the presence of soldiers at the exequies, whom Ambrose asks not to be ungrateful to Theodosius' sons and to show them the loyalty that they owed their father.[57]

In the opening chapters of the oration and especially in the excursus on "the finding of the cross" there are recurrent allusions to Theodosius' efforts to thwart challenges to his sovereignty. The usurpers over whom the emperor had triumphed a few months before his death were Eugenius and his supporters Flavianus and Arbogast, who had sought the support of the pagan aristocracy and had fought for the traditional gods against Theodosius' false god.[58] We cannot help but be reminded that the clash with non-Christians, the death of Eugenius,

---

53 See H. Pétré, "Misericordia. Histoire du mot et de l'idée du paganisme au christianisme," *REL* 12 (1934) 376–89 at 387.

54 *Obit.Theod.* 3 (*CSEL* 73.372).

55 L. Cracco Ruggini, "Il 397: l'anno della morte di Ambrogio," in L.F. Pizzolato and M. Rizzi (eds.), *Nec timeo mori: Atti del Congresso internazionale di studi ambrosiani nel XVI centenario della morte di sant'Ambrogio (1997)* (Milan, 1998) 5–29 at 13, states that *Obit.Theod.* above all supported the general Stilicho, who had entrusted Ambrose with the demanding *laudatio* before the court and claimed to have received from Theodosius, on the latter's deathbed, the order to watch over Honorius and Arcadius as a *parens*.

56 *Obit.Theod.* 4 (*CSEL* 73.373).

57 *Obit.Theod.* 10–11 (*CSEL* 73.376–7). See Biermann, *Die Leichenreden*, 182.

58 According to M. Forlin Patrucco, "Il tema politico della vittoria e della croce in Ambrogio e nella tradizione ambrosiana," in R. Cantalamessa and L.F. Pizzolato (eds.), *Paradoxos Politeia: Studi Patristici in onore di Giuseppe Lazzati* (Milan, 1979) 406–18 at 410–11, in the eyes of the pagans the battle had taken on the character of a final clash between Christianity and paganism. Virius Nicomachus Flavianus consulted the oracles, which predicted the end of Christian *superstitio*. When the clash was imminent, he had large statues of Jove placed on the altars at the sides of the valley of the *Frigidus* and in front of the army standards depicting Hercules. See also Ernesti, *Princeps christianus*, 209.

and the suicide of Flavianus lurk in the background.[59] Theodosius' death just a few months later could once again give hope to people who were not receptive to the idea of a Christian emperor or who would be eager to take advantage of the young Honorius.[60] Moreover, Ambrose evidently wanted to reach a wide and varied audience[61] and hoped that the underlying message of his oration would reverberate in the weeks following 17 February 395. This explains why he at first skilfully evokes the virtue that allowed the Christian Theodosius to be the perfect emperor (according to the Senecan template) and why he then broadens his scope by affirming the theoretical reasons for which a Christian emperor might realize the pagan ideal of the perfect emperor. In short, *Obit.Theod*, addresses the pagan and Christian worlds simultaneously and acknowledges the legitimacy of the Empire and its institutions while at the same time emphasizing the new faith's centrality to the destiny of every man. It simultaneously avoids the extremes of questioning the traditional virtues of the citizen and the emperor or of embracing the traditional cults. *Obit.Theod.*, composed as it was in the wake of Frigidus and of the emperor's death, captures the uncertainties of a historical moment in which the risk that Honorius' youthful inexperience might have compromised the integration of Christianity into imperial institutions, thereby undermining the achievements that Ambrose had attained under Theodosius. In other words, *Obit.Theod.* is not so much an assertion of a new ideology (that of the Romano-Christian Empire) as it is a tactical political proposal for a dynamic equilibrium between the two worlds (clearly in favour of the Christian one). This happened at a difficult moment for civil and religious institutions, in which the phase of euphoria over the triumph of Christianity was ending and the phase of the more laborious consolidation of the successes won under Theodosius was beginning.[62]

---

59 N.B. McLynn, *Ambrose of Milan: Church and Court in a Christian Capital* (Berkeley, 1994) 355, states: "The *Frigidus* was probably refought many times that winter in the taverns and regimental messes of Milan, for Arbogast's officers could be expected to resist the 'official version,' which made their general a treacherous murderer and a reckless instigator of civil war. This delicate situation helps explain the muted tone of Theodosius' victory celebrations, one of prayerful regret rather than triumphalism."

60 Aiello, "Il tempo del potere," 120–22.

61 To read Consolino, "L'*optimus princeps*," 1043, one gets the impression that the positive qualities of Theodosius evoked by Ambrose might also find the approval of a non-Christian.

62 Cracco Ruggini, "Il 397: l'anno della morte," 12: "Teodosio come persona, il vescovo di Milano se lo era già lasciato alle spalle; e la sua attuale preoccupazione era quella d'impostare al meglio i problemi politici del presente, che si preannunciavano gravi in una fase tutta nuova di crescente instabilità."

Chapter 4

Haec quibus uteris verba: The Bible and Boethius' Christianity*

Danuta Shanzer
University of Illinois, Urbana-Champaign

Sibboleth? Shibboleth? Pronunciation matters, as the Ephraimite spies found to their cost in Judges 12.[1] And vocabulary matters too. Augustine pointed out how the Christian, as opposed to the philosopher, had to speak *ad certam regulam*.[2] From the start Christians felt the need to confess, to cry out *Christianus sum* and be counted—and to recognize one another.[3] They also had to negotiate a strange, authoritative, and constantly-to-be-cited book whose language was distinctive at best, substandard and obscure at worse. Even in the second century AD there were authors who bellowed their Christianity and their Bible.[4] But until Christianity became the norm, Christians-in-the-making and Christians who needed to communicate with literate non-Christians had to tread carefully around obviously Christian and biblical speech. This

---

* This piece was written at the same time as I was preparing "Interpreting the *Consolation*," in *The Cambridge Companion to Boethius*, ed. John Marenbon (Cambridge 2009) 228–254. There is some necessary overlap between my discussions of Boethius and the Bible here and his Christianity there. I would like to thank the members of my Fall 2006 seminar on the *Consolation* for their patience, Howard Jacobson, as always, for his advice and scholarship, and Ralph Mathisen, for always keeping me on track. On 17 June 2008 Henry Chadwick died. This piece is dedicated to his memory. He was for 30 years a mentor, and my guiding light in Boethian studies.

1 Judg. 12:5–6: *Dic ergo "sebboleth" quod interpretatur spica. Qui respondebat "tebboleth," eadem littera spicam exprimere non valens. Statimque adprehensum iugulabant in ipso Iordanis transitu.*

2 Aug. *Civ.Dei* 10.23: *Liberis enim verbis loquuntur philosophi, nec in rebus ad intelligendum difficillimis offensionem religiosarum aurium pertimescunt. Nobis autem ad certam regulam loqui fas est, ne verborum licentia etiam de rebus quae his significantur, impiam gignat opinionem.* The passage was appositely cited by C. Mohrmann, "Le problème du vocabulaire chrétien: éxpériences d'evangélisation paléo-chrétiennes et modernes," in Eadem, *Études sur le latin des chrétiens* (Rome, 1958) 113–22 at 114.

3 See Min.Fel. *Oct.* 9.2: *Occultis se notis et insignibus noscunt*; and 31.8: *Sic nos denique non notaculo corporis, ut putatis, sed innocentiae ac modestiae signo facile dinoscimus.* The *notaculum corporis* has been interpreted as the sign of the cross, but the context implies an allusion to circumcision.

4 Tertullian, for example, as an "in your face" Christian.

paper provides a case study of one problematic author—Boethius, who was keenly aware of vocabulary, style, and audience[5]—and of his last work, the *Consolation of Philosophy*. Some unusual features of his language will be outlined, and two solutions proposed. One will have to do with where and when he was working. The second may tell more about him. The question of audience, however, still remains.

Boethius Responds to a Biblical Quotation

Cons. 3.12.22–5 represents the culmination of Boethius' discussion of the *summum bonum*:

> Est igitur summum, inquit, bonum quod regit cuncta ***fortiter suauiterque disponit.*** tum ego: quam, inquam, me non modo ea quae conclusa est summa rationum, ***uerum multo magis haec ipsa quibus uteris uerba delectant*** ut tandem aliquando stultitiam[6] magna lacerantem sui pudeat!
>
> "It is therefore," she said, "the highest good that rules all things **strongly and arranges all things sweetly.**" Then I said, "How much not just the sequence of arguments that has been brought to a close delights me, but **much more so the very words you use**, so that finally the foolishness that rends great things is ashamed of itself."[7]

Boethius here reacts to the one undisputed biblical quotation in the *Consolatio*, that is, of Wis. 8:1 (*adtingit enim a fine usque ad finem* ***fortiter et disponit omnia***

[5] Boeth. *Trin.*, proem: *Idcirco stilum brevitate contraho et ex intimis sumpta philosophiae disciplinis novorum verborum significationibus velo, ut haec mihi tantum vobisque, si quando ad ea convertitis oculos, conloquantur.*

[6] Given its negative valuation this cannot be the Pauline Christian *stultitia* (1 Cor. 1:19–23) that is opposed to the *sapientia huius mundi* that is foolishness with God. See 1 Cor. 3:19, and, for its application, Lact. *Div.inst.* 5.12.4: *Si uobis sapientes uidemur, imitamini, si stulti, contemnite aut etiam ridete, si libet: uobis enim stultitia nostra prodest. quid laceratis? quid adfligitis? non inuidemus sapientiae uestrae: hanc stultitiam malumus, hanc amplectimur, hoc nobis credimus expedire, ut uos diligamus et in uos ipsos qui odistis omnia conferamus.* Instead, Boethius must intend the *stultitia* that is the perennial opponent of the *sapiens*. J. Gruber, *Kommentar zu Boethius, De Consolatione Philosophiae*, 2nd ed. (Berlin, 2006) 308 rightly cites *Cons.* 1.3.5: *Meam scilicet criminationem uererer et quasi nouum aliquid accideret perhorrescerem? nunc enim primum censes apud improbos mores lacessitam periculis esse sapientiam? nonne apud ueteres quoque ante nostri Platonis aetatem magnum saepe certamen cum* ***stultitiae temeritate*** *certauimus eodemque superstite praeceptor eius Socrates iniustae uictoriam mortis me astante promeruit?*

[7] J.C. Relihan, *Boethius. The Consolation of Philosophy* (Indianapolis, 2001) 86 translates: "Now at long last they make the stupidity that rips great things apart ashamed of itself."

suaviter).[8] Aside from this one, none of the other alleged biblical allusions or echoes in *Consolatio*[9] is "hard" or can be made to stick, though they range from Genesis to Revelation.[10] One scholar argued that, although Boethius did not *quote* the Bible, he was quite familiar with it.[11] Those bent on confirming biblical credentials have fallen victim to various methodological fallacies.

Since "quotation" is being problematized one might begin with a more nuanced list of some of the important types.[12] Listed below are some forms of quotation, citation, reminiscence, and allusion:

- Explicitly flagged with intent to enable identification of precise quotation and original context (= previous citation)
- Not flagged or discreetly flagged, but nonetheless precise: "Peek-a-boo."[13]

---

8 LXX Sap. 8:1: διατείνει δὲ ἀπὸ πέρατος ἐπὶ πέρας εὐρώστως καὶ διοικεῖ τὰ πάντα χρηστῶς. This passage is hardly cited in the eastern tradition: only five occurrences besides the LXX in the *TLG* (twice in Eusebius and once in Origen).

9 See the *apparatus fontium* of Fortescue, Klingner, and Bieler (Moreschini does not provide one) and C.J. De Vogel, "Boethiana II," *Vivarium* 10 (1972) 1–40.

10 See L. Bieler (ed.), *Anicii Manii Severini Boethii Philosophiae Consolatio. CCSL* 94 (Turnhout, 1984) 109 (*Index locorum sacrae scripturae*). Many of these are discussed by De Vogel, "Boethiana II." P. Courcelle, *Les lettres grecques en Occident de Macrobe à Cassiodore* (Paris, 1948) 302, rightly characterizes many of them as "très douteuses." The passages, plus a few additions, are listed in Appendix 2.

11 De Vogel, "Boethiana II," 17: "The text of the Bible must have been quite familiar to the author. He does not actually *quote* it, but he does have it in his mind, and its words and expressions occur to him in writing his last work as naturally as any very familiar and cherished text would present itself to any person writing such a work under such circumstances."

12 The subject is often treated purely with reference to two authors: see G.N. Knauer, *Psalmenzitate in Augustins Konfessionen* (Göttingen, 1955), and Idem, *Die Aeneis und Homer: Studien zur poetischen Technik Vergils, mit Listen der Homerzitate in der Aeneis* (Göttingen, 1964). For some modern treatments of reference and allusion, see R. Herzog, *Die Bibelepik der lateinischen Spätantike: Formgeschichte einer erbaulichen Gattung* (Munich, 1975) 185–211, and K. Smolak, "Beobachtungen zur Darstellungsweise in den Homerzentonen," *JbOB* 28 (1979) 29–49 at 42, for the Christian reception of classical epic; and S. Hinds, *Allusion and Intertext: Dynamics of Appropriation in Roman Poetry, Roman Literature and Its Contexts* (Cambridge, 1998), for imitation in classical Roman poetry. For the technology of coincidence and intention and precedence, see D.R. Shanzer, "Editions and Editing in the Classroom: A Report from the Mines in America," in B. Merta, A. Sommerlechner, and H. Weigl (eds.), *Vom Nutzen des Edierens: Akten des internationalen Kongresses zum 150-jährigen Bestehen des Instituts für Österreichische Geschichtsforschung, Mitteilungen des Instituts für Österreichische Geschichtsforschung* (Vienna, 2005) 355–68, for bibliography and methodology.

13 A version of "mit der Bildung kokettierende Distanzierung" of Herzog, *Die Bibelepik der lateinischen Spätantike*, 189.

Under this heading should go deliberate examples of "interpolation"[14] and contrast imitation that produce a *Verfremdungseffekt*.[15]

- Vaguer with intent to provide recognizable coloration or flavor, but not necessarily invoke a precise passage
- Allusion with careful rewording or disguise (neutralization or dissimulation)
- Deliberate distancing[16]
- "Bleed through," "seepage," or *lapsus*, where the author is not aware that a cat has poked its nose out of the bag[17]

Boethius' Religious Affiliation

No one can seriously accuse Boethius of polytheism,[18] and no one any longer disputes his Christianity.[19] So this is not a rehashing of the old debate, resolved by the discovery of the *Anecdoton Holderi*,[20] about whether he was the author of the

[14] "Interpolation" per K. Thraede, "Epos," in *Reallexikon für Antike und Christentum* (Stuttgart, 1962) 983–1042 at 1011–12.

[15] Akin to the type of paraphrase discussed by H. Hagendahl, "Methods of Citation in Post-Classical Latin Prose," *Eranos* 45 (1947) 114–28 at 126: "Paraphrase of the kind I have illustrated is nothing but a veiled allusion. It calls for public attention, hardly less than the verbal quotations from poetry many authors like to insert, without indicating that they are quotations."

[16] Where the author makes it clear that he and his are not part of whatever phenomenon he is citing or attesting. A pejorative example may be found in Aug. *Conf.* 1.13: *Aeneae nescio cuius errores*. For a few examples from problematic characters such as Boethius, see Calc. *In Tim.* 127: *De his potestatibus quae* ***dii putantur*** *locutus*. Also Calc. *In Tim.* 132: *Quos* ***Hebraei vocant*** *sanctos angelos*; and 135: *Ultro etiam plerumque laedunt; tanguntur enim ex vicinia terrae terrena libidine habentque nimiam cum silva communionem, quam malignam animam* ***veteres vocabant****. Hos quidem et huius modi daemonas proprie vocant desertores angelos; quibus nulla quaestio referenda est super nomine*. Also more explicitly Amm. 14.9.7: *Post haec indumentum regale quaerebatur et ministris fucandae purpurae tortis confessisque pectoralem tuniculam sine manicis textam Maras nomine quidam inductus est,* ***ut appellant Christiani, diaconus***. On Ammianus' distancings, see E.A. Thompson, *The Historical Work of Ammianus Marcellinus* (Cambridge, 1947) 114 and the contribution by Weisweiler in this volume (Chapter 27). For examples from Boethius's *philosophica*, see Courcelle, *Lettres grecques*, 302 n.6.

[17] The concept is invoked in the case of a similar problem in H. Jacobson, "Artapanus Judaeus," *JJS* 57.2 (2006) 210–21 at 216.

[18] See A. Hildebrand, *Boëthius und seine Stellung zum Christentume* (Regensburg, 1885) 79, and the smiling question of G. Boissier, "Le Christianisme de Boèce," *JS* (1889) 449–62 at 449.

[19] For fairly recent bibliography and positions, see J. Gruber, "Boethius 1925–1998. Teil II," *Lustrum* 40 (1998) 199–259 at 232–35.

[20] H. Usener, *Anecdoton Holderi: ein Beitrag zur Geschichte Roms in ostgothischer Zeit* (Bonn, 1877).

Opuscula Sacra. He was.[21] Nor am I raising, for the moment, the problem of the putative trajectory of his faith.[22] He has been described by Courcelle as someone who is tailoring his Christianity to his Platonism and vice versa.[23]

A New Problem

It is time to shift the question from the rather crude what Boethius *is*, to what Boethius *does* and *why*.[24] It is a different question about his Christianity that this paper will raise, namely his relationship with the Bible. First, a summary of his profile: a Christian who on occasion engaged in theological controversy, a philosopher, and the author of four theological-philosophical tractates that make minimal or no allusion to the Bible.[25]

---

[21] E.K. Rand, "Der dem Boethius zugeschriebene Traktat de fide catholica," *JbKP* 26 (1901) 401–61 at 407; Courcelle, *Lettres grecques*, 301.

[22] Already raised by Bovo of Corvey in the early 10th century. See H. Chadwick, *Boethius, the Consolations of Music, Logic, Theology, and Philosophy* (Oxford, 1981) 247. This includes extreme paganism, for which see A. Momigliano, "Cassiodorus and the Italian Culture of his Time," *PBA* 41 (1955) 207–45 at 213: "Many people have turned to Christianity for consolation. Boethius turned to paganism. His Christianity collapsed—it collapsed so thoroughly that perhaps he did not even notice its disappearance." It also includes representatives of more modern compromises, described by J. Marenbon, *Boethius*, Great Medieval Thinkers (New York, 2003) 156, as "Christianizers" (e.g., Klingner), "Augustinians" (e.g., Chadwick), "Hellenists" (e.g., Courcelle), and Marenbon himself (*Boethius*, 158), who sees the work as a dialogue between a Christian (Boethius) and a non-Christian (Philosophy).

[23] See Courcelle, *Lettres grecques*, 302–3. He raises an interesting point; why are we not asking the same questions about Synesius, Aeneas of Gaza, or Ps.-Dionysius? Courcelle notes *lapsus* betraying both the Christian and the pagan.

[24] Fine early work such as C. Mohrmann, "Some Remarks on the Language of Boethius' 'Consolatio Philosophiae'," in J.J. O'Meara and B. Naumann (eds.), *Latin Script and Letters A.D. 400–900: Festschrift Presented to Ludwig Bieler on the Occasion of His 70th Birthday* (Leiden, 1976) 54–61, and De Vogel, "Boethiana II," concentrated on proving that he was a Christian. Here the issue is what sort of a Christian he was and, perhaps, why. Chadwick, *Boethius*, 249, rightly separates man from work, saying, "The *Consolation* is a work written by a Platonist who is also a Christian, but it is not a Christian work."

[25] None in the *De Trinitate*, the *Utrum Pater et filius*, the *Quomodo substantiae*, and minimal in the *Contra Eutychen*. In the last's praef., *tandem igitur pulsanti animo fores et veritas inventa quaerenti* may echo Matt. 7:7 and Luke 11:9. "Knock and it shall be opened." In the body of the treatise there is some allusion to promises made to Abraham and David (p. 104 Loeb) and one citation of John 3:13: *Non ascendit in caelum, nisi qui de caelo descendit*. For the status of the *De fide*, see Appendix 1 below.

He has been praised as a man living in a time warp, the last truly learned product of Classical culture.[26] He emerges as even odder, however, if considered in his contemporary social-religious (as opposed to purely theological-religious) context. How and why does a documented sixth-century Christian avoid biblical language without explicitly problematizing it, as did Jerome and Augustine?[27] Why does a theologian fueling contemporary ecclesiastical politics (that is, the Acacian Schism) have no interest in the *verba* of the Bible?

Cons. 3.12 provides a springboard to explore what is both a literary-historical and a historical question. Before eventually returning to the point of departure for a more specific suggestion about the passage, let us begin by illustrating some of Boethius' strategies in the contested *Consolation*, what he does with the Bible and Christian *Sondersprache*.

Strategies: What Boethius does with the Bible and Christian Sondersprache

Neutralization

We see clear strategies of neutralization. Boethius rewrites and de-Biblicizes: for example, *lux inaccessibilis* > *lux inaccessa*[28] or the wise man building on a rock (*Cons*. 2 M 4), which studiously avoids the ecclesiological *petra* of Matt. 7:24. Boethius says that he will use the term *deus* that all use for "whatever it is that causes created things to last and to be moved."[29] No Trinity appears; all is lowest common denominator.[30] What does he gain by his socio-linguistic strategy of neutralization?[31] Obviously it permits him to maintain some sort of firewall between his philosophical speech and his religious writing.[32] He recognized

---

[26] E.K. Rand, *Founders of the Middle Ages* (Cambridge, MA, 1928; reprint, Dover, 1957) 156, 158 and 161 is representative.

[27] Jer. *Ep*. 22.30; Aug. *Conf.* 3.4.8–9.

[28] See *Cons*. 5.3.34: *illique* ***inaccessae luci*** *prius quoque quam impetrent ipsa supplicandi ratione coniungi*; cf. 1 Tim. 6:16: *Qui solus habet inmortalitatem,* ***lucem*** *habitans* ***inaccessibilem***. See F. Klingner, *De Boethii consolatione philosophiae* (Berlin, 1921) 101; De Vogel, "Boethiana II," 6.

[29] *Cons*. 3.12.8: *Hoc, quidquid est, quo condita manent atque agitantur usitato cunctis vocabulo deum nomino.*

[30] Contrast *Trin*. 1 on Christian *religio* (claimed by many) and Catholic faith about the Trinity.

[31] Mohrmann, "Some Remarks on the Language of Boethius," 303 on his "linguistic neutrality."

[32] See, for example, P. Courcelle, *La Consolation de philosophie dans la tradition littéraire: Antécédents et postérité de Boèce* (Paris, 1967) 342, and De Vogel, "Boethiana II," 2.

the distinction.[33] That he was driven by a desire to separate faith and reason is supported by the end of *Cons.* 3.12.35, where he insists on arguing purely from internal proofs without recourse to *rationes extra petitae.*[34]

Re-Possession or Blissful Ignorance?

But there are more puzzling features of his language that go beyond neutralization or firewalls. He takes a term that had a special meaning in Christian thought, namely the "second death" of Rev. 20:14 and 21:8,[35] and uses it as a Classical conceit for the death constituted by oblivion.[36] Is he bulling ahead like those who refuse to be politically correct and use "his" instead of "his/her," or is he simply unaware of the passage from Revelation?

---

[33] See *Trin.* 6, where he provides extra support to a doctrine (*sententia*) that is *fidei fundamentis sponte firmissimae.* Also: *Utrum pater fin. Haec si se recte et ex fide habent, ut me instruas, peto; aut si aliqua re forte diversus es, diligentius intuere quae dicta sunt et fidem si poterit rationemque coniunge.*

[34] *Atque haec nullis extrinsecus sumptis, sed ex altero altero fidem trahente insitis* ***domesticis****que probationibus explicabas*; and *Cons.* 3.12.38: *Quodsi* ***rationes*** *quoque* ***non extra petitas,*** *sed intra rei quam tractabamus ambitum collocates agitavimus, nihil est quod ammirere, cum Platone sanciente didiceris cognates de quibus loquuntur rebus oportere esse sermones.* The allusion is to Timaeus 29b: ὡς ἄρα τοὺς λόγους, ὧνπέρ εἰσιν ἐξηγηταί, τούτων αὐτῶν καὶ συγγενεῖς ὄντας· τοῦ μὲν οὖν μονίμου καὶ βεβαίου καὶ μετὰ νοῦ καταφανοῦς μονίμους καὶ ἀμεταπτώτους—καθ’ ὅσον οἷόν τε καὶ ἀνελέγκτοις προσήκει λόγοις εἶναι καὶ ἀνικήτοις.

[35] Rev. 20:14: *Haec* ***mors secunda*** *est stagnum ignis*; and 21.8: *Stagno ardenti igne et sulphure quod est* ***mors secunda.*** See, for example, quite early Min.Fel. *Oct.* 8.5: *Mori post mortem timent.*

[36] *Cons.* 2.M.7.25: *Cum sera vos rapiet hoc etiam dies/iam vos secunda mors manet.* Here is not what G.B. Pighi, "Latinità cristiana negli scrittori pagani del IV secolo," in *Studi dedicati alla memoria di Paolo Ubaldi* (Milan, 1937) 41–72 at 57, would call a "retorsione polemica," but rather either blissful ignorance or no sense that the use of what has become a theological term of art would cause a problem. Even Hildebrand, *Boëthius*, 143, notes that he does not use the term in the Christian sense.

Avoidance and Seepage

And there is avoidance. He studiously avoids "creator."[37] He clearly dislikes what has happily been christened "baptized Latin."[38] Nonetheless, *creatus* "bleeds through" once, and a few other likely Christian expressions too.[39]

"Double Transparence"

At the beginning of the third century, even after the Biblicist Tertullian, there was still a need for the Classicizing Minucius Felix, to whom Boissier long ago rightly compared Boethius.[40] Fontaine cleverly emphasized Minucius' desire to focus on the interface between Christianity and the Stoicizing monotheism by creating a style with what he calls "double transparence."[41] And this is what Boethius does with various important types of theological material: for example, martyrdom,[42]

---

37 Rand, "Der dem Boethius zugeschriebene Traktat," 407; Hildebrand, *Boëthius*, 87, noted that *conditor* was his favourite word, and that he used *auctor* once and *sator* and *princeps rerum*. For a similar strategy in Dracontius, see W. Speyer, "Der Bibeldichter Dracontius als Exeget des Sechstagewerkes Gottes," in G. Schöllgen and C. Scholten (eds.), *Stimuli: Exegese und ihre Hermeneutik in Antike und Christentum: Festschrift für Ernst Dassmann* (Münster, 1996) 464–84 at 469.

38 The fortunate phrase, cited at J. Schrijnen, *I caratteri del latino cristiano antico*, ed. A. Traina, trans. S. Boscherini, Testi e manuali per l'insegnamento universitario del latino (Bologna, 1977) 22–3, may be his own, since it does not appear as such in A.F. Ozanam, "Comment la langue latine devint chrétienne," in *La Civilisation au cinquième siècle* (Paris, 1894) 117–48, to whom he seems to be attributing it.

39 Hildebrand, *Boëthius*, 89, notes *creatis a se rebus* in *Cons*. 3.11.33. Also *Cons*. 5.6.47: ***Humiles** preces*; 5.3.35: *Vnicum illud inter homines deumque **commercium** sperandi scilicet ac deprecandi siquidem iustae **humilitatis** pretio inaestimabilem vicem divinae gratiae promeremur* with the commentary of Mohrmann, "Some Remarks on the Language of Boethius," 304. For the absence of the *aqua humiliationis* in pagan thinking, see Hildebrand, *Boëthius*, 140, citing Aug. *Enarr.Ps*. 31.18 and A. Quacquarelli, "Spigolature boeziane," in L. Obertello (ed.), *Atti del congresso internazionale di studi boeziani* (Rome, 1981) 227–48 at 245. *Humilitas* was already ascribed to Moses in Num. 12:3. For prayer as *sacrum commercium*, see M.F. Herz, *Sacrum Commercium* (Munich, 1958).

40 Boissier, "Le Christianisme de Boèce," 19–39.

41 J. Fontaine, *Aspects et problèmes de la prose d'art latine au troisème siècle: La genèse des styles latins chrétiens* (Turin, 1968) 103 and 11. My colleague Maryline Parca kindly explains that "transparent" is used in the sense of "dont le sens caché se laisse deviner" (as in "une allusion transparente")—hence "with a double hidden meaning." The latter passage, a discussion of Min.Fel. *Oct*. 31.1–7, merits comparison with Boissier, "Le Christianisme de Boèce," 454, who points out that everything in Boethius seems to be Classical, even things one might be tempted to think Christian, such as the *Cons*. 2.4.29 on those who bought victory through death.

42 *Cons*. 2.4.29: *Quodsi multorum scimus beatitudinis fructum non morte solum verum etiam doloribus suppliciisque quaesisse*; and 4.6.42: *Nonnulli venerandum saeculis*

asceticism,[43] supplicatory prayer,[44] hell and purgatory,[45] and creation.[46] In all of these we see, *at very best*, syncretistic paraphrase.

But Minucius wrote before the Great Persecution, at a time when Christians were very much a minority. Boethius lived in the sixth century. By this time there no longer was any pagan Latin vs. Christian Latin, but a "*lingua commune*."[47]

Some Possible Answers to the Cultural Question

Have we spent too much time looking at the work of "this last Roman, whose gaze was so profoundly retrospective"[48] as a cento of Classical influences[49] and therefore not been sufficiently surprised by how he shies away from the Bible, because we are evaluating him as if he had lived many centuries before? And do we thereby posit a Boethius who is simply doing his own thing in the west in stark contrast to other contemporary Christian writers?

Sometimes there is a strict separation of secular and sacred writings, and nothing Christian appears in a secular genre, while Christian content is apparent in religious writings. More often there is no firewall, and Christian material appears passim, even in historically secular genres. In some cases we have to assess questions of relative freedom, how secular a bishop such as Sidonius is prepared to be in comparison to one such as Ennodius. Secular writers such as Dracontius and Dioscorus of Aphrodito[50] with their legal professions are under different constraints and obey different rules. But even the latter do not conceal Christian affiliations.[51]

Boethius, as Rand noted,[52] was writing a theodicy from prison, and his project is in some ways comparable to Dracontius'. Here is a similar case, the Roman aristocrat imprisoned by barbarian king for some treasonable panegyric or

---

nomen gloriosae pretio mortis emerunt, quidam suppliciis inexpugnabiles exemplum ceteris praetulerunt invictam malis esse virtutem.

43 Martyrdom and asceticism in *Cons.* 3.11.32: *Nam saepe mortem cogentibus causis, quam natura reformidat, voluntas amplectitur, contraque illud quo solo mortalium rerum durat diuturnitas, gignendi opus, quod natura semper appetit, interdum cohercet voluntas.*

44 *Cons.* 5.3.33, with the fine discussion by De Vogel, "Boethiana II," 4–5.

45 See *Cons.* 4.4.22–3, with Courcelle, *Lettres grecques*, 302, on Neoplatonic narratives about the *supplicia animarum*.

46 *Cons.* 3.M.9.

47 Pighi, "Latinità cristiana," 41.

48 Chadwick, *Boethius*, 251.

49 Courcelle, *Lettres grecques*, 278, calls it a "travail de dissection."

50 L.S.B. MacCoull, *Dioscorus of Aphrodito: His Work and His World* (Berkeley, 1988).

51 Ibid., 152.

52 Rand, *Founders of the Middle Ages*, 160.

correspondence writes from prison. The parallels are not perfect, because unlike Dracontius in the *Satisfactio*, Boethius did not entreat his ruler for freedom. Instead he delivered the impassioned unrepentant apologia of *Cons.* 1.4. It is in comparison to Dracontius' *Satisfactio* though, with its Classical rhetorical argument and its Christian exempla, that the profoundly non-Christian character of the *Consolatio* emerges even more clearly. It is one thing to see no Christianity in texts where no Christian discourse is necessary or expected, but in the case of a theodicy written in face of imminent death and Last Things, some theological-religious response is expected, and the absence thereof is marked. Part of the absence is a personal religious question. But the possibility of an Ostrogothic cultural microclimate is also worth exploring as a possible explanation.

Italy lacked a literary later fifth century of the sort Gaul enjoyed. Nonetheless, it seems to have staved off (till the later sixth century) the sort of highly proto-medieval pastoral culture that we can see in Gaul (for example, Cassian).[53] Fontaine noted the distinctions between secular and ecclesiastical education, and I have myself argued the case for a different, more urbane and secular Italian culture in Ostrogothic Italy.[54] Italy's churchmen were worldly, more so even than Sidonius.[55] While the Gauls were instituting Rogations, mortifying their flesh, and getting ready for *their* sixth century—Gregory of Tours, and endless miracles of exorcism—things looked rather different south of the Alps.

It is not difficult to find partial contemporary *comparanda* in Boethius' own circle for his strategies of neutralization and resistance to talking the Bible loud and clear. Cassiodorus in addressing him uses a Classical (Odysseus) and a biblical exemplum of the power of music (David), but does so in such a way that the latter is trimmed of most explicitly Christian language.[56] The same applies to two allusions to exorcism, one in the *Variae*[57] and a second in the later *De Anima*.[58]

---

[53] For Greek culture in Ostrogothic Italy, see still Courcelle, *Lettres grecques*, 257–312.

[54] D.R. Shanzer, "Latin Literature, Christianity, and Obscenity in the Later Roman West," in N. MacDonald (ed.), *Medieval Obscenities* (Woodbridge, 2006) 179–202 at 182–5.

[55] One has only to think of Ennodius' more scurrilous *carmina* (including his epigram on Boethius) and Pope Symmachus's "Conditaria" ("Spice Girl!"). To elucidate the latter's *nom de guerre* compare Apul. *Met.*1.7: *Quae dulce* ***condiens*** *et ollam et* ***lectulum*** *suave quatere novi.* There is also, of course, the elegist Maximianus and his Boethius—as pander. See D.R. Shanzer, "Ennodius, Boethius, and the Date and Interpretation of Maximianus's Elegia III," *RFIC* 111 (1983) 183–95.

[56] *Verum ut et nos talia exemplo sapientis Ithaci transeamus, loquamur de illo lapso caeli psalterio, quod vir toto orbe cantabilis ita modulatum pro animae sospitate composuit, ut et his hymnis et mentis vulnera sanentur et divinitatis singularis gratia conquiratur. en quod saeculum miretur et credat: pepulit Davitica lyra diabolum.*

[57] *Var.* 2.40: *Mentis vulnera sanentur ... pepulit Davitica lyra diabolum.*

[58] *De anima* 13: *Tales animae (Domino praestante) etiam* ***noxiis spiritibus*** *imperant; et illi, quos mundus patitur infestos, a creatura minore superantur. Adhuc in corpore*

The *De anima* itself is a fine para-philosophical document in which to study an author himself in religious transition.[59] Take *De anima* 9 on the origin of the soul, which begins with a citation of Gen. 2:7. It explicitly mentions original sin and ends with the following indication that what went before was a (pleasant theological) digression:

> Suavis quidem nimium mihi facta digressio est, dum suspiciones improbas amovere contendo, sed dum ad aliud tendimus, hic dicere multa non possumus. Restat nunc ut ordinem et propositum prosequentes, de sede animae dicere debeamus.
>
> Certainly I have made this pleasant digression while attempting to remove wicked suspicions, but as we are moving on to other matters, we cannot say much here. It remains now that following our order and purpose we should speak concerning the seat of the soul.

Christ is mentioned only six times (*De An.* 6[1], 9[2], 17[2], and 18[1]). So this is a partial analogy for what Boethius is trying to do.

We have more concrete evidence in the 18 biblical passages used in all of the *Variae*, 14 from the Old Testament.[60] Likewise in the way an anonymous quaestor edited an *Anagnosticum* of Theoderic's of 501 to remove biblical allusions.[61] That the monarch used biblical *exempla* is likewise suggested by Ennodius *Vita Epiphani* 132 with its allusion to Saul and Agag. The statistics for "God words" in the *Variae* are likewise telling.[62] Most telling of all: there is no example of *Christus*.[63] Theoderic's official letters prefer to allude in only the vaguest way

---

positae, fortiores sunt angelis malis; adhuc indutae carne iubent ***potestatibus aereis****; et quorum tentationibus non cedunt, eis divina virtute dominantur.*

59 See J.J. O'Donnell, *Cassiodorus* (Berkeley, 1979) 105, for a date of 538/40.

60 Three are from Matt. and one from 1 Tim. See the index in *CCSL* 96.179.

61 See S.J.B. Barnish, *The Variae of Magnus Aurelius Cassiodorus Senator* (Liverpool, 1992) xxix, for the *Anagnosticum Regis* in *MGH.AA* 12.424 that seems to have been reworked by a quaestor (not Cassiodorus) in the *Praeceptio Regis* of 1 October 501 on p. 423. The Quaestor removed Theoderic's biblical allusions. Little is left but neutral expressions such as *deo auspic*e (p. 424.9).

62 *Deus* (1), *dei* (5), *deo* (112), but usually in phrases such as *deo adiuvante/propitio*, *deum* (1), *creator* (2), *numen* (2) of pagan deities. *Christianus* appears twice, in *Var*. 4.22.6 and 11.2.27. *Catholica* once in *Var*. 11.2.22.

63 These figures are closely in line with those of the *Codex Theodosianus*, where a glance at O. Gradenwitz, *Heidelberger Index zum Theodosianus* (Berlin, 1925) 34, shows many instances of *Christani*, but none of *Christus*. At 61 can be found frequent instances of *deus*, and at 65 can be found hits for *divinitas* and *divinus*. Boissier, "Le Christianisme de Boèce," 461, compared Aug. *Conf.* 9.4.7, where Alypius disdained to name Christ in early writings in order to maintain the flavor of the "cedars of the *gymnasia*."

to "the divine."[64] This culture would eventually produce the last biblical epicist, Arator. The comparison is not precise, but one can contrast two different cultures in Gaul: first, Clovis, Catholic to Catholic, threatening the bishops of Aquitaine, *apostolica sede dignissimis*, with a pointed quotation from Gen. 18:23 (*perit iustus cum impio*).[65] Second, the Burgundian epistolary conventions (admittedly with a bishop writing), where a study of conventional expressions for "God" (*protegente/favente/propugnante/propitio*, and so forth) suggests an overwhelming preference for *Christus*.[66]

Ostrogothic Italy faced major theological disagreement, but largely achieved tolerance.[67] Witness the following famous statements from the *Variae*: *Religionem imperare non possumus, quia nemo cogitur ut credat invitus* (2.27.2), and: *Nam cum divinitas patiatur diversas religiones esse, nos unam non audemus imponere* (10.26).[68] And one might speculate that here, rather than bandying biblical passages as Arians and Catholics did in the Burgundian kingdom,[69] the rivals, attempting to live in concord, avoided troublesome terms—such as *Christus*—and preferred the Old Testament to the New.[70] If one thinks of a hierarchy of generality from

---

[64] The preference is overwhelmingly for the vaguer *divin**. There are 140 hits for various forms of the word, including *divina lectio* in *Var.* 4.39.5 and 9.25.72. There are interesting plurals, e.g., *Var.* 5.1.23: *Praestent divina concordiam.*

[65] The letter (507/11) is edited by A. Boretius in *Capitularia Regum Francorum* 1, *MGH.LS* 2.1 (1883) 1–2.

[66] These are in many cases personal letters, not official correspondence written for a second party to a third party. We may, however, by studying one correspondent, viz. Sigismund, see what may be significant variation in *Ep.* 23, which uses only *deus* expressions, whereas all the others liberally deploy *Christus* ones. *Ep.* 23 is difficult to date, and could conceivably pre-date the prince's conversion to Catholicism, even though he is called *pietas vestra* in it. Gundobad, who never converted, receives the same (largely ecclesiastical) honorific in *Ep.* 6.44. See D.R. Shanzer and I.N. Wood, *Letters and Selected Prose of Avitus of Vienne* (Liverpool, 2002) 399. The *Epistulae Austrasicae* might also be called into service. Theudebald, for example uses *Christus* liberally to Justinian in *Ep.Austr.* 18.

[67] *Anon.Vales.* 12.60. One should consider the (apocryphal) reverse discrimination allegedly exhibited by Theoderic when he killed a Catholic deacon for converting to Arianism to secure advancement. The episode is discussed by J. Moorhead, *Theoderic in Italy* (Oxford, 1992) 93 and 96. For Theoderic's policy about Arian churches, see Courcelle, *Consolation de philosophie*, 206.

[68] From a letter of Theodahad's to Justinian. Justinian seems to have intervened with an earlier Ostrogothic ruler about the treatment of a Catholic convert from Arianism, one Ranilda. For Theoderic's tolerance, see B. Saitta, "Religionem imperare non possumus," *QC* 8 (1986) 63–88.

[69] Shanzer and Wood, *Letters and Selected Prose of Avitus of Vienne*, 227–30.

[70] See above n. 63 for the statistics from the *Variae*. O'Donnell, *Cassiodorus*, 107 ("What image of religious peace there was in Italy is at least partly a creation of the tacit

(1) *religio* to (2) *Christiana religio* to (3) *Catholica fides*, many denizens of Ostrogothic Italy may have sought to function at level 1 or 2 whenever possible.

Why Boethius Is Pleased that Philosophy Quotes Sapientia?

Why, though, do Philosophy's *verba* at *Cons.* 3.12 give Boethius pleasure?[71] Rand thought the resemblance to Sapientia coincidental.[72] Souter raised the possibility that Boethius knew the passage from Augustine,[73] and Cabaniss saw here a reminiscence of the Great Advent Antiphon, *O Sapientia.*[74] For de Vogel "the text of Sapientia is not so much quoted as used freely in the manner of a literary reminiscence."[75] Not so. This is the one moment in the *Consolatio* when a clear biblical signal is intentionally transmitted and received. Wis. 8:1 was rarely cited until "discovered" by Augustine and used *frequently,* identifying the Wisdom of God with Christ.[76] Boethius instead equated Sapientia with the governing

---

agreement of all concerned to say nothing about the subject in public") picks up on the silence, but seems to underplay any genuine tolerance.

[71] One wonders whether somehow or other Boethius might not have been remembering Aug. *Ord.* 2.20.31 (in response to a compliment from Alypius): *Accipio ista, inquam, libenter—neque enim me tam* ***uerba tua****, quae uera non sunt, quam uerus in uerbis animus* ***delectat*** *atque excitat.* But perhaps this sort of compliment is just a rhetorical commonplace or (sometimes) ploy? See Min.Fel. *Oct.* 14.3: *Et quamquam magnum in modum me subtili varietate* ***tua*** *delectarit* ***oratio****, tamen altius* ***moveor****, non de praesenti actione, sed de toto genere disputandi.*

[72] E.K. Rand, "On the Composition of Boethius' 'Consolatio Philosophiae'," in M. Fuhrmann and J. Gruber (eds.), *Boethius* (Darmstadt, 1984) 249 77 at 274 n.111.

[73] A. Souter, "Review of Weinberger," *CR* 49 (1935) 209–10.

[74] J.A. Cabaniss, "A Note on the Date of the Great Advent Antiphons," *Speculum* 22 (1922) 440–42.

[75] De Vogel, "Boethiana II," 34–5.

[76] See, for example, Serm. 174 (*PL* 38.940.19): *Christus est certe uirtus et sapientia dei; de qua dicitur,* ***attingit a fine usque ad finem fortiter, et disponit omnia suauiter****.* Three passages in Augustine also contain forms of *reg**. See Aug. *Enarr.Ps.* 32.2.1.5: *Non adtendat quia inferiora sunt, sed quia et regi et gubernari non possunt, nisi ab illa sapientia,* ***quae adtingit a fine usque ad finem fortiter, et disponit omnia suauiter****. non enim caelestia* ***regit****, et terrena deserit; aut non illi dicitur: quo abibo a spiritu tuo, et a facie tua quo fugiam?* Aug. *Serm.* 52: *Nihil facere patrem sine filio, quia omnia per ipsum facta sunt; nec quod factum est* ***regi*** *sine filio, quia ipse est sapientia patris,* ***attingens a fine usque in finem fortiter, et disponens omnia suauiter****.* Aug. *C.Faust.* 23.10: *Ista omnino non capitis, quomodo dei uerbum, dei uirtus atque sapientia et in se manens et apud patrem et uniuersam creaturam* ***regens pertendat a fine usque ad finem fortiter et disponat omnia suauiter****.* D. Winston, *The Wisdom of Solomon* (Garden City, NJ, 1979) 67, says that he quotes *Sapientia* 800 times.

summum bonum. Why do Philosophy's words from and about Sapientia applied to the *summum bonum*, God, give him pleasure?

The phrase *haec quibus uteris verba* suggests three *prima facie* meanings. The first, "these Christian words you use," seems unlikely, for Boethius *auctor* and prisoner, as we saw, studiously avoids openly Christian terminology. The second, "these biblical words you use," is subject to the same objection. The third possibility is "these words from *Sapientia* that you use." Here, perhaps, may be the key to understanding the passage.

Some allusions in Boethius are mere touches. Others go deeper and invoke and even import the contexts of their original sources, for example, ἐξαύδα, μὴ κεῦθε νόῳ.[77] The textual context of the quotation from *Wisdom*, immediately clarifies its appeal to Boethius. *Wisdom* has strong protreptic and consolatory credentials. It is concerned with the fate of the δίκαιος.[78] The passage immediately preceding Philosophy's quotation describes God's gift of *scientia vera* (Wis. 7:17), the natural scientific knowledge that Boethius knew from his youth,[79] all taught by *Sapientia vera*.[80] Sapientia is an emanation of God (Wis. 7:25). Sap. 8:2, *hanc amavi et exquisivi a iuventute mea*, could not better characterize Boethius' youthful bent for the pursuit of wisdom. Solomon, philosopher-king, is the speaker in *Wisdom*, a fact that may resonate with Boethius' self-righteous mention of Plato's philosopher-kings.[81] And Philosophy herself was probably alluding to Sapientia as *nostra dux* in a difficult passage in *Cons*. 1.[82] Add to this the presence of *stultitia* as an opposing force, and we are again back in the Old Testament Sapiential

---

[77] See *Cons*. 1.4.1, where the motherly Philosophy quotes to her nursling Boethius *Il*. 1.363, describing the goddess Thetis' address to her unhappy son Achilles, as discussed by G.J.P. O'Daly, *The Poetry of Boethius* (London, 1991) 70.

[78] *Wis*. 4:7, 17; 5:1, 16.

[79] See *Cons*. 1.M.2.6–23 and *Cons*. 1.3.2: *Nutricem meam, cuius ab adulescentia laribus obversatus fueram, Philosophiam.*

[80] *Wis*. 7:21.

[81] *Cons*. 1.4.5: *Atqui tu hanc sententiam Platonis ore sanxisti beatas fore res publicas si eas vel studiosi sapientiae regerent vel earum rectores studere sapientiae contigisset.*

[82] *Cons*. 1.3.13: *Qui si quando contra nos aciem struens ualentior incubuerit,* ***nostra quidem dux*** *copias suas in* ***arcem*** *contrahit, illi uero circa diripiendas inutiles sarcinulas occupantur. at nos desuper irridemus uilissima rerum quaeque rapientes securi totius furiosi tumultus eoque uallo muniti quo* ***grassanti stultitiae*** *aspirare fas non sit.* Gruber, *Kommentar zu Boethius*, 114 takes *nostra dux* as Philosophy herself. But passages that speak of the *arx sapientiae* suggest that Sapientia herself may be the *dux*. See for example, *Ciris* 12: *Si me iam summa* ***Sapientia*** *pangeret* ***arce*** *(quattuor antiquis heredibus est data consors)*; Max.Taur. *Serm*. 92.47: *In sublimi quadam* ***arce sapientiae***; Aug. *Lib.arb*. 3.24.82: *sicut enim nullus mortalium fit sapiens nisi ab stultitia in sapientiam transeat ipse autem transitus si stulte fit non utique bene fit, quod dementissimum est dicere; si autem sapienter fit iam erat sapientia in homine antequam transisset ad sapientiam, quod nihilominus absurdum est; ex quo intellegitur esse medium quod neutrum dici potest, ita et* ***ex arce sapientiae*** *ut ad stultitiam primus homo transiret, nec stultus nec sapiens ille*

tradition, with Proverbs 8 and its personification of Wisdom and Proverbs 9:13 with its Woman of Folly, the *mulier stulta et clamosa*.

The author of the definitive commentary on *Wisdom* speaks of its titular heroine thus: "The central figure which strides across the book is Sophia or Dame Wisdom, appearing at first under a variety of names (chap. 1), then gradually coming into sharper focus, until she begins to dominate the stage completely (6:12 ff.), but then again receding into the background and merging almost imperceptibly with the deity, only to emerge one last time in full power under one of her alternate titles (18:15)."[83] Newman has written some very interesting pages in her *God and the Goddesses* about how the personified Scriptural goddess Wisdom is transmitted, how she initially is affiliated with Christ,[84] then with Mary,[85] but always also, from the start, features in an ethical didactic tradition in which she is herself, but linked to *artes* and virtues.[86] *Mutatis mutandis* all of this should sound oddly familiar.[87]

So what does it mean when a personified figure called Philosophia, defined by Boethius as the *amor sapientiae*,[88] quotes an Old Testament verse about personified Wisdom, and identifies the *summum bonum* with her? Should we look east, to the Orthodox theology that identified Christ with the Holy Wisdom who presided in

---

transitus fuit; Paul.Nol. *Ep.* 16.11: *Tua uero mens, quae ignita de caelesti semine diuinum iam spirat ardorem, in* ***ipsam arcem sapientiae*** *Christum fide praeuia dirigatur.*

83 Winston, *The Wisdom of Solomon*, 34.

84 B. Newman, *God and the Goddesses: Vision, Poetry, and Belief in the Middle Ages* (Philadelphia, 2003) 194–5.

85 Ibid., 196–205.

86 Ibid., 190–244, but esp. 192. On p. 193 Newman points out the logical endpoints of the first two options: the feminization of Christ and the divinization of Mary.

87 And adamantly anti-Augustinian. See D.R. Shanzer, "Licentius's Verse Epistle to Augustine," *REAug* 37 (1991) 110–43 at 142 and Eadem, "Augustine's Disciplines: *Silent diutius Musae Varronis*?," in K. Pollmann and M. Vessey (eds.), *Augustine and the Disciplines* (Oxford, 2005) 69–112 at 104–5 and 110.

88 See his *In Isagogen* 1.3: *Est enim philosophia amor et studium et amicitia quodammodo sapientiae, quae nullius indigens, vivax mens et sola rerum primaeva ratio est. est autem hic amor sapientiae intellegentis animi ab illa pura sapientiae illuminatio et quodammodo ad se ipsam retractio et advocatio, ut videatur, studium sapientiae studium divinitatis et purae mentis illius amicitia. Haec igitur sapientia cuncto equidem animarum generi meritum suae divinitatis inponit et ad propriam naturae vim puritatemque reducit.* Also of course Aug. *Conf.* 3.4.8: *Amor autem sapientiae nomen graecum habet philosophiae.*

the Great Church in Constantinople?[89] Or to an Anician "special relationship?"[90] Or can we see this as a "peek-a-boo" citation taking us back to that ultimate fusion cuisine that was Hellenistic Judaism in its interface with Greek philosophy?[91] As we so tiresomely often see with Boethius, there are two diametrically opposite readings. But his Wisdom and his personified Philosophy have taken on far fleshier and present flesh than his more distant deity. To support the second alternative one could adduce another passage, *Cons.* 1.1.3, where Philosophy, by alluding to her dress that she wove with her own hands, implicitly identifies herself with the Neoplatonic Athena-Minerva.[92] Furthermore, a Christological interpretation would require Boethius to know something of biblical exegesis—of which we have little or no evidence.[93]

We may end with how Boethius patterns. He never engages in clear distancing terminology of the "as the X say (not the author)".[94] Nor does he explicitly show his colors and put himself inside Christianity in the *Consolatio*. While there are plausible Christian fillips or allusions, one must ask whether they are intentional

---

[89] For the eastern identification of Wisdom with Christ, see J. Meyendorff, "Wisdom-Sophia: Contrasting Approaches to a Complex Theme," *DOP* 41 (1987) 391–401 at 392. For some of the Arian-Catholic problems caused by this identification when carried over to the exegesis of Prov. 8:22–3: κύριος ἔκτισέν με ἀρχὴν ὁδῶν αὐτοῦ εἰς ἔργα αὐτοῦ, πρὸ τοῦ αἰῶνος ἐθεμελίωσέν με ἐν ἀρχῇ, see J. Meyendorff, "L'iconographie de la Sagesse divine dans la tradition byzantine," *CahArch* 10 (1959) 259–77 at 260, and Idem, *Byzantine Theology: Historical Trends and Doctrinal Themes* (New York, 1974) 21.

[90] F. Troncarelli, *Tradizioni perdute: la Consolatio philosophiae nell'alto medioevo* (Padua, 1981) 67–70.

[91] See E. Schürer, *The History of the Jewish People in the Age of Jesus Christ (175 B.C.–A.D. 135)*, rev. ed. by G. Vermes, F. Millar, and M. Goodman (Edinburgh, 1986) 568–71; B.L. Mack, *Logos und Sophia: Untersuchungen zur Weisheitstheologie im hellenistischen Judentum* (Göttingen, 1973).

[92] *Cons.* 1.1.3: *Vestes ... quas, uti post eadem prodente cognovi, suis manibus ipsa texuerat. Il.* 5.733–5: Αὐτὰρ Ἀθηναίη κούρη Διὸς αἰγιόχοιο/ πέπλον μὲν κατέχευεν ἑανὸν πατρὸς ἐπ' οὔδει/ ποικίλον, ὅν ῥ' αὐτὴ ποιήσατο καὶ κάμε χερσίν with Klingner, *De Boethii consolatione philosophiae*, 117. Quoted by Procl. *Parm.*, p. 851.36 and Procl. *In Tim.*, vol. 1, p. 167.18 with the explanation τὸν μὲν γὰρ πέπλον, ὃν αὐτὴ ποιεῖ καὶ ὑφίστησι ταῖς ἑαυτῆς νοήσεσι, τὴν νοερὰν αὑτῆς σοφίαν ἀκουστέον.

[93] Quacquarelli, "Spigolature boeziane," 241, argues for one in the *Contra Eutychen*.

[94] These are the sort of passages that scholars must examine carefully when dealing with somewhat murky characters such as Ammianus Marcellinus or Calcidius. For Ammianus' distancings, see Pighi, "Latinità cristiana," 49–53 and above n. 16. At p. 54 he speaks of "certa precauzione linguistica." In Calcidius' case the debate has concerned his religious affiliation: pagan, Christian, or Jew. For some of his techniques, see Calc. *In Tim.* 127: *De his potestatibus quae dii putantur locutus*; 132: *Quos Hebraei vocant sanctos angelos*; 135: *Vltro etiam plerumque laedunt; tanguntur enim ex vicinia terrae terrena libidine habentque nimiam cum silva communionem, quam malignam animam veteres vocabant. Hos quidem et huius modi daemonas proprie vocant desertores angelos; quibus nulla quaestio referenda est super nomine.*

"peek-a-boos" (such as the one discussed) or seepages that bled through *malgré lui*.[95] Even more interesting are his avoidances, the usages that bypass the Christian *Sondersprache* and permit him to be read as a pagan,[96] or ones that permit that famous double transparency, where various sorts of readers can see what they choose. All of this could add up either to fence-sitting or to preservation of "deniability" on his part. If we prefer the "double transparence," we must ask ourselves who his two audiences were.[97] Here it is tentatively suggested that the places where he seems to be shooting for the lowest common denominator between any theistic system (*religio*) and where we see glaring absences (for example, Christ), he may reflect, even in his final work, the discourse that helped keep Ostrogothic Italy tolerant for so long. As for New Testament Christianity—he avoids it and at one crucial moment has his eye on a more ancient and, for him, more potent syncretism.[98]

---

[95] The source criticism needs to be redone and then analyzed with a more literary-critical eye.

[96] E.g. *Cons.* 1.4.17: *sacrarum aedium*; and 1.4.36: *sacras aedes* (for *ecclesiae*).

[97] A problematic question, given the *Consolatio*'s status as a last work. Earlier on we have some (perhaps formulaic) indications of *ignava segnities* and *callidus livor* among the theological public in *Trin.*, praef.

[98] He was someone whose primary interest was in knowledge and Wisdom, not in any sort of religious narrative. His more probable Bible quotations reflect this interest. See *Eutych. ad Nest.*, praef. (above n. 26) echoing Matt. 7:7. and Luke 11:7. Also *Cons.* 4.3.5: *Quantumlibet igitur saeviant mali* ***sapienti*** *tamen* ***corona*** *non decidet, non arescet.* See Appendix 2, below.

Appendix 1: A *corollarium*, as Philosophy Would Put It,[99] about the *De Fide*

The authorship of the *De Fide*, the one tractate that makes extensive reference to biblical matters and salvation history, is doubtful. It has become fashionable again[100] to regard it as authentic, but anyone who wishes to do so really must address the issues raised in Rand's Munich dissertation of 1901.[101] Even Chadwick fails to do so[102] and likewise Gallonier.[103] This is perhaps due to Rand's own (premature) recantation.[104] One might go further and argue that its extensive dependence on Augustine and likewise its level of open allusion to the Bible are both features that set it strongly apart from Boethius' genuine writings. Its very use of the Bible is strong evidence *against* its authenticity. Nonetheless, it clearly emerged from Boethius' milieu and probably from within his circle, whether Deacon John was its author or not.[105]

[99] *Cons.* 3.10: *Et pulchrum, inquam, hoc atque pretiosum siue porisma siue corollarium uocari mauis.*

[100] Courcelle, *Lettres grecques*, 301 n., noted (in 1948) that it was generally considered unauthentic.

[101] See Rand, "Der dem Boethius zugeschriebene Traktat," 28–36, particularly for the non-subject specific grammatical and stylistics, which can be especially probative, because they are not context-dependent.

[102] H. Chadwick, "The Authenticity of Boethius' Fourth Tractate, *De fide catholica*," *JThS* 31 (1980) 368–77, and Chadwick, *Boethius,* 175–80, ignore Rand's penetrating stylistic arguments, likewise Rand's point that Boethius did not believe in creation ex nihilo and the author of the *De fide* did (*De fide* 1.57: *Eumque cum omnino non esset fecit ut esset;* contrast *Cons.* 3.M.9.4–5). See Rand, "Der dem Boethius zugeschriebene Traktat," 425–7. At 79 Chadwick should have discussed the clear allusions to purgatorial punishment in the *Cons.* (4.4.22–3). One might also mention the orthodoxy of *De fide* 114–22 about original sin and allusion to Pelagianism in contrast to the perfectibility of man that seems to be implied throughout the *Cons.*

[103] A. Gallonier, *Boèce: Opuscula sacra*, 1 (Louvain-la neuve, 2007) 29 n.75.

[104] Rand, *Founders of the Middle Ages*, 156–7.

[105] As Rand, "Der dem Boethius zugeschriebene Traktat," 443–5, ingeniously suggests, is another matter!

Appendix 2: Alleged Biblical Echoes

List originally from Fortescue, printed by Bieler, and discussed by De Vogel:

Invalid

Cons. 3 M.9.7: *(tu cuncta superno) ducis ab exemplo, pulchrum pulcherrimus ipse.*
Gen. 1:26: *Faciamus hominem ad imaginem et similitudinem nostram.*
Wis. 2:23: *Quoniam deus creavit hominem inexterminabilem et ad imaginem suae similitudinis fecit illum.*[106]

Cons. 2.2.8: *Cum te matris utero natura produxit, nudum rebus omnibus inopemque suscepi.*
Job 1:21: *Nudus egressus sum de utero matris meae et nudus revertar.*[107]

Cons. 5. 6.48: *Ante oculos agitis iudicis cuncta cernentis.*
Esth. 16:4: *Sed dei quoque cuncta cernentis arbitrantur se posse fugere sententiam.*[108]

*Cons.*4.3.5: *Quantumlibet igitur saeviant mali sapienti tamen corona non decidet, non arescet.*
Ps. 89:6: *Mane quasi herba transiens..ad vesperam conteretur atque siccabitur.*

Cons. 2.7.20: "*'Intellexeram' inquit, 'si tacuisses'.*"
Prov. 11:12: *Qui despicit amicum suum indigens corde est. vir autem prudens tacebit.*

Cons. 2.7.20: "*'Intellexeram' inquit, 'si tacuisses'.*"
Prov. 17:28: *Stultus quoque si tacuerit, sapiens putabitur et si conpresserit labia sua intellegens.*[109]

Cons. 3 M.9.7: *Similique in imagine formans.*
Wis. 2:23: *Quoniam deus creavit hominem inexterminabilem et ad imaginem suae similitudinis fecit illum.*

---

106 De Vogel, "Boethiana II," 12, thinks it weak.

107 Ibid., 13 thinks it weak.

108 See Curt. 9.11.4: *Cuncta cernentis e ripa*; Luc. 4.699: *Cernit cuncta*; Manilius, 4.194: *Qui possint cernere cuncta.*

109 De Vogel, "Boethiana II," 13, thinks it stronger.

Cons. 2.7.20: *Intellexeram, si tacuisses.*
Sir. 20:6–7: *Est autem tacens non habens sensum loquellae..homo sapiens tacebit usque ad tempus.*

Cons. 4.3.5: *Quantumlibet igitur saeviant mali sapienti tamen corona non decidet, non arescet.*
Jer. 13:18: *Quoniam descendit de capite vestro corona gloriae vestrae.*

Cons. 3.10: *Huc omnes pariter venite capti.*
Matt. 11:28: *Venite ad me omnes qui laboratis et onerati estis.*[110]

Cons. 1.1.9ff.: *Hae sunt enim quae infructuosis affectuum spinis uberem fructibus rationis segetem necant hominumque mentes assuefaciunt morbo, non liberant.*
Matt. 13.22ff. Parable of the Sower[111]

Cons. 3.12.18: *Si quidem detractantium iugum foret, non obtemperantium salus.*
Matt. 11:29–30: *Tollite iugum meum super vos, et discite a me... et invenietis requiem animabus vestris. Iugum enim meum suave est, et onus meum leve.*

Cons. 1.1.28: *Hae sunt enim quae infructuosis affectuum spinis uberem fructibus rationis segetem necant hominumque mentes assuefaciunt morbo, non liberant*
Mark 4:18: The Parable of the Sower is at Mark.4:2–9

Cons. 3.10.25: *Omnis igitur beatus deus. Sed <deus> natura quidem unus; participatione vero nihil prohibet esse quam plurimos.*
John 10:34: *Nonne scriptum est in lege vestra quia ego dixi dii estis.*

Cons. 3 M. 9.28: *Principium, vector, dux, semita, terminus idem.*
John 14:6: *Ego sum via et veritas et vita.*

Cons. 4.1.6: *Si, uti tu aestimas, in tanti velut patris familias dispositissima domo vila vasa colerentur, pretiosa sordescerent.*
Rom. 9:21–3: *An non habet potestatem figulus luti ex eadem massa facere, aliud quidem vas in honorem, aliud vero in contumeliam.*[112]

Cons. 4.1.6: *Si, uti tu aestimas, in tanti velut patris familias dispositissima domo vilia vasa colerentur, pretiosa sordescerent.*

110 Hildebrand, *Boëthius*, 143.

111 De Vogel, "Boethiana II," 14, thinks it a good parallel.

112 Ibid., 16 does not accept it.

2 Tim. 2:20: *In magna autem domo non solum sunt aurea et argentea, sed et lignea et fictilia, et quaedam quidem in honorem, quaedam autem in contumeliam?*[113]

Cons. 4.6.55: *Dumque ea quae protulit in sui similitudinem retinere festinat.*
Phil. 2:7: *Sed semet ipsum exaninavit formam servi accipiens in simulitudinem hominum factus.*

Cons. 4.6.55: *Dumque ea quae protulit in sui similitudinem retinere festinat.*
James 3:9: *Et in ipsa maledicimus homines qui ad similitudinem dei facti sunt.*

Cons. 1 M 5.35: *Clara tenebris iustusque tulit crimen iniqui.*[114]
1 Pet. 3:18: *Iustus pro iniustis.*

Cons. 3.10.25: *Omnis igitur beatus deus. Sed <deus> natura quidem unus; participatione vero nihil prohibet esse quam plurimos.*
2 Pet. 1:4: *Vt per haec efficiamini divinae consortes naturae.*

Cons. 3 M 9.27: *Tu requies tranquilla piis, te cernere finis.*[115]
Rev. 1:8: *Ego sum a et o, principium et finis.*

Cons. 5 M 2.11: *Quae sint quae fuerint veniantque.*
Rev. 1:8: *Qui est et qui erat et qui venturus est.*[116]

Possible

Cons. 1.3.6: *Praeceptor eius Socrates iniustae* ***victoriam mortis*** *me adstante promeruit.*
1 Cor. 15:54–5: *Absorpta est* ***mors in victoriam****. ubi est,* ***mors, victoria tua****? ubi est mors stimulus tuus?*[117]

---

[113] Ibid. considers it a "vague literary reminiscence, if there is any at all."

[114] Hildebrand, *Boëthius*, 143, notes that he uses it of himself, not of the Son of God. Ibid., 15–16, thinks it might seem plausible, but that the context is quite different and that it has nothing to do with Christ's suffering.

[115] The only deity called *finis* in the classical Latin tradition is wittily Terminus. See Ov. *Fast*. 2.45. Numerous Christian texts, however, address God as *finis*, and the locution, though probably Christian, need not be biblical.

[116] A familiar combination, known since Homer. See *Il*. 1.70: ὃς ᾔδη τά τ' ἐόντα τά τ' ἐσσόμενα πρό τ' ἐόντα.

[117] This must be what Chadwick, *Boethius,* 249 intends. Gruber, *Kommentar zu Boethius*, 109 cites instead 1 Jn. 5:4 and Apoc. 17:14. This passage is not in Bieler.

Cons. 4.6.54: *Neque enim fas est* ***homini*** *cunctas divinae operas machinas vel ingenio comprehendere vel* ***explicare sermone.***
Eccl. 1:8: *Cunctae res difficiles non potest eas* ***homo explicare sermone.***[118]

Valid

Cons. 4.3.5: *Quantumlibet igitur saeviant mali* ***sapienti*** *tamen* ***corona*** *non decidet, non arescet.*
Prov. 14:24: ***Corona sapientium*** *divitiae eorum, fatuitas stultorum inprudentia*
(also Eccl. 1:22: *Corona sapientiae timor domini*).[119]

Cons. 2 M 4.15: *Humili domum memento certus figere* ***saxo.***
Matt. 7.24: *Omnis ergo qui audit verba mea haec et facit ea adsimulabitur viro sapienti qui aedificavit domum suam super* ***petram.***

Cons. 5.3.34: *Illique* ***inaccessae luci*** *prius quoque quam impetrent ipsa supplicandi ratione coniungi.*
1 Tim. 6:16: *Qui solus habet inmortalitatem,* ***lucem*** *habitans* ***inaccessibilem.***

Certain

Cons. 3.12.22: *Est igitur summum, inquit, bonum quod regit cuncta* ***fortiter suauiterque disponit.***
Wis. 8:1: *Adtingit enim a fine usque ad finem* ***fortiter et disponit omnia suaviter.***[120]

---

118 De Vogel, "Boethiana II," 14, thinks it less convincing. The parallels for the three words together in the same context are many, e.g. Cass. *De an*. 15.77: *Opinari quidem possumus spiritalis* ***homo*** *quarum causarum delectatione saginetur, sed quis sit ille suauitatis modus, sicut legitur, nec mente potest intellegi nec* ***sermonibus explicari.***

119 This definitely looks like a Christian (and probably Biblical) expression. The first example of *corona and sapien** is in Tertullian. See also Meth. *Symp*. 9–10: τοῖς ἀμιάντοις τῆς σοφίας ἀναδήσασα πετάλοις.

120 De Vogel, "Boethiana II," 13, thinks it strong.

PART II
Power Over the Divine: Porphyry, Iamblichus, and the Struggles for the Philosophical Tradition

Chapter 5

The Power of Religious Rituals: A Philosophical Quarrel on the Eve of the Great Persecution

Elizabeth DePalma Digeser
University of California, Santa Barbara

Although Eunapius places him firmly within the Plotinian line of succession in the fourth century,[1] Iamblichus' doctrines on the human soul and the inherent power of ritual or religious acts for all souls set him sharply at odds with the views of both Plotinus and Porphyry.[2] Disagreements between Iamblichus and Porphyry have been recognized since antiquity,[3] but the implications of their rupture have never been explored. This is partly because historians have only recently come to grips with Iamblichus' standing as a philosopher in his own right rather than as some late antique mystic and charlatan.[4] The differences between Iamblichus, Porphyry and Plotinus are many, but I shall concentrate on one, namely Iamblichus' argument that no soul had the power on its own to return to its divine source without the human person's participation in religious rituals involving matter. Shaw has referred to this claim as Iamblichus' "*via universalis*," and it depends—in part—on Iamblichus' conviction that all human souls have somehow fallen away from the divine realm. As I shall show, such a contention flew in the face of Plotinus' and Porphyry's convictions that there was no common path for both philosophers and ordinary people to follow in their quest to return to their divine source. I shall argue that Iamblichus' articulation of his *via universalis* in the treatise that now goes by the name *On the Mysteries* prompted a wide-ranging response from

---

1 Eun. *VSoph.* 1.5.1–10 (457–61).

2 This is true even though Iamblichus' theology depends heavily on Plotinus. G. Shaw, "Eros and Arithmos: Pythagorean Theurgy in Iamblichus and Plotinus," *AncPhil* 19 (1999) 121–43 at 124.

3 E.g., David, *In Porphyrii Isagogen commentarium* (*In Porph.Is.*) p. 92.3, ed. A. Busse (Berlin, 1904); Marinus *VProcl.* 26; J. Bidez, "Le philosophe Jamblique et son école," *REG* 32 (1919) 29–40 at 36.

4 G. Fowden, *The Egyptian Hermes* (Princeton, 1986), and G. Shaw, *Theurgy and the Soul: The Neoplatonism of Iamblichus* (University Park, PA, 1995), established that, "theurgy was a philosophically sophisticated response to social and philosophical challenges faced by Platonists of the fourth century." Cf. Shaw, "Eros and Arithmos," 124.

Porphyry in which he marshaled a variety of arguments and evidence against the existence of any such universal path, including Christianity. I shall suggest that a disagreement within the late third-century philosophical community—over the value and power of traditional religious rituals for a philosopher's soul—produced the texts that fueled the flames of the Great Persecution. This argument will begin with a brief description of the ways in which Porphyry's and Iamblichus' careers intersected and then will move on to an exploration of Iamblichus' universal theology, and conclude with an account of Porphyry's wide-ranging response.

Iamblichus and Porphyry were near contemporaries[5] and associates. Iamblichus was a student of Anatolius, the Aristotelian and Pythagorean scholar who was later the bishop of Laodicaea;[6] their association probably took place in Alexandria.[7] The destruction in 273 of Alexandria's Bruchion quarter, home to the library and many philosophical schools, may explain why Anatolius and his student separated, the former for Caesarea and the east, Iamblichus, now a mature man, approximately 30 years old, for the west.[8] There, probably in Rome, Iamblichus "attached himself"

---

[5] The date for the Syrian philosopher's birth is now accepted as ca. 242 or even 240, which means that only some 15 years separated him and Porphyry. The *Suda* seems to suggest that Iamblichus' date of birth was 280, but the portrait of Iamblichus preserved in Stobaeus' letters (erroneously attributed to Julian) led Bidez, "Le philosophe Jamblique et son école," 29–40, to push the date back by 30 years. Subsequently Alan Cameron, "The Date of Iamblichus' Birth," *Hermes* 96 (1968) 374–6, noticed that, since Iamblichus' son Ariston had married Amphiclea, a member of Plotinus' circle, by the year 300 (Porph. *VPlot.* 9.3–5), an even earlier date, i.e. ca. 242, should be posited. Cameron's arguments have been widely accepted: see J. Dillon (ed.), *Iamblichi Chalcidensis in Platonis Dialogos Commentaria* (Leiden, 1973) 6–7; B. Dalsgaard Larsen, "La place de Jamblique dans la philosophie antique tardive," in H. Dörrie (ed.), *De Jamblique à Proclus*, Entretiens sur l'antiquité classique (Geneva, 1975) 1–34 at 3; T.D. Barnes, "A Correspondent of Iamblichus," *GRBS* 19 (1978) 99–106.

[6] Eus. *HE* 7.32.6–13, 20–21. Eunapius' high regard for Anatolius (*VSoph.* 5.2 [458]), "who ranks next after Porphyry" (Ἀνατολίῳ τῶν κατὰ Πορφύριον τὰ δεύτερα φερομένῳ), together with the bishop's proficiency in Aristotelian and Pythagorean thought support this identification. P. Athanassiadi, "The Oecumenism of Iamblichus: Latent Knowledge and Its Awakening," *JRS* 85 (1995) 244–50 at 244, 246; J. Dillon, "Iamblichus of Chalcis (c. 240–325 AD)," *ANRW* 2.36.2 (1987) 862–909 at 866–7; J.A. Philip, "The Biographical Tradition: Pythagoras," *TAPA* 90 (1959) 185–94 at 190 n.5; Dalsgaard Larsen, "La place de Jamblique," 4. A. Smith, "Porphyrian Studies since 1913," *ANRW* 2.36.2 (1987) 717–73 at 745 n.157, while not closing off the possibility, is more cautious.

[7] Dalsgaard Larsen, "La place de Jamblique," 3–4; Athanassiadi, "The Oecumenism of Iamblichus," 245–6. Dillon, "Iamblichus of Chalcis," 867, however, advocates Caesarea.

[8] Anatolius is known to have participated in a lively defense of the Bruchion quarter (Eus. *HE* 7.32.6–13, 20–21), which S.I. Oost, "The Alexandrian Seditions under Philip and Gallienus," *CPh* 56 (1961) 1–20, dates to the early 260s, but C. Haas, *Alexandria in Late Antiquity* (Baltimore, 1997) 28, 366 n.18, links with the quarter's involvement with Zenobia in 273. The Museon was in the Bruchion, but after Aurelian's troops engaged with rioters in the 270s, the area was left in ruins (Amm. 22.16.15).

to Porphyry,[9] now in his middle forties. Iamblichus may have known about Porphyry through Anatolius, to whom Porphyry dedicated his *Homerica Zêtêmata.*[10] At the very least, Iamblichus was probably interested in Porphyry as the repository of the texts and doctrines of the venerable Plotinus, clearly the most distinguished Platonist of his age.[11] For whatever reason, a strong "tutorial bond" seems not to have formed between the two philosophers,[12] although initially they apparently had an amicable relationship, with Iamblichus being the recipient of Porphyry's *Peri tou gnôthi seauton.*[13]

At some unknown date, Iamblichus decided to return to Syria,[14] probably to set up his own school. Some of those around Porphyry may have decided to depart with him. A cryptic note in John Malalas has been taken to mean that Iamblichus may next be traced in Daphne, during the reigns of Galerius and Maxentius (which Barnes suggests might rather be Maximin Daia).[15] This information potentially places him in the city during the problem with the auspices in 299 that led to the purge of Christians from the imperial army and court (Lact. *Mort.pers.* 10).[16] At some later date, Iamblichus moved to Apamea, where he seems to have lived out the rest of his life.[17] In any case, by the time he moved there, Porphyry was probably dead.[18]

Iamblichus set out the views that I shall discuss in the work often called *On the Mysteries*, but that really bears the title, *The Reply of the Master Abammon*

---

9 Eun. *VSoph.* 5.1.2 (458). Dalsgaard Larsen, "La place de Jamblique," 3; Athanassiadi, "The Oecumenism of Iamblichus," 245; Barnes, "A Correspondent of Iamblichus," 105; E. Zeller, *Die Philosophie der Griechen in ihrer geschichtlichen Entwicklung*, vol. 3.2 (Leipzig, 1868) 612 n.1.

10 Dillon, "Iamblichus of Chalcis," 866–7; Smith, "Porphyrian Studies since 1913," 745 n.157.

11 Porph. *VPlot.* 20; Eun. *VSoph.* 4.1.1–3.1 (456–7).

12 Athanassiadi, "The Oecumenism of Iamblichus," 244–5; A. Smith, *Porphyry's Place in the Neoplatonic Tradition. A Study in Post-Plotinian Neoplatonism* (The Hague, 1974) xvii with n.18.

13 Stob. 3.21.26 (p. 579.21–2 Hense) apud Smith, *Porphyry's Place*, xvii n.18; Bidez, "Le philosophe Jamblique et son école," 32.

14 Barnes, "A Correspondent of Iamblichus," 105; Dillon, *Iamblichi Chalcidensis*, 9–14; Dalsgaard Larsen, "La place de Jamblique," 4; J. Vanderspoel, "Iamblichus at Daphne," *GRBS* 29 (1988) 83–6 at 84.

15 Joh. Mal. 12.47 (312). Barnes, "A Correspondent of Iamblichus," 105; Dillon, "Iamblichus of Chalcis," 870; Dalsgaard Larsen, "La place de Jamblique," 4, and Vanderspoel, "Iamblichus at Daphne," 83–5.

16 E.D. Digeser, "An Oracle of Apollo at Daphne and the Great Persecution," *CPh* 99 (2004) 57–77.

17 Ps. Julian, *Ep.* 78.

18 Suid. s.v. "Porphyrios."

to the Letter of Porphyry to Anebo.[19] As is clear from the title alone, something had motivated Porphyry to write to this Anebo, and Iamblichus himself assumed responsibility for the response. Saffrey argues that Anebo was a one-time student of Porphyry who had joined up with Iamblichus.[20] The surviving fragments of Porphyry's letter—most of which come from Iamblichus' treatise—seek information about the claim that a wide variety of rituals might produce theophanies or some form of divine manifestation; but they also show the elder philosopher increasingly troubled by the theological and metaphysical claims that were being used to justify the use of these rituals within philosophical circles.[21] This quest for information produced Iamblichus' *On the Mysteries*, a sarcastic and often mean-spirited treatise, that in answering Porphyry's questions criticizes him for failing to think properly about how the divine works through the material world, and for failing to be properly informed regarding the subjects about which he asks.[22] In particular, as Shaw observes, Iamblichus thought that the gods had established "a 'universal way'" but that "Porphyry had simply failed to notice."[23]

The difference between Iamblichus, Plotinus, and Porphyry over the nature of the soul is important. Whereas Porphyry—with Plotinus—believed that part of the human soul remained in contact with the divine,[24] Iamblichus believed that all souls were in some respect cut off from the divine realm.[25] Iamblichus posited three types of soul: material, intermediate, and noetic—the last of which was extraordinarily rare.[26] Since he believed that the "completely embodied" soul "projects its *logoi* into the phenomenal world," in his view, the soul "could recover its 'original' [i.e. divine] 'nature' only by *ritually* appropriating" the "natural correspondences" to these *logoi*—their *analogoi*—which was done through ritual acts.[27]

Throughout *On the Mysteries*, Iamblichus sets out his *via univeralis* by setting ritual practices (Hermetic and Chaldaean, especially, but also Greek) into a Pythagorean framework to achieve the Plotinian goal of the return of the soul to its

---

19 Greek text and translation from E.C. Clarke, J.M. Dillon, and J.P. Herschbell (eds.), *Iamblichus de mysteriis* (Leiden, 2004).

20 H.D. Saffrey, "Abamon, pseudonyme de Jamblique," in R.B. Palmer and R. Hamerton-Kelly (eds.), *Philomathes: Studies and Essays in the Humanities in Memory of Philip Merlan* (The Hague, 1971) 227–39 at 232.

21 Cf. Porph. *Aneb.* apud Eus. *PE* 5.7; Saffrey, "Abamon," 233; Shaw, "Eros and Arithmos," 128.

22 H.D. Saffrey, "Relecture de Jamblique, *De mysteriis*, VIII, chap. 1–5," in S. Gersh and C. Kannengiesser (eds.), *Platonism in Late Antiquity* (Notre Dame, IN, 1992) 157–71 at 171.

23 Shaw, "Eros and Arithmos," 125.

24 Plotinus, *Enn.* 4.3.12.1–13; 1.1.12.24–32; Porph. *Sent.* 29.

25 Iambl. *Comm. in Tim.* fr.87.18–22.

26 *Myst.* 219.8; 230.18.

27 *Myst.* 233.7–16; Shaw, "Eros and Arithmos," 127, see also 131–2, and J.F. Finamore, "Plotinus and Iamblichus on Magic and Theurgy," *Dionysius* n.s. 17 (1999) 83–4.

source. Unlike Plotinus, however, he is also concerned with the souls of ordinary people and sees few practical differences between all types of souls.[28] The gods, Iamblichus believed, had established the rituals by which souls could return to their origins, and these procedures had been preserved among "the sacred races of the world"—especially the Assyrians (that is, Chaldaeans), the culture associated with the *Chaldaean Oracles,* and the Egyptians, associated with the wisdom of Hermes and praised even by Plotinus.[29] By "integrating Pythagorean doctrines with traditional rites of sacrifice and divination,"[30] Iamblichus produced "the most comprehensive and systematic development of Pythagorean teachings in antiquity," according to Shaw and O'Meara.[31] In particular, his use of Pythagorean mathematics and his familiarity with Hermetic doctrine allowed Iamblichus to unburden matter of the evil associations which many Platonists had attributed to it, including Plotinus himself to some extent.[32] In Iamblichus' view, a life embodied in matter was not something "to be nobly endured"—as Porphyry or Plotinus might have it[33]—but was instead an opportunity for the soul to "participate in theophany."[34] On this basis Iamblichus constructed his *via universalis* by integrating religious ritual and theology, even though he presented his own system as only articulating what the gods themselves had long revealed.

Having started from the premise, in answer to Porphyry's doubts, that any ritual that had the power to produce a genuine theophany was authoritative or god-given, Iamblichus then reasoned that participation in such rituals was the one means by which fallen human souls could regain contact with the divine. Most scholars use the term "theurgy" to describe the rituals to which Iamblichus was so devoted, but it is important to realize that Iamblichus himself broadened this terminology—first deployed in the second-century *Chaldaean Oracles*—to apply to *all* rituals regardless of origin that could be identified as divinely ordained.[35] The value that Iamblichus placed on theurgy (or "god-work") as opposed to theology (or "god-talk") is clear in his attitude toward philosophers who hold themselves aloof from ritual practice. "The Greeks," Iamblichus argued, "had alienated themselves from

---

28 Shaw, "Eros and Arithmos," 125, 128. H.D. Saffrey, "Les néoplatoniciens et les Oracles chaldaïques," *REAug* 27 (1981) 209–25 at 217.

29 Shaw, "Eros and Arithmos," 125–6, 128.

30 Ibid., 129.

31 D.J. O'Meara, *Pythagoras Revived: Mathematics and Philosophy in Late Antiquity* (Oxford, 1989) 30; Shaw, "Eros and Arithmos," 129.

32 Shaw, "Eros and Arithmos," 129. C. Van Liefferinge, *La Théurgie des Oracles Chaldaïques à Proclus* (Liège, 1999) 91.

33 E.g. Plotinus, *Enn.* 4.4.44.7–25.

34 Iambl. *VPyth.* 130, 229; Shaw, "Eros and Arithmos," 130.

35 As A. Camplani and M. Zambon, "Il sacrificio come problema in alcune correnti filosofiche di età imperiale," *AnnSE* 19 (2002) 59–99 at 87, 90, point out, Iamblichus (*Myst.* 2.9) expands the concept of theurgy, making it include even rites that the *Chaldaean Oracles* themselves reject, including traditional cult. Cf. Van Liefferinge, *La Théurgie*, 91, 208–9.

the divine life by setting *themselves* up [i.e., as opposed to the gods] as authorities, preferring to 'talk about' gods [*theologia*] rather than worship and experience them."[36] For Iamblichus, however, the "way back to the gods" was "revealed in the hieroglyphs of nature," not only the minerals, plants, animals, seasonal changes, and traditional rites "that celebrate" the gods "through song, prayer, dance, [and] images," but also through "the divine numbers."[37] Plotinus too had, "acknowledged the presence of the gods in the world and referred to their traces as moving 'letters' written in the heavens and in nature," and he had attributed powers to stones and herbs.[38] But for Iamblichus, these were the *necessary* media through which a theurgist might bring a particular soul back to the gods after diagnosing the specific *analogia* that each soul required for its return.[39] Iamblichus also believed that, despite each soul's estrangement from the God who is over all things, every soul had an "innate knowledge of the gods" which derived from its "desire for the good," a desire that even Plotinus had acknowledged.[40] Accordingly, in his view, theurgy moved human beings out of their heads and toward divine life.[41]

Although Iamblichus taught that there were three types of souls, each "self-alienated" to a different degree and each requiring a different form of theurgic worship,[42] from the standpoint of material ritual practice he did not really differentiate these types of souls very strongly. Clearly, for Iamblichus, "material souls," the "vast majority" of people, those "who follow nature and fate, should perform material worship." These "perform material theurgies employing objects that correspond to the suffering of their own alienation,"[43] rites involving "dead bodies, animal blood and eating victims, as well as the use of stones, plants and other material *synthemata*."[44] But intermediate souls—the type of soul a philosopher might have—should *also* perform material rites, Iamblichus claims, along with rites involving immaterial elements.[45] For Iamblichus, *any* soul that did not honor these gods and daemons would remain "subject to their rule" and so

36 *Myst.* 259.5–19. For example, in Iamblichus' eyes, "nature revealed the traces of … divine life, but Greek intellectuals like Porphyry could no longer see it." Shaw, "Eros and Arithmos," 125–6 (emphasis added).

37 Shaw, "Eros and Arithmos," 126.

38 *Enn.* 3.3.6.18–20; 4.35.69–70; Shaw, "Eros and Arithmos," 127.

39 *Myst.* 42.9–15; 233.7–16; 229.3–7; Shaw, "Eros and Arithmos," 128.

40 *Enn.* 3.6.17–18, 25–9; 3.3.7; 4.35.13; Shaw, "Eros and Arithmos," 123, 126–8.

41 Shaw, "Eros and Arithmos," 126. For similar points of view, see Plotinus, *Enn.* 5.5.12.12–13 and *OrChald.* 43–4 in R. Majercik (ed.) *The Chaldaean Oracles: Text, Translation and Commentary* (Leiden, 1989).

42 *Myst.* 220.6–9; Shaw, "Eros and Arithmos," 131.

43 Shaw, "Eros and Arithmos," 132.

44 *Myst.* 217.14–218.9; 233.9–12; Shaw, "Eros and Arithmos," 132; cf. also Idem, *Theurgy and the Soul*, 21–57, 162–9; B. Nasemann, *Theurgie und Philosophie in Jamblichs De mysteriis* (Stuttgart, 1991) 231–82.

45 Shaw, "Eros and Arithmos," 131–2.

could not return to the divine.[46] In Iamblichus' system even the extraordinarily rare noetic souls, those "liberated from the constraints of nature," living "according to Nous alone," needed material ritual in their early human lives, before "they attain[ed] to the unitary worship of the One only" at the end of their lives and could then perform both immaterial and noetic rituals.[47] Not only did Iamblichus unite all three types of souls by a common need to participate in material ritual, but he also hinted that a complete return to the divine might be possible even for those who possess the humbler form of soul,[48] a claim that Porphyry would roundly have rejected. In short, throughout the *De mysteriis*, "Iamblichus' entire effort is to demonstrate the superiority of theurgy over philosophy,"[49] of divinely oriented action (*theourgia*) over divinely oriented speculation (*theologia*).

Anyone familiar with Porphyry's thought can already see how Iamblichus' *On the Mysteries* would have deeply offended his philosophical sensibilities: Iamblichus had rejected his view that part of the human soul remained in contact with the divine, that philosophical speculation was divinizing in itself, and that the souls of ordinary people might have the same potential for returning to their source as souls who lived as much as possible by intellect alone. Moreover, as Shaw observes, "While Plotinus showed" respect for, but "little interest in public worship or divinational practices, Iamblichus venerated such traditional forms of religious piety as receptacles to preserve our contact with the gods."[50] Iamblichus also explored certain implications within Plotinus' thought.[51] His presumption to speak *for* and to go beyond Plotinus in these ways would have been highly disturbing to Porphyry, because it gravely undermined what he understood to be Plotinus' legacy, which he would soon seek to preserve and to defend in his edition of the *Enneads* and the *Life of Plotinus* that introduced it.

It is clear, however, that Porphyry's response to Iamblichus went far beyond his assertion of Plotinus' authority and his own privileged role in maintaining Plotinus' legacy. I suspect that a significant number of Porphyry's treatises from the *Philosophy from Oracles* to *On Images* should be seen as a response to Iamblichus' position. I shall, nevertheless, concentrate on Porphyry's *On the Return of the Soul.* The fragments that are cataloged under this title are cited verbatim only in Augustine, and it is in this work that Porphyry's response to Iamblichus is easiest to see. Although it is possible to date securely neither Porphyry's *Letter to Anebo*

---

46 *Myst.* 218.8–11; cf. 228.19–229.13.

47 *Myst.* 225.1–5; cf. 219.8; 230.18 and Shaw, "Eros and Arithmos," 131–3. See also Iambl. *De phys.num.* 126 and *VPyth.* 11, 93, 147.

48 Camplani and Zambon, "Il sacrificio come problema," 91.

49 Saffrey, "Relecture de Jamblique," 171.

50 Shaw, "Eros and Arithmos," 128.

51 A.H. Armstrong, "Tradition, Reason and Experience in the Thought of Plotinus," in *Atti del Convegno internazionale sul tema Plotino e il Neoplatonismo (Roma, 5–9 ottobre 1970)* (Rome, 1974) 171–94 at 187 = Idem (ed.), *Plotinian and Christian Studies* (London, 1979) no. 17; Shaw, "Eros and Arithmos," 123 n.8.

nor Iamblichus' *On the Mysteries*, several scholars have noticed that Porphyry's treatise *On the Return of the Soul* takes firm positions on issues that perplexed him when writing the letter to Anebo.[52] Accordingly, it is possible to argue that Porphyry wrote the letter to Anebo before setting out his own ideas about the soul's return in *On the Return of the Soul*, a work that scholars have long thought he wrote in his later years.[53] Moreover, although few scholars have followed O'Meara in thinking that the *Philosophy from Oracles* and the *On the Return of the Soul* are the same treatise, it is now more generally accepted that they share common themes, adopt a common perspective and probably were written in the same period, toward the end of Porphyry's life in the late 290s.[54] What is particularly interesting about both treatises is that they firmly reject the notion that there is one path along which all souls must travel in their return to the divine, and their claims that different paths lead different types of souls to different heavenly spheres. This aspect of these texts is usually discussed within the context of Porphyry's criticisms of Christianity—which indeed is an important theme in the surviving fragments attributed to each title. I suggest that Porphyry developed these arguments against Christianity's being a *via universalis* as part of his campaign against Iamblichus' notion that there could be *any* one path appropriate for all souls.[55] Evidence for this reaction on Porphyry's part comes not only from his explicit statement that he had searched unsuccessfully all known religious practices for a *via universalis*, but also from his quite specific delineation of the kinds of practices that bring different types of souls closer to the divine, and from his sophisticated use of theophanies in the fragments attributed to both titles as the source of what he calls *theosophy* or divine *wisdom* (as opposed to philosophy, theology, or theurgy)—a point that exceeds the scope of this paper.

It is a commonplace among scholars of early Neoplatonism that Porphyry looked for, but did not find a "universal way of salvation," as Augustine puts it in the *City of God* when reporting on Porphyry's research for the *On the Return of the Soul*.[56] As Courcelle noted long ago, the central theme of this work of Porphyry is "*omne corpus fugiendum est*,"[57] a theme that could just as easily embrace Porphyry's treatise *On Abstinence*, and, like the other work, is antithetical to Iamblichus' position regarding all souls, but especially the philosophical soul,

---

52 P. Hadot, "Citations de Porphyre chez Augustin. A propos d'un ouvrage récent," *REAug* 6 (1960) 205–44 at 213; Saffrey, "Les néoplatoniciens," 217.

53 J.J. O'Meara, *Porphyry's Philosophy from Oracles in Augustine* (Paris, 1959); Hadot, "Citations de Porphyre," 205–44.

54 T.D. Barnes, "Monotheists All?" *Phoenix* 55 (2001) 142–62.

55 Smith, *Porphyry's Place*, 139.

56 Aug. *Civ.Dei* 10.32; Smith, *Porphyry's Place*, 136.

57 Porph. *Regr.* apud Aug. *Civ Dei.* 10.29; P. Courcelle, "Nouveaux aspects du platonisme chez Saint Ambrose," *REL* 34 (1956) 220–39; Idem, "Le colle et le clou de l'âme dans la tradition néo-platonicienne et chrétienne (*Phédon* 82e; 83d)," *RBPh* 36 (1958) 72–95.

in *On the Mysteries*. This theme, Courcelle continues, works toward Porphyry's overriding goal of freeing the soul from materiality in order to enable its return to the divine (hence the title of the treatise).[58] The only path that truly frees the soul, in Porphyry's view, is the *verissima philosophia* that he has found with Plotinus,[59] a final return to God and the Empyrean celestial sphere that was granted to only a small number according to the strength of their intellect.[60] Indeed, as Courcelle astutely observes, the expression "*verissima philosophia*" implies that there are different philosophical claims at stake.[61] On the basis of parallels with Macrobius (*Somn.* 1.3.18), Origen (*In Ioh.* 1.8), Methodius (*Symp.* 9), Eusebius (*PE* 7.8.39), and Lactantius (*Div. inst.* 3.1.3), Courcelle argues that, for Porphyry, one reason this path was not universal was that it was occluded by the fog of our corporeal nature, which could only evaporate when the human soul regained its eyes—through philosophy—so that truth could be revealed unveiled and bare in its beauty.[62] Unlike Iamblichus, Porphyry thought that only philosophy could achieve an end to metempsychosis and a return of the soul to the highest possible celestial sphere, the Empyrean realm.[63] For those who live according to their intellectual soul (*anima intellectualis*), this philosophical return must begin with "the practice of virtue," but is only potentially in view when the soul of a person who has attained the higher virtues takes up philosophy and practices the theoretical virtues.[64] Philosophers, both actual and potential, should respect traditional rituals, but not to the extent that they embrace their materiality.[65] In short, for the philosopher, religious ritual involving matter was devoid of any power to return his or her soul to its source.

Porphyry's arguments against Iamblichus, that differently oriented souls must take different routes to reach the sphere of heaven suited to their capacity, were not only the subject of *On the Return of the Soul* but were probably the subject of the *Philosophy from Oracles* as well. Several scholars have attempted to map out Porphyry's system; the most recent to do so is Simmons, who draws substantially on the work of Smith. Smith's work was path-breaking, but his habit of framing Porphyry's religious system as one of multiple paths to salvation depending on

58 P. Courcelle, "Verissima philosophia," in J. Fontaine and C. Kannengiesser (eds.), *Epektasis. Mélanges patristiques offerts à Jean Daniélou* (Paris, 1972) 653–9 at 653.

59 Ibid., 659; Saffrey, "Les néoplatoniciens," 215. Cf. Courcelle, "Verissima philosophia," 655, for the history of this concept, from Plato's *Ep.* 7.326b and *Rep.* 7.521c, through Clement of Alexandria.

60 Porph. *Regr*. apud Aug. *Civ.Dei* 10.29.11; Courcelle, "Verissima philosophia," 658. For celestial spheres, see M.B. Simmons, "The Eschatological Aspects of Porphyry's Anti-Christian Polemics in a Chaldaean-Neoplatonic Context," *C&M* 52 (2001) 193–215.

61 Courcelle, "Verissima philosophia," 659.

62 Ibid., 656.

63 *Regr.* apud Aug. *Civ.Dei* 10.30.

64 Porph. *Sent.* 34; Smith, *Porphyry's Place*, 135.

65 Porph. *Abst.* 2.2, 4, 43; *Marc.* 18–19.

which part of the soul it "saved" uses terminology that seriously distorts the issue.[66] Simmons, however, rightly perceives that Porphyry actually advocated three separate paths which led the soul to three separate celestial destinations—an observation that accords nicely with Arnobius' allusion to the new men (*viri novi*), now identified as Porphyrians, who had been advocating a three-fold system.[67] The first path, of course, as all agree, is philosophy which can lead souls living by their intellectual capacity to rest with God.

Porphyry's second path, as Simmons and many others have observed, is theurgy, a path along which souls living by their spirited capacity might purify themselves and in so doing reach a higher heavenly sphere at death than they otherwise would have. For those who lived according to their spirited soul (*anima spiritalis*), Porphyry conceded that theurgy might be of some limited use in producing *phantasia* that would connect people with the gods and lead their souls to the ethereal sphere after death.[68] Here, unlike Iamblichus, Porphyry seems to be using the term in the more limited sense in which it appears in the *Chaldaean Oracles*.[69] For Porphyry, the soul's experience in the ethereal realm might advantage it during its continued quest—in its next life—to return to its source.[70] Porphyry's position on theurgy, however, dramatically contradicts Iamblichus in several ways: First Iamblichus insists that such rituals produced genuine theophanies and consequently epiphanies. Second, unlike Iamblichus, Porphyry "saw no reason" at all "why the philosopher ... should bother to participate in the theurgic rites pertaining to his lower soul,"[71] because virtue could do just as much for the spirited soul as theurgy could.[72] Just as a soul oriented toward intellect might rise to a higher sphere through philosophy and a soul oriented toward its spirited part might, through theurgy, elevate itself after death, so, I would argue, a soul oriented toward its appetites might at least direct itself toward divinity by participating in the religious practices of its native people. This is not the place to sketch out Porphyry's third path completely, but the evidence points clearly in this direction. For example, Arnobius suggests as much in saying that people

---

66 Saffrey, "Les néoplatoniciens," 215, makes a similar mistake.

67 Arn. *Nat.* 2.13; P. Courcelle, "Les sages de Porphyre et les *viri novi* d'Arnobe," *REL* 31 (1953) 257–71; E.L. Fortin, "The *Viri novi* of Arnobius and the Conflict between Faith and Reason in the Early Christian Centuries," in D. Neiman and M. Schatkin (eds.), *The Heritage of the Early Church: Essays in Honor of the Very Reverend Georges Vasilievich Florovsky* (Rome, 1973) 197–226.

68 Porph. *Regr.* apud Aug. *Civ.Dei* 10.9; Saffrey, "Les néoplatoniciens," 215; Smith, *Porphyry's Place*, 135.

69 Camplani and Zambon, "Il sacrificio come problema," 90–91.

70 E.D. Digeser, "Porphyry, Lactantius, and the Paths to God," *StudPatr* 38 (2001) 521–8.

71 Smith, *Porphyry's Place*, 136; Saffrey, "Les néoplatoniciens," 216.

72 *Sent.* 34f.

connected to the *viri novi* are advocating the use of Etruscan rituals:[73] for Romans these would be among the oldest rites associated with their polity. Second, this thesis accords with Berchman's insights about Plotinus' and Porphyry's approach to images. He reads both as thinking that something of the divine is communicated even to the ordinary soul who gazed upon a beautiful image,[74] a glimmer of insight and a connection that might lead the ordinary soul perhaps to the realm above the moon after death—from which it might be in a better position to climb even higher during its next earthly sojourn.[75]

The *via universalis* that Iamblichus set out in *De mysteriis* seems to have directly motivated Porphyry to respond in turn with his threefold paths to different celestial spheres in *On the Return of the Soul* and the *Philosophy from Oracles*. At the same time as he was arguing against Iamblichus' claim that religious rituals had the power to return all souls to the divine, Porphyry was also evidently intent on undermining claims made by *any* system that purported to provide a universal path to the God above all things. We know from Augustine that Porphyry explored Christianity as part of this search, and also—from the same source—that he found it lacking. Scholars have long recognized that Porphyry's *On the Return of the Soul* and *Philosophy from Oracles* take a strong position against mainstream Christianity. Among other things they argue that Jesus was a very pious man but not divine, and that Christians make a grave error in worshipping his human soul.[76] From Porphyry's *On Abstinence* we know that such inappropriate devotions were instrumental in attracting demons to the polity.[77] This was especially the case if such devotions were accompanied by material acts, such as the eucharist undeniably was.[78] In Porphyry's view, the attraction of demons into a city might, in turn, produce any number of ills from famine to plague to civil strife—precisely the charges laid against Christians during the Great Persecution.[79] Moreover, just

---

73 Arn. *Nat.* 2.62 See also Garth Fowden, "Late Antique Paganism Reasoned and Revealed," *JRS* 71 (1981) 178–82 at 181.

74 R. Berchman, "*Arcana Mundi* between Balaam and Hecate: Prophecy, Divination, and Magic in Later Platonism," in D. Lull (ed.), *SBL Seminar Papers* (Atlanta, 1989) 107–85.

75 Digeser, "Porphyry, Lactantius, and the Paths to God," 521–8. Simmons, "The Eschatological Aspects," 196, identifies virtue as the third path for the soul. But in the passage he cites (Aug. *Civ.Dei* 10.28), Porphyry is really describing how the virtue of continence purifies the philosopher, negating his need for theurgy. This is the entire message of *On Abstinence* as well as the fragments of *Regr.* that Augustine preserves in *Civ. Dei* 10.23 and 10.9, and it is made clear in the *Sentences* as well.

76 E.D. Digeser, "Lactantius, Porphyry and the Debate over Religious Toleration," *JRS* 88 (1998) 129–46.

77 *Abst.* 2.37, 40.

78 Porph. apud Eus. *PE* 5.1.

79 See Arn. *Nat.* 1.1 and E.D. Digeser, "Lactantius, Eusebius and Arnobius: Evidence for the Causes of the Great Persecution," *StudPatr* 39 (2006) 33–46.

as Porphyry had attacked Iamblichus' *via universalis* through a careful exegesis of the divine oracles upon which his claims were based, he *also* applied this technique to undermine a wide variety of Christian claims, from Old Testament prophecies used to predict Jesus' advent, works, and divine identity, to New Testament testimony on Jesus' salvific mission. In this effort, Porphyry not only challenged the credibility of the Gospel accounts by calling attention to discrepancies and non sequiturs within and between them. But he also challenged the sophisticated allegorical techniques that scholars such as Origen had applied to the Hebrew Bible in their attempt to produce a Christian philosophy that surpassed and was "truer" than its Platonist precursor. Porphyry pursues these analyses in passages that are now grouped under the name of *Against the Christians*. Whatever their name, it is clear that they had the same agenda as *On the Return of the Soul*, namely to undermine Christianity's claim to being a *via universalis*—or really to its being any viable path at all in its mainstream form.[80]

By the turn of the fourth century, Porphyry's arguments against "mainstream" Christianity, a product of his campaign to preserve Plotinus' *verissima philosophia* from Iamblichus' universalizing innovations, had started to circulate widely. We know, for example, that some of Porphyry's arguments found their way to Antioch where an anonymous Hellene used them in public debates against local Christians.[81] Arnobius, Lactantius, and Eusebius all connect Porphyry's arguments in *Against the Christians*, *On the Return of the Soul*, and *The Philosophy from Oracles* with the charges and attitudes that culminated in Diocletian's edicts against the Christians in 303.[82] Although Iamblichus was no great lover of Christians himself,[83] it is ironic that Porphyry's wide-ranging response to his position on the universally salvific power of religious ritual did nothing at all to quell the popularity of the younger philosopher's school, but indirectly helped to fan the flames of the Great Persecution.[84]

---

80 E.D. Digeser, "Porphyry, Julian, or Hierokles? The Anonymous Hellene in Makarios Magnês' *Apocriticus*," *JThS* n.s. 53 (2002) 466–502.

81 Ibid. 466–502.

82 Digeser, "Lactantius, Eusebius and Arnobius," 33–46.

83 *Myst* 3.31.179–180; 10.2.

84 *Sent.* 34f.

Chapter 6

Subjugating the Divine: Iamblichus on the Theurgic Evocation

Sergio Knipe
Cambridge University

At the close of the third century, the Neoplatonist philosopher Iamblichus was met with an unexpected intellectual challenge in the form of a fictional epistle from his one-time master, Porphyry of Tyre. In the *Letter to Anebo* (*Epistula ad Anebonem*), Porphyry had addressed a series of queries to an (imaginary) Egyptian priest with the purpose of drawing attention to what he perceived to be serious religious *aporiai*. Porphyry was especially concerned with the problem of theurgy, a doctrine that Iamblichus keenly advocated. While similarly voicing his respect for the "perfect" theurgic art (which allows man to receive holy visions of the gods and embark on the path to εὐδαιμονία),[1] Porphyry argued that the priest Anebo was misrepresenting theurgy by defending senseless practices such as blood sacrifice and the use of βάρβαρα or ἄσημα ὀνόματα.[2] The one issue which proved most irksome for Porphyry was that of the alleged control or subjugation of the divine at the hands of Egyptian theurgists. According to Iamblichus, Porphyry complained: "A thing that very much troubles me is this: how does it come about that we invoke the gods as our superiors, but then give them orders as if they were our inferiors?"[3]

Porphyry's question about ritual coercion is largely rhetorical: an interrogative denunciation, it points to what the philosopher regarded as a significant inconsistency in the theory and practice of theurgy. Iamblichus, instead, read the *Letter to Anebo* as a challenge to his own doctrinal system, and fashioned a polemical response to Porphyry's query. "Une apologie de la théurgie,"[4] On the Mysteries of Egypt (*De mysteriis Agyptiorum*) was composed

---

1 Porph. *Aneb.* 2.6b, 14a, 18–19.

2 *Aneb.* 2.3a, 8b, 10. On the theurgic use of βάρβαρα / ἄσημα ὀνόματα, consider M. Hirschle, *Sprachphilosophie und Namenmagie im Neuplatonismus: Mit einem Exkurs zu "Demokrit" B 142* (Meisenheim am Glan, 1979) 45–8; F. Graf, *Gottesnähe und Schadenzauber: Die Magie in der griechisch-römischen Antike* (Munich, 1996) 195–8; P. Struck, "Speech Acts and the Stakes of Hellenism in Late Antiquity," in M.W. Meyer and P.A. Mirecki (eds.), *Magic and Ritual in the Ancient World* (Leiden, 2001) 386–406 at 391–6.

3 Iambl. *Myst.* 181.2–3. Cf. Porph. *Aneb.* 2.3a–b, 8a–c.

4 H.D. Saffrey, "Analyse de la réponse de Jamblique à Porphyre, connue sous le titre: *De mysteriis*," *RSPh* 84.3 (2000) 489–511 at 490.

by Iamblichus around the year 300 under the pseudonym of Abamon (or Anebo's superior in rank).[5] The treatise was conceived as a reply to the *Letter to Anebo*[6] and a way to counter Porphyry's "entire subversion of all the ceremonies of religion."[7] Iamblichus' response to Porphyry in *Mysteries* initiated, "one of the more fascinating debates of the late antique world, one that involved social, intellectual, and existential questions with significant consequences … for all thinkers of Late Antiquity."[8] In addressing the difficult issue of how theurgists might legitimately claim to control higher forces, *Mysteries* also provides what is perhaps the most articulate pagan reflection on the origins, nature, and limits of supernatural, ritual power.

Iamblichus first developed his critique of Porphyry's view of theurgy in book 3 of his treatise, which focuses on divination. Here the author disputes Porphyry's claim that the use of symbols and characters at the hands of Egyptian theurgists is irreligious and absurd. He draws a distinction between real theurgists on the one hand, and illegitimate practitioners on the other:

> When you say "those who stand on characters" (οἱ ἐπὶ χαρακτήρων στάντες) you have put your finger on nothing less than the cause of all evils concerning these practices [theurgic invocations]. For certain persons, disdaining the entire task of effective contemplation (τὴν ὅλην πραγματείαν τῆς τελεσιουργοῦ θεωρίας), both in regard to the one who invokes and to the one who enjoys the vision (περὶ τε τὸν καλοῦντα καὶ περὶ τὸν ἐπόπτην),[9] and disregarding the order of the ritual and the most sacred and extensive perseverance in labours over a long period of time, reject sacred laws and prayers and other holy preparations and believe that standing on characters alone is sufficient.[10]

---

5 On the authorship and dating of *Mysteries* see E.C. Clarke, J.M. Dillon, and J.P. Hershbell (eds.), *Iamblichus: De Mysteriis* (Leiden and Boston, 2004) xxvii–xxx.

6 As H.D. Saffrey notes (in "Analyse"), a better title for *Mysteries* would be, "*Réponse à Porphyre*." Concerning the date of Porphyry's *Letter to Anebo* see E.C. Clarke, *Iamblichus' De Mysteriis: A Manifesto of the Miraculous* (Aldershot, 2001) 6. For an analysis of the close parallels between *Mysteries* and the *Letter to Anebo* see E.C. Clarke, J.M. Dillon, and J.P. Hershbell (eds.), *Iamblichus: De Mysteriis* (Leiden and Boston, 2004) Introduction (with further bibliographical references).

7 Iambl. *Myst.* 230.11: τὸ παράπαν τὴν ὅλην ἀνέστρεψεν ἁγιστείαν.

8 G. Shaw, "Divination in the Neoplatonism of Iamblichus," in R.M. Berchman (ed.), *Mediators of the Divine: Horizons of Prophecy, Divination, Dreams and Theurgy in Mediterranean Antiquity* (Atlanta, 1998) 225–67 at 228.

9 Regarding the use of the term κλήτορες (callers) in theurgy, see H. Lewy, *Chaldaean Oracles and Theurgy: Mysticism, Magic and Platonism in the Later Roman Empires* (Paris, 1978) 467–71.

10 *Myst.* 131.3–9. Cf. Porph. *Aneb.* 2.2e. All passages quoted from *Mysteries* are based on Clarke, Dillon, and Hershbell, *Iamblichus: De Mysteriis*; all translations from the Greek are my own.

When read in the wider context of *Mysteries*, the distinction Iamblichus draws in this passage between legitimate and illegitimate theurgy can be seen as a theoretical justification of the supernatural, coercive power of theurgy against the scepticism of those who, like Porphyry, would seek to question it. In this respect, Iamblichus' distinction between legitimate and illegitimate ritual practice holds the key to the issue of the theurgic coercion of supernatural forces. But in order to appreciate the significance of Iamblichus' ideal of ritual legitimacy, it is necessary first to consider the doctrinal framework in which it was formulated. The best gateway into the teaching of *Mysteries* is found in the very semantics of the term "theurgy."

As "divine action" or "divine work" situated on a ritual plane, theurgy ultimately aimed at spiritual transcendence or the liberation of the soul.[11] According to *Mysteries*, this goal cannot be achieved by means of intrinsic human virtue and wisdom, since "even the perfect soul is imperfect with respect to divine activity." Rather:

> The successful accomplishment of divine actions is given only by the gods. Otherwise it would not at all be necessary to worship the gods, but, following this reasoning, divine blessings would exist for us of themselves without the performance of ritual.[12]

Theurgy, in *Mysteries*, primarily consists of the successful performance of specific ritual practices made possible by the aid of the gods. To be more exact, what makes it possible for the theurgist to free his own soul through ritual practice is a force permeating the cosmos, a universal φιλία which holds the universe together.[13] Iamblichus describes the cosmos (τὸ πᾶν) as "a single living being (ἓν ζῷον)" whose parts are "spatially distinct, but, through the possession of one nature, hasten to each other."[14]

The author of *Mysteries* explains that, "since it was necessary that earthly things not be deprived of participation in the divine, the earth received a certain share in divinity, capable of receiving the gods."[15] The particular portions of the earth which allow the material world to enter directly in contact with the divine are σύμβολα (symbols) and συνθήματα (tokens): these elements possess an

---

[11] Pierre Hadot provides a useful definition of theurgy as, "une technique révélée par les dieux eux-mêmes pour permettre à l'homme d'entrer en contact avec eux." See P. Hadot, "Théologie, exégèse, révélation, écriture dans la philosophie grecque," in M. Tardieu (ed.), *Les Règles de l'interprétation* (Paris, 1987) 13–34 at 27.

[12] *Myst.* 149.11–17. Cf. *Myst.* 47.11–48.3.

[13] See *Myst.* 211.

[14] *Myst.* 195.10–12.

[15] *Myst.* 233.6–8.

affinity with the gods who engendered them,[16] and reveal the divine order of the cosmos.[17] Iamblichus mentions σύμβολα and συνθήματα as being present in certain incantations, concoctions, ineffable names, melodies, and traced characters; but also in stones, herbs, animals, sticks, pebbles, incense, water, walls, and phallic objects.[18] Theurgy is the art by which symbols and tokens are used to free oneself "from the fate of the processes of generation (τῆς γενεσιουργοῦ μοίρας) and from a society dependent on the body (τῆς ἀντεχομένης τῶν σωμάτων κοινωνίας)":[19]

> The theurgic art, recognising this principle [of φιλία], and generally, in accordance with the properties of each one of the gods, having discovered receptacles adapted to them, often brings together stones, plants, animals, aromatic substances, and other sacred, perfect, and godlike objects of a similar kind, and from all these produces an integrated and pure receptacle (ὑποδοχὴν ὁλοτελῆ καὶ καθαράν).[20]

Through the ritual use of divine symbols, according to Iamblichus, the theurgist is able to transcend his own mortality and to attain a higher level of being. If human nature is commonly "inhabiting the borderland" between a confined terrestrial existence and higher realms,[21] the presence of divinity in matter allows the theurgist to attain a higher ontological status:

---

16 See *Myst.* 119.6–7: "Whatever happens to possess a likeness to the gods directly participates in them."

17 Iamblichus writes (*Myst.* 65.7–8) that "the inexpressible is expressed through ineffable symbols." See too G. Shaw, *Theurgy and the Soul* (University Park, PA, 1995) 162, 164.

18 See *Myst.* 38.10–39.1, 118.13–119.7, 133.13–134.7, 141.11–142.3, 157.8, 233.9–13, 235.5–11.

19 *Myst.* 220.2–3.

20 *Myst.* 233.9–13. Exactly what form the "perfect and pure receptacle" of the soul would take is impossible to determine. According to a recent attempt at reconstruction, the theurgic process would purify the body of the soul, described as an aetheric and luminous vehicle (αἰθερῶδες καὶ αὐγοιδὲς ὄχημα: *Myst.* 132.10) and breath (πνεῦμα: *Myst.* 125.5). In the process, the theurgist would assume a divine appearance and be conjoined with the Demiurge (*Myst.* 184.3–6, 292.4–14); freed from all passions and untouchable by evil spirits (*Myst.* 178.8–16), he would turn into a vehicle for the manifestation of divinity in the physical world. See Iamb. *Comm. in Tim.* fr.81, 84; Shaw, *Theurgy*, 51.

21 See A.C. Lloyd, *The Anatomy of Neoplatonism* (Oxford, 1990) 123; H.D. Saffrey, "Les livres IV à VII du *De Mysteriis* de Jamblique relus avec la Lettre de Porphyre à Anébon," in H.J. Blumenthal and E.G. Clarke (eds.), *The Divine Iamblichus: Philosopher and Man of Gods* (Liverpool, 1993) 144–58 at 152: "La condition de l'homme est double: il peut s'élever par l'intellect dans le ciel des dieux immatériels, il peut rester lié au corps et possédé par la matière."

> The whole of theurgy presents a twofold character. On the one hand, it is performed by men, and as such preserves the order possessed by our nature in the universe; on the other, it controls divine symbols (τὸ δὲ κρατυνόμενον θείοις συνθήμασι) and in virtue of them is conjoined to higher powers, and directs itself harmoniously in accordance with their dispensation, which enables it quite properly to be surrounded with the external form of the gods (τὸ τῶν θεῶν σχῆμα περιτίθεσθαι).[22]

As Shaw suggests, because the human soul in Iamblichean metaphysics exists in a fallen condition, theurgic elevation can be accomplished only through a metaphysical leap: "to become a vehicle of divine action" the soul must "step outside itself."[23] It is this very notion which Iamblichus seeks to convey when he suggests that "by virtue of the sacred liturgy" the theurgist "is established within the gods and united to them."[24] The theurgist who undergoes this process of ontological elevation then:

> invokes as his superiors the powers of the universe, since the one making the invocation is a man, yet in a sense also commands (ἐπιτάττει) them, since by means of the ineffable symbols, he is clothed in the shape of the gods (τὸ ἱερατικὸν τῶν θεῶν πρόσχημα).[25]

The challenge Iamblichus' theory of theurgy poses to the pious scepticism of Porphyry is conspicuous: while the author of the *Letter to Anebo* implied that coercion of the divine is something which theurgy cannot achive—and ought not attempt—in the above passage Iamblichus appears to be arguing that ritual subjugation can and does take place. If read out of context, Iamblichus' conclusions regarding the ritual effectiveness of theurgic power can be seen to reinforce Porphyry's negative stereotype of specific theurgic practices (as exemplified by Anebo); *prima facie*, the Iamblichean doctrine of theurgy appears both religiously problematic and socially dangerous.

Despite the secretive nature of theurgic practice, it is clear that Iamblichus was treading on dangerous terrain when claiming that the theurgist could command supernatural powers through the use of symbols. In formulating certain claims, the author of *Mysteries* was exposing himself to accusations of attempting to compel and manipulate the divine through ritual: Iamblichus, in other words, was exposing himself to charges of sorcery—a serious crime under Diocletian.[26]

---

22 *Myst.* 184.1–6.

23 Shaw, "Divination," 249.

24 *Myst.* 47.6–7.

25 *Myst.* 184.7–10.

26 On the suppression of the magical arts under Diocletian see M.T. Fögen, *Die Enteignung der Wahrsager: Studien zum kaiserlichen Wissensmonopol in der Spätantike* (Frankfurt, 1993) esp. 63–9.

No doubt, the ways in which acts of ritual compulsion were exercised in "magical" practices—what Greek sources describe as γοητεία[27]—appear remarkably similar to the methods Iamblichus describes in relation to theurgy. Like the theurgist, the γόης or magician knew words and actions—the so-called "binding formulas" or "words which compel" (ἐπανάγκοι)[28]—through which he could evoke and compel supernatural powers.[29] Both in magical papyri and in ancient sources critical of γοητεία, practitioners are described employing formulae to evoke demons that are then put to use in various ways.[30] By means of *uoces magicae*, for instance, a sorcerer could evoke a helper or πάρεδρος—a god or angel, or more commonly a demon—which was forced to serve him as a slave.[31]

Given the conspicuous similarities between theurgy and magical, "goetic" evocation, it is not surprising that a philosopher with a Platonist background such as Porphyry would wish to express criticism of those theurgic practices he perceived

---

[27] Γοητεία, like the related term μαγεία, was employed as a polemical category and a dismissive label for those ritual practices deemed dangerous or inappropriate. On the origin, use, and meaning of Greek and Roman terms pertaining to magic and sorcery, see J.N. Bremmer, "The Birth of the Term 'Magic'," *ZPE* 126 (1999) 1–12; G. Luck, "Witches and Sorcerers in Classical Literature," in V. Flint et al. (eds.), *Witchcraft and Magic in Europe: Ancient Greece and Rome* (London, 1999) 93–158 at 98–107; N. Janowitz, *Magic in the Roman World: Pagans, Jews, and Christians* (London, 2001) 9–16; M.W. Dickie, *Magic and Magicians in the Greco–Roman World* (London and New York, 2001) 135–41 and 224–9. For a recent overview of the (problematic) use of the term "magic" as a descriptive label in contemporary academic discourse, see S. Noegel, J. Walker, and B. Wheeler (eds.), *Prayer, Magic, and the Stars in the Ancient and Late Antique World* (University Park, PA, 2003) Introduction; S. Trzcionka, *Magic and the Supernatural in Fourth–Century Syria* (London and New York, 2007) § 2.

[28] See Graf, *Gottesnähe*, 181 and 199.

[29] While not all ritual action described in the *Greek Magical Papyri* is coercive in nature, much of it undoubtedly is. See F. Graf, "Prayer in Magical and Religious Ritual," in C.A. Faraone and D. Obbink (eds.), *Magika Hiera: Ancient Greek Magic and Religion* (New York, 1991) 188–213; Dickie, *Magic*, 16, 26, 202. More significantly, forceful (and hence sacrilegious) subjugation of the divine was considered to be one of the defining characteristics of γοητεία. See Graf, *Gottesnähe*, 198–201; S. Pulleyn, *Prayer in Greek Religion* (Oxford, 1997) 93–5; Luck, "Witches," 96 and 102; J. Braarvig, "Magic: Reconsidering the Grand Dichotomy," in D.R. Jordan, H. Montgomery, and E. Thomassen (eds.), *The World of Ancient Magic: Papers from the First International Samson Eitrem Seminar at the Norwegian Institute at Athens, 4–8 May 1997* (Bergen, 1999) 37–40.

[30] Libanius, for instance, relates (*Decl.* 41.29) how "demons of the worse kind, whose nature it is to work evil, take delight in the mystic rites performed by these magicians and help them in their dread doings which are fraught with ruin to mankind."

[31] See Graf, *Gottesnähe*, 88, 93, 99, 176; L. Ciraolo, "Supernatural Assistants in the Greek Magical Papyri," in M. Meyer and P. Mirecki (eds.), *Ancient Magic and Ritual Power* (Leiden, 1995) 279–95.

to be akin to sorcery,[32] and that by contrast, someone like Iamblichus, who wished to employ specific ritual methods while maintaining a respectable, philosophical approach to religion, would be forced to justify his theurgic technique in order to render it acceptable. In the late third and early fourth century, the risk of conflating theurgy with sorcery was certainly a distinct possibility—Porphyry himself was well aware that "one person's philosopher might be another's *magus*."[33] Because "rituals that claim to reveal divinity on earth can look to outsiders as if their purpose is to manipulate that same divine power,"[34] Iamblichus' attempt to justify the notion of theurgic evocation came to play a prominent role in his doctrinal system. Only by defining the theurgic process of evocation and subjugation in philosophically acceptable terms could Iamblichus hope to justify the use of ritual techniques that would otherwise be dismissed as mere acts of manipulative magic.

Iamblichus' solution to the challenge of advocating the theurgic subjugation of higher powers while seeking to avoid charges of magic was to draw a distinction between the proper, theurgic use of symbols and an illegitimate use of the kind made by "those who stand on characters." The crucial factor that distinguishes the two uses of symbols, as explained in *Mysteries*, lies in the very process of elevation and transformation which the theurgist undergoes. According to Iamblichus, the theurgist who follows the appropriate order of the ritual will be able to attain a higher ontological status; but it is only once the theurgist has reached this higher status that he will he be able, if necessary, to command and even threaten lesser deities such as the "irrational genus of δαίμονες without judgment."[35] An important point raised in *Mysteries* is that the theurgist cannot command the gods, because the gods cannot be duped or constrained.[36] But if the theurgist can constrain δαίμονες, it is because, "through arcane symbols, he, in certain respects, is invested with the sacred form of the gods."[37] The theurgist's threats to δαίμονες, in Iamblichus' words, serve to reveal "the magnitude and quality of the power which he possesses through a union with the gods, and which

32 Already Plato had voiced his disdain for the γόης, while Porphyry's own master Plotinus had accused the Gnostics of foolishly attempting to subjugate higher powers. See Plato, *Soph.* 234a–35a; *Resp.* 413b–d and 598d; *Meno*, 80b; *Grg.* 483e; Plotinus, *Enn.* 2.9.14.1–8; H. Remus, "Plotinus and Gnostic Thaumaturgy," *LThPh* 39 (1983) 13–20.

33 J. Rives, "Magic in Roman Law: the Reconstruction of a Crime," *ClAnt* 22 (2003) 313–39 at 325. Cf. Porph. *Reg.* 289 F. Less than a century after Porphyry's death, theurgy was intentionally (and polemically) conflated with magic by Augustine (*Civ.Dei* 10.9), who talked of "that which they call either by the more despicable name of goetic magic or by the more honourable one of theurgy."

34 Janowitz, *Magic*, 1.

35 *Myst.* 182.2: ἀλόγιστον καὶ ἄκριτον γένος. Cf. *Myst.* 246.5–11.

36 *Myst.* 45.4–5: "A divine nature is incapable of being allured, is impassive and uncompelled."

37 *Myst.* 184.9–10.

he obtains from the knowledge of ineffable symbols."[38] The theurgist can only exercise a coercive power over certain supernatural creatures because he has transcended his own mortality. Once the theurgist has attained a supra-human status, he can command δαίμονες because he finds himself on the same level as the gods: theurgists "empowered by divine symbols" are "established within the gods and united to them."[39]

Iamblichus' solution to the doubts first raised by Porphyry, then, is based on the notion that legitimate theurgic power derives from the one factor that distinguishes it from magic: divine support. Iamblichus' ritual system, to quote Dufault, "saved religious practice from an accusation of magic by placing ritual agency in the hands of the divine."[40] As Iamblichus emphasizes in *Mysteries*, in order to reach the elevated status from which it is possible to evoke and compel δαίμονες, the theurgist must first make use of formulae (σύμβολα and συνθήματα) that derive their power from the gods, by will of the gods. The theurgist never acts against the will of the gods: "the divine … is not forced into service through the ritual. Rather, the divine responds to an invocation out of overflowing benevolence."[41] In this respect, the theurgic rite is a paradoxical process. On the one hand, like γοητεία, it can be said to work "automatically," because symbols "by themselves, perform their own work without our thinking, and the ineffable power of the gods to whom these symbols relate, recognizes, by itself, the proper images of itself, and it is not awakened to this by our thinking."[42] On the other hand, the theurgic process of spiritual elevation depends, just like prayer, on the grace (χάρις) of the gods.[43] As Johnston suggests, Iamblichean "theurgy" is not to be translated as "working *upon* the gods," but rather as "being worked upon *by* gods," for "the theurgist's method of summoning the gods, like the *symbola*, was bestowed upon him by the gods themselves."[44]

By contrast, Iamblichus explains that "those who stand on characters," those who do not follow theurgy and make inappropriate use of symbols, will never

38 *Myst.* 247.3–5. Cf. *Myst.* 246.12–247.2: "The theurgist, through the power of arcane symbols, commands cosmic entities, no longer as man, nor as employing a human soul; but as existing superior to them in the order of the gods, he makes use of threats greater than are consistent with his own proper essence."

39 *Myst.* 47.6–7.

40 O. Dufault, "Magic and Religion in Augustine and Iamblichus," in R.M. Frakes and E.D. Digeser (eds.), *Religious Identity in Late Antiquity* (Toronto, 2006) 59–84 at 76.

41 P. Struck, "The Poet as Conjurer: Magic and Literary Theory in Late Antiquity," in L. Ciraolo and J. Seidel (eds.), *Magic and Divination in the Ancient World* (Leiden, Boston, and Cologne, 2002) 119–31 at 124. Cf. Shaw, *Theurgy*, 111.

42 *Myst.* 97.4–7.

43 See Pulleyn, *Prayer*, 93–5, 98.

44 S.I. Johnston, *Hekate Soteira* (Atlanta, 1990) 86–7. Cf. P. Athanassiadi, *La lutte pour l'orthodoxie dans le platonisme tardif de Numénius à Damascius* (Paris, 2006) 41 n.33.

attain a higher status from which any evocation and control of δαίμονες is possible. Rather, these individuals will fall prey to their own illusion:

> All those who are guilty of crime and fall upon and assault the divine in a lawless and disorderly way are not able to attain to the gods due to the slackness of their energy or deficiency of their inherent power. And on account of certain defilements they are excluded from association with pure spirits but are joined to evil spirits; and being filled by them with the worst possession, they become wicked and unholy, glutted with licentious pleasures, filled with evil, and affect habits foreign to the gods.[45]

In the eyes of Iamblichus, the un-orderly, inappropriate performance of theurgy represents a manipulative, forceful act: like any act of sorcery, it is simply a "performative self-assertion"[46] devoid of χάρις and religious effectiveness.

What Iamblichus' division between legitimate and illegitimate theurgy ultimately suggests is that at the basis of the philosophical conflict between Porphyry and Iamblichus lies the delicate issue of supernatural, ritual power. What was crucial for the two philosophers was the question of *who* exercised this supernatural power and *in what way*. As has been observed, the debate between Iamblichus and Porphyry, which "raised the question of divine causation in ritual in a more demanding and explicit way than traditional religion,"[47] "reveals critical issues concerning the role and significance of ritual for all thinkers in Late Antiquity."[48] Iamblichus' reply to Porphyry points to a central concern of all holy men, that of distancing themselves from accusations of ritual manipulation by proving that the religious power they embrace is divinely inspired and hence legitimate.[49] In addressing Porphyry's doubts and in formulating a defence of specific practices, the author of *Mysteries* was at the same time defending himself against possible accusations of sorcery. Aware that the ritual techniques which he advocated might be seen as futile attempts to manipulate the divine in ways which were absurd and hubristic for a Neoplatonist philosopher, Iamblichus set out to prove that the true origins of the theurgist's power, unlike that of

---

45 *Myst.* 176.11–177.3. Cf. *Myst.* 182.11–13 and 191.4–8.

46 E. Thomassen, "Is Magic a Subclass of Ritual?," in D.R. Jordan, H. Montgomery, and E. Thomassen (eds.), *The World of Ancient Magic: Papers from the First International Samson Eitrem Seminar at the Norwegian Institute at Athens, 4–8 May 1997* (Bergen, 1999) 55–66 at 64.

47 A. Smith, *Philosophy in Late Antiquity* (Abingdon and New York, 2004) 82.

48 G. Shaw, "Containing Ecstasy: the Strategies of Iamblichean Theurgy," *Dionysius* 21 (2003) 53–87 at 54.

49 The assumption here is that, "spiritual force must be under the direction of true religion and those in authority, not summoned up by magic or the incantation of a powerful name" (F.E. Brenk, "In the Light of the Moon: Demonology of the Early Imperial Period," *ANRW* 2.16.3 [1986] 2068–2145 at 2115).

magicians, lay in divine authority. In *Mysteries*, Iamblichus argued that the divine is not forced into service through the theurgic ritual, but that it responds to the practitioner out of overflowing benevolence;[50] and that when compulsion *does* come into play, as in the case of the evocation of δαίμονες, it is justified by the supra-human and godly status which the theurgist has acquired by grace of the gods.

[50] See Shaw, *Theurgy*, 111; C. van Liefferinge, *La Théurgie: Des oracles Chaldaïque à Proclus* (Liège, 1999) 57; Struck, "The Poet," 124.

Chapter 7
Arbiter of the Oracular: Reading Religion in Porphyry of Tyre*

Aaron P. Johnson
University of Chicago

In antiquity, the oracular—the mantic, the prophetic—was something that could scarcely be contained by civic or religious authorities. Indeed, the oracular continued to spill out and overflow whatever limits might be carefully laid around it. Channels of the prophetic and divinatory remained unpredictable in their currents and continued to challenge the authority of governing bodies from archaic Athens[1] to Augustan Rome,[2] Antioch in the time of Licinius,[3] or again in the time of Valens,[4] and beyond. Like sparks flashing across a darkened forge,[5] oracular activity leapt forth in myriad insuppressible directions under the blows of institutional hammering, scattering bits of numinosity and divine presence into the daily activities of both urban and rural populations across the ancient and late ancient Mediterranean.

---

* This paper has benefited a great deal from comments of the participants at the Shifting Frontiers Conference in Boulder, Colorado, especially Gillian Clark, Heidi Marx-Wolff, and Beth Digeser, as well as from subsequent conversations with Richard Sorabji, Timothy Barnes, and Ilinca Tanaseanu-Doebler. The illuminating work of Aude Busine, which I now consider to be the most important modern treatment of the *Phil.Orac.*, came to my attention only after the original presentation of this paper. I am grateful for her incisive criticisms and discussion, both in person and correspondence, during the course of my revisions.

[1] E.g., Onomacritus under the Peisistratids, see Hdt. 7.6.3; J. Dillery, "Chresmologues and *Manteis*: Independent Diviners and the Problem of Authority," in S.I. Johnston and P. Struck (eds.), *Mantikê: Studies in Ancient Divination* (Leiden, 2005) 167–231 at 189–92.

[2] Suet. *Aug.* 31; cf. the burning of oracular books during the Second Punic War as recounted by Livy 25.12.2.

[3] Eus. *HE* 9.3, 11.5–6; *PE* 4.2.11; A.P. Johnson, *Ethnicity and Argument in Eusebius'* Praeparatio Evangelica (Oxford, 2006) 160–62.

[4] Amm. 29.1–2; Lib. *Or.* 1.3, 119; Zos. 4.15; J. Matthews, *The Roman Empire of Ammianus* (London, 1989) 219–25; N. Lenski, *Failure of Empire: Valens and the Roman State in the Fourt Century* (Berkeley, 2002) 218–34; D. Potter, *Prophets and Emperors* (Cambridge, MA, 1994) 179–82.

[5] The metaphor used here is altered from that found in the Babylonian Talmud, *Shabbat* 88a *Sanhedrin* 34a.

The conjunction of religion with writing—the oracular with the textual—marked the attempt to control and delimit such otherwise uncontrollable movements of the divine and social spheres,[6] while at the same time exhibiting a new profusion of the oracular within a new medium. Writing allowed the fiction of containing the loquacity of the divine voices that chattered forth from within caves and sacred springs, echoed from the mouths of once mute statues, whispered in dreams, pierced the air in the frenzied screams of prophetesses, or drummed stone tables in the clickety-clack of dice. A prominent feature of the personnel at Apollo's oracles of Delphi, Didyma, and Claros were the diligent scribes who fixed the sometimes incoherent babblings of the god's inspired mouthpiece in a readable if not more understandable form.[7] Written oracular and divinatory texts—those of the free-wheeling diviner Bacis and his circle,[8] the officially inscribed stelai at the Asclepieion of Epidaurus (in the classical period),[9] the responses of Apollo's great prophetic centers (extant in a number of literary and epigraphic forms), the pillars of carefully organized divinatory responses connected to dice-throwing in Asia Minor,[10] the Sibylline Oracles guarded safely by the *XV viri sacris faciundis*,[11] or the divinely inspired number system of the *Sortes Astrampsychi*[12]—all marked the attempts by a literate, and hence narrow, section of society to funnel the slippery and sometimes messy flow of divine utterance into manageable units. Even though writing functioned in differing ways in the examples just enumerated, its use in oracular and divinatory contexts remained a means of establishing fixity and limits to what could be heard of the divine voice.

It is against this backdrop of what may be termed the textualization of the oracular that we must view the intriguing and frustratingly fragmentary remains of Porphyry of Tyre's *Philosophy from Oracles*, a text written sometime in the latter half of the third (or early fourth) century[13] that survives only within the pages of its

---

6 Cf. Dillery, "Chresmologues and *Manteis*," 167–231.

7 See A. Busine, *Paroles d'Apollon: Pratiques et traditions oraculaires dans l'Antiquité tardive* (Leiden, 2005) 50–54.

8 See Hdt. 8.20.2, 77.1–2, 96.2; 9.43.2; Dillery, "Chresmologues and *Manteis*," 179–81.

9 L. LiDonnici, *The Epidaurian Miracle Inscriptions* (Atlanta, 1995).

10 See F. Graf, "Rolling the Dice for an Answer," in Johnston and Struck, *Mantikê*, 51–97.

11 See E. Orlin, *Temples, Religion and Politics in the Roman Republic* (Leiden, 1997) 76–115.

12 See D. Frankfurter, *Religion in Roman Egypt* (Princeton, 1998) 179–84; Idem, "Voices, Books, and Dreams: The Diversification of Divination Media in Late Antique Egypt," in Johnston and Struck, *Mantikê*, 233–54 at 246–7.

13 Our only firm evidence for the date of the *Philosophy from Oracles* is the terminus ante quem of its Christian respondents in the second decade of the 4th century (certainly Eus. *PE*, and possibly Lact. *Div.inst.*, Arn. *Adv.nat.*, and Ps.-Justin [= Marcellus] *Exhortation to the Greeks*). Eun. *VSoph.* 4.1.11 (457), suggests ("probably … so it seems …")

Christian opponents. It is fortunate that Porphyry, the author of the greatest literary attack against Christianity in antiquity,[14] had fomented such ire and created such resentment among some of the most formidable and erudite Christian thinkers of Late Antiquity that they chose to quote often lengthy portions of his works in their retaliatory tirades. The *Philosophy from Oracles* now totals roughly 56 pages in the recent Teubner edition of his fragments[15] and derives primarily from Eusebius' *Praeparatio Evangelica*[16] and Augustine's *City of God*,[17] while John Philoponus,[18] Firmicus Maternus,[19] and the so-called *Tübingen Theosophy*[20] fill up the remainder of our fragmentary fund. In spite of the work's later misfortunes, it is clear that the original treatise in three books[21] centered upon the philosophical appropriation of a collection of oracles of varying provenance: from the Apollo at Didyma[22] to the likes of Hecate, Serapis, and Hermes—possibly produced in "free-lance"

---

that Porphyry wrote a book on oracles in his youth, claiming that this book contained a special oracle addressed to him; it is most economical to take this as a reference to the *Philosophy from Oracles*, as G. Wolff, *Porphyrii de Philosophia ex Oraculis Haurienda Librorum Reliquiae* (Berlin, 1856) 38.

14 Fragments of his *Contra Christianos* were first collected by A. von Harnack, *Porphyrios, "Gegen die Christen," 15 Bucher: Zeugnisse, Fragmente und Referate*, Abhandlungen der königlichen preussischen Akademie der Wissenschaften, philosophisch–historische Klasse, Nr. 1 (Berlin, 1916), and Idem, *Neue Fragmente des Werks des Porphyrius gegen die Christen*, Sitzungsberichte der Akademie der Wissenschaften zu Berlin, Phil.-hist. Klasse (Berlin, 1921). They have since been variously supplemented or questioned. For the hypothesis that the *Philosophy from Oracles* is to be equated with the *Against the Christians*, see P.F. Beatrice, "Towards a new edition of Porphyry's fragments against the Christians," in M.O. Goulet-Caze et al. (eds.), ΣΟΦΙΗΣ ΜΑΙΗΤΟΡΕΣ, *"Chercheurs de Sagesse," Hommage a Jean Pépin* (Paris, 1992) 347–55; Idem, "On the Title of Porphyry's Treatise Against the Christians," in G.S. Gasparro (ed.), *Agathe Elpis:, Studi storici-religiosi in onore di Ugo Bianchi* (Rome, 1994) 221–35. For critique of Beatrice's thesis, see the perceptive discussion of R. Goulet, "Hypothèses récentes sur le traité de Porphyre *Contre les chrétiens*," in M. Narcy and E. Rebillard (eds.), *Hellénisme et Christianisme* (Lille, 2004) 61–109.

15 A. Smith, *Porphyrius: Fragmenta* (Leipzig, 1993) 351–407, which supersedes Wolff, *Philosophia ex Oraculis* (though Wolff's introduction and comments remain useful).

16 Fr.303–5, 307–24, 326–31, 333–6, 338–41, 347–50; and from Eus. *DE*, fr.345.

17 Fr.343–44c, 345a–346; and from Aug. *De Consensu Evangelistarum*, fr.345c.

18 Fr.330a, 332, 337, 340a, 341a, 342.

19 Fr.306.

20 Fr.325, 325a.

21 For the number of books, see Wolff, *Philosophia ex Oraculis*, 39. Beatrice's attempt ("Towards a new edition," 351–2) to resuscitate the hypothesis of at least ten books based upon two corrupt manuscript witnesses—to support his theory that the *Phil.Orac.* is Porphyry's work against the Christians—fails to meet the points raised by Wolff.

22 See H.W. Parke, *The Oracles of Apollo in Asia Minor* (London, 1985) 205–6.

divinatory sessions.[23] In what follows, I wish to address the issues of the specific context within which the *Philosophy from Oracles* may have functioned (especially as they can be determined from its preface) and what this may tell us about the ways in which power and religion intersected in the pages produced by the literary industry of this philosopher and man of letters. Indeed, before we can attempt to situate this treatise within a historical and political schema (an issue that recently has received a spate of renewed interest as the *Philosophy from Oracles* has been repeatedly associated with the outbreak of the Great Persecution),[24] the immediate social context and audience must be assessed. Even if the dating and possible imperial connections remain allusive, a greater appreciation may be gained for the ways in which the text located itself amid, and was formative of, relations of power within late antique discourses of religion.

Of the four fragments belonging to the work's preface, the first three (303–305FF Smith) give a good indication of the general purpose Porphyry had in mind when drafting it, as well as the context within which he intended it to be used. The first of these should be quoted in full:

> The present collection (*sunagōgē*) will contain a record of many of the teachings according to philosophy, since the gods prophesied that they possessed the truth. And I shall briefly adjoin a useful discussion (*chrēstikē pragmateia*), which is profitable for contemplation and the remaining purification of life. What benefit the collection (*sunagōgē*) has they will especially know who are giving birth to truth[25] and have ever prayed to obtain a manifestation from the gods, and so

[23] See Busine, *Paroles d'Apollon*, 246–56. On "freelance" divination, see P. Athanassiadi, "Dreams, Theurgy and Freelance Divination: The Testimony of Iamblichus," *JRS* 83 (1993) 115–30. With regard to the general structure of the whole *Philosophy from Oracles*, the reconstruction by Wolff, *Philosophia ex Oraculis*, 40–43, is suspect; see Busine, *Paroles d'Apollon*, 240.

[24] The assumption of a date early in Porphyry's career, i.e., before his move to Rome to study under Plotinus (AD 262/3), by Wolff (*Philosophia ex Oraculis*, 38: based on the evidence of Eunapius, the absence of any trace of Plotinian doctrine, the failure to commend the Orphic [i.e., vegetarian] lifestyle, the adoption of common religious usage, and lack of philosophical maturity) and J. Bidez (*Vie de Porphyre* [Leipzig, 1913] 14–19: based on Eunapius and the "oriental" orientation of the fragments) had been generally followed until the argument for a date connected with the outbreak of the Great Persecution was forcefully made by E.D. Digeser, "Lactantius, Porphyry, and the Debate over Religious Toleration," *JRS* 88 (1998) 129–46; following P.F. Beatrice, "*Antistes Philosophiae*: Ein christenfeindlicher Propagandist am Hofe Dioketians nach dem Zeugnis des Laktanz," *Augustinianum* 33 (1993) 31–47. Most recently, this dating has been subjected to a post-colonialist reading in J. Schott, "Porphyry on Christians and Others: 'Barbarian Wisdom,' Identity Politics, and Anti-Christian Polemics on the Eve of the Great Persecution," *JECS* 13 (2005) 277–314. The reading of the fragments offered here avoids the issue of dating and is equally applicable to an early or a late date.

[25] The metaphor is Platonic, see Plato, *Symp.* 206d; *Phdr.* 251e; *Resp.* 6.490b.

> receive rest from difficulty (*aporia*) through the trustworthy teaching of those who have spoken.[26]

The term *sunagōgē*, which appears twice in this passage, while being the expected word to describe any collection of oracles,[27] also recurs with some frequency in post-classical Greek in a pedagogical context.[28] In any given field of learning, whether mathematics, medicine, or philosophy, a teacher could collect significant passages from the corpus under discussion for the purposes of reading them with a small circle of students, offering explanatory comment or emphasizing key features of the text as he saw fit. Such a text-based climate is readily envisioned for the erudite sensibilities of the schoolroom of Porphyry's early teacher at Athens, Longinus the philologist ("a living library and walking Museum"),[29] as a report of the conversation at a party celebrating Plato's birthday reveals: Longinus' students and other guests devoted their night to recherché rivalry in their skill at detecting plagiarism of word or idea in earlier authors.[30] Strikingly, a deep bookish haze also lingered over the lectures of the mystical Plotinus. His teaching was thoroughly grounded in the texts of Plato and his commentators, both middle Platonists and Peripatetics,[31] while more open-ended explorations of philosophical issues were merely interruptions in the exegetical activity of Plotinus' teaching, as the impatient Thaumasius attempted to remind the master after a three-day investigation with Porphyry of the relation between soul and body.[32] The pedagogy of Plotinus was not only grounded in the reading of texts; it resulted in the production of texts as well, for the treatises that would eventually be compiled and edited as the *Enneads*

---

26 Porph. *De phil.or.* 303F Smith, = Eus. *PE* 4.6.2–4.7.2: ἕξει δὲ ἡ παροῦσα συναγωγὴ πολλῶν μὲν τῶν κατὰ φιλοσοφίαν δογμάτων ἀναγραφήν, ὡς οἱ θεοὶ τἀληθὲς ἔχειν ἐθέσπισαν· ἐπ' ὀλίγον δὲ καὶ τῆς χρηστικῆς ἁψόμεθα πραγματείας, ἥτις πρός τε τὴν θεωρίαν ὀνήσει καὶ πρὸς τὴν ὅλην κάθαρσιν τοῦ βίου. ἣν δ' ἔχει ὠφέλειαν ἡ συναγωγὴ μάλιστα εἴσονται, ὅσοιπερ τὴν ἀλήθειαν ὠδίναντες ηὔξαντό ποτε τῆς ἐκ θεῶν ἐπιφανείας τυχόντες ἀνάπαυσιν λαβεῖν τῆς ἀπορίας διὰ τὴν τῶν λεγόντων ἀξιόπιστον διδασκαλίαν. Translations here and throughout are my own.

27 See the survey of oracular collections at Wolff, *Philosophia ex Oraculis*, 43–56. For a list of related terminology, see H.G. Snyder, *Teachers and Texts in the Ancient World* (London, 2000) 231 n.31. An excellent survey of approaches to teaching texts is offered by J. Mansfeld, *Prolegomena: Questions to be Settled before the Study of an Author, or a Text* (Leiden, 1994).

28 More immediately, see Longinus, *De fin.*, praef., apud Porphyry, *VPlot.* 20.58, 86.

29 Eun. *VSoph.* 4.1.3 (456); cf. Porph. *VPlot.* 14.18–20; J. Pépin, "Philologos/Philosophos," in L. Brisson et al. (eds.), *Porphyre: La vie de Plotin* (Paris, 1992) 2.477–501.

30 Porph. *Philologos Akroasis*, frs. 408–10 Smith (= Eus. *PE* 10.3.1–25).

31 Porph. *VPlot.* 14.10–16; Snyder, *Teachers and Texts*, 115–18; A. Grafton and M. Williams, *Christianity and the Transformation of the Book* (Cambridge, MA, 2006) 29–40; J. Dillon, "Philosophy as a Profession in Late Antiquity," in S. Swain and M. Edwards (eds.), *Approaching Late Antiquity* (Oxford, 2004) 401–18 at 401–6.

32 Porph. *VPlot.* 13.10–17.

were initially his lecture notes.[33] Apparently, both master and pupils were engaged in the incessant rhythm of reading and writing, exegesis and editing.

For both the novice and the more advanced student in Platonic philosophy, collections of texts were a staple of the Plotinian school. Learning the great truths to which Platonism pointed depended upon learning to read well. The assumption that a student could begin reading the works of the great philosopher with an untutored eye and be heedless of an appropriate order in reading his corpus had emphatically been rejected long before Plotinus began teaching in Rome. A profusion of isagogic literature had arisen to aid students of philosophy and other scientific fields in grappling with the immensity of learning a body of writings or a domain of knowledge.[34] *Eisagōgai* or "introductions" embraced a broad range of form (epitomes, thematic surveys, selections, collections, or even biographies),[35] but their aim was singular: to introduce the novice to the elements requisite for rightly approaching the topic at hand. A *sunagōgē* could, therefore, function as an *eisagōgē* within a particular curriculum.[36] Introductory collections of key passages from the works of Plato, for instance, assisted the aspiring student of Platonic philosophy in making sense of what would have seemed an overwhelming mass of intricate argumentation complicated by the dialogic form and literary artistry of the great philosopher.

That the *sunagōgē* of Porphyry's *Philosophy from Oracles* functioned in a similar way to these pedagogical collections is indicated by a statement in the preface that has been misunderstood largely because of its infelicitous translation by its sole English-language translator, Gifford (as well as Zink in his French translation for the Sources Chrétiennes series).[37] The term *chrēstikē pragmateia* is rendered by Gifford as "the practice of divination." The more common meaning

33 Porph. *VPlot.* 4.10–11; 5.5–6, 60–61; 16.9–12.

34 See Mansfeld, *Prolegomena*; A.P. Johnson, "Eusebius' *Praeparatio Evangelica* as Literary Experiment," in S. Johnson (ed.), *Greek Literature in Late Antiquity: Dynamism, Didacticism, Classicism* (Aldershot, 2006) 67–89.

35 Porphyry himself contributed to many of these forms, as his corpus attests: the *VPlot.* (which served as an introduction to his edition of Plotinus' *Enneads*); *eisagōgai* on logic, categorical syllogisms and particular texts (e.g., Ptol. *Apotelesmatica*); *sunagōgai* on rhetorical questions and oracles (i.e., the *Phil.orac.*); commentaries, in a range of forms including question-and-answer, on a great number of philosophical and scientific texts (from Plato, *Tim.* and Arist. *Cat.* to Ptol. *Harm.*); *zētēmata* on passages from Homer or on issues such as psychology or rhetoric. For more details see the conspectus of works at Smith, *Porphyrius*, l–liii.

36 Cf. B.D. Larsen, *Jamblique de Calchis: Exégète et philosophe* (Aarhus, 1972) 67–71.

37 E.H. Gifford, *Eusebius, The Preparation for the Gospel* (Oxford, 1903; reprint Eugene, OR, 2002) 1.157 ("practice of divination"); O. Zink, *Eusèbe de Césarée, La Préparation Évangélique, Livres IV–V, 1–17, SCh* 262 (Paris, 1979) 123 ("l'activité prophétique"); see also, A. Smith, "Porphyrian Studies Since 1913," *ANRW* 2.36.2 (1987) 717–73 at 735 ("ritual practices"). For an interpretation similar to the one I offer here,

of the adjective *chrēstikē* is "useful" (from *chraomai*, to furnish what is needful). While "of divination" or "oracular" is a possible rendering (from *chraō*), it is attested infrequently enough that it is omitted in LSJ,[38] making it best to opt for the more common meaning here.[39] To strengthen the argument, Porphyry claims that he will add the *chrēstikē pragmateia* only "briefly" (*ep' oligon*) to his record of the teachings of the oracles. If our fragments are representative of the work as a whole, then verbatim quotations of various oracular responses make up the bulk of the *Philosophy from Oracles*, and hence are not brief at all. The qualifier "briefly" can hardly be applicable to the subject of the entire treatise. Furthermore, an adjective meaning "useful" better corresponds to the following verb: his "useful discussion" will be profitable (*onēsei*) for contemplation and will benefit (*ōpheleian*) the person who is giving birth to truth. Finally, even if there was justification for taking *chrēstikē* as "divinatory," problems remain for Gifford's rendering of *pragmateia*: if it is divinatory "practice" in particular to which the phrase refers—that is, to the binding of a divine being to specific animate or inanimate mouthpieces and drawing out the prophetic utterance by compulsion (and not oracular "material" in general)—then it is difficult to argue from what remains of his treatment of the topic that Porphyry deemed such practices to be beneficial from the point of view of philosophy.[40] All of these difficulties are alleviated if we reject Gifford's translation and take Porphyry as referring to his own brief addition of "useful discussion" pertaining to salient features of the oracles he cites.

I belabor the issue of how we ought to construe *chrēstikē pragmateia* because, being couched as it is within his opening programmatic statements, which serve to highlight the overall character of the *Philosophy from Oracles*, these lines signal a firmly pedagogical approach to his treatment of the oracles. As in other isagogic compilations, Porphyry is here promising to offer his own brief explications of issues arising from his source-texts in the process of training an apprentice reader in how to read well, what to look for, and what overarching framework ought to guide his or her understanding of inspired utterances. And indeed, this is precisely what we find in the fragments. After quoting a hexameter oracle of Hecate,[41] for

though with slightly different (i.e., non-isagogical) implications, see Busine, *Paroles d'Apollon*, 256–8.

38 One might rather expect *chrēsmōdikē*, *mantikē*, *chrēstēriōdēs*, or the like.

39 *Pace* Zink, *Eusèbe de Césarée*, 122 n.1, and Goulet, "Hypothèses Récentes," 65 n.12.

40 See, e.g., his opening remarks in 347F Smith. Porphyry's own attitudes in the fragments dealing with the use of magic and sacred bindings in the context of divination deserve careful analysis on their own terms, as well as in their relationship to his statements regarding divination elsewhere (e.g., *Abst.* 2.51–52).

41 "Nothing among the immortal gods in vain or fruitlessly / Did Hecate ever speak to wise prophets, / But descending from her father, from a more sovereign mind, / She ever illumines with truth, and cunning remains steadfast about her / Having come with unbreakable words. / Therefore invoke [me] with a binding; for you bring me / A goddess

instance, who claims in the last line to be "the ensouler of the cosmos," Porphyry adds: "And perhaps the soul [is] tri-formed and tripartite because of this: there is on the one hand the courageous part, and on the other the appetitive part, whence also it is said to be near the amatory parts" (308F Smith = Eus. *PE* 5.6.2–5.7.2). Given that the oracle's emphasis seems to be primarily on the fearsome power of Hecate's words (though we must be cautious here, as we may not have the entire utterance, nor are we given any clues as to its provenance, context, or the initial question to which it responds), the remarks by Porphyry, focusing as they do upon the latent psychology he claims to have found in the oracle, are striking and even bewildering. While we may be missing part of Porphyry's comments—he only mentions two parts of the soul, the courageous and appetitive; where is the third?—it is clear that a reader of this oracle would need the guidance of a wise teacher not only to locate the respective parts of the soul behind elements in the oracular verses but also to recognize that these verses can tell us about the parts of the soul at all. The soul only occurs in verbal form (*psychōsai*) in the final line. Shuddering at the forceful burst of Hecate into human affairs and her gripping command to invoke so powerful a deity, the philosophical novice required the firm direction of a mature philosopher to catch the rays of deeper truth about the soul glinting from the "ensouling" of the final line,[42] or again from the "paternal mind" of the third.[43]

In fragment 314, he introduces another oracle:

> Accordingly, after the things spoken about piety, we should record what things they have given in oracular response about their worship, of which we partially anticipated and showed in the [teachings] about piety. This is the oracle of Apollo, [which] at the same time contains also the division of the order of the gods. (314F Smith = Eus. *PE* 4.8.4–4.9.2)

Then follows an oracle detailing various sacrificial procedures in 28 hexameter verses.[44] Porphyry's exposition of the oracle is given as fragment 315 (= Eus. *PE* 4.9.3–7), one of the longest quotations of Porphyry's own words among the

---

that is great enough to ensoul the most-high cosmos." The oracle is considered spurious at Wolff, *Philosophia ex Oraculis*, 102, and nn. ad loc.

42 On the identification of Hecate with the hypostasis of Soul, see S.I. Johnston, *Hekate Soteira* (Atlanta, 1990) 153–63.

43 On the "paternal mind" in Chaldean thought, see ibid., 50.

44 The oracle is considered spurious at Wolff, *Philosophia ex Oraculis*, 102, and nn. ad loc. Wolff's judgment (p. 100) that Porphyry was honest, but gullible and easily deceived by the fraudulent oracles of others may be unfair. He was an astute whistle-blower on the forgeries in other religious traditions (e.g., Gnostics [*VPlot.* 16.14–18], and Christians [*C.Christ.* fr.43 Harnack]). I doubt that Porphyry was concerned with the authenticity of the oracles here (and in any case, what criteria would he have used in judging the authenticity of one's experience of a freelance divination session?), but rather with their amenability

fragments, in which he ignores much that might interest the modern student of Greek sacrificial practices and instead focuses almost exclusively on the ways in which the details of the oracle presume a strict division of heavenly and chthonian deities, with further subdivisions of the chthonians into sub-terrestrial (also called netherworldly), super-terrestrial, and merely terrestrial.[45] His exposition is supplemented with brief extracts from other oracles (or later lines of the earlier quoted oracle?) and at points his style resembles a commentary consisting of lemmata followed by brief explanation: "[the victims must be] black: for such is the naturally dark earth. [There must be] three: for three is the symbol of the bodily and earthy [element]." His gaze, however, remains firmly fixed on tracing the theological hierarchy evident in the oracular utterance.

Examples of his persistently expository style could be multiplied. Throughout the *Philosophy from Oracles*, Porphyry offers careful observations of features that a less philosophically trained reader might overlook. The points that Porphyry emphasizes are not always those that seem most obvious in the oracles: theological hierarchy, especially the place and function of daemons within that hierarchy;[46] the limits of divinatory practice;[47] the nature of Christ;[48] and the importance of barbarian wisdom.[49] These concerns may, of course, be more indicative of the Christian sources for these fragments than of Porphyry's overall purposes, though the issues of theological hierarchy[50] and barbarian wisdom[51] recur in Porphyry's other less fragmentary works, most notably in his *On Abstinence*. Additionally, it remains difficult to ascertain his particular reasons for quoting some oracles, especially since the expository notes have not survived in nine of them; but there is a strong impression that the work is rooted in a systematizing effort to find—or provide—a theological framework behind the details of the various oracles.

The budding student of philosophy, faced with the flourishing of oracular utterances beginning in the third century,[52] may well have wondered how such phenomena related to the higher theological teachings of the philosophers. The collection of oracles arranged in the *Philosophy from Oracles* thus marks

---

to his philosophical system. He allowed his readers' belief in the oracles in order to direct them beyond the oracles themselves to deeper theological or metaphysical truths.

45 On this fragment, see Busine, *Paroles d'Apollon*, 259–61.

46 See fr.307, 314–15, 325–28, 344.

47 See fr.322, 331–2, 337–42, 347, 350; cf. *Abst.* 2.52.

48 See fr.343, 345–6.

49 See fr.323–4, 346.

50 See e.g. *Abst.* 2.34–42.

51 See e.g. *Abst.* 1.14.4; 2.26.1–5; 2.61.7; 3.16.3; 4.6.1–18.6; *Styx* 375F Smith (= Stob. 1.3.96); *Comm. in Tim.* fr.28 Sodano (= Proclus, *Comm. in Tim.* 64a).

52 On the increased importance of oracles in the late 3rd and early 4th centuries, see Parke, *Oracles of Apollo*, 95, 97–103; E.D. Digeser, "An Oracle of Apollo at Daphne and the Great Persecution," *CPh* 99 (2004) 57–77.

an attempt at inculcating a method of reading oracular utterances that finds a Platonizing systematic theology behind the poetic cadence of the oracles.

But how does one legitimize such reading strategies? What motivates a hearer of oracles to seek out a philosophical master who might offer guidance in the reading of their written forms? This point bears consideration in light of the remaining fragments of Porphyry's preface, which offer clear statements identifying his prospective audience. In the second fragment he writes:

> Whatever you do, make it your aim neither to publicize these things nor to cast them before the uninitiated for the sake of glory, gain, or some other impure flattery. For, there is a danger not only to you when you transgress these commands but also to me who easily trusted in one who could not guard my kindness. It must be given to those who have set their life on the salvation of their souls. (304F Smith = Eus. *PE* 4.7.2–4.8.1)

Apparently, the master reader was not taking all comers to his school of right reading.[53] His *sunagōgē* was meant only for those initiated into the philosophic quest of spiritual salvation. A small coterie of students committed to the pursuit of wisdom was envisioned, rather than the open-door policy that we are told Porphyry's own teacher, Plotinus, maintained.[54] Indeed, Firmicus Maternus, before his conversion to Christianity, lauded Porphyry as being a model of guarding the secrets of hidden wisdom and standing in an honorable line of philosophical masters—including Orpheus, Pythagoras and Plato—known for their exclusionary practices in sharing the way of wisdom with others.[55] Such esoteric practices were grounded in the oracles themselves: the prophetic words were meant to conceal deeper truths and hidden meanings inaccessible to all but the select few who had been sufficiently trained in their proper interpretation. Porphyry accordingly remarks in the third fragment of the preface: "It is necessary for me to conceal these things that are more unspeakable than unspeakable things;[56] for the gods did

---

[53] See Busine, *Paroles d'Apollon*, 288. J.-L. Cherlonneix, "L'intention religieuse de l''ésotérisme platonicien'," in L. Brisson et al. (eds.), *Porphyre: La vie de Plotin* (Paris, 1992) 2.416, too easily dismisses Porphyry's warning as "la vaine comédie de la discrétion des lecteurs par l'auteur," supposing it to be a work of his youth. For a sensitive and suggestive treatment of philosophical esotericism in the Empedoclean / Pythagorean tradition (in which Porphyry no doubt placed himself), see P. Kingsley, *Ancient Philosophy, Mystery, and Magic* (Oxford, 1995) 359–70.

[54] See *VPlot.* 1.5–19; 14.20–5.

[55] Firm. Mat. *Math.* 7.1.1–3. Such elitism is common in Porphyry's thought, see *Abst.* 1.27.1, 52.3–4; 2.3.1–2, 40.5; 4.9.10, 18.4–7; *Marc.* 15–16, 30. On the other hand, he must have had something to say to a broader audience, though what precisely that may have been is unclear; see Eun. *VSoph.* 456.

[56] The phrase seems to be derived ultimately from Soph. *Oed.tyr.* 465.

not prophecy about these things openly, but through riddles (*ainigmata*)" (305F Smith = Eus. *PE* 4.8.2).

The presence of riddles within the oracles, which were gateways to higher knowledge, required the help of expert exegetes who could locate and unlock the doors to truth.[57] Not everyone was able to read the oracles at this level, and a philosophically enlightened master able to aid in such reading was rare indeed. But the very nature of the oracles required this sort of mastery. The understanding of the oracular presumed in Porphyry's work created a space, both social and discursive, in which religion dispersed relations of power. The fixity imposed on the effusiveness of the oracular by the collection, arrangement, and exposition of written oracles formed a system of theological understanding with its attendant categories and demarcation of the divine domain ("this is the division of the order of the gods …").[58] This fixity, however, did not preclude the need for spiritual authority and textual mastery. Accessibility to the truth of fluid utterance, though captured within the cages of the written, remained elusive. The written oracular collections offered salvation of souls within an exclusionary pedagogy with Porphyry as the master reader. Porphyry's assumption of the presence of *ainigmata* in the oracular texts—an assumption nearly ubiquitous in antiquity—combined with his compilation of a *sunagōgē* of oracles, presented a powerful claim to his position as an arbiter of the oracular.

We might conclude from such a picture painted by a philologist-turned-philosopher that Porphyry's *Philosophy from Oracles* stands in a long line of repetitive instantiations of what seems typical of an "age of anxiety" and loss of rationality. Yet Porphyry's task of teaching an esoteric wisdom hidden in the cracks of oracular ambiguity stretches back to philosophers of a much earlier era, such as Pythagoras, Empedocles, and Plato.[59] Porphyry is therefore hardly unique in this regard. Nor is he unique in his teaching methods. As I remarked already, teaching a small group of elite students how to read a text well was an integral part of teaching how to think and live well within the philosophical circles of the Hellenistic and Roman periods. It is, rather, in his placement of an oracle collection within a philosophical curriculum that Porphyry seems unique among

---

[57] Cf. the rhetorical question: "Then will the symbols of the sacrifices need to be expounded clearly to the man of good understanding?" (315 Smith = Eus. *PE* 4.9.3–7). For *ainigmata* in oracles, see the valuable work of P. Struck, *Birth of the Symbol* (Princeton, 2004) 162–203; Idem, "Divination and Literary Criticism?" in Johnston and Struck, *Mantikê*, 147–65. For *ainigmata* in philosophical literary criticism, see Struck, *Birth of the Symbol*, esp. 71–5; L. Brisson, *How Philosophers Saved Myths* (Chicago, 2004) esp. 56–106; G. Stroumsa, *Hidden Wisdom: Esoteric Traditions and the Roots of Christian Mysticism* (Leiden, 1996) 11–26; and, as always, R. Lamberton, *Homer the Theologian: Neoplatonist Allegorical Reading and the Growth of the Epic Tradition* (Berkeley, 1986) esp. 108–33.

[58] Fr.314–15 Smith.

[59] See Kingsley, *Ancient Philosophy*, 359–70.

pagans. As the oracular sun of Apollo was about to set on the temples of Didyma, Claros, and Delphi, Porphyry unwittingly showed his students an enlightened way of understanding the oracles for a new age of pagan religious practice and reflection by evoking a theological and philosophical system from the oracles as part of a pedagogy of the initiated.

The *Philosophy from Oracles* finds its closest parallel in Christian isagogic literature which provided training in the prophetic oracles of the Hebrews to those seeking the salvation of their souls.[60] Christian teachers, from Clement of Alexandria and Origen to Eusebius, Cyril of Alexandria, and Junillus Africanus, had developed texts that could function within a curriculum of sacred Scriptures and taught students to read the writings of the Hebrews in such a way as to discover the Christological truth hidden within.[61] When Porphyry drafted his oracular collection, relations of power were being drawn not only between the poles of the written and the uttered, the fixed and the fluid, the master and the student, but also between the ancient wisdom of the pagan oracles and the novel foolishness of the Christians. Porphyry situated his work strategically within the embattled contestation over truth and its channels of enunciation by producing a rival oracular pedagogy for the initiated, promising the hope of salvation to those already pregnant with truth.

Whether or not the *Philosophy from Oracles* was written—or read—at the behest of persecuting emperors in the early 300s, which seems unlikely,[62] Porphyry's Christian opponents had reason to worry about this text and the

---

[60] See Busine, *Paroles d'Apollon*, 292–3, for the suggestive idea that the *logia* of the title of Porphyry's work was meant to counter Christian reliance on the Hebrew *logia* as the repository of ancient wisdom. While certainty is impossible, it does seem likely that Christians at least took it this way. H. Lewy's claim (*Chaldean Oracles and Theurgy* [Le Caire, 1956] 8) that the *logia* are the Chaldean Oracles is questioned, probably rightly, by Busine, *Paroles d'Apollon* , 200–202, 247; E.R. Dodds, "New Light on the *Chaldean Oracles*," *HTR* 54 (1961) 263–73.

[61] For the connection between education and the rise of the biblical commentary, see F. Young, *Exegesis and the Formation of Christian Culture* (Cambridge, 1997). On Eusebius' *Praeparatio Evangelica* as an educational text, see A.P. Johnson, "Eusebius' *Praeparatio Evangelica* as Literary Experiment." For a more direct juxtaposition of Porphyry and Eusebius' *General Elementary Introduction*, see Idem, "Eusebius as Educator: The Context and Importance of the *General Elementary Introduction*," in S. Inowlocki and C. Zamagni, (eds.), *Reconsidering Eusebius* (Leiden, forthcoming); for Cyril, see J.D. Cassel, "Cyril of Alexandria as Educator," in P.M. Blowers et al. (eds.), *In Dominico Eloquio* (Grand Rapids, MI, 2002) 348–68. For Junillus, see M. Maas with E.G. Mathews, *Exegesis and Empire in the Early Byzantine Mediterranean: Junillus Africanus and the Instituta regularia divinae legis* (Tübingen, 2003).

[62] See C. Riedweg, "Porphyrios über Christus und die Christen: *De Philosophia ex Oraculis Haurienda* und *Adversos Christianos* im Vergleich," in *L'Apologétique chrétienne gréco-latine à l'époque prénicénienne*, Entretiens sur l'antiquité classique, 51 (Geneva, 2005) 151–98; Goulet, "Hypothèses récentes."

pedagogy within which it was meant to function. An apocryphal tale mentions that Porphyry's anti-Christian stance may have resulted from his rough treatment by Christian thugs in Caesarea, for he bore on his body the blows of that conflict.[63] The body of his writings, too, endured the assaults of Christian battery: the now-fragmentary condition of his *Philosophy from Oracles* stands as a vivid memorial to the struggle over the oracular, the textual, and the education of the wise.

[63] Soc. 3.23.37–9 (= 9T Smith); cf. Niceph. Call. *HE* 10.36 (*PG* 146.561A). Though late, the episode cannot be easily dismissed: the report is based upon evidence from Eusebius, who as a local Caesarean was well placed to gain reliable information. Porphyry himself claims to have met Origen in his youth (*C.Christ.* fr.39 Harnack [= Eus. *HE* 6.19.5]), and Caesarea is as probable a location for their meeting as any other. Porphyry received the curious epithet "Bataneotes" in later 4th-century sources (*Test.* 16 Harnack [= Joh. Chrys. *Hom.* 6.3]; *C.Christ.* (?) fr.21A Harnack [=Jerome, *Comm. in Gal.*, prol. (*PL* 26.310C)]; *C.Christ.* (?) fr.65 [= Anastasius Sinaita, *Hodegos* 13]); Batanea was about 15 miles from Caesarea and Porphyry's family may have owned an estate there, where he may have spent time in his youth (cf. Bidez, *Vie de Porphyre*, 5–8). This evidence exhibits the likelihood that Porphyry did at least visit Caesarea in his youth; a story could easily have been invented later by Christians whom he encountered there when he had gained notoriety for his anti-Christian writings later in life. While all of this remains conjectural, there are ultimately no firm grounds to reject the possibility of a conflict, verbally or physically violent in nature, between Christians and the soon-notorious critic of their Scriptures.

PART III
Emperors and the Deployment of Religious Power

Chapter 8

Church, State, and Children: Christian and Imperial Attitudes Toward Infant Exposure in Late Antiquity*

Judith Evans Grubbs
Washington University, St. Louis

The abandonment of newborn infants (called "exposure" from the Latin *expositio*, "placing out") has long been the subject of scholarly discussion. In the later empire there is a significant amount of source material for infant exposure, especially from both legal and Christian perspectives. Emperors from Constantine to Justinian attempted to restrict and penalize the practice, in contrast to earlier Roman law. And Christian apologists denounced the heartlessness of pagan parents who abandoned the fruits of their own sexual activity. This paper looks at the intersection of these imperial and ecclesiastical attitudes toward infant exposure and at the role of the church and of individual Christians in shaping imperial attitudes and responses.

Legal and Social Attitudes before Constantine

Infant exposure was a fact of life in Greco-Roman antiquity. At a time when effective contraception was unavailable and abortion was as dangerous for the mother as for the fetus, exposure provided an easy and socially accepted means of population control. Although modern scholars often equate exposure with infanticide (and no doubt in many cases the result was the same—death for the newborn), neither those who exposed their infants nor the public authorities perceived it in such simple terms. For there was always the chance that the baby would be picked up and reared by someone else and could eventually be reclaimed by its original parent. Unrealistic as this scenario appears, it did occur.[1] Many *expositi* not only were rescued, but were eventually reclaimed by those who had abandoned them.

---

* This paper draws from a forthcoming book on parent–child relations in Roman law from Trajan to Constantine (to be published by Oxford University Press), which provides more detailed treatment of the evidence presented here.

1 J. Boswell, *The Kindness of Strangers: The Abandonment of Children in Western Europe from Late Antiquity to the Renaissance* (New York, 1988) 53–137. Though often inaccurate in interpreting the legal evidence, Boswell's study is extremely important.

No doubt this happened in only a small minority of cases, but frequently enough for the law to take an interest. Often when an abandoned infant was reared by someone else, there would be legal problems if the child's *paterfamilias* (either a biological father or the master of a slaveborn child's mother) tried to recover his child later, sometimes after many years. Conflicts would arise between the biological father's right of *patriapotestas* and the legally invalid but still compelling arguments of the rescuer, who could claim to have saved the child from death.

In most cases, the fate of an exposed infant who survived would be slavery; picking up an *expositus* and hiring a wet nurse for him was cheaper than buying an older slave, and after five or six years the child could begin to repay the cost of rearing by running errands and doing light chores. Modern historians recognize exposure as a significant source of the slave supply under the empire, though the proportion of *expositi* among the slave population is debatable.[2]

Imperial law before Constantine neither penalized nor promoted the abandonment of newborn infants. Legal sources of the first three centuries enunciate two fundamental principles: (1) *patria potestas*, the extensive legal authority granted to a *paterfamilias*, endured even after a father or slaveowner had knowingly exposed a child under his power, and therefore the *paterfamilias* could reclaim the *expositus* at any later time; and (2) freeborn children who were exposed and rescued, and then raised as slaves, still retained their right of free birth (*ingenuitas*), and could recover that freedom by proving their original birth status. Of course, proof of birth status would usually be extremely difficult, often impossible, especially for the exposed children themselves if they were held in slavery. They would need to have an *adsertor*, an advocate who could bring the claim for them before a judge in an action for freedom (*causa liberalis*).[3] A father or slavemaster would also have to present some proof of the child's identity in order to assert paternal power. Despite the obstacles to successful recovery of birth status, imperial rescripts from Trajan to the Tetrarchy show that such claims

[2] Boswell, *Kindness of Strangers*, 111–14; I. Bieżuńska-Małowist, "Die Expositio von Kindern als Quelle der Sklavenbeschaffung im griechisch-römischen Ägypten," *JWG* 2 (1971) 129–33; J. Ramin and P. Veyne, "Droit romain et société: les hommes libres qui passent pour esclaves et l'esclavage volontaire," *Historia* 30 (1981) 472–97 at 475–8; W.V. Harris, "Child-Exposure in the Roman Empire," *JRS* 84 (1994) 1–22 at 18–19; Idem, "Demography, Geography, and the Sources of Roman Slaves," *JRS* 89 (1999) 62–75 at 73–4 refutes W. Scheidel, "Quantifying the Sources of Slaves in the Early Roman Empire," *JRS* 87 (1997) 156–69, who argued that Harris overestimated the contribution of *expositi* to the slave population.

[3] See W.W. Buckland, *The Roman Law of Slavery* (Cambridge, 1908; reprint. New York, 1969) 672–5; G. Vismara, "Le *causae liberales* nel tribunale di Agostino vescovo di Ippono," *SDHI* 61 (1995) 365–72.

were often made before local judges, provincial governors, and even the emperors themselves.[4]

Societal awareness of the possible fate awaiting exposed children is suggested by one of the *controversiae* argued in the rhetorical schools of the early empire: a rescuer of *expositi* has crippled them and put them out to beg, on the assumption that people will give them more money out of pity. The argument revolves around whether the rescuer is harming the state by his actions, and even those who argue against him admit that what he did was not against the law. Moreover (according to the declaimers, who of course were focusing on the shocking and sensational in their rhetorical exercises) people do give money to the mutilated beggars in the fear that the children they rejected at birth may be among them.[5]

A few moralists did speak out against exposure. Musonius Rufus, a Roman Stoic philosopher of the first century, objected strongly to attempts by parents to limit their offspring and applauded the sight of large families.[6] Musonius' contemporary, the Jewish philosopher Philo of Alexandria, also criticized the practice of infant abandonment.[7] Even more outspoken were the Christian apologists, especially Justin Martyr and the north Africans Tertullian and Lactantius.[8] But by and large people in the Roman world, while being aware that freeborn infants were abandoned by their parents, would have gone along with the assertion by one of the speakers in a rhetorical school, that *expositi* "are of no account; they are slaves."[9] The position of enslaved freeborn *expositi* points up a basic contradiction in Roman law and society: the notion of the pre-eminence of *ingenuitas* existed side by side with tolerance of exposure of freeborn infants who, if they survived, were likely to end up as slaves.

Late Roman Legislation on Abandoned Infants

Pre-Constantinian imperial legislation on *expositi* was set forth in the form of rescripts, sent in response to imperial officials (like Pliny the Younger) who needed guidance in deciding claims for freedom under their jurisdiction, or to private individuals who had petitioned the emperor regarding their own situation.

---

4 Pliny, *Epp.* 10.65–6 (ca. 110); *CJ* 8.51.1 (a. 224); *CJ* 5.4.16 (tetrarchic); cf. *D* 40.4.29 (Scaevola, 2nd century).

5 Sen. Mai. *Controv.* 10.4. See A. Parkin, "'You do him no service': An Exploration of Pagan Almsgiving," in M. Atkins and R. Osbourne (eds.), *Poverty in the Roman World* (Cambridge, 2006) 60–82 at 71–3.

6 Muson. 15 ("Should every child that is born be raised?") edited and translated by C. Lutz, "Musonius Rufus: 'The Roman Socrates,'" *YClS* 10 (1947) 3–147 at 99–101.

7 Philo, *The Special Laws* 3.20 (110–19), in F.H. Colson (trans.) *Philo*. Loeb Classical Library (Cambridge, MA, 1929) 7.544–51; cf. Boswell, *Kindness of Strangers*, 147–9.

8 See the third section of this essay, "Christianity and the Law."

9 Sen. Mai. *Controv.* 10.4.13.

Emperors dealt with exposure on an ad hoc basis, in response to competing claims to children who had been picked up. Modern scholars have debated whether Roman law made reclamation of freedom by an enslaved *expositus* contingent on repayment of *alimenta* (expenses incurred in rearing) to the rescuer.[10] Policies differed from province to province, and depended on the governor hearing a case for freedom, or on the emperor who had been approached by petition. That different provinces had different policies in the early second century is clear from Pliny's correspondence with Trajan over claims to freedom that Pliny had to judge as governor of Bithynia and Pontus.[11] Since the compilers of the Justinianic corpus of Roman law retained only the pre-Justinianic legislation that was consonant with sixth-century law, evidence for fluctuations in imperial policy in the second and third centuries has disappeared. Nevertheless, it does seem that until the fourth century the basic principles of *patria potestas* and *ingenuitas* were always maintained.

Beginning with Constantine, *leges generales* set forth policy on *expositi* that was supposed to apply to all cases, although as was the case with the pre-Constantinian rescripts, these laws no doubt responded to actual situations. Constantine's approach marks a dramatic change from that of earlier emperors in more than form, however. By placing the need to rescue abandoned infants above the claims of *ingenuitas* and *patria potestas*, Constantine legitimized the rearing of *expositi* as slaves, even when they were freeborn.

Constantine's legislation frequently dealt with issues of status, including the enslavement of freeborn people and the procedures for reclaiming freedom through a process *de liberali causa*.[12] Constantine also addressed the phenomenon of parents selling or pledging their freeborn children into slavery, especially when the reason for getting rid of a child was poverty or the fear of starvation. In 322, after receiving a report that provincials in Africa, "oppressed by need of sustenance and lack of support," were selling or pledging their own children, Constantine ordered officials in the African provinces to provide grain to needy parents immediately from imperial storehouses: "For it is totally alien to our *mores* to allow anyone to be consumed by hunger or to break forth in an unworthy deed."[13] Another law enacted a year later began by declaring: "Such great weight was placed on liberty by our ancestors that fathers, to whom was granted the right of life and power of death over their children, were not permitted to snatch away

---

[10] See E. Volterra, "L'efficacia delle costituzioni imperiali emanate per le provincie e l'istituto dell'*expositio*," in *Studi di storia e diritto in onore di Enrico Besta* (Milan, 1939) 449–77; M.B. Fossati Vanzetti, "Vendita ed esposizione degli infanti da Costantino a Giustiniano," *SDHI* 49 (1983) 179–224 at 182–7.

[11] Pliny, *Epp.* 10.65–6. Extant 3rd-century rescripts: *CJ* 8.51.1 (a. 224), a slaveborn *expositus*; *CJ* 5.4.16 (tetrarchic), a freeborn girl.

[12] *CTh* 4.8.5 (to Maximus, urban prefect, a. 322). There were eight Constantinian laws under this title, but *CTh* 4.8.1–3 are lost and 4.8.4 and 4.8.8 are fragmentary.

[13] *CTh* 11.27.2 (a. 322), to Menander (office unknown).

liberty," and ruled that the claim to freedom of someone enslaved as a minor was not impaired if he continued to serve as a slave after turning 25, as long as he was ignorant of his true status.[14] That law does not say how a young person would have fallen into slavery, but the most likely possibility was sale by parents or long-term "rental of services," which often ended in de facto servitude.[15] A Constantinian law of 329, however, accepts the reality of the sale of freeborn infants by parents under pressure of poverty.[16] This appears to mark a sharp departure from earlier Roman law, which considered the sale of freeborn people, including a father's sale of his own children, to be invalid—nevertheless, a private rescript from early in Constantine's reign provided a precedent.[17] Probably Constantine was legalizing only the sale of neonates, who might otherwise be killed by their parents, whereas the sale of other freeborn people, including older children, remained illegal.[18]

Probably also in 329, Constantine enacted a measure intended to deter parents from getting rid of their infant children, whether by exposure or outright infanticide. The law as it is preserved in the *Theodosian Code* opens dramatically: "Let a law be published throughout all the cities of Italy, written on bronze or wax tablets or on linen cloths, which shall keep the hands of parents from parricide and turn their desire to the better." The law's recipient, the praetorian prefect Ablabius, is enjoined to speed supplies of food and clothing to needy parents, "since the rearing of infant children cannot bear delays."[19] Unlike the complex alimentary schemes to encourage rural Italians to rear their children enacted by the emperor Trajan more than two centuries earlier—which seem to have lapsed during the economic troubles of the third century—Constantine's measure was a one-time emergency measure probably intended to meet a temporary crisis, most likely a food shortage.[20] Its main interest—apart from the list of the materials used for publication of an imperial law—is the identification of the killing of an infant by its parents as *parricidium*. The classical definition of parricide covered a child's

---

14 *CTh* 4.8.6 (to Maximus, urban prefect, a. 323). See M. Humbert, "Enfants à louer ou à vendre: Augustin et l'autorité parentale (Ep. 10* et 24*)," in *Les lettres de Saint Augustin découvertes par Johannes Divjak* (Paris, 1983) 189–204 at 200–201.

15 Another possibility is sale by kidnappers, for which see *CTh* 9.18.1 (to the Vicar of Africa, a. 315) and Aug. *Ep.* 10*.

16 *CTh* 5.10.1 (18 August 329, from Serdica) "to his Italians." A different version appears at *CJ* 4.43.2 under the same date, "to his provincials." See J. Evans-Grubbs, *"Munita Coniugia": The Emperor Constantine's Legislation on Marriage and the Family* (diss. Stanford Univ., 1987) 197–200, and Eadem, "Constantine and Imperial Legislation on the Family," in J. Harries and I. Wood (eds.), *The Theodosian Code: Studies in the Imperial Law of Late Antiquity* (London and Ithaca, 1993) 120–42 at 134–5.

17 *Frag. Vat.* 34 (subscribed 21 July 313), to Flavia Aprilla.

18 R. Martini, "Sulla vendita dei neonati nella legislazione costantiniana," in *Atti del VII Convegno dell'Accademia Romanistica Costantiniana* (Perugia, 1988) 423–32.

19 *CTh* 11.27.1 (to Ablabius, probably a. 329).

20 For discussion, see Evans Grubbs, *"Munita Coniugia,"* 183–7.

killing of a parent, but not the death of a newborn at the hands of a *paterfamilias*.[21] Nonetheless, when Constantine had revived the ancient penalty for parricide in 318, he had also included the killing of a child by a parent.[22] Therefore the rhetorical flourish of the alimentary law of 329 was not inappropriate.

In 331, Constantine went beyond temporary measures and laid out a permanent policy on *expositi* that was intended to apply to all cases where an abandoned newborn had been picked up by someone other than the person who exposed it:

> Whoever should take up a boy or a girl thrown out of its home with the agreement and knowledge of its father or master, and should bring it up to strength with his own sources of support (*alimenta*), shall keep the same child under the same status, which he wished to consider it when it was taken up to his home, that is whether he should have preferred it to be his son or his slave (*sive filium sive servum*): and all unease should be completely removed about reclamation by those who knowingly, by their own will, threw out from their home recently born slaves or children.[23]

This can be seen as a merciful measure: Constantine was discouraging parents from exposing their children by depriving them of future power over them. Nevertheless, the status implications for those who had been exposed by their parents were serious: no longer could a freeborn *expositus* who was brought up as a slave by his rescuer reclaim his freeborn status. Possibly parents who had abandoned their baby could recover it if they reimbursed its rescuer for the costs of rearing. In his legislation allowing impoverished parents to sell their newborn infants, Constantine explicitly allowed redemption of the child later if the parents paid the buyer the fair value of a slave child.[24] But those who had picked up an abandoned baby might not want to part with it later, particularly if they had brought the *expositus* up as their own child. In such cases, fathers or former owners had no legal right to reclaim their child, having lost their *potestas* when they made the decision to expose.

Constantine did not prohibit infant exposure, but only penalized it by loss of *patriapotestas*. This policy was repeated in a law of Valentinian of 374, unfortunately only extant in a truncated version in the *Code of Justinian*.[25] Less

21 *D* 48.9.1 (Marcian) provides the classical definition according to the *lex Pompeia de parricidiis*.

22 *CTh* 9.15.1 (to Verinus, vicar of Africa, given 16 November 318, received at Carthage 19 March 319).

23 *CTh* 5.9.1 (to Ablabius, praetorian prefect, 17 April 331), my translation.

24 *CTh* 5.10.1 and *CJ* 4.43.2 (a. 329); see above.

25 *CJ* 8.51.2 (to Petronius Probus, praetorian prefect, 5 March 374). The second sentence of *CJ* 8.51.2 is identical to the beginning of *CTh* 5.9.2 (Honorius, a. 412). Most likely Justinian's compilers fused the two laws (Fossati Vanzetti, "Vendita ed esposizione," 215–16).

than a month earlier Valentinian had decreed a capital penalty for anyone who killed an infant.[26] Not that this stopped people from abandoning infants, as is clear from a repetition of Valentinian's law 38 years later by Honorius:

> We leave no means of recovering to masters or to patrons (of *coloni*) if friendly goodwill and pity have gathered up those who were exposed to death in some way. For he will not be able to call his own one whom he scorned when it was perishing, as long as the signature of a bishop as witness has followed, about which there can be absolutely no delay for the purpose of security.[27]

The rescuer of an *expositus* should immediately get the written testimony of a bishop in order to secure his claim to the child. Although the text of the law as it appears in the *Theodosian Code* mentions only slave or *coloni* infants, the original law may also have mentioned freeborn infants abandoned by their parents.

This is the first extant law to suggest the involvement of Christian clergy in the recovery of *expositi*. Nonetheless, the laws as preserved in the *Theodosian* and *Justinianic Codes* have been abbreviated, and it is not impossible that the earlier legislation of Constantine or Valentinian mentioned church officials. Constantine had granted new powers to Christian clergy in laws allowing manumission in church and granting bishops judicial authority (the *audientia episcopalis*).[28]

The version of Honorius' law preserved in the *Theodosian Code* does not provide details, but two canons from a church council held at Vaison 30 years later set out the procedure for claiming an abandoned child. "According to the statutes of the most faithful, pious and revered emperors," whoever picked up an *expositus* was to inform the church and receive an attestation of this. The finding of an infant was to be announced publicly from the altar of the church on Sunday, and the person who had abandoned the child had 10 days in which to come forth to claim it. If the child was claimed, the rescuer was to give it back and accept either monetary recompense for having provided 10 days of mercy, or eternal grace in heaven. If no one claimed the child after 10 days, it was (presumably) the rescuer's to do what he wished with, and anyone who later tried to reclaim the child or bring a false accusation (of kidnapping) against the rescuer was to be "struck with ecclesiastical punishment as a homicide." The clerics who met at Vaison made this policy in response to complaints arising "from all" that exposed infants were not picked up, even though people felt pity for them, because potential rescuers feared malicious prosecution (*calumnia*) by the exposers.[29] The canon's reference to

---

26 *CTh* 9.14.1 (also to Petronius Probus, posted 7 February 374).

27 *CTh* 5.9.2 (to Melitius, praetorian prefect, 19 March 412), my translation.

28 On manumission, see *CJ* 1.13.1 (a. 316); *CTh* 4.7.1 (a. 321). On *audientia episcopalisi*, see *CTh* 1.27.1 (a. 318?); *Sirm.* 1 (a. 333).

29 Council of Vaison (442) canons 9 and 10, in C. Munier (ed.), *Concilia Galliae A.314–A.506, CCSL* 148 (Turnhout, 1963) 100–101. See Fossati Vanzetti, "Vendita ed esposizione," 216–18; Boswell, *Kindness of Strangers*, 172–3.

imperial law indicates that the council was knowingly reinforcing and supporting the legislation of Honorius and his predecessors. But unlike imperial law, the Gallic church's solution was to allow a short period of time for regretful parents or masters to come forward and reclaim the child, and after that to ensure there could be no case against a rescuer who chose to adopt or enslave an *expositus*.[30]

Christianity and the Law

Although we do not hear of church involvement in the rescue and redistribution of *expositi* until the fifth century, the practice mentioned in Honorius' law and in the canons of Vaisons may have begun much earlier in Christian communities. From the second century on, Christian writers denounced the practice of infant exposure and accused pagans of refusing the responsibility of child-rearing while at the same time indulging in sex—for which, Christians thought, the procreation of children was the only excuse. Justin Martyr, who lived and taught at Rome in the mid-second century, claimed that abandoned children generally met one of two fates: they either died or were picked up by others and used for prostitution (that is, as slaves prostituted by their rescuers). Justin devoted far more attention to the second possibility; that exposure might result in death was apparently considered less likely or less shocking. Other apologists repeated Justin's objections and stressed the horrific possibility that dissolute parents might unknowingly commit incest with the children they had abandoned years before.[31]

But the most sustained and impassioned attack on infant exposure came from Lactantius, the North African Christian teacher of rhetoric. In book 6 of his *Divine Institutes*, written in the early fourth century, Lactantius condemned all killing of man by man, including public executions and even military service. Then he explicitly equated exposure with murder:

> What about those, whom a false sense of duty (*pietas*) drives to expose? Those who throw their own offspring to the dogs for booty, and, as far as they are able, kill them more cruelly than if they had strangled them, cannot be considered innocent, can they? Who would doubt that he is impious, who offers an opportunity for another's mercy? Even if what he wanted should happen to (his child), that it be reared, he has certainly delivered his own flesh and blood either to slavery or to the brothel … [He recalls the possibility of incest, with Oedipus as an example.] … Therefore it is as wicked to expose (*exponere*) as to kill.[32]

---

30 Boswell, *Kindness of Strangers*, 202–4 and 217–18, cites early medieval formularies from Anjou and Tours providing the "form letter" used in securing the rescuer's claim. A similar formula may have already been in use in the 5th century.

31 Justin, *1 Apol.* 27 and 29; also in Tert. *Apol.* 9.17, cf. 9.7; Min. Fel. *Oct.* 30.2; and other apologists.

32 Cf. *Sent. Pauli* 2.24.10 (= *D* 25.3.4) for similar language.

> But parricides complain of their straitened means; they claim that they cannot supply enough for bringing up many children—as if either means are in the power of those who possess them, or God does not every day make poor men from rich and rich men from poor. Therefore if anyone cannot bring up his children on account of poverty, it is better that he refrain from intercourse with his wife than corrupt the works of God with criminal hands.[33]

Lactantius' denunciation could be taken as merely inflamed rhetoric with little or no impact on real life. But Lactantius was not simply a teacher and writer of Christian handbooks. He held the chair of rhetoric in the imperial capital of Nicomedia under Diocletian, and when the persecution of Christians began, he went west and at some point became tutor to Crispus, Constantine's eldest son.[34] Although he first wrote the *Divine Institutes* before meeting the emperor, in a later "edition" of the work he added addresses to Constantine, as the first emperor to adopt Christianity.[35] Two manuscripts of the *Divine Institutes* contain these addresses, at the beginning of the first six books and the end of the seventh.[36] Digeser has suggested that Lactantius gave readings from the *Divine Institutes* at Constantine's court and at that time added the personalized addresses to the emperor.[37] And if Constantine did stay up late at night reading Christian treatises, as Eusebius claims he did, surely Lactantius's handbook was among them.[38]

Although little of Constantine's legislation on family matters was inspired by "Christian" ideas, it can be argued that the legislation on *expositi* is among the small number of such laws.[39] The law of 331 contains some unusual language not otherwise found in legal texts; this led Volterra to suggest that it had been drafted in an ecclesiastical environment rather than the imperial chancellery, although this

---

33 *Div.inst.* 6.20; cf. 5.9, my translation.

34 On Lactantius, see E.D. Digeser, *The Making of a Christian Empire: Lactantius and Rome* (Ithaca and London, 2000).

35 The "first edition" of the *Div.inst.* dates between 303 and 310. The date of the "second edition" is in dispute. E.D. Digeser, "Lactantius and Constantine's Letter to Arles: Dating the *Divine Institutes*," *JECS* 2 (1994) 33–52, suggests the Constantinian dedications were added between 310 and 313.

36 Long invocations at *Div.inst.* 1.1.13–16 and 7.27.2; briefer addresses at *Div.inst.* 2.1.2, 3.1.1, 4.1.1, 5.1.1, 6.3.1.

37 Digeser, "Lactantius and Constantine's Letter to Arles," 51; cf. Digeser, *Making of a Christian Empire*, 134.

38 Eus. *VConst.* 4.29; cf. 4.17.

39 J. Evans Grubbs, *Law and Family in Late Antiquity: The Emperor Constantine's Marriage Legislation* (Oxford, 1995) 317–21, argues that Constantine's marriage legislation was not significantly influenced by Christianity. Eadem, "Constantine and Imperial Legislation," 135–6, tentatively suggests Christian influence on *CTh* 5.9.1.

is unlikely.[40] Some scholars[41] have even seen echoes of Lactantius in Constantine's law ordering aid to needy families where children were at risk.[42]

But the emperor was not motivated solely, or even primarily, by religious considerations; this is not a "Christian" law. Constantine, like Roman lawmakers before him, was most concerned with sorting out legal confusion over the status of abandoned infants. Other Constantinian laws display great concern with preserving status boundaries and penalize unions between men and women of very disparate social and legal status.[43] It is therefore ironic that by permitting the rescuer of an *expositus* to rear the infant as either a slave or as the rescuer's own child, Constantine was actually enabling possibly drastic change of status. For under his law it was possible for a freeborn *expositus* to be legally enslaved, or for a slaveborn infant to be brought up as free with full inheritance rights from his or her rescuer.

In fact, Lactantius would not have approved of Constantine's solution, since it explicitly granted rescuers of exposed babies the right to rear them as slaves, thus raising the old Christian fear of slave prostitution and unintended incest. But even Lactantius would agree that denying a *paterfamilias* the right to recover his child might encourage potential rescuers who would no longer have to worry about losing their investment, and could also discourage parents from exposing in the first place.

Christians themselves rescued abandoned infants as an act of charity. The care of widows and orphans had always been a matter of community concern among Christians, and this included the raising of children who for some reason had been deprived of their natural parents. Augustine remarks that "Now and then even those whom their parents have cruelly exposed to be reared by whoever wants them, are sometimes collected by holy virgins and are offered by them for baptism."[44] One such virgin was Macrina, the sister of Basil of Caesarea and Gregory of Nyssa. When she died, the virgins in the monastic home that she headed grieved loudly, calling upon her as mother and nurse. "They were those whom she had taken up

---

40 E. Volterra, "Intorni ad alcune costituzioni di Costantino," *RAL* 13 (1958) 61–89 at 80–87. Volterra, "L'efficacia delle costituzioni," had suggested *CTh* 5.9.1 was a forgery.

41 E.g., J. Vogt, "Zur Frage des Christlichen Einflusses auf die Gesetzgebung Konstantins des Grossen," in *Festschrift für Leopold Wenger* (Munich, 1945) 2.118–48 at 139–40; and F. Amarelli, *Vetustas-Innovatio: Un'antitesi apparente nella legislazione di Costantino* (Naples, 1978) 123–4. Others disagree: e.g., Martini, "Sulla vendita dei neonati," 431–2.

42 Cf. *CTh* 11.27.1: *subolem quam pro paupertate educare non possit*, with *Div.inst.* 6.20: *si quis liberos ob pauperiem non poterit educare*; and the equation of *parricidium* and *expositio* in both.

43 Evans Grubbs, *Law and Family*, 261–316.

44 *Ep.* 98.6 (*CSEL* 34.527–8), written 408, to bishop Boniface.

when they had been thrown along the roads in time of famine, and tended and fostered and led by the hand to the holy and spotless life."[45]

At the same time, church leaders, including Macrina's brother Basil, called for ecclesiastical penalties for women who abandoned or killed their offspring.[46] In the east, institutions to house and care for orphans, including those abandoned by their parents, had existed since at least the mid-fifth century. The most famous was the Orphanotropheion, already well-established when it was mentioned in a law of Leo I and perhaps in existence by the mid-fourth century.[47] Such an institution would have taken in children whose parents were dead and who had no relatives to take care of them, and might include those abandoned at birth. Laws of Justinian in the sixth century also refer to more specialized orphanages called *brephotropheia*, intended for newborn infants, in both Constantinople and the provinces.[48] These were part of a highly developed system of charitable care in the Byzantine empire, promoted by the emperors and administered by the church.

In 529, Justinian overturned all previous regulations on the status of *expositi*. Henceforth all abandoned infants, whatever their status at birth, were to be considered freeborn and to have full capacity to receive under a will.[49] Moreover, *expositi* could not be enslaved by their rescuers. This rescinded Constantine's law (*CTh* 5.9.1) of two centuries earlier, which was therefore not included in the *Code of Justinian*. Among other officials responsible for enforcing this law were Christian bishops, in keeping with Justinian's policy of drawing on ecclesiastics to help further imperial law.[50] Justinian was not entirely successful, however. In 541, he received a report from the church of Thessalonika that people who had been left at the churches as newborns were being reclaimed years later as slaves. He had to issue a new law stating that all *expositi* were free, regardless of proof of ownership by those bringing claims. Anyone who brought such a claim, Justinian declared, was to be subjected to the ultimate penalty (death), so that others would

---

45 Greg. Nys. *VMacrinae* 26.30 (*SCh* 178.232).

46 Council of Elvira (Spain, early 4th century), cans. 63 and 68 (Hefele-Leclerq 1.1.256 and 258); Council of Ancyra (314), can. 21 (Hefele-Leclerq, vol. 1.1.323); Bas. *Ep.* 188, can. 2 and *Ep.* 217, can. 52; cf. *Ep.* 199, can. 33, from the so-called "canonical epistles" of Basil of Caesarea, in R.J. Deferrari (ed.), *Saint Basil: The Letters*, 3 vols. (Cambridge, MA, 1926–30), 3.20–23 (can.2), 244–5 (can. 52), 124–5 (can. 33).

47 *CJ* 1.3.34 (a. 472). See T.S. Miller, *The Orphans of Byzantium: Child Welfare in the Christian Empire* (Washington, 2003) 52–5.

48 Just. *Nov.* 7 and 43; see Miller, *Orphans of Byzantium*, 154–5. There is, however, no mention of *brephotropheia* after the 6th century.

49 *CJ* 8.51.3 (a. 529); cf. *CJ* 1.4.24. See Fossati Vanzetti, "Vendita ed esposizione," 222–4.

50 See C. Humfress, "Law and Legal Practice in the Age of Justinian," in M. Maas (ed.), *The Cambridge Companion to the Age of Justinian* (Cambridge, 2005) 161–84 at 178–80.

become more sensible. Judges who ignored or agreed to circumvent the law were fined five pounds of gold.[51]

Possibly, because they forbade or restricted reclamation of *expositi* by those who had abandoned them, these laws did make some parents or slaveowners think twice about exposure. Impoverished parents may have turned instead to selling newborns, which was legal under Constantine's law. And the establishment of a mechanism by which abandoned infants could be claimed by others could have encouraged desperate parents to choose exposure rather than outright infanticide. Of course, neither imperial legislation nor Christian prescriptions could end infant exposure. On the contrary, the safety net provided by well-meaning Christians and state institutions may have unwittingly promoted abandonment. One does not have to accept Boswell's equation of the medieval practice of oblation with ancient exposure to understand that parents who believed they could not afford to bring up all their children would take advantage of Christian charity and leave their unwanted newborns at nearby churches, as at Thessalonika.

This is borne out by studies of abandonment in later periods, which have shown how even the most well-meaning provisions for dealing with the problem can have "unintended consequences."[52] In early modern Italy, foundling homes were established to deal with the increasing number of abandoned children in Italian cities, and the practice spread to other European countries.[53] But the accessibility of such homes, particularly those with anonymous admissions, unwittingly promoted abandonment by those who previously would not have resorted to it. Financially pressed married couples used the homes to place their legitimate children, hoping that the infants could be kept alive until the family could afford to care for them. In fact, however, the vast majority of children in foundling homes soon died. These homes eventually disappeared in the late nineteenth and early twentieth centuries, because most children left there were actually legitimate. But similar "unintended consequences" occur in the United States today as a result of the so-called "safe haven" laws, which designate certain places, such as hospitals or police stations, where unwanted infants can be left without risk of criminal charges for murder or abandonment. A recent analysis of such laws (now passed in almost every state) concludes that some parents who would otherwise have kept their babies are taking advantage of the law and that many do not use the designated locations but

---

51 *Novel* 153 (a. 541).

52 The phrase is that of Ransel in L.A. Tilly, R.G. Fuchs, D.I. Kertzer, and D.L. Ransel, "Child Abandonment in European History: A Symposium," *JFH* 17 (1992) 1–23; also Boswell, *Kindness of Strangers*, 427.

53 See D.I. Kertzer, *Sacrificed for Honor: Italian Abandonment and the Politics of Reproductive Control* (Boston, 1993); V. Hunecke, "The Abandonment of Legitimate Children in Nineteenth-Century Milan and the European Context," in J. Henderson and R. Wall (eds.), *Poor Women and Children in the European Past* (London and New York, 1994) 117–35; and P.P. Viazzo, "Family Structures and the Early Phase in the Individual Life Cycle," in Henderson and Wall, *Poor Women and Children*, 32–50.

continue to leave newborns in dumpsters or other dangerous places.[54] Imperial and ecclesiastical attempts to discourage and regulate infant abandonment probably also had such "unintended consequences."

Conclusion

More significant than the putative effectiveness of these measures, however, is the fact that they were taken at all. Late Roman emperors, including Justinian, were responding to actual social problems, and their policies should be considered in multiple contexts: the late antique practice of enacting general legislation to cover situations that previously had been handled on an ad hoc basis; the Christianization of late Roman society; and the social and economic conditions of Late Antiquity. But there is reason to think that the denunciations of *expositio* made by Christian writers like Lactantius at least indirectly influenced imperial policy. Certainly Justinian was acting on religious as well as legal principles.[55] Infant abandonment was one issue on which church and state could agree and work together. Christians wanted to prevent the death or prostitution of vulnerable children, and the law was anxious to eliminate conflicts over ownership and the status of *expositi.* Late Roman emperors and Christian clergy agreed that infant exposure was a matter of social and moral concern and worked together to ameliorate the problem.

---

[54] See "'Unintended Consequences': Safe Haven' Laws are Causing Problems, Not Solving Them" E.B. Donaldson Adoption Institute 10 March, 2003 at http://www.adoptioninstitute.org/whowe/lastreport_coverpage.html (accessed 29 August 2007).

[55] Cf. Humfress, "Law and Legal Practice," 167–8. After completing this paper, I read a recently published article by J.C. Tate, "Christianity and the Legal Status of Abandoned Children in the Later Roman Empire," *Journal of Law and Religion* 24 (2008) 101–19. Tate is doubtful about Christian influence on Constantine's legislation; rather, he believes the impact of Christianity in regard to the legal status of abandoned children begins with the legislation of Honorius (*CTh* 5.9.2 [a. 412]; and *Sirmondian Constitution* 5 [a. 419]).

Chapter 9
Imperial Politics at the Court of Theodosius II

Hugh Elton
Trent University

An incident at the imperial court in Constantinople in 433 allows us to examine the complexity of imperial government in the mid-fifth century. The delegates to the Council of Ephesus in 431 had divided into pro- and anti-Nestorian groups, led by the patriarchs John of Antioch and Cyril of Alexandria respectively. The dispute was only resolved after Theodosius II negotiated an agreement between the two patriarchs via the Formula of Reunion in 433. However, some bishops remained recalcitrant, in particular those in the provinces of Cilicia. Theodosius now tried to use secular power to restore church unity by ordering the Cilician bishops to recognize John, or be exiled. This order was protested by the eastern praetorian prefect, Taurus, who warned that it would affect the flow of taxes from the region. Taurus' challenge to the emperor prompts questions about how Theodosius II made decisions, how government worked in Constantinople, and the interrelationship of civil, military, and religious leaders. All of this activity in Constantinople was driven by and had an impact on events in the provinces.

Some of these themes have been examined recently by Millar in *A Greek Roman Empire*, a work focusing more on the machinery of government than on the practicalities of politics. Kelly's *Ruling the Later Roman Empire* offers other ways to consider many of these themes, though with a similar focus on machinery and bureaucracy. And there is the approach of Brown in *Power and Persuasion in Late Antiquity*, with a focus on personal connections.[1] My approach to this incident concentrates on the mechanics of decision-making at the court of Theodosius. Although some attention has been paid to the court, much remains to be said.[2]

---

[1] *ACOec.* 1.4, nr.212; F. Millar, *A Greek Roman Empire: Power and Belief under Theodosius II (408–450)* (Berkeley, 2006), 221; C. Kelly, *Ruling the Later Roman Empire* (Cambridge, MA, 2004); P. Brown, *Power and Persuasion in Late Antiquity* (Madison, WI, 1992) 66.

[2] A.D.E. Cameron, "The Empress and the Poet: Paganism and Politics at the Court of Theodosius II," *YClS* 27 (1982) 217–89; J. Harries, "*Pius princeps*: Theodosius II and Fifth-Century Constantinople," in P. Magadalino (ed.), *New Constantines* (Aldershot, 1994) 35–44; J.A. McGuckin, "Nestorius and the Political Factions of Fifth-Century Byzantium: Factors in his Personal Downfall," *BRL* 78 (1996) 7–22; B.K. Ilski, "Der schwache Kaiser

In the fifth-century east, Roman imperial power was physically centralized in the person of the emperor, usually to be found in the Great Palace in Constantinople. The Palace was a large walled compound containing a number of different buildings. It was usually entered through the main gate at the north-east, later known as the Chalke—though we know little about this before its Anastasian rebuilding—immediately after which lay the barracks of the *scholarii*. The *consistorium* was on the east side of this first courtyard, presumably named for the meetings that took place there. Past these official areas were the private apartments of the emperor. The palace complex is best seen as a combination of imperial residence and government offices, so cannot simply be interpreted as either a public or private space, while access to certain areas such as offices and churches probably varied according to the time of day.[3]

Although power was centralized in the person of the emperor, as in all complex organizations most of the business of governing the Roman empire was done in the course of meetings. Most imperial officials lived outside the palace and thus could have bumped into each other as they came to meetings along the roads leading there, particularly the Mese, at the palace gate itself—where most probably dismounted from horses and carriages—or on various paths within the palace complex. There would have been further encounters as officials waited for meetings to start, after meetings, and at services in the Great Church opposite the palace gate, at Hagia Irene, or at St. Stephen, built by the emperor's sister Pulcheria inside the palace ca. 428.[4]

So, at the moment in 433 when Taurus was protesting Theodosius' order, what other things might have been discussed by leading Romans as they assembled at the palace? Topics could have included several military issues: for example, the situations on the eastern frontier with the Persians, on the Danubian frontier with the Huns, and in Africa with the army there under Aspar's command. Relations with the western empire could have been under discussion, including the recent victory of Bonifatius over Aetius at Rimini, the death of the former from wounds, and the latter's flight to the Huns. So too, one might have mused over the long-awaited marriage of Valentinian III to Theodosius' daughter Eudoxia and whether it would ever come off. The ongoing fallout of the Council of Ephesus and questions about the appointment of the bishop of Constantinople would also have come up: should Proclus have been preferred to Maximian? Western ecclesiastical affairs might also have been mentioned, since the bishop of Rome, Sixtus III, had planned a synod in July 433 to examine relations between western and eastern churches. Domestic issues could have been discussed, such as the fire which damaged the imperial city

---

Theodosios," in L.M. Hoffmann and A. Mouchizedeh (eds.), *Zwischen Polis, Provinz und Peripherie* (Wiesbaden, 2005) 3–23; K. Chew, "Virgins and Eunuchs: Pulcheria, Politics and the Death of Emperor Theodosius II," *Historia* 55 (2006) 207–27.

[3] C. Mango, *The Brazen House* (Copenhagen, 1959), 22–30; J. Bardill, "The Great Palace of the Byzantine Emperors and the Walker Trust Excavations," *JRA* 12 (1999) 216–30.

[4] Theoph. *AM* 5920.

in August 433, or the ongoing compilation of the *Codex Theodosianus*. But gossip probably took priority—a decade later rumours of an affair between Paulinus and Eudocia certainly set tongues wagging. We cannot show that all or even any of these issues was discussed, but they would undoubtedly have been on the minds of the men at and around these meetings.

Although all major decisions were theoretically taken by the emperor only after discussion with advisers, the absolute nature of imperial authority meant that any decision could be influenced by anyone who could reach the ruler. Too often, however, both ancient and modern historians have exaggerated such personal influences and suggested that the emperor was dominated by eunuchs, women, or barbarian generals. Theodosius' purported susceptibility to the influence of eunuchs is notorious: "since he had been brought up under the thumbs of eunuchs, he was open to their every demand." This entry in the *Suda*, possibly derived from Priscus, is confirmed by a statement of Isidore of Pelusium in a letter to Antiochus, *praepositus sacri cubiculi* in 421, which claimed that Antiochus controlled the empire. The conventional explanation of this dominance is that the *praepositus* controlled the access of individuals to the emperor's household.[5] If this were true, Isidore's flattery was to be expected, but since Sozomen, Socrates, Theodoret, and Philostorgius all said nothing of Antiochus, one wonders how literally Isidore and the *Suda* should be taken. The emphasis on reaching the emperor in his apartments also ignores the fact that he was not cocooned there.[6] Although the *praepositus* could grant or restrict access to the imperial household, he could not isolate the emperor. Theodosius met officials and aristocrats at meetings of the senate, at the consistory, and in church; Socrates says that he regularly discussed scriptural matters with bishops.[7] Theodosius also met his subjects on many public occasions. In Constantinople, we hear of assaults on the emperor because of a grain shortage, of the presentation of a giant apple to him, and of his attendance at beast hunts and chariot races.[8] He also left the city on a few occasions, for example he was at Chalcedon in 431, at Cyzicus in 436, and a law of 443 noted that when, "we were making a passage through the municipality of Heraclea, we were moved to great compassion by the petitions of the citizens of the aforesaid municipality."[9]

---

5 A.H.M. Jones, *The Later Roman Empire: 284–602: A Social, Economic, and Administrative Survey* (Oxford, 1964) 338–41; K. Hopkins, "The Political Power of Eunuchs," in *Conquerors and Slaves* (Cambridge, 1978) 172–96; J. Bardill and G. Greatrex, "Antiochus the *praepositus*: a Persian Eunuch at the Court of Theodosius II," *DOP* 50 (1996) 171–97; M. Heil, "Perser im spätrömischen Dienst," in J. Wiesehöfer and P. Huyse (eds.), *Eran und Aneran* (Stuttgart, 2006) 143–80 at 170–74.

6 *Suda* Θ.145; cf. Joh.Ant. fr. 288 (Roberto); Isid. Pel. *Ep.* 1.36; cf. Joh.Mal. 14.15, 19.

7 Soc. 7.22, 23.

8 Assault: Marc.Com. s.a. 431. Apple: Joh.Mal. 14.8. Beasts: Soc. 7.22. Other petitions: Theod. *HE* 5.23.

9 Chalcedon: S. Wessel, *Cyril of Alexandria and the Nestorian Controversy: The Making of a Saint and of a Heretic* (Oxford, 2004) 255; Cyzicus: Marc.Com. *s.a.* 436;

Isidore's flattery also ignores another group that had great influence on the emperor, his relatives. Like the eunuchs, Theodosius' sisters Pulcheria, Marina, and Arcadia and Theodosius' wife Eudocia could also provide personal access to the emperor. According to Sozomen, Pulcheria, "governed the Roman empire excellently and with great orderliness," an impressive feat for a woman "not yet 15," but as with Antiochus, not all authors report the same things and Socrates and Theodoret mention only her piety and not her control of the empire.[10] Generalizations aside, a good illustration of the realities of the power of an Augusta can be found in the case of Porphyry of Gaza.[11] When Mark the Deacon and Porphyry were trying to force the closure of a pagan temple in Gaza in 401, they sailed to Constantinople. Instead of appealing to the emperor himself, they met with the city's bishop John Chrysostom. John was unable to reach the emperor directly, supposedly because the empress Eudoxia had blocked his access, but thought he could use one of her eunuchs, Amantius, to move things along. As bishop of Constantinople, it is more likely that John thought this was the best way to move the petition forward, not that he could not actually get access to the emperor. Amantius brought Porphyry to Eudoxia who then mentioned the request to Arcadius. The emperor rejected her request because he did not want to take any action that might impede the flow of taxes from the city. This implies that a direct approach would also have been rejected. When Eudoxia gave birth to Theodosius soon afterward, she was able to win permission that a petition, coincidentally that of Porphyry, be granted by the newborn infant. Though the anecdote is deployed by Mark the Deacon to show the effectiveness of Porphyry's lobbying, it also demonstrates Arcadius' concern to privilege tax collection and order over the promotion of Christianity.

Apart from eunuchs and princesses, barbarian generals could also influence the emperor. Aspar exercised considerable power in his role as *magister militum* between 431 and 471 even though he was an Alan and Arian, while Plinta, *magister militum in praesenti* between 419 and 438, despite being a Goth and a heretic, was, according to Sozomen, "the most powerful of those then in the palace."[12] This is also to ignore the major role played by eastern praetorian prefects, such as Taurus, who, as we have seen, had direct access to the emperor, or Cyrus, who was exiled because of his popularity, or Anthemius, who was regent at the beginning of Theodosius' reign.[13]

If we merely accept what our contemporary primary sources say about these men and women influencing or controlling the emperor, we end up with an empire

---

Heraclea: *Nov.Theod.* 23.1.

10 K. Holum, *Theodosian Empresses: Women and Imperial Domination in Late Antiquity* (Berkeley, 1982) esp. 95–6; Soz. 9.1; echoed by Philost. 12.7.

11 Marc.Diac. *VPorph.* 37–48.

12 Soz. 7.17.4.

13 Soc. 7.1.1.

ruled by (to borrow Synesius' description of Arcadius) a "jellyfish."[14] However, this model of individuals dominating the emperor and thus the empire should be treated with caution. Take the case of Plinta, who was reported to be the most powerful of those in the palace at the same time as Antiochus was said to have run the state. The number of different individuals with different types of influence over the emperor suggests that the situation was more complex. A model focusing on any single individual influencing the emperor also ignores the effects of the remaining representatives of the government. The anecdotes about Taurus and Porphyry confirm that these were highly relevant. Another example of government at work is provided by an edict of Theodosius showing the ex-praetorian prefect Florentius advocating the banning of pimps from the imperial city. Since these men paid the *collatio lustralis*, Florentius offered to pay the tax himself, thereby pre-empting likely objections from both the *comes sacrarum largitionum* (whose office received the money) and the praetorian prefect (who collected it).[15] Without this sort of pre-emption, this give and take between the various arms of the government, such measures would have encountered difficulties. An edict issued to the eastern praetorian prefect in September 440 abolished certain privileges for imperial officials, but it took a second edict of December 440 to clarify that the first did not include soldiers. Jones suggests that, "this law cannot have been discussed in any kind of cabinet where the *magistri militum* would certainly have objected," but it is just as likely that the problems with the interpretation of the edict only became apparent once it had been promulgated.[16] These two situations thus suggest a model of government far more complex than one of simple influence on the emperor by a few individuals close to him.

Although Theodosius II is often presented as a cipher, he was well aware of the manoeuvring that took place to influence him. An edict of 415 insisted that delegations to the emperor were permitted only following a meeting of the local council, and that free delegations would not be permitted access. The effort was to reduce the number of independent embassies from competing factions. When, in late 430, Cyril of Alexandria addressed separate letters to the emperor and to Eudocia and Pulcheria, Theodosius wrote back and asked if he were trying to sow dissension. And when the praetorian prefect Cyrus received acclamations from the crowd in the Hippodrome following his rebuilding of Constantinople's walls, he was concerned, fearful of seeming to the emperor to have gained too much influence. His subsequent exile to Cotyaeum suggests that his fear was founded in a clear understanding of the realities of contemporary politics.[17]

We must also be aware of the power of literary models which generally argue that emperors were not bad, merely poorly advised, while many of the advisers

---

14 Syn. *De regno*, 14D.

15 *Nov. Theod.* 18 (a. 439); Jones, *Later Roman Empire*, 431–2.

16 Jones, *Later Roman Empire*, 339–40; *Nov. Theod.* 7.2–3; cf. cascading privileges shown by *CT* 6.25.1, 6.24.8, and 6.24.9

17 *CTh* 12.12.15 (a. 415); *ACOec.* 1.1.1 nr.20; Joh.Mal. 14.15–16.

were, by ancient definitions, automatically pernicious, being as they were women, eunuchs, or barbarians.[18] In the case of hagiography, it was in the interest of the authors to claim that their subjects had influence over the emperor. The scale of any of these interventions, however, was limited and, despite the assertions of Isidore of Pelusium or Sozomen, eunuchs and princesses were not involved in government. They could often obtain favours, but this seems little different from secular appeals from individual communities to the emperor like those received by Theodosius at Heraclea. These could be dealt with without taking up much time of the ranking officials. But even the performance of favours, as the case of Porphyry shows, was not always successful. A similar example is an imperial rejection of a request that a group of merchants on Pulcheria's estates should be exempt from the *collatio lustralis* in 418, a request presumably put forward by Pulcheria herself. Theodosius was only 16 years old at the time, making it likely that someone else in the palace was watching the accounts and denied the request for exemption.[19]

Moreover these favours should not be confused with the importance to the empire of religious disputes, Hunnic or Persian wars, or internal challenges to imperial power. With the ossification of the senate and the consistory, strategic decision-making in the mid-fifth century was the domain of what was termed in 446 the "leading men of the palace" (*proceres palatii*). This is perhaps best thought of as an informal grouping of high-ranking military and civil officials—at this point, the bishop of Constantinople was not a regular member of this group. "Those in the emperor's presence" would probably better reflect the reality than "council."[20] Probably the best example of how this group worked can be found in the plan to assassinate Attila in 449. According to Priscus, the *spatharius* Chrysaphius, on his own initiative, used a private audience with the Hun Edeco to concoct a plan to assassinate the Hunnic leader. Once Chrysaphius had a plan, he approached Theodosius who summoned Martialis, the *magister officiorum*. After a short discussion, the plan was put into operation.[21] This sounds similar to the description of Taurus' intervention in 433, "entering the imperial presence" (*intrans vero in principem*).[22] His protest is more likely to have entered the historical record from an opinion expressed at a meeting rather than from a private encounter between the two.

This background informs our understanding of the events surrounding the opening anecdote.[23] When Nestorius was made bishop of Constantinople in

[18] Hopkins, "Political Power," 173–4; my thanks to Danuta Shanzer for discussion of this point.

[19] *CTh* 13.1.21.

[20] *CJ* 1.14.8; cf. Prisc. fr.9.1.

[21] Prisc. fr.11.1.

[22] *ACOec.* 1.4, nr.212.

[23] For background, see Wessel, *Cyril of Alexandria*, 138–80. For the post-Ephesus date of the cult of the Theotokos, see B.V. Pentcheva, *Icons and Power: The Mother of God in Byzantium* (University Park, PA, 2006) 15–16.

428, he inherited a squabble over whether Mary could be called Mother of God (Theotokos). Nestorius' actions to limit the term drew the attention of Cyril, bishop of Alexandria, who issued Twelve Anathemas. The refutation of these by Theodoret of Cyrrhus set up a conflict between the churches of Alexandria and Antioch. To resolve the debate, Theodosius summoned an ecumenical council to meet at Ephesus in June 431. The Council began in confusion, and Cyril was able to exploit the late arrival of the bishops supporting Nestorius, led by John of Antioch, to have Nestorius deposed. Theodosius' response to this situation has been interpreted as showing the influence of monks. The arrival of the archimandrite Dalmatius, accompanied by a large crowd, at the imperial palace at the end of June 431 caused a sensation in Constantinople. Having entered the palace, Dalmatius showed the emperor the letter he had received from Cyril at Ephesus, recording the deposition of Nestorius.[24] But this sort of intervention could only occur rarely. Dalmatius caused a sensation precisely because he had not left his cell in forty-eight years—a similar shock was caused by Daniel the Stylite's descent from his column during the reign of Basiliscus. Perhaps more importantly, although Nestorius and Dalmatius both asserted that Dalmatius' intervention was successful, the intervention was not followed by any imperial action.[25] Similarly, a public demonstration at the Great Church in early July 431 may have had an impact on Theodosius, but such performances had to be orchestrated and were probably not seen as spontaneous by any of the actors.[26] Although Nestorius was unpopular, the Council of Ephesus was not just about him. For Theodosius, a solution to the problems raised by Nestorius was not necessarily the same as a solution to the problems raised by Cyril—though Cyril would have seen things differently. John of Antioch and the eastern bishops arrived at Ephesus, they held a separate counter-synod which deposed Cyril.[27] Both groups reported to the emperor and continued to meet in July. Cyril sent letters to various court officials as well as to the emperor and Pulcheria.[28] Theodosius confirmed the deposition of Cyril, and then considered further what was to be done about these issues. In other words, despite the claims for influence made by partisans, contemporaries, and later writers, neither Dalmatius nor Pulcheria actually succeeded in changing Theodosius' mind.

At the end of July 431, Theodosius summoned a small group of bishops to meet him at Chalcedon in September. Cyril knew that Theodosius had not yet made up his mind and so hoped to create a favourable climate of opinion at court. Dalmatius was encouraged to see the emperor again and Cyril sent out a slew

---

24 Letter: *ACOec.* 1.1.2 nr.67. Meeting: *VDalmatii* 13–15 (*AASS* Aug. 1.218–24).

25 D. Caner, *Wandering, Begging Monks: Spiritual Authority and the Promotion of Monasticism in Late Antiquity* (Berkeley, 2002) 217–23; Wessel, *Cyril of Alexandria*, 163–5; Nestorius, *Bazaar of Heracleides*, trans. G.R. Driver, and L. Hodgson (Oxford, 1925) 272–7.

26 *ACOec.* 1.1.3 nr.86; Holum, *Theodosian Empresses*, 170–71.

27 *ACOec.* 1.1.5 nr.119–24.

28 *ACOec.* 1.1.5 nr.161–2.

of presents. Bribing decision-makers directly was counter-productive so presents were sent not to imperial officials but to the wife of the eastern praetorian prefect and many of the palace eunuchs. Although Cyril presumably tried to be discreet, enough people talked that three contemporaries, Theodoret, Nestorius, and Acacius of Beroea, claimed that Cyril had conquered through bribery.[29] Although all were opponents of Cyril, we do have a preserved gift list, albeit from a dossier of anti-Cyrillian documents.[30]

Theodosius heard further submissions in person at Chalcedon in September 431 before confirming the exile of Nestorius and reinstating Cyril. As the bishops returned home, more meetings were generated with synods taking place in Cilicia I and II that confirmed the provinces' opposition to Cyril and the Anathemas.[31] More negotiations followed, and by April 433 Theodosius had been able to produce the Formula of Reunion which both John and Cyril were prepared to sign. They both made concessions, but some of John's bishops thought he had gone too far and refused to recognize him. Meanwhile, a baffled Succensus of Diocaesarea in Isauria wrote to Cyril, asking him to explain his position.[32]

Theodosius now ordered the *quaestor sacri palatii* Domitianus to tell the Cilician bishops to recognize John or be exiled. Taurus opposed this order and warned that it would cause disturbances, stating that "as Thrace is, Cilicia will be," and thus the flow of taxes from the region would be reduced.[33] Our source for these events is a letter from bishop Meletius of Mopsuestia to his metropolitan Maximinus of Anazarbus. Meletius later went into exile rather than accept John, so his version of events and approval of Taurus' actions may have been self-serving. But we cannot say why Taurus acted. It may have been out of religious principles, which is certainly the way that Meletius presented it, but Taurus might also have been genuinely concerned about tax collection, after all the responsibility of his office. The constant petitions for tax relief were probably an endless source of frustration, whether received via the emperor as shown by the Porphyry anecdote, or via other imperial officials, like the *cubicularius* Domninus, who also received gifts from Cyril in 431 and is attested in 427/429 in connection with a case before the court of the *comes sacrarum largitionum* over harbour taxes from Mylasa in Caria.[34] This pressure on Taurus was probably heightened by an edict of 22 April 433 which granted tax remissions for five years.[35] So there are two plausible reasons for Taurus to have acted as he did, but we cannot say whether he was moved by faith, duty, or both. Meletius may also have had different views of Taurus since a

29 Theodoret: *ACOec.* 1.1.7 nr.69. Nestorius: *Bazaar*, 272. Acacius: *ACOec.* 1.4 nr.80.

30 *ACOec.* 1.4 nr.294; Wessel, *Cyril of Alexandria*, 258, 262.

31 *ACOec.* 1.4 nr.199, 202 (Cilicia I), 200–201 (Cilicia II)

32 Cyril, *Epp.* 45, 46 = *ACOec.* 1.1.6 nr.171–2.

33 *ACOec.* 1.4 nr.212.

34 *CIL* 3.7152 = *AE* 2001.1850, as well as probably *CIL* 3.7151.

35 *CTh* 11.28.16.

letter from John to Taurus in 434 asked for help against "a few unruly men," which probably included Meletius.[36]

Meletius' letter also shows how modern attempts to compartmentalize religion and politics, though they supposedly make events easier for historians to analyse, consistently fly in the face of ancient behaviour. John of Antioch was not the only bishop to ask for help from state officials as shown by the numerous secular addressees of the correspondence of Nilus, Isidore, Firmus, and Theodoret. Holy men wrote to imperial officials because imperial officials were intimately involved in what are traditionally termed "religious" affairs. Candidianus, the *comes domesticorum*, presided over the Council of Ephesus. Domitianus, the *quaestor sacri palatii*, wrote to Helladius urging him to take communion with John of Antioch.[37] And Aristolaus, the *tribunus et notarius* who had managed the negotiations over the Formula of Reunion, also attended a synod of Cilicia I in Tarsus in 434/5 where the bishops were asked to acknowledge John's acceptance of the Formula.[38] Some acceded, but we have a letter from the *magister militum* Dionysius ordering the governor of Cilicia II to exile Meletius of Mopsuestia to Melitene, and Zenobius of Zephyrium in Cilicia I was also exiled.[39] A less subtle view of the overlap is offered by the statement of Nestorius to Theodosius on his appointment in 428: "Give me, emperor, the earth purged of heretics, and I will give you heaven in return. Help me put down the heretics, and I will help you put down the Persians."[40]

The problem posed by some Cilician bishops refusing to acknowledge their patriarch thus had wide ramifications. The importance and desired resolution to the problem could be different for emperor, empress, eunuch, prefect, general, and bishop. Theodosius probably desired unity, but was less worried about which form of religious thought dominated, whereas Pulcheria was perhaps engaging in a vendetta against Nestorius. For Dionysius, it may just have been a tedious bureaucratic process and Taurus may have been concerned only with the tax process. John of Antioch and Meletius may have seen this as a struggle for authority or as one to avoid damnation. In all these cases, we need to allow not only for differing perspectives and multiple interests but also for inconsistencies within individual points of view and the fact that opinions changed over time: Taurus may have been moved by both religion and taxes. Theodosius moved from backing Nestorius to rejecting him. And although the original dispute over Nestorius was purely theological—albeit reflecting political rivalries between the bishops of Constantinople, Antioch, and Alexandria—Taurus' response to Theodosius shows that contemporaries expected local populations to react to these events.

36 *ACOec.* 1.4 nr.211.

37 *ACOec.* 1.4 nr.213.

38 *ACOec.* 1.4 nr.281.

39 *ACOec.* 1.4 nr.279.vi, vii.

40 Soc. 7.29.

The court of Theodosius was not static, though there were few direct challenges to imperial power. Nor did Theodosius remain the same, for he changed from a child of six at his accession to sole rule to a man of 48 at his death. He has often been seen as a survivor rather than an actor, but his survival against a backdrop of the constant rise and fall of individual ministers suggests that he was more in control than has been assumed. The narrative sources present the story in terms of individuals because it is easier—and in many ways more exciting—to tell stories about evil eunuchs with shining pates, glamorous princesses with clandestine love affairs, and skin-clad barbarian generals. But if this version of history is privileged, it means overlooking the fact that it was Theodosius II, the longest reigning Roman emperor, who managed relationships between these individuals.

Chapter 10
"The Trembling of Cain": Religious Power and Institutional Culture in Justinianic Oath-Making

Charles Pazdernik
Grand Valley State University

In April of 535 Justinian promulgated an ambitious program of administrative reform that was intended to minimize pretexts for graft on the part of provincial office-holders by altering the terms of their appointment and remuneration. Among its provisions was the (re)institution of a loyalty oath, the text and details of which have been preserved in the *Corpus iuris civilis*.

This oath represents an audacious attempt to redeploy religious capital in order to augment imperial authority and to reinforce the governmental compact in Late Antiquity which legitimated the monopolization of power in the person of the monarch. The dire imprecations it contained were intended to impress upon both the emperor's functionaries and his citizens at large the reciprocal obligations that bound together ruler and subject, ruler and official, and subject and official.[1] At the same time, Justinian's deployment of the power of religion in this arena extended well beyond the gaudy prospect of divine retribution for official wrongdoing: it also represented an effort, in the first place, to mobilize ecclesiastical resources in seeking to rein in and to supervise the imperial administration; in the second place, it stood among a number of wide-ranging and consequential measures that progressively transformed the institutional culture of that administration by importing and imposing distinctively Christian models of service to the community and the delegation of authority. Chief among these was the characterization of the performance of official duties as a species of δουλεία or servitude, a concept that

[1] It may be compared with the terms of other loyalty oaths, which assert a commonality of interests between emperors and subjects: see N.G. Svoronos, "Le serment de fidélité à l'empereur byzantin et sa signification constitutionnelle," *REByz* 9 (1951) 106–42 = Idem, *Études sur l'organisation intérieure, la société et l'économie de l'Empire byzantin* (London, 1973) vi, esp. 106–9, 135, 139; P. Herrmann, *Der römische Kaisereid* (Göttingen 1968), esp. 21–44, 66–89; J. Le Gall, "Le serment à l'empereur: une base méconnue de la tyrannie impériale sous le Haut-Empire?" *Latomus* 44 (1985) 767–83; R. Scharf, "Conobaria 5 v. Chr.—Der erste römische 'Kaisereid'," in P. Defosse (ed.), *Hommages à Carl Deroux* (Brussels, 2003) 415–24.

in the medieval Byzantine period could encompass any obligation performed on behalf of the emperor.[2]

We can assess the nature of the governmental compact at the turn of the sixth century by examining two moments from the Byzantine *Book of Ceremonies* that are attributable to Peter the Patrician.[3] On 9 April 491 the emperor Zeno died in his bed.[4] That evening the people and the soldiers (ὁ δῆμος, οἱ στρατιῶται) gathered in the hippodrome and began clamoring for a new emperor. Meanwhile the officials, the senators, and the patriarch (οἱ ἄρχοντες καὶ οἱ συγκλητικοὶ καὶ ὁ ἐπίσκοπος) had assembled in the portico at the front of the Great Triclinium of the palace. They unanimously recommended that the Augusta Ariadne, wife of Zeno and daughter of Leo I, should appear in the imperial box at the hippodrome and address the crowd. She duly presented herself, clad in the imperial *chlamys*, in the company of high officials and attendants and the patriarch, Euphemius, with the remainder of the court arrayed below in order of rank. Having been immediately acclaimed and repeatedly entreated with calls for "an orthodox emperor for the world," she congratulated the people, through a spokesman, for their nobility of character in preserving good order. In response (*De cer*. 1.92 [419.4–7 Reiske]):

> παρὰ πάντων ἐβοήθη· "ἡμεῖς δοῦλοι τῆς αὐγούστης· εὐσεβῆ Κύριε, ζωὴν αὐτῇ· πολλὰ τὰ ἔτη τῆς αὐγούστας· Ἀριάδνη αὐγούστα, σὺ νικᾷς· Ῥωμαίων βασιλέα τῇ οἰκουμένῃ."

---

[2] J.H. Pryor, "The Oaths of the Leaders of the First Crusade to Emperor Alexius I Comnenus: Fealty, Homage—πίστις, δουλεία," *Parergon* 2 (1984) 111–41, esp. 123–4. The identification of this phenomenon as the adoption of an "oriental usage" (M. Guarducci, "Teodosio rinnovatore di Corinto," in J. Bingen, G. Cambier, and G. Nachtergael, [eds.], *Le monde grec: Hommages à Claire Préaux* [Brussels, 1975] 527–34, at 531) is questionable, but detailed examination of it is beyond the scope of this study. Compare H. Köpstein, "Zum Fortleben des Wortes δοῦλος und anderer Bezeichnungen für den Sklaven im Mittel- und Neugriechischen," in E.C. Welskopf (ed.), *Soziale Typenbegriffe, III. Untersuchungen ausgewählter altgriechischer sozialer Typenbegriffe* (Berlin, 1981) 319–53, esp. 322, 325 and nn.17–21, 36; Eadem, *Zur Sklaverei im ausgehenden Byzanz* (Berlin, 1966), esp. 33–4; O. Treitinger, *Die oströmische Kaiser- und Reichsidee* (Darmstadt, 1956), esp. 228 and n.84; A. Kazhdan, "The Concepts of Freedom (*eleutheria*) and Slavery (*douleia*) in Byzantium," in G. Makdisi, D. Sourdel, and J. Sourdel-Thomine (eds.), *La notion de liberté au Moyen Age: Islam, Byzance, Occident* (Paris, 1985) 215–26, esp. 219–20; for the Near Eastern background, see A. Missiou, "Δούλος τοῦ βασιλέως: The Politics of Translation," *CQ* 43 (1993) 377–91.

[3] See J.B. Bury, "The Ceremonial Book of Constantine Porphyrogennetos," *EHR* 22 (1907) 209–27 and 417–39.

[4] *De ceremoniis* 1.92 (417.15–425.21 Reiske). See J.B. Bury, *History of the Later Roman Empire from the Death of Theodosius I to the Death of Justinian, 395–565* (London, 1923) 1.429–32; G. Dagron, *Emperor and Priest: The Imperial Office in Byzantium* (Cambridge, 2003) 65–8; F.K. Haarer, *Anastasius I: Politics and Empire in the Late Roman World* (Cambridge, 2006) 1–6.

> All shouted: "we are the δοῦλοι of the Augusta! Blessed Lord, life for her! Many years for the Augusta! Ariadne Augusta, you are victorious! [We seek/implore/demand(?)] an emperor of the Romans for the world!"

The empress responded that in anticipation of their requests (or demands: πρὸ τῶν ὑμετέρων αἰτήσεων, 419.7–8) she had placed the nomination in the hands of the officials and the senate, who with the concurrence of the army and in the presence of the holy gospels and the patriarch should render a decision pleasing to God without enmity or favoritism or regard to any private interest. In the meantime the people must remain quiet until after Zeno's funeral.

The crowd roared its assent, but also seized the moment to demand the ouster of "the thieving Prefect of the City" (420.13–16). In her response Ariadne rejoiced that she had once again anticipated the people's request, having already replaced the objectionable official.[5]

In the end the officials and the senate, with the cooperation of the patriarch, reposed the nomination in Ariadne herself, who selected (and subsequently married) Anastasius. The account is a remarkable testament to a shared investment in the maintenance of public order by rulers and the ruled. Ariadne's role as a source of both legitimacy and continuity from previous reigns was critical to maintaining that order.

But the episode also recognizes a number of stakeholders in the decision: the people and the army as represented by the civilians[6] and soldiers present in Constantinople, whose ratification of the nomination is crucial and whose capacity for disorder serves as an implicit check upon decision-makers; the patriarch, whose participation in the proceedings is carefully noted (together with the presence of the holy gospels) and seems to serve to guarantee the integrity of those proceedings, and who functions as an intermediary between the empress and the administration; and the administration itself, the officials and the senate, who perform an essential role in orchestrating a successful resolution of the crisis while remaining effectively behind the scenes.[7] For her part, the empress intercedes only at the instigation of the administration and demonstrates her willingness to rely upon their advice, while at the same time holding them accountable to the public.[8]

---

5 He might have been an Isaurian: Bury, *History*, 1.403 n. 3.

6 Including, but presumably not limited to, members of the circus factions. See A.D.E. Cameron, *Circus Factions* (Oxford, 1976) 261–70, esp. 263 n.2.

7 Dagron, *Emperor and Priest,* 67, observes: "a new power structure, with two poles constituted by the Hippodrome, where the soldiers were present alongside the people, and the palace, where the civil and military dignitaries deliberated …"

8 Compare A. McClanan, *Representations of Early Byzantine Empresses* (New York, 2002) 65–92, esp. 67–8, who does not discuss the account of *De cerimoniis* but credits Ariadne with "dazzling alacrity" (68) in securing the accession of Anastasius. Speculation about behind-the-scenes maneuvers was bruited in antiquity, as Haarer, *Anastasius*, 1–6, notes.

The imperial office itself remains in principle an elective, public trust exercised in the public interest; legitimacy inheres in the processes through which the people, the army, and other stakeholders achieve consensus in the selection of the imperial candidate, and thus make manifest the operation of divine providence in appointing a ruler for the world; the investiture of an emperor effects a conferral of power by subjects upon the ruler they have created, who rules not as a popular representative but as an absolute monarch. The crowd's acclamation of Ariadne with the words, "we are the δοῦλοι of the Augusta," immediately after it has been congratulated for maintaining good order in spite of the absence of an emperor, must accordingly represent an act of empowerment on the part of the crowd, a recognition and ratification of Ariadne's role in providing for continuity of government.

So too once the crowd has made an emperor, its constituents signal their recognition and ratification of that fact and their subservience to the absolute power that they have ratified and conferred by declaring themselves to be δοῦλοι. In similar fashion upon the investiture of Anastasius the crowd declares, "have mercy on your δοῦλοι" (*De cer*. 1.92 [425.3 Reiske]).

Now for the second moment from the *Book of Ceremonies*. At the accession of Justin I on 9 July 518 (following a rather less orderly selection process than that of Anastasius)[9] we find the following exchange (*De cer*. 1.93 [429.17–430.15 Reiske]):

> Imperator Caesar Justin, victorious, ever Augustus [declared]: "Having attained the throne by the will of Almighty God and by your unanimous choice (τῇ τοῦ παντοδυνάμου Θεοῦ κρίσει, τῇ τε ὑμετέρᾳ κοινῇ ἐκλογῇ), we call upon celestial providence (τὴν οὐράνιον πρόνοιαν)."
>
> All cried: "Well-being to the world (τῇ οἰκουμένῃ). As you have lived, so rule. Well-being to the state (τῇ πολιτείᾳ). Heavenly βασιλεύς, preserve the earthly one. Justin Augustus, you are victorious. Many years for the new Constantine. We are the δοῦλοι of the βασιλεύς."
>
> Imperator Caesar Augustus: "May [God], through his grace, enable us to achieve everything that is beneficial to you and to the commonwealth (ὑμῖν τε καὶ τῷ δημοσίῳ)."
>
> All shouted: "Son of God, have mercy on him! You have elected him (σὺ αὐτὸν ἐπελέξω)! Have mercy on him! Justin Augustus, you are victorious," and other things of that sort.
>
> Imperator Caesar Augustus: "Our concern is to provide you, by divine providence (θείᾳ προνοίᾳ), with every kind of prosperity, and to safeguard each one of you with all benevolence, affection, and tranquility."

9 *De ceremoniis* 1.93 (426.1–430.21 Reiske, esp. 426.3–6). See Bury, *History* 2.16–18; A.A. Vasiliev, *Justin the First* (Cambridge, MA, 1950) 68–74; Dagron, *Emperor and Priest*, 68–9.

> All cried: "Worthy of the throne! Worthy of the Trinity! Worthy of the City! Many years for the emperor. [Grant us] honest officials for the world (ἁγνοὺς ἄρχοντας τῇ οἰκουμένῃ)," and other things of that sort.

The affirmation by the assembled people that they are δοῦλοι of the emperor is predicated upon the emperor's acknowledgment that his elevation to the imperial office proceeds from both the divine will and the unanimous choice of the people. This confirms the nature of the imperial office as a public trust exercised on behalf of, and in the interest of, the people; the people in turn confirm that they have vested their sovereignty in the person of the emperor by recognizing his mastery. This affirmation of δουλεία on the part of the masses is therefore understandable only in the context of this reciprocal, and profoundly legitimizing, acknowledgement of mutual dependency and obligation between the emperor and his subjects.

Such moments, at least as they are represented in the *Book of Ceremonies*, represented a crystallization of complete understanding and unmediated accord between the emperor and his subjects. Yet at the same time they evinced a latent awareness of the fact that most interactions between the emperor and his subjects were mediated and indirect, and were therefore subject to the machinations of imperial officials whose interests might not align with those of emperor and subject. This awareness of the crucial mediating role of such officials is discernible in the concluding plea tendered by the assembled masses: "[grant us] honest officials for the world."

We have already seen how, during the interactions that preceded the elevation of Anastasius, the people successfully pressed their demand for the ouster of "the thieving prefect of the city." Harries and others have demonstrated how adroitly imperial subjects in Late Antiquity participated in a "culture of complaint" that expected emperors to be responsive to the protestations of their subjects, particularly where official wrongdoing was concerned. Harries characterizes the central paradox of later Roman government as a tension between autocracy and populism: "Imperial rule ... was both autocratic and populist. As imperial rule became more overtly autocratic, so, increasingly, the emperor became the avowed champion of the *populus*, who had once vested authority in him,—*against his own servants*."[10]

This formula captures admirably two of the dynamics that are operative in the accession narratives just examined. Of particular interest then is the manner in which emperors deployed the power of religion in seeking to legitimate their mastery by demonstrating a positive duty to act in the public interest. In this connection the role played by officials in mediating interactions between the emperor and his subjects presented both a difficulty and an opportunity: on the one hand, the cohesion and collective self-interest of the imperial administration functioned as one of the few effective checks upon an emperor's autonomy short

---

[10] J. Harries, *Law and Empire in Late Antiquity* (Cambridge, 1999) 215 (emphasis added).

of outright rebellion and usurpation;[11] on the other, demonstrating mastery over his officials was one of the most formidable gestures available to an emperor in order to display his ability to govern in the public interest and thus to justify the governmental compact that created him.

Justinian in particular appears to have broken new ground in articulating a strictly instrumental function for imperial officials that stressed their role in perpetuating this characteristically late Roman political and religious synthesis: the emperor was at once the counterpart of the Almighty, inasmuch as his earthly realm was a mimesis of the kingdom of heaven, and yet also accountable, at least in principle, for his use of the powers jointly delegated to him by God and the Roman people. Subjects, in acknowledging themselves to be δοῦλοι of the emperor, demonstrated their confidence that he, both directly and by means of his officials, would govern in their interest. In faithfully serving the mutual interests of the emperor and his subjects, imperial officials advertised not only the unique and providential nature of an emperor's election in conferring authority and legitimacy but also his, as well as their own, investment in the greater public good. The expectation that an official ought to conduct himself as the emperor's δοῦλος merits special consideration because it suggests how such an idiom of official identity in the sixth century might have evolved out of the long-established Christian appropriation and transvaluation of the language of servitude and submission to connote delegated authority and power by association.[12]

But in acknowledging themselves to be δοῦλοι of the emperor, officials in the sixth century were capable of eliciting a variety of responses. The novelty of Justinian's approach can be gauged by the intensity of the reaction it provoked. As Kelly has shown, Justinian's attempts to reorder relationships between the imperial center and the administration threatened the entrenched interests of imperial officeholders.[13] Accordingly, those changes were apt to be stigmatized by traditionalists like Procopius of Caesarea and John Lydus as tokens of imperial aggrandizement and unalloyed despotism.[14]

---

[11] C. Kelly, *Ruling the Later Roman Empire* (Cambridge, MA, 2004), esp. 28–31, 190–92.

[12] See, inter alios, D.B. Martin, *Slavery as Salvation: The Metaphor of Slavery in Pauline Christianity* (New Haven, 1990); I.A.H. Combes, *The Metaphor of Slavery in the Writings of the Early Church: From the New Testament to the Beginning of the Fifth Century* (Sheffield, 1998). Detailed examination of these issues is beyond the scope of the present study.

[13] Kelly, *Ruling the Later Roman Empire*, esp. 71–81. See also now P. Sarris, *Economy and Society in the Age of Justinian* (Cambridge, 2006), esp. 200–227: "the explicit targeting of members of the aristocracy as villains in much of [Justinian's reform] legislation is highly significant, as, at a rhetorical level, it served to distance the person of the emperor, in whose voice the legislation spoke, from the power and abuses of the aristocracy" (211).

[14] See in particular Proc. *Anec.* 30.21–30, and Joh. Lyd. *De mag.* 1.6.

The dossier of documents preserved as Justinian's *Novel* 8, promulgated on 17 April 535, illustrates the various ways in which religious capital was deployed in order to augment imperial authority.[15] As in the account of the accession of Anastasius, the ecclesiastical establishment and the gospels themselves are mobilized in order to guarantee the integrity of official conduct. The proceedings that mark the investiture of officials are solemnized and sanctified by elaborate oaths and vivid curses. Most remarkably, there is an elaborate effort to invest the scripted word of the enacting legislation itself with the sacrosanctity of a holy object.

Novel 8 initiated an ambitious program of provincial reorganization that was extended by further legislation in May (*Nov.* 24–7) and July (28–9) of that year, and in March (30–31), May (102), and June (103) of the following year, and that aimed at consolidating provincial administration and enhancing both the authority and the accountability of governors relative to other civil and military officials operating in the provinces and to local centers of power.[16] Its central object was to prohibit so-called *suffragia*, fees payable in consideration for an official appointment, in particular for a provincial governorship.[17] In the fourth century emperors had attempted to stamp out the trafficking of offices *per suffragia*, but eventually extended legal protection to the practice, elements of which were incorporated into Justinian's *Codex*. In *Novel* 8 Justinian repudiated the practice and criticized his predecessors for relying upon *suffragia* as a source of revenue, which in turn provided pretexts for official corruption, including bribery and extortion.

Included in the dossier comprising *Novel* 8 are a constitution addressed to John the Cappadocian as praetorian prefect of the east, the text of an edict addressed to archbishops and patriarchs throughout the world, the text of an edict addressed to the inhabitants of Constantinople, a detailed schedule of fees to be paid by provincial governors upon their appointment to office, a constitution copied to

15 See G. Kolias, *Ämter und Würdenkauf im früh- und mittelbyzantinischen Reich* (Athens, 1939) 43–67; A.H.M. Jones, *The Later Roman Empire 284–602*, vol. 1 (Oxford, 1964) 394–5; D. Liebs, "Ämterkauf und Ämterpatronage in der Spätantike," *ZRG* 95 (1978) 158–86; R. Bonini, "Note sulla legislazione giustinianea dell'anno 535," in G.G. Archi (ed.), *L'imperatore Giustiniano storia e mito* (Milan, 1978) 161–78; Idem, *Ricerche sulla legislazione giustinianea dell'anno 535: Nov. Iustiniani 8. Venalità delle cariche e riforme dell'amministrazione periferica*, 3rd ed. (Bologna, 1989), esp. 22–34; R. Haase, *Untersuchungen zur Verwaltung des spätrömischen Reiches unter Kaiser Justinian I* (Wiesbaden, 1994), esp. 15–74.

16 See M. Maas, "Roman History and Christian Ideology in Justinianic Reform Legislation," *DOP* 40 (1986) 17–31; C. Roueché, "Provincial Governors and Their Titulature in the Sixth Century," *AnTard* 6 (1998) 83–9.

17 On the origin of the expression, see Kelly, *Ruling the Later Roman Empire*, 158–65, 211–12, and 293–4 n. 79; C. Collot, "La pratique et l'institution du *suffragium* au Bas-Empire," *RD* 43 (1965) 185–221; G.E.M. de Ste. Croix, "*Suffragium*: From Vote to Patronage," *BJS* 5 (1954) 33–48.

Dominic as praetorian prefect of Illyricum, and the formula of an oath to be sworn by provincial governors at the time of their appointment.

In the constitution addressed to John the Cappadocian, Justinian expatiated upon his unstinting efforts to relieve his subjects of undue care and anxiety, something that became for him a recurring theme. Nor did he mince words about the cause of this solicitude: thanks to the depredations of provincial governors determined to realize a profit on the *suffragia* they paid in consideration for their offices, public revenues could not be extracted without resorting to an inexpedient level of compulsion. Reform was intended to realize a realm filled with docile taxpayers, whose remittances were being put to good use in the recovery of the West (*Nov. Just.* 8.10.2 [74.27–34 Schöll-Kroll]):[18]

> nor have we been content to overlook the diminution of Roman territory, but have recovered the whole of Libya and reduced the Vandals to servitude (καταδουλωσάντων), and hope to acquire and accomplish, with God's help, many more things still and even greater than this—for which it is fitting that public taxes be paid unfailingly, ungrudgingly, and at the prescribed times.

To this end, provincial governors were required to swear an oath to the effect that, just as they had received their positions *sine suffragio*, they would claim no perquisites apart from those allowed by law, administer their offices with clean hands, and make themselves accountable *deo et nobis* (7, 8.1). When appointments were made outside of the capital, oaths were to be sworn in public assemblies in the presence of the bishop and other local grandees (14, *iusiur.*). Officials were carefully instructed to deal with taxpayers in a paternal spirit (8.pr., *iusiur.*), while an ex-governor who abandoned his province prior to the expiration of the 50-day period during which he had to make himself available for prosecution was to be hunted down "just as if he were the vilest of slaves (ἀνδράποδα)" (8.1). Significantly, the legislation provided that a corrupt governor was to be held accountable to three distinct constituencies: to the inhabitants of his province in a local proceeding presided over by the bishop for the recovery of what he had extorted; to the emperor himself for additional punitive action; and to heaven itself on account of violating his oath (9).

Through such measures Justinian manifested his solicitude for the afflicted, whom God had entrusted to his care, emulating divine benevolence in showing them mercy: "Therefore, as far as we are concerned, let this law be consecrated to God, since we are omitting nothing beneficial which occurs to us for the well-being of our subjects" (*Nov. Just.* 8.11 [75.10–13 Schöll-Kroll]).

Notice of the new measures was to be forwarded to the bishops, who like the praetorian prefects were instructed to publish them (10.1, edict), ideally by having them engraved upon tablets and set up at the entrances of their churches, and to report any acts of official malfeasance lest the bishops make themselves liable for

---

[18] On taxation, see Sarris, *Economy and Society*, passim.

punishment from on high for injustices committed within their dioceses. Rapp points to these provisions as evidence of Justinian's increasing reliance upon the episcopate: "by requiring the bishops to keep an eye on the civil administration, Justinian treated them, in effect, as his personal agents with direct and immediate access to his court."[19]

Yet even as Justinian was intent upon co-opting ecclesiastical authority for the sake of accountability in the civil administration, he was keen as well to enhance the sacrosanctity he claimed for his own legislation. Such a motivation seems to lie behind the following provision in Justinian's edict to the bishops (*Nov. Just.* 8 edict [79.9–13 Schöll-Kroll]):

> ἐπειδὰν δὲ ὁ νόμος δημοσίᾳ προτεθείη καὶ ἅπασι γένοιτο φανερός, τηνικαῦτα ληφθεὶς ἔνδον ἀποκείσθω ἐν τῇ ἁγιωτάτῃ ἐκκλησίᾳ μετὰ τῶν ἱερῶν σκευῶν, οἷα καὶ αὐτὸς ἀνατεθειμένος θεῷ καὶ πρὸς σωτηρίαν τῶν ὑπ' αὐτοῦ γενομένων ἀνθρώπων γεγραμμένος.

> Once this law shall have been displayed in public and become manifest to all, then let it be taken within and deposited in the most holy [part of the?] church together with the sacred utensils, since it too has been dedicated to God and written for the salvation of the human beings created by him.

Something more than the preservation of an official copy for archival purposes[20] seems to be operative here. There is no suggestion in any of the enacting constitutions for the preceding portions of the *Corpus iuris civilis* that such measures should observed in the case of the *Codex* or the *Digest*. Instead, the analogy with the sacred utensils in the cathedral treasury implies that the written text of the constitution itself is to be approached as a sacred object and as the locus of a holiness that is distinct from, although scarcely incompatible with, the sacredness that inheres in any imperial utterance or enactment.

The emperors Theodosius II and Valentinian III had already imposed an oath upon provincial governors in 439, and their constitution was incorporated into Justinian's *Codex* (9.27.6). As preserved there, that oath contained (1) a statement that the nominee had not given anything, and had not agreed that he or anyone on his behalf would give anything in the future, in exchange for his appointment to office, and (2) a promise that he would accept nothing other than his statutory emoluments either during or after his term of office. A fourfold penalty bolstered the impending threat of divine retribution should anyone, by violating his oath, prove unmindful of the fear of God (*divini timoris contemnendo iureiurando ... immemorem*, 9.27.6.1).

---

19 C. Rapp, *Holy Bishops in Late Antiquity: The Nature of Christian Leadership in an Age of Transition* (Berkeley, 2005) 277; E. Stein, *L'histoire du Bas-Empire* (Paris, 1949) 2.399–400.

20 As Rapp, *Holy Bishops*, 262, suggests.

The Justinianic oath contained these elements, but required in addition (3) an affirmation that the nominee was of the orthodox faith, (4) a promise that he would be most assiduous and equitable in the performance of his duties and in the supervision of his subordinates, particularly with respect to the collection of taxes, as well as (5) an imprecation that if he should violate his oath he would experience the fate of Judas and the leprosy of Gehazi and the trembling of Cain (τὴν μερίδα τοῦ Ἰούδα καὶ τὴν λέπραν τοῦ Γιεζὶ καὶ τὸν τρόμον τοῦ Καΐν, *Nov. Just.* 8 *iusiur.* [91.10–12 Schöll-Kroll]).[21]

Justinian's *Novel* 8 appears to be the earliest attested instance in which the so-called "Judas curse," that would go on to exercise a considerable influence over the imagination of both the Byzantine east and the medieval west, appears in an official document.[22] Its general effect was to abjure greed and treachery, and it is especially apt in this context that the curse invoked the figure of Gehazi, the treacherous servant of Elisha in 2 Kings (5:1–27) who illicitly elicited from Naaman the Aramean gifts in exchange for a service that Elisha had performed gratuitously.

When Procopius, in the *Secret History*, takes Justinian to task for first trafficking in offices, then forbidding the practice, and then trafficking once again, he repeatedly stresses not only the Justinianic oath, but also the curses it contained and the written character of the enactment (21.16–19):

> But afterward he wrote (ἔγραψε) a law that all those seeking offices should swear that they would themselves be innocent of all theft, and that they would neither give nor receive anything for the sake of the office. And he laid upon them all of the curses which have been invoked by men of the most ancient times, lest anyone should depart from what had been written (ἥν τις τῶν γεγραμμένων ἐκβαίη). But when the law had been in force not yet a year, he himself, ignoring what had been written and what had been accursed (αὐτὸς μὲν τῶν γεγραμμένων καὶ κατηραμένων ὀλιγωρήσας) and the disgrace concerning these things, proceeded all the more fearlessly to negotiate the prices of offices, not in secret, but in the public space of the market-place. And those who purchased the offices proceeded, in spite of their oath, to plunder everything even more than before.

Here Procopius is zeroing in with characteristic precision upon the regime's attempts to redeploy religious capital in order to augment imperial authority. His indictment of Justinian's impiety and hypocrisy in disregarding the scripted letter (τὰ γεγραμμένα) of his law as well as the oaths and the curses it contained is all the more pointed when one takes into account Justinian's own insistence in

---

[21] Compare *CJ* 1.27.1.17, 1.27.2.12, 17 (a. 534); *Nov. Just.* 17.3 (a. 535), 80.6, 82.7 (a. 539), 124.1 (a. 545), 161.1 (a. 574).

[22] H. Martin, "The Judas Iscariot Curse" *AJPh* 37 (1916) 434–51; A. Taylor, "The Judas Curse" *AJPh* 42 (1921) 234–52.

Novel 8 upon the sacrosanct character of the written text of his constitution and its assimilation with the sacred objects in a cathedral treasury. Perhaps Procopius is therefore acknowledging, and reacting against, the apparent novelty of Justinian's elaborate attempt to compel reverence for this showpiece legislation.

The preamble of the Justinianic oath invoked heavenly witnesses who complement the ecclesiastical, official, and civic figures who were expected to attend an investiture ceremony. It also stated in the starkest terms the ethic of selflessness and diligence that Justinian proposed to inculcate in the administration (*Nov. Just.* 8 *iusiur*. [89.45–90.8 Schöll-Kroll]):

> I swear, on the occasion of [my entry into the] office bestowed upon me by their piety, by almighty God, his only-begotten son our lord Jesus Christ, and the Holy Spirit, by the holy and glorified mother of God, Mary ever-virgin, by the four gospels which I hold in my hands, and by the holy archangels Michael and Gabriel, that I shall preserve a pure conscience and genuine servitude (γνησία δουλεία) toward our most consecrated and august masters (δεσπόται) Justinian and his consort Theodora; and that I will undertake every burden and labor with sincere goodwill and without any guile in the office entrusted to me by them on behalf of their empire and government (ὑπὲρ τῆς αὐτῶν βασιλείας καὶ πολιτείας).

The δουλεία Justinian demanded from his loyal officials is therefore qualitatively different from the δουλεία offered up by the assembled people at imperial accessions and other moments of unmediated contact between rulers and subjects. To the extent that the latter represents the conferral and the acknowledgment by subjects of the mastery of the emperor whom they have created, the former demonstrates an emperor's determination to exercise that mastery over functionaries whom he has created in order to serve the mutual interests of himself and his subjects. It is understandable how the one proceeds from, and is entailed by, the other, if one understands the imperial office to have been conferred upon its recipient with the expectation that good government in the public interest would result.

Roueché suggests that *Novel* 8 and Justinian's provincial reorganization more generally is a reflection of real anxiety about the effectiveness of central government and the extent of its control.[23] The need to forge a new consensus about the nature and purposes of government was correspondingly acute. The scale of Justinian's ambitions, moreover, demanded administrative efficiencies which encroached upon the cherished prerogatives of imperial officials and challenged their sense of continuity and exceptionalism.

The evident concern to advertise these convictions not only in the capital but also in the provinces also accords well with the message that *Novel* 8 is at such pains to communicate: that just as Justinian has assumed all of the cares

23 Roueché, "Provincial Governors," 89.

and burdens of his subjects, for whose welfare God and the constitution of the Roman state had made him uniquely responsible, so too has the emperor allotted those burdens to his faithful servants, his γνήσιοι δοῦλοι,[24] who embody the same public-spiritedness.

24 The expression is post-classical, in fact patristic—though not biblical—in origin, and is well glossed by John Chrysostom, with reference to the apostolate and ministry of Paul, in his homilies on the Pauline letter to the Philippians (*Ep. ad Phil.* 1.1 [*PG* 62.181–2]). Examples of such expressions within the patristic corpus may be multiplied.

Chapter 11

Power from Humility: Justinian and the Religious Authority of Monks

Hartmut Leppin
Goethe Universität, Frankfurt am Main

In recent years, Justinian has attracted a great deal of scholarly attention, and an important focus has been his religious policy. Theologians have drawn a much more nuanced picture of the dogmatic conflicts in his reign, and historians have underlined how important religious issues were for his perception of reality and, thus, for his politics.[1] It has also become clear that even what modern people would call "personal piety" was central to Justinian's imperial self-presentation. In many respects, he styled himself a holy man.[2] His religious politics give the impression of being the work of a tyrant: it is well known that he oppressed and offended various priests and bishops, most notoriously Pope Vigilius, in the course of the Constantinopolitan synod of 553. Additionally, he disciplined monks by means of far-reaching legislation that aimed at controlling their monasteries and removing ascetics from the public sphere. In Justinian's eyes, their main task was to pray for the government and to obtain God's mercy for the empire and its pious emperor.[3]

Observations of this kind potentially obscure another element of the emperor's habitus: his reverential attitude toward individual monks and other people who could be deemed holy men. There can be no doubt that Justinian was persuaded by monks when he adopted the Theopaschite formula and that monks exerted a heavy influence on the Constantinopolitan synod of 536. Less acknowledged, however, is his extremely respectful treatment of monastics. A closer look at the sources reveals that this is well attested in the hagiographic lives of contemporary saints (for example in *Lives of the Eastern Saints* of John of Ephesus or the *Life of Sabas* by Cyril of Scythopolis), but also in less obvious sources such as Procopius' *Anecdota*. Passages from these texts, which tell about the dealings between Justinian and certain monks, provide significant details about the interaction between the

1 H. Leppin, "(K)ein Zeitalter Justinians—Bemerkungen aus althistorischer Sicht zu Justinian in der jüngeren Forschung," *HZ* 284 (2007) 659–86.

2 M. Meier, *Das andere Zeitalter Justinians: Kontingenzerfahrung und Kontingenzbewältigung im 6. Jahrhundert n. Chr.*, 2nd ed. (Göttingen, 2004) 101–82.

3 Cf. C. Rapp, *Holy Bishops in Late Antiquity: The Nature of Christian Leadership in an Age of Transition* (Berkeley, 2005) 279. This aspect is discussed in detail by A. Hasse-Ungeheuer, *Das Mönchtum in der Religionspolitik Kaiser Justinians I.* (forthcoming).

emperor and ascetics. Although the character of the encounters differs widely—the attitudes of the monks towards the Neo-Chalcedonian emperor range from benevolence to hostility—they share a common pattern which is revealing. The following will offer an examination of four such passages in order to demonstrate how they offer a deeper understanding of Justinian's self-presentation.

The first scene is perhaps the most famous one: the encounter between Sabas and Justinian in 530, as narrated by Cyril of Scythopolis.[4] Cyril (ca. 524–568/9) was a Neo-Chalcedonian author living as a monk in Sabas' Great Laura near Jerusalem. He wrote several *Vitae* of Palestinian monks which colorfully depict their way of life.[5] The most important one is that of the founder of his monastery, Sabas, who on two occasions travelled to the court in Constantinople acting as the emissary of the Church of Jerusalem.[6]

He visited Justinian in the year 531.[7] Their first encounter is described by Cyril at length. When the emperor learns about the saint's plan to present him with a petition from the patriarch, he sends imperial galleys to transport him and distinguished clerics to the court. The monk is treated like an official guest of high rank, with the exception that he is escorted by clerics instead of magistrates. When Sabas is ushered into the palace, the emperor—and only the emperor—sees the grace of God in him immediately:

> As he (Sabas) entered the palace with the said bishops and came within the curtain, God opened the emperor's eyes: he saw the radiance of divine favour in the shape of a crown blazing forth and emitting sunlike beams from the head of the old man. Running up, he greeted him with reverence (προσεκύνησεν), kissing his Godly head with tears of joy; on obtaining his blessing, he took from his hand the petition from Palestine and pressed him to go in and to bless the Augusta Theodora.[8]

---

4 For this episode see C.J. Stallman-Pacitti, *Cyril of Scythopolis: A Study in Hagiography as Apology* (Brookline, MA, 1991) 32–4; J. Patrich, *Sabas, Leader of Palestinian Monasticism: A Comparative Study in Eastern Monasticism, Fourth to Seventh Centuries* (Washington, 1995) 313–19; Rapp, *Bishops*, 270–72; K. Trampedach, "Reichsmönchtum? Das politische Selbstverständnis der Mönche Palästinas im 6. Jahrhundert und die historische Methode des Kyrill von Skythopolis," *Millennium* 2 (2005) 271–96 at 279–84.

5 D. Krueger, "Writing as Devotion: Hagiographical Composition and the Cult of Saints in Theodoret of Cyrrhus and Cyril of Scythopolis," *ChHist* 66 (1997) 707–19.

6 J. Binns, *Ascetics and Ambassadors of Christ: The Monasteries of Palestine 314–631* (New York, 1994) 174.

7 For the date (April–September 531), see D. Hombergen, *The Second Origenist Controversy: A New Perspective on Cyril of Scythopolis' Monastic Biographies as Historical Sources for Sixth-Century Origenism* (Rome, 2001) 75 n.92.

8 Cyr.Scyth. *VSabae* 71, trans. R.M. Price, *Lives of the Monks of Palestine by Cyril of Scythopolis* (Kalamazoo, MI, 1991) 183.

The meeting between these two men is characterized as a kind of role reversal. While the Roman subjects were expected to do *proskynesis* before the emperor, Justinian himself performs this gesture before the monk, although he does not kiss the hem of the monk's garment. It is little wonder that Justinian demonstrates his willingness to grant the petition carried by Sabas.

So far, this text may be regarded as having little worth as a source for the behaviour shown by the historical Justinian. It could just as easily represent the imagination of a monk who wanted to illustrate the charisma of a revered saint. Interestingly, however, Cyril's description portrays Sabas' dealings with Theodora evolving in a less satisfactory way:

> The elder went in and was received with joy by the Augusta, who greeted him respectfully and made this request: "Pray for me, father, that God grant me fruit of the womb." The elder answered: "God the Master of all will guard your empire." The Augusta said again, "Pray, father, that God give me a child." The elder said in reply: "The God of glory will maintain your empire with piety and victory." The Augusta was grieved at his not granting her request.[9]

Although the empress does not fail to show respect, Sabas' encounter with her differs significantly from his meeting with Justinian. There is no mention of tears and no sign that the empress recognizes "the radiance of divine favour" in the monk. Justinian shows his readiness to fulfil the monk's wishes, while Sabas declines to pray that the empress will give birth to a child.

Although this parley cannot have been heartening in the eyes of the imperial couple, nothing more happens. Sabas is neither pestered by the courtiers to give in to Theodora's requests, nor is he disciplined. He is merely asked by his companions why he has acted in such a way and justifies his response with Theodora's heretical convictions.

Cyril assigns all the blame for her infertility to Theodora herself, but the orthodox emperor also suffers from childlessness and must be disappointed by Cyril's denial to grant his blessing. Nevertheless, the monk continues to enjoy the emperor's utmost reverence: Sabas is allowed to lodge in the palace; all his desires are fulfilled splendidly; Justinian even accepts his rejection of financial support for his monasteries, but agrees to grant his plea to construct or restore churches, a hospital, and even a fortress against the Saracens.[10] The emperor for his part is promised that his empire will regain the west,[11] but the monk does not make any mention of a child being born. As Cyril's narration is nuanced and does not ignore

---

[9] Ibid.

[10] For one project, which is also known from Procopius and from archeological remains, see Y. Tsafrir, "Procopius and the 'Nea' Church in Jerusalem," *AntTard* 8 (2000) 149–64.

[11] For the prophecy, see G. Filoramo, "Profezia e politica nelle 'Storie monastiche' di Cirillo di Scitopoli," *CrSt* 20 (1999) 521–44, 533–4; Hombergen, *Cyril*, 75–6.

the discord between the monk and the emperor, it is highly probable that the text is more than a pious fiction. It must reflect a certain aspect of Justinian's conduct, albeit in stylized form.

This suspicion can be corroborated by an episode handed down by Procopius of Caesarea in his notorious *Anecdota*, which adopts, as is well known, an extremely critical stance toward Justinian. Whatever Procopius' religious affiliation, one thing is clear: he writes in the classical historiographical tradition and thus in a manner completely different from hagiography. In his *Anecdota* he sets out to depict Justinian as a demon eager to destroy mankind. This is made explicit in the central chapter containing the following paragraph:[12]

> They also say that a certain monk, very dear to God, at the instance of those who dwelt with him in the desert, went to Constantinople to beg for mercy to his neighbours who had been outraged beyond endurance. And when he arrived there, he forthwith secured an audience with the Emperor; but just as he was about to enter his apartment, he stopped short as his feet were on the threshold, and suddenly stepped backward. Whereupon the eunuch escorting him, and others who were present, importuned him to go ahead. But he answered not a word; and, like a man who has had a stroke, staggered back to his lodging. And when some followed to ask why he acted thus, they say he distinctly declared he saw the King of the Devils sitting on the throne in the palace, and he did not care to meet or ask any favour of him.[13]

The reader, be he pagan or Christian, learns that not only people from Procopius' world of court politics (and intrigue) but also a monk loved by God abhorred this emperor. There are several parallels with the anecdotes narrated by Cyril. Procopius remarks that the anonymous monk is ushered to the emperor without delay, not by bishops, however, as in Sabas's case, but by a eunuch, as was customary. His subsequent behaviour is then extremely offensive, for he retreats when he is already on the threshold of the throne room. Yet nobody attacks him physically, nobody forces him to return, nobody punishes him; he is only asked to state his reasons.

Procopius obviously did not consider it necessary to explain the situation. Although his broader narrative depicts Justinian as being generally brutal and reckless, there is no sign here of any violent action by the emperor or his entourage, of the sort that a reader of the *Anecdota* might expect. Obviously such mild comportment should in no way be regarded as surprising. The emperor's

---

[12] For the general interpretation of this chapter, see A. Kaldellis, *Procopius of Caesarea: Tyranny, History, and Philosophy at the End of Antiquity* (Philadelphia, 2004) 154–7.

[13] Proc. *Anecd.* 12.24–6, translation from R. Atwater (trans.), *Procopius, Secret History* (Ann Arbor, 1961); cf. http://www.isidore-of-seville.com/library-procopius/secrethistory-2.htm.

restrained behaviour is neither criticized nor praised by Procopius but is simply taken for granted.

John of Ephesus is the third author to be discussed here. Although a leading Miaphysite in the age of Justinian, he maintained close contacts with the court. His *Lives of the Eastern Saints*, which he wrote in Syriac, contains several encounters between Justinian and holy monks. Two examples will be under investigation here, starting with Z'ura.[14] When the stylite is forced to climb down from his pillar, he decides—on his own initiative—to go to Constantinople to address the emperor in person, with ten of his disciples in tow. In Constantinople, the monk is expected nervously. Justinian gives ܐܣܦܠܝܐ (ἀσφάλεια) to the senators;[15] the chief men, literally the "heads," and the bishops are assembled. When Z'ura arrives, the Chalcedonian dogmas are expounded to him coaxingly (ܡܦܝܣܐܝܬ: *PO* 17.23),[16] but Z'ura reacts aggressively and attacks the emperor in an extremely harsh address, with παρρησία – the Greek word written in Syriac letters (ܦܪܗܣܝܐ) is often used as a loan word. The emperor's reaction is illuminating:

> When the emperor by reason of the fear of him feared to lay a hand on the blessed man on account of the divine *parrhesia* which he possessed, he was excited by his rage, and clenched his fist as tightly as he could in violent rage and struck himself upon the breast and said: "You are apostates and corrupters, and the synod is true, and I will not consent to hear these things against it from you any more, and, if you were true men, God would show me a sign by your hands. And he who anathematizes the synod contends with his life." (*PO* 17.24)

Two things in this passage are noteworthy. First, the emperor, who had kept quiet up to this point, utters a threat, but does not act violently. One even gets the impression that John wants to depict the emperor as a harsh ruler but is not able to ascribe any brutal deed to him. Secondly, the emperor indicates how in his view a monk can prove his holiness by working a miracle. According to John, Z'ura is not impressed by the emperor's rebuke:

---

14 Joh.Eph. *VSS.Or.* 2 (PO 17.21–6). The edition and translation used here are E.W. Brooks (ed. and trans.), *John of Ephesus Lives of the Eastern Saints*, 3 vols. PO 17–19 (Turnhout, 1923–25). See S. Ashbrook Harvey, *Asceticism and Society in Crisis: John of Ephesus and Lives of the Eastern Saints* (Berkeley and Los Angeles, 1990) 84–5.

15 It is unclear what is meant by this. Brooks, *John of Ephesus*, 22, translates "precaution," but perhaps ἀσφάλεια is to be understood here in the sense of "safe-conduct"; cf. H.G. Liddell and R. Scott, *A Greek-English Lexicon*, 8th ed. (Oxford, 1985) s.v. 2.

16 Brooks characteristically casts doubt on the text here, but this word is perfectly understandable against the background of Justinian's general behaviour on such occasions, see H. Leppin, "Zu den Anfängen der Kirchenpolitik Justinians," in H.U. Wiemer (ed.), *Staatlichkeit und politisches Handeln in der römischen Kaiserzeit* (Berlin, 2006) 187–208 at 188–9. In this article I argued that the emperor spoke himself; this, however, is improbable, see p. 23, v. 5ss. I am grateful to A. Hasse-Ungeheuer for this hint.

> On all this commotion taking place great terror overwhelmed all the magnates; but the blessed man, when he saw that he (the emperor) had decreed death against anyone who anathematized the synod, was kindled with zeal and his heart became hot within him as it is written and fire seized his body, and immediately he went straight against him and said: "The synod which divided Christ our Lord is anathematized not only by us, but also by the angels of heaven. And, since you seek a sign, by believers signs are not required; but the Lord will not show you a sign outside you, but in your own self." And so [Justinian] went on with violent rage, while threats were also being forged against the blessed man.

Justinian's threats are not put into effect. The monk is harried, yet there is no retribution. A reader who was versed in the Old Testament might have expected harsh measures, because in this tradition (bad) kings—most notoriously Ahab—often reacted brutally to the provocations of prophets. Although John makes evident how enraged Justinian is, not even he affirms that the emperor misuses his power against the monk. In the end, however, a terrible miracle is worked as if to fulfill Justinian's own provocation:

> But after a day the sign for which he (Justinian) asked appeared in him according to the blessed man's saying, in that he was smitten upon his head and his understanding was taken away; and a fearful swelling covered him, until human shape was not recognised.

Regardless of what happens to Justinian, he takes no reprisal against Z'ura, who, thanks to Theodora's intercession, later heals Justinian and spends several years in Constantinople enjoying considerable respect among the inhabitants. To summarize, there is a fierce argument between emperor and monk, yet, although the emperor is surrounded by dignitaries and surely also guards, Z'ura is never attacked violently. He can voice his reprimands but remains unharmed. John attributes this to the respect a person like Z'ura engendered in his opponents through his frankness und fearlessness, yet the incident and John's retelling of it reveals again a pattern of behaviour in Justinian seen elsewhere: he avoids any harassment of holy men.

An even more extreme case in John's *Vitae* is offered in the second example treated here: Mare the Solitary,[17] who dwells in Egypt, is expelled from his cell by Chalcedonians. As a result, he decides to go up to Constantinople in order to reprimand the imperial couple. He attacks both of them with such an unbelievable rudeness that John does not dare to write down his words. He does, however, depict the reaction of the emperor and the empress:

> But, when he sternly rebuked the royal pair, as we had said with such *parrhesia* and sternness … they as by the grace of God accepted it from him humbly

[17] Joh.Eph. *VSS.Or.* 37 (PO 18.630–34). See Ashbrook Harvey, *Asceticism*, 85–6.

> (ܡܟܝܟܐܝܬ) and with fear without violent action, as from a great man and a perfect solitary, especially because they saw the *parrhesia* of his speech, that he spoke and rebuked and reproved courageously and without fear not being frightened by the crown or alarmed by the purple, and they said: "This man is in truth a spiritual philosopher." (*PO* 18.631)

The frankness itself attests to Mare's holiness in John's interpretation. The monk's dishevelled appearance, as described admiringly by John, has the same function. Thereupon John returns to the emperor's reaction:

> When the victorious king observed these things, he greatly wondered at him and gave him a promise that he would do for him whatever he commanded; and yet more the believing queen held him as a great and righteous man, and continued entreating him to remain with her in the palace that he might speak to her words of profit. (*PO* 18.632)

Nevertheless, the holy man remains true to himself, merely repeating his rebukes. Not even the fact that the empress adheres to the same dogmatic faction as he calms him down. When the deeply impressed empress offers him a centenarian of gold (about 32kg), he throws it away, demonstrating his indifference to material goods as well as his strength. Consequently, the encounter seems to end in a parting of the ways:

> And after answering her with many stern words which we refrain from recording he (Mare) left her and went out; and she remained in distress and fear, and she and all her chamberlains as well were wondering at the man's bodily strength … insomuch that the story was heard over the whole palace and over the whole of this city, and was spoken of with astonishment by many persons. (*PO* 18.633)

Mare retreats to a mountain near Constantinople while the empress continues to seek contact with him. Again, a belligerent monk can leave the palace without hindrance and without any harassment.

As with the other episodes discussed in this paper, so also with both of the stories told by John of Ephesus: one cannot be sure about the historicity of the events, but this is not especially important for the argument advanced here. What becomes clear once more is that an author who on the whole depicts Justinian in a very negative way—and who admires monks—still concedes implicitly that Justinian did not apply physical violence toward hostile monks, even if their behaviour was outrageous. This is not ascribed to the empress's influence, but deemed a result of Justinian's personal attitude.

The main interest of the four scenes lies in the fact that they represent descriptions given by authors whose attitudes to politics and religion diverge widely: Cyril of Scythopolis was a Neo-Chalcedonian, John of Ephesus a Miaphysite, and Procopius a historian who probably was a Christian but wrote a traditional, non-Christian discourse. All of them agreed that Justinian behaved in a reverential, humble way, even if this characterization was not in keeping with the general tendency of their narratives. Given this intersection, it seems acceptable to assume that Justinian as a historical person in principle behaved as they described.

The common pattern in the emperor's behaviour can be described as follows. Holy monks were always greeted with reverence. Their comportment might be provocative to varying degrees, but even Justinian's worst enemies portrayed him not as a cruel tyrant intent on taking revenge but rather as tolerant of rebukes and even slander while expressing threats only occasionally and without putting them into practice. It is well known that Justinian did not spare monks completely from the harsh reprisals to which he often resorted; Z'ura, who was causing unrest in Constantinople, suffered exile in the end. Nevertheless, this was legitimized by a synodical decision, which, significantly, was promoted by other monks and did not result from offences against the emperor.[18] In personal encounters with holy men, Justinian adopted the habitus of reverence and even humility.

Yet was this attitude really something new? Obviously, emperors typically acted with reverence toward monks; in the Christianized empire it was to be expected that high-born persons behaved in this manner. The difference in Justinian's instance becomes clear by comparing these episodes with yet another from Cyril's work. About twenty years before his voyage to Justinian, under the reign of Anastasius (491–517), Sabas had already paid a visit to an emperor's court.[19] Although Anastasius was a Miaphysite, and thus a theological opponent of Sabas, there are several parallels between the encounters, as described by Cyril, which the hagiographer obviously intended his readers to detect. In both cases, the emperor is respectful toward the monk; he is eager to see him and recognizes his spiritual qualities immediately; Sabas even meets Anastasius' wife (53), who in this case shares his same dogmatic convictions (53); and Jerusalem is a main theme in both discussions between emperor and monk. Yet there are significant differences, as well: not every request by Sabas meets with success. More importantly, Anastasius greets Sabas with apposite honours, but completely within the traditional forms. Not the emperor, but the monk performs the *proskynesis* (51). It is obvious that this was the usual pattern and that even a renowned monk did not decline to accept the rules of the court, which were reversed by Justinian himself when he recognized the spiritual authority of Sabas.

Why did this emperor decide to show himself as a humble person in front of the ascetics? Why did he ignore the insults of these monks? Why was he willing to suffer such treatment even in a confrontation with monks who were heretics in his eyes? Justinian's behaviour is perhaps unique in its consistency, but it must be interpreted against the background of his era and the constraints this imposed even

[18] Just. *Nov*. 42.3. John of Ephesus has him retreat because he is begged to do so by the imperial couple.

[19] Cyr.Scyth. *VSabae* 51. For this episode see Stallmann-Pacitti, *Cyril*, 28–31; Patrich, *Sabas*, 311–13.

upon rulers. Late antique Christian emperors were confronted with expectations that were ultimately contradictory. On the one hand, they were under the traditional obligation to defend the unity of the empire, and on the other hand, they had to do what they could to maintain Christianity in their empire. Otherwise they risked losing God's favour. Obviously, emperors strove to unite the empire politically as well as religiously. This proved to be impossible, however, because in the eyes of contemporary Christian authorities only one among the many dogmas could be true and merited support, and this necessarily endangered the unity of the empire where several confessions competed.[20]

Holy persons, who were typically monks,[21] could help to diminish the impact of these fissures because their demeanour and power confirmed their saintliness independently of their dogmatic orientation; no sincere Christian could avoid showing reverence for them. Yet it was difficult to integrate them in the power structure of the empire. Due to their ascetic authority,[22] they were allowed—and even expected—to provoke others through their behaviour. *Parrhesia* was accepted, and practically appreciated in their case, particularly frankness shown against the powerful; in the Syriac tradition rudeness counted almost as a virtue. Since this was well established, any resistance on the part of the emperor could only make things worse, for he would have shown that he was not disposed to suffer the legitimatized behaviour of holy men. For the emperor to use physical violence in order to assert his position did not make any sense here. On the contrary, martyrdom would only have enhanced the authority of the monks and shown the emperor to be a persecutor. This would be dangerous for him, because a late antique emperor, although he had considerable resources at his disposal, needed to gain acceptance[23] among the population, particularly in the capital, among the soldiers, and among the elite. All of those groups were overwhelmingly

[20] For the concept of the so-called Mosaic distinction in monotheistic religions—which engenders the assumption that there is only one true religion—and its consequences, see J. Assmann, *Die Mosaische Unterscheidung oder der Preis des Monotheismus*, 3rd ed. (Munich, 2004).

[21] Humility was not restricted to his contacts with monks. The *VAgap.* (59) in the *Liber pontificalis* even affirms that Justinian prostrated himself in front of the pope (L. Duchesne [ed.], *Le Liber pontificalis: texte, introduction et commentaire*, 2 vols. [Rome, 1886–92] 287–8). See for this passage Leppin, "Kirchenpolitik," 202.

[22] For monastic authority and its diverse aspects, cf. Rapp, *Bishops*, passim.

[23] For the concept of acceptance, which seems to be chiefly discussed in German research, see e.g. S. Diefenbach, "Frömmigkeit und Kaiserakzeptanz im frühen Byzanz," *Saeculum* 47 (1996) 35–66; Idem, "Zwischen Liturgie und *civilitas*: Konstantinopel im 5. Jahrhundert und die Etablierung eines städtischen Kaisertums," in R. Warland (ed.), *Bildlichkeit und Bildort von Liturgie* (Wiesbaden, 2002) 21–47; M. Meier, "Die Demut des Kaisers: Aspekte der religiösen Selbstinszenierung bei Theodosius II. (408–450 n. Chr.)," in A. Pečar and K. Trampedach (eds.), *Die Bibel als politisches Argument: Voraussetzungen und Folgen biblizistischer Herrschaftslegitimation in der Vormoderne* (Munich, 2007) 135–58.

Christian during the age of Justinian and would have disapproved of any limitation on the monks' right to use their *parrhesia*.[24]

The emperor, though, could not concede much ground to defiant monks; he had to maintain his imperial authority which also extended to religious issues. Given that Justinian saw himself as having been enthroned by God and felt increasingly competent to pronounce on dogmatic issues—going so far as to write dogmatic treatises himself—he clearly felt that he enjoyed a degree of spiritual and dogmatic authority. Although he had no ascetic authority, in some ways he yearned for it. As a result, Justinian was forced to find a strategy by which to compete with monks in their own sphere of pious behaviour without being at a disadvantage from the outset. It was clear that he was not able to work miracles and that he was not supposed to appear in public wearing the bedraggled garments of an ascetic, with the exception of certain days on which he might lead penitential processions.[25] Here, self-humiliation came into play, because in a Christian context humble behaviour could always lend authority and could lend even more authority to high-ranking Christians who were not normally expected to humble themselves in this way.

When humility was shown by the emperor, this was the only way to defuse the attacks of the monks, for a humble emperor was a most impressive figure precisely because the whole notion seemed so paradoxical. In a certain sense Justinian turned the tables on the monks. Interestingly, his humbleness never went so far as to make the emperor accept the theological position of heretical monks. Justinian may have been influenced in theological conflicts by monks whom he used as councillors, but as far as we can see the reasons for following them lay in convincing dogmatic arguments, not in personal authority based on asceticism.

Justinian thus had a clear concept of how to navigate his confrontations with even the rudest of monks without losing face and without creating the impression of being a persecutor. He reacted to the humiliations inflicted on him by monks not with violence, but by humbling himself all the more. Precisely the fact that he endured humiliation patiently enabled Justinian to compete with the monks' authority in their own field and, as a result, he did not feel obliged to give in to the monks in every regard. Humility was an element Justinian added to the emperor's arsenal of power and, in the end, this strengthened his position toward holy men.

---

24 See e.g. D. Krueger, "Christian Piety and Practice in the Sixth Century," in M. Maas (ed.), *The Cambridge Companion to the Age of Justinian* (Cambridge, 2005) 291–315.

25 M. Meier, "Kaiserherrschaft und 'Volksfrömmigkeit' im Konstantinopel des 6. Jahrhunderts n. Chr. Die Verlegung der Hypapante durch Justinian im Jahr 542, "*Historia* 51 (2002) 89–111; more generally, see B. Croke, "Justinian's Constantinople," in M. Maas (ed.), *The Cambridge Companion to the Age of Justinian* (Cambridge, 2005) 60–86 at 77–8.

PART IV
Ecclesiastical Hierarchies and the Limits of Religious Power

Chapter 12
Currencies of Power: The Venality of Offices in the Later Roman Empire*

Sabine R. Huebner
Columbia University

In the early fifth century, the Roman poet Claudius Claudianus wrote a virulent invective against Eutropius, the infamous eunuch and chamberlain of the emperor Arcadius, in which he attacked with bitter sarcasm the latter's practice of selling his influence for money:

> All the country between the Tigris and Mount Haemus he [Eutropius] exposes for sale at a fixed price, this huckster of empire, this infamous dealer in honours. This man governs Asia for which his villa has paid. That man buys Syria with his wife's jewels. Another repents of having taken Bithynia in exchange for his paternal mansion. Fixed above the open doors of his hall is a list giving the provinces and their prices: so much for Galatia, for Pontus so much, so much will buy one Lydia. Would you govern Lycia? Then lay down so many thousands. Phrygia? A little more.[1]

Payments and gifts in exchange for favors and advancement were already a well-established practice under the Principate and one of many tactics for establishing and maintaining networks of influence.[2] This practice assumed a different form during Late Antiquity in that the government became involved in it and aimed to control it directly, as Kelly has shown.[3] From the second half of the fourth century on, we encounter an official acknowledgement in Roman law of the fact

---

* I am very grateful to the editors Noel Lenski and Andrew Cain and many other participants of the Shifting Frontiers conference for valuable comments and suggestions. I would also like to thank Richard Payne, Irene Sanpietro, and James Tan for further comments and help with my English.

1 *In Eutrop.* vv. 190–210, trans. M. Platnauer, *Claudian* (Cambridge, MA, 1922) 1.155.

2 W. Goffart, "Did Julian Combat Venal Suffragium? A Note on *C.Th.* 2.29.1," *CPh* 65 (1970) 145–51, at 150; W. Schuller, "Kaiser Julian und der Ämterkauf," in R. Günther and S. Rebenich (eds.), *E fontibus haurire: Beiträge zur römischen Geschichte und zu ihren Hilfswissenschaften* (Paderborn, 1994) 197–201.

3 C. Kelly, *Ruling the Later Roman Empire* (Oxford, 2004).

that powerful men sold their influence (*suffragium*) for money to those who sought offices.[4] Even though the emperors disapproved of this practice[5] and insisted that the candidate's integrity outweigh any payment (*non ambitione vel pretio, sed probatae vitae et amplitudinis tuae solent testimonio promoveri*),[6] payments of money in return for offices were nonetheless a daily occurrence in Late Antiquity.[7] There can be no doubt but that things such as social origin, higher education, genuine merit, and influential connections remained important currencies of power in Late Antiquity.[8] Be that as it may, the role of monetary payments in obtaining office in the imperial civil service was, according to Kelly, central to the shift from the early imperial administration to the late Roman bureaucracy. From the account of John Lydus, who tells us about his career in the office of the praetorian prefecture in the early sixth century, we know that, apart from bribing influential men in return for recommendations, a new appointee usually was expected to pay a considerable sum to the retiree.[9] In addition, the new appointee paid a fee to the official who issued the formal certificate of appointment, and it was necessary to offer money to the magistrate responsible for maintaining the department's personnel registers.[10] It is therefore no wonder that Laniado commented wryly: "In a certain way, this principle (of election according to merit) is foreign to the mentality of the late empire."

Interestingly, the same is true for the clergy in the later Roman empire: venality went hand in hand with competition for office. In this article I shall examine the mechanism that was at play in the recruitment of the Christian clergy in the fifth and sixth centuries. This investigation, it is hoped, will yield further insight into not only the social composition of the later Roman clergy and the structure and workings of late antique society in general, but also the interplay between power and religion at this time.

---

4 *CTh* 2.29.1 (a.362) and *CTh* 2.29.2 (a.394). Cf. *CJ* 1.3.46.2 (a. 530); *CJ* 8.13.27 (a.528). Cf. Goffart, "Venal Suffragium"; A.H.M. Jones, *The Later Roman Empire 284–602: A Social, Economic, and Administrative Survey* (Cambridge, 1964, reprint. Norman, OK) 1.391–6: G.E.M. de Ste. Croix, "*Suffragium*: From Vote to Patronage," *BJS* 5 (1954) 33–48; C. Collot, "La pratique et l'institution du *suffragium* au Bas-Empire," *RD* 43 (1965) 185–221. The general aim was to cut out the middleman; cf. Kelly, *Later Roman Empire*, 163.

5 See Goffart, "Venal Suffragium," 146, for the evidence.

6 *CJ* 9.27.6.pr. (a.439).

7 Goffart, "Venal Suffragium," 150.

8 Eun. *Hist. frg*. 72.1 (R.C. Blockley, *The Fragmentary Classicising Historians of the Later Roman Empire* [Liverpool, 1985] 2.116–19), cf. K.G. Holum, *Theodosian Empresses: Women and Imperial Dominion in Late Antiquity* (Berkeley, 1982) 100–101.

9 Cf. J.B. Bury, *History of the Later Roman Empire, 395–565* (London, 1923) 2.360–61; J.A.S. Evans, *The Age of Justinian: The Circumstances of Imperial Power* (London, 1996) 44; Kelly, *Later Roman Empire*, 66–7.

10 Cf. Kelly, *Later Roman Empire*, 161.

Definition of a Career in the Clergy

A novel of Justinian tells us that many clerics from all over the eastern empire were eager to be relocated to the church of the patriarch in Constantinople and to be supported by some kind of patronage (διὰ τινος προστασίας).[11] Networks of influence and favor as "the most effective currencies of power"[12] had always been a distinctive mark of Roman society, and we see these networks of personal favors at play also in clerical circles, notably in the many letters of recommendation written by influential figures such as Basil of Caesarea, Synesius of Cyrene, and Theodoret of Cyrrhus to their peers for the purpose of securing promotions and advantages for their subordinates, families, and friends.[13]

The career of the presbyter Paulus, who appears in the *Life of Theodore of Sykeon*, may be taken as one such example of promotion to the patriarch's church through patronage.[14] Paulus was originally from Lycaonia where he held the position of presbyter in a local monastery. The protagonist of the *Life* was his patron Theodore, the ascetic saint and bishop of Anastasiupolis who enjoyed close connections with the patriarch of Constantinople and was held in high regard by the emperor. When Theodore brought his influence to bear on behalf of Paulus, the latter was relocated and obtained the position of presbyter at the Church of Mary at Sycae, one of the four churches that constituted the patriarch's establishment at Constantinople. This move is characterized in the saint's *Life* as an important career step, even though Paulus remained in the same ecclesiastical rank. Apparently this was the case because the rank of his new church increased his influence and social prestige enormously. In fact, his position at the patriarch's church later led to his promotion to a bishopric in Isauria.[15]

The attractions of a position at the church of Constantinople were obvious. Just as the young and ambitious John Lydus was eager to leave his hometown Philadelphia for the empire's capital in order to find a position in the imperial bureaucracy, so also many well-educated clerics from the provinces wished to come to Constantinople,[16] the political and religious center of the eastern

---

11 Just. *Nov.* 3.2 (a.535).

12 Kelly, *Later Roman Empire*, 130.

13 Cf. Kelly, *Later Roman Empire*, 160.

14 *VTheod.Syc.* 81; cf. E.A.S. Dawes and N.H. Baynes, *Three Byzantine Saints: Contemporary Biographies of St. Daniel the Stylite, St. Theodore of Sykeon and St. John the Almsgiver* (London, 1948) 144–5.

15 *VTheod.Syc.* 81; cf. S. Huebner, *Der Klerus in der Gesellschaft des spätantiken Kleinasiens* (Stuttgart, 2005) 230.

16 Cf. *Council of Antioch*, can. 11 (Mansi 2.1313); *CJ* 1.3.43 (a.529); Just. *Nov.* 67.3 (a.538); K.L. Noethlichs, "Anspruch und Wirklichkeit. Fehlverhalten und Amtspflichtverletzungen des christlichen Klerus anhand der Konzilskanones des 4. bis 8. Jahrhunderts," *ZSRG.K* 76 (1990) 1–61, at 48; Huebner, *Klerus in Kleinasien*, 253.

Roman empire.[17] Analogous to the benefits afforded by an office in the imperial bureaucracy, proximity to the patriarch offered ways of increasing one's social prestige and enhanced one's chances of career advancement. An example is the fact that, as with the presbyter Paulus in the saint's *Life*, many of the provincial bishops previously had held a position in the patriarch's clergy in Constantinople.[18] In addition, clerics at the main church received considerably higher stipends than their provincial counterparts. The emperor Justinian therefore saw in the flooding of clerics into the main church at Constantinople a sign of their greediness and profit-seeking.[19] Moreover, apart from their regular stipends, clerics at the main church had more opportunities to exact fees from the faithful who required their services. As in the imperial bureaucracy, it had become routine in the sixth-century church for the clergy to expect payments of money for almost every task they performed, such as when assisting in ordinations, performing baptisms or the Eucharist, conducting burials, and administering justice.[20]

But even if the main church represented the *non plus ultra* for every clergyman, an office at the church of a provincial metropolis or another wealthy see was also much sought-after, some more and some less, depending on the rank and wealth of the respective bishopric. The great differences between sees in the wealth, size, and number of their subordinate churches, and thereby the income and amount of stipends the clerics received, become obvious in another Justinianic novel, *Nov.* 123.3 (a.546). It is unique in the degree of information it provides on church finances, yet it has been almost completely neglected in scholarly debates about the church in Late Antiquity. In this edict Justinian ranked all the bishoprics of the eastern empire in seven different categories based on their yearly income. The four eastern patriarchates constituted the first class; their income was not specified but it amounted to several hundred pounds of gold per year. Below them were the sees that enjoyed annual revenues of more than thirty pounds of gold. These were the churches of the metropoleis, the bishops in the provincial capitals, and some other very wealthy bishoprics. The third group comprised all those bishoprics that had an income between ten and thirty pounds of gold. Then followed the sees that had an income between five and ten pounds of gold, between three and five, and between two and three. The seventh and last group covered all those bishoprics that had an income of less than two pounds of gold per year.

An example of a poor see is the little Isaurian hill town Meloe on the south coast of Asia Minor. In the early sixth century its bishop Musonius received only six solidi per year. Summoned before the patriarch of Antioch because he had acted as a moneylender, Musonius excused his engagement in this improper worldly occupation on the grounds that he could not make ends meet otherwise.

---

17 Cf. Kelly, *Later Roman Empire*, 192–3.

18 Huebner, *Klerus in Kleinasien*, 253–4.

19 Just. *Nov.* 3.2 (a.535).

20 Huebner, *Klerus in Kleinasien*, 176–7; cf. Kelly, *Later Roman Empire*, 64–5, for the imperial bureaucracy.

When he was further accused of questionable conduct by a priest of Antioch, he defended his usury: "By God, what do you care, you who receive the stipends of Antioch, while I have nothing in my city, not so much as six solidi?" Apparently this priest of the patriarch's church of Antioch had a much higher income than his colleague who held a minor bishopric.

The Social Composition of the Clergy

If the town's bishop could not live off the local church's stipend, we should assume that his clergy most probably received next to nothing for their daily maintenance. From the surviving documentary sources we know that the clergy in the small provincial towns usually continued to pursue their worldly occupation after taking office in the church—and not only the lower ranks but also the deacons and presbyters. Extraordinarily well documented in this respect is the clergy of Korykos, a thriving little seaport on the Cilician coast in southern Asia Minor. The inscriptions from Korykos, dating from the fourth to sixth centuries, inform us about priests who worked as goldsmiths, tailors, potters, carvers of gems, or money-lenders; archpresbyters who were blacksmiths and butchers, deacons who were active as entrepreneurs and silver-smiths; sub-deacons who were cider merchants or flue-knotters. Readers are attested as wine merchants and cobblers, and ecclesiastical gravediggers as millers and innkeepers.[21] The evidence from outside Cilicia and Asia Minor shows us that in this respect the social composition of the clergy was not specific to this region but rather typical for the clergy in the small towns and villages of the Roman east. Papyri from Egypt tell of priests, deacons and lectors as bakers, weavers, tailors, dyers and tanners, potters, blacksmiths, silversmiths, goldsmiths, nailers, carpenters, saddlers, stonecutters and masons, and even as camel drivers.[22] Furthermore, the hagiographic sources, which give us a glimpse into the everyday life of the clergy in the small towns and villages, reveal that many clerics earned their living as humble craftsmen or traders.[23] That many members of the clergy continued to work in trades is confirmed also by the legal sources, namely the constitutions of the emperors.

21 *MAMA* 3.682 (Samuel, reader and wine dealer); *MAMA* 3.463 (John, subdeacon and knotter of fishing nets); *MAMA* 3.760 (subdeacon and cider dealer); *IK* 30 (Keramos),195 (Alexander, deacon and contractor); *MAMA* 3.336 (Eugenius, priest and goldsmith); *MAMA* 3.582 (Marinus, priest and tailor of sails); *MAMA* 3.643 (Paulus, priest and potter); *MAMA* 3.676 (Romanus, priest and moneychanger); *SEG* 27.1292 (Theodore, archdeacon and blacksmith). For further references, see Huebner, *Klerus in Kleinasien*, 131–2.

22 G. Schmelz, *Kirchliche Amtsträger im spätantiken Ägypten nach den Aussagen der griechischen und koptischen Papyri und Ostraka* (Munich, 2002) 232–41.

23 Leontius, *VIoh.El.* 44A; cf. Dawes and Baynes, *Three Byzantine Saints*, 253–4; Cyr.Scyth. *VSabae* 78 (ed. E. Schwartz [Leipzig, 1939]); Greg.Naz. *Epp.* 9, 98; Bas. *Ep.* 198.1; see also Huebner, *Klerus in Kleinasien*, 132.

These relieved clerics, their wives, and servants from the labors that the guilds had to perform[24] as well as from the *collatio lustralis*, that is the business tax, that every tradesman and craftsman had to pay.[25]

> The Emperor Constantius greets the clergy: According to the sanction which you are said to have obtained previously, no person shall obligate you and your slaves to the new tax payments, but you shall enjoy exemption. Furthermore, you shall not be required to receive quartered persons, and if any of you, for the sake of a livelihood, should wish to conduct business, they shall possess immunity.[26]

This law from 343 explicitly states that clerics continued in their worldly business for the simple reason that they had to make a living (*alimoniae causa*). These privileges were reaffirmed in 357,[27] but then temporarily revoked at the end of the fourth century, apparently because this exemption was a major draw for businessmen to escape tax burdens by seeking clerical office.[28] Justinian's *Codex* included only the laws from 343 and 346 and thereby relieved again all clerics from the *collatio lustralis*, implicitly stating that even in the middle of the sixth century many clerics were engaged in worldly professions.[29]

If even many bishops' churches were too poor to provide their clergy with adequate maintenance, poorer still were the churches and chapels in the free villages and those on the estates of the great landowners that had been erected by the local population or by the landlords for their dependent *coloni*. The clerics recruited from the local rural population[30] might have received their share in kind from the humble offerings of the faithful, but in general they had to continue to

---

24 For these *munera sordida*, see Jones, *Later Roman Empire*, 2.858–9; Huebner, *Klerus in Kleinasien*, 134.

25 For this tax, see Jones, *Later Roman Empire*, 1.431–4; Huebner, *Klerus in Kleinasien*, 133–4.

26 *CTh* 16.2.8 (a.343), trans. Pharr, with modifications.

27 *CTh* 16.2.14 (a.357); cf. already *CTh* 16.2.2 (a.313) which implicitly included the clergy's liberation from any tax, and also *CTh* 16.2.10 which exempted the clerics from tax payments and menial public services and probably dates to the year 320. See also K.L. Noethlichs, "Zur Einflussnahme des Staates auf die Entwicklung eines kirchlichen Klerikerstandes," *JAC* 15 (1972) 136–53 at 140; Huebner, *Klerus in Kleinasien*, 135–6.

28 *CTh* 13.1.16 (a.399); cf. Huebner, *Klerus in Kleinasien*, 135–7.

29 *CJ* 1.3.1 (= *CTh* 16.2.8 [a.343]); also *CJ* 1.3.2 (= *CTh* 16.2.14 [a.357]). Cf. Noethlichs, "Einflussnahme," 140 n.12, who holds the view that it had become "undenkbar" that clerics were active as *negotatiores* by the 6th century.

30 According to imperial law, clergy should be ordained from among landholders in the village where the church was located, so that they could continue working their land as well as continue paying the poll tax and providing special services (*CTh* 16.2.33 = *CJ* 1.3.11 [a.398]); see also *CJ* 1.3.16 (a.409) and Just. *Nov.* 123.17 (a.546); cf. Huebner, *Klerus in Kleinasien*, 124–8.

plough their land in order to make a living. A certain Fronto, a priest of the village Malos in Galatia in the early fourth century, grew fruits and vegetables and sold his produce at the farmers' market in Ancyra.[31] From the *Life of St. Hypatios*, set in fifth-century Phrygia, we learn that many clerics were too exhausted from their work in the field to meet their obligations in the church.[32] According to the papyri, most of the clerics in the Egyptian villages also seem to have earned their living by farming.[33] The documentary evidence therefore shows on the one hand that clergymen were recruited from the lower and middle classes of their communities—farmers, small traders, and craftsmen—and on the other hand that it was necessary for them to continue in their former occupations even after taking office since the stipend they received from their church was not sufficient for their livelihood.[34]

We encounter a completely different situation for the clergy at the major churches, especially those of the patriarchs in Constantinople, Antioch, or Alexandria, for which our literary sources provide the most valuable evidence. This reveals that the clergymen there had come from the social elite: they were the sons of well-to-do curiales or high officials in the imperial bureaucracy. These clerics had often enjoyed a higher education in law, philosophy, or rhetoric. Some were renowned for their literary works and others had previously served in the army or imperial administration.[35] In an episode of the *Life* of Saint John the Almsgiver, this patriarch of Alexandria in the early seventh century welcomed the Syrian bishops who had fled from Syria to Egypt during the Persian invasion. He encouraged his clergy to support these fugitives threatened with impoverishment:

> When he learnt that some of the bishops staying in Alexandria were in need, he summoned the richer members amongst the leading clergy and when he had brought them together he exhorted them with many counsels and then laid down

[31] For references, see W.M. Ramsay, *Cities and Bishoprics of Phrygia, Being an Essay of the Local History of Phrygia from the Earliest Times to the Turkish Conquest*, 1.2 (Oxford, 1895–97) 521.

[32] Callin. *VHypatii* 1.4.

[33] E. Wipszycka, *Les ressources et les activités économiques des églises en Égypte du IVe au VIIIe siècle* (Brussels, 1972) 81–2; Schmelz, *Kirchliche Amtsträger*, 211–12, 218–20.

[34] J.-U. Krause has come to similar conclusions about later Roman Gaul, Italy and Spain. After examining the social origins, level of education, and economic situation of the clergy, and the relationship between the bishop and his clerics, he thinks that the clergy were recruited from the lower and middle social strata of their local communities. See "Überlegungen zur Sozialgeschichte des Klerus im 5./6. Jh.n.Chr.," in Idem and C. Witschel, *Die Stadt in der Spätantike—Niedergang oder Wandel? Akten des internationalen Kolloquiums in München am 30. und 31. Mai 2003. Historia Einzelschriften 190* (Stuttgart, 2006) 413–39.

[35] For the evidence from the sources and further literature, see Huebner, *Klerus in Kleinasien*, 249–52.

> that they all, and he himself first of all, should pay one pound of gold a year [that is, 72 solidi] to their poverty-stricken colleagues. He made a similar arrangement for the needy priests and deacons and the rest of the clergy of the Church, freely granting to each in every rank a certain sum of gold yearly corresponding to the particular labour of his own station so that his wants might be satisfied.[36]

Seventy-two solidi constituted a sum that was sufficient to support seven or eight families for a year. Some of these clerics were thus very prosperous if they could afford to give away annually this amount of money. Either the stipend they received from the church was considerable or, more probably, their origins were in much higher social strata than those of clergy in the provincial towns and villages and consequently they were already very well-to-do prior to taking office. The latter seems indeed to have been the case. From the literary sources we know that many clerics at the patriarchs' churches came from curial or cohortal families, that they had enjoyed a higher education, had been active as lawyers or orators, or had held a position in the imperial administration.[37]

How to Make a Career in the Clergy?

No one who fulfilled the entry requirements for the clergy was banned from climbing the career ladder and obtaining a position at the church of the patriarch or even the patriarchal throne itself. In a law of 534 Justinian established several criteria that assessed the suitability of an episcopal candidate: he should be free from any obligations to serve as *curialis* or *cohortalis*; a longstanding member of the secular or monastic clergy; should not have wife nor offspring; should not have purchased his office; should have knowledge of the holy dogmas and be willing to devote his entire life to the service of God.[38] As I shall show, there would seem to have been three other criteria that, although they were not made explicit in either imperial legislation or the canons of the church councils,[39] were nonetheless essential for those who wished to make a career in the clergy: level of education, wealth, and quality of social connections. The degree to which one was able to fulfill these determined one's chances of appointment and promotion.

As it was in the imperial service, so also in the late antique clergy: with power, influence, and imperial privileges came competition for office, and with competition came venality. We encounter attempts to acquire religious office through payment,

---

36 Leon. *VIoh.El.* 6; cf. Dawes and Baynes, *Three Byzantine Saints*, 213.

37 For the considerable costs of a higher education, which was the precondition for attaining such positions, see R. Cribiore, *The School of Libanius in Late Antique Antioch* (Princeton, 2007) 112.

38 Just. *Nov.* 6.1–7.

39 J.D. Harries, "Resolving Disputes: The Frontiers of Law in Late Antiquity," in R. Mathisen (ed.), *Law, Society and Authority in Late Antiquity* (Oxford, 2001) 68–82 at 68.

a process branded "simony" after Simon Magus, right from the beginning of the Christian church:

> When Simon saw that the Spirit was given at the laying on of the apostles' hands, he offered them money and said, "Give me also this ability so that everyone on whom I lay my hands may receive the Holy Spirit." Peter answered: "May your money perish with you, because you thought you could buy the gift of God with money!"[40]

It therefore comes as little surprise that simony became a more pressing problem from the fourth century onward as the church and its clergy began to rise in power and gain imperial privileges. An example from fourth-century Cappadocia illustrates this point. Basil of Caesarea, having heard that his *chorepiskopoi* had accepted money in return for ordinations, addressed a vituperative letter to them and threatened them with excommunication.[41] Later church canons repeated the same threats against those who either paid for or accepted money in return for ecclesiastical office.[42] From the later fifth century onward the sale of offices and bribery among the clergy were also topics addressed in imperial law: whoever dared to buy or sell an office lost his position in the church and was charged with *publicum crimen* and *laesa maiestas*.[43]

Nevertheless, with the growing power of the Christian church in worldly affairs, the charging of payments in return for office became commonplace, and eventually even became sanctioned, constituting as it did a counterpart to the payments which were due for obtaining office in the imperial bureaucracy, as we saw earlier.[44] Around the middle of the sixth century Justinian, while he continued to disapprove of the venality of clerical offices,[45] officially legitimized consecration fees payable to the ordaining bishop and to the assisting clergy.[46] From the text of the novel it becomes clear that Justinian did not introduce these

---

40 Acts 8:18–20.

41 Bas. *Ep.* 53; cf. also Pall. *Dial.* 89.

42 *C Chalc.* 2 (Mansi 7.357–60 [a.451]). In the great synod of Constantinople in 459 the patriarch Gennadius published his *Epistula Encyclica* against the practice of simony in the conferring of holy orders (Mansi 7.911–20).

43 *CJ* 1.3.30 (a.469); *CJ* 1.3.41.19–21 and 23 (a.528); Just. *Nov.* 6.1.5 (a.536); Just. *Nov.* 123.2 (a.546); cf. Noethlichs, "Anspruch und Wirklichkeit," 23–4; Huebner, *Klerus in Kleinasien*, 171–2.

44 For investiture fees for pagan priesthoods, see W.H. Willis and K. Maresch, *The Archive of Ammon Scholastikos of Panopolis (P.Ammon). Vol. I: The Legacy of Harpocration* (Opladen, 1997) 33; Kelly, *Later Roman Empire*, 200–201.

45 Just. *Nov.* 6.1.5 (a.536).

46 Just. *Nov.* 123.3, 16 (a.546). For papyrological evidence for ordination fees, see E. Wipszycka, *Études sur le christianisme dans l'Égypte de l'antiquité tardive* (Rome, 1996) 210–11.

fees but rather he aimed at regulating payments upon appointment and promotion and, by setting upper limits, he hoped to enforce imperial control over these transactions. According to this edict, candidates for bishoprics were expected to pay ordination fees, the amount of which depended on the income of their future church. These ordination fees ranged from several hundred solidi at the wealthiest sees to 50 solidi at smaller ones. Candidates for the throne of the patriarch were expected to pay 1,440 solidi, but not more, to the ordaining bishop and his staff. For the throne of a metropolitan bishop, a candidate was not to pay more than 400 solidi. An episcopal candidate at a minor see in the provinces was to pay no more than 50 solidi.

For the clerics below the episcopate there were consecration fees, and here too Justinian defined upper limits: these fees should not exceed the amount the candidate was to receive annually from his church as a stipend.[47] So, the amount of these ordination fees depended on several factors, first of course on the ecclesiastical rank at which the candidate was aiming, and second on the wealth of the church to which he was going to be ordained, since the clergy's stipends constituted a certain percentage of the church's total income.

Not only did the ordaining bishop and his clergy expect payments, but so did the candidate's future colleagues. If the candidate refused to pay, his senior colleagues would withhold his salary and not take him on as a new member. Justinian denounced this practice of demanding fees at any church other than the main church of Constantinople.[48]

Down to the sixth century, church councils and imperial law had always condemned the giving of gifts in return for ordinations. Justinian, however, not only allowed the church to levy consecration fees, but he also sanctioned the signing over to the church of parts or all of a candidate's property. Even though this rule prevented individual clerics from selling offices for their personal profit, it did not prevent the most prosperous and generous candidates from gaining preference. Justinian excused this new regulation by affirming that these payments should not be regarded as purchase (ἀγορασία) but rather as donation (προσφορά).[49] Regardless of the emperor's rhetoric, there can be no doubt but that this ruling encouraged the consecration of that candidate who offered the most generous donation. And by contrast with ordination fees, for which Justinian was zealous to set upper limits, the sky was the limit for these so-called "donations."

As Kelly has shown with regard to the imperial civil service, the emperors, far from condemning payments, even favored them upon appointment because these fees supplemented official salaries and raised the general state revenue.[50] The same applies for payments of money upon appointment for an office in the church. Ordination fees supplemented the stipends of the bishop and his clergy

47 Just. *Nov.* 123.16 (a.546).

48 Just. *Nov.* 56 (a.537); 123.16 (a.546).

49 Just. *Nov.* 123.3, 16 (a.546).

50 Kelly, *Later Roman Empire*, 164.

without burdening the church's revenues. The custom of signing over a proportion of one's property to the church in return for an office increased the latter's wealth even more directly.

The emperors, however, apparently aimed at cutting out the middleman by regulating these payments through official action. While the paying of regular fees to certain officials and gift-giving to the church in general were welcome,[51] all kinds of arrangements involving a broker who sold his influence for money were declared illegal. Justinian's novel speaks of the middleman (ὁ μέσος) who arranged the deal between the one who gives (ὁ διδούς), that is, the candidate who wished to be ordained, and the one who takes (ὁ λαμβάνων), that is, the bishop who carried out the ordination.[52] All three parties involved, according to Justinian, should lose their priestly offices.

It becomes apparent from the evidence adduced here that over the course of the fifth and sixth centuries a change in the perception of simony had taken place and that payments for obtaining office in the clergy had become widespread and accepted. Only those payments that were made to individuals who sold their power and influence to the highest bidder were still outlawed. Payments to officials who assisted in the appointment of future colleagues that did not transgress certain upper limits and payments of any amount to the church as an institution rather to an individual were perfectly legitimate and even encouraged.[53]

What is especially striking is that payments for a given church office were apparently no longer a matter of shame or embarrassment in the sixth century but rather were openly conducted and broadly accepted as a strategy for obtaining office. Requesting a payment from a candidate became so pervasive that the fact that someone did not have to pay these fees was regarded as a high distinction. For instance, the *Life of Saint Nikolas of Sion* stresses that the archbishop did not demand any payment when he ordained Nikolas a reader because he recognized that his character was filled with divine grace (τὸν χαρακτῆρα τοῦ παιδὶου πλήρη χάριτος ὄντα) and that he was to become the chosen instrument of God (σκεῦος ἐκλογῆς).[54] Here we observe a noticeable shift from the fourth century, when Basil the Great had reproached his *chorepiskopoi* for taking money in return for ordinations, to the sixth century, when fees and gifts in exchange for clerical offices became an everyday affair.

---

51 Just. *Nov.* 123.3 (a.546).

52 Just. *Nov.* 123.2 (a.546).

53 Just. *Nov.* 123.3, 16 (a.546).

54 I. and N.P. Sevcenko, *The Life of Saint Nicholas of Sion* (Brookline, MA, 1984) 24–5 § 5: ἐχειροτόνησεν αὐτὸν τῇ τάξει τῶν ἀναγνωωστῶν, μὴ λαβὼν παρ' αὐτοῦ χειροτονὶας ἕνεκεν τὸ σύνολον.

Conclusions

There were many prerequisites to obtaining high positions within the church, including wealth, higher education, influence, and connections, similar to those that contributed to the advancement of secular careers. As for a secular career, the payment of fees and the giving of gifts in order to obtain a position gained importance in the sixth-century church. Traditional means of influence such as powerful patrons and friends and high social status did not vanish or lose their importance; the payment of money, however, had become available as "an alternative method of establishing priority among those pressing for access."[55] And not only in practice but also in attitude; here we can identify assimilation to the secular administration. As the imperial legislation and saints' lives show, monetary exchanges used as a means to gain access to the clergy were conducted openly and conversed about without shame. There is the same striking transparency as in the secular administration, "an unabashed openness" about the sale of offices.[56] Acquiring an office in exchange for payment of money was no under-the-table deal but had become an established practice used to increase church revenues and regulate access to the clergy, a process which might have been related to the increasingly and explicitly political role the bishop and his clergy attained in the towns and villages over the course of the late fifth and especially the sixth centuries.[57] Furthermore, I have argued that it was not his rank in the church's institutional hierarchy that was decisive for a cleric's degree of power, social prestige, and income, but rather the church to which he belonged. A reader at the main church of Constantinople was considered to be of much higher social standing, origin, and education and received much greater emoluments than a presbyter of a minor provincial town.[58]

The clergy of Late Antiquity has often been described as a melting-pot standing outside society, a uniform and homogeneous class in which all differences as regards secular status were evened out by the time of ordination. The clergy indeed represented a profession that was open to all ranks of late antique society, and men from almost all levels of society could be found in it. However, it would be wrong to assume that the clergy was unaffected by secular social hierarchies. It has not been previously acknowledged that there were enormous social differences between the clergy at the metropolitans' and patriarchs' churches and the clergy

---

[55] Kelly, *Later Roman Empire*, 182.

[56] Kelly, *Later Roman Empire*, 177.

[57] A.M. Cameron, *The Mediterranean World in Late Antiquity, AD 395–600* (London, 1993) 62–6; J.H.W.G. Liebeschuetz, *The Decline and Fall of the Roman City* (Oxford, 2001) 137–68; Idem., *Decline And Change in Late Antiquity: Religion, Barbarians and Their Historiography* (Aldershot, 2006) 145, 160–61; Huebner, *Klerus in Kleinasien*, 96–102.

[58] For a discussion on how this affected the clergy as a community, see Huebner, *Klerus in Kleinasien*, 255–6, 267–8.

in the provincial towns and villages, and that above all secular virtues such as lofty social origins, wealth, and powerful connections were decisive for obtaining positions of power and influence in the clerical hierarchy. The clergy therefore should be regarded as an institution that was tightly interwoven with the secular social structure of later Roman society.

Chapter 13

Religion and Power in the Early Thought of John Chrysostom

Justin Stephens
Metropolitan State College, Denver

The year 378 was an important turning point in the career of John Chrysostom. Having rigidly devoted himself to monasticism for six years, he returned to his native Antioch and resumed a career in the church.[1] Later that same year, or early in the next, he composed the *Discourse on the Blessed Babylas*, a Christian apology centered upon the story of a third-century bishop and martyr of Antioch.[2] An examination of this work within the context of Chrysostom's early career reveals that he had well-developed ideas regarding the relationship between temporal and spiritual authority even at this early stage of his development.

The early years of Chrysostom's career are less well known than his tenure as bishop of Constantinople (s.397/398–404). During those stormy years, Chrysostom was twice exiled following multiple confrontations with the emperor Arcadius and his wife Eudoxia, and ultimately, he died weakened as a result of his exile and these confrontations. In current scholarship, the early political thought of Chrysostom has largely been absent from the discussion of his downfall.[3] Instead,

---

1 For Chrysostom's life and career, see J.N.D. Kelly, *Golden Mouth: The Story of John Chrysostom, Ascetic, Preacher, Bishop* (Ithaca, 1995); R. Brandle, *Johannes Chrysostomus: Bischof-Reformer-Märtyrer* (Stuttgart, 1999); C. Tiersch, *Johannes Chrysostomus in Konstantinopel (398–404): Weltsicht und Wirken eines Bischofs in der Hauptstadt des Oströmischen Reiches* (Tübingen, 2002); W. Mayer, "Progress in the Field of Chrysostom Studies (1984–2004)," in *Giovanni Crisostomo: Oriente e Occidente tra IV e V secolo, XXXIII Incontro di Studiosi dell'Antichità Cristiana, Augustinianum 6–8 maggio 2004, Roma* (Rome, 2005) 9–35.

2 Joh.Chrys. *De s.Bab.* 41. All citations are from M.A. Schatkin, C. Blanc, and B. Grillet (eds.), *Jean Chrysostome Discours sur Babylas, Introduction, texte critique, traduction et notes. SCh 362* (Paris, 1990). Translations follow M.A. Schatkin and P.W. Harkins (trans.), *Saint John Chrysostom Apologist*. FOTC, 73 (Washington, DC, 1985). Schatkin and Harkins, *Apologist*, 15–16, dates this work to 378. Kelly, *Golden Mouth*, 41, dates it to 379.

3 For a more in-depth discussion of the historiography on this subject see J. Stephens, *Ecclesiastical and Imperial Authority in the Writings of John Chrysostom: A Reinterpretation of his Political Philosophy* (diss: Univ. of California, Santa Barbara, 2001).

the prevailing view is that he was an ascetic with little interest in politics.[4] For example, Liebeschuetz describes him as a "non-political bishop, who was careful to keep completely clear of involvement in secular political controversy."[5] This conclusion is in danger of overlooking important events that suggest otherwise. Additionally, it underestimates the difficulty of separating "secular" from "religious" events in this period. An examination of the *Discourse on the Blessed Babylas* reveals that Chrysostom's views regarding the authority of the bishop need to be reintegrated into any attempt to understand fully his later career.[6]

The circumstances surrounding Chrysostom's return to Antioch in 378 were shaped in part by the Battle of Adrianople in August of that same year. In the wake of the Arian emperor Valens' death, the western emperor Gratian issued a decree of religious toleration.[7] This allowed Antioch's Nicene bishop Meletius to return from exile and it may have played a role in Chrysostom's decision to return to the city as well. Valens' death also led to the appointment of Theodosius I as emperor in early January 379. Because Theodosius' reign marked an end to imperial support for Arian Christianity and the "triumph" of Nicene Christianity, it is now easy to overlook the turmoil of the second half of the fourth century. It is important to remember, however, that neither Chrysostom nor his contemporaries could have predicted the permanence of Theodosius' policy.[8] Born about 349,

---

4 C. Baur, *John Chrysostom and His Time*, 2 vols., trans. M. Gonzaga (Westminster, 1959). Brandle, *Johannes Chrysostomus*; J.B. Bury, *History of the Later Roman Empire* (London, 1923; reprint. New York, 1958) 1.138–160; J. Quasten, *Patrology* (Westminster, MD, 1950–60) 3.424–8.

5 J.H.W.G. Liebeschuetz, *Barbarians and Bishops: Army, Church and State in the Age of Arcadius and Chrysostom* (Oxford, 1990) 189.

6 The general lack of attention paid to Chryosostom's political thought has been partially addressed in recent years. See K. Groß-Albenhausen, *Imperator christianissimus: Der christliche Kaiser bei Ambrosius und Johannes Chrysostomus* (Frankfurt, 1999) 144–207; F. Santovito, "Ambrogio e Chrisostomo conscienza critica della Chiesa del IV secolo di fronte al potere politico," *Nicolaus* 12 (1985) 67–181; O. O'Donovan and J. Lockwood O'Donovan (eds.), *From Irenaeus to Grotius: A Sourcebook in Christian Political Thought* (Grand Rapids, 1999) 89–103. Of these scholars, only Groß-Albenhausen examines the role that Chrysostom's early beliefs played in his later difficulties as bishop of Constantinople, but ultimately dismisses (p. 207) the importance of his thought upon his later actions.

7 N. Lenski, *Failure of Empire: Valens and the Roman State in the Fourth Century* (Berkeley and Los Angeles, 2002) 262–3; R.M. Errington, *Roman Imperial Policy From Julian to Theodosius* (Chapel Hill, 2006) 171–211.

8 See R.M. Errington, "Christian Accounts of the Religious Legislation of Theodosius I," *Klio* 79 (1997) 398–433. Errington argues that Theodosius' religious legislation had much less of an impact than is traditionally assumed. He looks at late fourth- and early fifth-century sources which paid little attention to Theodosian laws to support his view. Errington's argument helps to underscore the fact that contemporaries of Theodosius, such as Chrysostom, did not immediately recognize the significance and permanence of Theodosius' reign.

Chrysostom had lived through the reigns of the Arian emperor Constantius II (337–61), the pagan emperor Julian (361–63), and the Arian emperor Valens (364–78). As a result of the religious beliefs of these rulers, imperial religious policy had shifted dramatically during Chrysostom's early years, but in no case was it supportive of Nicene Christianity.[9]

The potential for conflict between Christianity and imperial authority is central in the *Discourse on the Blessed Saint Babylas*. It begins with an argument that Christianity is superior to paganism and continues with the story of Babylas, a Bishop of Antioch, who was martyred by an unnamed emperor in the third century (§§ 1–21; 23–66). The majority of the work deals with the fate of Babylas' remains under Julian and culminates with a description of the disasters that befell Julian, following his removal of these remains from the temple of Apollo at Daphne (§§ 66–127).

In the early part of the work, Chrysostom's comparison of Christianity with paganism outlines an understanding of the proper relationship between church and empire. Paganism had all the advantages of imperial support, according to Chrysostom, and in fact it depended upon this support for its survival. The rapid decline of the numbers of pagans and the pagan religion following Constantine's conversion was, for Chrysostom, evidence that paganism was false and that it depended upon state support. By contrast, the success of Christianity in the face of imperial opposition proved the truth of its doctrine (42.2). He made this distinction even more pronounced by arguing that Christianity benefited from imperial opposition.[10] The belief that Christianity was impervious to shifts in imperial religious policy suggests that Chrysostom viewed the church and empire as distinct institutions. Because he saw the church as being independent, the bishop's authority was ultimately independent from the emperor and the empire as well.

The authority of bishops relative to that of emperors is a prominent theme in Chrysostom's retelling of the story of Babylas. In his version, an unnamed emperor murdered the child of a foreign king who had been given as a hostage to the emperor in order to secure a peace treaty (§ 23.1). Following his murder of the child, the emperor "rushed to the church of God" (§ 27.12). When he reached it, Babylas threw him out "with the calmness and fearlessness of a shepherd who separates a mangy and diseased sheep from the flock" (§ 30.16). Chrysostom emphasizes the significance of this event to his audience saying that "the subordinate [Babylas] gave orders to the chief, and the subject judged the ruler [emperor] of all and cast the vote which condemned him" (§ 31.1).

Chrysostom then highlights the dramatic scene that must have occurred when the emperor, "appearing more dignified from his clothes, purple robe, and the gems spread all across his right hand," approached the church with his large number of

---

9 R. Wilken, *John Chrysostom and the Jews* (Berkeley, 1983) 29–33.

10 See also: Joh.Chrys. *Adversus oppugnatores vitae monast. Lib. II* (*PG* 47.344.9); trans. David G. Hunter, *A Comparison Between a King and a Monk—Against the Opponents of the Monastic Life* (Lewiston and Queenston, 1988).

attendants.[11] The emperor's magnificence is contrasted with the bishop's "modest bearing, simple dress, contrite soul, and spirit free from arrogance" (§ 33.3). While most people would have been intimidated by the arrival of an emperor, Babylas was unimpressed and refused to let the emperor enter the church (§ 35.1). In Chrysostom's view, Babylas' actions matched the boldness of both Elijah and John the Baptist (§ 34.17). The source of this courage was his need to vindicate "the outraged laws of God" (Ibid.). In the process, he "established for us certain rules and principles, which might serve as guidelines for our conduct in similar situations in the future" (§ 39.10).

After a digression comparing Babylas to Diogenes the Cynic, Chrysostom further explains how Babylas's actions benefited both Christians and later bishops.[12] "[He] emboldened future priests and intimidated future emperors," showing that the "one appointed to the priesthood is a more responsible guardian of the earth and what transpires upon it than the one who wears the purple" (§ 51.1). Finally, Babylas showed that the power of the priesthood was so great that one's life must be surrendered rather than allow it to be diminished, as no priest could overlook "the violation of the laws of God (§§ 51.6–20: τῶν θείων νόμων)." The emperor, however, was less sympathetic toward Babylas' stance than was Chrysostom. He "put the saint in irons" and threw him into prison where he was eventually executed (§ 54.4).

At the very end of the piece, after describing the disasters that plagued Julian, Chrysostom returns to the theme of Babylas as a model bishop:

> He defended the outraged laws of God (τοῖς τοῦ θεοῦ νόμοις) exacted proper punishment in behalf of the deceased; showed the great gulf between priesthood and kingly office … taught emperors not to carry their authority beyond the measure given them by God; and showed bishops how they ought to exercise this office. (127.4)

This passage is central to understanding Chrysostom's view of the office of bishop and the relationship between imperial and ecclesiastical authority. The conflict between Babylas and the emperor is portrayed as a struggle over divine laws that, for Chrysostom, governed the proper actions of both bishop and emperor. A related and crucial point is that bishops were the ultimate interpreters of divine law. As such, the bishop determines the boundaries of his own authority. Moreover, the

---

11 *De s.Bab.* 32.8. On Chrysostom's fondness for this type of comparison between emperors and priests, see K. Setton, *Christian Attitude Towards the Emperor in the Fourth Century* (New York, 1967) 187–9. For other examples see Joh. Chrys. *De perf. car.* 6 (*PG* 56.286–7); *C. Anom.* 12.4 (*PG* 48.809); *Expos. in Ps.* 109.6 (*PG* 55.274).

12 *De s.Bab.* 40–49. Chrysostom argues that Babylas' boldness of speech (παρρησία) was much greater than Diogenes' confrontation with Alexander, because Babylas' speech served a higher purpose whereas Diogenes simply confronted the Macedonian for selfish reasons.

authority of bishops, because it rests in part upon divine laws, is superior to the authority of emperors.[13]

The *Discourse on the Blessed Babylas* makes it clear that emperors who opposed Christianity, such as Julian and the anonymous emperor in the story of Babylas, were on Chrysostom's mind upon his return to Antioch in 378. It is very likely as well that he had in mind the recently deceased Valens who had supported Arianism and opposed Nicene Christianity.[14] Even though another non-Christian emperor, or another Arian emperor, never materialized, Chrysostom's views held the potential for conflict, because he outlined clear boundaries for the authority of emperors and bishops. In the Christian empire of the late fourth century, however, distinguishable boundaries between religion and politics were often non-existent.

A good example of how religion and politics could become easily intertwined occurred in the aftermath of the 387 Riot of the Statues.[15] Following the announcement of a new imperial tax in Antioch, statues and imperial portraits were damaged, a riot ensued, and many of its participants were arrested and executed. Defacing the imperial visage was a serious offense, and the Antiochenes had every reason to believe that worse punishment was yet to come. In an effort to assuage the emperor, Antioch's bishop Flavian departed for the capital only days after the riot. After a tense three weeks that included an investigation of events by imperial officials sent by Theodosius, and a meeting between Flavian and the emperor, news of Theodosius' clemency reached Antioch.

That Flavian felt it necessary to intercede following a riot over taxes and that Theodosius was willing to receive his embassy both point to the fluid boundaries between politics and religion in the fourth century. Even more significant is the manner in which Chrysostom interpreted the events. Unlike the story of Babylas, which was set in the distant past, Flavian's embassy was a real historical event with the authority of both the emperor and bishop on display.

In his capacity as a priest, Chrysostom managed the congregation while Flavian was away.[16] In a homily delivered just after Flavian had departed, only days after

---

13 For a good discussion of the spiritual and ascetic basis of the authority of the bishop in Late Antiquity, see C. Rapp, *Holy Bishops in Late Antiquity: The Nature of Christian Leadership in an Age of Transition* (Berkeley, 2005) 3–22, 56–154.

14 For Valens' opposition to monks and Nicene Christianity, see N. Lenski, "Valens and the Monks: Cudgeling and Conscription as a Means to Social Control," *DOP* 58 (2004) 93–117. He makes a strong case that book 1 of *Adversus oppugnatores vitae monasticae* dates to the reign of Valens (p. 103–7) and that Chrysostom was reacting to Valens' persecution of monks.

15 F. van de Paverd, *St. John Chrysostom: The Homilies on the Statues* (Rome, 1991); R. Browning, "The Riot of AD 387 in Antioch: The Role of the Theatrical Claques in the Later Empire," *JRS* 42 (1952) 13–20; D. French, "Rhetoric and the Rebellion of AD 387 in Antioch," *Historia* 47 (1998) 468–84.

16 Joh. Chrys. *Homilae XXI de Statuis ad populum Antiochenum habitae* (*PG* 49.15–222). Cf. *NPNF* 1.9.317–489. Traditionally, there are 21 homilies associated with the Riot

the riot, Chrysostom made clear the role he envisioned for Flavian: "The sacred laws (οἱ ἵεροι νόμοι) take and place under his hands even the royal head." He added that "when there is need of any good thing from above, the emperor is accustomed to fly to the priest: but not the priest to the emperor."[17] Additionally, Chrysostom claimed that, compared to the emperor, the priest had greater weapons, and the right to speak freely.[18]

The twenty-first homily, *In Episcopi Flaviani reditum*, delivered roughly five weeks later, about two weeks after the pardon had reached Antioch, provided Chrysostom with an opportunity to explain fully the role that Flavian had played in the successful outcome of events. He says that Flavian told Theodosius to consider:

> what it is for all posterity to hear it reported, that when so great a city had become liable to punishment and vengeance, when all were terrified, when its generals, magistrates and judges were all in horror and alarm and did not dare to utter a word on behalf of the wretched people, a single old man, invested with the priesthood of God, came and moved the heart of the Monarch ... and that the favor which he bestowed upon no other of his subjects, he granted to this one old man, being actuated by a reverence for God's laws (τοῦς τοῦ θεοῦ νόμους)![19]

Chrysostom went on to relate another of Flavian's arguments: "Some when they go on an embassy bring gold, and silver, and other gifts of that kind ... But I come into your presence with the sacred laws (ἱέρων νόμων); and instead of all other gifts, I present these; and I exhort you to imitate your lord ..."[20] In both of these instances, Flavian's knowledge of divine law is given as the reason for his ability to convince Theodosius to spare the Antiochenes further punishment.

When taken together, the examples of Babylas and Flavian point the way toward a re-thinking of Chrysostom's career in Constantinople. In both cases, Chrysostom outlined a very broad notion of the authority of bishops based in part upon their knowledge of "divine law." Divine law in these instances can be defined as general principles derived from the Scriptures, which prescribe a code for proper human behavior. The office of bishop gave its holder both the right to interpret these principles and the duty to defend them. Chrysostom's belief that bishops defined the limits of their own authority, and his belief that episcopal authority was greater than that of the emperor were consistent in his early thought.[21]

---

of the Statues, but the first homily was actually delivered before it took place, leaving 20 homilies related to events surrounding the riot.

17 Joh. Chrys. *Ad pop.* 3.2 (*PG* 49.50). This third homily was the first delivered following the departure of Flavian; cf. *Ad Pop.* 3.1 (*PG* 49.48).

18 *Ad pop.* 3.2 (*PG* 49.38).

19 *Ad pop.* 21.4 (*PG* 49.219).

20 *Ad pop.* 21.3 (*PG* 49.219).

21 For a clear expression of this view, see Joh.Chrys. *De sacerd.* 3.5 (*SCh* 272.148).

Once in Constantinople, he was not afraid to act upon these views.[22] In the year 400, the Gothic general Gainas entered the capital with his army of 35,000 troops.[23] Soon afterward, Gainas asked Arcadius to allow one of the city's churches to be used for Arian services. In the face of an immediate military threat, Arcadius agreed to the demand and asked Chrysostom for his cooperation. Chrysostom, however, refused the request immediately and instead demanded to meet with both Gainas and Arcadius. According to Sozomen, when he, along with a group of bishops he had assembled, met with Gainas and Arcadius in the palace:

> He spoke at length in the presence of the emperor and Gainas, reproached the latter with being a stranger and a fugitive, and reminded him that his life had been saved by the father of the emperor, to whom he had sworn fidelity, as likewise to his children, to the Romans, and to the laws, which he was striving to make powerless. When he had made this speech he showed a law which Theodosius had established, forbidding the heterodox to hold a church within the walls.[24]

Chrysostom followed his rebuke of Gainas with a speech to Arcadius in which he exhorted the emperor to "maintain the laws which had been established against heretics; and told him that it would be better to be deprived of the empire than to be guilty of impiety by becoming a traitor to the house of God."[25] Surprisingly, given the tension of the situation, both Gainas and Arcadius acceded to the bishop's demands. Thus, according to Sozomen, Chrysostom boldly rebuked both the emperor and the general and was successful in thwarting the effort to secure a church for Arian use.

At first glance, Chrysostom's boldness seems almost reckless given the power of Gainas at the time. Moreover, it is hard to believe that he would have gone against not only a powerful general, but also the emperor who had been constrained to appoint him. His actions, though, make perfect sense when we consider his views on the authority and duty of the bishop outlined in his early writings. Like Babylas and Flavian, he was standing his ground in defense of divine laws; this was his right, and duty, as a bishop. In short, this confrontation provided Chrysostom with the opportunity to act upon his views regarding the authority of the bishop.

This lone example underscores the importance of evaluating Chrysostom's actions as bishop of Constantinople in light of his views regarding the authority of the bishop. One obstacle that has kept scholars from seeing Chrysostom in this light has been the attempt to distinguish definitively between the categories of "religious" and "secular." This false dichotomy has muffled the ambiguity of the relationship between politics and religion in the late fourth century. Boundaries

22 For Chrysostom's career in Constantinople, see Kelly, *Golden Mouth*, 145–285; J.H.W.G. Liebeschuetz, "The Fall of John Chrysostom," *NMS* 29 (1985) 1–31.

23 Kelly, *Golden Mouth*, 156–62.

24 Soz. 8.4.

25 Ibid.; cf. Theod. *HE* 5.32.

between the two spheres had never been fully distinct in the Roman Empire, but with the emergence of the Christian church as a political force in the later fourth century, these lines became even less clear.[26] Emperors were often directly involved in religious matters (for example, theological debates), and bishops increasingly played a role in a wide range of matters that the modern world would deem political. Chrysostom's use of Babylas as a model for future bishops, his understanding of Flavian's embassy to Theodosius, and his confrontation with the emperor and Gainas reveal the limits of these categories for understanding Chrysostom, and certainly do not fit with the traditional view of the younger John as an ascetic who allegedly had little interest in politics. Rather, they point toward a coherent view of episcopal authority formed by Chrysostom already while he was in Antioch, and acted upon when he became bishop of Constantinople.

[26] P. Brown, *Power and Persuausion in Late Antiquity: Towards a Christian Empire* (Madison, WI, 1992); H.A. Drake, *Constantine and the Bishops: The Politics of Intolerance* (Baltimore, 2000) 35–113; E.D. Hunt "The Church as a Public Institution," in A.M. Cameron and P. Garnsey (eds.), *The Cambridge Ancient History* (Cambridge, 1998) 13.238–72.

Chapter 14

"The truth shall make you free": Augustine on the Power of Religion*

Gillian Clark
University of Bristol

It would be surprising if Augustine, bishop of Hippo, did not have something to say about the power of religion. Religion was his life, he experienced its power over himself and others, and unlike many philosophers he actually had some power: not very much, but some. Defining power is always a problem. Plato's dialogue *Gorgias* asked the key question: do people really have power if they do not in fact achieve what they want, especially if, as Plato thought, what they really want to achieve is the real good, not what seems good to them? One recent study of power, by a theologian who has also been a bishop, works with the minimal suggestion that, "to have power is to be able to make a difference in the world."[1] This does not solve the problem, because everything we do makes a difference to the world. But some people have a choice to make a particular difference, and some differences are of more interest to historians because they have more impact on people's lives.

Augustine the bishop did not exercise the most obvious kind of power: immediate physical force, *vis*. He did not command troops, and unlike some bishops, he chose not to deploy monks or committed followers as an immediate strong-arm demonstration of the power of religion.[2] But he did have *potestas*, authorized power to take actions that had an effect in Roman law. This is not the same as making things happen, but societies work because most people accept the orders of those in power. In everyday speech, Augustine not only had *potestas*, he was a *potestas*. His contemporary Ambrosiaster, commenting on Paul's advice (Rom. 13:1) to "let every soul be subject to the more exalted powers," observed that "*potestates* are people who manage human affairs with some kind of status."[3] Paul said, "There is no *potestas* except from God, and those there are, God set in order": in Latin translation from Paul's Greek, *non est potestas nisi a Deo; quae*

* Especial thanks to Sam Clark for a philosopher's perspective on power.

[1] S. Sykes, *Power and Christian Theology* (London, 2006) 7.

[2] In H.A. Drake (ed.), *Violence in Late Antiquity: Perceptions and Practices* (Aldershot, 2006), see esp. B.D. Shaw, "Bad Boys: Circumcellions and Fictive Violence," 179–96.

[3] *Exp. ad Rom.* 64: *Potestatibus, id est, hominibus res humanas cum aliquo honore administrantibus.*

autem sunt, a Deo ordinatae sunt.[4] When Augustine called such power *ordinata potestas*, he meant that it was part of the *ordo*, the social and political structures that determine who gives orders and who takes them. He thought that this giving and taking of orders by individuals was the central fact about rule, whether in monarchy or democracy, nation or empire, and he saw *ordo* not just as Roman social rank, but as the order that is intrinsic to the universe.[5]

As the duly ordained, *ordinatus*, priest and then bishop of Hippo, Augustine had the power to include people in the church community by baptism, give them status within it by ordination, exclude them from it by excommunication, and order the punishment of delinquent clergy or monks by immediate physical force, specifically by beating. This sounds impressive, but in practice all such actions could meet with resistance. Augustine was opposed by some of his own clergy and episcopal colleagues, not to mention the Donatists who said he was not in fact the authorized ecclesiastical power in the diocese of Hippo.[6] As bishop, Augustine also made decisions in civil cases and could ask the local governor to enforce them.[7] He remarked that, "both parties love the judge before he judges," but this power to judge ensured that in many cases there would be someone who suspected the bishop of bias or corruption (*En.Ps.* 25.2.13). Official *potestas* coexisted with the "soft" power of persuading people to want the same things.[8] *Potentia*, the less acceptable face of soft power, could make things happen by influence and deals, while *auctoritas*, the acceptable face, could make things happen by reputation. Often *auctoritas* resulted from authorized power, as in the case of senior statesmen, but it could also come from acknowledged expertise. Augustine's letters, especially those to his long-term friend Alypius, show him trying to use the soft power of contacts and persuasion, but not to bribe or threaten. Some bishops also had financial power in the form of charitable funds and potential donors, but Augustine's church at Hippo was not well endowed.[9]

---

4 Many English translations of Paul's Greek give the impression that he meant "God ordered that there should be powers" or "The people in power are there by God's orders."

5 R.A. Markus, *Saeculum: History and Society in the Theology of St. Augustine*, rev. ed. (Cambridge, 1988) 72–104.

6 On problems with clergy, see J.J. O'Donnell, *Augustine, Sinner and Saint: A New Biography* (London, 2005) 164–9. On Donatists, see E.M. Atkins and R.J. Dodaro (eds.), *Augustine: Political Writings* (Cambridge, 2001) 128–203.

7 J.C. Lamoreaux, "Episcopal Courts in Late Antiquity," *JECS* 3 (1995) 143–67; N. Lenski, "Evidence for the *Audientia Episcopalis* in the New Letters of Augustine," in R.W. Mathisen (ed.), *Law, Society and Authority in Late Antiquity* (Oxford, 2001) 83–97.

8 On varieties of power see S. Lukes, *Power: A Radical View* (London, 1974); S. Clark, *Living Without Domination* (Aldershot, 2007) 66–73.

9 S. Lancel, *St. Augustine*, trans. A. Nevill (London, 2002) 235–45.

These familiar varieties of power interacted with the personal authority of ascetic lifestyle to establish the spiritual power of the holy bishop.[10] He was seen as being closer to God than ordinary people were and less vulnerable to human needs and failings. As such, he was a powerful spiritual patron with influence (so to speak) at the court of heaven, and his authority had to be respected. Augustine did not deploy this kind of power. Even if he had wanted to claim such personal holiness, he had to be wary of looking ascetic, because he was still living down his years as a Manichaean. Everyone expected Manichaeans to be pale from fasting (Jer. *Ep.* 22.13), whereas Augustine, according to his friend Possidius (*VAug.* 22), had simple tastes but provided meat for guests or for those recovering from illness, and always had wine on the table. Besides, Augustine knew that matching food intake to physical need is not a simple matter of diet: as he said, Esau had an inordinate desire for lentils (*Conf.* 10.31.46). His particular strength was not austerity but the power of the word, written or spoken, in persuasive rhetoric to move his hearers or in precise formulation of arguments. If he had been told about the power of discourse to shape experience, he might have murmured "if only."[11] But even when he could not change the law or the way that people behaved, he might convince a Roman official that the law had been broken or that mercy should be shown in enforcing it against heretics or illegal slave-traders.[12]

All of these powers, even if limited and often frustrated, are instances of the power of religion in that they depend on the acknowledged status of a Christian bishop, which is one clear difference between Late Antiquity and earlier Roman history. But the main trend of Augustinian scholarship in the last two decades has been to change our perspective on "the towering figure of Augustine" who dominated the theological landscape in late antique North Africa and has dominated western Christian theology ever since. Augustine provided the word for these changes: *retractationes*, reconsiderations. Their effect overall is to confirm his own claim that he had very little power:

> It is often said of me, "Why is he going to that *potestas*? What does a bishop want with that *potestas*?" But you all know that your needs make me go where I do not want to go, and watch, and stand at the door, and wait while worthy and unworthy people go in, and be announced, and finally get in, and put up with snubs, and ask, and sometimes succeed and sometimes go sadly away. (*Serm.* 302.17)

Augustine, according to the recent *retractationes*, lacked contacts and influence in political or ecclesiastical networks. His appointment to the chair of rhetoric

---

[10] C. Rapp, *Holy Bishops in Late Antiquity: The Nature of Christian Leadership in an Age of Transition* (Berkeley, 2005).

[11] On the power of discourse see A.M. Cameron, *Christianity and the Rhetoric of Empire* (Berkeley, 1991).

[12] Atkins and Dodaro, *Political Writings*, 61–99.

at Milan did not show a provincial reaching the centre of empire through sheer ability; it had more to do with the limited field that year and with the manoeuvres of Symmachus as prefect of Rome. In any event Milan, as Augustine soon realized, was a backwater. He did not become a protégé of Ambrose; he was not offered a position on the African estates that belonged to the Milan diocese; he did not even take letters of commendation back to Africa. Hippo was a large but not a major diocese, and Augustine's church was in the minority there. His influence did not reach further than Carthage. Beyond Africa, Paulinus of Nola, who was kind to everyone, was one of the few who had read or even heard of Augustine, and most of those few disagreed with him. It is Augustine's books that give the impression of the towering figure.[13]

We know now that we do not know Augustine, we know Augustine's books. A new biography insists that we remember how carefully Augustine constructed himself as a publication record, not as a "living, breathing, quarrelling cleric."[14] Possidius, Augustine's apparently simple friend, added a *Life of Augustine* to deploy the publication record against local opposition, constructing Augustine as an authoritative theologian who never changed his mind or wrote something he later regretted.[15] There are many *retractationes* in the revised edition of the most influential modern biography, and one of the most endearing concerns Augustine the "old bishop," the "severe and aggressive figure of authority" who sent a *frisson* through readers of the 1967 version.[16] Brown reflects: "Since then I have come to know bishops. Some can be saintly; many are really quite nice; and most are ineffective."[17]

Even so, Augustine had some power and he often had to deploy it because otherwise people would be in danger, from militant Donatists or from barbarians or from slave-traders, from physical violence or from soul-destroying doctrine. His reflections on the use of power come from this experience.[18] He did not develop political theories. Over the centuries, many readers of *City of God* have tried to derive theories about the power of the church in relation to the state, but all of them rest on selective reading and system-building.[19] Augustine said that the city of God is the community of all those, angels and humans in every time and

---

13 N. McLynn, "Augustine's Roman Empire," in M. Vessey, K. Pollmann, and A. Fitzgerald (eds.), *History, Apocalypse and the Secular Imagination: New Essays on Augustine's City of God* (Bowling Green, OH, 1999) 29–44; O'Donnell, *Augustine*.

14 O'Donnell, *Augustine*, 319.

15 E.T. Hermanowicz, *Possidius of Calama: A Study of the North African Episcopate in the Age of Augustine* (Oxford, 2008).

16 P. Brown, *Augustine of Hippo: A Biography*, rev. ed. (London, 2000) 197.

17 Brown, *Augustine*, 492.

18 Atkins and Dodaro, *Political Writings*, xi–xii.

19 H.A. Deane, *The Political and Social Ideas of St. Augustine* (New York, 1963); E. TeSelle, *Living in Two Cities: Augustinian Trajectories in Political Thought* (Scranton, PA, 1998).

place, who want what God wants; the city of this world is the community of all those, angels and humans in every time and place, who want what they want (*Civ. Dei* 14.28). Citizenship is determined by love. It follows that the city of God is not coextensive with the institutional church and that the city of this world is not coextensive with the current organization of secular power. In this life, the two cities are intermixed, and we do not know who belongs to which: citizens of God's city may hold office in the state and citizens of the earthly city may be members of the church (1.36). If that is the case, spiritual power cannot be called in to judge and validate secular power.[20]

Augustine did not develop political theories, but he did think about the problems of power-relationships between human beings and about the power of religion to transform or distort human lives. His own power was the power of religion in that it depended on his status in the Christian religion, at a time when the ruling power gave formal recognition to that status and when many individuals were prepared to declare themselves Christian. Many historians think that there is no difference between spiritual and temporal power; that religion is one more way of exercising power, either cynically or in self-deception; and that it is alarmingly successful in controlling people, uniting them against other groups, and motivating them to kill and die in the belief that God will reward them. Too many recent events have shown that religion still does this, or rather that people still do it "in the name of religion."[21]

Augustine also thought that religion can be a way of exercising power and of motivating people to kill and die. He thought this about the statesmen who used Roman religion to control their people, and about the Roman pursuit of glory and empire. Romans, he said, believed that glory came from victory and that their empire was given by the gods, but there was a high cost in bloodshed, whether the blood was Roman or foreign. Great men are like gladiators who fight and win, and their amphitheatre is a world filled with corpses (3.14); empire depends on aggression, either that of the empire-builder or that of the opponent whose aggression is resisted (4.16). But Augustine distinguished false religion, which is dangerous because it worships dangerous beings, from true religion, which worships the true God. In *City of God*, he argued that the power of religion varies with what the religion does, and what it does varies with what it worships. Book ten asks how the angels want us to "maintain *religio* and *pietas*": the answer is that, unlike the harmful demons who want worship for themselves, the angels want us to worship God. But Augustine did not have a distinctive word for this worship. He used *religio* both for the true religion, that is the Christian religion, and for the false religion of his pagan opponents. When he meant the Christian religion, he always added "our" or "true" or "Christian" to the noun *religio*, because neither Latin nor Greek had a word that specifies the worship of the true God. He

---

[20] R.W. Dyson, *The Pilgrim City: Social and Political Ideas in the Writings of St. Augustine of Hippo* (Woodbridge, 2001); Sykes, *Power*, 37–8.

[21] K. Ward, *Is Religion Dangerous?* (Oxford, 2006).

explained (10.1) that all the possible words had too wide a range of meaning. The Greek Scriptures, which he regarded as authoritative (18.42), used *douleia* for service to people and *latreia* for service to God. But if *latreia* is translated by Latin *cultus*, that word applies also to respect for people, living or dead, and even to agriculture. *Religio* appears to mean specifically the *cultus* of God and is therefore used to translate Greek *threskeia*, but *religio* also extends to human obligations, as does *pietas*, which is used to translate Greek *eusebeia*; indeed, both *pietas* and *eusebeia* are used of charitable actions. That, Augustine suggested, is why the Scriptures sometimes use *theosebeia*, "god reverence," instead of *eusebeia*, "good reverence." But Latin does not have a word for either and in order to be clear it must use *cultus Dei*.

This is one of the occasions in *City of God* on which Augustine drew on his earlier career as a *grammaticus*, a teacher of literature, to explain why the text used one word rather than another. According to Augustine's argument, unless religion is the worship of the true God and human obligations spring from that worship, the power of religion is undeniable but also damaging. False religion is indeed "service," but in the sense of "servitude," *douleia*: it is enslavement to demonic powers who demand worship for themselves and get it by the use of fear and deception. These powers deluded or terrified the statesmen who devised Roman religion. King Numa, who was credited with establishing the majority of Roman cults, wrote an explanation of their underlying causes which he was too frightened either to reveal or to destroy. So he ordered the book buried with him, and when it was rediscovered, the Senate ordered it burned (7.34). The key question about Roman religion is who or what receives service and reverence from this system of myths and images and rituals.

In many cases, Augustine argued, false religion honours dead rulers whom the people believed to be gods. He encountered this "Euhemerist" theory of religion both in Cicero (*Nat.deor.* 1.119) and in Varro whom he took as the leading authority on Roman religion. He did not discuss Euhemerus in detail, on the grounds that his predecessors had done so (6.7), but there are many examples of deified rulers in *City of God* 18.[22] Here Augustine, with acknowledgement to Varro (18.2), provided a rapid survey of world history in relation to biblical history. Where biblical history showed God's people protected and liberated and sometimes deservedly punished by the true God, world history showed the people of Sicyon and Argos and Egypt and Latium offering cult and sacrifice to benefactors who had died or to even less plausible deities. The power of this religion depends on belief in these gods, and what it does is to make people carry out pointless rituals or, more usefully, follow examples of outstanding achievement. Earlier in *City of God* Augustine cited Varro's remark that it is useful to cities if brave men believe they are descended

[22] The predecessors included Lactantius (*Div.inst.* 1.11.33), but Augustine did not acknowledge his debt to Lactantius: see further P. Garnsey, "Lactantius and Augustine," in A. Bowman, H. Cotton, M. Goodman, and S. Price (eds.), *Representations of Empire: Rome and the Mediterranean World* (Oxford, 2002) 153–79.

from gods, even though they are not, and commented: "You see what scope it offers for falsehood? We may conclude that many sacred, supposedly religious, claims could have been invented, where lies are thought to benefit citizens, even on the subject of the gods" (3.4).

In most cases, Augustine concluded, false religion honours not dead mortals but demons, that is, supernatural beings who do not intend good, but whom the true God, for inscrutable reasons, permits to have some power, especially over those who deserve it (7.35). The power of the demons is limited in time and extent, especially in the case of the demons who are Roman gods, the "little tiny gods with their little tiny tasks" (7.2) recorded by Varro. Augustine happily reported examples of Varro's extreme polytheism. It takes three gods to look after a door and eight to bring a corn-ear to fruition (4.8). On the wedding-night (6.9) the bedroom is full of them, and they leave nothing for the bridegroom to do himself. These gods of Rome, according to Augustine, want people to believe that the Roman empire is the greatest ever demonstration of the power of religion: Rome worships her gods and the gods make the empire grow and prosper. But the gods cannot even decide who is responsible for what or control their "little tiny tasks." Bearded Fortune cannot make beards grow (6.1). If Augustine's opponents argue that all these gods are aspects of Jupiter, they involve their greatest god with the most squalid and trivial aspects of existence (4.12–13).

The gods of Rome, according to Augustine, want worship for themselves, and that is how Christians recognize them as the fallen angels who do not want to do the will of God and want to draw others into their own wretchedness (7.33; 11.1). God has permitted them some power, and they use it to get what they want. They want worship incorporating sex and violence in rituals such as those performed by the Galli who lacerate and even castrate themselves (6.10), and in stage shows enacting sexy and violent stories about the gods; they do not care whether the stories are true or false. Varro assigned stage shows to the *Res Divinae* ("Divine Matters") section of his *Roman Antiquities*, not by his own judgement but because that is where he found them, for stage shows were part of the practice of religion (4.1; 4.26). Varro himself knew better, for he said that "poetic theology" is fictitious and misleading (6.5). By "poets" Varro—like Aristotle—meant dramatists, so by "poetic theology" he meant stories about the gods presented by dramatists.[23] But, Augustine argued, Varro could not plausibly distinguish his category of poetic theology from his category of civic theology, that is, the myths and rituals offered by the city. Civic theology used the same representations of the gods as poetic theology did; moreover, it was the city that offered stage shows to the gods (6.7).

This religion, according to Augustine, has the power to entrap and corrupt those who practise it. Civic ritual did not teach people about the gods, so the people were left to learn from stage shows, which offered them examples of gods behaving

[23] T.P. Wiseman, *Roman Drama and Roman History* (Exeter, 1998) 18–19.

badly.[24] The stage shows were sexually explicit and morally corrupting; the gods enjoyed this and it kept their worshippers corrupt. Varro openly disapproved of poetic theology but was too afraid of the demons, or of the people, to say openly what he could only hint about the gods of Rome (6.2). He did not have the truth that could make him free, so he colluded with other statesmen in the deception of the Roman people (6.6; 4.27). The power of Roman religion does not expand and sustain Rome's empire, it deludes and enslaves Rome's people with the collaboration of Rome's leaders. "A fine religion! The weak take refuge there in hope of liberation, and when they seek the truth that shall make them free, it is thought expedient for them to be deceived" (4.27).

True religion, by contrast, liberates people from deception and compulsion and empowers them to serve the true God. For Augustine, that is the overwhelming power of religion. Varro betrayed in his *Antiquities* the awful truth he was too afraid to speak, that Roman religion was a human construct. He said he wrote the "Human Matters" section before the "Divine Matters" section, just as the painter comes before the painting and the builder before the building (6.4). But true religion is not a human construct, it is divine revelation. Varro rejected poetic theology and thereby also invalidated the images and rituals of Roman civic theology. But Christians have divinely inspired scriptures, which reveal both the truth about God and the appropriate ways of worshipping God (7.32). Christians do not have to separate belief from practice or teach educated Christians to reject the beliefs of uneducated Christians.

So far, so good, but Augustine was always conscious of living in a fallen world, where the liberating power of true religion is not always evident. Ignorance and weakness obstruct our efforts to do God's will. Our bodies do not respond to rational control. God provided natural hierarchy and cooperation, but now there is dominance and subjection. Power can be used for good, to protect and provide for the weak, but domination is the desire to be *dominus*, to be the master of slaves who must obey orders, as distinct from the father of the household who serves those he commands (19.14; 19.16). At school Augustine read Sallust, who identified *libido dominandi*, the lust for domination, as a driving force in the acquisition of empire (Sall. *Cat.* 2.2). He extended Sallust's concept beyond politics, arguing that *libido dominandi* is inherent in fallen human nature and distorts households as well as political communities. Everyone naturally wants peace, but in a fallen world it is Roman peace—that is, pacification, in which subjects will follow orders without rebelling. Wars are fought to achieve such peace. Even political rebels want that kind of peace among their associates and their families. The extreme case is Virgil's solitary monster Cacus, who has no one under his orders but still wants to be at peace with his own body (19.12). But what power can achieve peace? Some people use physical force, *vis*; some learn the power of persuasion to subdue or

24 See further G. Clark, "Augustine's Varro, and Pagan Monotheism," in S. Mitchell and P. Van Nuffelen (eds.), *Monotheism between Pagans and Christians in Late Antiquity* (Leuven, forthcoming).

redirect the force of others. Earthly peace should be an "ordered concord in giving and obeying orders" both in household and in city (19.14; 19.17), and to maintain that concord we must have recognized power-structures, *ordo*, and authorized power, *ordinata potestas*.

Now *ordo* is in itself a good thing, a gift of God who orders the universe. According to the gospel of Luke (4:5–6), the devil claimed to be the source of political power. "He showed [Jesus] all the kingdoms of the earth in a moment of time, and said 'I will give you this universal power and the glory of the kingdoms, for they are handed over to me, and I give them to whom I choose.'" But it is never wise to believe the devil. Augustine thought that all rulers, even the bad ones, have their power with God's permission and for God's hidden purposes (4.33; 5.21). He did not think that power is in itself demonic or that pride results from something wrong in the one who loves power or in power itself; rather, the fault lies in the soul that perversely loves its own power (12.8). People who have power think about it differently from those who do not; belief that there is something inherently wrong with power is usually found in people who have no power.[25] Christians are confronted by Christ's renunciation of power, his silence at his trial, and his acceptance of suffering and death. But they are also confronted by Christ's use of power. One of Augustine's own *retractationes* (1.13.6) corrects his assertion in *True Religion* (16.31) that "Christ did nothing by force [*vis*], but everything by persuasion and advice." Christ, he noted, used a *flagellum*, a scourge, to drive the money-changers out of the Temple, and he drove out unclean spirits "not by the persuasion of speech but by the force of power (*vi potestatis*)." He acknowledged that power, even in the form of force, can be used to maintain or restore peace and to rescue people from physical or spiritual danger.[26] Good men do not seek to rule far and wide, but when they do, it is a blessing for their subjects (*Civ.Dei* 4.15; 5.19). The problem with power, including authorized power, is that all human beings are hampered by ignorance and weakness. We do not know enough about ourselves and our motives, and we know still less about other people and the effects of our actions on them. A Roman governor ordering interrogation under torture, or physical punishment of a convicted person, does not know whether the accused is really guilty or what level of punishment will change his behaviour; the result may be the death by torture of an innocent human being.[27] A bishop preaching to his congregation or writing a treatise does not know whether his message has been received and understood, or whether the audience that shouts "Bravo! Bravo! (*euge, euge*)" is concerned with rhetoric rather than content (*Conf.* 10.36.59). Augustine's experience as a teacher was that he did not in fact teach

---

25 Sykes, *Power*, viii–ix.

26 G. Clark, "Rod, Line and Net: Augustine on the Limits of Diversity," in K. Cooper and J. Gregory (eds.), *Discipline and Diversity*, special issue *Studies in Church History* 43 (Woodbridge, 2007) 80–99.

27 G. Clark, "Desires of the Hangman: Augustine on Legitimized Violence," in Drake, *Violence*, 137–46.

his students: he said things, and sometimes they recognized that what he had said was something they knew (*De mag.* 46). By analogy, if his audience was indeed transformed by the word of God, it was not Augustine's discourse that empowered them.

The holders of power do not know the effects of their actions, nor can they be sure of their own motives:

> It is necessary for us, because of responsibilities in human society, to be loved and feared by people. So the enemy of our true happiness attacks, baiting his traps with "Bravo, bravo!" … so that we will enjoy being loved and feared, not for your sake, but in your place. (*Conf.* 10.36.59)

This is the third of the three great temptations that Augustine saw at work in human life: "lust of the flesh, and lust of the eyes, and pride of life" (1 John 2:16). He interpreted the first two as desire for physical or for intellectual satisfaction, for having things or knowing things, and he saw the third as an even greater challenge. To paraphrase what he said in *Confessions* (10.37.60): I can find out how dependent I am on material goods by getting rid of them and seeing how much I mind, but I cannot find out how dependent I am on approval ratings without changing my behaviour so that I do not get any, and this would not be a good idea, especially for someone who has some power. Augustine was confident that true religion, worship of the true God, will help us to act rightly, but he thought that even true religion is no guarantee that we will do so, or that we will achieve our aim. In *City of God* he argued that there are reasons why good rulers may be defeated and bad ones may be victorious. We do not know the hidden purposes of God, but we can learn that a "happy" ruler is a just and merciful ruler who acts in the love of God, not a ruler who has a long and triumphant reign (5.17, 24–25). Good rulers are beneficial for their subjects, but it does not greatly matter who has *imperium*, which is the power to give orders and have them obeyed. It does not greatly matter whether a people rules others or is ruled by others, provided that the ruling power does not obstruct the true religion; and even if it does, there are splendid examples of dying for the sake of true religion, and it does not greatly matter how people die. Even so, people who have power must use it as best they can, ignorant and weak though they are, for the sake of others. To be *innocens*, harmless, it is not enough to refrain from doing harm (19.16). The judge cries out to Heaven: "Deliver me from my necessities!" (19.6), but the necessities remain. The job still has to be done, or imperfect human peace and order becomes even more imperfect.

Historians too might say that the job still has to be done. Augustine alerted us to the uncertain motives of human action and the limitations of human power, but how can we integrate these questions about the power of religion in human lives into our study of events and ways of thinking? They are like so many of the philosophical problems raised by reflection on history, for example that there is no such thing as an event: we choose narratives to select events from the flow, and our chosen metaphors shape our understanding.[28] All of this is true, but what can be done, after acknowledging the problem, but to try to stay aware and to go on writing, or alternatively to stop writing history? We do not know whether people deluded themselves about what they did or whether and how God was at work in and through them, but most historians now would argue that these questions are not part of their job, and that supernatural explanations are not part of history.

Augustine said that he was not writing history in *City of God,* because if he did, he would be nothing other than a historian (3.18). He did not mean to disparage history, as if he had written "nothing more than a historian." Rather, he was aware that the research and writing of history was a full-time task he could not combine with his other duties, as secular historians disagree on so much (18.40). It is often noted that he made very few references to the history of his own times, or indeed to any history after the end of the New Testament. The main reason for this is that he engaged with writers his opponents recognized as authorities, in order to show that their own *auctores* contradicted their claim that Rome had suffered since Christian neglect offended Rome's gods (4.1). These *auctores* were all classical authors from the time before Christ: Terence, Sallust, Cicero, and Virgil from the school curriculum, and Varro as the authority on religion cited by schoolteachers who expounded these texts. But there is another reason. Augustine believed that the prophecies recorded in the Old Testament, both verbal prophecy and prophetic event, had been fulfilled in the life of Christ. When the scriptural narrative ended, how could he select the continuing strand of *sacra historia*, the sacred history of God's dealings with humanity?[29] The city of God and the city of the world are intermixed, not neatly separated like the *canones* of Eusebius. We do not know who belongs to which city, and membership of one or the other city is much more important than who gives or takes orders within transient social and political structures. If Augustine was right, history in the sense of *res gestae*, things that have been done, is interesting only when it can be used to demonstrate the justice and mercy of the true God or the folly of claiming that Roman gods extended and maintained Rome's empire. But even then we do not know how history exemplifies the power of true or false religion over human beings.

As Augustine insisted, the heart is known only to God. We do not know the true motives of people who have power or the effects of their actions on the relationships of other human beings with God. We do need to consider how things get done in this imperfect world and how they were done by people who had an empire to run and a diocese to manage. There were people to be protected, certainly by the preaching of true doctrine but also by persuading the local governor, using contacts, checking on the state of the law, and recognizing when it was "time to sail" and send a delegation from Africa to the imperial court. The power of the true God is at work in everything and we can do nothing without it, but we cannot know where and how it works. The power of religion is evident in the power of

28 N. Morley, *Writing Ancient History* (London, 1999).

29 On history and prophecy, see Markus, *Saeculum*, 1–21.

religious leaders to muster support and influence politics, to exclude others from religious community, and to persuade people to change their lives; in the writing of history, it is a category of human power. Augustine's life and writings act as a reminder of the power of true religion.

Chapter 15
"Our own most severe judges": The Power of Penance in the Eusebius Gallicanus Sermons

Lisa Bailey
University of Auckland

Late antique Christians generally agreed that penance was powerful. They did not always agree, however, on who had control over that power: the clergy, the laity or God alone. The sermons of the Eusebius Gallicanus collection offer a fresh perspective on the difficulties pastors faced when exhorting their congregants to do penance and reveal the variety of ways in which they responded to the challenge.

Sin posed a problem. It threatened the coherence and identity of the Christian community, yet sinners could not simply all be excommunicated—there would quickly be no community left from which to exclude them. This became a more obvious issue over time. By the fifth and sixth centuries most Christians were baptized as infants. Whereas Constantine and many of his contemporaries had delayed baptism for fear of subsequent sin, that option was no longer available to those born into the faith. The church had to find a way to allow sinners to be, and stay, within the church.[1]

Augustine of Hippo was one of the most influential figures advocating an "incorporative" vision of the church.[2] Faced with Donatists who desired a church without blemish, Augustine argued that this was impossible—that sin was an inevitable part of the human condition. Anyone who lived even a moment after

---

[1] On this change see P. Brown, "Pelagius and his Supporters: Aims and Environment," *JThS* n.s. 19 (1968) 93–114 = Idem, *Religion and Society in the Age of Saint Augustine* (London, 1972) 199–207; A. Fitzgerald, *Conversion through Penance in the Italian Church of the Fourth and Fifth Centuries: New Approaches to the Experience of Conversion from Sin* (Lewiston, PA, 1988); G. Strousma, "From Repentence to Penance in Early Christianity: Tertullian's *De paenitentia* in Context," in J. Assmann and G. Strousma (eds.), *Transformations of the Inner Self in Ancient Religions* (Leiden, 1999) 167–78; E. Rebillard, *In hora mortis: évolution de la pastorale chrétienne de la mort aux IVe et Ve siècles dans l'Occident latin* (Rome, 1994) 129–67.

[2] P. Brown, *Augustine of Hippo: A Biography* (London, 1967) 212–25.

baptism was tainted by it.[3] But to Augustine's way of thinking, the inevitability of sin did not diminish its force. Sins might only be small but, as he put it, enough drops of water can cause a flood and enough grains of sand can form a landslide.[4] Small, inevitable daily sins were still a problem. They infected the soul of the Christian and the moral integrity of the community. Being cleansed of them required constant vigilance. Public penitential humiliation, however, was reserved for serious sins and prominent sinners.[5] To provide ablution for everyday sins, pastors instead developed an everyday penance—one that all Christians, they argued, could and should perform.

Scholars have recently made this "everyday penance" central to revised views of the remission of sins in Late Antiquity.[6] Augustine's ideas have been considered to mark a definitive break with early Christian treatments of sin, and their broad influence has been noted and traced.[7] Augustine does not, however, provide a complete picture. The sermons in the Eusebius Gallicanus collection reveal a different approach to that taken by the bishop of Hippo. The pastoral application of penance in these sermons was neither groundbreaking nor revolutionary, but it reveals some of the difficulties pastors faced in implementing Augustine's ideas. The sermons therefore provide an illustrative counterpoint to Augustine's picture of the power dynamics in Christian communities.

The Eusebius Gallicanus is a collection of 76 sermons, attributed in some manuscripts to a mysterious Eusebius but actually the work of a number of different fifth-century Gallic preachers.[8] Faustus of Riez is the only one of these contributors who can be identified with certainty—the others remain anonymous, and authorship issues are complicated by the selective plagiarism of the works of earlier preachers. The 76 sermons were compiled in the sixth century and edited and rewritten to a degree not now recoverable. They appear to have been

---

3 Aug. *Serm.* 9.17–19, 58.10, 181; Brown, "Pelagius," 199–201; Rebillard, *In hora mortis*, 151–7.

4 Aug. *Serm.* 9.17, 56.12, 179A.6.

5 M. de Jong, "Transformations of Penance," in F. Theuws and J. Nelson (eds.), *Rituals of Power from Late Antiquity to the Early Middle Ages* (Leiden, 2000) 185–224 at 190.

6 See, e.g., de Jong, "Transformations"; R. Meens, "The Frequency and Nature of Early Medieval Penance," in P. Biller and A.J. Minnis (eds.), *Handling Sin: Confession in the Middle Ages* (Woodbridge, 1998) 35–61; K. Uhalde, *Expectations of Justice in the Age of Augustine* (Philadelphia, 2007) 105–34.

7 See, e.g., P. Brown, "The Decline of the Empire of God: Amnesty, Penance and the Afterlife from Late Antiquity to the Middle Ages," in C.W. Bynum and O. Freedman (eds.), *Last Things: Death and the Apocalypse in the Middle Ages* (Philadelphia, 2000) 41–59; Rebillard, *In hora mortis*; R.H. Weaver, *Divine Grace and Human Agency: A Study of the Semi-Pelagian Controversy* (Macon, GA, 1996).

8 For a fuller account of the authorship issues and history of the collection, see L. Bailey, "Building Urban Christian Communities: Sermons on Local Saints in the Eusebius Gallicanus Collection," *EME* 12 (2003) 1–24 at 3–6.

put together as a "preaching guide," and the collection includes sermons for all the major feasts and standard homiletic topics, as well as a number of "sample" introductions preachers might use when addressing different audiences. Clergy who lacked rhetorical training or the skills of composition could use it to produce homilies in good style, and the church could be sure of their doctrinal orthodoxy.

The collection was a success. It was widely dispersed and extensively plagiarized. There are 447 surviving manuscripts that contain sermons from the collection. The Eusebius Gallicanus, in other words, was popular, influential, and represented a common style of preaching. It reveals how clergy who were not great rhetors or saintly theologians, and who needed someone else to write sermons for them, might have approached penance. They are neither original nor brilliant, but they show the late antique Gallic clergy "at work" trying to create a Christian community. They are texts that are fascinating because they are unremarkable.

At the heart of the Eusebius Gallicanus approach to penance is an emphasis upon the role of the laity in expiating their own sin. If you accuse yourselves, the author of Eusebian sermon 64 informs his congregants, "justice is born out of sins ... here, therefore, we should condemn our faults and offenses through daily emendation and contrition; we should be our own most severe judges and we should anticipate the judgment of the future examination through full satisfaction. Here, daily tears and daily weeping should blot out what would be consumed by the eternal fire."[9] The preacher of Eusebian sermon 26 emphasizes how the Ninevites averted God's punishment through their acts of penance. He imagines God speaking thus to the sinner: "What you admit is grave in yourself, I will kindly forgive; what you sadly accuse yourself of, I will gladly absolve; what you recall in public, I will disregard in eternity. And because you have anticipated my sentence through your penance, I will resheath my sword."[10] The collection's sermons are filled with judicial imagery, applied to ordinary Christians for themselves and by themselves. The author of sermon 26 goes on to instruct that he who would "be pleasing to God" should be "his own witness, accuser, and judge, under the judgment of a private examination."[11] Two sermons in the Eusebian collection, in variations on the same passage, urge members of their community to "condemn

9 *Eus.Gall.* 64.11, 13 (*CCSL* 101A.734–5): *Accusanti se, iustitia nata est de peccatis... Hic ergo culpas offensasque nostras quotidiana emendatione et contritione damnemus; ipsi in nobis seuerissimi iudices simus, et plena satisfactione futuri examinis sententiam praecurramus. Hic deleat quotidianus gemitus et quotidianus fletus, quidquid concrematurus erat ignis aeternus.* All subsequent Latin quotes from the Eusebius Gallicanus come from *CCSL* 101–101A.

10 *Eus.Gall.* 26.5: *Quod tu in te seuerus agnoscis, ego propitius ignoscam... quod tu recordaris in publicum, ego obliuiscar in aeternum. Et quia per paenitentiam tuam praeuenisti sententiam meam: recondam gladium meum.*

11 *Eus.Gall.* 26.5. The passage in full reads: *Qui placiturus est deo: ipse sibi displicet; ipse sibi quodammodo, sub priuatae cognitionis sententia, et testis et accusator et iudex est.*

ourselves" and "accuse ourselves daily to our judge."[12] The author of sermon 64 approvingly offers the example of the publican who was his own accuser and judge and who beat his breast to punish himself.[13] The sinner is exhorted to pre-empt the role of God by presiding over his own personal "last judgment" in this life. Other Eusebian preachers used metaphors of introspection and medical examination to convey the same idea. We must inspect ourselves inwardly, the preacher of sermon 14 urges and gauge our own deficiencies.[14] We should do within ourselves, the author of sermon 45 tells his audience, what doctors do externally.[15] The role of specialist was thereby absorbed by the laity. The intervention of pastors was cut out of the expiatory process almost entirely.

The contrast with Augustine of Hippo brings out the distinctive flavour of this approach. In the sermons of Augustine, the image of the doctor was used of the pastor or of God, rather than of the sinner.[16] Augustine did use judicial imagery in his preaching. In sermon 20, for example, he tells his congregants to "let your sin have you as its judge, not as its defending counsel."[17] He did not come close, however, to matching the enthusiasm of the Eusebian preachers for the image. In his model of pastoral care, power remained in the hands of God or in the hands of the pastor as his mediator. Self-judgment or self-healing were not presented as options.

There is a theological component to this difference. Augustine believed that salvation was brought about by unmerited grace from God rather than by human action. According to this logic, penance could not expiate sin. He exhorted his congregants to penance not in order to perform reparation, but merely to show awareness of their own sinfulness and to demonstrate their hope for redemption. Augustine recommended to his congregants what Straw has described as "active passivity": actively hoping to receive grace, but passively accepting what comes.[18] The role of lay penitential action in such a schema was severely circumscribed. The central act Augustine therefore urged upon his congregants was prayer—in particular, the recitation of the *pater noster* and its plea for forgiveness. "You are cleansed every day from light and minor sins through your prayers, if you say

---

12 See *Eus.Gall.* 4.6 and 60.8.

13 *Eus.Gall.* 64.10.

14 *Eus.Gall.* 14.7.

15 *Eus.Gall.* 45.2–3. See also Caes.Arel. *Serm.* 189.2, 197.2.

16 Aug. *Serm.* 2.3, 15A.8, 16B.1, 20.1, 87.13, 97A.1, 113A.13, 126.4, 174.6, 175.2, 176.4.

17 Aug. *Serm.* 20.2 (*PL* 38.139): *Peccatum tuum judicem te habeat, non patronum.* Trans. E. Hill, *The Works of Saint Augustine: A Translation for the Twenty-First Century* (Hyde Park, NY, 1990–) 3.2.16. For other instances where Augustine employed judicial imagery, see *Serm.* 9.2, 13.1 and 49.5, although these cases do not relate to penance and expiation.

18 C. Straw, "Augustine as Pastoral Theologian: The Exegesis of the Parables of the Field and Threshing Floor," *AugStud* 14 (1983) 129–51 at 147.

from the heart, if you say truthfully, if you say in faith, 'Forgive us our debts, as we too forgive our debtors.'"[19] For Augustine this prayer, representative as much of a mental state as of an actual action, is the key to the penitential lifestyle. He gave it far more attention than any of the other "traditional" expiatory acts such as fasting, almsgiving or lamentation.

Like some other Gallic clergy, however, the Eusebius Gallicanus preachers appear to have found Augustine's approach unsatisfactory in pastoral terms. They did not openly debate or disagree with him. They simply took a different approach. Their exhortations to expiation place far more emphasis on human action. They instructed their audience to *earn* their salvation. Anyone who dies immediately after receiving baptism, the preacher of sermon 29 tells his audience, will go to the last judgment with unstained innocence. All others require continued effort to ensure their victory. God banishes the blemishes on our hearts through baptism, the preacher of sermon 20 notes, "but it is necessary that we exert ourselves, lest we should pollute again that which he purified, lest we should tear open the wounds which he healed, lest he should have to boil out of us again in the fires of hell that which he once washed away in the waters of baptism."[20] Prayer is not the central penitential act in such an approach and the *pater noster* scarcely features. It is action and effort that take centre stage in the Eusebian exhortations to expiation.

This divergence from the approach of Augustine must be set against a background of debate in Gaul over some of his views. The existence of a divisive "semi-Pelagian controversy" has been convincingly downplayed by recent scholarship.[21] It remains clear, however, that some of Augustine's ideas made people uncomfortable, and that this discomfort was most evident in fifth-century Gaul. A number of Gallic monastics and pastors felt uneasy about Augustine's insistence that unmerited grace alone ensures salvation and that human beings have no control over their own eternal fate.[22] The corollary of this—that forgiveness of sin is always available and does not depend on meritorious action—also was controversial. The life-long recalcitrant sinner who begs for penance on his

---

19 Aug. *Serm.* 179A.6: *Et quodammodo in orationibus vestris a cottidianis levibus minoribusque peccatis cottidie purgamini, si ex animo dixeritis, si veraciter dixeritis, si fideliter dixeritis: "Dimitte nobis debita nostra, sicut et nos dimittimus debitoribus nostris* (Matt. 6:12)." (*Miscellanea Agostiniana* 1.679). Trans. Hill, *Works*, 3.5.311.

20 *Eus.Gall.* 20.4: *Sed opus est ut ita elaboremus: ne, quod ille abluit, nos iterum polluamus; ne rescindamus uulnera quae ille sanauit; ne, quod semel in nobis diluit unda baptismi, rursum excoquere necesse habeat ignis inferni.*

21 See Weaver, *Divine Grace*; C. Tibiletti, "Rassegna di studi e testi sui 'semipelagiani'," *Augustinianum* 25 (1985) 507–22; T.A. Smith, *De gratia: Faustus of Riez's Treatise on Grace and its Place in the History of Theology* (Notre Dame, 1990).

22 On the mixed reception of Augustine in Gaul, see R.W. Mathisen, "For Specialists Only: The Reception of Augustine and his Teachings in Fifth-Century Gaul," in J.T. Lienhard, E.C. Muller, and R.J. Teske (eds.), *Augustine: Presbyter Factus Sum* (New York, 1993) 29–41.

death-bed, Augustine argued, should be granted it. Gallic bishops, Faustus of Riez among them, expressed doubt about the efficacy of such last-minute repentance.[23] These issues go some way to explain the difference in approach. Theological divergence, however, was only one factor at work.

More important was the practical position in which clergy found themselves. Augustine was an unusual figure. He built up, over his lifetime, a network of powerful supporters and a reservoir of moral authority. Even he, however, struggled at times to assert his pastoral power.[24] Most clergy had far less behind them when they spoke. When they emphasized the role of the laity as their own judges, therefore, the Eusebius Gallicanus preachers shifted a pastoral burden from their own shoulders. "Even when the pastor is absent," the author of sermon sixty-three informs his congregation, "fear of the future judgment should be there, a very sharp anxiety about the eternal necessities should be there, and even if he is absent, who can urge you on to fulfilling the act of daily redemption, man, who stands alone before the tribunal of God with his deeds, should urge himself on."[25] Congregants were instructed to internalize judgment and circumscribe their own lives before clerical intervention was even necessary. This is not to say that the clergy did not have power in such a model of expiation. They set the parameters, defined the grounds and exerted considerable pressure. All of this power, however, was indirect. It did not rest upon the charisma of the pastor, nor did it emphasize his role as a mediator. It was difficult to challenge and it suited the kinds of preachers who relied upon pre-prepared sermon texts to carry them through the liturgical year.

How this difference played out in practice becomes clear through further comparison of the pastoral directions of Augustine and the Eusebius Gallicanus preachers. Because he argued that sin is inevitable and that human beings are entirely dependent upon the unmerited mercy of God to achieve salvation, Augustine focused his pastoral energies on combating despair. For him, penance is a sign that forgiveness is always possible. So long as the sinner lives, no matter

---

[23] Gallic bishops were rebuked by Pope Innocent in 405 (*Ep.* 6.2) and by Pope Celestine in 428 (*Ep.* 4.2) because they refused to grant penance to the dying on the grounds that redemption of their sins had not yet been, and could not be, properly earned. In *Ep.* 5, Faustus claimed that death-bed penance would not deceive God if sinners had not made genuine efforts in life to rid themselves of sin. See C. Vogel, *La discipline pénitentielle en Gaule des origines à la fin du VIIe siècle* (Paris, 1952) 49–51; D.J. Nodes, "*De subitanea paenitentia* in the Letters of Faustus of Riez and Avitus of Vienne," *RecTh* 55 (1988) 30–40; and G. Weigel, *Faustus of Riez: An Historical Introduction* (Philadelphia, 1938) 89–90.

[24] Witness, for example, his conflicts with the congregation as evidenced in Aug. *Serm. Dolbeau* 2. On this theme see Gillian Clark's essay in this volume (Chapter 14).

[25] *Eus.Gall.* 63.6: *Itaque, etiam quando pastor absentat: praesens sit futuri iudicii timor, praesens sit mordacissima aeternarum necessitatum sollicitudo; atque, etiamsi deest qui perurgere possit ad implenda quotidianae redemptionis officia, perurgeat se homo ipse qui solus stabit ante tribunal dei cum actibus suis.*

how wicked their crimes, God can grant absolution. No one should assume that damnation is certain and indulge in sin thinking that all is lost anyway. The wages of the worker are not dependent on how long he works.[26]

Augustine recognized the danger of complacency. He knew that some Christians might interpret his reassurances as a license to sin and delay penance deliberately until death was near.[27] In sermon 20, he struggles to combat such thinking. "Now God has promised to pardon all who turn away from their sins," he pictures the sinner thinking to himself, "the very day they are converted he will forget all their iniquities. So I will do whatever I want, and whenever I want to I will have a conversion, and what I have done will be blotted out." The pastor does not deny that the claims of the sinner are true. All Augustine can respond with is a threat that time may run out. "No-one has promised you that you are going to be alive tomorrow."[28] Nonetheless, Augustine insists that even a deliberately delayed penance or confession may be sufficient to ensure the expiation of sin.[29] Despair is a more pressing pastoral threat to the bishop of Hippo than excessive confidence.

The Eusebius Gallicanus preachers, by contrast, were far more worried about combating security. We need to beware, warns the author of sermon 33, "lest either pernicious relaxation should trip us up on the left, or ruinous pride on the right."[30] Repentance should happen now, the preachers repeatedly urge, while there is still time and in case of sudden death. Penance will not be possible in the afterlife, and the sinner will regret not having taken the opportunity easily within his grasp. "And therefore, dearly beloved, let us convert ourselves to the better while the remedies are still within our power."[31] Whatever we do not redeem here, deceived by a fatal security, the preacher of sermon 27 insists, we will carry with us into the presence of the saints and of the judge.[32] "And thus, through present mortification, the sentence of future death is anticipated."[33] In the time

---

26 For these arguments, see Aug. *Serm. Dolbeau* 14.6, *Serm.* 87.4–9, 335M.5. He is evoking Matthew 20:1–16.

27 Aug. *Serm.* 229E.2: *Dicimus unde nobis cottidie dimittantur; sed non ideo debemus in flagitiis, in sceleribus, in criminibus quasi securi requiescere.* (*Miscellanea Agostiniana* 1.469). See also Aug. *Serm.* 20.3, 352.9.

28 Aug. *Serm.* 40.5 (*PL* 38.245): *Crastino die te victurum nemo tibi promisit.* Trans. Hill, *Works,* 3.2.222–3. See also Aug. *Serm.* 9.2, 17.6, 352.9.

29 Aug. *Serm.* 20.3.

30 *Eus.Gall.* 33.5: *Ne nos aut in sinistra perniciosa remissio aut in dextera ruinosa supplantet elatio.* See also *Eus.Gall.* 14.7.

31 *Eus.Gall.* 6.8: *Et ideo, carissimi, conuertamus nos ad meliora dum in nostra sunt potestate remedia.* See also *Eus.Gall.* 27.8, 45.1. Compare the parallel passages in Caes. Arel. *Serm.* 167.8, 189.1, 197.1, 206.3.

32 *Eus.Gall.* 27.8.

33 *Eus.Gall.* 45.1: *Ac sic: mortificatione praesenti, futurae mortis sententia praeuenitur.* Compare further parallels in Caes.Arel. *Serm.* 189.1 and 197.1.

to come, it will no longer be possible to perform good works or to redeem sin.[34] "No emendation will be possible there, no prayer will have any force."[35] Those sinners would want to return, if they could, not to joys, not to lusts, not to sins, but to penance and the labours of emendation, and salubrious lamentation. We are granted a period of unknown brevity, "to cure stains, wash faults, heal the things of the past, consider the things of the future, and make undone the things which are done."[36] The pressure of this responsibility is intense. Furthermore, the Eusebian preachers made clear what is at stake by emphasizing the horrors awaiting the damned. In sermon 6, for example, the flames of hell lick the bones of sinners, torture their thoughts, and enter into their very marrow.[37] The "unquenchable fire" will extinguish in hell, the preacher warns, whatever penance has failed to correct on earth. "The burning pit of hell will be opened and there will be a descent, but no return."[38] "Too late" sinners will lament their failure to repent and to avert these horrors through alms and tears.[39] There is nothing comparable in the sermons of Augustine.[40] The Eusebian preachers tried to ensure that their congregants felt the full weight of their freedom and its attendant responsibility.

These two pastoral styles are not in conflict. Both are orthodox and both have precedent within the Christian tradition. They reveal, however, different constructions of power in the relationship between pastor and congregant. Two case-studies clarify the nuances of emphasis in the Eusebius Gallicanus collection. The stories of the "good thief" (Luke 23:39–43) and the Ninevites (Jon. 3–4) were standard penitential *exempla*. They could be spun, however, to support a variety of pastoral points. The story of the conversion of the thief on the cross and his immediate salvation was used by preachers who followed Augustine's lead to rebut both despair of redemption and the Pelagian position that grace must be merited by human action. The story demonstrated, in their telling, that sincere death-bed repentance is sufficient to expiate sin and that hope is available until the very last moment. Peter Chrysologus, for example, used the example of the thief to restore hope—he "broke into paradise" at the last moment, when there no longer seemed time—and to recommend that all Christians likewise undertake penance on their death-bed.[41]

---

34 *Eus.Gall.* 45.7, 61.9, 64.12.

35 *Eus.Gall.* 74.7: *Non ibi emendatio poterit, non ualebit oratio.*

36 *Eus.Gall.* 74.8: *Nos ergo, <...as> adhuc etsi incerta breuitate conceditur curare maculas, lauare culpas, subuenire praeteritis, consulere futuris, et facere infecta de factis.*

37 *Eus.Gall.* 6.6.

38 *Eus.Gall.* 6.6: *Ardens inferni puteus aperietur; descensus erit, reditus non erit.* Compare Caes.Arel. *Serm.* 167.5. This translation is based in part on that by M.M. Mueller, *Saint Caesarius of Arles: Sermons*, Fathers of the Church 47 (Washington, 1964) 406.

39 *Eus.Gall.* 6.6 and 6.7. Compare Caes.Arel. *Serm.* 167.7.

40 Brown, "Decline," 61.

41 Pet.Chrys. *Serm.* 60 (*PL* 52.365). The passage reads: *si latro in ipso momento mortis paradisum invasit, et vitam vobis, in articulo temporis quam quaeritis, quis negabit?* Trans.

The Eusebius Gallicanus sermon that treats the good thief begins with a similar point. His absolution, the preacher argues, "was done for the consolation and hope of all the people."[42] However, the preacher of this sermon also implies that this grace was not wholly unmerited. "But not without reason did he merit so much."[43] The thief believed in Jesus with a praiseworthy faith, even as the apostle Peter denied him.[44] God filled him with the Holy Spirit, and "thus he joined grace to merit."[45] The thief earned salvation, according to the Eusebian preacher, through the rapidity and utter perfection of his belief. This was not Augustine's view of unmerited grace.

Moreover, whereas other late antique preachers used the thief as an argument against despair, the author of the Eusebian sermon focused on ensuring that he would not be an excuse for confidence. He expressed his anxiety that hearing this story might make someone feel "secure" or "relaxed," that they might say to themselves: "I see in what a short space of time the crimes of the thief were remitted, and so they will also be cancelled for me."[46] The devil introduces such security, the preacher warns, in order to bring you to ruin. Just like Augustine, the Eusebian preacher worries that the sinner is taking a risk—he or she might die before being presented with the chance to repent. But he goes further than this. "It is hateful to God," he warns, "when man sins freely, relying on a penance reserved for old age …" "Artifice is not admitted to salvation."[47] The thief did not deliberately put off redemption, but grasped at it the moment he knew of it. "He neither delayed knowing the time of salvation, nor deceitfully arranged the remedies for his condition at the last unhappy moment, nor saved up the hope of his redemption until the desperate end."[48] The Eusebian preacher does not deny the possibility of death-bed remission, but he casts serious doubt upon its efficacy. The story of the good thief is therefore spun as a warning against the last-minute "unmerited" penance which it seems to support.

The story of the Ninevites, who repented and were spared the destruction that threatened them, was more problematic for preachers following Augustine's lead. The wording of the passage, suggesting that the Ninevites' penance caused God

---

Fitzgerald, *Conversion*, 311. See also Pet.Chrys. *Serm.* 42, 61, 125, 167 and discussion in Rebillard, *In hora mortis*, 181–4, 226.

42 *Eus.Gall.* 24.2: *Vt consolatio ac spes fieret totius populi.*

43 *Eus.Gall.* 24.2: *Sed non sine causa tantum meruit.* The phrase is repeated in 24.3.

44 *Eus.Gall.* 24.3.

45 *Eus.Gall.* 24.4–5: *ita gratiam adiungit ad merita.*

46 *Eus.Gall.* 24.8: *Video sub momento, uideo sub exiguo spatio latroni crimina sua fuisse donata, et mihi resoluta.*

47 *Eus.Gall.* 24.8: *Odibile est apud deum, quando homo, sub fiducia paenitentiae in senectute reseruatae, liberius peccat.... ars non admittitur ad salutem.*

48 *Eus.Gall.* 24.9: *Ille nec salutis tempora sciens distulit, nec remedia status sui in momenta ultima infelici fraude disposuit, nec redemptionis suae spem in desperationis nouissimum reseruauit.*

to change his mind, was difficult to reconcile with a model in which salvation and damnation were both predestined and unmerited. In his preaching, Augustine used them as an example of those who did not despair but he did not dwell on the passage or choose to explore its implications.[49]

For the preacher of Eusebian sermon 26, however, the Ninevites are a useful model of successful penitential action and of the power of the faithful to act toward their own salvation. "Where are those," he challenges sceptics, "who deny the remedy of penitence ...?"[50] The example of the Ninevites ought to remove any doubt that God hearkens to human supplication. "Therefore, every one of the faithful should not doubt that the sacrifice of requests, the burnt offering of prayers and the sacrifice of tears can immediately rise up to the divine presence."[51] When God rebuked Jonah for his anger, the preacher maintains, he was also rebuking those who refused to believe in the redemptive power of penitence. "Therefore the Ninevites, through penance and abstinence, caused the ruin of imminent anger from above to be suspended, and with children and cattle abstaining equally, they turned back, as I said, the blow coming forth from the Lord and the judgment about to fall upon them."[52] The emphasis throughout is upon the action of the citizens. It is their penitence which brings about their redemption. The preacher does not claim that these deeds forced God's hand, but he tells his congregants that through the actions of the Ninevites severity was strongly urged toward clemency.[53] The Ninevites showed, in the Eusebian reading, that effort was worthwhile, and could bear fruit.

Theology played a role here, but pastoral care was the determining factor. Augustine's "active passivity" was almost unpreachable. The bishop of Hippo tried, as did others, but it could be a struggle to motivate a congregation while maintaining that their efforts were effectively irrelevant. What we see in Gaul in the fifth and sixth centuries, therefore, was not so much a theological disagreement with Augustine as a pastoral response to his ideas. Furthermore, although the Eusebian preachers, and those who used the collection, appear to have shifted power into the hands of the laity, appearances can be deceptive. As they removed some of the pastoral burden from themselves, they also increased the pressure on

---

49 Aug. *Serm.* 361.20 (*PL* 39.1610). Trans. Hill, *Works*, 3.10.238. See also Aug. *Serm.* 72A.1, 346A.3, 351.12; *Serm. Dolbeau* 5.2. For Augustine's avoidance of the Ninevites in treatises on grace, see Weaver, *Divine Grace*, 179. He gives them careful exegesis in *Civ.Dei.* 21.24.

50 *Eus.Gall.* 26.1: *Vbi sunt: qui negant remedia paenitentiae ...?*

51 *Eus.Gall.* 26.3: *Inter haec fidelis quisque non dubitet: hostias precum, holocausta uotorum, sacrificia lacrimarum ad diuinum familiariter ascendere posse conspectum; ecce ad aurem domini, gemitus etiam brutorum animalium peruenerunt.*

52 *Eus.Gall.* 26.4: *Ergo Niniuitae, per paenitentiam atque abstinentiam, irae desuper imminentis suspenderunt ruinam; et paruuli ac pecora, pariter abstinentes, egressam a domino plagam atque sententiam iam cadentem, ut sic dixerim, retorserunt.*

53 *Eus.Gall.* 26.5: *Secundum haec ualde ad clementiam diuinam seueritas inuitatur.*

their congregants. This may have been a more realistic option for many clergy than the shouldering of burden undertaken by Augustine.

Penance could result from external coercion—public humiliation as a weapon of social control. But it did not function this way in late antique Gaul. Instead what we see is internal coercion. Pastors tried to make their congregants restrict their own actions, thoughts, and behaviours—they hoped that judgment could be internalized. This was an indirect imposition of power which appealed to clerics otherwise without strong coercive mechanisms. If the laity could be made into their "own most severe judges," the task of Gallic pastors became somewhat easier.

PART V
Constantine and the Power of the Cross

Chapter 16
Solar Power in Late Antiquity

H. A. Drake
University of California, Santa Barbara

Despite what its title may suggest, this chapter is not about environmentalism, although it is in a way about a renewable resource. Its aim is to evaluate the role of the sun god in the religious development of the emperor Constantine—an exercise that may also prove useful for reflecting on the strengths and weaknesses of the positivist approach to history. The long-standing question concerning Constantine's conversion has been reinvigorated by the work of the German scholar Peter Weiss.[1] With meticulous scholarship, Weiss has convincingly connected textual and numismatic evidence for Constantine's famous vision of the cross to a celestial event known as a "solar halo phenomenon." Simply put, these events occur when sunlight is refracted through ice crystals in the high atmosphere. They take a number of forms, including "light pillars," single-ring (or 22°) haloes and, in their most spectacular form, double-ring (46°) haloes.[2] Weiss has carefully analyzed a passage in the Latin panegyric of 310 in which Constantine is said to have made a detour on his route from the battlefield to a temple of Apollo, probably that of Apollo Granus in Vosges, and there to have seen a vision of the god Apollo—the so-called "pagan vision." Weiss demonstrated how the orator could well have been referring to a vision seen *before* Constantine had entered that temple, and argued that this vision was, in fact, the cause of that detour.[3] Combining this analysis with the fact that halo phenomena occur most often in late winter or spring and connecting this with the timing of Constantine's march, Weiss concluded that this vision was the only one that Constantine ever had, that it occurred in 310, and that it was, in fact, a solar halo phenomenon.

Weiss's study has met with decidedly different reactions in the scholarly world. Anglo-Saxon scholars have generally embraced it, while Weiss himself laments

---

1 P. Weiss, "Die Vision Constantins, " in J. Bleicken (ed.), *Colloquium aus Anlass des 80. Geburtstages von Alfred Heuss*, Frankfurter althistorische Studien 13 (Kalmunz, 1993) 143–69. Citations are to, and English quotations from, the translation by A. Birley, "The Vision of Constantine," *JRA* 16 (2003) 237–59. On Constantine and the sun god, see nn. 19 and 20 below.

2 Weiss, "Vision," 240–45.

3 Weiss, "Vision," 249. On the oration, see Jacqueline Long's essay in this volume (Chapter 17).

that his own colleagues in Germany have been more standoffish.[4] By itself, the halo phenomenon does not explain either the reason for these differing reactions or the originality of Weiss's argument. A.H.M. Jones, relying on a more dated scientific study, made the same suggestion more than half a century ago.[5] But Weiss is the first to make a systematic attempt to correlate this phenomenon with contemporary evidence. Using his readings, we can now agree that there is no substantive difference between the two most important Christian accounts of this event, the dream story in Lactantius and the vision story in Eusebius.[6] Although Lactantius' account is chronologically earlier than Eusebius, it narrates an experience Constantine had some two years later than the halo vision, prior to the battle for Rome in 312, when Constantine grasped the full import of the sign he had seen. When Lactantius writes that Christ instructed Constantine to mark his soldiers' shields with a *caelestis signum dei*, the phrase should not be taken to mean some generic "heavenly sign of god," but as a specific reference to the "sign of god" that Constantine had seen "in the heavens."[7]

Weiss's study of the coinage is particularly impressive, especially for the way he rationalizes the seemingly arbitrary use of asterisks—which would now equate with a solar symbol—and an infrequent but puzzling reverse from the 320s (see Figure 16.1) that shows the sun god standing amid a set of four interlocking Xs, with a legend that reads VIRT(us)-EXERC(itus). These lines have been traditionally, but not very convincingly, identified as the gates of an army camp; Weiss suggests that they were meant to signify a radiate cross.[8]

Not all of Weiss's evidence is equally conclusive. Coin images were open to multiple interpretations, and even this coin with the mysterious Xs could be interpreted very differently, for example as an elaborate acrostic for the fifth anniversary of Constantine's son Constantine II, the tenth of Crispus and the twentieth of Constantine himself.[9] Similarly, many of the traits that Weiss finds unique to Constantine—his sense of divine mission and use of light imagery, for instance—are likely just a trick of the sources, since the documentation for this emperor's reign is so much more substantial than that for any of his immediate predecessors. For example, one fragment we do have indicates that Aurelian believed his power had come directly from a divine source, and it would be foolish to discount the divine ties Diocletian established through his Jovian and Herculian dynasties.[10]

---

4 In an addendum to the English translation, see Weiss, "Vision," 257–9.

5 A.H.M. Jones, *Constantine and the Conversion of Europe*, rev. ed. (1948; reprint. New York, 1962) 85; also E.R. Dodds, *Pagan and Christian in an Age of Anxiety: Some Aspects of Religious Experience from Marcus Aurelius to Constantine* (Cambridge, 1965) 47.

6 Lact. *Mort.pers.* 44.5; Eus. *VConst.* 1.28.2.

7 Weiss, "Vision," 246.

8 Weiss, "Vision," 251. For the coin, *RIC* 7.507 Thessalonica 71 and pl. 16.

9 I am grateful to Linda Hall for this suggestion.

10 A.D. Nock, "*A Diis Electa*: A Chapter in the Religious History of the Third Century," *HThR* 23 (1930) 251–74, at 263–4: "There may be anticipations of the theory of divine

Figure 16.1 Reverse of bronze follis of Constantine: VIRT(us)- EXERC(itus) with Sol Invictus standing atop a series of interlocking Xs. *RIC* 7.507 Thessalonica 71 pl.16. Photo by The British Museum. Used by permission.

There are other ambiguities. By equating wreaths with solar haloes, one possible translation of the Latin *corona*, Weiss is able to make powerful connections. Thus, when the orator in 310 speaks of Apollo offering Constantine "laurel garlands (*laureas*), each one bearing the sign of thirty years [of rule]," he was actually—to Weiss—referring to the *coronae* in the halo phenomenon Constantine had just witnessed.[11] But statues of Apollo Granus, the deity worshipped in this part of Gaul, regularly show the god holding a victory wreath,[12] and the orator's further claim that Constantine recognized his own features in this vision (*Vidisti teque in illius specie recognouisti*), a claim strikingly manifested in the famous jugate bust of Constantine and Apollo struck for Constantine's meeting with Licinius in Milan

choice to be found in the epithets *pius*, *felix*, *invictus*, on coins of the early third century after Christ, but the first explicit formulation of it would appear to be the work of Aurelian, who told the troops they were in error if they supposed the choice of rulers to rest with them: god had given him the purple and fixed the length of his rule." The fragment Nock cited is from the anonymous continuator of Dio Cassius, *fr.*105. apud Müller, *FGH* 4.197. A. Ehrhardt drew a connection between Constantine and a vision attributed to Alexander the Great in Ps.-Callisthenes 1.33 in *Politische Metaphysik von Solon bis Augustin* (Tübingen, 1959) 2.262 n.4.

[11] *Pan.Lat.* 6(7).21.3–5. Weiss, "Vision," 247: "Often enough in Latin literature halo-rings are called crowns (*coronae*)."

[12] G. Woolf, "Seeing Apollo in Roman Gaul and Germany," in S. Scott and J. Webster (eds.), *Roman Imperialism and Provincial Art* (Cambridge, 2003) 139–53. More generally, P. Boyancé, "L'Apollon solaire," in J. Heurgon et al. (eds.), *Mélanges d'archeologie, d'épigraphie et d'histoire offerts à Jérôme Carcopino* (Paris, 1966) 149–70.

three years later,[13] makes a more literal reading of this account at least equally plausible. Indeed, the basic sense of *corona*, "wreath," suggests that the symbols on Constantine's coins are just that—signs of traditional votive offerings. It is true that the "double corona" to which Weiss points on a coin from 324 is rare, but this is at least partially because the number of emperors celebrating 20 years of rule is rare.[14] Weiss also points to Cyril of Jerusalem's famous letter to Constantine's son, Constantius II, in 351 (discussed in Chapter 18 of the present volume by Drijvers). As Weiss argues, Cyril's description of the appearance of a cross in the sky above Jerusalem also fits the criteria for a halo phenomenon.[15] But it does not confirm widespread knowledge of Constantine's vision. In fact, it does just the opposite, for Cyril is at pains to contrast this omen with Constantine's discovery of a cross *in the ground*, a reference to the construction of the Holy Sepulchre.[16] If this passage indicates anything, it is that Cyril knew nothing at all about Constantine's vision in the sky.

There is no need to take anything away from the brilliant work Weiss has done of connecting the dots. Locating Constantine's vision in 310 and doing so in a way that convincingly demonstrates how the dream story of 312 would be an elaboration of that same event puts to rest a long-standing and utterly unnecessary controversy over the priority of "pagan" versus "Christian" visions.[17] What must

---

13 *RIC* 6.227–8.

14 For examples, see C.E.V. Nixon and B.S. Rodgers, *In Praise of Later Roman Emperors: The Panegyrici Latini* (Berkeley, 1994) 248 n.92.

15 Weiss, "Vision," 259. On the date, see E. Bihain, "L'épitre de Cyrille de Jérusalem à Constance sur la vision de la Croix. Tradition manuscrite et édition critique," *Byzantion* 43 (1973) 264–96. For other sightings, see J. Vogt, "Berichte über Kreuzeserscheinungen aus dem 4. Jahrhundert n. Chr.," *AIPhO* 9 (Mélanges H. Grégoire 1) (1949) 593–606.

16 *Epistola ad Constantium imperatorem* (*PG* 33: 1165–76, at 1168): "For if in the days of your Imperial Father, Constantine of blessed memory, the saving wood of the Cross was found in Jerusalem (divine grace granting the finding of the long hidden holy places to one who nobly aspired to sanctity), now, Sire, in the reign of your most godly Majesty, as if to mark how far your zeal excels your forebear's piety, not from the earth but from the skies marvels appear: the trophy of the victory over death of our Lord Jesus Christ, the Only-begotten Son of God, even the holy Cross, flashing and sparkling with brilliant light, has been seen at Jerusalem." Trans. L.P. McCauley and A. Stephenson, *The Works of S. Cyril of Jerusalem*, The Fathers of the Church 64 (Washington, 1970) 232. For 351 instead of 350 as the year, see T.D. Barnes, *Athanasius and Constantius: Theology and Politics in the Constantinian Empire* (Cambridge, MA, 1993) 107. See also O. Irshai, "Cyril of Jerusalem: the Apparition of the Cross and the Jews," in O. Limor and G. Stroumsa (eds.), *Contra Iudaeos: Ancient and Medieval Polemics between Christians and Jews* (Tübingen, 1996) 85–104.

17 The debate was touched off by H. Grégoire, "La 'conversion' de Constantin," *RUB* 36 (1930) 231–72 at 256–7. See further W. Seston, "La vision païenne de 310 et les origines du chrisme constantinien," *AIPhO* 4 (Mélanges F. Cumont) (1936) 373–95; A. Brasseur, "Les deux visions de Constantin," *Latomus* 5 (1946) 35–9; P. Orgels,

be noted, however, is that Weiss may have connected more dots than he needed to: to paraphrase Freud, sometimes a wreath is merely a wreath. The problem starts with the way he builds all of Constantine's career around the vision of 310. Consider just one passage in his argument:

> It is now possible to trace Constantine's unique and unshakeable conviction back to its roots: to the epiphany of the *summus deus* that actually took place, which both he and his army witnessed, which promised him victory, intimated that he would achieve sole power, and confirmed this, with victory after victory.[18]

With these and similar statements strewn throughout his text,[19] Weiss comes dangerously close to making everything in Constantine's career depend on this one experience, and this tendency, in turn, seems to explain the varied reception of Weiss's argument. For scholars trained in the positivist tradition, his study provides a convenient explanation for the traditional story line. But it also leads to a certain amount of reductionism that would set Constantine scholarship back a good 50 years.

The problem can be illustrated by posing a simple counter-factual: suppose Constantine had never seen this halo phenomenon. Is it conceivable that, had this chance sighting not occurred, there would have been no triumphant march from

"La première vision de Constantin (310) et le temple d'Apollon à Nîmes," *BAB* 5, ser. 34 (1948) 176–208; E. Galletier, "La mort de Maximien d'après le Panégyrique de 310 et la vision de Constantin au temple d'Apollon," *REA* 52 (1950) 288–99; B.S. Rodgers, "Constantine's Pagan Vision," *Byzantion* 50 (1980) 259–78. Weiss's derivation of "labarum" from Celtic terminology was anticipated by J.J. Hatt, "La vision de Constantin au sanctuaire de Grand et l'origine celtique du Labarum," *Latomus* 9 (1952) 427–36. J. Ferguson suggested a derivation from "soldiers' slang" in M. Green and J. Ferguson, "Constantine, Sun-Symbols and the Labarum," *DUJ* 49 (1987) 9–17 at 14.

18 Weiss, "Vision," 251 = Idem, "Die Vision," 161–2: "Die unverwechselbare, unverrückbare Grundüberzeugung Constantins läßt sich endlich auf ihre Wurzel zurückführen: die tatsächliche 'Epiphanie' des sonnenhaften *invictus summus deus*, die ihm und seinem Heer galt, die Sieg versprach, die Allherrschaft andeutete, und die sich Sieg um Sieg aufs neue verifizierte."

19 See, e.g., Weiss, "Vision," 238 = Idem, "Die Vision," 144: "totally unheard of" (völlig ungewöhnlich); ibid. 247 = Idem, "Die Vision," 157: a "sudden change of direction" (plötzliche Wende); ibid. 250 = Idem, "Die Vision," 161: "it [is] possible for the first time to get behind the 'Constantine mystery,' to understand why this emperor, as a complete exception, was filled with such a deep-seated religious conviction, so singular a sense of mission ..., why it was that he never tired of claiming divine guidance, and how that influenced his drive to achieve sole power" (Erst damit läßt sich besser hinter das Rätsel "Constantin" kommen, läßt sich verstehen, warum dieser Kaiser als die große Ausnahme von einer derart tiefsitzenden religiösen Überzeugung und einem singulären Sendungsbewusstsein erfült war … warum er sich unermüdlich göttlicher Führung rühmte, und wie das alles auf den Impetus einwirkte, mit dem er die Alleinherrschaft erstritt).

Britain to the Hellespont, no sense of divine mission, no fateful union between Christian church and Roman state? Is it conceivable that Constantine never would have taken on his wars with Maxentius and Licinius or opened the corridors of power to Christian participation? And if all this is so, then what is the practical difference between a chance sighting and a miracle?

Put in this way, the reason for the different reactions to Weiss's argument becomes clear: for all its brilliance, it stumbles on the issue of causality. Its effect is simply to transpose the traditional miracle event from 312 to 310 and to give it an explanation more suitable to modern tastes in evidence. It puts more explanatory weight on the halo phenomenon than it can possibly bear, and, in its own way, is as reductionist, and as unsatisfying intellectually, as the traditional miracle story that it seeks to explain away.

What is missing from Weiss's study is context. To evaluate his conclusions, we need to look at the way that the symbols of cross and sun could be adapted to the very different goals of contemporary commentators. We also need to look at continuities in Constantine's behavior, the role of political ideology, and the widespread influence of solar imagery.[20]

This is not as easy a task as it may seem. Constantine's association with the sun god after 310 is easy to document in a variety of ways, ranging from his long series of SOLI INVICTI COMITI coins and the remarkable medallion struck in Milan in 313 with Constantine and the sun god in joint profile, to his ambiguously worded Sunday law that created a legal holiday on "the day of the revered Sun" (*dies venerabilis Solis*), to the statue of Apollo Helios on which he had carved his own features and placed atop the porphyry column he erected to grace his new capital.[21] In the final months of Constantine's reign, Eusebius of Caesarea still found it prudent to use the image of him driving the sun's chariot in an official oration, about the same time that the former advocate Firmicus Maternus sent up a prayer to the Sun in order to:

> vouchsafe that Constantine the Most Great Princeps and his unconquered children, our lords and Caesars, rule over our children and our children's

---

20 As done, for instance, by O. Nicholson in "Constantine's Vision of the Cross," *VChr* 53 (2000) 309–23, by connecting the vision with contemporary Christian expectations about the Last Days.

21 For the coins, see P. Bruun, "The Disappearance of Sol from the Coins of Constantine," *Arctos* n.s. 2 (1958) 15–37, and Idem, *RIC* 6.61–4; M. Wallraff, "Constantine's Devotion to the Sun after 324," *StudPatr* 34 (2001) 256–69. On the statue, see T. Preger, "Konstantinos-Helios," *Hermes* 36 (1901) 457–69, and G. Fowden, "Constantine's Porphyry Column: The Earliest Literary Allusion," *JRS* 81 (1991) 119–31. On Constantine's Sunday law of 321 (*CTh* 8.1), see K. Girardet, "Vom Sonnen-Tag zum Sonntag. Der Dies solis in Gesetzgebung und Politik Konstantins d. Gr.," *ZAC* 11 (2007) 279–310. Girardet demonstrates Christian influence on the law despite its ambiguous wording, and also traces it to an original that may have been issued a decade earlier.

children through endless ages so that, freed from all misfortune, the human race may enjoy everlasting peace and prosperity.[22]

But tantalizingly little is known of Constantine's development prior to 310, other than that it lasted substantially longer than he would have us believe.[23] Eusebius remembered seeing him riding at Diocletian's side when the emperor marched through Palestine, probably in 297 or 298, from which it would appear that Constantine held a place of honor at Diocletian's court and was being groomed for a leadership position.[24] The effort made by Constantius I to have his son on hand for what proved to be a fatal campaign in Britain—even if not as dramatic as it became in subsequent retellings[25]—underlines this sense of imperial ambitions, as does his subsequent marriage to the daughter of the western Tetrarch Maximian in 307.

22 Math. 1.10.14: *Constantinum maximum principem et huius invictissimos liberos, dominos et Caesares nostros, consensu uestrae moderationis et dei summi obsecuti iudicio perpetua his decernentis imperia, facite etiam nostris posteris et posterorum nostrorum posteris infinitis saeculorum continuationibus imperare, ut omni malorum acerbitate depulsa humanum genus quietae ac perpetuae felicitatis munera consequatur.* Trans. J.R. Bram, *Ancient Astrology, Theory and Practice* (Park Ridge, NJ, 1975) 30. For Eusebius, see *Laus Constantini* 3.4: "having harnessed as it were, under the self-same yoke the four most noble Caesars as horses in the imperial chariot, he sits on high and directs their course by the reins of holy harmony and concord; and himself everywhere present and observant of every event, thus traverses every region of the world." On this passage, see now I. Tantillo, "Attributi solari della figura imperiale in Eusebio di Cesarea," *MedAnt* 6 (2003) 41–59.

23 Constantine liked to claim that he was "just a kid" (κομιδῆ παῖς ἔτι) at the time of the Great Persecution (see Eus. *VConst.* 2.51), and orators indulged him with compliments about his youthful appearance, but other sources indicate that he would then have been well into his twenties and perhaps older (for instance, Eusebius says at *VConst.* 1.4 that Constantine ruled 30 years and lived twice as long, which would put his birth in the 270s). There were, of course, obvious political advantages to be gained by claiming to have been "out of the loop" during that time. On Constantine's youthful image, see R.R.R. Smith, "The Public Image of Licinius I: Portrait Sculpture and Imperial Ideology in the Early Fourth Century," *JRS* 87 (1997) 170–202 at 185.

24 At *VConst.* 1.19, Eusebius writes that he first saw Constantine as he passed through Palestine riding at Diocletian's right side. The occasion, presumably, was connected with Diocletian's campaign in Egypt to suppress a revolt in Alexandria, hence 297 or 298: T.D. Barnes, *The New Empire of Diocletian and Constantine* (Cambridge, MA, 1982) 54–5. Lact. *Mort.pers.* 18.10 claims that Constantine attained the rank of *tribunus ordinis primi* in Diocletian's *comitatus*.

25 Lact. *Mort.pers.* 24 provides the elements of a thriller with Constantine avoiding capture by hamstringing the post horses en route and arriving just in time at his father's death-bed. For a more sober account, see T.D. Barnes, *Constantine and Eusebius* (Cambridge, MA, 1981) 27. It should be said, however, that this story shows up in a variety of sources and source traditions, so it was clearly at the very least something Constantine himself propagated.

That wedding was important because it helped to solidify Constantine's claim to the purple, giving him a tie of his own to Maximian's Herculian dynasty. One hint about Constantine's religious interests is provided by the orator at that wedding, who pictured Constantius as beaming down on the ceremony from his place in the chariot of the sun,[26] a seemingly irrelevant detail unless the orator wanted to call attention to an association with that deity. Another hint comes from Lactantius, who claimed that Constantine's first act on assuming power in 305 was to permit Christians to worship their God.[27]

These are tiny, but consistent pieces of data that indicate Constantine's attraction to the sun and his interest in Christians both antedated 310.[28] A closer look at the panegyric of 310 allows us to broaden the context to include political developments. As Weiss notes, the orator strategically placed his account of the "pagan miracle" at the end of his panegyric. But two bombshells preceded it. The first he placed at an equally strategic point, right at the beginning of his oration (2.1): the news that Constantine had a heretofore unknown relationship to the third-century emperor Claudius Gothicus (268–70). At this point, the orator waxes lyrical about Constantine's superior lineage, his greater right to rule—"No chance agreement of men, nor some unexpected consequence of favor, made you Emperor," he proclaims. This was a not-so-subtle swipe at the criteria of the Tetrarchy.[29] The second bombshell comes after predictable praise for the deeds and virtues of father and son: it seems that Constantine, however reluctantly, had had to put to death old Maximian, his father-in-law and the founder of the Herculian dynasty.[30]

---

26 *Pan.Lat.* 7(6).14.3: *O felix in imperio et post imperium felicior! Audis enim profecto haec et vides, diue Constanti, quem curru [et] paene conspicio, dum uicinos ortus repetit occasu, Sol ipse invecturus caelo excepit.* Eusebius used a similar image for Constantine almost 30 years later, *Laus Constantini* 3.4. On indications of Constantine's later policies, cf. S. MacCormack, "Latin Prose Panegyric," in T.A. Dorey (ed.), *Empire and Aftermath* (London, 1975) 154: the orator "introduced and pointed to themes which turned out to be of great importance in Constantine's later policy."

27 Lact. *Mort.pers.* 24.9: *Suscepto imperio Constantinus Augustus nihil egit prius quam Christianos cultui ac deo sui reddere. Haec fuit prima eius sanctio sanctae religionis restitutae.* ("The first act of Constantine Augustus on assuming imperial power was to restore the Christians to their worship and their God. This was the first measure by which he sanctioned the restoration of the holy religion.") Trans. Creed; cf. T.D. Barnes, "Lactantius and Constantine," *JRS* 63 (1973) 29–46 at 46.

28 As A. Alföldi, *The Conversion of Constantine and Pagan Rome*, trans. H. Mattingly (1948; reprint. Oxford, 1969) 14, observed: "All that we know of the development of the youthful Constantine shows that his decisive step had many preparatory stages and a long history behind it."

29 *Pan.Lat.* 6(7).3.1, trans. Nixon and Rodgers.

30 The orator indicates how sensitive the subject is at *Pan.Lat.* 6(7).14.1, where he asks for a nod from Constantine before proceeding. On Maximian's death, cf. Lact. *Mort. pers.* 30.

There is no need to rehearse the disastrous instability of the third century to see that Maximian's demise made for an untidy situation. It sent Constantine scrambling for cover. We cannot fully appreciate the accomplishments of his reign if we ignore how tenuous his hold on power was in 310.[31] With this context in mind, the orator's intent is clear: he begins and ends his panegyric with alternative claims for Constantine's legitimacy. If we are to understand Constantine's situation, we have to give as much attention to the descent from Claudius Gothicus as to the vision experience.

This vulnerability is one of the reasons that locating a halo phenomenon in that year makes so much sense. But the ancients were not unfamiliar with halo phenomena; as Weiss himself notes, they regularly took them as portents of war and regime change.[32] So we still have to ask why the sun was so powerful an image to Constantine that he read the phenomenon differently.

Solar imagery is unquestionably a key to unraveling the skein of Constantine's religious development. The sun has always been a powerful symbol for monotheistic thought because it illustrates how a single deity can be everywhere at once and also bring good things to humans without being contaminated by contact with imperfect nature—a major sticking point, as we know, for critics of Christian teaching, who had difficulty contemplating the proposition that the Supreme Being of the universe had undergone the indecencies of human birth.[33] The sun was central to the thinking of the first known monotheist, the pharaoh Ikhnaton, who ruled Egypt in the fourteenth century BC. Plato made the sun the visible symbol of the ideal Good, and Constantine's nephew Julian made it the

---

31 As observed long ago by O. Seeck, *Geschichte des Untergangs der antiken Welt*, 3rd ed. (Stuttgart, 1897 [1910]) 1.105–6.

32 Weiss, "Vision," 244–5, with references. See further J.S. Hanson, "Dreams and Visions in the Graeco-Roman World and Early Christianity," *ANRW* 2.23.2 (1981) 1395–427.

33 An example of anti-Christian argument can be found in the 2nd-century polemicist Celsus, whose criticisms survive in the rebuttal written half a century later by Origen. See Origen, *C.Cels.*, esp. 6.73. Ikhnaton's sun is illustrated on his throne, found in the tomb of his son-in-law and successor, Tutankhamon. See also his "Hymn to Aton," trans. J.A. Wilson, *Ancient Near Eastern Texts Relating to the Old Testament*, ed. James Pritchard, 2nd ed. (Princeton, 1955) 370–71. In general, E. Hornung, *Akhenaten and the Religion of Light*, trans. David Lorton (Ithaca, NY, 1999). The locus classicus for Plato is *Resp.* 6.508B–E. For Christian use of solar imagery, see now M. Wallraff, *Christus Verus Sol: Sonnenverehrung und Christentum in der Spätantike*, Jahrbuch für Antike und Christentum Ergänzungsband 32 (Münster, 2001).

centerpiece of the alternative state religion he tried to create in 361.[34] The Sun has even shown up in mosaics on the floors of late antique synagogues in Judaea.[35]

By the fourth century, imperial ideology made a connection to a special divine source, a *comes*, an essential prerequisite for rule.[36] In the course of the third century, Sol Invictus had emerged as the most popular of these *comites*. From mid-century on, emperors depicted themselves wearing the solar helmet, and in the 270s, Aurelian installed Sol Invictus in the Roman pantheon. Most importantly, one of the emperors who issued these Sol coins was also Constantine's new ancestor, Claudius Gothicus.[37] When Diocletian revamped his Tetrarchy around the lines of traditional gods, creating the Jovian and Herculian dynasties, Sol lost this privileged place. Weighing Constantine's newfound allegiance to the Sun god together with his newfound lineage shows that both were part of a program to redraw the lines of legitimacy to pre-Tetrarchic boundaries.

Christians were very adept at incorporating symbols of other religions into their own teaching; it would be astonishing if they had not found a way to do so with the sun. There is no need to rehearse the role the sun played in Christian apologetics, or in the thinking of Christian Platonists,[38] because there is an excellent, albeit

---

[34] P. Athanassiadi, "A Contribution to Mithraic Theology: The Emperor Julian's Hymn to King Helios," *JThS* n.s. 28 (1977) 360–71; J. Dillon, "The Theology of Julian's 'Hymn to King Helios,'" *Ítaca* 14–15 (1998–99) 103–15. For solar worship in Celtic Gaul and the Danubian regions that dates as far back as 1200 BC, see Green and Ferguson, "Constantine, Sun-Symbols and the Labarum."

[35] M. Dothan, *Hammath Tiberias: Early Synagogues and the Hellenistic and Roman Remains* (Jerusalem, 1983) 39–43. See also ibid., plan E (34–5) and pl.13; R. Hachlili, "The Zodiac in Ancient Jewish Art: Representations and Signification," *BASOR* 28 (1977) 61–77.

[36] A.D. Nock, "The Emperor's Divine Comes," *JRS* 37 (1947) 102–16. See further J. Straub, *Vom Herrscherideal in der Spätantike*, Forschungen zur Kirchen- und Geistesgeschichte 18 (Stuttgart, 1939; reprint. Darmstadt, 1964); F. Kolb, *Herrscherideologie in der Spätantike* (Berlin, 2000).

[37] See, for references, G.H. Halsbergh, *The Cult of Sol Invictus* (Leiden, 1972). Earlier, but still useful, is H. Usener, "Sol Invictus," *RhM* 60 (1905) 465–91; J. Gagé, *Apollon Romain, Essai sur le Culte d'Apollon et le Développement du "ritus Graecus" à Rome des Origines à Auguste*, Bibliothèque des Écoles françaises d'Athenes et de Rome 182 (Paris, 1955); H. Dörrie, "Die Solar-Theologie in der kaiserzeitlichen Antike," in H. Frohnes and V.W. Knorr (eds.), *Kirchengeschichte als Missionsgeschichte* (Munich, 1974) 1.283–92.

[38] In addition to Walraff, *Christus Verus Sol*, see two standard works by F.J. Dölger: *Sol Salutis, Gebet und Gesang im christlichen Altertum*, Liturgiegeschichtliche Forschungen 4–5 (Münster, 1920; reprint. 1972), and *Die Sonne der Gerechtigkeit und der Schwarze, eine religions-geschichtliche Studie zum Taufgelöbnis*, Liturgiegeschichtliche Forschungen 2 (Münster, 1918, reprint. 1971). On Christianity and Platonism more generally, see H.J. Blumenthal and R.A. Markus (eds.), *Neoplatonism and Early Christian Thought, Essays in Honor of A.H. Armstrong* (London, 1981); H.D. Blume and F. Mann (eds.),

not uncomplicated, piece of evidence for this Christian adaptation of Sol: the well-known image of Christus-Helios in the Tomb of the Julii, showing Christ riding in the solar chariot with the rays of his cross emanating from a solar disk.[39] These tombs were buried as part of the construction of St. Peter's basilica on the Vatican, traditionally attributed to Constantine and placed in the 320s, a date that Bowersock has argued is a good two decades premature.[40]

Platonismus und Christentum: Festschrift für Heinrich Dörrie, JACh Ergänzungsband 10 (Münster, 1983); T. Finan and V. Twomey (eds.), *The Relationship between Neoplatonism and Christianity* (Dublin, 1992); J. Pelikan, *Christianity and Classical Culture: The Metamorphosis of Natural Theology in the Christian Encounter with Hellenism* (New Haven, 1993). Lact. *Div.inst* 4.29 uses the image of the sun and its rays to express the relationship of God the Father to the Son. I am grateful to Elizabeth Digeser for this reference.

39 The basic work on the original excavations remains J.M. Toynbee and J. Ward-Perkins, *The Shrine of St. Peter and the Vatican Excavations* (New York, 1956); for "Christus-Helios," see 72–3, 116–17 and pl.32. More recent conservation efforts are detailed in A. Sperandio and P. Zander, *La tomba di San Pietro: Restauro e illuminazione della Necropoli Vaticana* (Milan, 1999); see 77 for a color illustration and 37 for a computer-generated enlargement.

40 G. Bowersock, "Peter and Constantine," in J.-M. Carrié et R. Lizzi Testa (eds.), *"Humana Sapit": Études d'antiquité tardive offertes à Lellia Cracco Ruggini* (Turnhout and Brussels, 2002) 209–17, has recently made a powerful case for postponing construction at least 20 years, to the reign of Constantine's son Constans (r. 337–50). The argument is cogent and deserves fuller treatment than it can receive here; but it should be noted that Bowersock places a good deal of weight on the assumption that such a foundation would have been prompted by a particular devotion to Peter on Constantine's part—a devotion that he rightly observes is nowhere attested in contemporary sources (see, e.g., 209, 215). But is this stipulation necessary? It is equally plausible to assume that Constantine was responding to an initiative from the bishop of Rome, as he apparently did when the bishop of Jerusalem asked for return of the site of the Holy Sepulchre: Constantine's letter to Macarius of Jerusalem. Eus. *VConst.* 3.30–32, is clearly a response to discoveries that had already been made, not the original order, which probably was prompted by a petition from Macarius, on which see H.A. Drake, "The Return of the Holy Sepulchre," *CHR* 70 (1984) 263–7. More generally, E.D. Hunt, "Constantine and Jerusalem," *JEH* 48 (1997) 405–24. Under this scenario, the groundwork may well have begun in connection with Constantine's vicennalian visit to Rome in 326, as frequently assumed, though it may well be that the church was not completed, or even begun, until much later—again, the Holy Sepulchre provides an analogy. For the Holy Sepulchre as constituting only a memorial over the tomb at the time of Constantine's death, see K. Conant and G. Downey, "The Original Buildings at the Holy Sepulchre in Jerusalem," *Speculum* 31 (1956) 1–48 at 45–7. This scenario would have the advantage of explaining how the endowments for this church listed in the *Liber Pontificalis* 34 (Pope Sylvester) could all have come from the eastern half of the empire—otherwise, as Bowersock notes (212, 216) a conundrum.

With his later dating, Bowersock sees the "Christus-Helios" mosaic as "yet another manifestation of Constantinian devotion to Sol Invictus,"[41] as it may well be. But people usually do not invest in expensive tombs with the foreknowledge that they are going to be destroyed, so a date for this representation no later than the early 320s, and conceivably much earlier, remains plausible. While it is, therefore, chronologically possible that the deceased had heard of Constantine's solar vision and wanted to advertise it, it is much more likely that we are looking at independent testimony to the ubiquitous power of the sun god. This is, in other words, one more example of a Christian who found his way to Christ via solar monotheism, as in all likelihood had Constantine himself.[42]

Because of the tangled scholarship on this subject, it is easy to be misunderstood, so two points need to be emphasized: this chapter is not saying Constantine was a political opportunist nor is it denying the strength of his religious convictions. Furthermore, this evidence has not been adduced to deny that Constantine witnessed a halo phenomenon. Rather, its aim has been to demonstrate how limiting it is to build our understanding of his reign around this one event. As a point in a continuum, the halo experience or, for that matter, the direct intervention of the hand of God, are both perfectly acceptable. But it is far more satisfying, and in the long run more useful, to situate Constantine's political and religious development in a context that does justice to the rich complexity of the political and religious currents of his day. This is a far better guide to understanding the momentous events of this reign than reliance on a single paranormal event, whether ordained by God or nature. A halo phenomenon, or any number of other omens, may have *confirmed* Constantine's belief in his mission, but they did not *create* it.

41 Bowersock, "Peter and Constantine," 217.

42 For another example, see Green and Ferguson, "Constantine, Sun-Symbols and the Labarum."

Chapter 17
How to Read a Halo: Three (or More) Versions of Constantine's Vision

Jacqueline Long
Loyola University Chicago

Light bends. Rays ignited in a sun spill from their course. They fall on objects, bounce, diffuse, and concentrate, until finally the lens of an eye collects them into focus and they are seen. When crystalline ice is suspended in air light strikes obliquely, it may cross the sky with a halo. Many cultures would identify a miracle: too splendid for human sentiment to want to assign to happenstance, too vast to corral within workaday sequences of causation. Even if the physics is understood, why should conditions align so perfectly? Weiss has made a persuasive case, confirming the suggestion more arbitrarily advanced before by Gwatkin and Jones, that just such a sight arrested Constantine once in the earlier years of his reign.[1] The habit of taking divine messages from meteorology readily made it seem portentous. Constantine and his contemporaries read significances they were able to deem appropriate. Disparate perspectives focused their views of the heavens and of contemporary politics. Refractions converged. They generated Constantine's charisma in no less multiply contingent and, in its way, miraculous a fashion than the physics of the celestial blazon itself.

The earliest account was rendered by a rhetor of Autun speaking at the city-anniversary of the Gallic capital Trier in 310.[2] The holiday brought citizens and rulers together to share pleasure, exchange congratulations, and thereby renew their commitment to common purposes. A speaker's art could win him recognition and credit toward his own objectives, the more effectively if he could strengthen everyone's assurance. The emperor occupied the focal point of collective hopes. Yet Maximian, the emperor who had longest survived as the Gauls' protector, recently lay dead after a contest of authority with his son-in-law, Constantine,

[1] P. Weiss, "The Vision of Constantine," trans. A.R. Birley, *JRA* 16 (2003) 237–59, expanded from Idem, "Die Vision Constantins," in J. Bleicken (ed.), *Colloquium aus Anlaß des 80. Geburtstages von Alfred Heuß*, Frankfurter althistorische Studien 13 (1993) 143–69.

[2] *Pan.Lat.* 6(7); C.E.V. Nixon and B.S. Rodgers, trans. and comm., *In Praise of Later Roman Emperors: the Panegyrici Latini*, with the Latin text of R.A.B. Mynors (Berkeley, 1994). On panegyrists' role generally, see Nixon, "Latin Panegyric in the Tetrarchic and Constantinian Period," in B. Croke and A.M. Emmett (eds.), *History and Historians in Late Antiquity* (Sydney, 1983) 88–99.

who now alone was present as emperor among them. The speaker had to rouse confidence afresh.

The traditional format of a comprehensive encomium made it possible to re-write Constantine on a new basis, as if current political realities alone had situated him in the firmament of Roman power. The speaker dated Constantine's merits from a new origin, proclaiming it a surprise: "most people up to now perhaps do not know, but those who love you know it most, from the famous divinized Claudius ancestral kinship runs into you."[3] Constantine's father Constantius added glory to this doubly deep imperial lineage. It legitimated Constantine's own rise, according to the panegyrist. It launched his narration. Constantine came to Constantius' side. The father crossed "the inmost threshold of the world" to join the council of the gods. He sanctioned his son's succession. His soldiers acclaimed it. Constantine punctiliously referred it to his constitutional superiors. He triumphantly defended Gaul. The speaker accorded unqualified approval to the carnage of defeated enemies in all three generations—by Claudius of Goths, by Constantius of Alamanns, by Constantine of Franks—as assuring Roman dominance. Now, he declared, Constantine was building up a permanently aggressive position in the form of a bridge at Cologne.

Tightly interlocking Constantine's early accomplishments with the novel claim that he descended from Claudius as well as from Constantius yielded advantageous suggestions. The continuum of three generations extended the line of victories for which Constantine could be given credit: the longer pattern could support citizens' hopes more securely. Their desire to continue expecting success could also help seduce them to attribute the victories' reality to the false ancestry. Constantine's power would seem the more autonomous.

Fusing ancestry and early achievements, standard divisions of formal panegyric, also gave the speech a strong continuity, so that what the speaker next described as Maximian's treacherous machinations could seem an even more alien interruption roiling its momentum. The speaker hesitated (*Pan.Lat.* 6[7].14). Looking to Constantine, he suspended his hearers' attention. The performance transposed an element of the interpretation of events the panegyrist was advancing and set up Constantine to act it out: he cued Constantine to nod and let the speech proceed undisturbed by the sudden crisis, just as he asserted Constantine saved his citizens from the disruption Maximian caused:

> When you were bent on this sort of measures for the advantage and honor of the state, revolutionary agitations demanded your attention—acts of that man whom it most befitted to support your successes. How am I to speak about him? Almost up to this moment I hesitate. I await counsel from the nod of Your Divinity.

[3] *Pan.Lat.* 6(7).2.1–2. No consideration validates this genealogy as fact: R. Syme, "The Ancestry of Constantine," in *Bonner Historia-Augusta Colloquium 1971*, Antiquitas Reihe 4.11 (Bonn, 1974) 237–53 = Idem, *Historia Augusta Papers* (Oxford, 1983) 63–79.

Art gave the audience an echo of the experience it claimed to represent, Constantine's majestic control.

Constantine's lineage and rise having constructed his legitimacy positively, lively narration in the next section of the panegyric complementarily demolished any authority Maximian once retained. By pretending to excuse Maximian's actions as the work of arbitrary fate, the speaker obviated explanation. The excuse did not stop him from decrying betrayal of gratitude, partnership, kindred, oaths to gods, and leadership of Gallic armies: he coolly made Constantine the anchor of loyalty rather than Maximian, for all that Maximian had been Constantine's father-in-law, the senior Tetrarch to endow him with the title Augustus, and his armies' earlier emperor-general. The speaker's indignation extended righteousness to Constantine's soldiers with the claim they loyally, eagerly strove to vindicate him. The reversal was completed when Constantine was said to have spared Maximian, but the gods avenged him "even against your will" (*Pan.Lat.* 6[7].20.4).

Finally the speaker showed the promise Maximian had failed to nullify as re-confirmed. Northern barbarians took advantage of Constantine's absence in the south while facing Maximian, but a single day after Constantine began to hasten back north to crush them, he received word they were pacified again. He turned aside, apparently from the planned march, to make thank-offerings "in the place where you had bent your route to the most beautiful temple in the world, or rather to the god in his presence, as you saw" (*Pan.Lat.* 6[7].21.3). The very simplicity of this assertion took peculiar emphasis. Whereas the speaker made a virtue of necessity in claiming Constantine's Claudian ancestry was formerly an intimate secret, now he declared, "you saw, I believe ... but why do I say, 'I believe'? You saw!" (*Pan.Lat.* 6[7].21.4). He contrasted his credence starkly against the absolute assertion. Deference to the emperor is courtly. But the speaker had already showily deferred to Constantine in introducing the topic of Maximian; repeating the device would show his resource exhausted. Moreover, his speech now sought its climax. It needed to carry the audience powerfully into the conviction of a secure future. Deference to Constantine alone would prop their hopes on the private experience of a single man. Yet if, as Weiss's identification of Constantine's solar vision entails, the festival crowd included members of that army of witnesses who, unlike the panegyrist, saw the solar halo together with Constantine on their march, invoking Constantine's knowledge implicitly invoked theirs. The listeners' experience, integral to the speaker's proof, could carry their confidence as the festival required a panegyric to do. The speaker's deference to their involvement in the miracle secured their complicity as he solicited their emotions.

The speaker identified the dazzling spectacle as Apollo and Victory offering Constantine laurel garlands each of which promised 30 years of rule (*Pan.Lat.* 6[7].21.4). Nestorian longevity, a Classical point of reference the speaker tagged explicitly, conjured hopes for stability. Maximian's 20 years as Augustus, though tailed by unrest, long exceeded most of his predecessors and saw Gaul recovering from some half-century's worth of invasion, civil war, and brigandage. Yet another decade still for Constantine would prolong security. The triple unit also echoed the three Claudian generations the speech claimed Constantine represented. Various Classicisms joined Nestor in connoting golden traditions of literarily-handled history. Of the divine sponsors the speech identified, Victory matched the context of martial celebration. The Greek and Roman sun-god Apollo was nominated by Constantine's detour. He also fit the speech's resonance with the age of Augustus, peace supervening on civil war,[4] just as the speaker recalled Caesarian and Pompeian forces clashing at Marseilles when Constantine's army besieged Maximian. Final opportunity, Apollo possessed a sacred spring and grove at Autun: the solar halo not only united the audience in memory and hope, but also gave the speaker a tie to subjoin his appeals on behalf of his home-community, sons, and pupils. The miracle was a new fact of Constantinian image-making; the matrix in which the speaker displayed it turned it also to his own artistic and material aims. Constantine bore the festival's social contract to return his approval.

Sol Invictus was a familiar military patron of Roman emperors, but on Constantine's coinage the god apparently recalled the solar halo as a special pledge.[5] Constantine's distinctive military emblem, the *labarum*, could be read as a solar emblem.[6] More broadly too, for example, the "prompting of divinity" (*instinctu divinitatis*) the Senate honored on the triumphal arch it dedicated to Constantine in 315, commemorating his conquest of Rome in 312, suggests the idea was kept current that Constantine served divine will with "his mind's immensity" (*mentis magnitudine*) and enjoyed divine support.[7]

Constantine took over Maxentius' monumental public building-projects in the heart of Rome, added another set of imperial baths, and dedicated immense churches around the periphery.[8] Magnificence beamed in all the projects: in order to cast himself as a liberator, Constantine had to outdo the "tyrant" he suppressed. Especially in the ancient capital, to which all Roman audiences might look, opulence advertised Constantine's grandeur. His Christian building became assimilated to imperial standards. Christians eagerly read endorsement.

Lactantius, formerly the Latin rhetor of Diocletian's capital Nicomedia, throughout his monograph *On the Deaths of the Persecutors* contrasted Constantine

---

4 B.S. Rodgers, "Constantine's Pagan Vision," *Byzantion* 50 (1980) 259–78.

5 Cf. P. Bruun, "The Disappearance of Sol from the Coins of Constantine," *Arctos* n.s. 2 (1958) 15–37 = Idem, *Studies in Constantinian Numismatics* (Rome, 1991) 37–48; T. Grünewald, *Constantinus Maximus Augustus: Herrschaftspropaganda in der zeitgenössischen Überlieferung*, Historia Einzelschrift 64 (Stuttgart, 1990); M. Wallraff, "Constantine's Devotion to the Sun after 324," *StudPatr* 34 (2001) 256–69.

6 H.A. Drake, *Constantine and the Bishops: the Politics of Intolerance* (Baltimore, 2000), 201–4, with references.

7 *CIL* 6.1139 = *ILS* 694; Grünewald, *Constantinus*, 78–86; L.J. Hall, "Cicero's *instinctu divino* and Constantine's *instinctu divinitatis*," *JECS* 6 (1998) 647–71.

8 M.J. Johnson, "Architecture of Empire," in N. Lenski (ed.), *The Cambridge Companion to the Age of Constantine* (Cambridge, 2006) 278–97 at 280–90.

to his targets.[9] Like the Gallic panegyrist, Lactantius described Constantine's trip from Galerius' court to Constantius' in 305 as marvelously fast. But where the panegyrist emphasized Constantius' joyous transmission of authority to his son, Lactantius crafted a thriller (Lact. *Mort.pers.* 24.3–8): Constantine slipped away from the persecutor-Augustus in the dead of night and emptied the post-stations of their horses behind him so that pursuit could not follow. The speedy journey evidently claimed a place in public knowledge about Constantine,[10] but different authors gave it different significance. Lactantius blackened Galerius. Spontaneously jealous malevolence toward Constantine personalized his alleged arbitrarily malicious will to destroy Christians. Both ascribed emotions interpreted Galerius' acts for the sake of Lactantius' narration. Even if hatred was an easy inference for contemporaries to draw, observers at the moment might more reasonably have supposed Galerius resented a son of his fellow-emperor because he had more distant relatives and allies of his own to promote (cf. Lact. *Mort. pers.* 18.8–14). It took a Christian hindsight from beyond Constantine's first pro-Christian acts to connect him with Galerius' persecutorial zeal.

When Lactantius termed Constantine's putting an end to the persecution of Christians in Constantius's territories "his first sanction on the restored holy religion,"[11] partisanship obviously globalized the extent of restoration aggressively. But Lactantius did not align his Constantine wholly with his own primarily religious interests. According to Lactantius, Maximian's revolt and attempt to assassinate Constantine were driven by treachery, lust for power, malice, and violence—flaws of the old persecutor rather than virtues of his intended victim. Constantine necessarily figured in this action, but merely instrumentally. At its denouement two Vergilian tags focused all attention on Maximian's stupefaction when he was caught and on his choice of suicide by hanging.[12] The haughty persecutor had become abject. With triumphant scorn Lactantius emphasized Maximian's title *maximus imperator* and his 20 years of rule. He became the first of the final persecutors to die. Lactantius' transition immediately following underlined the Christian god's vindication: "from him God, the avenger of religion

---

9 J.L. Creed (ed., trans., comm.), *Lactantius: De Mortibus Persecutorum* (Oxford, 1984).

10 Phot. *Bibl.* 62 summarized a two-book "history" of Constantine by Praxagoras of Athens, *FGrH* 2.B 219.3; *Origo Constantini* 2; Eus. *VConst.* 1.20–21; Aur. Vict. *Caes.* 40.2; [Aur. Vict.] *Epit.* 41.2; Zos. 2.8.3.

11 Lact. *Mort.pers.* 24.9. Cf. T.D. Barnes, *Constantine and Eusebius* (Cambridge, MA, 1981) 28; Drake, *Constantine*, 171.

12 Lact. *Mort.pers.* 30.5: *haeret manifestarius homicida et mutus stupet, quasi "dura silex aut stet Marpesia cautes"*; cf. Verg. *Aen.* 6.471 (of Dido's stoniness toward Aeneas's apology in the Underworld): *postremo datur ei potestas liberae mortis, "ac nodum informis leti trabe nectit ab alta"*; Verg. *Aen.* 12.603 (of Amata's suicide). Lactantius shifts Vergil's representation of extreme emotional states in women from pathos to disparagement of a military man.

and his own people (*deus religionis ac populi sui vindex*), transferred his eyes to the other Maximian [Galerius]" (Lact. *Mort.pers.* 31.1).

Lactantius credited Constantine with warning Maximin from renewing Galerius' persecutions after his gruesome death; Maximin, however, proceeded by subterfuge (Lact. *Mort.pers.* 37.1). Constantine's removal of Maximian's portraits, Lactantius gloated, entailed removing Diocletian's too so that the senior ex-Augustus despaired and died forlorn.[13] But Lactantius did not claim Constantine displayed either animus against Diocletian or religious intent. When he fully enrolled Constantine in Christianity's cause, he identified the initiative as its god's. He stated that the night before Constantine's army met Maxentius's near the Milvian Bridge, a dream advised Constantine to mark his shield with "the celestial sign of god" and he complied "by means of a crosswise X, the top of its head bent round, mark[ing] Christ" (Lact. *Mort.pers.* 44.5). Although Lactantius's awkward wording makes the monogram hard to picture, let alone how it might have been thought to resemble a solar halo, Weiss is right to urge that Lactantius's term "celestial sign" literally fit what the pagan panegyrist of 310 affirmed Constantine's solar vision to constitute, with only the god adjusted.[14] Solar imagery was acceptable to Christians.[15] It is likely enough that Constantine put out some story of his sign's being authorized by dream and halo at the time he adopted it. In the run-up to battle, when morale looked most eagerly for assurance, the earlier miracle could seem renewed by the nocturnal message and in its turn add the impact of a shared, waking experience to the dream's private injunctions.[16] As late as 321, Nazarius in his panegyric for Constantine's sons' quinquennalia recurred to the battle of 312 and counted heavenly armies on Constantine's side (*Pan.Lat.* 4[10].14.1–16.2, 29.1): divine support at the Milvian Bridge became canonical in popular understanding. Lactantius fit the emblem to a specifically Christian reading and appropriated credit for the victory to his god. The closer the connection with his god's support, the more this success might outshine any thought the persecutions abashed Christianity. Lactantius could only blur his partisan appraisal by relating his sacred sign to a vision seen years before.

Lactantius was telling a collective Christian story.[17] He put the Tetrarchic persecution into a sequence of Christian deaths under the authority of Roman

---

13 Lact. *Mort.pers.* 42.1–3. On the date, see T.D. Barnes, "Lactantius and Constantine," *JRS* 63 (1973) 29–46 = Idem, *Early Christianity and the Roman Empire* (London, 1984) no. 6.

14 Weiss, "Vision," 246.

15 Drake, *Constantine*, 129–32, 202–3; O. Nicholson, "Constantine's Vision of the Cross," *VChr* 53 (2000) 309–23.

16 On the efficacy credited to supernatural intervention by Constantine's contemporaries, see R. MacMullen, "Constantine and the Miraculous," *GRBS* 9 (1968) 81–96 = Idem, *Changes in the Roman Empire* (Princeton, 1990) 107–16.

17 R. Van Dam, "The Many Conversions of the Emperor Constantine," in K. Mills and A. Grafton (eds.), *Conversion in Late Antiquity and the Early Middle Ages*

emperors beginning with Jesus' own under Tiberius and Peter's under Nero. Constantine contributed vitally to reversing the Great Persecution, but Lactantius did not portray him as acting alone. In his account Constantine's visionary dream was paralleled by the dream in which an angel instructed Licinius to have his soldiers recite a monotheistic prayer before they fought with Maximin's (Lact. *Mort.pers.* 46.2–11). Where Constantine's vision was realized in an obscurely twisted monogram, Licinius relayed ten sentences of dictated text: the second miracle by which the Christian god redeemed his people dominated the tale. Lactantius observed the parallel by which Maximin like Maxentius was to be defeated on the anniversary of his reign, so that an extra day might escalate narrative tensions. Lactantius described all of Licinius's campaign against Maximin with more circumstantial detail. Although the superior rank the senate voted Constantine when he took Rome put his name at the head of the "Edict of Milan," Licinius ordered the letter to be publicly displayed after he defeated Maximin (Lact. *Mort.pers.* 48.1, 2): his voice spoke the direct quotation of the document.[18] Climactically, Maximin was the last of the persecutors to die. In the denouement of his death and of the work as a whole Licinius was the one to extirpate the families of Diocletian and of the other persecutors: Lactantius declared their utter destruction marked his god's final triumph (*hoc modo deus universos persecutores nominis sui debellavit, ut eorum nec stirps nex radix ulla remaneret*, Lact. *Mort. pers.* 50.1). Lactantius portrayed Diocletian's daughter and wife with apparent sympathy when they were harried by Maximin (Lact. *Mort.pers.* 39–41), but the pathos was opportunistic. Just as when the panegyrist of 310 praised Claudius, Constantius, and Constantine for slaughtering Rome's enemies indiscriminately, Lactantius expected his Christian audience to regard violence as justified if the victorious inflictor supported their side. Lactantius did not heroize Licinius or Constantine individually. He diverted triumphal imagery to his addressee Donatus and his sufferings as a confessor (Lact. *Mort.pers.* 16.3–11). Donatus displayed the human courage of his faith against oppression, but Lactantius declared he wrote so that he might show how his god demonstrated power by reversing the oppression (Lact. *Mort.pers.* 1.1–7, 50.1, 52.1–5). Constantine and the memory of his miracle became one element in the demonstration.

(Rochester, NY, 2003) 127–51, made a similar point about Eusebius's account of Constantine in his *Ecclesiastical History*. He contrasted the *Vita Constantini* comparably with the account below.

[18] H. Grégoire drew support from Lactantius in crediting Licinius, rather than Constantine, with the initiative in pro-Christian policy in the 310s: "La 'conversion' de Constantin," *RUB* 36 (1930) 231–72; Idem, "Eusèbe n'est pas l'auteur de la 'Vita Constantini' dans sa forme actuelle et Constantin ne s'est pas 'converti' en 312," *Byzantion* 13 (1938) 561–83; Idem, "La vision de Constantin 'liquidée'," *Byzantion* 14 (1939) 341–51. Grégoire's argument broke down, but J. Bleicken, *Constantin der Große und die Christen*, Historische Zeitschrift Beihefte15 (Munich, 1992) 13–33, has revived elements of it with nuance.

Eusebius of Caesarea, by contrast, in his *Life of Constantine* rendered Constantine a heroic and exemplary Christian.[19] Like both the panegyrist of 310 and Lactantius, Eusebius derived Constantine's imperial right from Constantius. Lactantius praised Constantius by contrast with his colleagues but admitted he destroyed church buildings in the persecutions (Lact. *Mort.pers.* 15.7); Eusebius claimed Constantius deliberately promoted confessing Christians in his service and dismissed lapsarians (Euseb. *VConst.* 1.16). He identified Constantius as a monotheist and located Christian worship at his court (Euseb. *VConst.* 1.17.3). The serene harmony with divinity Eusebius claimed for Constantius, paradoxically more like the pagan panegyrist's version than that of Eusebius's fellow-Christian, reproduced the traditional encomium's principle that virtue is pedigreed. Constantine himself, however, was raised in the palace of his enemies, an analogy Eusebius drew to Moses (Euseb. *VConst.* 1.12).[20] As in Lactantius, God delivered Constantine. But where Lactantius' dramatic action sketched the urgency of Galerius' threat, Eusebius' god inspired Constantine's perceptiveness and made him a collaborative subject of divine will (Euseb. *VConst.* 1.20). He sped to his father. Constantius declared him his heir. Constantine stepped forth in the purple. His father's people, not only the army, received him joyfully (Euseb. *VConst.* 1.22.1). God's choice was effected, Eusebius concluded, rightfulness meeting consent.

All three authors falsely suggested Constantine arrived at Constantius' side just before he died authorizing his succession; in fact they campaigned together in Britain through the summer of 305 before Constantius fell ill and died in July 306.[21] Eusebius also telescoped the time between Constantine's elevation and his assault on Rome. He stated Constantine recognized that because "the tyrant" employed magic he would need more than military support, and he considered carefully which god would aid him most dependably (Euseb. *VConst.* 1.27). History and logic recommended the god his father had honored. Constantine accordingly prayed and sought further revelation. He was answered doubly. First, he and a company of soldiers on campaign with him saw "lying over the sun a light-formed trophy of a cross, with writing attached to it saying, 'prevail by this!'" (Euseb. *VConst.* 1.28.2). He puzzled for a long time, then in his sleep "God's Christ" instructed him to use the image as a talisman. Whereas Constantine's dream in Lactantius revealed divine will just in time to catch up Constantine as its agent, Eusebius traced Constantine along the trajectory of a pious quest. According to this version, Constantine rationally connected religion and power, he sought divine guidance, he received it first in a mysterious form that publicly pre-ordained him, and finally

---

19 A.M. Cameron and S.G. Hall (trans. and comm.), *Eusebius: Life of Constantine* (Oxford, 1999).

20 C. Rapp, "Imperial Ideology in the Making: Eusebius of Caesarea on Constantine as 'Bishop'," *JThS* n.s. 49 (1998) 685–95; Cameron and Hall, *Eusebius*, 35–9.

21 *Origo* 4. *Pan. Lat.* 6[7].7.5, following reference to Constantius's final campaign, death-bed, and will for the succession (6[7].7.1–4), blurred the sequence.

he was blessed by a direct, explicit revelation that gave him the means of his success. Eusebius, like the panegyrist of 310, called attention by hesitating at the vision's marvelousness. But he deferred to Constantine's authority on the basis of the emperor's own oaths and victorious record, by ancient standards external proofs rather than mere personal assertion (Euseb. *VConst.* 1.28.1; for example, Arist. *Rh.* 1.15). In order to describe the form of Constantine's sign, Eusebius cited the public manifestation Constantine made of it in the gold and jeweled *labarum* and the emperor's helmet-badge (Euseb. *VConst.* 1.31). In the retrospect of a biography, the emperor's public emblems and success reified his averrals. After he had committed himself to the revealed sign, Constantine found experts to teach him about this faith (Euseb. *VConst.* 1.32). When he defeated Maxentius, he offered prayers of thanksgiving and publicly monumentalized his divine support (Euseb. *VConst.* 1.39.3–40.2). Eusebius reported Constantine's solar vision as a process carrying him through this first chapter of his reign: he grew into his mission. Over the remaining course of the *Life*, Constantine elevated Christianity to be, as Eusebius represented it, the pre-eminent religion of his realm, and he modeled imperial piety for his Christian successors.[22]

Constantine's vision of the solar halo served each author differently, according to historical and literary circumstances. In the face of all too continual foreign invasion, with a former defender recently fallen amid internal disputes, a panegyric's traditional victory-symbols promised cultural continuity under a new but enduringly rooted leader. In Lactantius' invective history of his faith's casting off of oppression, god's mark seals the armies he chose. Eusebius's hagiographic biography could instruct the first Christian emperor's heirs in his legacy of religious validation. Each time the celestial light flashed on Constantine. He himself projected the halo variously throughout his reign. By a constructive, polysemous miracle, it continued to meet dynamic needs. Constantine's image in memory became composed of its different reflections.

[22] Drake, *Constantine*, 389–92.

Chapter 18
The Power of the Cross: Celestial Cross Appearances in the Fourth Century

Jan Willem Drijvers
University of Groningen

In the fourth century the image of the cross developed rapidly from a symbol of disgrace into the Christian symbol par excellence. The cross could be seen everywhere: it was depicted on coins, houses, sarcophagi and weapons, sewn on clothes, and tattooed on bodies. The sign of the cross was thought to have healing power, to offer protection against evil, and to be able to ward off demonic forces.[1] Not only was the symbol of the cross considered to have these powers but so also were its relics. Around the year 330 a piece of wood considered by Christians to be the cross on which Christ had suffered and died was alleged to have been found in Jerusalem by Helena, the mother of Constantine the Great.[2] This relic, preserved in the Church of the Holy Sepulchre, had been venerated in Jerusalem on Good Friday and during the feast of the Encaenia in September since at least the mid-fourth century.[3] Pieces of the wood from the cross were quickly distributed over the Roman Empire and were not only preserved in churches but also carried around by Christians on their persons.[4] Gregory of Nyssa reports that

---

1 P. Stockmeier, *Theologie und Kult des Kreuzes bei Johannes Chrysostomos: Ein Beitrag zum Verständnis des Kreuzes im 4. Jahrhundert*, Trierer Theologische Studien 18 (Trier, 1966) 212–17.

2 On the discovery of the cross and the origin of the cult of the cross, see e.g. S. Borgehammar, *How the Holy Cross was Found: From Event to Medieval Legend* (Stockholm, 1991); J.W. Drijvers, *Helena Augusta: The Mother of Constantine the Great and Her Finding of the True Cross* (Leiden, 1992); H.A. Pohlsander, *Helena: Empress and Saint* (Chicago, 1995) 101–16.

3 *It. Eger*. 36.5–37.5, 48.2. On the Encaenia, see M.A. Fraser, *The Feast of the Encaenia in the Fourth Century and in the Ancient Liturgical Sources of Jerusalem* (diss. Univ. of Durham, 1995); accessible at http://www.encaenia.org/.

4 On the distribution of relics and the cult of the cross, see A. Frolow, *La relique de la Vraie Croix: Recherches sur le développement d'un culte* (Paris, 1961); H.A. Klein, *Byzanz, der Westen und das "wahre" Kreuz: Die Geschichte einer Reliquie und ihrer künstlerischen Fassung in Byzanz und im Abendland* (Wiesbaden, 2004). See also A.J. Wharton, *Selling Jerusalem: Relics, Replicas, Theme Parks* (Chicago, 2006) 12–15 and 18–22.

his sister Macrina carried a relic of the cross in an iron ring, apparently to be used as a talisman in order to ward off danger, demons, and enemies.[5] John Chrysostom observed that many tried to get their hands on a relic of the cross and that both women and men enclosed splinters of it in gold and wore them as a piece of jewellery.[6] However, the cross was more than a talisman, a symbol of protection against sickness, evil, and demons, or a nice decorative trinket to wear. It was first and foremost a sign that brought victory and power for Christianity and unity to the Christian community and that distinguished Christians from others. For Cyril, bishop of Jerusalem in the second half of the fourth century, the cross was the apex of his theological system: it was the glory of the catholic Church, a source of illumination and redemption, the end of sin, the source of life, a crown of honour instead of dishonour, the basis of salvation, the indestructible foundation of the faith, the sign of the Second Coming of Christ, and the symbol that brings the faithful together. It warded off those who objected to the Christian faith, even as eternal fire awaited those who denied it.[7]

This article focuses on the cross as a symbol of victory and power. This being a rather broad subject, it will focus on celestial appearances of luminous crosses in the fourth century and the way in which they can be viewed as reflecting the power of Christianity. The sources inform us about three heavenly staurophanies in the fourth century: that at the Milvian Bridge before Constantine's decisive battle against Maxentius on 28 October 312, that in Jerusalem above Golgotha extending to the Mount of Olives on 7 May 351, and a third in Jerusalem in May 363.[8] Most attention will be devoted to the two appearances in Jerusalem, which are less well-known than Constantine's famous vision before his decisive encounter against Maxentius.

---

5 *VMacrinae* 30 (*SCh* 178.238–43). F.J. Dölger, "Das Anhängekreuzchen der hl. Makrina und ihr Ring mit der Kreuzpartikel: Ein Beitrag zur religiösen Volkskunde des 4. Jahrhunderts nach der Vita Macrinae des Gregor van Nyssa," *Antike und Christentum* 3 (1932) 81–116.

6 Joh. Chrys. *Iud. et Gent.* 10 (*PG* 48.826).

7 *Catech.* 13.1, 4, 6, 19, 20, 22, 36, 37, 38, 40, 41; 15.22. P.W.L. Walker, *Holy City, Holy Places? Christian Attitudes to Jerusalem and the Holy Land in the Fourth Century* (Oxford, 1990) 256–7, 328; A. Doval, *Cyril of Jerusalem, Mystagogue: The Authorship of the Mystagogic Catecheses* (Washington, 2001) 181–3; J.W. Drijvers, *Cyril of Jerusalem: Bishop and City* (Leiden, 2004) 156–8.

8 Since J. Vogt, "Berichte über Kreuzeserscheinungen aus dem 4. Jahrhundert n. Chr.," *AIPhO* 9 (1949) 593–606, the cross's appearances in Jerusalem have received only sparing scholarly attention.

Rome AD 312

The account of Constantine's vision before the Battle of the Milvian Bridge is probably the most famous story from Eusebius' *Life of Constantine*.[9]

> About the time of the midday sun, when day was just turning, he said he saw with his own eyes, up in the sky and resting over the sun, a cross-shaped trophy formed from light, and a text attached to it which said "By this conquer." Amazement at the spectacle seized both him and the whole company of soldiers which was then accompanying him on a campaign he was conducting somewhere, and witnessed the miracle.[10]

This story, which has received considerable scholarly attention, became widely known and was integrated into the *vitae* of and legends about Constantine. It was also included in the legends of the finding of the True Cross[11] and found expression in the visual arts.[12] Many consider Constantine's vision of 312 to represent the moment of his conversion to Christianity.[13] Even though that may be questioned—his conversion was more likely a gradual process—the vision was an important event in his stand towards Christianity and an evident turning-point in the history of western civilization. In the period immediately following 312 the emperor granted Christians freedom of religion, he took measures favourable to Christians such as exemption from *munera* for the clergy, and he made Christianity visible in the urban landscape by building churches. Eusebius' narrative, however, raises many questions. One of them is why we have only a very brief account of the events leading up to the decisive battle against Maxentius from Lactantius, writing in 315, which speaks of only a dream and the chi-ro sign,[14] while Eusebius offers a

---

[9] *VConst.* 1.27–32 and the commentary by A.M. Cameron and S.G. Hall, *Eusebius. Life of Constantine* (Oxford, 1999) 204–13.

[10] *VConst.* 1.28.2. Translations follow Cameron and Hall. On supernatural or divine interventions in terrestrial affairs and on Constantine's various visions, R. MacMullen, "Constantine and the Miraculous," *GRBS* 9 (1968) 81–96, remains standard.

[11] See, e.g., S.N.C. Lieu, "From History to Legend and Legend to History: The Medieval and Byzantine Transformation of Constantine's Vita," in Idem and D. Montserrat (eds.), *Constantine: History, Historiography and Legend* (London and New York, 1998) 136–76; Idem, "Constantine in Legendary Literature," in N. Lenski (ed.), *The Cambridge Companion to the Age of Constantine* (Cambridge, 2006) 298–321.

[12] E.g. Piero della Francesca's fresco "Constantine's dream," which is part of his fresco cycle on the Legend of the True Cross in the church of San Francesco in Arezzo, or Bernini's equestrian statue of Constantine seeing the celestial cross at the Vatican.

[13] E.g. T.D. Barnes, *Constantine and Eusebius* (Cambridge, MA, 1981) 271; C.M. Odahl, *Constantine and the Christian Empire* (New York, 2004) 106; N. Lenski, "The Reign of Constantine," in Idem (ed.), *The Cambridge Companion to the Age of Constantine* (Cambridge, 2006) 59–90 at 71.

[14] Lact. *Mort.pers.* 44.5–6.

much more elaborate report of these events from the end of the 330s that includes a vision, a dream, and a cross-shaped saving sign? And why did Eusebius not include this story in his *Ecclesiastical History*, the last edition of which probably dates from 325?[15] A possible answer is that the story as told by Eusebius in the *Life of Constantine* only developed after 325 when Constantine had become more engaged with the issue of how he wished to be remembered by posterity, a concern that is attested in his foundation of Constantinople and his pre-arranged burial in the Church of the Apostles there. Eusebius' narrative of the miraculous vision and conversion may well have been part of the emperor's efforts to mould the image he wished to project to future generations; the narrative would thus reflect Constantine's desire for ideal self-representation as an exemplary Christian ruler. It is also possible that the story was composed in response to negative reports about Constantine and his choice to convert which circulated in pagan circles.[16] That Constantine was responsible for the account of the events before the battle against Maxentius is attested by Eusebius who mentions that he knew the story because it was told to him by the emperor himself who confirmed it with oaths.[17] It seems therefore that the narration of vision, dream, and conversion in the *Life of Constantine* is a constructed and retrospective interpretation composed by Constantine himself for the sake of his own self-representation and remembrance.[18] Various elements have been combined in this construct: the vision, which probably goes back to some kind of solar revelation Constantine is alleged to have had at the Apollo temple at Grand in 310;[19] the dream, of which Lactantius has the earliest, account; and the labarum, which Constantine had fashioned after his vision and dream.

---

15 T.D. Barnes, "The Editions of Eusebius' Church History," *GRBS* 21 (1980) 191–201; R.W. Burgess, "The Dates and Editions of Eusebius' *Chronici Canones* and *Historia Ecclesiastica*," *JThS* 48 (1997) 471–504 at 483 and 501–2. It is generally held that Eusebius did not include the vision story in his *Church History* because he was not well informed about western affairs and did not know the story.

16 E.g. Jul. *Caes.* 336A–B; Zos. 2.29. See in general F. Paschoud, "Zosime 2.29 et la conversion de Constantin, " *Historia* 20 (1971) 334–53 = Idem, *Cinq études sur Zosime* (Paris, 1975) 24–62.

17 *VConst.* 1.28.1.

18 This is not to deny that some portentous event happened before the battle against Maxentius, but to assert that the story about it was deliberately elaborated and embellished over the years. See, for instance, R. Van Dam, "The Many Conversions of the Emperor Constantine," in K. Mills and A. Grafton (eds.), *Conversion in Late Antiquity and the Early Middle Ages: Seeing and Believing* (Rochester, NY, 2003) 127–51. The vision may have been a solar halo, on which see P. Weiss, "The Vision of Contantine," *JRA* 16 (2003) 237–59. Cf. H. Singor, "The Labarum, Shield Blazons, and Constantine's *Caeleste Signum*," in L. de Blois et al. (eds.), *The Representation and Perception of Roman Imperial Power* (Amsterdam, 2003) 481–500. For Constantine's vision as solar vision, see M. Wallraff, *Christus Verus Sol: Sonnenverehrung und Christentum in der Spätantike* (Münster, 2001) 127ff.

19 *Pan.Lat.* 6.21.4–5.

This labarum is elaborately described by Eusebius (*VConst.* 1.31). It was of cruciform design with the chi-rho symbol on the top of the vertical pole; from the transverse bar hung a cloth decorated with precious stones and interwoven with much gold; this bore the portraits of the emperor and, following their accession, his sons. Eusebius calls it a saving sign used for protection against enemies. But it is also a sign of victory, because it was the labarum and the copies made of it which was carried as a military standard in front of his troops. This cross-shaped victory sign brought protection against hostile forces, brought Constantine his triumphs, and is clearly presented as a Christian symbol of power over Constantine's enemies.

Constantine's vision before the battle at the Milvian Bridge was known also in eastern versions. The Judas Kyriakos legend of the beginning of the fifth century, for example, reports how in his war against the northern barbarians—Goths and Sarmatians—Constantine saw along the banks of the Danube on the night before the decisive battle:

> a miraculous light that shone above him in the shape of the cross and letters written by stars whose reading taught him: "'in this [sign] you will conquer." When he woke up and arose ... he fashioned [something] like the shape of the image that had appeared to him and he ordered that it would go out before him in the battle. Consequently, there was a great victory ...[20]

It is noteworthy that this eastern vision, which recurs in other sources as well,[21] became part of the legend of the discovery of the cross. This is understandable since in both myths the cross is presented as a symbol of victory: it brings Constantine victory over his barbarian enemies and its discovery symbolizes the defeat of Christianity's enemies.[22]

Jerusalem AD 351

On 7 May 351 there occurred the remarkable appearance of a luminous cross above Golgotha extending to the Mount of Olives.[23] The apparition lasted several hours and was observed by all the inhabitants of Jerusalem. It induced young and old,

---

[20] See H.J.W. Drijvers and J.W. Drijvers, *The Finding of the True Cross: The Judas Kyriakos Legend in Syriac: Introduction, Text and Translation, CSCO* 565, Sub. 93 (Louvain, 1997) 54.

[21] E.g. Soz. 1.8.9; *BHG* 364, 81r, 82r (= S.N.C. Lieu and D. Montserrat [eds.], *From Constantine to Julian: Pagan and Byzantine Views* [London, 1996] 127–8). See also A. Linder, "The Myth of Constantine the Great in the West: Sources and Hagiographic Commemoration," *Studi Medievali* 16 (1975) 43–95 at 63–4.

[22] Drijvers and Drijvers, *The Finding of the True Cross*, 21–2.

[23] The 7th of May became a day of annual commemoration for the Jerusalem Christians as evidenced in the local calendar, see *Arm. Lect.* No. LIV (*PO* 36.195).

men and women, local folk and foreigners, and pagans and Christians to praise the Lord and to pray at length at the holy places. We know of this staurophany from a letter by Cyril, bishop of Jerusalem (ca. 350–87), to the emperor Constantius II, which the bishop presumably sent shortly after the occurrence.[24] The letter was sent by Cyril as a "first offering," implying that this was the first contact between the bishop and the emperor, and received by Constantius at a crucial point in his reign, when the emperor was confronted with very serious problems.[25]

The letter serves several purposes. Although its addressee was the emperor, it was also clearly meant for Cyril's own community as well as for the other bishops of Palestine, in particular the metropolitan in Caesarea. The letter expresses loyalty to and praise for the emperor by the newly appointed bishop. Constantius is referred to explicitly several times and is called pious and benevolent towards the Church; indeed, the tone is almost panegyrical in its praise of the emperor. The apparition of the luminous cross in the sky above Jerusalem occurred at a convenient moment. Constantius had ongoing problems on the eastern frontier, and in the west his position was threatened by the usurpation of Magnentius. Analogous to Constantine's vision before his battle against Maxentius, the appearance of the cross in Jerusalem could be taken as a favourable premonition of victory for Constantius over Magnentius and his other foes. According to Cyril, Constantius had been shown to enjoy even greater favour from God than his father Constantine, for Constantine's piety was rewarded with the discovery of the saving wood of the cross in Jerusalem whereas Constantius' age witnessed miracles appearing not from the ground but in the heavens. The cross is called the trophy of victory,[26] and this victorious symbol is said to have been sent by God to the emperor as an obvious sign of his approval of Constantius' reign. The emperor could consider God his ally in his forthcoming confrontation with Magnentius.[27]

---

24 The standard edition of the letter was published by E. Bihain, "Épitre de Cyrille de Jérusalem à Constance sur la Vision de la Croix (*BHG* 3 413)," *Byzantion* 43 (1973) 264–96. See also Vogt, "Berichte über Kreuzeserscheinungen," 596–604; H. Chantraine, "Die Kreuzesvision von 351—Fakten und Probleme," *ByzZ* 86/7 (1993/94) 430–41; Drijvers, *Cyril of Jerusalem*, 50–53.

25 Soz. 4.5 informs us that the emperor received numerous reports about the occurrence, among them Cyril's letter.

26 *Ep. ad Const.* 3: νικῆς τρόπαιον.

27 Constantius and his generals roundly defeated Magnentius at the Battle of Mursa (28 Sept. 351), but it took another two years before the usurper was finally eliminated: see for example T.D. Barnes, *Athanasius and Constantius: Theology and Politics in the Constantinian Empire* (Cambridge, MA, 1993) Ch. 12; P. Barceló, *Constantius II and seine Zeit: Die Anfänge des Staatskirchentums* (Stuttgart, 2004) 92. Philost. *HE* 3.26 reports that, at the moment the cross appeared in Jerusalem, it was also seen by Constantius and his soldiers at Mursa. The chronological discrepancy was apparently not considered a problem. The appearance of the cross, undoubtedly inspired by Constantine's vision of the cross, is also presented by Philostorgius as a clear sign of Constantius' impending victory over Magnentius. See also Theoph. a.m. 5847 and *Cons. Const.* s.a. 351. Soc. 2.28.21–3

Apart from being a sign of divine support for the emperor, Cyril portrays the celestial cross as announcing the Second Coming, which is soon to take place in Jerusalem as prophesied:

> In accordance, Emperor most favoured by God, with the testimony of the prophets and the words of Christ contained in the holy gospels, this miracle has been accomplished now and will be accomplished again more fully. For in St. Matthew's Gospel the Saviour granted his blessed apostles knowledge of future events and through them foretold to their successors in the clearest of statements: "And then the sign of the Son of Man will appear in the sky" (Matt. 24:30).[28]

The Second Coming was an important theological theme in Cyril's *Catechetical Lectures*.[29] It is not surprising, therefore, that the apparition of the luminous cross in Jerusalem is also taken as a sign announcing the *adventus* of Christ. His Second Coming will deter and destroy Christianity's enemies. Although these foes are not specified, it has recently been argued that in particular the Jews are meant.[30] That is probable, all the more so because the celestial cross must have shone right above the Temple Mount which was situated between Golgotha and the Mount of Olives. However, the Jews were not considered by Cyril as Christianity's only adversaries. In his *Catechetical Lectures* Cyril warns his catechumens not only against the Jews, but also against pagans, heretics, Manichaeans, and a large variety of gnostic movements. These groups may also have been meant by Cyril in this letter. It is, however, evident that the celestial cross about which Cyril reports marked the beginning of the fulfilment of the eschatological future in which Christ would return and defeat the enemies of the Christian faith. In this context the cross clearly symbolizes power and victory. Moreover, Cyril's eschatological scheme emphasizes the centrality of Jerusalem.

---

connects the appearance of the cross with Gallus' arrival in Antioch as Constantius' newly appointed Caesar. See also H. Leppin, "Das Bild des Gallus bei Philostorg. Überlegungen zur Traditionsgeschichte," in D. Meyer (ed.), *Philostorge et l'historiographie de l'Antiquité* (forthcoming). I am grateful to Hartmut Leppin for providing me with a still unpublished version of this article.

28 *Ep. ad Const.* 6; trans. E. Yarnold, *Cyril of Jerusalem* (London, 2000) 70.

29 See his *Catech.* 13.41, 15.1 and 22.

30 O. Irshai, "Cyril of Jerusalem: The Apparition of the Cross and the Jews," in O. Limor and G.G. Stroumsa (eds.), *Contra Iudaeos: Ancient and Medieval Polemics between Christians and Jews* (Tübingen, 1996) 85–104 at 97. This article, on which a large part of my argument is based, is the most profound interpretation of Cyril's letter. However, it neglects Cyril's political propaganda for Jerusalem and its episcopal see. According to O. Nicholson, "Constantine's Vision of the Cross," *VChr* 53 (2000) 309–23, Constantine's vision of 312 should also be seen as an eschatological premonition.

Jerusalem was central to Cyril's actions, and he seized every opportunity to promote his episcopal see.[31] It therefore comes as no surprise that the letter is to a great extent self-serving. The bishops of Jerusalem cherished and propagandized Jerusalem's biblical past. Thanks to this the bishops at the Nicene Council decided that, recognizing "custom and ancient tradition," the bishop of Jerusalem was to have a position of honour at general church councils together with the bishops of Alexandria, Antioch, and Rome. However, in his own ecclesiastical province the bishop of Jerusalem was to remain subordinate to the jurisdiction of the metropolitan bishop in Caesarea.[32] This paradoxical situation was a source of tension between the bishops of the two sees, and it was reinforced by differences between Jerusalem and Caesarea concerning doctrinal matters: in general the bishops of Caesarea tended to favour Arian tenets whereas the Jerusalem bishops kept close to the Nicene Creed. Under Cyril, Jerusalem's history and holiness were promoted to the fullest. In his opinion Jerusalem's biblical past and the presence there of sacred sites visibly and tangibly connected with Christ's life and passion merited its recognition as an apostolic see and as the prime see within the ecclesiastical province of Palestine. In particular the cross was employed by Cyril to help Jerusalem gain a favourable position in its conflict with Caesarea.[33] In order to achieve his goals Cyril needed to gain the favour of the emperor, and "a manifestation of divine approval in Jerusalem might favorably dispose the emperor toward the city and its bishop."[34] This was all the more important because Acacius, the metropolitan bishop at the time, enjoyed great influence at the court in Constantinople.[35] By reporting an appearance of a celestial cross, Cyril intended to attract the emperor's attention to Jerusalem and to gain imperial favour in order to enhance the position of his own episcopal see vis-à-vis the metropolitan in Caesarea.

It is not known whether Cyril was inspired by the stories about Constantine's visions of the celestial cross either at Rome or on the Danube. Cyril does not refer to these, but this does not necessarily mean that he did not know about them; he might have refrained from mentioning them so as not to distract from the apparition in Jerusalem.

Cyril's *Letter to Constantius* thus portrays the cross as a symbol of power and victory. It will bring Constantius triumphs over Magnentius and his other foes. As an announcement of the Second Coming the cross is also a symbol of victory over the Jews and other non-Christians. In addition Cyril uses it as a symbol of

---

31 Drijvers, *Cyril of Jerusalem*, Ch. 6 "Promoting Jerusalem."

32 J.D. Mansi, *Sacrorum Conciliorum nova et amplissima collectio* (Florence, 1759) 2.671; K.J. Hefele, *A History of the Christian Councils from the Original Documents*. Vol. 1: *To the Close of the Council of Nicaea A.D. 325* (Edinburgh, 1894) 404–9.

33 Drijvers, *Cyril of Jerusalem*, 146–7 at 156; B. Bitton-Ashkelony, *Encountering the Sacred: The Debate on Christian Pilgrimage in Late Antiquity* (Berkeley, 2005) 57–62.

34 Barnes, *Athanasius and Constantius*, 107.

35 According to Soz. 4.23.1–2, Acacius had secured the favour of the emperor through court officials.

power to extend his episcopal reach and that of his see vis-à-vis his metropolitan bishop in Caesarea.

Jerusalem AD 363

In 363 Julian the Apostate started the restoration of the Jewish Temple in Jerusalem which had been demolished by Titus in AD 70. This restoration project was one of Julian's most remarkable endeavours and had a considerable impact. Even though the project was a complete failure and was abandoned at a very early stage, probably due to an earthquake, it elicited fierce reactions from Christian authors and had a great influence on the opinion formed of Julian's reign by his Christian contemporaries as well as by later generations.[36] The source material on the event is substantial and the first references in the sources are found already within a year of Julian's death on 26 June 363. The first to mention it were Ephrem Syrus and Gregory of Nazianzus—Ephrem in one of his hymns against Julian, and Gregory in his fifth *Oration* against the pagan emperor.[37] Both give a relatively detailed account of the restoration of the Temple, but Gregory is the only one

[36] On Julian's rebuilding of the Temple, see e.g. G.W. Bowersock, *Julian the Apostate* (London, 1978) 88–90, 120–22; G. Stemberger, *Jews and Christians in the Holy Land: Palestine in the Fourth Century* (Edinburgh, 2000) 201–16; Drijvers, *Cyril of Jerusalem*, chap. 5; H. Sivan, *Palestine in Late Antiquity* (Oxford, 2008) 204–10.

[37] Ephrem, *Hym.c.Jul.* 4.18–23. For an English translation, see S.N.C. Lieu, *The Emperor Julian: Panegyric and Polemic*, 2nd ed. (Liverpool, 1989). Greg. Naz. *Or.* 5.3–4. Gregory wrote his oration against Julian in the winter of 363–64 according to J. Bernardi, "Un réquisitoire: les invectives contre Julien de Grégoire de Nazianze," in R. Braun and J. Richer (eds.), *L'empereur Julien: De l'histoire à la légende (313–1715)* (Paris, 1978) 89–98. The event is also reported or referred to, though with less rage and more matter of factly, by John Chrysostom, Ambrose, and of course by the church historians Rufinus, Socrates, Sozomen, Theodoret, and Philostorgius: Joh.Chrys. *Adv.Iud.* 5.11 (*PG* 48.900–901); *Iud. et Gent.* 16 (*PG* 48.834–5); *S. Babyla* 22 (*PG* 50.567–8); *Exp. in Ps.* 110.5 (*PG* 55.285); *De Laud. Pauli* 4 (*PG* 50.489); *Hom. in Matt.* 4.1 (*PG* 57.41); *Hom. in Acts* 41.3 (*PG* 60.291–2); Amb. *Ep.* 40.12 (*PL* 16.1105); Ruf. *HE* 10.38–40; Soc. 3.20; Soz. 5.22; Theod. *HE* 3.20; Philost. 7.9. The best treatise on the available sources is by D.B. Levenson in his unpublished thesis, *A Source and Tradition Critical Study of the Stories of Julian's Attempt to Rebuild the Temple* (diss. Harvard Univ., 1979). An abridged version is presented in his "Julian's Attempt to Rebuild the Temple: An Inventory of Ancient and Medieval Sources," in H.W. Attridge, J.J. Collins, and T.H. Tobin (eds.), *Of Scribes and Scrolls: Studies on the Hebrew Bible, Intertestamental Judaism, and Christian Origins* (Lanham, 1990) 261–79. For a more elaborate synopsis, see now Idem, "The Ancient and Medieval Sources for the Emperor Julian's Attempt to Rebuild the Jerusalem Temple," *JSJ* 35 (2004) 409–60.

to report a celestial cross.[38] According to his account the Jews, who were full of hatred for Christianity, were incited against the Christians by Julian, who gave them permission to return to Jerusalem and to restore the Temple in order to re-establish the customs (that is, the sacrificial rituals) of their forefathers. The Jews immediately seized the opportunity. Even the women helped by assisting with the actual building work and parting with their jewellery, either in order to help finance the project or to make special silver tools for its implementation.[39] While the work was in full swing, storms suddenly blew up, and the earth began to tremble. The Jews tried to seek protection in the houses of God but, as if driven by an invisible force, their doors remained shut. Then a fire broke out from the foundations of the Temple that caused many Jews to be burned. Subsequently, there appeared a cross of light in the sky above Jerusalem and the sign of the cross appeared on the clothes and bodies of all those present.

The Christian sources display a hypersensitivity regarding the site of the Temple Mount and especially the attempted rebuilding of the Temple. Although extreme, the concern of the Christians is understandable. The empty space of the Temple Mount represented a tangible expression of the defeat and ruination of Judaism as prophesied by Christ. Had Julian's project succeeded, Christ's prediction that not one stone of the Temple would be left upon another (Matt. 24:2) and the premonition in the Book of Daniel (9:26–7) that the site of the Temple would remain desolate forever would have been proven wrong and the credibility of Christian claims severely damaged.

The failure of the project must have been a tremendous relief for Christians, in particular those in Jerusalem and its vicinity, since it constituted a clear sign that they, not the Jews, had God on their side and were His chosen people. The triumphal celestial cross was a clear sign of Christian victory over the Jews. It is therefore remarkable that there are no sources on the event from Jerusalem or Palestine, unless a letter attributed to Cyril of Jerusalem is considered as such. This letter, entitled "On how many miracles took place when the Jews received the order to rebuild the Temple, and the signs which occurred in the region of Asia," was discovered some 30 years ago in a Syriac manuscript (Harvard 99).[40] It is presented as an eyewitness account written immediately after the disastrous event. However, the letter is probably not genuine.[41] In its Syriac form it may have

---

38 Later the staurophany was also mentioned by Theod. *HE* 3.20.7; Philost. 7.9; Theoph. a.m. 5855. See also S. Heid, *Kreuz, Jerusalem, Kosmos: Aspekte frühchristlicher Staurologie* (Münster, 2001) 134–6.

39 According to Deut. 27:5 and 1 Kings 6:7, the use of iron in the construction of the altar was legally forbidden.

40 S.P. Brock, "A Letter Attributed to Cyril of Jerusalem on the Rebuilding of the Temple," *BSOAS* 40 (1977) 267–86 = Idem, *Syriac Perspectives on Late Antiquity* (London, 1984) no. 10.

41 Cf. P. Wainwright, "The Authenticity of the Recently Discovered Letter Attributed to Cyril of Jerusalem," *VChr* 40 (1986) 286–93, who argues that Cyril may very well

been composed in the fifth century. Even though Cyril was almost certainly not its author, the letter may have its origin in Jerusalem because it reveals detailed knowledge about the topography of the city and presents unique information about the actions of the Jerusalem Christian community.[42] The letter, addressed to "brethren, bishops, priests, and deacons of the Church of Christ in every district," is meant to inform these of the events that occurred in Jerusalem when the Jews intended to rebuild their Temple and of how the land was shaken, prodigies were witnessed, and fire consumed a great number of Jews as well as many Christians. As a consequence of these disasters the whole city, Jews and many pagans received the sign of baptism, such that there was no one in the city who had not received the sign of the living cross in heaven. Because of what had happened, the people thought that the day of resurrection had arrived. The sign of Christ's crucifixion was received by all, and "whosoever did not believe in his mind found his clothes openly reproved him, having the mark of the cross stained on them."

In Gregory's fifth *Oration* the celestial cross is the ultimate sign of victory over the Jews.[43] It leaves its brand-mark on the clothes and bodies of those who had witnessed the shining cross in the sky. Even though the letter allegedly by Cyril does not mention a celestial cross, this cross nevertheless is an expression of power and triumph. It is the marker of victory as the cross stained on the clothes of non-believers demonstrates. It is also, as in Cyril's letter to Constantius, the victorious sign which announces the Second Coming.

Conclusion

The three known celestial staurophanies from the fourth century reveal the cross as a symbol of power and victory. In Eusebius' narrative about Constantine's vision the cross is a clear sign of victory which brings the emperor his desired triumph over Maxentius. The appearance of the cross in Jerusalem in 351 is seen as a prediction of Constantius' victory over Magnentius and, perhaps even more importantly, as a premonition of the Second Coming signifying the Christian triumph over all non-

---

have been the author of the letter. See further J.W. Drijvers, "Cyril of Jerusalem and the Rebuilding of the Jewish Temple (A.D. 363)," in C. Kroon and D. den Hengst (eds.), *Ultima Aetas: Time, Tense and Transience in the Ancient World. Studies in Honour of Jan den Boeft* (Amsterdam, 2000) 123–35; Heid, *Kreuz, Jerusalem, Kosmos,* 137–9; Levenson, "The Ancient and Medieval Sources," 427–34.

42 Drijvers, *Cyril of Jerusalem*, 145–9.

43 During the 4th century and beyond the cross was increasingly employed as the symbol of victory over the Jews. The Judas Kyriakos legend (beginning of the 5th century), the best-known version of the legend of the discovery of the cross, is a good example of this. The finding of the cross by the Jew Judas (who converted to Christianity) is evidence that the Jews had killed Christ and that Christianity was victorious over Judaism; see Drijvers and Drijvers, *The Finding of the True Cross*, 28–9.

Christians, in particular the Jews. Moreover, the bishop of Jerusalem employed the cross in his conflict with his metropolitan bishop in Caesarea. The appearance of the cross in 363 which marked the end of the rebuilding of the Jewish Temple symbolized God's abandonment of the Jews in favour of the Christians and thus once again Christianity's triumph.

PART VI
Rome: The Center of Power

Chapter 19

Augures et pontifices: Public Sacral Law in Late Antique Rome (Fourth–Fifth Centuries AD)*

Rita Lizzi Testa
Università degli Studi di Perugia

This article deals with an aspect of late antique religion which is usually associated with impotence rather than power: the traditional state cults of Rome. It examines two of the four *amplissima collegia* of ancient Rome, that is the *collegium pontificum* and the *collegium augurum*, and asks specifically whether these continued to exercise a public function during the fourth and into the fifth centuries, a period that is conventionally associated with the inexorable Christianization of the city's religious institutions.

Some years ago Alan Cameron answered this question resoundingly in the negative. He asserted that members of the Roman nobility in the fourth century continued to hold the traditional priesthoods not through any attachment to the ancestral cults and still less with any intent to mount some final defense of their religion against a triumphalist Christianity, but rather only in order that these might serve as indicators of their elevated social position. Eminent aristocrats accumulated two or even three priesthoods. This, he argued, is evidence that the colleges to which they belonged no longer served any concrete function. Therefore, in his opinion, once the priesthoods had been deprived of public financing, they were abandoned. *Flamines* and *sacerdotales* linked to the imperial cult, who are attested in North Africa until the late fifth century, survived because, in contrast with Roman priests, they continued to have responsibilities and privileges. Even so, they lost any real religious functions.[1]

There is much that is defensible in Cameron's position. He is surely right that the simultaneous assumption of several priesthoods cannot be read in the same terms in which Bloch and Alföldi read it half a century ago.[2] In Cameron's spirited

* Remembering the friendly hospitality we all enjoyed in Boulder, let me express also my warmest thanks to Noel Lenski for his help with the English version of my paper.

[1] A.D.E. Cameron, "The Last Pagans of Rome," in W.V. Harris (ed.), *The Transformation of Urbs Roma in Late Antiquity* (Portsmouth, RI, 1999) 109–21.

[2] Their opinion is well known. See H. Bloch, "A New Document of the Last Pagan Revival in the West," *HThR* 38 (1945) 199–244; Idem, "La rinascita pagana in Occidente

study one can sense a strong desire to clear the field of any conception of the last pagans as "fearless champions … of traditional cults," a conception that had already been unsustainable by the time of the conference on *The Transformations of Urbs Roma in Late Antiquity* held in Rome in 1997. In response to one extreme interpretation, however, he has introduced another that harkens back to old models, and specifically those of Cumont and his followers who believed that Roman religion and its traditional cults had been doomed even before Christianity became widespread because they were no longer able to foster deep religious feelings within their followers. Working in this school, Bouché-Leclercq held that the official Roman priesthoods had become a sinecure devoid of religious activities or responsibilities.[3] As part of this tradition, Cameron's model is thus no less radical than Bloch's or Alföldi's.

Between the two extremes, however, there exists a yawning gap. The space it creates is interwoven with subtleties, legislative second thoughts, and continuities; it was open to those who, while remaining pagan, enjoyed the chance to express their own religious identity even despite the adoption of Christianity by the emperors. An unprejudiced assessment of the sources, unfettered by obsolete paradigms of mortal conflict between pagans and Christians, allows us to explore this space more thoroughly.

Certain assumptions, taken for granted by Cameron, can be shown to be weak even on a first reading. Take, for example, his assumptions about amassing multiple offices. To be sure, the fact that many nobles boasted two or more traditional colleges in their *cursus* cannot be interpreted as proof of a rise in the devotion of those Roman aristocrats who were still pagan. In itself, however, the same fact also cannot be considered proof of a diminution in their religious enthusiasm or of the disappearance of the concrete and substantive functions of the individual colleges. Even in the high empire, tenure in a priesthood amounted to a status symbol and, quite apart from feelings of devotion, which are always difficult to quantify, the members of the senatorial aristocracy strove to win as many priesthoods as possible. Seneca, for example, captures the lament of the aristocratic malcontent thus: "He gave me the praetorship, but I was hoping for the consulate; he granted me the twelve consular *fasces*, but he did not make me *consul ordinarius*; he desired that the year carry my name, but I have yet to attain

---

alla fine del secolo IV," in A. Momigliano (ed.), *Il conflitto tra paganesimo e cristianesimo nel secolo IV* (Turin, 1968) 199–224; A. Alföldi, *Die Kontorniaten* (Budapest, 1943), esp. chap. 4, which has been republished without corrections in A. and E. Alföldi, *Die Kontorniaten-Medaillons* (Berlin, 1990).

3 F. Cumont, *Les religions orientales dans le paganisme* (Paris, 1929); P. de Labriolle, *La réaction païenne* (Paris, 1934); A. Bouché-Leclercq, *Histoire de la divination dans l'Antiquité* (Paris, 1882) 4.285. Idem, *Manuel des Institutions romaines*, 2nd ed. (Paris, 1931) 555, argues that the only cult which was expanding was the imperial cult.

my goal of the priesthood; I've been co-opted into a priestly college, but why just one?"[4]

In addition, imperial inscriptions demonstrate that it was by no means exceptional for a Roman senator to hold two priesthoods, even if—in contrast with his late antique counterpart—he held only one of the four *amplissima collegia* (that is the *pontifices*, *augures*, *quindecemviri sacris faciundis*, and *septemviri epulonum*) in conjunction with one of the four *sodalitates* (*arvales*, *salii*, *luperci*, *fetiales*), or with a priesthood in the imperial cult.[5] Less common, but not impossible, was the assumption of three. Religious appointments were thus already a potent signal of the social prestige that an individual could enjoy.[6]

Other components played into the desire to assume a Roman priesthood. Around AD 102, having just learned that posts in two major colleges had become available, Pliny the Younger asked Trajan directly for the office of *augur* or *semptemvir*. His letter shows almost no trace of religious ardor. It argues instead that such a nomination would have confirmed Trajan's esteem for Pliny and that in his function as priest (whether *augur* or *septemvir*) Pliny could "pray to the gods officially on behalf of the emperor," which he had been able to do previously only as a private citizen.[7] The letter shows that the sense of hierarchy between the four *amplissima collegia*, which had been so strong in the Republican period, was beginning to vanish, with the exception of the ongoing primacy of the pontificate.[8] On the other hand, the letter confirms that, ever since the days of Augustus, who

[4] Sen. *De ira*, 3.2: *Dedit mihi praeturam, sed consulatum speraveram; dedit duodecim fasces, sed non fecit ordinarium consulem; a me numerari voluit annum, sed deest mihi ad sacerdotium; cooptatus in collegium sum, sed cur in unum?* See S. Orlandi, "Osservazioni prosopografiche sulle Vestali," *RPAA* 68 (1995–96) 359–71, esp. 359.

[5] G. Howe, *Fasti sacerdotum populi Romani* (Leipzig, 1904) remains useful, but for convenient prosopographical research and useful contextualization see now J. Rüpke, *Fasti sacerdotum: Die Mitglieder der Priesterschaften und das sakrale Funktionspersonal römischer, griechischer, orientalischer und jüdisch-christlicher Kulte in der Stadt Rom von 300 v.Chr. bis 499 n.Chr.,* 3 vols. (Stuttgart, 2005).

[6] Over three centuries, 13 nobles held three priesthoods simultaneously. From a new inscription it is possible to add L. Pomponius Horatia Bassus Cascus Scribonianus, who was *augur*, *fetialis*, *sodalis Titialis*: see S. Panciera, "Lucius Pomponius Horatia Bassus Cascus Scribonianus Luci Bassi consulis et Torquatae filius," in Idem (ed.), *Epigrafi, epigrafia, epigrafisti: Scritti vari editi e inediti (1956–2005) con note complementari e indici*, 3 vols. (Rome, 2006) 2.1029–46 at 1037.

[7] Plin. *Ep*. 10.13: *Cum sciam, domine, ad testimonium laudemque morum meorum pertinere tam boni principis iudicio exornari, rogo dignitati, ad quam me provexit indulgentia tua, vel auguratum vel septemviratum, quia vacant, adicere digneris, ut iure sacerdotii precari deos pro te publice possum, quos nunc precor pietate privata.*

[8] Fest. 198–200 describes the hierarchy of *rex sacrorum*, *flamen Dialis*, *flamen Martialis*, *flamen Quirinalis* and *pontifex maximus*: see F. Van Haeperen, *Le collège pontifical (3ème s.a.C.– 4ème s.p C.): contribution à l'étude de la religion publique romaine* (Brussels, 2002) 89–96.

had revitalized and restructured even the college of the *fratres Arvales* to serve the imperial cult, the performance of religious acts on behalf of the emperor had become one of the central functions for each of the four traditional colleges.[9] Here it helps to remember that the Roman emperor was never conceived of as an absolute divinity, as Christianizing approaches used to assume. Rather, he acquired divine status through the honors directed toward his persona.[10] Bearing this in mind, we can better understand the force of Pliny's request. Alongside the "weak" proposition that this would offer some confirmation of imperial favor, which he had already acquired just two years earlier with the ordinary consulship, the public prayers that he would be able to offer as *augur* constituted the "strong" motive for convincing Trajan to confer the priesthood upon him.

Pliny was even more explicit about why he had desired the augurate in a response he crafted to congratulations offered by Maturus Arrianus upon his receipt of the office. The appointment he had received proved the lofty esteem in which the emperor held him, but this was not like other honors:

> For the priesthood is an old-established religious office and has a particular sanctity in that it is held for life. There are other positions no less honorable, but they can be bestowed and taken away, whereas in this the element of chance is limited to the bestowal.[11]

Certain characteristics thus rendered each of the four Roman priesthoods particularly attractive for a senator in the early centuries of the empire: the fact that these honors were not limited in time qualified the *sacerdotium* as *insigne* and made those who held it *insignes*. Above all, however, according to Pliny, the fact that it was an ancient office strengthened its connection with the religious and the sacred (*cum priscum et religiosum tum hoc quoque sacrum plane*); whoever held it participated in this sacredness and was able to boast a privileged relationship with the divine; his prayers, being those of a public priest, would be efficacious enough to benefit the emperor more potently and thus make his cult more stable. Furthermore, in a religious system like Rome's, this public sacredness was able to be realized in concrete fashion thanks to the ability of the members of the

---

[9] M. Beard, J. North, and S. Price, *Religions of Rome*, 2 vols. (Cambridge, 1996) 1.192–6.

[10] K.K. Hersch, Review of I. Gradel, *Emperor Worship and Roman Religion*, *JRS* 95 (2005) 259–60.

[11] Plin. *Ep.* 4.8.1–2: *deinde quod sacerdotium ipsum cum priscum et religiosum tum hoc quoque sacrum plane et insigne est quod non adimitur viventi. Nam alia quamquam dignitate propemodum paria ut tribuuntur sic auferuntur, in hoc fortunae hactenus licet, ut dari possit.*

four *amplissima collegia* to guarantee the preservation of forms and traditional institutions as they had been handed down since antiquity.[12]

No late antique noble has left a document analogous to these letters of Pliny that could help us to understand what fueled people's desire to hold traditional priesthoods in the fourth century. Nevertheless, individuals did continue to assume them even though emperors from Constantine onward, with the brief exception of Julian, made ever clearer pronouncements of their personal preference for Christianity. We can be certain, however, that no Roman aristocrat of the fourth century would have added or subtracted any of the motivations Pliny expressed. They would not have disregarded the imperial esteem indicated by the grant of such priesthoods, regardless of whether the appointment was made directly by the emperor or the emperor simply ratified nominations submitted by the various colleges. Furthermore, since the high empire nothing had changed in regard to the length of the various public offices, so that even in the fourth century the four traditional priesthoods remained noticeably distinct from the magistracies or imperial *administrationes* precisely because they lasted a lifetime. As for the power associated with their antiquity, it is useful to recall that Q. Aurelius Symmachus mentioned this in his attempts to claim the absolute authority of Rome's traditional religion in contrast with the Christian religion.[13] At the same time, the dry language of imperial constitutions confirms that, even in the fifth century, this same antiquity appeared to be an asset capable of rendering statues and pagan temples worthy of preservation and even veneration. In so far as they were works of art, they had been rescued from the contamination of the abhorrent cults and, with a few rare exceptions, were judged worthy of being preserved from the ravages of time and from violent destruction.[14] Art, it seems, was nothing

---

[12] F. Jacques and J. Scheid, *Roma e il suo impero: Istituzioni, economia, religione* (Rome, 1982) 145–9, 153–4; J. Scheid, *La religione a Roma* (Rome, 1983) 8–11; G.J. Szemler, "Priesthoods and Priestly Careers in Ancient Rome," in *ANRW* 2.16.3 (Berlin, 1986) 2314–31.

[13] Symm. *Rel.* 3.8: *Si longa aetas auctoritatem religionibus faciat, servanda est tot saeculis fides et sequendi sunt nobis parentes, qui securi sunt feliciter suos*; cf. 3.10: *videro quale sit quod instituendum putatur; sera tamen et contumeliosa est emendatio senectutis.*

[14] Even emperors who developed a very strict policy against paganism did not forget the artistic value of the ancient temples and statues. Constans issued *CTh* 16.10.3 (a. 341); Theodosius I *CTh* 16.10.8 (a. 382): *simulacra feruntur posita artis pretio quam divinitate*; Honorius *CTh* 16.10.15 (a. 399): *sicut sacrificia prohibemus, ita volumus publicorum operum ornamenta servari*; cf. *CTh* 16.10.17–18. Notwithstanding the law which Theodosius II issued in Costantinople in 435 (*CTh* 16.10.25: *cunctaque eorum fana templa delubra, si qua etiam nunc restant integra, praecepto magistratuum destrui ... praecipimus*), in Rome the situation remained different: Majorian in 458 (*Nov.Mai.* 4) and even still Theodoric in 510–11 (Cass. *Var.* 3.31.3–4) ordered that the temples had to be preserved from destruction as they were public and artistic monuments. See C. Lepelley, "Le musée des statues divines. La volonté de sauvegarder le patrimoine artistique païen à l'époque théodosienne," *CahArch* 42 (1994) 5–15; J. Curran, "Moving Statues in Late Antique Rome: Problems of

less than the sister of antiquity, even still for Macrobius, who attributes to Vettius Agorius Praetextatus this very notion.[15]

Another point in Cameron's analysis requires further inquiry. The cause-and-effect relationship that he identifies between the measures taken by Gratian and the abandonment of the priesthoods by the aristocracy can hardly be viewed as having been automatic. To limit ourselves only to Roman augurs and pontiffs, we know the names of some nobles that continued to advertise their tenure in these priesthoods between 375 and 390/395. Leaving aside the first aristocrats in Bloch's list,[16] who died around 370–76 and must therefore have held their priesthoods in the first half of the fourth century,[17] it is clear that Q. Aurelius Symmachus, P. Ceionius Caecina Albinus, Virius Nicomachus Flavianus Senior, Vettius Agorius Praetextatus and Alfenius Caeonius Iulianus Kamenius assumed their priesthoods around 360. Q. Clodius Flavianus, however, who dedicated an *ara taurobolica* on 5 April 383, must have had yet to assume any *honores* since he was still very young and must have assumed all the priesthoods listed in the same year: *pontifex maior*, *quindecimvir*, *septemvir*, and *pontificium Solis*.[18] In the same

Perspective," *ArtH* 17 (1994) 46–58. A western senatorial influence can be identified in the issuance of these laws: see R. Lizzi Testa, "Paganesimo politico e politica edilizia: la 'cura Urbis' nella tarda antichità," in *Centralismo e autonomie nella tarda antichità. Categorie concettuali e realtà concrete. AARC XIII Conv. Intern. (Perugia 1–4 ottobre 1997)* (Naples, 2001) 671–707, and now C.J. Goddard, "The Evolution of Pagan Sanctuaries in Late Antique Italy (Fourth–Sixth Centuries AD): A New Administrative and Legal Framework. A Paradox," in M. Ghilardi, C.J. Goddard, and P. Porena (eds.), *Les cités de l'Italie tardo-antique (IVe–VIe siècle): Institutions, économie, société, culture et religion* (Rome, 2006) 281–308.

15 Macr. *Sat.* 1.5.4: *Nec insolenter parentis artium antiquitatis reverentiam verberemus*. New perspectives on the antiquarian interests in Late Antiquity can be found in C. Machado, "Religion as Antiquarianism: Pagan Dedications in Late Antique Rome," in J. Bodel and M. Kajava (eds.), *Dediche sacre nel mondo greco-romano: Diffusione, funzione, tipologie* (Rome, 2009) 331–54.

16 Bloch, "A New Document," 245; see also Idem, "Ein neues Zeugnis der letzten Erhebung des Heidentums," in R. Klein (ed.), *Das frühe Christentum im römischen Staat* (Darmstadt, 1971) 129–86 and the plate at the end of the volume.

17 Thus Memmius Vitrasius Orfitus, who disappeared around 370; Clodius Octavianus, who died in 371; L. Aurelius Avianius Symmachus, who died in 376.

18 *CIL* 6.501 = *ILS* 4149: *M(atri) d(eum) m(agnae) I(daee) / et Attidi sancto / Menotyranno, / Q(uintus) Clodius Flavianus / v(ir) c(larissimus), pont(ifex) maior, / XVvir s(acris) f(aciundis), / septem / vir epulonum, / pontifex dei Solis, / taurobolio criobo / lioque percepto / aramque dicavit, / nonis Aprilibus / FFll(aviis) Merobaude II / et Saturnino / cons(ulibus).* As is evident, this dedication mentions only priesthoods, without public offices. Onomastics indicates the dedicant's descent from a Clodius or a Flaviana. So too the presence in the *Phrygianum* of the dedication of Q. Clodius Hermogenianus Caesarius, *tauroboliatus* on the occasion of his urban prefecture in 374, a decade prior to Q. Clodius Flavianus, and of a *clarissima femina* who offered an altar for having repeated the *taurobolium* the same day as Q. Clodius Flavianus, might indicate that the dedicant was the

way L. Ragonius Venustus, who received the *taurobolium* and *criobolium* in 390 having already been *pontifex* and *augur*, must be the second—anonymous—son of Nicomachus Flavianus Senior.[19] The fact that his brother Nicomachus Flavianus Iunior did not hold any priesthood may then be less an objective fact than a false impression based on the simple failure to find inscriptions that mention them.

Similarly, inscriptions can offer only a partial impression of how deep into the fourth and fifth century the four priesthoods continued to be occupied. Pagan religious affiliations were usually recorded along with other public offices in the *cursus* of persons of importance. Such careers were usually inscribed on the bases of statues, dedicated either by the will of the senate or (in more exceptional cases) of the emperor, or (more frequently) by family members. At times these statues and their inscriptions were destined for public spaces like the *forum*, but more often they were reserved for the *atria* of *domus*, and if they appeared on funerary *tituli*, they were obviously destined for private spaces. By contrast, lists of offices and priesthoods held by an individual almost never appear in the dedications of buildings newly constructed or restored. There the name of the dedicant is followed only by an indication of the office he held at the moment when the public work was dedicated. Nor is this a question of a custom falling into desuetude with the advance of Christianity, but rather a practice generally followed throughout the course of the empire in response to precise rules on the control and limitation of individual power by an oligarchic group that was internally competitive and recognized the superiority of imperial authority alone.[20] Over the course of the fourth century, while honorific titles decrease almost to the point of disappearing by century's end, the quantity of dedications for public buildings remains relatively high.

It is sufficient to examine the provenance of the evidence assembled by Bloch to understand that we would have difficulty knowing the religious affiliations of the "last pagans" if the *taurobolium* altars of the *Phrygianum Vaticanum* had never been found. In these terms, it is undeniable that up to now the oldest public dedication mentioning a pagan priest is that of Avianius Symmachus inscribed on the base of a statue dedicated to him in the *forum* of Trajan at Rome.[21] Nevertheless,

---

son of these two: see R. Lizzi Testa, *Senatori, popolo, papi. Il governo di Roma al tempo dei Valentiniani* (Bari, 2004) 266.

19 *CIL* 6.503 = *ILS* 4151: *PLRE* 1 *Lucius Ragonius Venustus* 3. For the hypothesis that he was the other—anonymous—son of Nicomachus Flavianus Senior, see Lizzi Testa, *Senatori, popolo, papi*, 267 n.201.

20 See, e.g., the inscriptions of Lollianus Mavortius, PUR in 342, collected by A. Chastagnol, *Les Fastes de la Préfecture de Rome au Bas-Empire* (Paris, 1962) 114–21: the three inscribed bases of Pozzuoli give the *cursus* of this person (ibid. 117) while the dedication of the *statio aquarum* mentions only the office held in 328 of *curator aquarum et Minuciae* (ibid. 118). Similar examples could be added.

21 H. Niquet, *Monumenta virtutum titulique: Senatorische Selbstdarstellung im spätantiken Rom im Spiegel der epigraphischen Denkmäler* (Stuttgart, 2000) 178.

this datum cannot be interpreted as a sign of the disaffection of Roman aristocrats from the traditional priesthoods. It is not so much their mention in the *cursus* that falls away in the course of the second half of the fourth century as the honorific *tituli*—the type of inscription in which priesthoods were usually listed alongside public offices—which diminish markedly in this period. Paradoxically, if we knew Vettius Agorius Praetextatus only from the inscription he put up for the restoration of the *porticus deorum consentium* during his urban prefecture, we would think that he himself, while of course pagan and interested in the renovation of a temple building in ruins, held no religious priesthood.[22]

The haphazard nature of epigraphic evidence precludes a precise and documented reconstruction of the phenomenon of Christianization of the western senatorial class. Be that as it may, the need for certainties should not drive us to oversimplified schematism. Only because of a cursory reference in the *Vita Melaniae*, for example, do we know that Rufius Antonius Agrypnius Volusianus, the uncle of Melania the Younger, was still pagan in 436. Although an old hypothesis that he was a catechumen when he reached Constantinople has recently been revived, the bulk of the evidence concerning him confirms the generally accepted idea that he remained pagan throughout his life and converted only shortly before his death in 437.[23] The text of the *Vita Melaniae* identifies him as still pagan upon his arrival in the city, such that we must conclude that he agreed to become a catechumen only during his final illness and to receive baptism only the day before he expired in the arms of his niece—who wanted to have him take communion thrice—on the Feast of Epiphany in 437.[24] If Volusianus had reached Constantinople already a catechumen, there would have been little sense in the dialogue with his niece, who after having learned of his arrival in a letter and

---

22 *CIL* 6.102 = *ILS* 4003. For an analysis of the epigraphic corpus related to Vettius Agorius Praetextatus see M. Kahlos, *Vettius Agorius Praetextatus: A Senatorial Life in Between*, Acta Instituti Romani Finlandiae 26 (Rome, 2002) 216–25. Further considerations on the difficulty of deriving certain information on the religion professed by the senators of the city in this period from inscriptions in R. Lizzi Testa, "Dal conflitto al dialogo: nuove prospettive sulle relazioni tra pagani e cristiani in Occidente alla fine del IV secolo," in *Trent'anni di studi sulla tarda antichità: bilanci e prospettive (Napoli 21–23 novembre 2007)* (Naples, 2009) 167–90.

23 On the conversion of Volusianus see A. Chastagnol, "Le sénateur Volusien et la conversion d'une famille de l'aristocratie romaine au Bas-Empire," *REA* 58 (1956) 241–53, with important clarifications at Idem, *Les Fastes*, 276–9. M. Moreau, "Le dossier Marcellinus dans la Correspondance de saint Augustin," in *RecAug.* 9 (1973) 7–181, esp. 49–77 and 123–9, attributed to Volusianus and his group of friends a nuanced skepticism of religious discontent, without excluding the notion, advanced by others, that he moved in a circle of catechumens at Carthage. In examining the letters, however, Moreau admits beyond doubt that the friends of Volusianus and he himself were pagans, steeped in the neo-Platonism of a Porphyrian mould (123–9).

24 *VMel.* 4.50–5 (*SCh* 90.224–38); E. Clark, *The Life of Melania the Younger* (New York, 1984) 62–8 and commentary at 129–33; *PCBE* 2.2.2340–41.

knowing him still to be pagan had left Jerusalem suddenly in order to convert him and who upon reaching him made every effort to convince him to "free himself from the falsity of demons."[25]

Some passages in the *Vita Melaniae*, in turn, would seem to suggest even more radical hypotheses about the form in which his paganism had been expressed up to that point. In the text Volusianus begs Melania not to call the emperor's attention to him but to permit that his potential conversion should spring from an act of free will.[26] These words, put into Volusianus's mouth by the hagiographer rather than being a transcript of what Volusianus actually said, are meant to draw attention to the action of Gerontius' "champion of the faith," who was suddenly able to cause Volusianus' lifelong pagan stubbornness to waiver. Thus Volusianus, although still pagan, spoke like a Christian because divine grace had worked its power in him through the sanctity of Melania. Gerontius is obviously not Alessandro Manzoni, but the rhetorical artifices he adopts in describing the conversion of Volusianus are identical with those used in the conversion of the Innominato. It is difficult to say what actually happened. It is probable, however, that Volusianus chose to speak the language of his niece in order to prevent her from going through with her proposition to report his paganism to the emperor.

The meaning of this threat, furthermore, is far from clear. One wonders in particular how the emperor would have been able to compel a pagan senator who was still reluctant to become Christian to convert. Animal sacrifices and the entrance into temples had been forbidden several times, but no law up to that point had imposed Christianity on imperial functionaries or members of the senate, nor does it seem that the doctrine professed by an individual had any influence on imperial choices of functionaries.[27] The emperor would have been able to intervene officially only if Volusianus had continued to hold one pagan priesthood or another, all the while avoiding any public declarations about all the evils that had happened to the empire because of a religion like Christianity, which had distracted subject and emperor from the defense of the common good.[28] There is nothing to prevent us from speculating that Volusianus, who was born around

---

25 *VMel.* 4.53 (*SCh* 90.231–2).

26 *VMel.* 4.53 (*SCh* 90.232) = Clark, *Life of Melania*, 65: "I exhort your holiness not to take from me the gift of self-determination with which God has honored us from the beginning. For I am completely ready and long to wash away the stain of my many errors. But if I should do this by the command of the emperors, I would gain it as if I had come to it through force and would lose the reward of my free decision."

27 For the recruitment of court functionaries, see now M.G. Castello, "Cristianesimo e burocrazia tardoimperiale: La religiosità dei *magistri officiorum*," *CrSt* 26 (2005) 625–70.

28 Aug. *Ep.* 136.2. Further considerations on Volusianus as a stereotype for an entire generation of young aristocrats born in a world already potentially Christian, but in whom the disastrous sack of Rome provoked a crisis at the religious level, in R. Lizzi Testa, "La conversione dei 'cives', la evangelizzazione dei 'rustici': alcuni esempi fra IV e VI secolo," in *Città e campagna nei secoli altomedievali: LVI Settimana di Studio del CISAM (Spoleto 27 marzo–1 aprile 2008)* (Spoleto, 2009) 115–50.

375, might have been co-opted into one of the greater priestly colleges in the manner of Q. Clodius Flavianus and L. Ragonius Venustus, who in 383 and 390 respectively dedicated altars in the Phrygianum Vaticanum, perhaps at the same time they assumed public priesthoods.[29]

As Lepelley has recently suggested, during a long period in which phases of tolerance and intolerance alternated, notable citizens who were often still pagan chose neutrality in the face of pressures from the emperor and Christian bishops. Rather than provoking direct conflict they opted for different forms of accommodation. At Rome the members of the nobility continued to perform—as Vestals, pontiffs and augurs—certain traditional ceremonies that, without involving animal sacrifices or entrance into temples, were tolerated even after 391, whether because they were celebrated by elements of the aristocracy or because their "pagan" significance had been totally reabsorbed into their civic value. In the provinces, many notables maintained their own private cults; they continued to visit local temples too, but in ways that were neither illegal nor suspect; they offered dedications in which they advertised not their own priesthoods, but rather those of Roman senators, who lived among them in growing numbers, and were celebrated as *augures publici populi Romani Quiritium*.[30]

Alongside a careful examination of the attestations of *pontifices* and *augures*, which in Africa extend down to 375[31] and in Rome down to 390/395, we must investigate more closely the actual effect of Gratian's measures regarding such priesthoods. In fact, it is probable that these had less of a negative impact on the desire of late antique nobles to assume traditional priesthoods than was previously assumed, for their extent was much more limited than heretofore believed. Gratian's measures have been considered a decisive step toward the delegitimization of traditional paganism, above all because they have been spoken of almost always as part of some anti-pagan package that included the refusal of the title *pontifex maximus* and the removal of the altar of Victory from the *curia* of the senate. Gratian is thus supposed to have sapped traditional paganism's foundations by coupling actions of broader ideological scope with more concrete measures at the legislative level: public cult is said to have been deprived of state

---

[29] Above nn. 18–19.

[30] C. Lepelley, "Le lieu des valeurs communes: la cité terrain neutre entre païens et chrétiens au IVe siècle," in H. Inglebert (éd.), *Les idéologies civiques dans l'Antiquité grecque et romaine: Hommages à Claude Lepelley* (Paris, 2002) 271–85, esp. 275.

[31] On *augures* and *pontifices* in the African towns see X. Dupuis, "Les pontifes et les augures dans les cités africaines au Bas-Empire," in *Afrique du Nord antique et médiévale: Spectacles, vie portuaire, religions. Actes du Ve colloque international du CTHS (Avignon 1990)* (Paris, 1992) 139–51. Furthermore, in this region the nature of the documentation changes and the municipal *cursus*, which report the names of pontiffs and augurs in the 2nd and 3rd centuries, subsequently disappear almost entirely in favor of dedications of monuments that are usually less explicit on priestly offices held by the honoree (141–2).

financing; Vestals and all other priestly colleges are said to have had their fiscal immunities withdrawn, and temples their *fundi*.[32]

Recently, it has become necessary to refine our assumptions about the content of these provisions. The sources that offer evidence for Gratian's dispositions are few and vague. On the refusal of the title *pontifex maximus*, we have had to rely on a single reference in Zosimus.[33] By now Cameron has subjected the traditional interpretation of this passage to a healthy dose of skepticism, arguing that it was not a question of refusing the pontifical robe and the title. In fact, there was no specific pontifical robe in antiquity, and the college does not seem ever to have offered one to any previous emperor. The text may simply be developing a source—not a well-informed, Latin one, but a Greek antiquarian source—in which Gratian's refusal to accept the senate's requests about the pagan cults is described.[34]

As regards provisions pertinent to public cults, priestly colleges, and temples, the only truly useable evidence—apart from later references that have been entirely distorted by polemic[35]—is the third *Relatio* of Q. Aurelius Symmachus and the two related letters of Ambrose.[36] A summary of the facts related to the removal of the altar of Victory from the senate house is also given in a letter Ambrose wrote to Eugenius in 394.[37] No imperial constitution remains, however, in which the original imperial dispositions are given. Strictly speaking, Ambrose's first letter to Valentinian II is entirely generic because the bishop declares that he had just heard about the consistory's or senate's attempt to discuss Gratian's measures but

---

32 From G. Boissier, *La fin du paganisme: Étude sur les dernières luttes religieuses en Occident au IVe siècle* (Paris, 1891), to the recent J.H.W.G. Liebeschuetz and C. Hill, *Ambrose of Milan: Political Letters and Speeches* (Liverpool, 2005) 13–14 and 61, and even S. Mitchell, *A History of the Later Roman Empire, AD 284–641* (Oxford, 2007) 248, this traditional view is present in both general surveys and specific studies. Cf. A. Piganiol, *L'Empire chrétien (325–395)*, 2nd ed. (Paris, 1972) 250; A. Chastagnol, *La préfecture urbaine à Rome sous le Bas-Empire* (Paris, 1960) 157–60; D. Vera, *Commento storico alle* Relationes *di Quinto Aurelio Simmaco* (Pisa, 1981) 12–23, and almost all the recent bibliography on the subject.

33 Zos. 4.36.

34 A.D.E. Cameron, "The Imperial Pontifex," *HSCP* 103 (2007) 341–84, in whose opinion no Roman emperor refused the title, which nevertheless was changed from *maximus* (fatally compromised by its pagan connections) to *inclitus*: the emperor is celebrated as *pontifex inclitus* in an edict by Marcian and Valentinian III in 452 and in a letter from Anastasius to the senate of 516.

35 N. McLynn, *Ambrose of Milan: Church and Court in a Christian Capital* (Berkeley, 1994) 264.

36 Symm. *Rel.* 3: text, Italian translation and historical commentary in Vera, *Commento storico*, 23–53, 352–4, 390–94. An introduction, English translation, and notes of Ambr. *Ep.* 72(17), 73(18), and Symm. *Rel.* 3 can be found at Liebeschuetz and Hill, *Ambrose of Milan*, 61–94.

37 Amb. *Ep. extra coll.* 10(57); cf. Liebeschuetz and Hill, *Ambrose of Milan*, 255–61. Similarly Amb. *De obitu Val.* 19.

was still poorly informed about the content of that initiative.[38] Even if that was not entirely true—the letter contains some direct references to Symmachus' third *Relatio*—he had to be consistent with his own claims.[39] Over the course of the first letter, then, the requests metamorphose from a generic "to build altars and to finance profane sacrifices," to "give them privileges," and even "to build an altar and to furnish funds for the pagan sacrifices." Never is the altar described as the altar of Victory in the senate house, and never are the funds for the sacrifices defined in more precise terms.[40] There is also an allusion to the privileges requested for the Vestals, but it is too vague to be useful.[41] There is little difference in Ambrose's approach in the letter to Eugenius, where he does not so much describe the requests of successive senatorial embassies as he does his relationship with different emperors who had had to refuse their requests, in order to show that in the case of Eugenius he was threatening nothing different from what he did with previous emperors. He summarizes the contents of these requests in a few sentences, such as: "to give to the idols, and not to return to them," or "to raise altars to Gods, not to replace them."[42]

Even the second letter to Valentinian II, which Ambrose wrote with a copy of Symmachus' third *Relatio* in hand, is clear only about the kind of altar the pagan senators asked to restore in the senate house.[43] Regarding the other requests, the comparison between Symmachus' text and this letter confirms that Ambrose wished to use only generic terms. In particular, he describes Gratian's measures involving not only Vestals but also other pagan priests since he actually wanted to show that, if the emperor restored the previous *status religionum* as the senate had asked, he had to abolish the recent laws on Christian priests of curial origin and to allow Christian virgins the same privileges requested for the pagan Vestals.[44]

---

38 Amb. *Ep.* 72(17).10.

39 Ambrose surely knew Symmachus' *Relatio* when he wrote the first letter to Valentinian II, as can be seen from several passages: compare Symm. *Rel.* 3.3 with Amb. *Ep.* 72(17).2, which uses the same term, *dissimulatio*; Symm. *Rel.* 3.5 and Amb. *Ep.* 72(17).9, on the altar of Victory; Symm. *Rel.* 3.7, 10, 11, 13, 15 and Amb. *Ep.* 72(17).14, about the comparison between the Vestals and the virgins of God; Symm. *Rel.* 3.20 and Amb. *Ep.* 72(17).14, 16, for the imaginary speeches Gratian and Valentinian I directed to Valentinian II from heaven.

40 Amb. *Ep.* 72(17).2, 4, 9.

41 Amb. *Ep.* 72(17).14.

42 Amb. *Ep. extra coll.* 10(57).3–5.

43 Amb. *Ep.* 73(18).1.

44 The central section of the second letter to Valentinian II (*Ep.* 73[18].11–16) develops a comparison between the Vestals, who had lost their *alimenta publica* (Symmachus' *annonae*), and the Christian priests, who could not receive properties from widows (*CTh* 16.2.20 [30 July 370], 16.2.22 [1 December 372]) and had recently had to renounce their patrimony if they wanted to become clerics and enjoy fiscal immunities (*CTh* 12.1.99 [18 April 383], 12.1.104 [7 November 383]).

Nevertheless, from Symmachus' third *Relatio* we gather that Gratian had cancelled some privileges that had previously been enjoyed only by the Vestals: the first of these "prerogatives of the Vestal Virgins that had been removed" (*detracta praerogativa Vestalium virginum*) is a *stipendium castitatis*, a sort of pay (*peculium*) which they had received from the State since the creation of their college by the King Numa.[45] The second is fiscal immunity (which Symmachus describes as *vacatio muneribus*) guaranteed by all the emperors up to the time of Gratian "to the virginity consecrated to the public benefit" (*saluti publicae dicata virginitas*).[46] Saving the third privilege for the discussion which follows, we turn to the fourth privilege, "moderate board" (*victus modicus*), or also "food rations" (*alimenta, annona*), better defined as the "sanctified rations of virginity" (*sacra castitatis alimenta*) or "a ration common to the sanctified Virgins and people" (*annona communis sacris Virginibus cum populo*). This was a sort of subvention in foodstuffs given to the Vestals by the city food treasury (*arca frumentaria*).[47]

Only regarding the third privilege must we be skeptical, for in describing it Symmachus conflates Vestals and ministers: "Fiscal authorities also claim lands that the wills of those on their deathbed have bequeathed to the Virgins and the ministers."[48] We might be tempted to believe that the *ministri* in this sentence were all the pagan priests of Rome, but in late antique Latin the word *minister* was used increasingly to indicate religious functionaries lower than *sacerdotes*. Thus the distinction between *ministri* and *sacerdotes*, so typical of the pagan colleges, was adopted by the Christians, who used *minister* to refer only to functionaries at a level lower than that of priests.[49] Ambrose's description of this measure as if it were related to *sacerdotes et Vestales*—shifting the order of Symmachus' sentence and interpreting *ministri* as priests—was thus surely wrong.[50]

Gratian seems, therefore, to have done much less than he is usually credited with. The other privileges aside, the confiscation of the landed properties left in

---

45 Symm. *Rel.* 3.11: *honor solus est in illo veluti stipendio castitatis*; cf. Liv. 1.20: *iis (*scil. *virginibus Vestae) ut adsiduae templi antistites essent, stipendium de publico statuit.*

46 Symm. *Rel.* 3.11.

47 Symm. *Rel.* 3.15; cf. *Rel.* 37.2 for the role of *arca frumentaria.*

48 Symm. *Rel.* 3.13: *agros etiam virginibus et ministris deficientium voluntate legatos fiscus retentat.*

49 *TLL* s.v. *minister* (1000.23, 38); s.v. *ministra* (1004); A. Ernout and A. Meillet, *Dictionnaire étymologique de la langue latine* (Paris, 1959), s.v. *minister.* Many laws show that pagan and Christian *ministri* were considered different from the *sacerdotes*: e.g. *CTh* 16.10.14 for pagan *ministri*; 16.2.31, 41: *si episcopus vel presbyter, diaconus et quicumque inferioris loci Christianae legis minister*; 16.6.7: *eos, qui episcoporum seu clericorum vel ministrorum nomine usurpato*; for catholic *ministri*; 16.5.12, 13, 24, 36.2, 54.1 (heretic *ministri*).

50 Although frequently followed by modern scholars, the inversion of the two words is present only in Amb. *Ep.* 73(18).3: *quod sacerdotibus suis virginibusque vestalibus emolumenta tribuenda.*

testament to the Vestals and the ministers did not choke off funding to the ancient college but simply eliminated one source of financing, leaving it still with cash donations and landed rents from which to draw funds. *Praedia intercepta, non iura* commented Ambrose, obviously responding to the emphatic question of the senator, "Is not Roman religion within the purview of Roman law?"[51] Since the fiscal authorities did not confiscate all the Vestals' lands, but merely ordered that they should not receive other properties in future, this statement was probably not mockery on the part of Ambrose but a bitter admission that the provisions of Gratian were still too limited to give the *coup de grâce* to official state religion.[52]

The Function of Late Roman *augures* and *pontifices*

That Gratian's provisions limited the privileges of Vestals only is confirmed by the fact that it had little effect on the life of the Roman colleges. Indeed, the principal traditional priesthoods continued to function for at least another half-century after 382, both because they still had various other activities to perform and because nothing really stood in the way of the Roman aristocracy's holding of organized priesthoods as long as they continued to have interest in them. Let us examine first this second point. In his third *Relatio*, Symmachus suggested to Valentinian II:

> Let Your Eternity be reminded of different actions of that same emperor, which are more worthy of your imitation. He in no way diminished the privileges of the sacred Virgins, but filled the priesthoods with nobles, nor did he deny money contributions to the Roman ceremonies.[53]

Gratian's provisions cannot have provoked definitive changes in the relationship between the emperor and the four *amplissima collegia*. If they had, an urban prefect in 384 would never have dared to exhort the emperor to involve himself in the appointment of Roman priests.

Whatever the case, Gratian most certainly selected no priests given that Symmachus had to go back to Constantius II to find an example of this. Religious motives aside, however, it is probable that his involvement in this arena was simply not requested, whether because no post became vacant during his reign

---

[51] Amb. *Ep.* 73(18).16; Symm. *Rel.* 3.13: *ergo Romanae religiones ad Romana iura non pertinent?*

[52] For an examination of the texts and the historiographical tradition that these have spawned, see R. Lizzi Testa, "Christian Emperor, Vestal Virgins and Priestly Colleges: Reconsidering the End of Roman Paganism," *AnTard* 15 (2007) 251–62.

[53] Symm. *Rel.* 3.7: *Accipiat Aeternitas vestra alia eiusdem principis facta quae in usum dignius trahat. Nil ille decerpsit sacrarum virginum privilegiis, replevit nobilibus sacerdotia, Romanis caerimoniis non negavit impensas.*

(the positions were lifelong), or because Gratian himself never journeyed to Rome and everything was thus taken care of in his absence.[54] The same can be said of his father, who never paid a visit to the city and, even despite the tolerance that characterized his government, is not recorded as having appointed a single Roman priest.

The involvement of the Augustus, on the other hand, was not strictly necessary for the functioning of the principal Roman priesthoods. Just as Rome was governed for almost two centuries without the need for the physical presence of the emperor, having as it did its own prefects and senate in residence, so also the traditional priesthoods continued to co-opt their own members in the absence of the *princeps*. Attestation of imperial involvement in this arena had to be recollected from a distance of some years, but not so much because the traditional offices had been left empty in the absence of imperial involvement as because it was an imperial act and, like any other imperial act, it was necessary to emphasize its unusualness.

Indeed, the choice of new candidates for the four *amplissima collegia* had never been conceptualized as an exclusively imperial activity. The honor conferred on Octavian by the people in 29 BC allowing the emperor to appoint *ordinarii* or *supernumerarii* priests and even to vary the traditional number in each college had been special and extraordinary—despite the fact that Cassius Dio indicates that it had become common practice in the early third century.[55] Nevertheless he was able to perform this function only because he had become a member of the four religious colleges, and the same principle formally applied to his successors.[56] Even so, by virtue of his office in the priesthood the emperor was equally able to delegate this privilege at will.[57]

The election of *pontifices* and of other major priests depended first and foremost on the nominations made by the members of each college. The appointment of augurs, for example, included various procedures: each of the members of the augural college suggested a nominee for the post that had become vacant and vouched for his aptitude in an oath (*nominatio*); if accepted, the nominee was co-opted by the entire college (*cooptatio*) and then inaugurated (*inauguratio*) by one of the colleagues (in the case of Cicero, it was the same colleague who had nominated him); this member then became a sort of father for the new member

[54] There is no evidence for a visit to Rome, whether it is assigned to 376 (F. Paschoud, *Cinq études sur Zosime* [Paris, 1975] 65–79; Idem, *Zosime Histoire Nouvelle II* [Paris, 1979–89] 2.420), or to 382, see A.D.E. Cameron, "Gratian's Repudiation of the Pontifical Robe," *JRS* 58 (1968) 96–102. The passage that T.D. Barnes, "Constans and Gratian in Rome," *HSPh* 79 (1975) 325–33 at 328–30, adduces does not prove an actual visit; cf. McLynn, *Ambrose*, 88 n.37.

[55] Cass.Dio 51.20.3; cf. Beard, North, and Price, *Religions of Rome*, 1.192.

[56] Beard, North, and Price, *Religions of Rome*, 1.186.

[57] Cass.Dio 52.17.

(*parentis loco*).[58] In the period of the Republic such procedures were conducted through the intermediacy of the *comitia*.[59] During the high empire, the second phase of the election (*creatio*) of the priests was placed in hands of the senate, which allowed the emperor to exercise a decisive influence in his capacity as *princeps* of that body: the *comitia* had only to announce the names of the new members of the colleges (*renuntiatio*); finally they were co-opted by the colleges, who called them to the temples (*vocatio ad sacra*), probably in order to celebrate the different cults of each college.[60] The first phases, however, remained just as they were described by Cicero. Precisely because the appointments continued to be conducted within the individual colleges and to be confirmed by the senate at the *creatio* stage, all of this was able to operate without the presence of the emperor, which had always been both a stimulus and a burden.

In as far as he was not simply a *pontifex* but the *pontifex maximus*, the emperor also had the special assignment of choosing Vestals, *Flamines maiores* and the *Rex Sacrorum*.[61] As regards the first, a series of reforms changed the ancient procedure somewhat over time. In the early centuries of the empire, however, a selection from the candidates offered by the noble families occurred in the senate, where the emperor in his role as *pontifex maximus* "captured" the young woman, just as in remotest antiquity, and made her into a priestess of Vesta.[62] The priestess's consecration to Vesta was completed with the recitation of an archaic formula, the antiquity of which, rather than any particular sacrifice or rite, conferred

58 For *nominatio* and *inauguratio* see Cic. *Brut.* 1: *qua in cogitatione et cooptatum me ab eo* (scl. Q. Hortensius Hortalus, who was dead) *in conlegium recordabar, in quo iuratus iudicium dignitatis meae fecerat, et inauguratum ab eodem, ex quo augurum institutis in parentis eum loco colere debebam*. Cf. Liv. 10.8 and Suet. *Cl.* 22 for *nominatio*, and Liv. 40.42, 45.44 for *cooptatio*.

59 On those occasions, *comitia* were composed of only 17 *tribus*, which created (*creabant* or also *faciebant*) the priests. They would select these from candidates named by the pertinent colleges. The *Lex Domitia*, which established this rule in 104–103 BC, was abolished by Sulla and put in force again by Pompey in 63 BC, cf. J. Scheid, *Romulus et ses frères: Le collège des frères arvales, modèle du culte public dans la Rome des empereurs* (Rome, 1990) 202.

60 Most of these procedures are known from the evidence of the election of the *fratres Arvales*, on which see Scheid, *Romulus*, 199–201.

61 On the role of the *pontifex maximus* during the archaic and Republican period, see T. Mommsen, *Römisches Staatsrecht* (Leipzig, 1887) 2.25–6; G. Wissowa, *Religion und Kultus der Römer* (Munich, 1912) 487, 510. For the special relationship between the *pontifex* and the Vestals, often members of the same families, see Orlandi, "Osservazioni prosopografiche," 359–71.

62 Tacitus describes Tiberius and Nero electing Vestals. The words he uses confirm that the old procedure was still active: *post quae rettulit Caesar capiendam virginem in locum Occiae* (*An.* 2.86); *defunctaque virgo Vestalis Laelia, in cuius locum Cornelia ex familia Cossorum capta est* (*An.* 15.22).

sacredness.[63] Perhaps because the emperor was implicated in his role as *pontifex maximus*, Christians never criticized the *consecratio* of Vestals as scandalous or sacrilegious, even if they attacked them on many other grounds.[64] And virgins continued to be "captured" by the *pontifex maximus*—or his delegate—well into the fourth century. Indeed, in addition to the catalogue of priestesses of Vesta attested in inscriptions from the fourth century, the Vestal that cursed the sacrilegious act of Serena in the Roman temple of *Magna Mater* must have been "captured" by Constantius II in 357 during his visit to the city given that she is called "old" toward the end of the fourth or beginning of the fifth century.[65]

Even Prudentius records the conversion of a Vestal, indicating that the procedure for appointing these priestesses must have continued in force after the reign of Julian.[66] The passage from the *Peristephanon* may be questioned as relevant to its contemporary context considering that it attributes the desertion of the temple of Vesta, the decline of the temples, and the conversion of the *luperci, flamines* and *pontifices* to the effects of the martyrdom of Lawrence during the reign of Valerian in 258.[67] Nevertheless, the framework of the story is anything but purely imaginary. A careful analysis of the text leads to the conclusion that it describes the first sensational public conversions among members of the nobility,

63 Aul.Gell. 1.12, 14.

64 The main Christian cant against the Vestals is already evidenced in third-century apologetic: Min.Fel. *Oct.* 25.10; Tert. *ux.* 1.6.3–5; Tert. *De monogamia* 17.4; *exh.cast.* 13.1–2. Some of the same rhetoric appears in two Athanasian texts, which are known in Coptic and Syriac (*Sur la virginité: Lettre aux Vierges* and *Lettre à des vierges qui étaient allées prier à Jérusalem et étaient revenues*, CSCO 150–51 Scr.Copt. 19–20, 56.30, 57.1–2, 3–9, 10–13, 57.16–23) and is developed in Amb. *De virg.* 1.15 even before the two epistles related to the problem of the Altar of the Victory in the senate. See R. Lizzi, "Vergini di Dio-vergini di Vesta: il sesso negato e la sacralità," in S. Pricoco, *L'Eros difficile: Amore e sessualità nell'antico cristianesimo* (Rubbettino, 1998) 89–132, esp. 93–7.

65 Zos. 5.38.3–4. The episode is dated some years after the second visit of Theodosius I to Rome—in 394, even if this second trip could be a doublet of that in 389—and the Vestal who was πρεσβῦτις (40–50 years old) could have been a member of the college for some 30 years. On this incident, see F. Paschoud (ed.), *Zosime: Histoire Nouvelle* 3.1 *(Livre V)* (Paris, 1986) 258–66, and recently S. Conti, "Tra integrazione ed emarginazione: le ultime Vestali," *SHHA* 21 (2003) 209–22 at 218–20.

66 Prud. *Perist.* 2.527–8: *Aedemque, Laurenti, tuam / Vestalis intrat Claudia.*

67 Prud. *Perist.* 2.1–20; cf. 509–28 (trans. Thomson): "The death the holy martyr died was in truth the death of the temples. That day Vesta saw her Palladian house-spirits deserted and no vengeance follow. All the Romans who used to reverence Numa's libation-cup now crowd the churches of Christ and sound the martyr's name in hymns. The very ornaments of the senate, men who once served as *Luperci* or flamens, now eagerly kiss the thresholds of apostles and martyrs. We see distinguished families, where both sides are high-born, dedicate their dear ones, their noble children. The priest who once wore the head-bands is admitted to receive the sign of the cross and, Lawrence, a Vestal Claudia enters thy church."

who evidently renounced their pagan priesthoods in order to embrace Christianity no earlier than the reign of Theodosius I. The chronological inconsistencies and the poetic transformations worked by Prudentius were imposed on the story by the hymnography of martyrdom, so to speak; the euhemeristic cues in the presentation of paganism, also adapted from the literary tradition of the *Adversus nationes* dialogues against idolatry, were intended to exorcize the pagan cults by casting ridicule upon them as an expression of an archaic form entirely foreign to religious and philosophical conceptions in Late Antiquity. This poetic and apologetic overlay, however, should not induce us to believe that Prudentius was discussing some fossilized relic. Works like the *Peristephanon* and the *Contra Symmachum* were firmly anchored in reality: their goal was to placate the anxieties of the most radical Christians, while Honorius accepted the preservation and financing of the temples as public works as the price of insuring a politics of detente with the great senatorial landholders.[68]

It is of course difficult to identify the Vestal Claudia, who abandoned the hearth of Vesta and first entered the sanctuary of Lawrence, with any real historical personality. No Vestal, however, would have been able to enter a Roman church of that saint before Damasus erected over his ancestral house the Church of S. Lorenzo *in prasino*—that is, in the quarter that played home to the stalls of the Green faction.[69] The sanctuary of Lawrence cited in the poem may indicate the church *in agro Verano* and the entry of the converted Vestal her burial *ad sanctos*. If so, this Vestal may have been the Claudia of noble origin whose funerary inscription was found in the vicinity of the Basilica of S. Lorenzo Outside the Walls.[70] And thus her conversion would not necessarily date to a period so very distant from that in

---

[68] Even if no certain date is transmitted for the Hymn to Lawrence, there are two *termini post quem* for the text: Prud. *Perist.* 2.473–80 clearly alludes to the constitution sent by Theodosius to the PUR Albinus in February 391 (*CTh* 16.10.10), but Prud. *Perist.* 2.481–4 (*Tunc pura ab omni sanguine / tandem nitebut marmora. / Stabunt et aeria innoxia / quae nunc habentur idola*) can be compared with *CTh* 16.10.15 (Ravenna, 29 January 399): *Sicut sacrificia prohibemus, ita volumus publicorum operum ornamenta servari*), which threatens transgressors with harsh penalties. D.R. Shanzer, "The Date and Composition of Prudentius's *Contra Orationem Symmachi libri*," *RFIC* 117 (1989) 442–62, esp. 461 n.1, first isolated this passage as a reference to Honorius' law. *CTh* 16.10.15 (29 August, per Seeck) was preceded by *CTh* 16.10.17–18 (fragments of the same constitution, sent to the proconsul of Africa on 20 August), along the same lines. Cf. R. Delmaire, *Les lois religieuses des empereurs romains de Constantin à Théodose II (312–438). I. Code Théodosien Livre XVI. SCh* 497 (Paris, 2005) 450 and 452–4 with bibliography. In the first book of the *Contra Symmachum*, even the end of the speech attributed to Theodosius (1.501–5) reflects the politics of Honorius regarding temples and pagan statues.

[69] On the construction see R. Krautheimer and M. Pentiricci, "S. Laurentius in Damaso," in E.M. Steinby (ed.), *Lexicon Topographicum Urbis Romae* (Rome, 1993–99) 3.179–82; Lizzi Testa, *Senatori, popolo, papi,* 134–5.

[70] *ILCV* 1.163: *Claudia nobilium prolis generosa parentum / hic iacet. Hinc anima in carnem redeunte resurget / aeternis Christi munere bonis.* Cf. H. Leclercq, "Vestale

which Prudentius wrote. But even if it was actually Constantine who constructed the basilica above the crypt where the body of the saint was deposed,[71] that building did not become a focal point for the Christians of the city until Damasus increased its importance with his program of reviving the old martyr crypts, each of which he endowed with an inscription that identified the saint buried inside.[72]

The conversion of senators who held office as *luperci*, *flamines*, and *pontifices* reported in the *Peristephanon* thus indicates that, when Prudentius wrote his hymn to Lawrence, these priesthoods still existed at Rome. Certainly the *Lupercalia* continued to be celebrated down to the end of the fifth century, and Pope Gelasius, our source for this information, declares that it was not in his power to abolish it but only to forbid participation by Christians.[73] As has been recently suggested, we cannot be sure that they ceased to be celebrated even after the Pope excommunicated Andromachus with his letter.[74] As to *flamines* and *pontifices*, their presence was required in festivals such as the *Carmentalia*, *Quirinalia*, *Regifugium*, *Floralia*, and *Volcanalia*, which are cited both in the Calendar of 354 and in that of Polemius Silvius written in Gaul in 448/49.[75] If these ceremonies, like the *Lupercalia*, remained vibrant well beyond the end of the fourth century, the priests who celebrated them must also have continued to be nominated.

In possible contrast with the Vestals, for whom a rite of inauguration is not explicitly attested, once *flamines* and *pontifices* had been nominated, they had to be inaugurated.[76] According to Varro the inauguration occurred on the Capitoline in the

chrétienne," in H. Marrou (ed.), *Dictionnaire d'Archeologie chrétienne et de liturgie* (Paris, 1953) 15.2.2985–89, esp. 2988–9.

71 *Lib.Pont.* 1.18. The present Basilica of S. Lorenzo in Verano (or "Outside the Walls") is formed from the Pelagian-Honorian complex, since its architecture has been modified with the successive interventions of Pope Pelagius II (579–90) and Honorius III (1216–27): R. Krautheimer, W. Frankl, and S. Corbett, *Corpus basilicarum christianarum Romae*, 5 vols. (Vatican City, 1937–80) 2.1–146, esp. 20–23.

72 For stronger indications on the precise contemporary relevance of Prudentius's hymn in honor of Lawrence, see Lizzi Testa, "La conversione", 130–2.

73 Gelas. *Ep.* 100 (*Coll. Avel.* A13 = *SCh* 65.162–88). On the Pope's intentions see Gelas. *Ep.* 100.31.

74 N.B. McLynn, "Crying Wolf: The Pope and the Lupercalia," *JRS* 98 (2008) 161–75, argues that the festival was not celebrated by the *Luperci* of the ancient *sodalitas* but by professional actors. Nevertheless, the text shows that the patrons of the *Lupercalia* intended to introduce this reform for the first time (Gel. *Ep.* 100.16, 26–7), after a casual suspension (Gel. *Ep.* 100.12, 23): cf. Lizzi Testa, "La conversione", 138.

75 *Inscriptiones Italiae* 13.2.239 and 264; 241 and 265; 245 and 267; 253 and 271; 261 and 275. Cf. M.R. Salzman, *On Roman Time: The Codex-Calendar of 354 and the Rhythms of Urban Life in Late Antiquity* (Berkeley, 1990) 242–4.

76 Many scholars believe that Vestals did not have to be inaugurated, but those among them who wanted to go back to normal life—after 30 years of service—certainly had to be exaugurated: A. Bouché-Leclercq, "*Augures,*" in C. Daremberg and E. Saglio, *DAGR* (Paris, 1877–1919) 550–60 at 557 n.215. On *flamines* and the *rex sacrorum*, who were apparently

presence of the college of pontiffs, who were endowed with the right of *auspicium*, and with the cooperation of a single *augur*. The rite implied a consultation to determine the divine will by employing proper divinatory techniques.[77]

Because there is no reason to believe that the procedure was not preserved in Late Antiquity, Constantius II would presumably have had some scruples about being present at the *inauguratio* of new priests whose appointment he had approved. The harsh provisions he issued against paganism between 353 and 356, after the defeat of Magnentius, are in fact well known: he forbade the nocturnal sacrifices that had been restored by the usurper;[78] he ordered the general closure of temples and forbade sacrifices from being made;[79] and in an *edictum ad populum* he threatened with death any who practiced pagan cults, consulted with *haruspices*, astrologers, and diviners, or exercised magic arts and divination.[80] All who used to create disturbances with magic arts were stigmatized as perverted and worthy of being afflicted with a violent plague.[81]

By this point, it should be clear that Constantius II and other Christian rulers had a clear idea of the difference between the paganism of nocturnal rites, temple sacrifices, magic arts, haruspicy, and divination conducted for private purposes, and the actions fulfilled by the traditional religious colleges, which are nowhere abrogated openly in any constitution.[82] Furthermore, when some legal provision created confusion and uncertainty in this context, the senators hastened to demand

chosen from among three candidates (Tac. *An.* 4.16.2), we have sufficient evidence. On the *inauguratio* of *flamines*: Cic. *Phil.* 2.43; Liv. 27.8, 29.38, 37.47, 41.28, 45.15, Gaius *Inst.* 130: *Praeterea exeunt liberi virilis sexu de patris potestate si flamines Diales inaugurentur, et feminini sexu si virgines Vestales capiantur*; Ulp. tit. 10.5: *In potestate parentum esse desinunt et hi qui flamines Diales inaugurantur et quae virgines Vestae capiuntur* (in J.T. Abdy and B. Walker, *The Commentaries of Gaius and Rules of Ulpian* [Cambridge, 1885] 50 and 393). On *pontifices*: Liv. 30.26. Since the same ceremony is mentioned also for the *augures* (Liv. 27.36, 30.26; Cic. *Brut.* 1; Suet. *Cal.* 12) and for the *rex sacrorum* (Liv. 27.36, 40.42, 11: [*Pontifices*] *Cloelium Siculum inaugurarunt, qui secundo loco nominatus erat*; cf. Aul. Gell. 15.27) it is possible that all priests had to be inaugurated.

77 Varro, *Ling.* 5.47.

78 *CTh* 16.10.5 (a. 353).

79 *CTh* 16.10.4 (a. 356).

80 *CTh* 9.16.4, 16.10.6 (both a. 356).

81 *CTh* 9.16.5 (a. 356 or 357). For the possibility that the three last constitutions were part of a single *Edictum ad populum*, see P.O. Cuneo, *La legislazione di Costantino II, Costanzo II e Costante (337–361)* (Materiali per una palingenesi delle costituzioni tardo-imperiali 2.2) (Milan, 1997) 308–11. On Constantius II's legislation against magic, see Lizzi Testa, *Senatori, popolo, papi*, 222–9.

82 See now N. Belayche, "*Realia versus leges*? Les sacrifices de la religion d'état au IVe siècle," in S. Georgioudi, R. Koch Piettre, and F. Schmidt (eds.), *La cuisine et l'autel: Les sacrifices en questions dans les sociétés de la Méditerranée ancienne* (Turnhout, 2006) 343–70.

a return to the *status quo*.[83] Even the phrase "let the wicked profession of augurs and seers fall silent" (*augurum et vatum prava confessio conticescat*) from one of the most famous constitutions of Constantius II was in fact aimed at forbidding only private forms of divination and magic, which were considered inferior: as, for example, those types of popular divinatory practice, also termed *auguria*, that Peter Chrysologos saw still being practiced well into the fifth century.[84]

In this sense, while emperors were far removed from Rome, pagan senators distinguished with priestly offices continued to fulfill the various demands of their priesthoods, including divinatory activity connected with the *inauguratio* of priests chosen for posts that became vacant.[85] In Africa, the persistence of priests of the imperial cult well into the fifth century[86] may indicate that *pontifices* and *augures publici* continued to exist there too, for the former would have had to be formally inaugurated in the presence of and with the cooperation of municipal *pontifices* and *augures*. The priests of the imperial cult were charged with conducting ceremonies associated with a cult with which no emperor, would willingly have dispensed.[87] The existence of one implied the functioning of the other, unless we assume the priests were legally decoupled from their chief roles, a move that would also have delegitimized the cult they were charged with maintaining. It is known that by the middle of the fifth century African priests of the imperial cult were Christian, but even this fact does not confirm that the ancient ceremonial of *inauguratio* had been dismissed. The *patroni* of the *Lupercalia* at the end of the fifth century were also Christian—or at least they desired to be recognized as such.[88] Nevertheless, they were senators first, and, until the pope excommunicated one of them for his public declaration about the necessity to

83 An example is given by Valentinian I's "Edict of toleration," issued at the beginning of his reign as a means to nullify the religious excesses of Constantius II and Julian. This law is recalled by *CTh* 9.16.9 (29 May 371), which may have been elicited by the senatorial embassy of Praetextatus (Amm. 28.1.24–5). For the context, N. Lenski, *Failure of Empire: Valens and the Roman State in the Fourth Century AD* (Berkeley, 2002) 215; Lizzi Testa, *Senatori, popolo, papi*, 229–35.

84 *CTh* 9.16.4. Petr.Chrys. *Serm*. 18.9, 71.5; cf. G.A. Cecconi, *Commento storico al libro II dell'epistolario di Q. Aurelio Simmaco* (Pisa, 2002) 222.

85 An examination of the *augures*'activities up to the end of the 4th century, but omitting this aspect, is offered by F. Heim, "Les auspices publiques de Constantine à Théodose," *Ktema* 13 (1988) 41–53.

86 A. Chastagnol and N. Duval, "Les survivances du culte impérial dans l'Afrique du Nord à l'époque vandale," in *Mélanges d'histoire ancienne offerts à William Seston* (Paris, 1972) 87–118 and A. Chastagnol, "Sur les *sacerdotales* africains à la veille de l'invasion vandale," in A. Mastino (ed.), *L'Africa romana: Atti del V Convegno di Studio, Sassari 11–13 dicembre 1987* (Sassari, 1988) 101–10.

87 C.J. Goddard, "Les formes festives de l'allégeance au prince en Italie centrale, sous le règne de Constantin: un suicide religieux?," *MEFRA* 114 (2001) 1025–88.

88 Gelas. *Ep*. 100.3: *Quomodo autem non in hanc partem recidit qui cum se Christianum videri velit, et profiteatur, et dicat, palam tamen publiceque praedicare non*

propitiate the god Februarius, they did not realize that their public ceremonies, heavily laden with civic significance, were to be condemned.[89]

Inauguratio implied divinatory activities. According to Salvian of Marseille the practices of *auspicia* were still conducted in the mid-fifth century, with public consent from the consuls who would make predictions—*auguria*—based on the manner in which chickens ate their food and on the movement of birds.[90] Alongside Salvian's consuls, we must assume that the "technicians of *augurium*," that is the *pullarii* or the *augures* themselves who had always been considered "interpreters of Jupiter," continued the job of safeguarding the ancient rules of *auspicatio*.[91] A letter of Symmachus reinforces Salvian's testimony when he writes to Siburius jestingly that his friend's desire to return to the ancient usage of "just names" (*nuda nomina*) in the heading of letters represented a movement toward a rigid return to archaism (*vetustas*) that would ultimately end with the restoration to common usage of the "antique words with which the Salian priests sing and the augurs consult birds and the decemvirs established their tables" (*verba prisca quibus Salii canunt et augures avem consulunt et decemviri tabulas condiderunt*).[92] This phrase has been taken to demonstrate that the consultation of the flight of birds by the *augures* was considered an outmoded practice at this point.[93] On the contrary, it is worthy of note that, while Symmachus uses the perfect tense

---

horreat, non refugiat, non pavescat, ideo morbos gigni, quia daemonia non colantur, et deo Februario non litetur?

[89] They actually responded to the Pope that their festivals continued in the Christian age with Christian bishops: Gelas. *Ep.* 100.28: *Sed dicitis tot saeculis rem gestam non oportere secludi*; 29: *Sed dicis etiam christianis temporibus haec fuisse. Sed etiam illa aliquamdiu christianis quoque temporibus celebrata sunt: Numquidnam, quia sub primis praesulibus christianae religionis ablata non sunt, ideo sub eorum successoribus tolli minime debuerunt?*

[90] Salvian, *De gub.Dei* 6.12–13 (*SCh* 220.370–71): *Nec solum hoc sed sunt alia maiora. Quid enim? Numquid non consulibus et pulli adhuc gentilium sacrilegiorum more pascuntur et volantibus pinnae auguriae quaeruntur, ac paene omnia fiunt, quae etiam illi quondam pagani veteres frivula atque inridenda duxerunt? … Atque utinam sicut haec propter consules tantum fiunt, ita illos tantum incestarent propter quos fiunt! Illud est feralissimum et gravissimum quod, dum consensu publico aguntur, honor paucissimorum fit, crimen omnium, ac sic, cum singulis annis bini inaugurentur, prope est ut in omni mundo nullus evadat.* Cf. at the beginning of the fifth century, Prud. *Per.* 10.146–7: *cum consulatum initis, ut vernae solent, / (pudet fateri) farre pullos pascitis.* On the credibility of these references to divinatory activity from the early to mid 5th century, see Lizzi Testa, "La conversione," 135–6.

[91] Cic. *Leg.* 2.8.

[92] Symm. *Ep.* 3.44.1.

[93] The Italian translation of A. Pellizzari, *Commento storico al libro III dell'epistolario di Q: Aurelio Simmaco* (Pisa, 1988) 289 is misleading: "Se così grande è in te l'amore per l'antichità, ritorniamo allora con uguale zelo alle antiche parole con le quali i Salii *cantavano* e gli auguri *traevano* auspici e i decemviri fissarono le tavole della legge."

condiderunt for the activity of the decemvirs, who established the laws of the Twelve Tables, he uses the present for the activities of the *Salii*.

Strictly speaking, then, Symmachus does not prove that augural practice had been superseded in his day—and not even in limited fashion in the vocabulary used in rituals, as has been suggested[94]—but rather the opposite, that the *augures* had brought back into prominence the observations of *signa ex avibus*. That practice was the most ancient and most complicated to conduct, given the many varieties of observable birds, their appearance in a fixed part of the heavens, and the variety of signs that one could deduce from these.[95] Indeed, already in the late Republic it had fallen into disuse (by the standards of *coelestia auguria*, of *pedestria auspicia*, and of *signa ex diris*) and was superseded by auspices from chicken feedings" (*auspicia ex tripudiis* or, as Servius called them, *auspicia pullaria*) of the sort to which Salvian refers. This type of divinatory activity was much easier to manipulate, with the result that in the high empire it had become the only sort which was regularly employed in all circumstances.[96] Whatever the sort of *auspicia* still possible in the fifth century given the state of knowledge of the augural discipline, some senators felt free to conduct ancestral ritual practices publicly. They did it without intending to challenge the progressive Christianization of the society around them but rather with a concern to maintain their own identity as *periti* and *prudentes*, insofar as they were holders of powers of a juridical nature in sacred matters, rather than *sacerdotes* in the strict sense.[97]

The reference in the letter of Symmachus to the activity of the *Salii* still being conducted in his day calls to mind an inscription that records the restoration of the "residences of the Palatine Salian Priests" (*mansiones Saliorum Palatinorum*) during the promagistracy of Plotius Acilius Lucillus and Vitrasius Praetextatus. The hypothesis that this edifice had to postdate 382 because the *pontifices* completed it at their own expense is no longer tenable, for we have seen that Gratian's order on the financing of public cult probably pertained only to the Vestals and did not affect the other priestly colleges.[98] Nevertheless, because of the fact that the *pontifices* are here defined as *pontifices Vestae*, a title that seems to have appeared only after the death of Constantine, it is tempting to read the inscription against the background of Symmachus' words and to assume that the *pontifices* set themselves the task

---

94 E.g., by Cecconi, *Commento storico*, 222.

95 Bouché-Leclercq, s.v. *augures*, 555.

96 Signs could derive from each kind of bird, Cic. *Div.* 2.35; Fest. s.v. *tripudium*, 363. For *auspicia pullaria* see Serv. *Aen.* 6.198.

97 Cicero (*Div.* 2.34) terms the *augures periti* and *prudentes*.

98 *CIL* 6.2158 = *ILS* 4944: *mansiones saliorum Palatino / rum a veteribus ob armorum magnalium / custodiam constitutas longa nimis / aetate neglectas pecunia sua / reparaverunt pontifices Vestae / vv. cc. promagisterio Plotii Acilii / Lucili, Vitrasii Praetextati vv. cc.* One finds reference to Borghesi's hypothesis in the apparatus criticus.

of restoring the place where this ancient sodality kept the sacred shields (*ancilia* = *arma magnalia*) as part of its mandate to preserve Rome's most ancient rites.[99]

The custom, so frequent among the great senators of Late Antiquity, of holding more than one priesthood at the same time (even if never all four together), could also reflect the desire to assimilate oneself to the imperial model, considering that Augustus himself was the originator of this practice. Even more salient would have been the opportunity to retake control of those sectors of urban life that no longer interested the Christian emperor and thus to restore these to the control of the senate. By analogy, one thinks of the provision that restored to the senate the autonomous *auctoritas* of designating quaestors and praetors which is known from the fragmentary inscription carved on the base of the statue of Ceionius Rufius Albinus erected by decree of the senate.[100] The very indifference of Christian emperors to exercising effective control over the pagan colleges encouraged their aristocratic members not just to assume control of these priesthoods but also to apply the rules that regulated their activity with greater scrupulosity. The rigorist attitude assumed by Q. Aurelius Symmachus on a number of occasions demonstrates this. In an effort to prevent the Vestals from taking the initiative in erecting a statue of Vettius Agorius Praetextatus, who had recently died, he invoked ancient usage and referred to King Numa and Q. Caecilius Metellus Pius, considered *pontifex maximus* through antonomasia according to a tradition still alive in the fifth century. In the same letter, sent to Nicomachus Flavianus, Symmachus shows his fervor for consultations, both public and private, which he organized in order to avoid altering traditional procedures.[101]

With equal attention to rigor, Symmachus asked the urban prefect and then, upon learning that he was not competent in this matter, the vicar of Rome to put into effect the condemnation of a Vestal of Alba Longa who had been judged guilty of *incestum* in a trial (*inquisitio*) conducted by the pontifical college.[102] And he himself did not fail to recall Nicomachus Flavianus and even Vettius Agorius Praetextatus to their pontifical duties by exhorting them not to absent themselves from the meetings of the *pontifices*—where "many things must be deliberated" (*multa sunt deliberanda*)—and to aid him in the *pontificalis administratio* that he was responsible for in his role as monthly president of the college (*officium stati mensis*). Both of them, moreover, had been absent for reasons other than simple

[99] For the title of *pontifex Vestae*, which appears after Constantine, see Van Haeperen, *Le collège pontifical*, 85. The title *pontifices maiores* is already present under Trajan, when these wished to distinguish themselves from the *pontifices minores,* who were often equestrians. It became common only during the 3rd century; see Panciera, *Epigrafi*, 995.

[100] *CIL* 6.1708 = 31906 = *ILS* 1222 on which, see S. Mazzarino, *Il basso impero. Antico, tardoantico ed èra costantiniana* (Rome, 1974) 1.183–4 and 443–4 n.114.

[101] Symm. *Ep.* 2.36.3 with Cecconi, *Commento*, 266–81.

[102] Symm. *Ep.* 9.147–8; cf. S. Roda, *Commento storico al libro IX dell'epistolario di Quinto Aurelio Simmaco* (Pisa, 1981) 315–19.

ennui with the activities of the college, although normally this evidence is taken in precisely this sense.[103]

Beyond issuing their deliberations related to the control of the Vestals and to the management of their treasury, which was filled through funerary fines and through income from landed estates, the *pontifices* were charged with the oversight of funerary monuments, with the *inauguratio* of new priests, and with the care and restoration of cultic buildings.[104] They thus fulfilled a series of public tasks that had been their exclusive areas of competence in remote antiquity but that they had come to share with the urban prefect by virtue of their common understanding of sacral law.[105] There seem then to be solid grounds for the hypothesis that the maintenance of the ritual activities of *augures* and *pontifices* was not so much a religious issue *stricto sensu* as a question of the necessity to continue enforcing broad areas of public law. In ancient Rome, public law was not distinguished from pontifical or augural law.

This is also evident if we consider another activity in which the Roman *pontifices* and *augures* specialized in the early Republic: the *inauguratio* of public spaces, including those of temples and cities. Even Constantine used the services of a *pontifex* and *augur* to consecrate his new capital on the Bosphorus, whether we accept that the "Praitextatos" who performed the function of hierophant (= *pontifex*) in John Lydus was the then very young Vettius Agorius Praetextatus or an older relative of the same name.[106] The first Christian emperor also allowed *augures* and *pontifices* to play a role in the dedication of the temple that the people of *Hispellum* constructed in honor of the *gens Flavia*. In this case, a degree of uncertainty over the presence of both pagan priests might arise because of the

103 Symmachus asked Nicomachus Flavianus for help (*Ep.* 2.36.1), since the *officii pontificalis cura* occupied him so completely that he could not write as often as usual to Vettius Agorius Praetextatus (*Ep* 1.47.1). This delayed his return to Rome for the sake of his wife's illness (*Ep.* 1.48). On the procedure of the pontifical college's practice of electing a monthly president from among its members see Symm. *Ep.* 1.51.

104 Symm. *Ep.* 1.68, asking to his brother Celsinus Titianus, then *vicarius Africae* (and also *pontifex Vestae et Solis*) to help Rufus, treasurer of the college, inspect the local properties of the *pontifices*. *CTh* 9.17.2 (28 March 349) covers the pontifical oversight of funerary monuments.

105 Symmachus' letters about the Vestal Primigenia make it clear that the *pontifices* had to organize the inquiries and the structure of the process, but the Urban Prefect gave the final sentence and decided the penalty. That public tasks of *pontifices* and Urban Prefect also apparently overlapped in their oversight of funerary monuments and in decisions on the restoration of sacred buildings.

106 Lyd. *Mens.* 4.2: Sopatros the τελεστής performed the function of *augur* and Praetextatos the ἱεροφάντης acted as *pontifex*, see Mazzarino, *Il basso impero*, 1.99–150, esp. 122; L. Cracco Ruggini, "Il paganesimo romano fra religione e politica (384–394 d.C.): per una reinterpretazione del *Carmen contra paganos*," *MemAccLinc* 8 (1979) 3–143 at 131–41; A. Fraschetti, *La conversione: Da Roma pagana a Roma cristiana* (Rome, 1999) 65–70.

injunction put forth in the rescript that the place not be polluted with the frauds of a "contagious superstition" (*ne aedis nostro nomini dedicate cuiusquam contagiose superstitionis fraudibus polluatur*). Nevertheless, the intervention of both *augures* and *pontifices* was surely not judged as an act of *superstitio* by Constantine. Even so, the involvement of said *sacerdotes* is not specified in the inscription as such. Furthermore, because the building was an *aedes* and not a *templum*, some would have it that it could have been established with the *consecratio* of a pontifex and *dedicatio* of a magistrate, and without any necessity for an *inauguratio*.[107] Nevertheless, even when one wished to dedicate a building without making it into a *templum* in the technical sense, the construction needed to be preceded by a delimitation of the area, and this always implied the involvement of an *augur*.[108] This procedure was required not only in the inauguration of a new building, but also in the dedication of public buildings that had been restored: not so much because these were conceived of as the elimination of the old, which would have implied an *exauguratio*, as because the parts that had been added or rebuilt should not remain without consecration. A specific instance of such alterations to a previously inaugurated public space is attested in the movement of the *pomerium*: from Sulla to Aurelian, whoever wished to move the sacred boundary traced by the augur-king needed the participation of the *augures* whose solemn "augural imprecation" (*precatio auguralis*) is partially preserved by Festus.[109]

In the sixth century the procedure still had not changed. A passage in Justinian's *Institutes*, published in 533 following the outline of the *Institutes* of Gaius, reinforces the importance of the presence of *pontifices* in all types of consecration.[110] The text holds interest because it shows how institutions that were entirely pagan were subsumed into the codification of the sixth century with only minor changes of terminology. It was this process that some modern scholars believe led to the creation of a Roman Christian law, others to a "juridification" of Christianity or even of the Christian empire: "All institutions operate according to rules that come to constitute directives or provisions for conduct. Such rules do not change even when the recipients change if they are effective, sufficient, and opportune."[111] Between the fourth and sixth centuries the rules did not change: the

---

107 E. De Ruggiero, *Dizionario Epigrafico di Antichità Romane* (Rome, 1886–1994) 1.142, s.v. *Aedes*.

108 F. De Marini Avonzo, "Appendice," in R. Orestano, *Il problema delle fondazioni in diritto romano* (Turin, 1959) vii–viii.

109 Festus, s.v. *pomerium* 249; Bouché-Leclercq, s.v. *augures*, 558; P. Catalano, *Contributi allo studio del diritto augurale* (Turin, 1960) 327–9; A. Giardina, *L'Italia romana. Storie di un'identità incompiuta* (Rome, 1997) 117–38.

110 *Inst.* 2.1.8: *Sacra sunt, quae rite et per pontifices deo consecrata sunt, veluti aedes sacrae et dona, quae rite ad ministerium dei dedicata sunt, quae etiam per nostram constitutionem alienari et obligari prohibimus, excepta causa redemptionis captivorum.*

111 G. Crifò, "La Chiesa e l'Impero nella storia del diritto," in E. Dal Covolo and R. Uglione (eds.), *Cristianesimo e istituzioni politiche da Costantino a Giustiniano*

priests of the principal Roman colleges continued to apply them, and these were then replaced by Christian bishops who assumed the title *pontifices* from them.[112]

In late antique Rome, a city without an emperor, governed by a senate that was still in part pagan, the cooperation between *pontifices* and *augures* probably continued to manifest itself each time it was necessary to consecrate public spaces. In at least one case the sources offer ample support for this hypothesis, that is the inauguration of the Bridge of Valentinian (*pons Valentiniani*). Its dedication is recorded by Ammianus in his description of the prefecture of L. Aurelius Avianius Symmachus and is confirmed by an inscription carved on a white marble pedestal of considerable dimensions which acted as the base of a column of the monumental entry arch for the bridge on the side of the Campus Martius.[113] The inscription makes it clear that the bridge was dedicated by Avianius Symmachus, not however in the course of his urban prefecture of 364–65 but rather "with the honor having been deferred" (*honore delato*) for some time afterward. Analyzing the information furnished by Ammianus, that of the inscriptions, and other sources pertinent to the ancient structure, the dedication seems to be datable to 368 and not, as is commonly assumed, before the proclamation of Gratian as Augustus in 367. The occasion was rather the *quinquennalia* of Valentinian and Valens beginning on 26 February 368: thus Ammianus' notice that the dedication of the bridge occurred with great celebration by the people, *magna civium laetitia*, would seem to be confirmed.[114]

If this was in fact the year in which Valentinian I's bridge was inaugurated, we cannot underestimate the role played by Vettius Agorius Praetextatus, urban prefect until the end of 367, in helping to make the rites and ceremonies connected with the *vota* for the imperial jubilee particularly solemn. Given the strong bonds that united him with the family of the Symmachi, it should not surprise us that he left the honor of dedicating the bridge to Avianius Symmachus after he had laid down the urban prefecture.[115] Their friendship aside, juridical and sacral scruples must also have played a role. The dedication of a space and a building

(Rome, 1997) 171–96 at 179: "Tutte le istituzioni operano secondo regole che vengono a costituire direttive e misure di comportamento. Tali regole non cambiano quando pur cambiassero i destinatari se sono efficaci, adeguate, opportune."

112 I. Kajanto, "Pontifex Maximus as Title of the Pope," *Arctos* 15 (1981) 37–52.

113 Amm. 27.3.3–4; *CIL* 6.31402 = *ILS* 769: ... *Dedicandi operis honore delato iudicio princip(um) maximor(um)/ Lucio Aurelio Avianio Symmacho v. c. ex praefectis urbi*. G. Alföldy, "Iscrizione commemorativa del restauro del Ponte di Valentiniano," in S. Ensoli and E. La Rocca (eds.), *Aurea Roma: Dalla città pagana alla città cristiana. Catalogo della Mostra (Roma, Palazzo delle Esposizioni, 22 dic.– 20 apr. 2001)* (Rome, 2000) 460–61 and n.61. For analysis of the remaining inscriptions from the bridge, which were found in the bed of the Tiber at the end of the 19th century, see Lizzi Testa, *Senatori, popolo, papi*, 447–54.

114 A. Chastagnol, "Les quinquennalia de Valentinien Ier et Valens," in *Mélanges à Pierre Bastien* (Wetteren, 1987) 255–66.

115 Lizzi Testa, *Senatori, popolo, papi*, 399–411.

was, as we have seen, at least down to Justinian, an act regulated by public law that implicated sacred law (*ius sacrum*) insofar as this followed the "custom of the ancestors" (*mos maiorum*). The principle is recorded in the *Digest*, where it is stated that the power of consecration, meaning any sort of dedication implying a consecration, pertained to the emperor—evidently by virtue of his role as *pontifex maximus*—or to whomever he wished to delegate this power (*potestas*).[116] Given that Valentinian I was in Trier and thus needed to transfer the power of dedication (*potestas dedicandi*) to others in keeping with the norms of public law, Avianius Symmachus, who was the colleague of Praetextatus both in the pontifical college and in the quindecimvirate, was chosen. In his role as *pontifex maior*, he would have been able to perform the rites of *consecratio*, after which Praetextatus himself, as urban prefect and above all *augur*, would have completed the *inauguratio* of the reconstructed bridge.

The cooperation of these two aristocrats assured the highest degree of solemnity for the celebratory festival: Valentinian I was not bothered by the fact that *pontifices* and *augures* still completed traditional ceremonies in christening a public work in his name. The two senators, for their part, did not have any particular notion of anti-Christian struggle in their observance of the ancient procedures. On the contrary, a desire to preserve the rules of ancient law, still considered sacred, lived on in them. Its sacrality was linked to its public nature more than to any connection with the divinities of the traditional pantheon. Acting thus, Avianius Symmachus, Vettius Agorius Praetextatus, the Andromachus excommunicated by Gelasius, and however many others like them who continued to preserve venerable traditions in the context of the stable noble families, were not simply cooperating in the preservation of pagan religion, they were expanding the frontiers of the profane with the goal of keeping the sacred rules of civic life from changing.

---

[116] *D.* 1.8.9.1 (Ulpian): *loca publica tunc sacrum fieri posse, cum princeps ea dedicavit vel dedicandi dedit potestatem.*

Chapter 20
Imagining the Capitolium in Late Antiquity

Lucy Grig
University of Edinburgh

Let us begin with a vision of late antique Rome as seen through the eyes of an outsider, albeit an outsider with a difference: the emperor Constantius II, visiting Rome for the first time in 357, as reported by that artful observer Ammianus Marcellinus. Ammianus tells us that when Constantius arrived in Rome he headed, in considerable pomp, to the Forum Romanum. His (and our) vista of the city is given from the Rostra:

> So then he entered Rome, the home of empire and of every virtue, and when he had come to the Rostra, and saw the most renowned Forum of ancient dominion, he stood amazed, and on every side on which his eyes rested he was dazzled by the concentration of marvellous sights.[1]

After the emperor had finished addressing the senate and people, he treated himself by feasting his eyes on a panorama of the city. The reader follows Constantius' gaze, which is sweeping and seemingly from on high.[2] At first sight it is an omniscient, totalizing view, but also, clearly, deeply partial and subjective.[3]

> Then, as he surveyed the sections of the city and its suburbs, lying within the summits of the seven hills, along their slopes, or on level ground, he thought that whatever first met his gaze towered above all the rest. (Amm. 16.10.14)

The first monument that Ammianus observes through Constantius, and the reader through Ammianus, is the Capitolium: "[He saw] the sanctuaries of Tarpeian Jove,

---

[1] Amm. 16.10.13. This and other translations from Ammianus are taken from J.C. Rolfe (trans.), *Ammianus Marcellinus*, vol.1 (Cambridge, MA, 1982).

[2] Compare the panorama in Claud. *De VI Cons. Hon.* 39–52, in which the vantage point is explicitly located as the—imperial and divine—Palatine Hill.

[3] Urban theorists have stressed the polyvalency of the city and its representation. E.g., J. Raban, *Soft City* (Glasgow, 1974) 242: "There is no single point of view from which one can grasp the city as a whole." All individual vistas are partial, but when the gaze belongs to the emperor there is an added power dynamic: imperial power can impose its own vision of things upon its subject.

so far surpassing [sc. other structures] as divine things surpass those of earth."[4] The Capitolium is peerless, the model by which all other monuments are judged, the marker of venerability and greatness.[5] It is also only the first monument to be name-checked in an intriguingly partial cityscape, one which is securely "pagan" and early imperial.[6] After viewing this parade of wonders, the emperor concludes, awed and amazed, that Rome is impossible to describe adequately:

> So then, when the emperor had viewed many objects with awe and amazement, he complained of Fame as either incapable or spiteful, because while always exaggerating everything, in describing what there is in Rome, she becomes shabby. (Amm. 16.10.17)

And herein, it is suggested, lies the greatness of Rome.

There is no visual image surviving from antiquity that seeks to depict a cityscape of Rome: no totalizing bird's eye view of the city. This may not be by chance. Recently Favro has argued that ancient Rome, as the *caput mundi*, consistently resisted visual encapsulation, or "iconicity," that is to say, no single image could stand for Rome.[7] Totalizing views were for subject nations; indeed, in Ammianus' account (16.10.4) the iconicity works the other way round: the Roman baths are described as being "as big as provinces" (*lavacra in modum provinciarum exstructa*). There is, of course, one striking exception: the Severan Forma Urbis Romae, which presented the architectural ground plan of the entire city in bird's eye view. This image was presented on a staggeringly monumental scale and impressed the viewer with a scrupulous attention to the city's glorious complexity.

If there was one site, one building in Rome that could serve as an icon—or, more accurately, as a *metonym* for both city and empire—it was the Capitolium, the temple of Jupiter Optimus Maximus and the Capitoline Triad. This temple remained throughout antiquity the largest and most splendid of Rome's temples. First built in the sixth century BC, it was the focus of splendid donations and lavish improvements, its last (and most splendid of all) major reconstruction being undertaken by Domitian after a fire in AD 80. The temple was a key focus of Roman religious and political life: as the site of the swearing-in of the year's consuls, on occasion serving as a meeting place for the senate, and, perhaps most famously of all, acting as the final destination for the triumphal procession and its culminating sacrifice. The exemplary status of the Capitoline temple in antiquity

---

4 Amm. 16.10.14.

5 Cf. Amm. 22.16.12; Aus. *Ord.* 19.15–18; Cass. *Var.* 7.6.1.

6 The other buildings detailed are the imperial baths, the Colosseum, the Pantheon, the Temple of Venus and Rome, the Forum of Peace, the Theatre of Pompey, and the Odeon and Stadium of Domitian (Amm. 16.10.14).

7 D. Favro, "The iconiCITY of ancient Rome," *JUH* 33 (2006) 20–38, at 34.

is highlighted by the fact that even the most grandiose temples built by Roman emperors never surpassed it in size.

Over and over again in Latin literature the Capitolium serves as *the* key topographical location, metonymically functioning *as* Rome. Firstly, the Capitolium stands synedochically for the Capitoline Hill as a whole[8] and was used interchangeably as such in antiquity and even still today.[9] More generally the Capitoline stands for the well-being and longevity of Rome, as stated by Vergil: "As long as the house of Aeneas shall dwell on the Capitoline's unshaken rock, and the father of Rome hold sovereign sway (*imperium*)" (*Aen.* 9.448–9). Furthermore, the Capitolium is frequently used as a metonym for *imperium*, especially in early imperial texts,[10] while the famous gilded roof of the Capitolium is clearly to be associated with the notion of an *aurea Roma*, even in Late Antiquity.[11]

The status and symbolic value of the famous temple were clearly far more complex in a newly Christian empire than they had been previously. The notorious role of the temple as final destination of the triumph, for instance, lay in abeyance since the reign of Constantine. Here the situation is muddy, for the date of the first "refusal" is much debated, with 313, 315, and 326 all having been proposed.[12] Zosimus places it in the context of his highly tendentious account of Constantine's conversion in 326 (Zos. 2.29.5). This would put the omission at the time of the celebrations of the emperor's vicennalia, which does now indeed seem the most plausible occasion.[13] In any case, the scandal caused by this "snub" is generally considered to be reflected in the hostile account of Elagabalus' refusal to ascend to the Capitol and assume the usual vows on the Kalends of January (*SHA Hel.* 15.7).[14]

---

8 The topography of the ancient *mons Capitolinus* was somewhat complex and incorporated two summits, the *Arx* and the *Capitolium*, with a saddle between the two known topographically as *inter duos lucos*.

9 More rarely the designation *in Capitolio* can also refer to an administrative and topographical region, that is, part of the Augustan *regio* IV.

10 For instance, Tac. *Hist.* 3.72 describes the Capitolium as the *pignus imperii* (pledge or guarantor of empire). See further C. Edwards, *Writing Rome: Textual Approaches to the City* (Cambridge, 1996) 69–95.

11 This is a well-known Augustan topos that is associated most famously with Ovid (e.g., *Fast.* 6.73–4), but also found more generally in moralizing Latin of the early empire (e.g. Sen. *Controv.* 1.6.4; Sil. *Pun.* 3.622–4). Ausonius' short but sweet description of Rome as part of his catalogue of cities (*Ord.* 1) is telling: "First among cities, the home of gods, is golden Rome."

12 Scholarship here is voluminous, but for useful discussion, summary, and bibliography see F. Paschoud, *Zosime, Histoire nouvelle* (Paris, 1971–89) 1.234–40, and A. Fraschetti, *La conversione: Da Roma pagana a Roma cristiana* (Rome, 1999) 9–63.

13 The case for 326 has recently been strengthened with reference to Libanius *Or.* 19.19: H.-U. Wiemer, "Libanios und Zosimus über den Rom-Besuch Konstantins I. im Jahre 326," *Historia* 43 (1994) 469–94.

14 See for instance L. Cracco Ruggini, "Elagabalo, Costantino e i 'culti siriaci' nella Historia Augusta," in G. Bonamente and N. Duval (eds.), *Historiae Augustae colloquium*

The role and meaning of the Capitolium in Late Antiquity were controversial and contested, as this paper will demonstrate. What is clear, as we shall see, is the continuing potency and centrality of the temple in both the imaginative and real topography of late antique Rome.[15] It is in this context that one of the most eloquent (if unreliable) commentators on the late antique city of Rome, St. Jerome, chose to proclaim the languishing of the gilded temple par excellence on more than one occasion. In 393 he wrote: "The Capitolium is dingy (*squalet Capitolium*), the temples of Jupiter and their ceremonies have perished" (*Adv. Iov.* 2.38). Almost a decade later (ca. 401–2) he warmed to this theme again: "The golden Capitol is dingy, all the temples in Rome are covered with soot and spiders' webs".[16]

Unsurprisingly, Jerome was not the only Christian writer to exploit the metaphorical potency of such an image. Paulinus of Nola imagined the Capitolium as shaken by the power of Christianity:

> The holy chorus strikes the heavens with the praise of our eternal Lord and the Capitol's heights tremble with the shock (*incusso Capitolia culmine nutant*). In deserted temples the decaying images shake, buffeted by sacred voices and overthrown by the name of Christ.[17]

While such claims are clearly polemical and should be seen as examples of performative rhetoric, Jerome, in particular, has been taken surprisingly seriously by a number of scholars. Consider, for instance, the entry on the temple of Jupiter Optimus Maximus Capitolinus in the *Lexicon topographicum urbis Romae*. The author notes that the temple was "recorded for its splendour and as such must have still been intact" in the second half of the fourth century, yet Jerome is adduced as a witness for its "state of abandonment" by the beginning of the fifth century.[18] In the absence of archaeological evidence to settle the issue, the testimony for this change remains of a literary nature. What this means is that we are being asked

---

Parisinum (Macerata, 1991) 123–46 at 139.

15 See here also A. Fraschetti, "Il Campidoglio: dal tardoantico all'alto medioevo," in *Roma nell'alto Medioevo: 27 aprile–1 maggio 2000* (Spoleto, 2001) 31–56.

16 *Ep.* 107.1: *Auratum squalet Capitolium, fuligine et aranearum telis omnia Romae templa cooperta sunt.*

17 Paul.Nol. *Carm.* 19.67–70. P.G. Walsh (trans.), *Poems of Paulinus of Nola*, Ancient Christian Writers 40 (New York, 1975) 133. There is some more plagiarism of Jerome here (*In Gal.* 2, praef.) as well as some interesting allusions to Verg. *Aen.* 2.338 and 2.629. Cf. a more playful reference to the dispossession of Jupiter from the Capitoline: Prud. *Perist.* 2.465–70, on which see D. Shanzer, "De Iovis Exterminatione," *Hermes* 114 (1986) 382–3.

18 S. De Angeli, "Iuppiter Optimus Maximus Capitolinus, Aedes (fasi tardo repubblicane e di età imperiale)," in E.M. Steinby (ed.), *Lexicon topographicum urbis Romae* (Rome, 1993–2000) 3.152–3: "ricordato per il suo splendore e pertanto doveva essere ancora intatto … stato di abbandono … incuria."

to compare the panegyrical testimony of Ammianus and Ausonius[19] on the one hand and the polemical claims by Jerome and Paulinus on the other. The critically minded historian might well conclude that reliable evidence for the actual state of the Capitolium in Late Antiquity is lacking.

In the search for more concrete testimony regarding the swift decline of the Capitolium we may turn to an intriguing case of alleged spoliation of the temple supposedly undertaken by Stilicho. The source for this allegation is Zosimus, who claims Stilicho ordered the stripping of the gilding on temple doors. An "oracle" was discovered underneath which read *misero regi servantur* (*rex* translated by Zosimus as *tyrannos*): these are reserved for an unfortunate king. This prophecy, Zosimus (5.38.5) reminds us, was to be realized in the way in which Stilicho lost his life. This is of course more than just a negative story about Stilicho, toward whom Zosimus is deeply hostile. It is a story with a moral, that impiety will be met with its just deserts. Moreover, it is paired with an account relating to Stilicho's wife Serena, who is alleged to have removed a necklace from the statue of Rhea in the temple of Magna Mater in Rome and who even attacked a Vestal Virgin who had dared to protest. This act of sacrilege was, like that of Stilicho, answered with divine vengeance: the wretched Serena died by strangulation, that is, she died by the neck on which she had impiously put the goddess' necklace (Zos. 5.38.2–4).

How seriously are we to take such stories? Zosimus' modern editor Paschoud, though admitting that various problems exist in both accounts, is nevertheless inclined to seek credibility for at least certain aspects of each.[20] I see no reason why we should be so generous: the role of the stories within the broader context of Zosimus' analysis is only too clear. The placement within his narrative of both episodes, for instance, is crucial: they are set in the context of Alaric's threat to Rome in 408 and are followed soon by two further related stories, the first of which focuses on the Capitolium.

We are told that the urban prefect Gabinius Barbarus Pompeianus, understandably anxious about the great peril faced by the city at this time, chose to consult experts in traditional religion in the hope of finding a solution. The experts in question, identified as Tuscans, claimed to have delivered the town of Narni from the barbarians through performance of the ancient rites. In the Roman case they counselled a public procession, at public expense, including the senate, up to the Capitoline (as well as to all the open spaces of the city), in order to perform all the "necessary" religious rites. Zosimus even alleges that the bishop of Rome Innocent I was happy to go along with the plan. But despite this supposed episcopal sanction, the senators themselves did not have the nerve, we are told, and thus the procession was cancelled and negotiations with the barbarians resumed (5.41.1–3).[21] The same story (more or less) is related by the ecclesiastical historian

19 Note the texts discussed above and cited at n. 5.

20 Paschoud, *Zosime*, 3.263–7.

21 We might wish to compare Ammianus' (19.10.4) story from 50 years earlier, in which the urban prefect of 359, Tertullus, had travelled to Ostia to perform sacrifice at

Sozomen (both authors rely on Olympidorus), though unsurprisingly Sozomen omits the claim that Innocent gave his consent to such shenanigans (9.6.3–6).[22] The moral of the tale is further signposted by Zosimus telling us that shortly after this episode, in order to raise the large ransom demanded by Alaric, statues of the gods—including even that of *Virtus*—were denuded of their jewels, resulting in a loss of courage and *virtus* amongst the Roman people (Zos. 5.41.6–7).

The details, grouping, and shaping of these stories clearly work to express Zosimus' view that the woes of Rome are to be understood as the natural consequence of the neglect, and indeed suppression, of the traditional cults, including the end of state subsidies and a lack of respect for statues.[23] Therefore, we find ourselves at the heart of the late antique debate about the causes of the fall of Rome. Nevertheless, the vital importance of the Capitolium, as citadel of the city, as both symbol and safeguard of its security, is evoked on a number of dates and occasions, certainly before Alaric was even on the mental horizon of the Roman elite.

During the debate over the Altar of Victory in 384 Symmachus took a hard traditional line and used the Capitol as a metonym for empire, seeing it, alongside the city walls, as representing both the city itself and its security. His aim was clear: to argue for the necessity of maintaining the traditional rites in securing Rome's safety. Symmachus imagines the figure of Roma standing before the emperor, declaring that:

> Through this worship I brought the whole world under the rule of my laws, these sacred objects drove Hannibal from our walls, the Gauls from the Capitol.[24]

Ambrose picks up this theme, quoting Symmachus' words in his own *Ep.* 18 to Valentinian II. The bishop makes mock of Symmachus' claims and argues that it was only due to the cackling of geese that the Gauls failed to penetrate into the *Capitolii secreta*. Ambrose sneers: "See what sort of protectors the Roman temples have. Where was Jupiter at that time? Was he speaking through the mouth of the goose?" (*Ep.* 18.5).

What Ambrose aimed to do in this text—as later Augustine would do so comprehensively in his *City of God*—was to uncouple the all-important link

---

the temple of Castor and Pollux in order to ease a food shortage; this, we are told, was successful inasmuch as the ships were then able to come in.

22 C. Pietri, *Roma christiana: recherches sur l'Église de Rome, son organisation, sa politique, son idéologie de Miltiade à Sixte III (311–440)* (Rome, 1976) 1.444, describes the involvement of Innocent as "parfaitement invraisemblable" but links the event with *CTh* 9.16.12 (1 February 409) ordering that books of *mathematici* be burned before the bishop and the practitioners themselves be expelled far from Rome.

23 Paschoud, *Zosime*, 3.282–4.

24 Symm. *Rel.* 3.9. Translation by B. Croke and J. Harries, *Religious Conflict in Fourth-Century Rome: A Documentary Study* (Sydney, 1982) 37.

between Roman power and Roman religion. Taking his cue from Symmachus, Ambrose in turn took up the voice of the goddess Roma[25] and argued that it was through arms and not *superstitio* that Rome had conquered the world. The Capitol looms large here as Roma speaks:

> Why do you stain me every day with the blood of innocent beasts? Trophies of victory are not to be found in the sinews of cattle but in the strength of the warrior. I conquered the world through a different discipline. Camillus went to war and brought back the standards taken from the Capitol, taking those who had vaunted their triumph on the Tarpeian rock; his military prowess overthrew men whom superstition had failed to dislodge. I need not mention Attilius who fought with death itself. Africanus won his triumph not among the altars of the Capitol but in the battle-lines of Hannibal.[26]

Ambrose, as much as Symmachus, highlights the continuing metaphorical significance of the Capitolium in Late Antiquity but brings us to a key development in its meaning. In earlier classical texts its significance is primarily as metonym for Rome as both city and empire. Indeed, this is the signification that Ambrose pointedly selects over a religious interpretation—contrasting, as we saw, the *Capitolio signa* with the *Capitolii aras*. However, in late antique Christian texts, the Capitolium increasingly takes on a new significance as the headquarters of "paganism," and thus, in the writings of Christian polemicists, as the heart of darkness. Long before the Christians had set their sights on earthly power, Tertullian claimed that—along with the amphitheatre, his principal target—"the Capitolium is the temple of all the demons" (*Spect.* 12). Later, Lactantius took on the traditional etymology of the Capitol[27] with his challenge to "the Romans": "Let the Romans then know that their Capitol, that is the chief head of their objects of public veneration, is nothing but an empty monument".[28]

Was this notion an entirely Christian, and false interpretation? According to Servius, "all of the images of the gods were worshipped in the Capitolium".[29] The Capitoline Hill was of course the site of a number of temples: a total of 27 are known from various sources, though we need not assume that

---

[25] The goddess Roma was appropriated by "pagans" and Christians alike, on several occasions in polemical contexts; see M. Roberts, "Rome Personified, Rome Epitomized," *AJPh* 122 (2001) 533–65.

[26] Amb. *Ep.* 18.7. Translation by Croke and Harries, *Religious Conflict in Fourth-Century Rome*, 42.

[27] A story that a human head was found during the digging of the foundations for the Capitoline temple is reported at Livy 5.54.7; Varr. *Ling.* 5.41; Dion.Hal. *Ant.Rom.* 4.59.1–61.2.

[28] *Div. inst.* 1.2.49: *Sciant ergo Romani Capitolium suum id est summum caput religionum publicarum nihil esse aliud quam inane monumentum.*

[29] *Aen.* 2.319: *In Capitolio enim omnium deum simulacra colebantur.*

all existed at the same time. As well as the temples of the Capitoline Triad and Juno Moneta there were temples and shrines to Jupiter Tonans, Fides, and many more, not to mention numerous statues and other monuments. This precinct, encompassing all of these different monuments, is referred to in the ancient sources as the *Area Capitolina*.[30] The dazzling gold of the temple of Jupiter Optimus Maximus stood as the apex of a dense concentration of religious sites, an area richly over-determined in historical and religious memory.

It is clear that the *Area Capitolina* still had a key role to play in civic life throughout the fourth century. Interestingly, despite his claims of the languishing of the Capitolium, Jerome provides crucial testimony here. In his *Ep.* 23, written in 384, he sneers at the recent death of the prominent arch-pagan Vettius Agorius Praetextatus.[31] He gloatingly juxtaposes the earthly glory from which the consul elect had fallen with his current hellish condition:

> He, who only a few days before, preceded by the insignia of all the highest magistrates, ascended to the Capitoline citadel as if triumphing over the defeated enemy, who the Roman people had welcomed with applause and stamping of feet.[32]

What exactly was Praetextatus doing on the Capitoline? It is unlikely that Jerome is referring to an actual triumph,[33] more likely he is playing up the triumphal associations of Praetextatus' procession for satirical effect.[34] That there was a religious—or from Jerome's point of view, "profane"—element to the procession

---

[30] See most comprehensively C. Reusser, "Area Capitolina," in Steinby, *Lexicon Topographicum*, 1.114–17.

[31] On Praetextatus, see now M. Kahlos, *Vettius Agorius Praetextatus: A Senatorial Life In Between* (Rome, 2002). The striking public reaction to Praetextatus' death is also mentioned by Symm. *Rel.* 10–12, 24, esp. 10.2. While Jerome does not often bother attacking pagans in his letters—indifferent Christians are far better targets for his score—Praetextatus merits the rare distinction of multiple mentions. He is held up as the ultimate example of the "pagan" in *C.Ioh.* 8: *homo sacrilegus ... idolorum cultor*. Here he mocks the grief of Praetextatus' widow, Fabia Anconia Paulina, and possibly refers to the funerary epigram she wrote for her husband (*ILS* 1259); see too *Ep.* 39.3.

[32] Jer. *Ep.* 23.3: *Ille, quem ante paucos dies dignitatum omnia culmina praecedebant, qui quasi de subiectis hostibus triumpharet Capitolinas ascendit arces, quem plausu et tripudio populus Romanus excepit.*

[33] A connection with the celebrations for the Sarmatian victories is just about possible: Symm. *Rel.* 47.1 refers to a *spectaculum triumphale*. See D. Vera, "Lotta politica e antagonismi religiosi nella Roma tardoantica: la vittoria Sarmatica di Valentiniano II," *Koinonia* 7 (1983) 133–55, esp. 140–42, suggesting a "pagan" polemical character to the event.

[34] As well as the comments given above, the reference to the *non palmatum consulem* (also at *Ep.* 23.3) makes the triumphal connection, the *tunica palmata* being the traditional dress of the triumphator—also, admittedly that of the late antique consul.

is underscored by his reference to the *tripudium*, an ancient dance traditionally performed as part of religious ritual. There is no reference, however, to the performance of any (illegal) sacrifice.

In 384 the symbolic topography of the Capitoline Hill presented a renewed traditionalist vision of Rome's central dyad of politics and religion. Praetextatus and his procession would have mounted the Clivus Capitolinus at the west end of the Forum. En route they would have taken in a number of shiny, recently restored temples: the Temple of Concord was probably restored during the late fourth century[35] and the Temple of Saturn definitely was.[36] Most relevant of all for Praetextatus would have been, just a few steps further up, the smart Porticus of the Consenting Gods, which he had restored with gusto during his tenure as urban prefect in 367.[37]

The identification of the anonymous *praefectus* targeted in the *Carmen contra Paganos* has been the subject of much debate.[38] The role of the Capitolium in this text, however, is beyond question. The poem begins by referencing the Capitolium as a key locus of paganism: "Tell me, you who worship the grove and cave of the Sibyl and the glade of Ida, the towering Capitol of the Thunderer (*Capitolia celsa Tonantis*)" (*Carm.* 1–2).[39] An association between the prefect and the Capitolium is stressed again in a troublesome line—the obscurity of which has led different scholars to propose various corrections—which refers to the anti-hero reaching the *Iovis solium*, the throne of Jupiter. Despite the problems of this line, a connection to Praetextatus' pseudo-triumph of 384 is not far-fetched.[40] What can be ascertained for sure is that the *area Capitolina* was still a key part of senatorial and ceremonial

35 A no longer extant inscription tells us that the senate carefully restored the temple after it collapsed due to old age: *CIL* 6.89.

36 *CIL* 6.937 = *ILS* 3326; see R. Pensabene, *Templo di Saturno, architettura e decorazione* (Rome, 1984) 152, who suggests a date of restoration between 360 and 380.

37 *CIL* 6.102 = *ILS* 4003.

38 Mommsen's original identification of the anonymous prefect with Virius Nichomachus Flavianus is argued for by J. Matthews, "The Historical Setting of the *Carmen Contra Paganos* (Cod. Lat. Par. 8084)," *Historia* 19 (1970) 464–79; Idem, "Symmachus and the Oriental Cults," *JRS* 63 (1973) 175–95 at 189. It has recently been reasserted by A. Coşkun, "Virius Nichomachus Flavianus, Der Praefectus und Consul des *Carmen Contra Paganos*," *VChr* 57 (2004) 152–78. However, the identification of Praetextatus is argued for by L. Cracco Ruggini, "Il paganesimo romano fra religione e politica (384–394 d. C.): per una reinterpretazione del Carmen contra paganos," *MemAccLinc 8 (1979)* 3–143, and again by Kahlos, *Vettius Agorius Praetexatus*, 163–8.

39 Translation by Croke and Harries, *Religious Conflict in Fourth-Century Rome*, 80.

40 The text as it stands (*Carm.* 26) makes little sense: *quem Iovis ad solium raptum tractatus abisset*. Moricca corrected the words as *qui Iovis ad solium raptum tractatus adisset* and interpreted them as referring to Praetextatus' glorious ascent to the Capitoline temple of Jupiter described by Jerome. *Tractatus* could indicate that the Roman people almost carried him to the Capitol: U. Moricca, "Analecta," *Didaskaleion* n.s. 4 (1926) 85–107 at 102. However, Matthews, "Historical Setting," 472, proposes *quem Iovis ad*

life in late fourth-century Rome, still crucially linked to Roman power, however much hardline Christian polemicists deplored this fact.

Although this paper has shown the continuing centrality of the Capitolium into the early fifth century, it is nevertheless clear that in time the ceremonial and civic practices of Praetextatus and his friends became distant memories. Even so, at the end of the fifth century Pope Gelasius I would still describe the Capitolium as the location for the celebration of "profane vanities" (*Ep.adv.Andr.* 28). Meanwhile, in a parallel development the remapping of the city in Christian hagiography was taking place. As a result of both of these processes the notion of the Capitolium as the heart of pagan darkness took on ever more dramatic colours. The key texts are the perennially enigmatic *Gesta martyrum*,[41] in a number of which we see the selection of the Capitolium as *the* paradigmatic site for the practice of a dramatically bloodthirsty paganism.

In the *Actus Sylvestri*[42] the emperor Constantine, suffering from leprosy, is ordered by the pontiffs to fill up a pool on the Capitoline hill with the blood of young boys. Luckily for the boys, the story has a happy ending: on his journey to the Capitoline Constantine is faced by the boys' mourning mothers, whose dramatic grief leads him to change his mind. The text tells us pointedly that he abandons his journey to the Capitoline and returns to his palace.[43] Shortly afterward, of course, Constantine swaps the pool of blood for the more salubrious font of baptism, administered by the titular hero Pope Sylvester, and completes his penance at the *confessio* of St. Peter.[44]

The Capitolium is the scene of miraculous events of perhaps a more familiar—or stereotypical—kind in several other *Gesta*. The Capitol is again set up in opposition to St. Peter's as the locus of healing in another story, this one recounted

---

solium raptum iactatis abisse and prefers to see *Iovis solium* as signifying Jupiter's throne in heaven rather than the material Capitolium.

41 See A. Dufourcq, *Étude sur les gesta martyrum romains* (Paris, 1886–1910), and for more recent approaches K. Cooper (ed.), *The Roman Martyrs and the Politics of Memory*, special issue *EME* 9 (2000), and K. Sessa, "Truth, Perception and the Pagan Body in the Roman Martyr Narratives," in A. Hopkins and M. Wyke (eds.), *Roman Bodies: Antiquity to the Eighteenth Century* (London, 2005) 99–110.

42 See recent work on the *Actus Sylvestri* by W. Pohlkamp, especially "Kaiser Konstantin und der christliche Kult in den Actus Silvestri," *FMS* 18 (1984) 357–400. See also G. Fowden, "The Last Days of Constantine: Oppositional Versions and Their Influence," *JRS* 84 (1994) 146–70, esp. 154–5. The text itself is best consulted in P. De Leo, *Ricerche sui falsi medioevali I: Il Constitutum Constantini: Compilazione agiografica del sec. VIII. Note e documenti per una nuova lettura* (Reggio Calabria, 1974) 151–221.

43 *Actus Sylvestri*, 161–3. Pohlkamp, "Kaiser Konstantin," 388–90, sees a clear connection between this conversion narrative and that of Zosimus.

44 The Capitoline makes a second appearance in another version of the *AcSylv.*, where it is the location of the cave of a dragon defeated by Pope Sylvester—otherwise this cave is located in the Forum Romanum: see W. Pohlkamp, "Tradition und Topographie: Papst Silvester I (314–335) und der Drache vom Forum Romanum," *RQ* (1983) 1–100.

by a new convert explaining his conversion. Hermes tells how, when his infant son had fallen ill, he and his wife brought him to the Capitoline temple, where sacrifices were offered and gifts made to the pontiffs. Despite their efforts, the child died. At the suggestion of the child's nurse, the grieving parents then took the baby to St. Peter's and made a declaration of belief in the Christian God, with the result that the child was brought back to life.[45] In the *Acts of St. Callistus*,[46] meanwhile, the Capitoline temple is the location of something of a divine showdown. First, the Christian God shows his displeasure at the Capitolium: part of the temple is burnt by a heavenly fire and the left hand of the statue of Jupiter falls to the ground. When expiatory sacrifices only provoke lightning, which kills four priests and strikes the altar of Jupiter, the Christians of Rome are blamed for this sacrilege and all Romans summoned *ad Capitolium*—and so the story goes on.

The main characters in these tales can sometimes have surprisingly familiar prosopographical resonances. For example, in the *Passio* of Anastasia[47] the heroine, the daughter of Praetextatus, is brought before the urban prefect Probus. Amid dire threats Anastasia is given a prospective husband, Ulpian, who is described as the *summus pontifex Capitolii*. Ulpian is mysteriously blinded and seeks healing at the Capitolium with the aid of sacrifices to the Capitoline Triad and the help of the *magnus pontifex*. The trio of "demons" say only that they are now constrained to serve the god Anastasia, and Ulpian, who dies shortly thereafter, will be with them forever in hell. On other occasions the traditional topography of the Capitoline hill is made use of. In the *passio* of Restitutus[48] the stubborn hero is brought to the Capitolium, where he too refuses to comply, insults the statue of Jupiter, and is beheaded beside the Capitoline temple, and his body thrown to the dogs near the triumphal arch *ad Palmam*.[49]

In these accounts it looks as if Tertullian's definition of the Capitolium won the day, but some contrasting early medieval texts show that eventually the Capitolium would be re-secularized and returned to its primary meaning as signifier for Roman power. In the earliest redaction of the *Mirabilia of Rome* (23) we find the following description:

> The Capitolium is so called because it was the head of the world, where consuls and senators once aboded to govern the earth. Its façade was covered with strong

45 *Passio SS. Alexander Pont., Eventio et Theodoulo pres.* in *AASS* 1.376–7.

46 *Acta Callisti*, in *AASS* 6.439–41. This tale contains as a character a consul called Palmatius, a name with obvious Capitoline associations.

47 *Pass.Anast.* The critical edition of this text is found in H. Delehaye, *Étude sur le légendier romain: les saints de novembre et décembre* (Brussels, 1936) 221–49.

48 *PassRest.*, in *AASS* 7.11–13.

49 For more examples of appearances of the Capitolium in the *Gesta Martyrum* see Fraschetti, "Il Campidoglio," 39–49. Others can be found by consulting the University of Manchester's "Roman martyrs database": http://distlearn.man.ac.uk/rome/romanmartyrs/index.php.

> high walls, rising above the top of the hill, and covered all over with glass and gold and marvellous carved work.[50]

The author further picks up the ancient designation of the *aureum Capitolium*, describing it as the location from which the whole world was ruled with *sapientia et decore*. The linkage of the Capitolium with government is heightened by its frequent association in medieval texts with meetings of the senate, and even with the transferral of the seat of imperial power from the Palatine to the Capitoline. The mythical status of the power associated with the Capitolium is again highlighted by its designation as the location of the *Salvatio civium*, a magical device incorporating images of the provinces of the Roman empire with a warning bell, which would ring indicating rebellion. By the eighth (?) century it seems the legendary Capitoline finally became successfully secularized and returned to its status as signifier for *imperium*, albeit in a radically different age.[51]

The potency of the image of the Capitolium did not die in the Middle Ages. In his memoirs Edward Gibbon tells how it was the sad state of the Capitolium that prompted his magnum opus:

> It was at Rome ... as I sat musing amidst the ruins of the Capitol, while the bare-footed friars were singing Vespers in the temple of Jupiter, that the idea of writing the decline and fall of the city first started to my mind.[52]

This is a great metaphor, but the account is not exactly accurate. When Gibbon visited Rome the Capitoline hill was adorned with the splendid piazza of Michelangelo and he remarked in his journals that, "the modern Capitol is still grand."[53] But the power of the metaphor of the ruined Capitolium was just too tempting to resist as the perfect ironic image with which to frame the composition and theme of his history.[54] Some more literally minded historians will conclude that the sheer metaphorical and metonymical power of the Capitolium has distorted our views of historical reality for too long while others will accept this "distortion" as a significant historical force in its own right. The contribution of this article has been to map more clearly the particular, peculiar, and historically contingent

---

[50] *Capitolium, quod erat caput mundi, ubi consules et senatores morabantur ad gubernandum orbem, cuius facies cooperta erat muris altis et firmis diu fastigium montis, vitro et auro undique coopertis et miris operibus laqueatis.* R. Valentini and G. Zucchetti (eds.), *Codice Topografico della Città di Roma* (Rome, 1940–53) 3.17–65.

[51] See C. Nardella, *Il fascino di Roma nel Medioevo* (Rome, 1988) 9–19, and Fraschetti, "Il Campidoglio," 49–51.

[52] J. Murray (ed.), *The Autobiographies of Edward Gibbon* (London, 1897) 302.

[53] G.A. Bonnard (ed.), *Gibbon's Journey from Geneva to Rome* (London, 1961) 239.

[54] See further P.B. Craddock, "Edward Gibbon and the 'Ruins of the Capitol,'" in A. Patterson (ed.), *Roman Images* (Baltimore, 1984) 63–82.

transformations of the Capitolium, the ultimate signifier for the ancient Roman relationship between power and religion.

Chapter 21

The Making of a Papal Rome: Gregory I and the *letania septiformis*[*]

Jacob A. Latham

University of California, Santa Barbara

In recent years, the phrase "Invention of Christian Rome" has been used to characterize the Christianization of Rome during the fourth and fifth centuries. The invention of Christian Rome appears to have consisted in the production of a Roman Christian culture modeled after, or rather cobbled together out of, classical Roman culture. For example, Trout argues that Pope Damasus' inscriptions honoring Rome's martyrs reimagined them in classical terms in order to invent a new vision of Rome's glorious past.[1] Similarly, Elsner maintains that the material evocations of the saints, who were to become the foci of cultic activity, created an alternative sacred topography by borrowing heavily from late classical visual and architectural traditions.[2] To this one may add the construction of monumental Christian basilicas, the forms of which were clearly classical.[3] Likewise, the development of a Christian institutional history in the Codex-Calendar of 354 was modeled after traditional Roman conventions of chronology and institutional memory.[4] In all cases—the Damasian *elogia*, late antique Christian art and architecture, the Calendar of 354—Christianity imagined its place in Rome, thereby re-imagining Rome by following a classical pattern.

* I would like to acknowledge Christine Thomas, Hal Drake, and Michele Salzman for their suggestions, which greatly improved this essay. In addition, I would like to acknowledge the assistance of Kristina Sessa and Patrick Geary as well as the insightful comments from the round-table, *Les frontières du profane dans l'Antiquité tardive: fêtes et cérémonies dans l'Antiquité tardives*, at the École française de Rome and the audience at Shifting Frontiers VII. Finally, I would like to thank the editors of this volume for their perceptive, detailed remarks.

1 D. Trout, "Damasus and the Invention of Early Christian Rome," *JMEMS* 33 (2003) 517–36.

2 J. Elsner, "Inventing Christian Rome: The Role of Early Christian Art," in C. Edwards and G. Woolf (eds.), *Rome the Cosmopolis* (Cambridge, 2003) 71–99.

3 H. Brandenburg, *Ancient Churches of Rome from the Fourth to the Seventh Century: The Dawn of Christian Architecture in the West*, trans. A. Kropp (Turnhout, 2005).

4 M.R. Salzman, *On Roman Time: The Codex-Calendar of 354 and the Rhythms of Urban Life in Late Antiquity* (Berkeley, 1990) 42–60.

Christianity attempted to rewrite the past in order to write itself into Roman history; this, in a word, is how Christian Rome was invented. This essay will treat a further stage of that process: no longer simply the invention of a Christian Rome, but the formation of a papal Rome.

A kind of *bricolage* of classical and Christian cultures characterized the invention of Christian Rome in the fourth and fifth centuries, whereas the exercise of an increasingly centralized authority, including the institution of processions, marks the making of a papal Rome in the sixth and seventh centuries.[5] Two spectacular penitential processions—*letaniae septiformes*, seven-fold processions, in which seven different groups gathered at seven different churches and marched to S. Maria Maggiore—stand near the beginning of this "second stage." These litanies embraced almost the entire city by making use of churches that were distributed throughout Rome. As the participants traversed the city, they took possession of Rome, even as the procession wove together Roman institutions and spaces into a singular Christian entity. The *letania septiformis* equally invented a new social and topographical image of Rome. However, this invention, even though it made use of a very traditional ritual form, owes a great deal less to classical antiquity, and so heralds a new stage in the history of the Christianization of Rome, one that might be better called "papalization."

On the one hand, processions, like poetic metaphors, are creative juxtapositions—an act of the imagination that sees one thing as another. The *letania septiformis* presented the social structure of late antique Rome as the Christian or Christianized categories by which it was organized. On the other hand, processions, like narrative, order and organize a confusing welter of urban experience. In a word, processions put the world in order. The *letania septiformis* also forged a series of Christian itineraries through the city, which seems to have served as the foundation for the later Einsiedeln Itineraries—a compilation of administrative but also symbolic routes through Rome that may have been used to orient pilgrims.[6] The *letania septiformis*, then, produced a Christian mental map of Roman society and Rome's topography.

---

[5] On the seventh century as the pivot of late antique/early medieval Rome, see R. Vielliard, *Recherches sur les origines de la Rome chrétienne: essai d'urbanisme chrétien* (Rome, 1959); T.F.X. Noble, "Rome in the Seventh Century," in M. Lapidge (ed.), *Archbishop Theodore: Commemorative Studies on his Life and Influence* (Cambridge, 1995) 69–87; Idem, "Topography, Celebration, and Power: The Making of a Papal Rome in the Eighth and Ninth Centuries," in M. de Jong, F. Theuws, and C. van Rhijn (eds.), *Topographies of Power in the Early Middle Ages* (Leiden, 2001) 45–91. See also J.A. Latham, *The Ritual Construction of Rome: Processions, Subjectivities, and the City from the Late Republic to Late Antiquity* (diss. Univ. of California, Santa Barbara, 2007) chaps. 4 and 6.

[6] See nn. 29–32 below for references on the Einsiedeln Itineraries.

The *letania septiformis*

The first of the two known *letaniae septiformes* took place in 590, shortly after a series of devastating floods had decimated the city. According to Gregory of Tours:

> The river Tiber covered the city of Rome with such floods that ancient temples fell down and the storehouses of the church were destroyed, with the loss of several thousand bushels of wheat … A pestilence soon followed, which men call the plague of the groin. Coming in the middle of the eleventh month [January 590], it first of all attacked Pope Pelagius … and swiftly quenched his life. After his death great destruction of the people was wrought by this plague. And because the church of God could not remain without a leader, the whole people chose the deacon Gregory.[7]

Even though not yet officially the bishop of Rome, the deacon Gregory quickly instituted a penitential procession by which the anger of God would be pacified. On a Sunday morning, quite possibly during Lent, he preached a homily calling the citizens of Rome to repentance. In this same sermon he also gave directions for a seven-fold litany to be performed on the next Wednesday at dawn after three days of prayer.[8]

---

[7] Greg.Tur. *HF* 10.1 (*MGH.SRM* 1.1.477): *Tanta inundatio Tiberis fluvius Romam urbem obtexerit, ut aedes antiquae deruerent, horrea etiam eclesiae subversa sint, in quibus nonnulla milia modiorum tritici periere ... Subsecuta est de vestigio cladis, quam inguinariam vocant. Nam medio mense XI adveniens, primum omnium iuxta illud ... Pelagium papam perculit et sine mora extinxit. Quo defuncto, magna stragis populi de hoc morbo facta est. Sed quia ecclesia Dei absque rectorem esse non poterat, Gregorium diaconem plebs omnis elegit*; cf. O.M. Dalton (trans.), *The History of the Franks by Gregory of Tours* (Oxford, 1927). This is the first *letania*, so long as this passage is not an interpolation, as is argued by O. Chadwick, "Gregory of Tours and Gregory the Great," *JThS* 50 (1949) 38–49 and A.H.B. Breukelaar, *Historiography and Episcopal Authority in Sixth-Century Gaul: The Histories of Gregory of Tours Interpreted in Their Historical Context* (Göttingen, 1994) 66–9. Cf. J. McClure, *Gregory the Great: Audience and Exegesis* (diss. Oxford Univ., 1978) app.1; M. Heinzelmann, *Gregory of Tours: History and Society in the Sixth Century*, trans. C. Carroll (Cambridge, 2001) 76–81 and 165–6; Latham, *The Ritual Construction of Rome*, chap. 5. On the flooding of the Tiber, see G.S. Aldrete, *Floods of the Tiber in Ancient Rome* (Baltimore, 2007).

[8] V. Saxer, "L'utilisation par la liturgie de l'espace urbain et suburbain: l'exemple de Rome dans l'Antiquité et le Haut Moyen Âge," in N. Duval, F. Baritel, and P. Pergola (eds.), *Actes du XIe congrès international d'archéologie chrétienne: Lyon, Vienne, Grenoble, Genève et Aoste (21–28 septembre 1986)* (Rome, 1989) 2.917–1033, here 962–3 n.129. J. Hill, "The *litaniae maiores* and *minores* in Rome, Francia and Anglo-Saxon England: Terminology, Texts, and Traditions," *EME* 9 (2000) 211–46 at 228 n.45, argues that Gregory of Tours may have Gallicized this *letania* based on the three-day Rogation parades.

The clergy along with the presbyters of the sixth region gathered at SS. Cosma e Damiano. All the abbots, together with their monks and the presbyters of the fourth region, met at S. Vitale. The abbesses and their congregations with the first-region presbyters collected at SS. Marcellino e Pietro. All children and the second-region presbyters assembled at SS. Giovanni e Paolo. The laymen with the seventh-region presbyters came together at S. Stefano Rotondo. Widows and the fifth-region presbyters congregated at S. Eufemia. Finally, married women and the presbyters of the third region convened at S. Clemente. From these seven different starting points, each of the seven cortèges wound their way through the city to S. Maria Maggiore.[9]

Thirteen years later, in 603, Gregory, now pope, preached a similar homily and again organized a seven-fold procession by which he hoped to secure God's mercy.[10] The reason for the second procession is not clear, though seeking relief from the outbreak of some sort of contagious illness such as malaria is likely.[11] Gregory delivered this second homily at S. Sabina on 29 August, asking that the litany take place the very next day rather than after three days of prayer and penance.[12]

> Let the procession of the clergy go out from the Church of Saint John the Baptist [the Lateran], that of men, from the Church of the blessed martyr Marcellus [on the Via Lata], that of the monks, from the Church of the blessed martyrs John and Paul, that of the nuns, from the Church of the blessed martyrs Cosmas and Damian, that of married women, from the Church of the blessed first martyr Stephen [S. Stefano Rotondo], that of the widows, from the Church of

---

[9] Greg.Tur. *HF* 10.1. The clergy most likely indicates the Lateran curia staff, while the presbyters were the priests of the other churches of Rome, on which see P. Llewellyn, *Rome in the Dark Ages* (London, 1970) 109–40; V. Saxer, "La chiesa di Roma dal V al X secolo: amministrazione centrale e organizzazione territoriale," in *Roma nell'alto Medioevo: 27 aprile–1 maggio 2000* (Spoleto, 2001) 2.493–637, 523–9 (clergy) and 563–71 (presbyters).

[10] D. Norberg (ed.), *S. Gregorii Magni Registrum epistularum, CCSL* 140–140A (Turnhout, 1982) 140.vi–vii (on the preservation of the homily in the epistolary register) and 140A appendix IX (*Denuntio pro septiformi letania* [text of sermon]).

[11] J.R.C. Martyn, "Four Notes on the *Registrum* of Gregory the Great," *Parergon* 19 (2002) 5–38 at 16–23, argues that Pope Gregory I considered the Emperor Phocas to be a plague and consequently this second performance of the procession sought protection from the emperor-plague. However, various contagious illnesses affected Rome regularly, even seasonally, on which see B. Shaw, "Seasons of Death: Aspects of Mortality in Imperial Rome," *JRS* 86 (1996) 100–138; R. Sallares, *Malaria and Rome: A History of Malaria in Ancient Italy* (Oxford, 2002); W. Scheidel, "Germs for Rome," in Edwards and Woolf, *Rome the Cosmopolis*, 158–76; L.K. Little (ed.), *Plague and the End of Antiquity: The Pandemic of 541–750* (Cambridge, 2007).

[12] Greg.Mag. *Reg.* app. IX.54–5 (sermon given *sub die IIII Kalendarum Septembrium indictione sexta*) and app. IX.38 (procession *crastina die*); Saxer, "L'utilisation," 963.

> the blessed martyr Vitalis [S. Vitale] and that of the poor and infants, from the Church of the blessed martyr Cecilia [in Trastevere].[13]

Both processions were similarly organized: four churches figured in both processions, SS. Giovanni e Paolo, SS. Cosma e Damiano, S. Stefano, and S. Vitale; and many of the same social divisions were followed—clergy, monks, nuns, married women, widows, laymen, and children. Most notably, the 590 performance did not include the poor, while the 603 procession eliminated the distribution of presbyters amongst each of the seven cortèges. Nevertheless, in both cases there were seven individual cortèges that formed one unified procession, but eight different categories by which the procession was organized.

The categories used to organize both processions articulate a radically Christian understanding of Rome. These categories are not neutral, analytic terms, but rather they re-describe Rome. More typically, in the sixth and seventh centuries, papal epistolary conventions described Roman society as consisting of the clergy, nobility, and the people.[14] Like the Damasian *elogia* and early Christian art, which combined classical and the Christian forms, the clergy were simply added to the head of a classical social order, the nobility and people, which is reminiscent of the ubiquitous SPQR, Senate and the Roman people. If the placement of the clergy at the head of a traditional social order was a more typical vision of late antique Christian Rome, then *letania septiformis* embodied a striking, unequivocal, and uncompromising Christian conceptualization of late antique Roman social structure.

The full complement of the Christian religious world—clergy, presbyters, abbots, abbesses, monks, and nuns—appeared in the seven-fold procession, comprising at least three out of the seven cortèges and even, according to Gregory of Tours, accompanying each and every group. Notably, in both performances of this procession the non-ecclesiastical and non-impoverished men participated in the procession simply as the laity or men without secular distinctions. Laywomen, however, participated as widows and wives.[15] Strangely, unmarried women

13 Greg.Mag. *Reg.* app. IX.46–53: *Letania clericorum exeat ab ecclesia Iohannis* (47) *baptistae, letania uirorom ab ecclesia sancti martyris Marcelli,* (48) *letania monachorum ab ecclesia beatorum martyrum Iohannis et (*49) *Pauli, letania ancillarum Dei ab ecclesia beatorum martyrum* (50) *Cosmae et Damiani, letania feminarum coniugatarum ab ecclesia* (51) *beati primi martyris Stephani, letania uiduarum ab ecclesia beati* (52) *martyris Vitalis, letania pauperum et infantium ab ecclesia beatae* (53) *martyris Ceciliae*; cf. J.R.C. Martyn (trans.), *Letters of Gregory the Great* (Toronto, 2004) 888.

14 On these conventions and how they changed, see C. Diehl, *Études sur l'administration byzantine dans l'exarchat de Ravenne (568–751)* (Paris, 1888) 304–18; E. Patlagean, "Les armes et la cité à Rome du VIIe au IXe siècle et le modèle européen des trois fonctions sociales," *MEFRM* 86 (1974) 25–62.

15 See K. Cooper, *The Virgin and the Bride: Idealized Womanhood in Late Antiquity* (Cambridge, MA, 1996), on the contest between wives and virgins.

would seem to have been excluded from the processions, though perhaps they accompanied the children. Finally, the Roman masses figured in this procession as the special object of pastoral care, the poor.[16] These Christian or Christianized social categories were then deployed in these processions so as to represent the entirety of Rome. In the collective formed by the procession, the totality of a Christian Rome marched through the city.

Not only did these processions attempt to construct a Christian Rome in a spectacular manner, but also the texts that describe them—the *Histories* of Gregory of Tours and the homily preserved in the epistolary register of Gregory I—arranged their participants in a hierarchical fashion. Such literary ordering is rather common in descriptions of rituals and so it need not correspond to historical reality.[17] However, according to MacCormack, in descriptions of *adventus* ceremonies "the people are enumerated in groups according to age on the one hand, and to official status on the other, and these were also the groupings according to which they would appear in a welcoming procession."[18] Thus literary description may be historically accurate. Nevertheless, I do not believe that the Gregorian texts so strictly correspond to a ritual reality. Rather, both texts imagine and present a proper hierarchical order that would not necessarily have been visible during the actual performance of the processions.

Gregory of Tours listed the seven groups in the following order: the clergy, abbots and monks, abbesses and nuns, children, laity (men), widows, and wives. The very order of the list privileged the ecclesiastical or religious bodies, men first, then women. The children were placed directly after the purely religious categories, as perhaps their relative innocence warranted a place before the politically and sexually entangled men and women. After the children came the laymen, then the two categories of women, the para-ecclesial widows and lastly the wives.[19] Not only did Gregory of Tours report this dream of a Christian city,

---

16 E. Patlagean, *Pauvreté économique et pauvreté sociale à Byzance, 4e–7e siècles* (Paris, 1977) 9–35; P.R.L. Brown, *Poverty and Leadership in the Later Roman Empire* (Hanover, NH, 2002).

17 On the relationship between ritual description and historical reality in the classical world, see e.g. M. Beard, "Writing Ritual: The Triumph of Ovid," in A. Barchiesi, J. Rüpke, and S. Stephens (eds.), *Rituals in Ink: A Conference on Religion and Literary Production in Ancient Rome* (Stuttgart, 2004) 115–26. For early medieval period, see P. Buc, *The Dangers of Ritual: Between Early Medieval Texts and Social Scientific Theory* (Princeton, 2001), tempered by G. Koziol, "The Dangers of Polemic: Is Ritual Still an Interesting Topic of Historical Study?" *EME* 11 (2002) 367–88. For the early modern period, see R. Darnton, *The Great Cat Massacre and Other Episodes in French Cultural History* (New York, 1984) chap. 3 "A Bourgeois Puts His World in Order."

18 S. MacCormack, *Art and Ceremony in Late Antiquity* (Berkeley, 1981) 21.

19 On the order of widows, see C. Carletti, "Aspetti biometrici del matrimonio nelle iscrizioni cristiane di Roma," *Augustinianum* 17 (1977) 39–51 at 46–7; J.-U. Krause, "La prise en charge des veuves par l'Église dans l'antiquité tardive," in C. Lepelley (ed.),

but he also organized it so that the Christian ecclesiastical elements were clearly favored.

The homily preserved in Pope Gregory's register of letters has a different order, one that perhaps more accurately reflected social status within the city. First come the clergy, followed by men, monks, nuns, married women, widows, and finally the children and the poor. The late sixth- or early seventh-century aristocracy may have been economically crippled by more than a half-century of war in Italy, but there were always powerful laymen at Rome, including Gregory himself before he entered religious life: this list, which places the men directly after the clergy, conforms to this fact. The emphasis on religious status reasserts itself after the men, as monks and nuns come next—betraying the pope's concern for ascetic practice. Interestingly, in his schema the married women are placed before the widows. The children and the poor come last, as one might have expected.

With the elevation of the position of men, still without titles, and the devaluation of children, the *letania* of 603 seems better to reflect the late sixth- or early seventh-century social map of Rome. Or rather, these *letaniae* do not reflect a social map, so much as they tried to create one. Whatever the pastoral intention of Gregory I, the processions produced a new vision of a Christian Rome. The seven-fold litany demonstrated how things ought to be, at least according to certain sectors of society, offering a specifically Christian vision of the world.[20]

The distribution of the participants in this way not only reflected a Christian image of Roman society, but it also helped to reify this image. More specifically, these processions demanded that their participants accept and perform a certain social identity. Most of these social identities might already have been accepted. For instance, one can imagine that the poor allowed themselves to be registered as such so as to qualify for assistance. The laymen, however, might not have been so compliant. Nevertheless, despite any protests the former aristocracy might have voiced, to be divided up in this way forced the participants to identify with the categories conferred upon them, however provisionally, if they wanted to be able to march with everyone else. In effect, these processions interpellated their participants. Interpellation may be best imagined as a scene in which a policeman hails someone, who then responds.[21] The hailed individual, who acknowledges that the call was really addressed to her, turns around, by which act she gains a social identity as subject to the law.[22]

La fin de la cité antique et le début de la cité médiévale (Bari, 1996) 115–26; E. Wipszycka, "La sovvenzione constantiniana in favore del clero," *RAL* ser. 9a 8 (1997) 483–98.

[20] On this aspect of ritual, see J.Z. Smith, *Imagining Religion: From Babylon to Jonestown* (Chicago, 1982) chap. 4 "The Bare Facts of Ritual"; Idem, *To Take Place: Toward Theory in Ritual* (Chicago, 1987) chap. 5 "To Take Place."

[21] L. Althusser, "Ideology and Ideological State Apparatuses," in *Lenin and Philosophy and Other Essays*, trans. B. Brewster (London, 1971) 127–188 at 162–3.

[22] According to J. Butler, *The Psychic Life of Power: Theories in Subjection* (Stanford, 1997), interpellation is "the process of becoming subordinated by power as well as the

In a similar manner, late antique participants in the *letania septiformis* recognized themselves in the call of the pope and gained a Christian social identity as part of a Christian collectivity, by accepting, again perhaps temporarily, the processional categories. During the course of the sermon, members of the audience had to acknowledge themselves as a member of the clergy, a presbyter, a monk, a nun, a layman, a widow, a wife, a child, or a member of the faceless "poor" in order simply to know where to go. This recognition interpellated each individual as a Christian social being.

Not only did the procession construct certain forms of subjectivity through a process of interpellation, but it also determined how the participants were to perform those subjectivities.[23] It was not sufficient simply to be a Christian subject, whether a monk or a nun, a layman or a widow: one had to be a Christian subject in a certain way. In the case of the *letania septiformis*, the newly interpellated Christian social being had to be penitent.

The demand for penance emerges clearly in the sermons in which the processions were announced. Pope Gregory I urged his listeners to "take refuge in the lamentations of penitence, while there is still time to weep before being struck down." He continued:

> Let us recall before our mind's eye whatever sins we have committed and let us punish our wicked deeds by weeping. "Let us come before his presence with confession," [Ps. 94:2] and as the prophet advises, "Let us lift up our hearts with our hands unto God," [Lam. 3:41] because to lift up our hearts unto God with our hands is to arouse the earnestness of our prayer with the merit of good deeds ...[24]

Penance for the Christian means to weep at the remembrance of sins. That is, in the face of horrible destruction and death, one was asked to think of oneself as guilty, as having already committed sins for which one, along with the entire city, was

---

process of becoming a subject" (p. 2), because for Althusser, "social existence, existence as a subject, can be purchased only through a guilty embrace of the law" (p. 112).

[23] In short, the *letania septiformis* also molded the mode of subjection, which M. Foucault, *The History of Sexuality: The Use of Pleasure*, vol. 2, trans. R. Hurley (New York, 1985) 27, defines as "the way in which the individual establishes his relation to the rule [here the demand to accept a certain identity] and recognizes himself as obliged to put it in practice." On Foucault's notion of *assujetissement*, see Butler, *Psychic Life of Power*, 83–105.

[24] Greg.Mag. *Reg.* app. IX.14–20: *Unusquisque* (15) *ergo nostrum ad paenitentiae lamenta confugiat, dum flere ante percussionem uacat. Reuocemus ante oculus mentis, quicquid errando commisimus, et quod nequiter egimus flendo puniamus.* Praeueniamus faciem eius in confessione [Psalm 94.2] *et, sicut propheta admonet,* leuemus corda nostra cum manibus ad Deum. [Lam. 3.41] *Ad deum quippe* (20) *corda cum manibus leuare est orationis nostrae studium cum merito bonae operationis erigere*; *Letters*, trans. Martyn, 887.

being punished. In this manner, late antique Christianity inflected, or perhaps even created, a certain kind of interior life, by instilling a sense of sin in the individual.[25]

The Christian subject, the participant in the procession, should have arrived at S. Maria Maggiore feeling ashamed and remorseful, after having spent the night (or three days) reflecting on his or her guilt. Shame, a penitential disposition, should then emerge from the interior, appearing as devout tears streaming down one's face. Of course, such an emotional state was most likely already present, particularly in 590 and probably also in 603. Apocalyptic exaggeration aside—a difficult issue as both Gregories entertained the notion of the impending apocalypse—Rome seems to have been truly devastated. In sum, the *letaniae* welded social positions and emotional states into specific forms of Christian subjectivity. At the same time, these Christian subjects were hierarchically organized into a vision of Christian Rome.

Making a Papal Rome

These processions constructed an image of Rome that made the city legible, understandable, and meaningful in Christian, ecclesiastical, and even papal terms. However, the impact of these processions was not confined to the realm of social knowledge. These processions also organized activity by creating an ordered set of itineraries through the city. More specifically and more practically, the processional image served as a cognitive map of Christian Rome, oriented by churches, by which one could negotiate the city.[26] As an ordering process, like narrative, processions could organize urban experience, a realm of activity to which processions remained connected as its ritualized form.[27] Consequently, ritual processions form a privileged set of urban spatial activities that are akin to ordinary habits, though they are elevated above them. This connection with habitual activity suggests that ritual processions can function as the paradigm for daily urban life. Most processions chart one pathway through the city, though a calendar of such processions may mark out a whole series of routes. By contrast, the *letania septiformis* knitted together seven different Christianized itineraries through the jumbled mass of late ancient Rome all at once, though admittedly, the *letania septiformis* seems to have been performed only twice. This limited iteration may have restricted its impact on urban habit—though its spectacularity and apocalyptic atmosphere may have compensated for this lack of repetition.

The itineraries of the seven-fold processions symbolically embraced Rome, even if not the city in its physical entirety, as at least one of the seven ecclesiastical

[25] C. Taylor, *Sources of the Self* (Cambridge, MA, 1989) chap. 7 "'In Interiore Homine.'"

[26] See K. Lynch, *The Image of the City* (Cambridge, MA, 1960) 1–14 and 123–8.

[27] M. de Certeau, *The Practice of Everyday Life,* trans. S. Randall (Berkeley, 1984) 91–110; C. Bell, *Ritual Theory, Ritual Practice* (Oxford, 1992) 69–93.

regions was omitted in each litany. One scholar has recently argued that the two *letaniae* constituted a pious itinerary followed by the faithful during their visits to Rome.[28] Though admittedly little evidence has been offered in support of this contention, some support may actually be found in the pilgrimage-guides of early medieval Rome. The earliest extant guides composed from the early seventh through the mid-eighth centuries offer lists of cemeteries and martyr basilicas and indicate along which street they lie.[29] Only in the mid-eighth century, with the appearance of an intramural guide known as *Istae vero ecclesiae intus Romae habentur,* were the churches within the walls given similar treatment.[30]

The most important intramural guide, the *Itinerarium Einsiedelnensis* from the late eighth or early ninth century (ca. 775–815), may have organized visits to Rome according to ecclesiastical customs.[31] The routes are indicated in an extremely formalized manner: after the title—listing the names of the extremities of the route written in large red letters—there are two columns of classical and Christian toponyms indicating what was found to the right and the left of the path. Rarely, a name appears in the center of the page; this means that the route passed through or under the place or monument, like a piazza or an arch. In total, the ten itineraries list more than one hundred buildings or places, almost evenly split between the Christian and the classical. Impressively, the itineraries attest to a confident papal control of the city, which encompassed Rome's classical past within its Christian present.[32] If the list of Roman bishops in the Codex-Calendar

28 J. Closa Farrés, "San Gregorio Magno y la evocación de la Roma cristiana," in *Gregorio Magno e il suo tempo: XIX incontro di studiosi dell'antichità cristiana in collaborazione con l'École française de Rome, Roma, 9–12 maggio 1990* (Rome, 1991) 2.183–97.

29 See R. Santangeli Valenzani, "Le più antiche guide romane e l'itinerario di Einsiedeln," in M. D'Onofrio (ed.), *Romei & Giubilei: il pellegrinaggio medievale a San Pietro (350–1350)* (Milan, 1999) 195–8, for a clear and intelligent discussion of these guides. For the dating of the itineraries, see H. Geertman, *More Veterum: Il* Liber Pontificalis *e gli edifici ecclesiastici di Roma nella tarda antichità e nell'medioevo* (Groningen, 1975) 198–203.

30 All of these texts are collected in F. Valentini and G. Zucchetti (eds.), *Codice topographico della città di Roma*, 4 vols. (Rome, 1940–53).

31 For the most recent edition of the *Itinerarium,* see G. Walser (ed.), *Die Einsiedler Inschriftensammlung und der Pilgerführer durch Rom* (Stuttgart, 1987). For analyses of the itineraries, see R. Santangeli Valenzani, "L'itinerario di Einsiedeln," in M. Stella Arena et al. (eds.), *Roma dall'Antichità al Medioevo: archeologia e storia nel Museo Nazionale Romano Crypta Balbi* (Milan, 2001) 1.154–9, upon whose admirable work I am largely dependent; F.A. Bauer, "Das Bild der Stadt Rom in karolingischer Zeit," *RQA* 92 (1997) 190–228; S. del Lungo, "La percezione dello spazio: gli itinerari urbani," in L. Pani Ermini (ed.), *Christiana loca: lo spazio cristiano nella Roma del primo millennio* (Rome, 2000) 231–8.

32 D. Bellardini and P. Delogu, "*Liber Pontificalis* e altre fonti: la topografia di Roma nell'VIII secolo," in H. Geertman (ed.), *Atti del colloquio internazionale Il* Liber

of 354, itself modeled after consular *fasti*, inaugurated a process of imagining *Christianitas* in terms of *Romanitas*, then these itineraries represent the end of that process, as the importance of the classical now depended upon the Christian.[33]

The blossoming of Christian processional activity at Rome that began with the two performances of the *letania septiformis* eventually culminated in the production of these itineraries, which functioned as something of a symbolic map of Rome. Certainly the pathways of the Einsiedeln Itineraries were not the direct result of these processions. But it does seem that the history of Roman Christian processional activity created the image and idea of Rome embodied in them. Christian processions served as the imaginative foundation upon which such detailed itineraries through the city were constructed.

This tradition of imagining Rome in symbolic terms dependent upon churches and other Christian institutions began after Gregory I, whose pontificate marks a watershed in the history of Christian processional activity at Rome. There were organized and formal processions prior to Gregory, like the procession of Pope Pelagius I in 554 and the *letania maior*, a penitential procession similar to the *letania septiformis* that seems to have existed prior to Gregory I.[34] But, beginning with Gregory I and continuing into the seventh century, Christian processional activity expanded greatly. In fact, by the end of the seventh century, the first regular system of Roman Christian processions had emerged.[35] It may be a coincidence that the first efforts to "map" a Christian Rome follow the full flowering of Christian processional activity, but there does seem to be a connection, even if the precise relationship is ultimately impossible to unravel.

No matter why they were chosen, the churches used in the *letania septiformis* would eventually figure prominently in a papal image of Rome, for every church, except SS. Marcellino e Pietro, figures in at least one of the itineraries.[36] With the *letania septiformis*, Gregory I invented a new Christian image of Rome—a novel social map of Rome dominated by the papacy and the church hierarchy. Thus Gregory I—even if he was not responsible for the expansion and systematization

---

Pontificalis *e la storia materiale (Roma, 21–22 febbraio 2002)* (Assen, 2003) 205–24.

33 Along these lines see further M. Lafferty, "Translating Faith from Greek to Latin: *Romanitas* and *Christianitas* in Late Fourth-Century Rome and Milan," *JECS* 11 (2003) 21–62. I would like to thank the editors of this volume for calling this essay to my attention.

34 L. Duchesne, (ed.), *Le Liber Pontificalis,* 2nd ed. (Paris, 1955) 62.2 (*VPelagii*). On the *letania maior*, see Greg.Mag. *Reg.* app. IV. On the development of Christian processions at Rome, see Latham, *Ritual Construction of Rome*, chap. 4.

35 J.F. Baldovin, *The Urban Character of Christian Worship: The Origins, Development, and Meaning of Stational Liturgy* (Rome, 1987) 158–66; Latham, *Ritual Construction*, chap. 6.

36 The Einsiedeln Itineraries call attention to the fact that most of the churches used in the two *letaniae* were sited along major and still usable roads, on hills, or at otherwise accessible locations despite the flooding. Many of these churches also possessed atria or large open spaces before their doors.

of the stational liturgy, that great mechanism of urban unity—accelerated the process of Christianization.[37] These same processions also interpellated those who would inhabit this new Christian Rome, forging Christian or Christianized social positions into subjectivities whose interior emotional states were equally determined by the performance of these penitential litanies. Eventually, after the regular and systematic performance of Christian processions, only organized during the course of the seventh century, a Christian cognitive map, which embraced the classical as part of Rome's now Christian heritage, would overlay the city. The two performances of the seven-fold procession did not lead directly to the Einsiedeln itineraries, but they did carve out Christian pathways through the center of Rome, laying a conceptual foundation upon which such a cognitive map of Rome could be built. In short, the *letania septiformis* marks an intensification of the process of Christianization: no longer a *bricolage* of the classical and the Christian in the invention of a Christian Rome, but rather a confident assertion of episcopal power in the creation of a papal Rome.

37 See Noble, "Topography, Celebration, and Power."

PART VII
The Power of Religion in the Barbarian West

Chapter 22
Ricimer's Church in Rome: How an Arian Barbarian Prospered in a Nicene World

Ralph W. Mathisen
University of Illinois at Urbana-Champaign

During the fifth century, western Masters of Soldiers, and especially the highest ranking one, the *patricius et magister utriusque militiae*, acquired inordinate amounts of authority. Many of these generals, including Stilicho, Sigisvult, Ricimer, Fl. Valila, Gundobad, and Odovacar, were of barbarian extraction. Modern studies focus almost exclusively on the secular side of the policies and activities of these barbarian generals, and scarcely any notice is taken of any religious affiliations or agendas they might have had.[1] Why is this? Did barbarians not have any religious interests? As these barbarians attempted to legitimate their personal authority in the context of the Roman world, government, and military, did not they, like Romans, see the political advantages to which religion could be put?

Barbarian Generals and Religion

In the fourth and early fifth centuries, barbarian generals represented the full spectrum of religious affiliation. Some, such as Richomer, Bauto, Arbogast, Fravitta, and Generidus, remained devoted pagans. Others, such as Gaïnas, were Arian Christians. And a surprising number, such as Victor[2] and Modares[3] in the east and Silvanus[4] in the west, were Nicenes. But by the early part of the fifth century, paganism was

---

1 E.g., J.M. O'Flynn, *Generalissimos of the Western Roman Empire* (Edmonton, 1983); H. Castritius, "Zur Sozialgeschichte der Heermeister des Westreichs. Einheitliche Rekrutierungsmuster und Rivalitäten im spätromischen Militäradel," *MIÖG* 92 (1984) 1–33.

2 A.H.M. Jones, J.R. Martindale, and J. Morris (eds.), *The Prosopography of the Later Roman Empire, Volume I. A.D. 260–395* (hereafter *PLRE* 1) (Cambridge, 1971) 957–9; he married Maouvia, the Nicene queen of the Saracens, and he and the Roman Saturninus competed to have monks live on their property.

3 *PLRE* 1.605.

4 Amm. 15.5.31: *Silvanum ... ad conventiculum ritus Christiani tendentem.*

a dead letter, and barbarian generals were nearly all Christian, some Arian, some Nicene. Nicenes included Merobaudes, Master of Soldiers in 443 and presumed to be a descendent of the fourth-century pagan Master of Soldiers Merobaudes; he is thought to be the Merobaudes who wrote an extant Nicene poem entitled *De Christo*.[5] Nicene generals, of course, would have been fully integrated into the religious mainstream of the empire and would have gained political legitimation through their Nicene affiliation. But Arian barbarian generals were on their own. No Nicene Roman was going to look favorably on their Arian practices. Nevertheless, eastern Arian barbarian generals interacted quite genteelly with Nicene Romans. The bishop of Rome Leo (440–61), for example, confidently expected that the eastern patrician and Master of Soldiers Aspar would uphold the cause of "orthodoxy" at the Council of Nicaea of 457, noting in a letter, "for the sake of the faith, we sent the required documents to the *vir magnificus*, the patrician Aspar."[6]

It is more difficult, however, to locate western Arian barbarian generals in Roman service who openly manifested their religious affiliations. The Visigoth Alaric, who was accompanied by the Arian bishop Sigesarius, is a special case because his western appointment was by the usurper Priscus Attalus.[7] More significantly, in 427 the barbarian Arian general Sigisvult was accompanied by the Arian bishop Maximinus when he undertook his expedition against the rebellious Count Boniface in Africa in 427—while in Hippo on Sigisvult's orders, Maximinus engaged in his famous debate with Augustine.[8]

Based on the extant evidence, the western barbarian general who manifested his religious affiliations most openly was the Patrician and Master of Soldiers Ricimer.[9] Between the death of Majorian and the accession of Anthemius, from 461 to 467, Ricimer behaved like a *de facto* emperor whether there was an emperor on the throne or not. For example, during the reign of Libius Severus (461–65), Ricimer sent out embassies and undertook military campaigns apparently on his own authority (Priscus, fr.29). In 464, he reportedly killed Beorgor king of the

---

[5] J.R. Martindale (ed.), *The Prosopography of the Later Roman Empire. Volume II., A.D. 395–527* (hereafter *PLRE* 2) (Cambridge, 1980) 758.

[6] Leo *Ep.* 153, *Accepimus dilectionis tuae* (*PL* 54.1123): *Ad magnificum virum patricium Asparem necessaria in causa fidei scripta transmisimus.*

[7] *PLRE* 2.47; see Zos. 5.48.1–3; Soz. 9.7.1–2.

[8] See R.W. Mathisen, "Sigisvult the Patrician, Maximinus the Arian, and Political Strategems in the Western Roman Empire ca. 425–440," *EME* 8 (1999) 173–96.

[9] For Ricimer, see, e.g., A.M. Papini, *Ricimero: L'agonia dell'impero romano d'Occidente* (Milan, 1959); L.R. Scott, "Antibarbarian Sentiments and the 'Barbarian' General in Roman Imperial Service: The Case of Ricimer," in *Actes du VIIe congrès de la Fédération Internationale des Associations d'Études Classiques* (Brussels, 1984) 2.23–33; L. Vassili, "Il comes Agrippino collaboratore di Ricimero," *Athenaeum* 14 (1936) 175–80; Idem, "La figura di Nepoziano e l'opposizione ricimeriana al governo imperiale di Maggioriano," *Athenaeum* 14 (1936) 56–66; and G. Lacam, *L'agonie de Rome: Ricimer, un barbare, maître de l'Occident (455–472)* (Paris, 1992).

Alans, an act that Count Marcellinus attributed to "king Ricimer."[10] After Severus' death, as will be discussed below, legislation continued to be issued in his name, very likely with the connivance of Ricimer.

In April of 467, a new emperor, Anthemius, arrived in Italy as the nominee of the eastern emperor Leo. Ricimer and Anthemius initially cooperated. Before the end of the year Ricimer married Anthemius' daughter Alypia, thus, in the manner of Stilicho, bringing him into the imperial family: any offspring of this union would have had a strong claim on the throne. But relations between the two deteriorated because both wanted to be in charge. In 470, civil war broke out and Ricimer withdrew to Milan, where he resumed his independent behavior: on one occasion, Ennodius noted, "Word was brought to Anthemius that a bishop of Liguria had arrived on an embassy, a man whom no one, howsoever eloquent, could adequately describe. But the emperor responded, 'Cleverly does Ricimer contend with me by means of his embassies; he sends such men to subdue by prayers those whom he provokes by injuries'." (*VEpiph.* 60–61)

Ricimer and His Church

Sometime between 459 and 471, Ricimer underwrote a mosaic in the apse of the present-day Church of S. Agata dei Goti in Rome. The dedicatory inscription, in gold letters, reads:

> FL^A•RICIMER• VI• MAG• VTRIVSQ• MILITIÆ• PATRICIVS• ET• EX• CONS•ORD• PRO•VOTO•SVO•ADORNAVIT•[11]

> *Flavius Ricimer, vir inlustris, magister utriusque militiae, patricius et ex consule ordinario, pro voto suo adornavit* ("Flavius Ricimer, an illustrious gentlemen, master of both services, patrician, and ex-ordinary consul, adorned [this church] according to his vow")

Ricimer's personal religious affiliation, which is not stated in any source, can be inferred from his Gothic and Suevic ethnicity. Given that the royalty of both

---

[10] Marc.Com. s.a.464: *Beorgor rex Alanorum a Ricimere rege occiditur*; also Cass. *Chron.* no. 1278: *His conss. rex Halanorum Beorgor apud Pergamum a patricio Ricimere peremptus est.*

[11] Preserved, e.g., in *Barb.lat.* 2161 f.86r; see C. Hülsen, C. Cecchelli, G. Giovannoni, U. Monneret de Villard, A. Muñoz, *S. Agata dei Goti* (Rome, 1924) 181–2, 192; J. Zeiller, "Les églises ariennes de Rome a l'époque de la domination gothique," *MEFRA* 24 (1904) 20–25 and 25 (1905) 127–46; and Idem, "Étude sur l'arianisme en Italie à l'époque ostrogothique et à l'époque lombarde," *MEFRA* 25 (1905) 127–46 at 130–31.

peoples was Arian, the presumption is that Ricimer, too, was Arian.[12] In addition, the Arian status of Ricimer's church is confirmed by its reconsecration as a Nicene church in honor of St. Agatha, a mid-third-century martyr of Catania in Sicily, in the late sixth century by Gregory the Great: it was called the *ecclesia Gothorum* in the *Liber pontificalis*, and Gregory himself referred to it as the *spelunca pravitatis haereticae* and the *Arianorum ecclesia*.[13]

Of course, simply because the church that Gregory rededicated in 594 was Arian during the sixth century does not necessarily mean that, regardless of Ricimer's Arian affiliation, it was Arian at the time of Ricimer. It could have become Arian during the Ostrogothic occupation of Rome (493–536), but even then one would have to explain why this particular church was chosen to be Arian in a city that never had a large Ostrogothic population. Nor would there necessarily have been any legal prohibitions against such a church, for a western law of 386 legalized the Arianizing formula of the Council of Rimini in 359, confirmed at Constantinople in 360, which declared the Son to be like the Father "according to the scriptures," and recently had been revalidated by its inclusion in the *Theodosian Code* in 438, providing a legal safety-valve for Arians who adhered to this formula even though it had been anathematized by the Nicene church.[14] Adherence to the Creed of Rimini then became the touchstone for the acceptability of barbarian Arianism in the Nicene world, as demonstrated by the canon of the Third Council of Toledo in 589, where the Visigoths renounced Arianism, anathematizing anyone who

---

[12] See Zeiller, "Églises," 21–2. A passage from Hyd. *Chron.* 232 (*Ajax, natione Galata, effectus apostata et senior Arrianus, inter Suevos regis sui auxilio hostis catholicae fidei et divinae trinitatis emergit*) sometimes has been taken to indicate that some of the Suevi converted to Nicene Christianity, but the Nicenes whom Ajax troubled were probably Romans.

[13] *Lib.pont.* 66 (L. Duchesne, *Liber Pontificalis: texte, introduction et commentaire*, 2 vols. [Paris, 1886–92] 1.312); Greg.Mag. *Reg.* 4.19 (a.594) (*CCSL* 140.237); also Greg. Mag. *Dial.* 30 (*PL* 77.288): *Arianorum ecclesia in regione urbis hujus quae Subura dicitur ... introductis illic ... sanctae Agathae martyrum reliquiis*. At the same time, another Arian church was dedicated to St. Severinus of Noricum: Greg.Mag. *Reg.* 3.19 (*CCSL* 140.165); see Hülsen et al., *S. Agata*, 26; M.C. Cartocci, "Alcune precisazioni sulla intitolazione a S. Agata della 'Ecclesia Gothorum' alla Suburra," in *Teoderico il Grande e i Goti d'Italia. Atti del XIII congresso internazionale di studi sull'alto Medioevo, Milano 2–6 novembre 1992* (Spoleto, 1993) 2.611–20 at 615.

[14] *CTh* 16.1.4 (a. 386): *Damus copiam colligendi his, qui secundum ea sentiunt, quae temporibus divae memoriae Constanti ... Ariminensi concilio ... decreta sunt*. See M. Weedman, "Hilary and the Homoiousians: Using New Categories to Map the Trinitarian Controversy," *ChHist* 76 (2007) 491–510, who overstates, however, the degree to which Homoians and Homoiousians "were not Arians." Note also that the opposition to an Arian church in Constantinople in 399 was not based on legal prohibitions but on popular opinion: see Zos. 5.20–22; Eun. *Hist.* fr.69.4; Philost. 11.8; Socr. 6.39; Joh.Ant. fr. 284 (Roberto); and Al. Cameron and J. Long, *Barbarians and Politics at the Court of Arcadius* (Berkeley, 1993) 224–39. In addition, the schismatic Novatians still had churches in Rome in the 420s (Socr. 7.12).

continued to adhere to the Creed of Rimini.[15] So, economy of hypothesis suggests that Ricimer decorated an Arian—in whatever form barbarian Arianism was manifested—church that then remained Arian until Gregory's rededication.

In addition, a question raised by Gregory's association of the church with St. Agatha is to whom it was dedicated in the time of Ricimer. To approach this question, we can turn to the iconography. Ricimer's inscription and mosaic were destroyed in the late sixteenth century when the apse vault collapsed; only some of the columns now remain from the fifth century.[16] But detailed notes and copies of the inscriptions and artwork were made shortly before the collapse by Alfonso Ciacconio and are preserved in manuscript *Vat.lat.* 5407 (see Figure 22.1).[17] The mosaic, reconstructed from Ciacconio's drawings, depicted Christ seated on a globe with the legend *salus totius generis humani* ("Salvation of the entire human race") and surrounded by the twelve apostles.[18] The mosaic's iconography suggests that Ricimer's church was dedicated to Christ the Savior, or to Christ and the Apostles.[19]

Arian Iconography

Two significant issues now can be addressed relating to Ricimer's decorative program. First of all, what, if anything, does it tell us about Arian iconography? And, secondly, what does it tell us about how Ricimer perceived his own position in late Roman religion, politics, and society? With regard to the first of these, we might ask whether barbarian Arians portrayed Christ in a manner that at all identified him as an Arian Christ as opposed to a Nicene Christ? This is a difficult question for at least two reasons. For one thing, there are very few surviving examples of Arian iconography, and this makes it difficult, or impossible, to make any generalizations about common characteristics. In addition, there is nothing in Arian theology that hints at how it might have been manifested in art. Indeed, by the Council of Rimini in 359, theological distinctions between Nicenes and Arians had been reduced to finer and finer points. And by the Council of Constantinople in 381, it was only the name of Arianism, not any particular theological attribute, that was condemned. So how, if at all, would the increasingly small theological distinctions between Nicene and Arian Christology have been reflected in the iconography, even if one were minded to do so?

15 *Conc.Tolet.III*, can.17 (*PL* 84.344): *Quicunque Ariminense concilium non ex toto corde respuerit et damnaverit, anathema sit.*

16 See E. Muntz, "The Lost Mosaics of Rome of the IV to IX Century (I)," *AJA* 2 (1886) 295–313 at 309.

17 See Muntz, "Lost Mosaics," 308; and M. Armellini, *Le chiese di Roma dal secolo IV al XIX* (Rome, 1942) 201–2.

18 C. Cecchelli, *Monumenti cristiano-eretici di Roma* (Rome, 1944) vii.

19 F.M. Clover, "Count Ricimer and the Church of the Holy Apostles'," in *Abstracts. Twenty-Second Annual Byzantine Studies Conference, October 24–27, 1996, The University of North Carolina At Chapel Hill* (Chapel Hill, 1996), suggests just the Apostles.

Figure 22.1 Collage of Ciacconio's drawings recreating Ricimer's mosaic. From Hülsen et al., *S. Agata dei Goti* (1924) pl.9.

The only way to identify any Arian iconographic markers is to look at surviving examples of Arian art and see if any differences can be detected. The best such examples come from two buildings in Ravenna, the Arian baptistery and the Church of S. Apollinare Nuovo. Many modern art historical surveys do propose to identify an Arian agenda of the Ravenna churches, but they do so by beginning with the assumption that there must have been an Arian agenda and then proceeding to find it. For example, some interpreters have confused Gothic Arianism with Nestorianism and supposed that Arianism was about the differentiation between a divine bearded Christ and a clean-shaven human Christ.[20] This assumption, of course, is not only simply mistaken but also neglects the fact that Nicene churches, too, used bearded and clean-shaven Christs. Attempts to find explicit Arian markers in the Ravenna artwork have not been convincing.[21] Indeed, one thing that can be said about Ostrogothic iconography is that the Ostrogoths' theological understanding of the relationship between the Father and Son in no way lessened their devotion to Christ. The original dedication of S. Apollinare Nuovo was to "our Lord Jesus Christ,"[22] and the baptistery, of course, focuses on Christ. This emphasis on Christ would have been the Arian way of saying, "this is our Christ," and that may have been as close as they ever came to making an iconographic statement about their views of Christ. Ricimer, therefore, was not the only Arian barbarian with a special attachment to Christ.

So just where did his program of church decoration fit into Ricimer's personal plans and goals? The standard work on S. Agata concludes that the mosaic had no overtly Arian characteristics.[23] This is consistent with the lack of overt Arian theology in the Ravenna mosaics and suggests that any analysis of Ricimer's goals for his church decoration should be sought in his political and social ambitions, not in any heavy-handed theological agenda. Now, Ricimer's dedication must have occurred between his consulate in 459 and his death in 472. At this time, Ricimer was the most powerful politician in Rome, and any analysis of his church

[20] N. MacGregor and E. Langmuir, *Seeing Salvation: Images of Christ in Art* (Yale, 2000): "the [heresy] that most affected visual art was Arianism" (80); the mosaics "distinguish the two (for the Arians) separable natures of Jesus Christ, human and divine" (81). Also O. von Simson, *Sacred Fortress: Byzantine Art and Statecraft in Ravenna* (Chicago, 1948) 73; and C. Ricci, *Ravenna* (Bergamo, 1912) 25.

[21] R.M. Jensen, "The Economy of the Trinity at the Creation of Adam and Eve," *JECS* 7 (1999) 527–46 at 528: "Attempts to distinguish something *particularly* Arian have been somewhat strained." More emphatic is A. Urbino, "Donation, Dedication, and *Damnatio Memoriae*: The Catholic Reconciliation of Ravenna and the Church of Sant'Apollinare Nuovo," *JECS* 13 (2005) 71–110 at 88: "There is no convincing evidence that Arian Goths … employed significantly different symbology or iconography in Italy as an expression of an Arian theology."

[22] Agnellus, *Lib.pont.eccl.rav.* 86: *Si diligenter inquisieritis, super fenestras invenietis ex lapideis litteris exaratum ita: Theodericus rex hanc ecclesiam a fundamentis in nomine domini nostri Iesu Christi fecit.*

[23] Hülsen et al., *S. Agata*, 25: "Il mosaico non aveva alcuna caratteristica ariana."

must be made in this context. So let us take a detailed look at the iconography of Ricimer's decoration and see whether it is possible to detect any connections with Ricimer's political programs.

Depiction of the Apostles

First, the apostles. They wear striped tunics, each bearing a so-called gammadia character (nine Ls, two Ns, and a gamma on Peter).[24] Six hold scrolls, Peter holds keys, and five have their right hands in various positions. Iconographically, the apostles of S. Agata are quite similar to those in S. Apollinare Nuovo—they hold scrolls, and their robes hang in a similar manner and are marked with gammadia. On the other hand, the S. Agata apostles do not have haloes. The general stylistic similarities also confirm the late antique date of the S. Agata mosaics. The apostles appear, from left to right, in the order: James son of Alphaeus, Simon the Zealot, James, Judas son of James, Philip, Paul, Peter, Andrew, John, Thomas, Matthew, and Bartholemew, with Paul and Peter in the positions of honor flanking Christ. S. Agata clearly uses the roster of apostles from the book of Luke as opposed to that from Matthew or Mark: it has Simon as the Zealot rather than the Canaanite and it includes Judas brother of James in place of Thaddeus.[25] For comparative purposes, the apostles in the Arian churches of Ravenna are not named, but the sixth-century mosaic of apostles in the Nicene Archepiscopal Chapel are and use a combination of the Matthew and Mark versions, citing Thaddeus and Simon the Canaanite. One can only speculate whether barbarian Arians had some preference for the gospel of Luke.

Depiction of Christ

The most noteworthy aspect of the artwork, it would seem, is the emphasis upon Christ, who sits on a globe, holding his right hand in benediction and a book—presumably the Bible—in his left hand (see Figure 22.2). The words in the book are illegible, but the reproduction does show seven lines per page plus a heading, a page or folio number in the upper right, and a shorter subscript on each page, for a total of ten lines of text per page, a number that seems rather too large for a mosaic, unless the lines in the original mosaic also were illegible. If the copy does represent an actual quotation, the latter would have been quite long. Christ's tunic bears the letter L (see Figure 22.3), like most of the other apostles, but Christ is the only figure with the nimbus, establishing his position superior to the apostles. The

24 For these characters, see J. Welch and C. Foley, "Gammadia on Early Jewish and Christian Garments," in J.F. Hall and J. Welch (eds.), *Masada and the World of the New Testament* (Provo, 1997) 252–8.

25 Luke 6:13–16; Matt. 10:1–4; Mark 3:13–19.

Christ-on-globe motif is striking.[26] It is known only in the western church. Its first appearance may be in S. Costanza in Rome, in an apse mosaic dated variously to the fourth, fifth, and seventh centuries depicting Christ, seated on a globe, handing a scroll reading *Dominus pacem dat* (not a Scriptural citation) to Peter.[27] The next (if not the first) attested use in Rome is at S. Agata in the 460s. It was used again in Rome above an arch in San Lorenzo Outside the Walls ca. 559/579, where Christ bears a scepter and is flanked by Peter, Paul, and local clerics, and yet again in Rome in the late sixth century in an apse at S. Teodoro, where Christ, again holding a scepter, is flanked by Peter, Paul, and two martyrs. Meanwhile, in Ravenna, an apse mosaic at S. Vitale dated ca. 540 shows Christ, with a zeta on his tunic, seated on a globe flanked by two angels and two bishops, but without any apostles. The last example, also ca. 540, comes from just across the Adriatic from Ravenna at Poreč, where a mosaic above an apse shows Christ flanked by all the apostles, just as at S. Agata, albeit with the apostles in a different order (Andrew, Peter, Paul, John, and so on). Given its use in Nicene churches, the Christ-on-globe motif cannot be considered to have had any specifically Arian associations. But its theme, emphasizing Christ's dominion over the earth,well could have appealed to a military man like Ricimer and resurfaces in the text that accompanies the Christ figure.

Figure 22.2 Close-up of the book held by Christ in the Ricimer mosaic. From Hülsen et al., *S. Agata dei Goti* (1924) pl.5 detail.

[26] For this motif, see Hülsen, et al., *S. Agata*, 34; J.M. Spieser, "The Representation of Christ in the Apses of Early Christian Churches," *Gesta* 37 (1998) 63–73 at 70: "The image of the lord seems more distant"; T.F. Mathews, *The Clash of Gods: A Reinterpretation of Early Christian Art* (Princeton, 1993).

[27] See D.J. Stanley, "The Apse Mosaics at S. Costanza," *RM* 94 (1987) 29–42 (on the restored sections), and Idem, "New Discoveries at Santa Costanza," *DOP* 48 (1994) 257–61; G. Mackie, "A New Look at the Patronage of Santa Costanza, Rome," *Byzantion* 67 (1997) 383–406; and P. Vallin, "Dominus pacem dat. A propos du mausolée de Constantina à Rome," *RSR* 51 (1963) 579–613.

Figure 22.3 Ciacconio's rendering of the figure of Christ in the Ricimer mosaic. From Hülsen et al., *S. Agata dei Goti* (1924) pl.5.

The inscription *salus totius humani generis* has received surprisingly little attention or commentary.[28] None of the discussants, for example, even suggests a source for the phrase, but a little investigation yields some interesting results. Although the words "*totius generis humani*" recur in many ecclesiastical contexts,[29] their use in a salvific context is much rarer and quite circumscribed, occurring primarily in northern Italy, between ca. 390 and 450. For example, at the end of the fourth century, Ambrose of Milan spoke of the death of Christ as being *pro totius humani generis absolutione* (*In Ps. 39*). Around 400, Chromatius of Aquileia preached: *Aduentus ergo Christi salus omnium gentium facta est, et totius generis humani redemptio* (*Serm.* 12). Just before 450, Peter Chrysologus of Ravenna spoke of the Virgin Mary bearing *totius generis humani ... fructus* (*Serm.* 142). And ca. 450, Maximus of Turin said in one sermon: *Per salvatorem ... totius generis humani sanatur infirmitas* (*Serm.* 43) and in another, using the same words as Ricimer's inscription, *totius generis humani salus redempta sit sanguine Salvatoris* (*Serm.* 48).[30] But these, of course, are all Nicene authors. Did Ricimer encounter this tag while having theological discussions with Italian ecclesiastics? Why not? If eastern Arian generals could engage in theological discussions, why not a western one? And if Ricimer picked up the concept of Christ as *salus totius humani generis* in a Nicene environment, it could not have had any specifically Arian connotations. But that does not mean that it could not have appealed to him nonetheless, especially if his intention also was to indicate that Christ was the savior of all of humanity, including barbarians.

Thus, the religious significance of Ricimer's iconography and text both were in the mainstream of Nicene culture. Ricimer was not, therefore, being openly provocative in his decoration. But his choices do reflect the typically Arian devotion to Christ, in this case a Christ who represented nothing less than world domination, a theme that one might suggest also was consistent with Ricimer's personal philosophy and inclinations. But if Ricimer's design and legend did not represent an overtly Arian program, it very likely did reflect his personal social and political agendas, and it is with these that the rest of this study will be concerned.

---

28 Hülsen, et al., *S. Agata*, 33, e.g., cites it without commentary.

29 See, e.g., Arnob. *Comm.Ps. 12* (*PL* 53.340): *In totius generis humani persona propheticum carmen exorat*; Marius Mercator (*PL* 48.932) spoke of salvation through Christ as being *pro redemptione totius humani generis*; *Brev.fid.adv.Ar.Haer.* (*PL* 13.665): *Vbi salus humani generis agitur, Patri et Filio copularetur*; Salvian, *Ad eccl.* 2.2: *Pendentem in patibulo humani generis salutem.*

30 The tradition continued in the 6th century, when Agnellus of Ravenna *Lib.pont. eccl.Rav.* 21 (*PL* 52.19) spoke of God as, *qui per sanctum Filium tuum totius generis humani salutem recuperasti.*

Church Dedications

It was not uncommon at this time for Roman senators and officials to underwrite the cost of church construction and to commemorate having done so in dedicatory inscriptions, often using language very similar to Ricimer's. Around 430, the empress Galla Placidia dedicated a church of John the Evangelist in Ravenna; one inscription read:

> To the sanctified and most blessed apostle John the Evangelist the empress Galla Placidia along with her son the emperor Placidus Valentinianus and her daughter the empress Justa Grata Honoria fulfill their vow for their liberation from the danger of the sea.[31]

At about the same time, the Master of Soldiers and Consul Felix and his wife Padusia underwrote "from their own funds" work in the Lateran basilica, "fulfilling their vow."[32] In the 460s, bishop Hilarus of Rome (461–68) sponsored two oratories in the same basilica, one of them to his "liberator" John the Evangelist.[33] And around the 470s, Attica, the wife of the patrician and Gallic prefect Magnus Felix, paid "from her own funds" for work in San Lorenzo in Damaso.[34]

Ricimer's example demonstrated that church dedication was not limited to Nicenes and Romans. Indeed, in 471 a Nicene Gothic general, the direct subordinate of Ricimer, the Master of Soldiers Flavius Valila *qui et* Theodobius, dedicated a church to St. Felix at Tivoli and bequeathed to the church the house of Iunius Bassus on the Esquiline Hill, which, probably still during the 470s, then was consecrated by Pope Simplicius (468–83) as a church of St. Andrew.[35] This church,

---

31 Agnellus, *Lib.pont.eccl.Rav.* 20.43: *Sancto ac beatissimo apostolo Iohanni evangelistae Galla Placidia augusta cum filio suo Placido Valentiniano augusto et filia sua Iusta Grata Honoria augusta liberationis periculum maris votum solverent*, referring to the fulfillment of a vow.

32 *ILS* 1293 = *ILCV* 68: *Flavius Felix, v.c., magister utriusque militia, patricius, et cons. ord. et Padusia eius illustris femina ejus uxor voti compotes de proprio fecerunt.* Felix and Padusia were murdered at Ravenna in 430: Prosp. s.a. 430, Hyd. *Chron.* 94 (430), Marc.Com. s.a.430, Joh.Ant. fr.293.1 (Roberto); *PLRE* 2.461–2.

33 Surviving inscriptions read for John the Evangelist: *liberatori suo beato Iohanni evangelistae Hilarus episcopus famulus XPI*, and for John the Baptist: *Hilarus episcopus dei famulus offert* (see Muntz, "Lost Mosaics," 305–70).

34 *ICUR* 2.151 no. 25: *Attica Felicis Magni clarissima coniunx sumptibus hoc propriis aedificauit opus.*

35 Tivoli: The *Carta Cornutiana* (Duchesne, *Liber Pontificalis,* 1.lcxlvii). Esquiline: *Lib.pont.* 49 (for discussion, see Duchesne, *Liber pontificalis*, 1.250). The elegiac dedicatory inscription of Simplicius begins: *Haec tibi mens Valilae decrevit praedia, Christe / cui testator opes detulit ille suas / Simplicius quae papa sacris caelestibus aptans / effecit vere muneris esse tui.* See H. Castritius, "Zur Sozialgeschichte der Heermeister des Westreichs nach der Mitte des 5. Jh.: Flavius Valila qui et Theodosius," *AncSoc* 3 (1972) 233–43.

later known as S. Andrea in Catabarbara (an acknowledgment of its barbarian connection), also had an apse mosaic of Christ accompanied by apostles, although in this case Christ was standing and there were only six apostles; one can only speculate as to whether Valila, mindful of Ricimer's decoration, had suggested the motif.[36] Both of these powerful barbarian generals thus were engaged in the kind of philanthropic work expected of high-ranking Roman aristocrats. And both also might have been engaging in games of philanthropic one-upmanship.

On the one hand, Valila would have been showing that he could be even more munificent toward the church than his barbarian superior officer. Indeed, these two barbarian generals also might have been competing for influence among the Christian barbarian population of Rome. Ricimer's church, the *ecclesia Gothorum quae fuit in Subora*, was located on a promontory of the Quirinal, ascending above the Suburra, which bordered on the *campus barbaricus*, the area between the Caelian and Esquiline hills which since the Antonine period had been the habitual residence of the emperor's barbarian guard.[37] The Arian church of St. Severinus also was located in the heart of the *campus barbaricus*. One might suggest that in Ricimer's time, his church would have been the center of Gothic religion and society in Rome and have served the same purpose as Gaïnas' church in Constantinople.[38] Was it the seat, one might ask, of an Arian bishop of Rome?[39] Ricimer's church, therefore, would have positioned him not only as the supreme military commander of the western Roman empire, but also as a Roman aristocrat sensitive to the religious needs of his Arian barbarian clients, who by participating in traditional Roman forms of Christian, albeit Arian, religious observance would themselves also have been integrated into Roman society and culture.

On the other hand, Ricimer may have been competing philanthropically not only with Valila, but also with other senatorial generals, such as his predecessor as patrician, Flavius Felix. Not only did Ricimer's dedicatory inscription mimic the parallel section of Felix's almost word for word, but the titulature of Felix's church dedication virtually duplicates that of his consular diptych. Unfortunately, no diptychs survive from Ricimer's consulate of 459, but if they did, they presumably would have read much like his church dedication.

---

36 S. Waetzoldt, *Die Kopien des 17. Jahrhunderts nach Mosaiken und Wandmalereien in Rom* (Munich, 1964) pl.15.

37 *Lib.pont.* 66; M.C. Cartocci, "S. Agatha Gothorum," *LTUR* (1993) 1.24–6; G. Tomassetti, "Il quartiere militare di Roma," *MDAIR* 17 (1902) 98. See also Cartocci, "Alcune precisazioni," 619; C. Ceccchelli, in Hülsen, et al., *S. Agata*, 26; Zeiller, "Églises," 24–7.

38 Ugonio mentions "fragmenti di scritture et epitafi in lingua gotica" (*Barb.lat.* 2160 f.119r; see Hülsen, et al., *S. Agata*, 181), although these are dismissed by Hülsen, et al., *S. Agata*, 27. See also Hülsen, et al., *S. Agata,* 28, for the suggestion that S. Agata was the *ecclesia Gothorum* of Rome, parallel to the *ecclesia Gothorum* of Ravenna and the "church of the Goths" in Constantinople.

39 Hülsen, et al., *S. Agata*, 26: see L.G. Marini, *I papiri diplomatici* (Rome, 1805) no.140, p.376, for an Arian bishop at Rome ca. 490. See also Zeiller, "Églises," 127–46.

Indeed, the question of consulates may provide some insight into Ricimer's decision to decorate the church. Ricimer never held a second consulate even though other powerful senators, including Stilicho, Aëtius, and Petronius Maximus, did so. It might be argued, for example, that Ricimer eventually saw the consulate as being beneath him and thus chose not to hold it. But Ricimer's use of Roman aristocratic status symbols in other regards suggests otherwise, and a look at the consular *fasti* is instructive.[40] A second consulate in 460 and 461, when the western consulate was in Majorian's gift, would have been unseemly so soon after the first one. As of 467, when Anthemius became emperor, the consulate for 468 and later was out of Ricimer's control. That leaves 462–67 as years when Ricimer could have held a second consulate. Emperors customarily assumed the consulate their first full year in office, hence 462 was reserved for Libius Severus, whose consulate was not even recognized in the east. The western nominee for 463, the distinguished senator Fl. Caecina Decius Basilius, was acknowledged in the east, suggesting that this choice was the result of some delicate negotiations. But for the next four years, no western consul was appointed at all, no doubt as a result of further disagreements with the east. And in 468, Anthemius was sole consul. So much, then, for Ricimer's opportunity to hold a second consulate and manifest his aristocratic status in traditional senatorial style. Thus, Ricimer's church decoration and inscription might have served as an ersatz for the second diptych that he could never circulate.

An even more immediate social and political context for Ricimer's church dedication might be sought in his marriage to Alypia in late 467. Not only does the marriage demonstrate that there was no religious prohibition against an Arian-Nicene marriage,[41] but the decoration of a church with iconography that had no Arian overtones also would have emphasized any claim Ricimer may have been making that his Arianism was "not a problem."

Ricimer's Pretensions

Ricimer's personal political agenda also can be detected in his choice of inscription. Even if the legend *salus totius generis humani* did not have specifically Arian associations, it could have had political implications, as suggested by a look at a reconstruction of Ricimer's mosaic that includes his dedicatory inscription, which, according to Ugonio, was placed underneath. Is it too much of a stretch to suggest that one could have read these inscriptions as *salus totius generis humani, Fl. Ricimer*? Before we dismiss such a suggestion out of hand—for who could have ambitions so grandiose as even to contemplate being thought of in the same terms as Christ—we might consider a few things (see Figure 22.4):

40 See R.S. Bagnall, Al. Cameron, S.R. Schwartz, and K.A. Worp (eds.), *Consuls of the Later Roman Empire* (Atlanta, 1987).

41 Also suggested by the betrothal of Patricius, the son of the Arian Aspar, to Leontia, daughter of the emperor Leo in 470, just three years later (*PLRE* 2.667, 842).

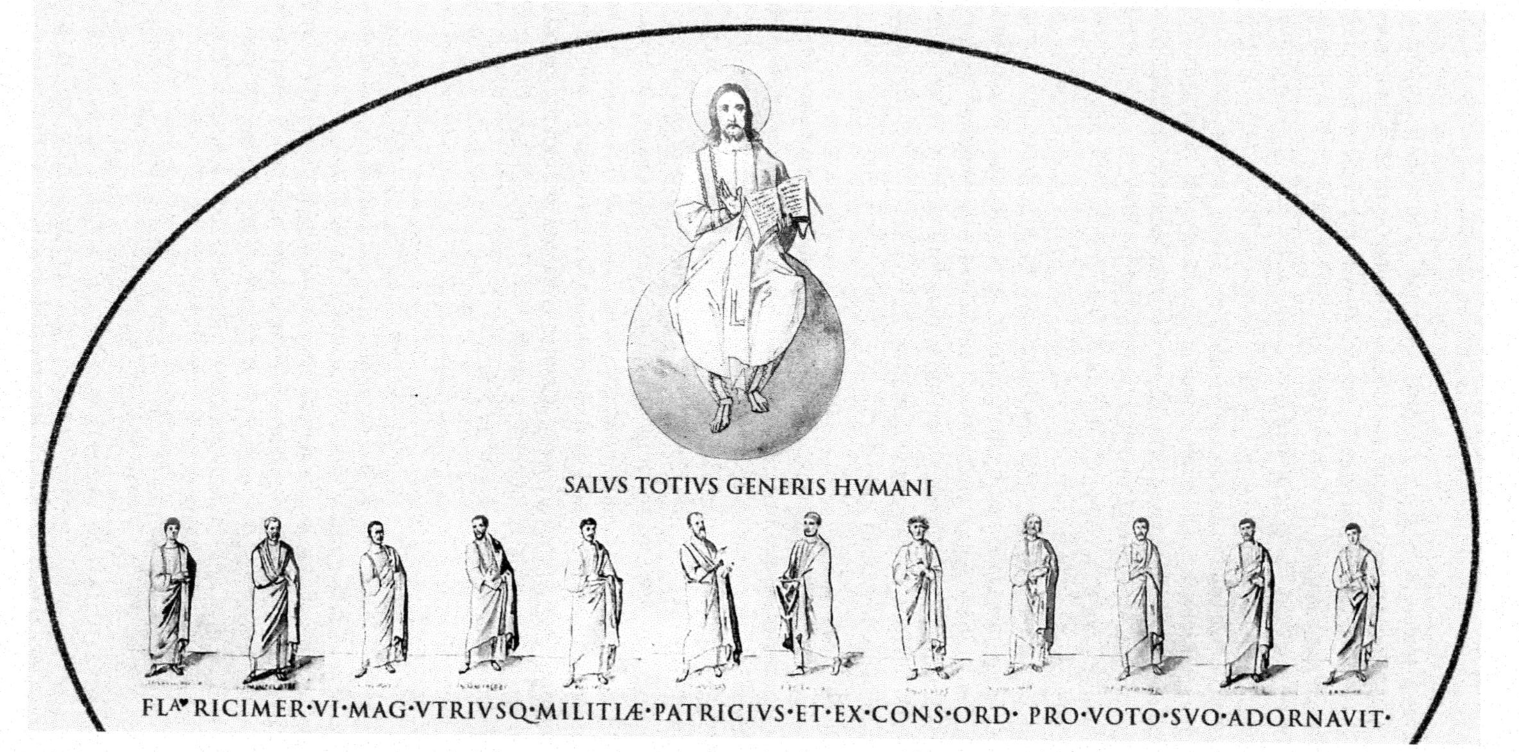

Figure 22.4 Reconstruction of how Ricimer's mosaic and inscriptions might have appeared in situ. Montage by D. Underwood. Used by permission.

1. There was a precedent for the use of such terminology to refer to emperors. The phrase *spes totius generis humani* was used to describe Constantine in a panegyric of AD 310.[42] This concept resurfaced around 400, with the emperor being referred to on the coinage as the *nova spes reipublicae*.[43] In addition, there was an earlier tradition of emperors being described specifically as the *salus generis humani*, as seen on coins of Vindex, Galba, and Trajan.[44] Its use in the fifth century to refer to Christ would have occurred against this backdrop of prior secular usage.
2. Even though Ricimer was not an emperor, he already has been seen to have assumed quasi-imperial powers both during and after the reign of Libius Severus. His aspirations to quasi-emperorship went well beyond being a power behind the throne and marrying an emperor's daughter. During either the reign of Severus or the succeeding interregnum, Ricimer dared to strike coins bearing on the obverse the portrait of Severus but on the reverse his own monogram, something that had been done in the past by legitimate emperors but which was completely unprecedented for someone who was not an Augustus or Augusta.[45] (see Figure 22.5) After his death, Ricimer's example was followed by other ambitious barbarians, who also put large monograms on the reverse of the coinage, including Odovacar, Theoderic, and even Ricimer's own nephew, the Burgundian king Gundobad.
3. Equally unprecedented, the Prefect of Rome Eustathius, probably during the reign of Severus, issued tesserae that cited Ricimer on equal terms with the two *domini nostri*, with a legend reading: "For the salvation of Our Lords [the emperors] and the patrician Ricimer, Plotinus Eustathius Prefect of the City, made this" (see Figure 22.6).[46] The expression *salvis d(ominis) n(ostris)* was customarily reserved for emperors. What makes this example even more striking is that other contemporary tesserae (that do not name Ricimer), including one of Severus and Leo that must date to the very same period, name the emperors, but on this one only Ricimer is named and not the emperors.[47] Again, it would not take much of a stretch of the imagination to read this inscription as *salvo domino nostro Ricimere*.

---

42 *Pan.Lat.* 12(9).9.4: *Spem totius generis humani et vota deceperas?*

43 See J.P.C. Kent (ed.), *The Roman Imperial Coinage. Volume X., The Divided Empire and the Fall of the Western Parts, AD 395–491* (London, 1994) 65, 242.

44 E.g., H. Mattingly, *Coins of the Roman Empire in the British Museum* (London, 1923) 1.cxcvi. And Nerva was referred to by Pliny the Younger (*Pan.* 6) as *parens generis humani*.

45 For illustrations, and the suggestion that the portrait on some of these coins represents Ricimer himself, see D. Woods, "A Misunderstood Monogram: Ricimer or Severus?," *Hermathena* 172 (2002) 5–21.

46 *ILS* 813: (recto) *SALVIS DD NN / ET PATRICI/O RICIMERE*; (verso) *PLOTINVS EVS/TATHIVS VC / VRB. PR. FECIT*; see *PLRE* 2.436 (no.13), dated only to 457/472.

47 E.g., *ILS* 811 (a. 461–5): (recto) *SALVIS DD NN / LEONE ET LIBIO / SEVERO PP AVG*; (verso) *CELIVS ACONIV[S] / PROBIANVS PRAE / PRAET FECIT*; and *ILS* 814 (a. 474/475): (recto) *SALVO DN / IVLIO NEPOTE / PP AVG;* (verso) *AVDAX VC / PRAEFECTVS / VRB FECIT.*

Figure 22.5 Copper coin bearing the portrait and title of Libius Severus on the obverse, but the monogram of Ricimer on the reverse. From Numismatik Lanz München, Auction 123, 30 (May 2005) no. 980.

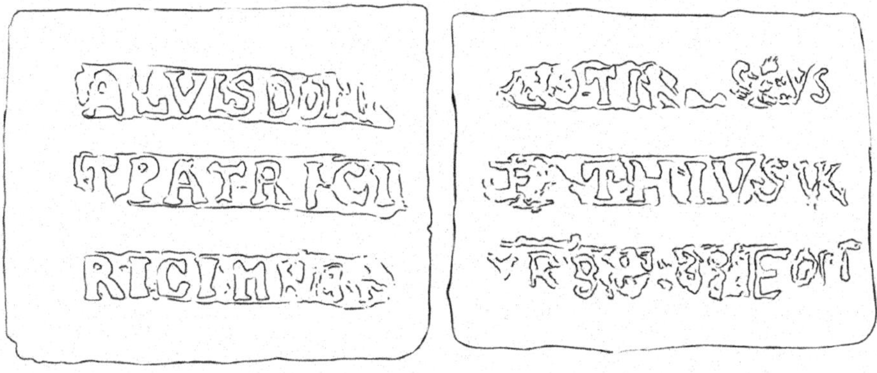

Figure 22.6 A tessera names Ricimer on equal terms with the emperors Severus and Leo. Drawing by D. Underwood based on Hülsen et al., *S. Agata dei Goti* (1924). Used by permission.

To return to the church inscription, one also cannot but note the parallelism between *salus totius generis humani* and *salvis ... patricio Ricimere* on the tessera. On the latter Ricimer was the salvation of the earthly Rome, and on the former Christ was the salvation of the entire human race. It would have been but a small conceptual step to view Ricimer, too, as the salvation of the human race. All of which suggests that Ricimer had an even higher opinion of himself than has been thought in the past.

So why, one might ask, did Ricimer not simply become emperor? Based, among other things, on a comment by Procopius, it has been assumed that his barbarian ancestry or his Arianism, if not both, disqualified him.[48] But there are

---

48 Proc. *Bell.* 3.3–7: "For Aspar himself, being an adherent of the Arian faith, and having no intention of changing it for another, was unable to enter upon the imperial office."

too many counterexamples to credit this assumption. The emperor Theodosius II and his progeny, for example, were the descendents of the Frank Bauto, putting paid to the notion that barbarian ancestry disqualified one from the emperorship. As for Arianism, this did not keep Priscus Attalus from being named emperor, albeit an illegal one, in 408, and Procopius' evidence is nuanced by another report that Aspar had in fact been offered the emperorship by the senate but declined with the reply, "I fear that through my example a precedent regarding the throne would be set."[49] Subsequently, in 469, Patricius, the son of Aspar, actually was named Caesar. To this list can be added Odovacar's proclamation of his son Thela as Caesar ca. 490 (Joh.Ant. fr.307 [Roberto]). So Arianism seems not to have been an insurmountable barrier to being emperor either.

Perhaps a more likely answer is that by his time, the office of western emperor was no great prize. Ricimer saw emperors come and saw them go. As a patrician, he had all the benefits of being emperor—issuing laws and coins, being cited on equal terms with the emperors, and marrying an emperor's daughter—without any of the drawbacks—being burdened by court ceremony and being a ready target for assassination, not to mention being faced with the need to appoint a new patrician who would immediately become his own rival. Ricimer's authority was more greatly legitimated as Patrician and Master of Soldiers, an office for which barbarian origin and Arian affiliations, far from being a possible hindrance, were virtually part of the job description.

But Ricimer's failure to become emperor should not be taken to mean that he did not think of himself as Roman. All of his activities, and in particular his church dedication, indicate that Ricimer perceived himself as a togate Roman senator, not as a skin-clad barbarian *rex*—a status that he clearly eschewed. During his tenure in office, Ricimer was scrupulously careful to maintain good relations with the Italian senators. The first Novel of Majorian, addressed to the senate of Rome, paid respect to the traditions of the senate at the same time that it acknowledged the status of Ricimer. Majorian began: "Know, O Conscript Fathers, that I have been made emperor by the decision of your election … The watchful care of military affairs will be Our concern, as well as the concern of Our Father, the patrician Ricimer."[50] Ricimer also supported the interests of the senate in legislation over which he had more direct control. The second Novel of Severus, issued more

---

[49] *Acta synod.habit.Rom. V* (*MGH.AA* 12.425) (AD 501): *Aliquando Aspari a senatu dicebatur, ut ipse fieret imperator, qui tale refertur dedisse responsum, timeo ne per me consuetudo in regno nascatur.* See *PLRE* 2.168, citing E. Stein, *Geschichte des spätrömischen Reiches vom römischen zum byzantinischen Staate (284–476 n. Chr.)* (Vienna, 1928) = *Histoire du Bas-Empire. Tome premier. De l'état romaine à l'état byzantine (284–476)*, trans. J.R. Palanque (Paris, 1959; reprint. Amsterdam, 1968) 1.353–4, who suggests a date in 457 between Marcian and Leo and assumes the offer came from the west, but this is by no means certain.

[50] *Nov.Mai.* 1 (11 January 458); trans. C. Pharr, *The Theodosian Code and Novels and the Sirmondian Constitutions* (Princeton, 1952) 551.

than a month after Severus' death presumably under Ricimer's authority, forbade children of slaves and *coloni* from escaping servitude by becoming members of *collegia*, a ruling that would have endeared Ricimer to the heart of any senatorial landowner.[51] In return, the senate supported Ricimer in his other emperor-making: Hydatius (*Chron.* 211) notes that in 461 "Severus was named emperor by the senate at Rome in the fifth year of the emperor Leo," and Malalas (*Chron.* 14.45 [375]) states that in 472 "Ricimer established Olybrius as emperor at Rome, with the approval of the senate," this while Anthemius was still in office. Individual senators also supported the patrician: John of Antioch (fr. 299 [Roberto]) mentions "Romanus, a good friend of Ricimer, who had held the office of master and was included among the patricians."

In this context, one could see Ricimer's church decoration as part of a policy of personal accommodation with the Italian senators. Rather than being an unsubtle barbarian who imposed his will by brute force, Ricimer cagily allied himself with the Italian aristocracy, shared their values, and protected their interests. By so doing, he was able not only to legitimate his authority but also to provide a model for barbarian potentates such as Odovacar and Theoderic for how to gain even greater legitimacy in the context of Roman traditions. Rather than laying claim to the emperorship, Ricimer preferred to assume the status of the most powerful senator in Rome. In doing so, he brought to its natural conclusion the process of increasing senatorial self-consciousness that had been building ever since the reign of Constantine. But at the same time, Ricimer also stayed true to his religious convictions. His choice of text and iconography in his church decoration, and the consistency between them, suggests that he also wanted to make a religious statement, to claim that his Christ was both the ruler of the world, signified by the globe, and the salvation of the world. In this regard, he also provided a model for barbarian rulers such as Theoderic for how to pursue an Arian architectural and artistic agenda in a Nicene world.

---

[51] *Nov.Sev.* 2 (25 September 465). The *Fasti vindobonenses priores* place the death of Severus on 15 August 465. Nor was Ricimer the only potentate jockeying for power in Rome after Severus' death. In November of 465, the bishop of Rome Hilarus made his own move to aggrandize his influence by summoning a council in Rome, the first Roman council for which the *acta* survive, in which he ostentatiously acknowledged appeals from bishops in Spain and Gaul.

Chapter 23
Gregory of Tours and "Arianism"

Edward James
University College Dublin

The apparent paradox that Gregory (bishop of Tours 573–94) thought it worthwhile combating Arianism in his *Ten Books of History*, even though he knew that Arianism was not a problem in Gaul and was, by the time he revised his *History*, no longer a problem in Spain either, has been addressed in a number of ways, none of them entirely satisfactory: it was a relic of his initial concerns when he began writing the *History* that was left in the text; it was a way of displaying his own theological credentials and proving his orthodoxy; it was an expression of his hostile feelings towards Spain; it was a reinforcement of the Catholic faith of his own congregation and, beyond that, of his readership. All of these explanations perhaps have an element of truth in them, but here I shall argue that the treatment of Arianism in his works should be seen more in terms of Gregory's representation of himself and of his own episcopal power.

It is always worth looking at how Gregory of Tours begins and ends each of the ten books of his *History*. He usually places an event at the start of a book in order to emphasize its significance. Often books end with deaths: St. Martin (book 1), King Clovis (2), King Sigibert (4), King Chilperic (6). Book 6 is framed by St. Salvius of Albi, as if to contrast Chilperic's ignoble end with Salvius' glorious life: at the very end of book 5 Salvius has a vision of the deaths of the two sons of Chilperic (an episode wrenched out of its chronological position, inasmuch as the deaths themselves had been mentioned 16 chapters earlier), while in the first chapter of book 7 Gregory recounts the holy life and glorious death of Salvius himself, deliberately contrasting them with the sordid death and wicked life of King Chilperic, "the Nero and Herod of our times,"[1] described in the preceding chapter. The start of books may record deaths too, like the death of Queen Clotild (4), but more frequently they record auspicious beginnings. Indeed, the death of Clotild should no doubt be seen in that light: her departure from this world, "full of days and rich in good works," is in marked contrast to the deaths of sinful kings that *end* books, and this clearly signifies a glorious *beginning* for her in the afterlife. Other beginnings are more obvious: the beginning of the reign of

---

[1] I use the edition of Gregory's writings in B. Krusch and W. Levison (eds.), *MGH. SRM*, vol. 1, part 1 (Hanover 1951) and B. Krusch (ed.), *MGH.SRM*, vol. 1, part 2 (Hanover, 1885; reprint. 1969); the translations from the *History* are taken from L. Thorpe (trans.), *Gregory of Tours: History of the Franks* (Harmondsworth, 1974).

Clovis's four sons (3.1); the beginning of the reign of the infant king Childebert II (5.1); the fateful change of alliance made by Childebert's advisors, which begins a new era in Frankish politics (6.1); the triumphal arrival of St. Salvius in Heaven (7.1); the triumphal arrival of King Guntram at the gates of Orleans (8.1); and the inauguration of Pope Gregory the Great (10.1).

The death in 586 of Leuvigild, the Visigothic king of Spain, is placed at the end of book 8—the only time a non-Frankish ruler is accorded this honor. It is only a brief notice, and it reports that "some say" that before he died he had repented of his heretical beliefs, that is, his Arianism.[2] At the beginning of book 9, we are informed that Leuvigild's son Reccared succeeded him and agreed to acknowledge his father's widow as his mother. That woman, Goiswinth, was also the mother of Brunhild, and therefore the grandmother of Gregory's own king at the time, the young Childebert II. Her wicked treatment of the Frankish princess Ingund, who had refused to convert to Arianism, is described by Gregory in a much earlier chapter (5.38). Reccared tried to make peace with the two Frankish kings, Childebert and his uncle Guntram. Childebert received the envoys kindly, but Guntram refused even to meet them. If the first chapter of book 9 records a new beginning, it is not a very auspicious one, and indeed its futility is underlined by the fact that at 9.16 Reccared sends envoys again, who meet with exactly the same reception from the two kings. But it is in the previous chapter, 9.15—and therefore in a much less prominent position in Gregory's book than 9.1—that Gregory does mention a genuine new beginning. Just ten months after his accession,[3] Reccared abandoned his Arian religion, received the chrism, and "confessed his belief in Jesus Christ, the Son of God, equal to the Father and the Holy Ghost" (9.15). The chapter ends, "This people of heretics (*populus hereticorum*) who lived in that province gave up their false belief and confessed the Trinity, one and indivisible." Gregory could easily have trumpeted this new beginning at 9.1, with a slight chronological adjustment of the kind in which he frequently indulged, but he took the decision instead to "hide" it in the middle of the book.

We might think that the *populus hereticorum* in question was the Visigoths, above all because all the modern scholarship describes this event as the "conversion of the Visigoths from Arianism to Catholicism." But Gregory does not say so, and his more attentive contemporary readers could have noticed that he had told them seven books earlier that the wicked Thrasamund, king of the Vandals, forced the entire population of Spain (*totam Hispaniam*) to be Arian, "by tortures and all sorts of executions" (2.2). Gregory was content to let his

---

[2] For the evidence that the Arian king was indeed softening his attitude to Catholicism towards the end of his life, see R. Collins, "King Leovigild and the Conversion of the Visigoths," in Idem, *Law, Culture and Regionalism in Early Medieval Spain* (Aldershot, 1992) 2.1–12.

[3] This detail of the timing is given in John of Biclaro's *Chronicle*: K.B. Wolf, *Conquerors and Chronicles of Early Medieval Spain* (Liverpool, 1999) 73.

readers think that the entire population of Spain was tainted by heresy thereafter,[4] for at one point he relates that he personally enquired from returning Frankish ambassadors "whether there was still any zeal for the Christian faith among the few Catholics who still remained in that country" (6.18), which is, as far as we can tell, a total misreading of the religious situation in Spain. Arianism does not appear to have been widespread among the Romans of Spain, who formed the great bulk of the population, and seems restricted to the descendants of those barbarians who had come into the peninsula in the previous century, above all the Visigoths and the Sueves, who were unlikely to have constituted more than 5 per cent of the population—although they no doubt constituted a much higher percentage of the elite.

The modern scholarly literature on early Arianism is considerable.[5] One of the most important conclusions, however, is that Arianism as such, as a unified and agreed set of doctrines, never really existed. Williams has suggested that "the time has probably come to relegate the term 'Arianism' at least to inverted commas, and preferably to oblivion … the sheer uselessness and inaccuracy of the word becomes clearer with every new piece of research in the period."[6] Gwynn has recently suggested that the idea that the orthodox faced one united heretical enemy was in a sense created in the polemical writing of Athanasius, for whom all of his enemies were "Eusebians," spiritual followers of Eusebius of Nicomedia, the first of Arius' prominent supporters. Indeed, with the reckless disregard of reason that characterizes much polemic, Athanasius first lumped them all together as followers of Eusebius, regardless of the diversity of their opinions, and then chided them for not following the teachings of their master with sufficient consistency.[7] In fact, saying that Christ was begotten of God the Father was common enough in the fourth century, and not necessarily an indication of "Arianism." Athanasius' own view about the equality of persons in the Trinity was no less controversial itself. Nevertheless, by the end of the fourth century, after several turbulent councils and much polemicizing, Athanasius's Trinitarianism was established as orthodoxy,

---

[4] On Gregory's views of Spain and the Visigoths in general, see E. James, "Gregory of Tours, the Visigoths and Spain," in S. Barton and P. Linehan (eds.), *Cross, Crescent and Conversion: Studies on Medieval Spain and Christendom in Memory of Richard Fletcher* (Leiden, 2008) 43–64.

[5] For Arius himself, see R. Williams, *Arius: Heresy and Tradition* (London, 2001); for a brief account of early Arianism, see R. Williams, "Arianism," in E. Ferguson (ed.), *Encyclopedia of Early Christianity* (New York, 1997) 107–11. For the Arian controversy, see R.P.C. Hanson, *The Search for the Christian Doctrine of God: The Arian Controversy 318–381* (Edinburgh, 1988); for the extended history of Arianism, see M. Wiles, *Archetypal Heresy: Arianism Through the Ages* (Oxford, 1996).

[6] Review of Hanson, *The Search for the Christian Doctrine of God*, in *SJT* 45 (1992) 102.

[7] D.M. Gwynn, *The Eusebians: The Polemic of Athanasius of Alexandria and the Construction of the "Arian Controversy"* (Oxford, 2007) 177.

and modified versions of "Arianism" (that is, subordination of Son to Father) were anathematized and thereafter adhered to only by small marginalized groups within the Christian Roman population of the empire. Williams notes that "by the time that the great upheavals with the empire were over, Arianism had been irrevocably cast as the Other in relation to Catholic (and civilized) religion."[8]

Arianism became a problem again because of its adoption by most of the barbarian peoples who entered the Roman Empire from 376 onwards. Indeed, by the year 500 these heretics were now in charge—and apparently permanently in charge—of former Roman provinces: of Italy, Spain, North Africa, and the whole of the southern part of Gaul. The situation only improved slightly when, in 507, Clovis, the Frankish king who recently had converted to Catholicism, announced, according to Gregory of Tours, "I find it hard to go on seeing these Arians occupy a part of Gaul," before taking over most of south-western Gaul from the Arian Visigoths (*HF* 2.36). The Byzantine victories over the Arian Vandals and Ostrogoths resolved the problem for North Africa and Italy, though shortly after the Byzantine victory over the Ostrogoths Italy was invaded by the Arian Lombards.[9] When Gregory began writing, the only Arian peoples of any significance were in Spain: the Sueves in Gallaecia and the Visigoths in the rest of the peninsula.

The modern scholarly approach to "Arianism"—the recognition, with Williams, that the word should be placed in inverted commas—is very relevant to an understanding of "Arianism" in Gregory's works. The inverted commas remind us that we are not necessarily dealing with a coherent theological system: what "Arians" had in common, above all, was their adherence to beliefs and practices of which the majority of churches disapproved. In fact, we know very little about the actual *beliefs* of "Arians" in Visigothic Spain, though we do know something about their practices.[10] It would seem that their services were conducted in Gothic,[11] which suggests that the basic difference between Arian and Catholic in Spain was an ethnic one; they believed in triple immersion at baptism; and they had a different style of tonsure—this may have been a deliberate effort to distinguish themselves.[12] As far as belief is concerned, Thompson suggested that the most striking difference between Catholic and Arian was that tolerance "appears to have run right through the Arian population." However, the only evidence Thompson is

[8] Williams, *Arius*, 1.

[9] But see S. Fanning, "Lombard Arianism Reconsidered," *Speculum* 56 (1981) 241–58.

[10] See E.A. Thompson, *The Goths in Spain* (Oxford, 1969) chap. 2, esp. 41.

[11] Though Thompson's declaration of that fact (*The Goths in Spain*, 41) is referenced by a footnote to E.A. Thompson, *The Visigoths in the Time of Ulfila* (Oxford, 1966) xiv n. 2, which notes that the evidence for this comes from two homilies by John Chrysostom in relation to the Goths in Constantinople, nearly two centuries before Gregory's time, and that some doubt that Chrysostom's reference is in fact to Gothic.

[12] See, in a different context, E. James, "Bede and the Tonsure Question," *Peritia* 3 (1984) 167–82.

able to adduce for this comes from a passage in Gregory's *History*, which I shall discuss below.[13] In reality, Arian "tolerance"—in short supply in Vandal Africa—may relate to their position as a religious minority in Spain, although it could have something to do with diversity of belief within "Arianism" itself.

It does seem very surprising that Gregory of Tours did not welcome the conversion of the Visigoths of Spain from Arianism to Catholicism with rather more enthusiasm, and indeed with something like the ecstatic joy of Pope Gregory the Great when he heard of this "new miracle of our days"—that is, when eventually, several years after the event, he actually was informed about it.[14] At least one might expect that the conversion to Catholicism be given more prominence in the structure of the *History*. It is almost as if it was unimportant for Gregory, which is surprising given his hostility to "Arianism"—stated and restated throughout the *History* and, indeed, in his other works as well. This apparent paradox needs to be explained; in the process the role of "Arianism" in Gregory's works, and above all in the *History*, needs to be re-examined.

Some years ago Wood suggested that "a narrative refutation of arianism [*sic*] may have been one of the original aims of Gregory's *Histories*."[15] Gregory had, after all, started the preface to book 1 by saying that his task would be to describe "the wars waged by kings against hostile peoples, by martyrs against the heathen, and by the churches against the heretics" (*HF* 1, prol.), and "Arianism" is in fact the only heresy he treats in any detail. In book 2 he describes "Arianism" among the Vandals, the Burgundians, and the Visigoths, and in each case he describes the persecution unleashed by the Arians against the Catholics. At the end of book 2, he tells of the determined struggle of the Frankish king Clovis to rid Gaul of Arians altogether. However, even though book 3 starts with Gregory's reiteration of his orthodox credentials in the preface, "Arianism" crops up again in the *History* only at rare intervals; as Wood notes, his "avowed concern with the relations of churches and heretics is forgotten."[16] And this is hardly surprising: "Arianism" had ceased to be a threat in Gaul even before Gregory's birth, so far as we can see, and we are left bemused as to why a "narrative refutation of arianism" could ever have been his stated objective.

One answer to this may well be, as Heinzelmann has suggested, that "Arianism" stands for all manifestations of heresy in Gregory's world and that it stands for "error" in a general sense rather than merely theological error. Heinzelmann draws our attention to St. Brice, St. Martin's successor as bishop of Tours, being falsely accused by his people of fathering a child, at the beginning of book 2 of the *History*. Although Brice performs a miracle to prove his innocence—and the month-old child pronounces him not to be his father—he is expelled from Tours

---

13 Greg.Tur. *HF* 5.43; see Thompson, *Goths in Spain*, 37.

14 Greg.Magn. *Ep.* 9.122 (*CCSL* 140A.673–4). Gregory I celebrates the conversion also in his *Dial.* 3.31 (*PL* 77.289–93).

15 I. Wood, *Gregory of Tours* (Bangor, 1994) 34.

16 Wood, *Gregory*, 35.

and a new bishop is chosen in his place, who subsequently acquires a successor. Both of these bishops died, and Brice was restored to his see. As Heinzelmann notes, this is paralleled by another story, in the middle of book 2, where Sidonius Apollinaris, bishop of Clermont, was persecuted by two of his priests. They took control of his income from him and reduced him to poverty. But one of them, on the eve of a further plot against the bishop, went into the lavatory and there died.

> From this we may deduce that this man was guilty of a crime no less serious than that of Arius, who in the same way emptied out his entrails through his back passage in the lavatory. This, too, smacks of heresy, that one of God's bishops should not be obeyed in his own church … (Greg. *HF* 2.23)

The other priest dropped dead too, at the height of his ambition, for he had managed to take over the property of the church on Sidonius' death. Both men, says Gregory, ended up in hell. The crime of the two priests, like the crime of the two bishops who succeeded the deposed Bishop Brice, resulted in death and in God's eyes—or at least in Gregory's—it was the equivalent of the crime of Arius. One could argue that it was only the disgusting manner of the priest's death that brought Arius to Gregory's mind, but to Heinzelmann it indicates the real nature of *haeresis*: heresy is not just a question of dogma, but an attack on the divine ordering of the world, crucial to which is the role of God's deputies, the bishops.[17]

After book 2, when "Arianism" does appear, it is linked to Spain. But, as we have seen in the case of the conversion of Reccared, Gregory does not take such opportunity as he had to record and to celebrate the refutation of "Arianism." He knows about the conversion of the Spanish Sueves of Gallaecia to Catholicism, for instance, because he talks about it in his *Miracles of St. Martin*, but the event does not figure in his *History* at all. The conversion of the Sueves is indeed a remarkably obscure event. Thompson remarked that apart from the fact that it happened, and its approximate date, "every circumstance is undescribed, every detail unknown, every question unanswered."[18] The history of the conversion of the Visigoths of Spain to Catholicism is better known, though that is not saying very much. Anyone familiar with Gregory of Tours will be worried at the emphasis modern historians of Spain have placed on Gregory's own evidence. But the unhappy fact is that much of what we know about Spanish "Arianism" does come from the unreliable, prejudiced, and not necessarily well-informed pen of Gregory. He alone, for instance, says that King Reccared's decision to convert

---

[17] M. Heinzelmann, "Heresy in Books I and II of Gregory of Tours' *Historiae*," in A.C. Murray (ed.), *After Rome's Fall: Narrators and Sources of Early Medieval History. Essays Presented to Walter Goffart* (Toronto, 1998) 67–82 at 73.

[18] These were the words that ended Thompson's conference paper in Dublin in 1975, which prompted Peter Brown to comment: "Edward, no one else could say so much so elegantly about so little." See E.A. Thompson, "The Conversion of the Spanish Suevi to Catholicism," in E. James (ed.), *Visigothic Spain: New Approaches* (Oxford, 1980) 77–92.

came after a meeting with his Arian bishops, which was followed by a meeting of the king with both Arian and Catholic bishops, who then debated the issue. The Spanish chronicler John of Biclaro presents it as a royal decision that was followed by Reccared persuading the Arian bishops to convert "through reason rather than force."[19] Again, it is Gregory alone who says that what actually persuaded the king was his realization that no Arian bishop had ever worked a miraculous cure. Gregory at this point relates how Reccared recalled that in his father's day an Arian bishop had once condemned a man to perpetual blindness by laying his hands on a blind man in an attempt to cure him. Gregory wrote that he had told the story elsewhere, as indeed he did in his *Glory of the Confessors*.[20] In this fuller version, it was King Leuvigild who challenged the Arian bishop to work a miracle, "just like those who call themselves Christians," and the bishop went away and bribed a fellow Arian with 40 gold pieces to claim that he had been cured by the bishop. But when the bishop laid his hands on the man's eyes, the man went blind and confessed that he had attempted to trick the king in return for money. The bishop was "a new Cyrola," says Gregory, and this epithet implies that either the story of Cyrola was well known or he expected readers of *Glory of the Confessors* to know the story related in book 2 of the *History*. Cyrola was an Arian bishop in Carthage living under the Vandal kings who had tried exactly the same trick—though the bribe cost him 50 gold pieces.[21]

The story of the Arian bishop under Leuvigild is not the only instance in Gregory's *Glory of the Confessors* of the falsehood of "Arianism" being exposed through some form of miracle-working. Gregory also tells the unpleasant story of a Gothic priest baptizing 20 children one Easter in a borrowed Catholic church, and because a Catholic priest decided to baptize some children at the same time in his own house, all 20 of the newly baptized Arians die within days (*Glor.conf.* 47). Gregory also relates the story of a heretic (presumably Arian), who is challenged to pick up a red-hot ring from a fire; he refuses to do it, but a Catholic does it without harm (*Glor.conf.* 14). This can be compared with another story in Gregory's *Glory of the Martyrs* in which a Catholic deacon challenges an Arian priest to a "trial by hot water." While the two were arguing about whether or not the Catholic had cheated by smearing ointment on his arm, another Catholic deacon came by and plunged his arm into the boiling water in order to pick out the ring. It took him an hour, but he retrieved the ring with no harm done to himself. The Arian tried it, and all the flesh fell off his bone. The details are clearly fantastical, but it may

---

19 Joh.Bicl. 85; Wolf, *Conquerors and Chronicles*, 73.

20 *Glor.conf.* 13. For translation see R. Van Dam, *Gregory of Tours: Glory of the Confessors* (Liverpool, 1988) 29.

21 Greg.Tur. *HF* 2.3. For some comment, see James, "Gregory of Tours, the Visigoths and Spain," 44–5; but see especially A. Cain, "Miracles, Martyrs, and Arians: Gregory of Tours' Sources for his Account of the Vandal Kingdom," *VChr* 59 (2005) 412–37.

have been based on a genuine challenge, and the story survives as the earliest occurrence of what later became a common European legal procedure of ordeal.[22]

In the *History*, therefore, there is very little about "Arianism" after the beginning of book 3. When it does crop up later in the *History* it is usually linked to the relations between the Frankish and Visigothic kings. As Gregory presents it, there was an interesting contrast between Catholic steadfastness and Arian wickedness. The first marriage alliance between Frank and Visigoth occurred early in the sixth century when the Visigothic king Amalaric—who came to the throne while still a boy, in 511—married Clovis' Catholic daughter Chrotechild. She refused to convert to Arianism, and Amalaric treated her badly until 531, when her brother Childebert invaded Visigothic territory and defeated Amalaric's forces, which led directly to Amalaric's assassination in Barcelona (Greg. *HF*. 3.10). Arian hostility to Catholicism had thus been punished by God. The next marriage alliance occurred much later, when the two Arian daughters of King Athanagild (Brunhild and Galswinth) married into the Frankish royal family. These women did not have Chrotechild's determination: they both converted to Catholicism after only a minor struggle. However, when Ingund, the Catholic daughter of Sigibert and Brunhild, married into the Visigothic royal family, she put up with much physical abuse yet still refused to renounce her Catholicism. On the contrary, she persuaded her Arian husband Hermenegild to become a Catholic—though that is a detail attested only in Gregory's *History* and not in our main Spanish sources.[23] It was convenient for Gregory to present this contrast—lukewarm and changeable Arians as opposed to the steadfast Catholics—but it is unlikely that he was massaging the truth very much.[24]

Two episodes in the *History* bring Gregory's views on Arianism into sharp relief. Both of them relate to the complex negotiations between the Franks and the Visigoths in the 570s and 580s, in which there was a good deal of traveling to and fro by envoys of both kings. In both of these episodes an envoy from King Leuvigild of Spain to King Chilperic stopped off in Tours, which at that time was in Chilperic's kingdom. In 580, the envoy was Agila (5.43) and in 584 it was Oppila (6.40). In both cases Gregory descends into a debate about Arianism. We may compare these two debates with the third theological debate Gregory describes, in 581, in which Gregory debates with a Jew called Priscus, who was

---

22 *Glor.mart.* 80. For translation see R. Van Dam, *Gregory of Tours: Glory of the Martyrs* (Liverpool, 1988) 104–5.

23 Greg.Tur. *HF* 5.38, 8.21 and 9.24.

24 There is much about the revolt of Hermenegild that is difficult to understand, and Gregory may have exaggerated the significance of Hermenegild's Catholicism. If it was a Catholic revolt against an Arian tyrant, it is very difficult indeed to understand the comment by the contemporary chronicler John of Biclaro that Hermenegild was incited to revolt by Goiswinth—who in Gregory's account is an implacable enemy of Catholicism. See Thompson, *Goths in Spain*, 66–7, and J.N. Hillgarth, "Coins and Chronicles: Propaganda in Sixth-Century Spain and the Byzantine Background," *Historia* 15 (1966) 483–508.

attached to Chilperic's court (6.5): it is comparable, because here too the main focus of the debate is on the nature of the Trinity.[25] They do actually link to the only other two debates in which Gregory describes his role: his argument with King Chilperic about the king's own views on the Trinity (5.44) and, towards the end of the *History*, his argument with his own priest about the nature of resurrection (10.13). Four out of the five theological debates in the *History* therefore deal with the Trinity, and it is the orthodoxy of his belief about the Trinity that Gregory stresses in the preface to book 1, in which he recites his own personal creed. As Van Dam has noted, the debates with Agila and Oppila deal with the Trinity but also touch on the resurrection, as Gregory warns Agila that belittling the Holy Spirit endangers his own resurrection, and as he hints that Oppila—with whom he debated at Easter—had denied the resurrection. And so in fact all five of these theological "digressions," as Heinzelmann calls them,[26] are interconnected. Moreover, this suggests perhaps that in Gregory's mind the dangers posed by Visigothic "Arianism" had ramifications within "Catholic" Gaul as well. I am not convinced that they are digressions; or, rather, I would say that it is not easy to see in Gregory's *History* what is digression and what is core, or, indeed, whether or not Gregory considered the "digressions" to be just as crucial to his purpose as his main narrative.

We must now turn to the possible relevance of these exchanges to the *Ten Books of History* as a whole. Agila was, according to Gregory, "of low intelligence, untrained in logical argument [and] distinguished by his hatred of our Catholic faith" (Greg. *HF* 5.43). What follows shows, presumably without conscious irony, that Agila was none of those things. Gregory presents him as a layman who has all the necessary biblical citations ready at hand, and who is smart, well-schooled in argument, and interestingly tolerant. Their debate starts with Agila noting that the Son and the Father cannot be equal when, at John 14:28, Christ is reported to have said "My Father is greater than I." This invites the counter-quotation "I and my Father are one" (John10:3). It is John who provides the keystone to this part of the debate as far as Gregory is concerned: "The Word was God. And the Word was made flesh and dwelt among us, by whom all things are made" (John1:1-3). The invocation of this biblical text compels Agila to move on to what he might have considered firmer ground, the role of the Holy Spirit. He was promised by the Son and sent by the Father, says Agila: clearly a subordinate person. "God is he who sends: he who is sent is not God." Gregory perhaps realized at this point that he had run out of biblical quotations and as a result pulled out his trump card,

---

25 I am indebted to the comments made on these three debates by R. Van Dam, *Saints and their Miracles in Late Antique Gaul* (Princeton, 1993) 106–9.

26 At least in Carroll's translation, M. Heinzelmann, *Gregory of Tours: History and Society in the Sixth Century* (Cambridge, 2001) 155. Heinzelmann's original word, "Exkurs," excursus, does not perhaps have the same weight: see Heinzelmann, *Gregor von Tours (538–594): "Zehn Bücher Geschichte". Historiographie und Gesellschaftskonzept im 6. Jahrhunderts* (Darmstadt, 1994) 138.

reminding the Arian that the perversion of Arianism is proved by the fact that Arius met his end in a lavatory. Agila responds mildly: "You must not blaspheme against a faith which you yourself do not accept" (Greg. *HF* 5.43). He ends by making a comment that Gregory thinks of as proving Agila's *stultitia*:

> It is no crime for one set of people to believe in one doctrine and another set of people to believe in another. Indeed it is a proverbial saying with us that no harm is done when a man whose affairs take him past the altars of the Gentiles and the Church of God pays respect to both. (5.43)

The debate descends to insult after that, but much later, Gregory tells us, when Agila was back in Spain, he fell seriously ill and decided to convert to Catholicism.

Four years later, the Spanish envoy Oppila, who brought many presents for Chilperic, arrived in Tours just before Easter. Gregory asked him if he was of our faith, *nostrae religionis*, and he replied that he believed what Catholics believe. But he did not take communion, and afterwards at supper in Gregory's house, Gregory pushed him. The envoy said that he believed that the Father, the Son, and the Holy Ghost were equal in power, but that he objected to the improper use of "glory." Gregory would say "Glory be to the Father, and to the Son, and to the Holy Ghost," while Oppila would say "Glory be to God the Father, through the Son."[27] The debate that followed was not presented as a discussion, as the one with Agila had been. Gregory lectured, Oppila raised one objection, Gregory lectured again, and the "debate" was over. Gregory pointed out Oppila's error: the doxology he recited denied the equality of the Son with the Father, whatever else Oppila might say to the contrary. Gregory suggests that Oppila use some ointment or other to wash away the blindness from his eyes, and that Oppila ought to do something about his ears, which were *oppilata*, or blocked up.

In the four years that elapsed between these two visits (from 580 to 584), changes seem to have been happening within Spanish Arianism that are apparently reflected in these two exchanges. The Arian Synod of Toledo in 580 had made minor concessions that made it easier for Catholics to convert. Rebaptism was no longer demanded, only the laying on of hands and the recitation of "Glory be to God the Father, through the Son."[28] In 582, Leuvigild moved towards orthodoxy on the Son while keeping to Arian doctrines on the Holy Spirit—although again Gregory is our only source for this.[29] One does wonder whether this information is based on what he had learned from Oppila in 584, rather than on any more solid information arriving from Spain. It is perhaps part of Gregory's intention to show the Arians as wavering in their views, unlike the rock-solid views of the Catholics,

---

27 Greg.Tur. *HF* 6.40. Thorpe mistranslates the crucial phrase as "and to the Son" rather than "through the Son."

28 See Joh.Bicl. 57.

29 Thompson, *Goths in Spain*, 85, seems prepared to accept Gregory's view, in *HF* 6.18.

just as he had emphasized what were to him the shockingly relativistic views of Agila, who was prepared to allow people to follow their own opinions.

What, then, is the function of these debates in Gregory's *History*? I do not see them, as Heinzelmann seems to, in terms of the theological aims of the work as a whole, although perhaps that is part of the answer. I prefer to see them more in terms of Gregory's representation of himself. Indeed, even though it has been argued that Gregory started writing his *History* while still a priest in Clermont, in the 560s and up to the time of his consecration as bishop of Tours in 573, I see much of his writing career as being preoccupied with the desire to bolster his position as bishop and to answer his "critics." Crucial to this interpretation are the circumstances related at 5.49. This is a difficult chapter to interpret because more than anywhere else in the *History* Gregory must have been inclined to offer rewriting and elision. There are two clerics called Riculf involved in conspiracy, a priest and a subdeacon. Their conspiracies may well have been quite separate from each other. The priest Riculf was conspiring with Count Leudast to accuse Gregory of slandering Queen Fredegund, his motive being to become bishop in Gregory's place. The subdeacon Riculf—and here we are relying on evidence that Gregory says was obtained under torture—was apparently out to remove Queen Fredegund herself. Chilperic's son Clovis would acquire a kingdom and assassinate his brothers. Leudast would obtain a dukedom and the priest Riculf the bishopric. And the subdeacon Riculf would be raised to the dizzy heights of archdeacon, second-in-command in the diocese. The conspiracy, or conspiracies, were unmasked, and the bishops wondered whether those who had accused Gregory falsely, namely King Chilperic and Bishop Bertram of Bordeaux, should not be excommunicated. The king blamed it all on Count Leudast, who was excommunicated and also subjected to a peculiar form of secular excommunication: Chilperic forbade anyone in the kingdom to take him into their house.

Upon Gregory's return to Tours, he found that the priest Riculf had installed himself as bishop. And only now do we learn that this same Riculf had been the archdeacon under Gregory's predecessor (and cousin) Eufronius. Riculf had been demoted when Gregory appointed Plato to that position: Plato, a close associate of Gregory's, had probably been brought with him from Clermont and installed in a senior position in Tours. Riculf had proposed to replace these interlopers from Clermont by home-grown talent. Gregory had him shut up in a monastery, although he later escaped to Nantes, where he was welcomed warmly by Gregory's enemy, Bishop Felix.

The accusation of slandering Fredegund—probably an easy enough accusation to substantiate, given the amount of libel against Fredegund to be found in the later books of Gregory's *History*—can thus be seen to be a convenient ploy on the part of the former archdeacon Riculf to recover the bishopric that he—and perhaps the previous bishop, too—rightfully considered his. And although Gregory makes fun of him for thinking of Gregory as a foreigner from Clermont—"the poor fool seems not to have realised that, apart from five, all the other bishops who held their appointment in the see of Tours were blood-relations of my family"

(Greg. *HF* 5.49)—it may well be that many of those in Tours were on the side of the would-be bishop Riculf.

In these circumstances—trying to hold on to a bishopric when many of his flock were hostile to him, and in particular doing it after 575, when the king who had recently appointed him was assassinated and he was now under the authority of his hostile brother, and possibly, indeed, of the man who had hired the assassins—Gregory would no doubt have thought of all possible means of survival. Building and repairing churches in Tours itself and in the whole diocese and using his family's wealth for various charitable purposes were obvious ploys. But it was important for him to present himself as the ideal bishop in other ways, and he could do that in part through his writings. He had to be seen to be an enthusiastic supporter of the local cult of St. Martin of Tours, and so he wrote his four books of the *Miracles of St. Martin*. He had to show himself to be a supporter of other local cults, and at the same time point out to people that he came from a family of bishops and saints: and so he wrote his *Life of the Fathers*. In the *History* he shows himself to be a loyal subject of Sigibert and his son Childebert II, and he presents himself as dealing firmly with King Chilperic and his widow Fredegund—and perhaps exaggerates the extent of his dislike of the king, who was assassinated in 584, in order to endear himself to those who had even less reason to like him.[30]

Furthermore, Gregory shows himself to be an able defender of orthodoxy, not just in his personal creed, which he lays out in the preface to book 1, but through descriptions of his actual encounters with the unorthodox (King Chilperic and his own priest), the Jews (Priscus), and the two Arians, Agila and Oppila. I doubt that these encounters, and Gregory's dexterity with biblical citation, were designed to impress a real theologian—not that there appear to be many of those in late sixth-century Gaul—but for members of his own potentially disloyal clergy they might have been reassuring. They had a bishop who knew his mind, and who knew his Bible, and who was certain in his defence of orthodoxy, not only in the face of Arians but in the face of any persons—and perhaps these existed in Gaul, too—who saw no harm in allowing "one set of people to believe in one doctrine and another set of people to believe in another."

[30] As G. Halsall argues in "Nero and Herod? The Death of Chilperic and Gregory's Writing of History," in K. Mitchell and I. Wood (eds.), *The World of Gregory of Tours* (Leiden, 2002) 337–50.

Chapter 24
The Imagery of Personal Objects: Hints of "Do-It-Yourself" Christian Culture in Merovingian Gaul?

Bailey K. Young
Eastern Illinois University

In 1971, in the course of a construction project in a Burgundian vineyard at Ladoix-Serrigny near Beaune, a striking object was recovered from a destroyed Merovingian grave. This plate-buckle depicts a bearded and haloed horseman directly facing the viewer, indeed staring intently at him or her (see Figure 24.1). In his left hand he brandishes some sort of spear and in his right hand an axe; he is seated on a serpentine mount with a prominent erection. To the rider's left appears an elongated, four-legged creature of some sort (dragon? bird?); to his right, above the horse's head, a type of chi-rho, which offers an omega suspended from the right arm and an alpha from the left. There is also an equal-armed, footed cross below the horse's mouth; the scutiform tongue-plate, by contrast, is engraved with a simpler type of chi-rho, an X crossing the long vertical stem. The bottom of the buckle plate is taken up with an inscription in carefully incised capitals, reading as follows on four lines:

> ⊦ LANDELINVS FICIT
> NVMEN
> QVI ILLA PVSSEDIRAVIT VIVA(t)
> VSQVI ANNVS MILI IN D(omin)O

A horizontal line divides the inscription into two registers, underlining NVMEN. The Landelinus plate-buckle was first discussed by Werner in 1976[1] and, more recently, by Treffort[2] and Gaillard de Sémainville.[3] Before we consider its

[1] J. Werner, "Zu den Knochenschnallen und Reliquarschnallen des 6. Jahrhunderts," in Idem (ed.), *Die Ausgrabungen in St. Ulrich und Afra in Augsburg 1961–1968* (Munich, 1977) 1.332–6 and 2 Taf.107.3.

[2] C. Treffort, "Vertus Prophylactiques et sens eschatologique d'un dépôt funéraire du haut Moyen Age: les plaques boucles rectangulaires burgondes à inscription," *ArchMéd* 32 (2002) 31–53.

[3] Only in 1996–97 was Henri Gaillard de Sémainville, then Director of Historical Antiquities for Burgundy, able to learn some details of the circumstances of the find and to

interpretation in more detail, let us sketch how it fits into the broader scholarly debate about the religious character of Merovingian civilization.

Salin, the dominant figure in Merovingian archaeology in France for half a century, concluded his four-volume synthesis *La civilisation mérovingienne* (*CM*) in 1959 with *Les Croyances*, a volume devoted to what material culture might be able to tell us about beliefs and religious practices in Merovingian Gaul.[4] His interpretative paradigm may be epitomized with his phrase "progressive fusion": the cultural systems (Germanic on the one hand, Gallo-Roman on the other), distinct around 500 when Clovis came to power, had fused sometime before the date when the Pippinids swept his dynasty aside (700/750). "Christianization" plays an essential role in the process of fusion so hypothesized. Gallo-Roman culture was essentially Christian—though not uniformly so—when it began to interact with the newcomers, who brought with them essentially pagan traditions.[5] *Les Croyances* examines a vast selection of objects—most of them "personal" in the sense that they once belonged to individuals and went with them to the grave—with the intention of finding in their imagery evidence of the interaction of these originally pagan and Christian iconographic traditions assumed to reflect distinct religious cultures which were slowly merging into one. For Salin, then, "paganism" was a religious and cultural reality to be taken into account for much, if not all, of the Merovingian period, and he appends to his book excerpts from a number of literary sources which he takes to support this view.

For Hen, such sources paint a "lurid picture of Merovingian paganism" and are deeply suspect for their self-interested Carolingian myth-making.[6] He believes a stricter study of the contemporary literary sources suggests that Merovingian culture was heavily Christian. Such evidence of pagan survival as can be found—such as practices stigmatized in the sermons of Caesarius of Arles—suggest that these were, at most, marginal phenomena.[7] Now I might be accused, in throwing emphasis on the contrasting views of the archaeologist and the textual scholar, of setting up a classic *dialogue des sourds*, but my intention is to suggest, with the help of a phrase borrowed from Smith's remarkable new cultural history of the early Middle Ages, that useful middle ground can indeed be found.

---

obtain permission from the owners to study it in detail. See H. Gaillard de Sémainville, "Nouvel examen de la plaque-boucle mérovingienne de Landelinus découverte à Ladoix-Serrigny (Côte d'Or): apocalypse et millénarisme dans l'art mérovingien," *RAE* 52 (2003) 297–328.

4 E. Salin, *La civilisation mérovingienne d'après les sépultures, les textes et le laboratoire*, vol. 4, *Les Croyances* (Paris, 1959).

5 For a critical discussion of Salin's views of Christian and pagan funerary culture, see B.K. Young, "The Myth of the Pagan Cemetery," in C. Karkov, K. Whickham-Crowley, and B.K. Young (eds.), *Spaces for the Living and the Dead: An Archaeological Dialogue* (Oxford, 1999) 61–85.

6 Y. Hen, *Culture and Religion in Merovingian Gaul, AD 481–751* (Leiden, 1995) 251–3; see also 197–206.

7 Ibid. 162–72 for Caesarius of Arles.

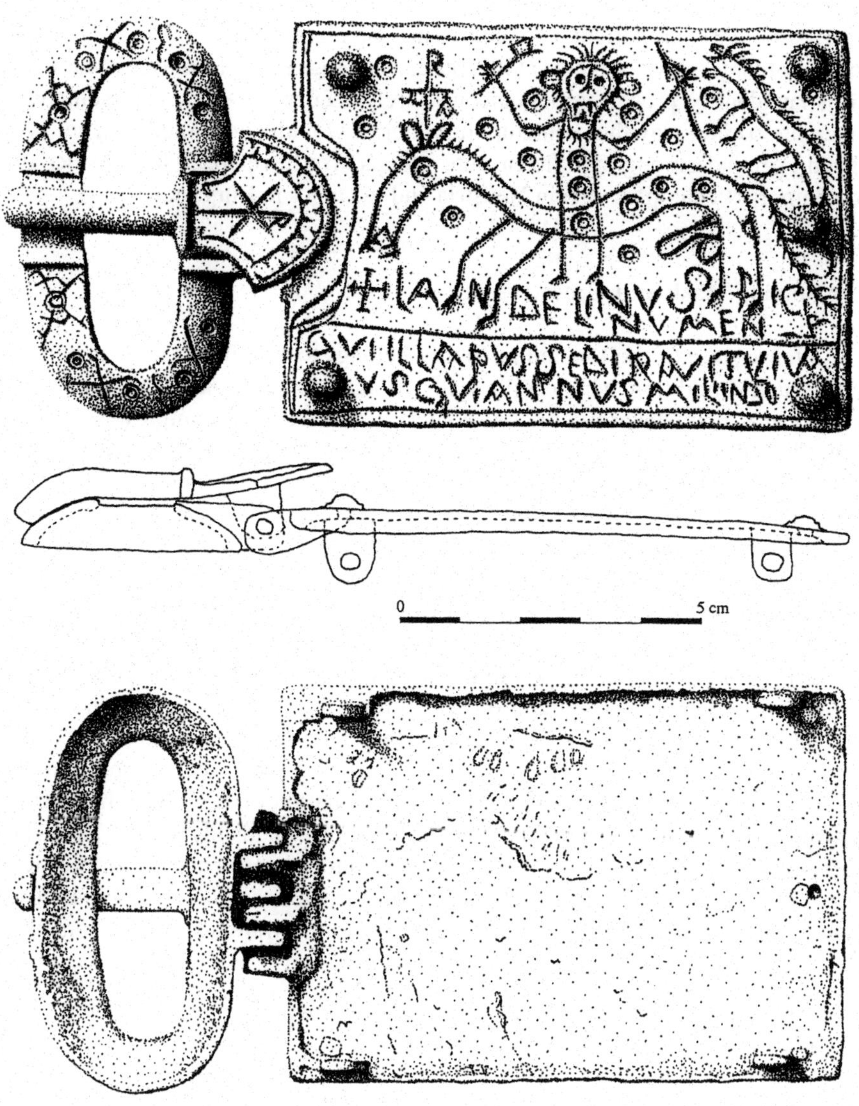

Figure 24.1 "Landelinus" plate-buckle, from Ladoix-Serrigny. Drawing of C. D'Arbaumont, SRA de Bourgogne. From H. Gaillard de Sémainville *RAE* 52 (2003). Used by permission.

I shall argue that what she calls "do-it-yourself" Christianity[8] helps us to understand the vogue, in the years around 600, for strongly religious imagery on a particularly important personal item, the plate-buckle. When seen in the context of larger developments at this time, these suggest that a new affirmation of Christian identity, probably spontaneous, surely uncoerced, and at least sometimes superstitious in a way that contemporary clerics would have called "pagan," was gaining ground among significant elite groups. We have space to consider two contemporary examples, one in Neustria and the other in Burgundy.

The Staring Mask and Cross

The intense stare of the Landelinus figure belongs to a well-known Merovingian iconographic tradition which Salin calls *la masque humaine.*[9] This sometimes appears in an unmistakably Christian context. Let us take the example of an artefact found in 1975 on the site of Saint-Pierre-de Montmartre (Paris), a Romanesque church with a Merovingian background (see Figure 24.2).[10] Surmounted by a cross that clearly expresses its Christian character, it proved to be the latest in a series known particularly in the Paris area. The object is a terra-cotta antefix, interpreted as having decorated a roof's edge. Salin's suggestion that it was intended as an apotropaic image evoking the power of Christ to keep demonic forces away from a sacred building or a tomb certainly fits the circumstances of this discovery.[11] He is also surely correct in pointing out that the staring mask derives from an old European iconographic tradition with strong religious overtones, dubbed the "exaltation of the head" by the Belgian scholar Lambrechts, who showed it to be an essential feature of La Tène art.[12] The staring mask features prominently in the Sutton Hoo burial (dated to the first quarter of the seventh century), ornamenting all sides of the so-called "whetstone," plausibly a kind of sceptre with strongly pagan overtones.[13] More to our point is its presence on various items of personal ornament in Merovingian Gaul, in particular displayed prominently on plate-buckles. The earliest examples of which I am aware are indeed somewhat

8 J.M.H. Smith, *Europe after Rome: A New Cultural History 500–1000* (Oxford, 2005) 229–39.

9 Salin, *Les Croyances*, 255–420 offers an extensive, well-illustrated commentary on "*figurations humaines.*"

10 B.K. Young, "Archaeology in an Urban Setting: Saint-Pierre-de-Montmartre," *JFA* (1978) 323, fig.5.

11 Salin, *Les Croyances*, 278–81, and pl.3.

12 P. Lambrechts, *L'exhaltation de la tête dans la pensée et dans l'art des Celtes* (Bruges, 1954).

13 R. Bruce-Mitford, "The Regalia," in *The Sutton Hoo Ship-Burial: Arms, Armour and Regalia* (London, 1978) 2.311–77. For detailed analysis of the human masks and their likely pagan significance, see 2.358–75 and pl.10–11.

pre-Merovingian. The staring mask at the center of the kidney-shaped buckle-plate from Haillot, in southern Belgium, dates to the mid-fifth century. There can be very little doubt, in my view, that Haillot was an early Frankish cemetery, and I would agree with Salin that its owner meant to protect himself with a tutulary image of supra-human power, whether or not it can be associated with a particular deity.[14]

Figure 24.2 Human mask and cross, terra-cotta antefix from Eglise Saint Pierre, Montmartre (Paris, France). Photo by P. Périn. Used by permission.

[14] Salin, *Les Croyances*, 261, fig.71. On Haillot, see J. Breuer and H. Roosens, "Le cimetière franc de Haillot," *AnnNamur* 48 (1956) 1–171.

It should not surprise us that belt buckles have often served as sites of prominent personal display—as rodeo-buckles continue to do in our own day. Bronze belt-sets with elaborate chip-carved decorations were a striking part of the uniform of "barbarian" soldiers in the late Roman military elite; they have been found in graves all along the *limes*.[15] An exquisitely crafted plate-buckle of pure gold is among the most splendid items accompanying the regal burial of Sutton Hoo.[16] But the dominant fashion as the Merovingian period opened was for cloisonné ornament: flashing red garnets cut to fit in cell patterns, the visual impact enhanced by the gold-foil under them. This cloisoné style, exemplified in the grave of Childeric (d. 481/2), remained in favor among the Frankish elite well into the sixth century.[17] Figurative imagery was not at first a usual feature with this style. This changed in the later sixth century, as the new Germanic animal-style art became fashionable with northern and western European elites; the Sutton Hoo plate-buckle offers a particularly sophisticated and well-studied example. Its Frankish equivalent comes from the grave of "Aregonde" (so identified by her ring), excavated in 1957 under the Saint-Denis basilica just north of Paris. Here the large rectangular buckle-plate hides, like Sutton Hoo, a number of Style II beasts in its gold filigree decoration. It also features the staring mask, here prominently displayed on the tongue-plate.[18] The mask's appearance, emphasized in the costume of a noble woman of the highest Merovingian elite, who was buried in an unambiguously Christian context, plausibly dates to around 580, the time so vividly described by Gregory of Tours, then writing his *Ten Books of Histories.*

The relatively precise dating of this grave, which now seems secure in the light of recent interdisciplinary research,[19] is of particular interest here because it fits with the rather narrow chronological bracket that can now be assigned with a great degree of confidence to another type of plate-buckle often displaying the staring mask, or the cross, or both, a type popular with the Neustrian elite. The mask stares out from the center of a round bronze buckle-plate from Corbie, north of Paris, while the tongue-plate presents an equal-armed cross; Salin comments that the mask motif is here

[15] L.-C. Feffer and P. Périn, *Les Francs: A l'origine de la France* (Paris, 1987) 64–9.

[16] Bruce-Mitford, *Sutton Hoo*, 2.536–64 and pl.20.

[17] P. Périn and M. Kazanski, "Das Grab Childerichs I," in K. Van Welck (ed.), *Die Franken: Wegbereiter Europas* (Mainz, 1996) 1.173–82, figs.121–2.

[18] M. Fleury and A. France-Lanord, *Les trésors mérovingiens de la basilique de Saint-Denis* (Woippy, 1998) describe the circumstances of the find and provide superb color reproductions of the artefacts.

[19] Périn has recently summarized a half-century of debate over its attribution to the mother of King Chilperic and its chronology, arguing convincingly that the date of the burial must be moved from 565/570 to ca. 580. See P. Périn and T. Calligaro, "La tombe d'Arégonde. Nouvelles analyses en laboratoire du mobilier métallique et des restes organiques de la défunte du sarcophage 49 de la basilique de Saint-Denis," *Antiquités Nationales* 37 (2006) 181–206 ; for the plate-buckle, see 197–9 and fig.19.

Christianized.[20] Périn has studied a particular group of these objects distinguished by their round buckle-plate and argues convincingly that they were made by one or two workshops in the Paris region, where most of them were found (see Figure 24.3).

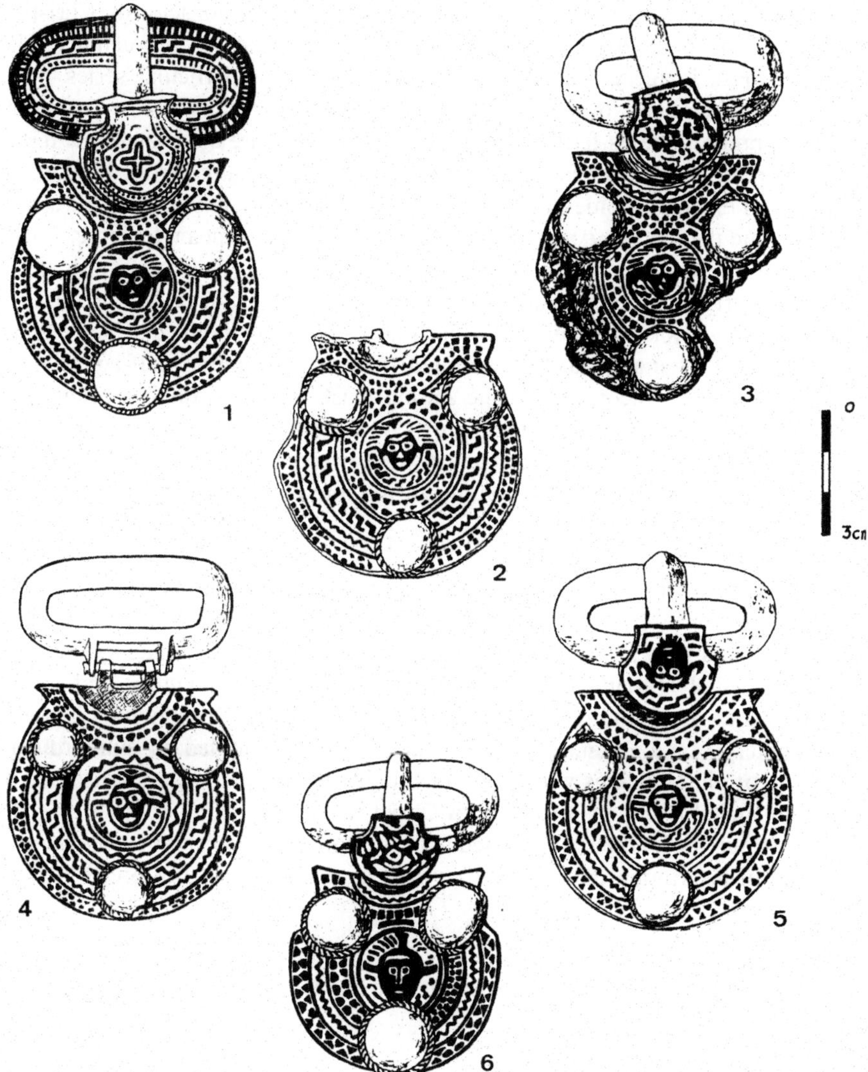

Figure 24.3 Round plate-buckles with mask and cross from the Carnavalet Museum (Paris, France). From P. Périn *BGASM* 14–15 (1973–74). Used by permission.

20 Salin, *Les Croyances*, 271, fig. 82.

His distribution map shows a striking concentration of findspots in what was, at the time of their deposition in graves, the heart of the Neustria of Fredegonde and Childebert II.[21] Although we are dealing with old finds that cannot, for the most part, be precisely identified with a particular grave and group of artefacts, I would argue that these plate-buckles are evidence of a fashion for consciously Christian imagery among the Neustrian elite around the turn of the seventh century. The cross and mask imagery was by no means limited to this particular series, or to the Neustrian heartland, or to this precise chronological bracket. In late sixth- and seventh-century contexts farther afield, these two motifs are associated in a decor whose Christian character is otherwise made more emphatic. From Frouard in Lorraine, for example, comes a tongue-plate where the mask has become the center of a cross and the letters IMMANUEL confirm that the image is meant to depict Christ himself.[22] From Limons in Auvergne a round gold brooch places the mask at the center of a chrism from whose arms hang the alpha and the omega; its pure Style II animal imagery—for example, pairs of boar heads—help to fix the date and exhibit Germanic taste.[23] It may plausibly be argued, then, that a vogue for self-consciously Christian imagery—incorporating the staring mask that so strongly evokes both pre-Christian traditions and contemporary non-Christian contexts such as Sutton Hoo—was reflected on personal ornament worn by some members of the Neustrian elite around 600, and the fashion continued well into the seventh century.

Plate-Buckles with Christian Figurative Imagery in Burgundy

The Landelinus buckle, with its elaborate Christian figurative imagery, belongs to a type called D-plate-buckles, dated to the later sixth century and to the seventh, which are found rather often in elite graves in the Burgundian *regnum*.[24] The cemetery of La Balme (La-Roche-sur-Foron) has yielded an extraordinary collection of plate-buckles with quite unambiguous Christian figurations. One of them unmistakably depicts the entry of Christ into Jerusalem.[25] Another presents two male figures with their arms raised in the gesture of prayer (orants) surrounded by a helpful inscription that reads: ACHVLAVS FECIT BENE IN SPE DOMINVS + IVSTINA

21 P. Périn, "Six plaques-boucles mérovingiennes de bronze à plaque ronde ornée d'un masque humain et de motifs géométriques du musée Carnavalet," in *BGASM* 14–15 (1973–74) 71–97, fig.6.

22 Salin, *Les Croyances*, 270–72, fig.84.

23 Ibid., 277 (misattributed to Linon instead of to Limons). For a color reproduction, see J. Hubert, J. Porcher, and W.F. Volbach (eds.), *Europe des invasions* (Paris, 1967) fig.293.

24 M. Martin, "Bemerkungen zu den frühmittelalterlichen Gurtelbeschlagen der Westschweiz," *ZSchwAKg* 28 (1971) 29–57.

25 M. Colardelle, *Sépulture et traditions funéraires du Ve au XIIIe siècle ap. J.C. dans les campagnes des Alpes françaises du Nord* (Grenoble, 1983) 111–14, fig.55.2.

O T C +. (*Iustina oro te Christe*) (see Figure 24.4).[26] The iconography has been much studied, by Salin among others.[27] The two figures on the Achulaus plate, for example, have been identified as the prophets Daniel and Habacuc, at the moment when the latter brought Daniel bread to nourish him in prison.

Figure 24.4 "Achulaus" plate-buckle from La Balme. From Treffort *ArchMéd* 32 (2002). Used by permission.

Figure 24.5 "Daniel and Habacuc" plate-buckle from the Febvre Collection (Chalon-sur-Saone?). From Treffort *ArchMéd* 32 (2002). Used by permission.

[26] Ibid., 114, fig.55.5. Also Treffort, "Vertus Prophylactiques," 54, figs.1, 5.

[27] Salin, *Les Croyances*, 310–24.

Let us pause for a moment to give further consideration to the theme of Daniel, by far the most common depicted on these Burgundian type D plate-buckles. An example from the Febvre Collection offers more refined treatment: in the central panel a rather naturalistic Daniel is shown having his feet licked by a pair of friendly lions, and man and beasts alike are marked with a cross. In the smaller panel Habacuc, also depicted with arms raised in prayer and like Daniel wearing a long tunic belted at the waist—a detail which suggests an iconographic filiation with Mediterranean Christian traditions—is shown with a pair of baskets to carry the bread with which he will nourish the imprisoned prophet. The inscription this time identifies the two: DANFE PROFETA ABBACU PROFETA (see Figure 24.5).[28] The eccentric spellings, rather contrasting with the graphic sophistication of the image, give something of a homemade flavor to this item. The association of visual image and text on this type of plate-buckle has recently been studied by Treffort.[29] She has identified about twenty examples with inscriptions, spread from Lake Geneva to the Saone River (see Figure 24.6).[30] Treffort's analysis confirms what I have just termed the homemade flavor of the inscriptions. Though the writing often frames the images on the rectangular buckle-plate, it can appear elsewhere as well, including on the back of the buckle-plate where it would have been invisible. Spellings are eccentric, as DAGNIHIL for Daniel, VENE for *bene,* FICIT for *fecit* (on the La Balme plate), and abbreviations occur (at La Balme: IVSTINA O T C +.). The form of the letters resembles those of lapidary inscriptions, as though these had served as models, but the style suggests the spoken language. Some of the inscriptions are what Treffort calls enigmatic or pseudo-epigraphic, without a decipherable literal meaning. But was the writing even meant to be read? Text here is not meant so much to communicate as to reinforce, quasi-magically, the power of the visual imagery. Why was Daniel the outstanding theme? As Salin had pointed out before Treffort, he occurs quite often in early Christian art as (1) the figure of the soul confronted by the greatest of perils who is saved by his faith in God's omnipotence; and (2) the prophet who most clearly prefigured the coming of Christ—Isidore of Seville, contemporary with the vogue for these plate-buckles, stressed this.[31] Daniel's name and example figure in the litany of *Commendatio animae*,[32] a text no doubt particularly familiar to Merovingian Christians.

---

28 Ibid., 316, pl.5. Also Treffort, "Vertus Prophylactiques," 54, figs.1, 8. Gaillard de Sémainville, "Nouvel examen," 298 n.3, disputes the attribution of this object to Chalon-sur-Saone, noting that it belonged to the Febvre Collection which seems to have included many items from Franche-Comté.

29 Treffort, "Vertus Prophylactiques," 39–47.

30 Ibid., fig.3.

31 Salin, *Les Croyances*, 337–40, quoting a passage from Isid. *In lib.vet.et nov.testam. Prooemia*, 59 (appended text 313).

32 Ibid., 341 n.1 (quoting from F. Chabrol and H. Leclercq (eds.), *Dictionnaire d'archéologie chrétienne et de la liturgie* (Paris, 1920–21) 4.436.

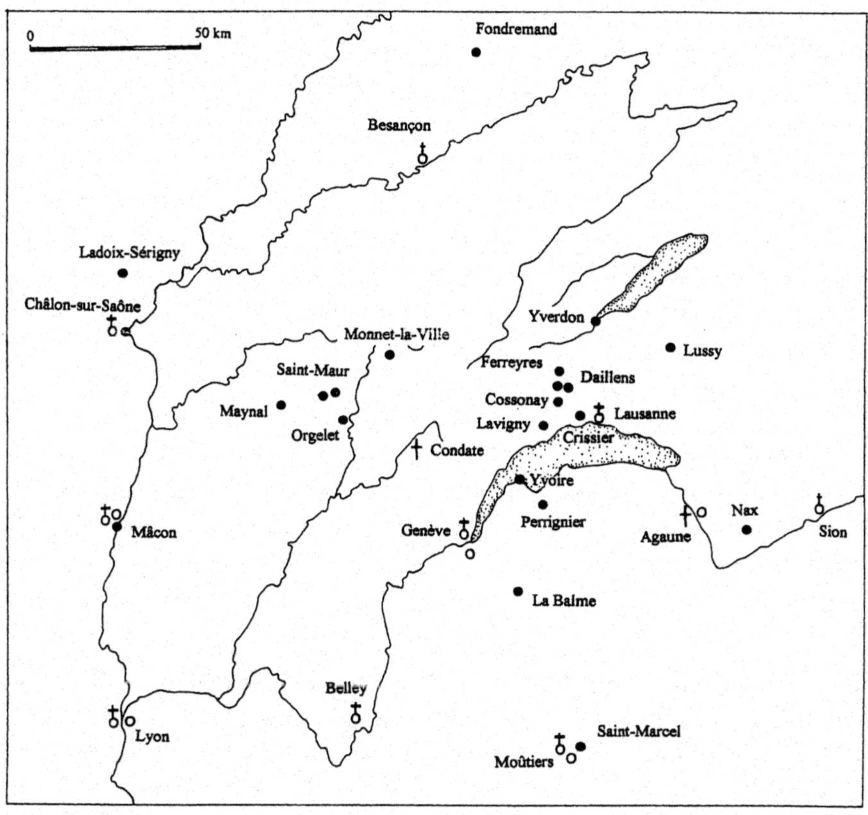

Figure 24.6 Location map of plate-buckles with inscriptions found in Burgundy. From Treffort *ArchMéd* 32 (2002). Used by permission.

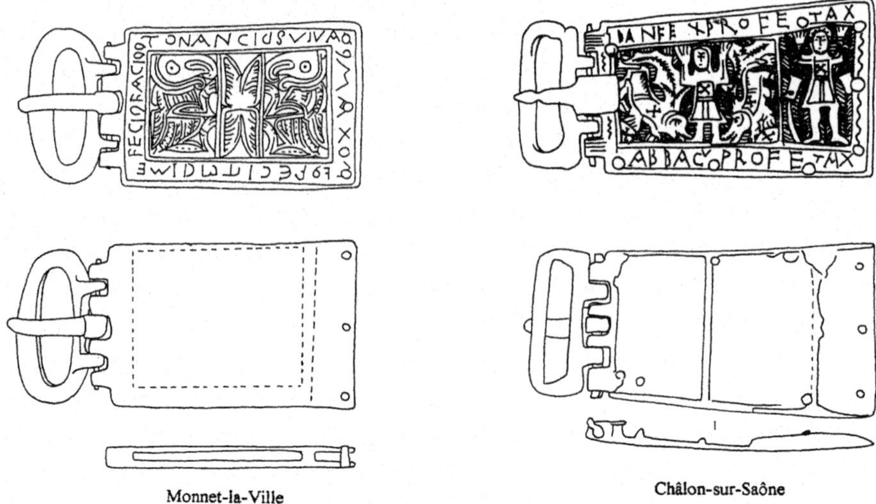

Figure 24.7 Plate-buckles with hidden reliquary compartments from Monnet-la-Ville and Chalon-sur-Saone(?), Burgundy. From Treffort *ArchMéd* 32 (2002). Used by permission.

A closer look at the Daniel/Habacuc "PROFETA" plate-buckle reveals further clues about its function: it has a secret compartment where one could carry a hidden relic—perhaps a piece of cloth, or even a small bone or a sliver of bone.[33] (see Figure 24.7) Werner first studied the corpus of such very personal, portable reliquaries,[34] and Treffort illustrates four examples among the Burgundian group—in one, from a recent, controlled excavation (Monnet-la-Ville), laboratory analysis showed traces of cotton fiber, a fabric that must have been imported into Merovingian Gaul, perhaps from Egypt.[35] She also points out that in other cases, where there was no compartment, a thin organic relic such as a bit of cloth could have been inserted between the back of the buckle plate and the leather of the belt. Hence, she thinks, this type of plate-buckle should be regarded as a phylactery, and thus she agrees with the general tenor of Salin's insistence that imagery on Merovingian personal ornament often had a tutelary function.

But she is able to raise new questions and to push his conclusions a bit farther. Who made these buckles? Under what sort of theological control? For whom? And why? She is helped by the fact that the inscriptions rather often name names. Sometimes it is clearly the owner's name, such as IVSTINA on the La Balme plate, but surprisingly often the artisan is named, again at La Balme: ACHVLAVS FECIT. The people named are both men and women (Justina again), lay (as she must be) and also

33 Treffort, "Vertus Prophylactiques," fig.5.

34 Werner, "Zu den Knochenschnallen."

35 Treffort, "Vertus Prophylactiques," 45–7 and fig.5.

clerics. The Yverdon plate-buckle reads *Willimeres fecit fib(u)la Polemico clerico* (Willemer made this buckle for the cleric Polemicus). Was Willimer an independent entrepreneurial craftsman? Were the dynamic Burgundian monasteries of the day, Saint-Maurice d'Agaune or Condate, perhaps involved in this production? The evidence of a score of objects, widely varying among themselves in technical quality and in theological sophistication, is not sufficient to enable us to venture a firmer reply than this: the plate-buckles were clearly made for members of the elite who were concerned about protecting themselves spiritually. Treffort offers this interesting phrase: these artefacts suggest "an individualized conception of salvation."[36] Many of our examples, she points out, that were found—when we know much about context, and we now know more than Salin thanks to the last 50 years of research—come from rural, as yet unchurched cemeteries. Churches, and clergy ready to confer sacraments, were not yet common outside the towns, and a Christian might face death suddenly, at any time. The possessor of a Daniel buckle reinforced by a relic, inscribed with an acclamatory formula of salvation empowering the *commendatio animae*, would be ready to set in motion the process of salvation without the need for clergy. Smith's phrase "do-it-yourself Christianity" seems apt here.

In his study—the most complete to date—of the Landelinus plate-buckle Gaillard de Sémainville conveys valuable details about the context of the discovery, details learned from interviews with the owners and other witnesses when he was Director of Historical Archaeology for Burgundy.[37] The buckle's owner, since he wore a scramasax, was doubtless an elite male, and the grave was part of a large rural cemetery in use both well before and after it had been dug. In arguing that the horseman is meant to represent the Christ of the Apocalypse, Gaillard de Sémainville agrees with Treffort,[38] but his analysis goes much farther by insisting on the very particular, scarcely orthodox, and culturally ambiguous character of the object taken as a whole, text and imagery. The overall composition is clear enough: the Triumphant Christ is depicted as St. John's Revelation had predicted, with (to his right) the symbols of salvation—the Chrismed cross with the Alpha and Omega—and (to his left) the Beast. Landelinus, however, drew with great originality on various scriptural as well as iconographic traditions in rendering sometimes surprising details. The halo is inspired by the radiant diadem of late Roman art and reflects Revelation 19:12; the intense stare here translates the "flaming eyes"; the extended ears are a way of suggesting Christ's power to hear everything, while his mouth presents not a smile but two vertical fangs which translate the verse "From his mouth darts a sharp blade to strike the pagan nations ..." (Rev. 19:15) (see Figure 24.8 detail). The fierce nature of this image is strongly emphasized by the weapons he brandishes, and Gaillard de Sémainville is the first to insist, I believe, on their particularly Frankish character. The war-axe in the right hand, sometimes called

36 Ibid., 49: "une conception individualisée du salut."

37 Gaillard de Sémainville,"Nouvel examen," 298 n.2 and 319–22.

38 Treffort, "Vertus Prophylactiques," 47.

a francisca, was for the Franks a weapon of choice; and Gaillard de Sémainville was surely right that it is not a spear in the left hand but an angon, something like a harpoon, a weapon associated with elite warriors in Clovis' time.[39] Even without the inscription the image is quite unique, though parallels can be found for various aspects taken separately. A horseman with upraised arms, in some cases armed with a lance, is a not uncommon motif on a kind of openwork bronze disc called a *rouelle*.[40] There is, to my mind, a necessarily ambiguous iconographic and religious penumbra surrounding such figures. Salin shows that the mounted horseman appears not only in pre-Christian iconography but in contemporary non-Christian contexts as well, such as on a disc from Vendel, in Sweden, which likely depicts Woden with his pet crows.[41] The specific iconography might well have been inspired by a Christian artefact, but that does not make its intention here Christian. Gaillard de Sémainville points to a gold bracteate from Gudbrandsdalen in Norway as being thematically close to the Ladoix-Serrigny buckle and perhaps inspired in part by Christian imagery adapted to evoke a pagan monster-battling myth.[42] The creators of the imagery on these personal objects could choose from the various traditions known to them the right elements to meet a specific demand.

Two of Landelinus' choices demand further comment. Why depict the horse with a prominent erection? This, like the fangs, like the big ears, like the weapons and, indeed like the chi-rho, is a symbol of vitality and power. Gaillard de Sémainville has even found a parallel: an ithyphallic, armed figure of Christ himself trampling a serpent.[43] And what about the word NVMEN, given such prominence on a line by itself? Gaillard de Sémainville proposes that it designates the power of Christ, although he reports the suggestion of Dierkens that "*numen* can also designate the object itself, an artefact provided with divine, indeed magic, powers."[44] I believe that Gaillard de Sémainville and Treffort would agree with me that the purpose here was to create an object of practical power. Treffort indeed suggests that, even without a hidden hinged compartment, the plate-buckle could have concealed, between the leather of the belt and the back of the buckle-plate, a relic such as a bit of cloth or a fragment of text, and Gaillard de Sémainville agrees that this is quite likely. He also rejects Werner's suggestion that a painting in a church or monastery, some form of "official" Christian art, inspired the iconography. Not only does the warlike—and sexual—emphasis of the imagery argue against this idea, but so does the forthright millenarist inscription.

39 Gaillard de Sémainville,"Nouvel examen," 306 and figs.3 and 5. For the weapons, see also Feffer and Périn, *Les Francs*, 88–90.

40 Salin, *Les Croyances*, 286–94.

41 Ibid., fig.102.

42 Gaillard de Sémainville,"Nouvel examen," 316 and fig.10.1.

43 Ibid., 314–15 and fig.9. The object is a terra-cotta plaque from Grésin, in central France, dated to the 4th or 5th century.

44 Ibid., 301–2 and n.8.

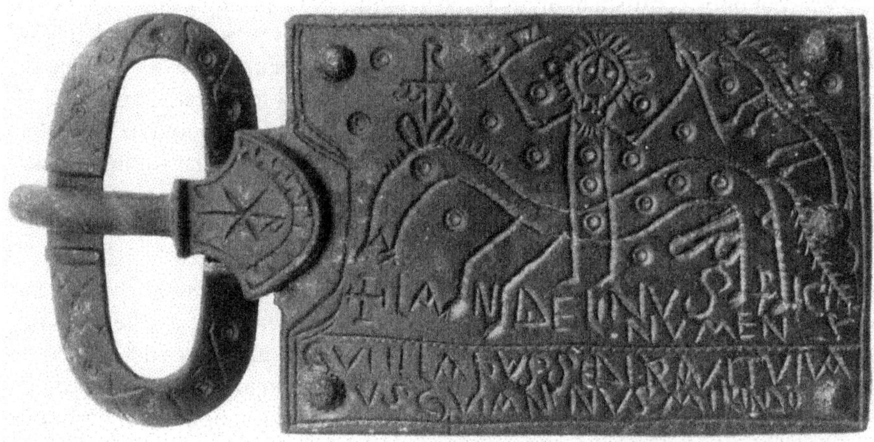

Figure 24.8 Detail of "Landelinus" plate-buckle, from Ladoix-Serrigny. From H. Gaillard de Sémainville *RAE* 52 (2003). Photo by H. Gaillard de Sémainville. Used by permission.

Millenarism had become theologically incorrect in the western church following an attack by Saint Augustine.[45] Clearly this did not perturb Landelinus, who was not only a craftsman of great self-confidence—look at the prominence of his signature—but also well versed both in scripture and in eclectic iconographic traditions. His concern was to tailor his work for a client who was, Gaillard de Sémainville has now plausibly established, a member of the local warrior elite in the Burgundian kingdom. This man wanted to be as sure as he could be that when his time came, priest or no priest, Apocalypse impending or not, he would be ready for the coming of that horseman.

The Landelinus plate-buckle offers a valuable corrective to the usual perception, ingrained in the sources written by clerics, of "conversion" as a top-down process deemed successful when the institutional Church could claim control of the meaning of its specific manifestations. The apocalyptic message, fashioned from bits of sacred text and of numinous iconography rooted alike in Christian and non-Christian traditions, was clearly not controlled or approved by any orthodox religious authority. In this sense it fits Smith's imaginative suggestion of a "do-it-yourself" phase within the centuries-long conversion process, where individuals cobbled together pieces from the various sacred traditions within their environments to suit their needs, rather like the *bricolage* pieces of some modern artists. The text on this plate-buckle asserts Landelinus as the author of the *bricolage*, but we cannot know whether he, as much artist as craftsman, was full master of the message or responded as best he could to the specific requirements of a patron. Was he a craftsman perhaps associated with a monastery who did some private work on the side? An independent smith who traveled about in search of commissions? We cannot know, but we can note that in contrast with the cross-and/or mask round plate buckles of the Paris region, serially produced in workshops, this was clearly a custom-made item. Its unique blend of naive and sophisticated imagery is forceful testimony to the eclectic traditions present within the religious imagination of the Frankish elites in the days of the mission of Saint Columbanus.

---

45 Ibid., 318. On the history of early Christian millenarian thinking, see J. Delumeau, *Mille ans de bonheur* (Paris, 1995). See also Josef Lössl's essay in this volume (Chapter 2).

PART VIII
The Power of Religion in the Communities of the East

Chapter 25
Antioch and the Intersection between Religious Factionalism, Place, and Power in Late Antiquity*

Wendy Mayer
Australian Catholic University

Antioch is a city that in Late Antiquity was the centre of military administration for the eastern frontier, the seat of civic administration for the vast diocese of Oriens, the provincial capital of Syria, at times the residence of the eastern emperor and his court, and an important conduit of trade from Syria and the far east to Constantinople and the west. As such, economic, administrative, imperial, and military power were a prominent part of its identity. It was home to a substantial Jewish community, one of the oldest Christian sees, and a city in whose Olympic games, civic calendar, and private life the influences of Greco-Roman cults long persisted. As a result, religious pluralism was a dominant part of its landscape. It also had a long history of factionalism within its Christian community that reached extremes in the fourth and sixth centuries, making it inevitable that at Antioch the domains of religion and power would at times merge to a point where the boundary between the two became difficult to determine. In this article two examples of how these two domains could overlap are explored by showing how place—more specifically religious buildings—could play a role in the discourse of power.

The Cult of Babylas and the Power of Place

The first case study begins with the martyrdom of a local Antiochene bishop, Babylas, in the mid third century.[1] At the time the martyr's body was buried locally, most likely in the common cemetery.[2] The cemetery lay outside the southern walls

* This article is the product of a Fellowship in Byzantine Studies at Dumbarton Oaks (2006–7). It constitutes part of the research for a larger project conducted in collaboration with Pauline Allen of the Centre for Early Christian Studies, Australian Catholic University, concerning the Christian churches in Antioch from 300 to 638.

1 Babylas was killed at Antioch ca. 250 under the emperor Decius (249–51).

2 While the sources do not explicitly tell us this, this is the most logical conclusion given the cluster of Christian martyr burials situated in that location by the time of Julian.

of Antioch alongside the road leading up to its suburb Daphne.[3] Daphne was the site of a number of important temples—in particular to Apollo and Zeus[4]—contained at least one significant Jewish healing shrine and a synagogue,[5] and was the site of a variety of festivals or spectacles with their origins in Greco-Roman cults.[6] Almost a century after Babylas' death, during the reign of Constantius II, the caesar Gallus (351–54) had the body disinterred and the relics translated to Daphne to a martyrium that had been built within the *temenos* of the temple of Apollo.[7] Whether the martyrium had been purpose-built to house the relics of Babylas or was a building already under construction that was taken over for this use after Gallus' arrival, its location was clearly a political choice, since it violated a long-standing taboo on the burial of bodies in sacred spaces and was a direct insult to the cult of Apollo.[8] Sozomen attributes the decision to Gallus' Christian background, his reverence for those martyred for the faith, and a desire to purify Daphne of "pagan" superstition.[9] Implicit in his attribution of this motive is a

---

See P. Franchi di Cavalieri, "Il κοιμητήριον di Antiochia," *ST* 49 (1928) 146–53; and G. Downey, "The Shrines of St. Babylas at Antioch and Daphne," in *Antioch-on-the-Orontes*, vol. 2 *The Excavations of 1933–1936* (Princeton, 1938) 45–8.

[3] See *Antioch-on-the-Orontes*, 2.215 plan 1, where the excavations of the 1930s confirm burials near the southern end of the city, some 500–700m to the left of the Daphne gate as one exits the city.

[4] See Lib. *Or*. 11.236. For temples of Hecate and Nemesis, see Joh.Mal. 12.38. For a temple of Artemis, see Joh.Mal. 10.9 and 11.11, which claims that both Tiberius and Trajan built one but is most likely confused.

[5] See Joh.Chrys. *Adv.Iud.* 1 (*PG* 48.852.1–8 and 855.59–61), with reference also to the Temple of Apollo.

[6] On the Maiuma, held in honour of Dionysus and Aphrodite, see G. Greatrex and J.W. Watt, "One, Two or Three Feasts? The Brytae, the Maiuma and the May Festival at Edessa," *OC* 83 (1999) 1–21; and Lib. *Or*. 41.16, who refers to a festival of five or more days at Daphne which may be the same. The quadrennial Syrian Olympics, of which the last 15 days were held in the stadium in Daphne, were dedicated to Zeus. See Joh.Mal. 12.38. Joh.Chrys. *In S. Julianum* (*PG* 50.672.36–45 and 673.57–674.1) refers to a well-attended festival at Daphne that involves troupes of dancing men, eating, and bawdy songs.

[7] For the argument that the martyrium was situated within the *temenos* rather than simply being adjacent to the temple precinct, as is commonly supposed, see D. Woods, "Malalas, 'Constantius', and a Church-inscription from Antioch," *VChr* 59 (2005) 54–62, esp. 60.

[8] See U. Volp, *Tod und Ritual in den christlichen Gemeinden der Antike* (Leiden, 2002) 255–6.

[9] Soz. 5.19.12. Gallus' motivation may well have been less noble and have been more closely allied to a desire to elevate his own authority at Antioch over against that of Constantius. On the troubled relations between Constantius and Gallus, and between Gallus and the citizens of Antioch, see C. Vogler, *Constance II et l'administration impériale* (Strasbourg, 1979) 84–93.

discourse of power—in this case the power of the martyr's relics as a purifying force that expels non-Christian supernatural entities.[10]

The way in which the overwhelmingly Christian sources frame these events is particularly instructive. That Gallus' choice of Babylas was perceived by them as a political act is indicated by the events that follow.[11] When the neo-pagan Julian became emperor and was resident at Antioch in 362–63 he is said to have attributed the failure of the famed oracle of Apollo at Daphne to the relics of Babylas. This is peculiar when it is considered that within the eight years between Babylas' translation and Julian's arrival other bodies had been buried alongside Babylas in the martyrium.[12] Ignoring the fact that the removal of a single body would have failed to cleanse the temple precinct of pollution, the ecclesiastial historians nonetheless claim that it was only the extraction of Babylas upon which Julian insisted.[13] This singling out of Babylas serves to emphasize his status as a martyr and to demonstrate his symbolic significance for the local Christian communities. That the other bodies are so cavalierly dismissed most likely indicates that they were simply those of ordinary citizens who had elected to be buried next to the martyr following the practice of *depositio ad sanctos*. The episode concludes with yet another political act—the triumphant *adventus* of the saint as the relics were escorted from the martyrium in Daphne back to the common cemetery, accompanied by the chanting of a psalm verse with obvious anti-pagan, and therefore anti-imperial, overtones.[14]

That the Christian community viewed these events as the triumph of the power of one deity (the Christian God) over the powerlessness of another (Apollo) and of a champion of the faith (a powerful martyr) against an impious—and therefore impotent—emperor becomes even clearer when we look at their framing of what then happened to the temple of Apollo. Preaching some 20 or more years after these events, the Antiochene priest John Chrysostom describes a lightning strike which instantly incinerated the cultic statue in the temple of Apollo, calling it an act of God and thus constructing the ruined temple as a permanent symbol of the powerlessness of paganism and the adjacent, thriving martyrium, with its carefully preserved empty space, as a potent symbol of Christianity's triumph.[15] This is in marked contrast to Ammianus Marcellinus' description of the same event.[16] In his account Julian suspected the Christian community of having started the fire and, in retaliation, closed down the Great Church, their main centre of worship. That is, it was not to a powerful divine act, but simply a political human act, to

[10] For this idea see Volp, *Tod und Ritual*, 249, 259, 262–3, and 269–70.

[11] In addition to Soz. 5.19, see also Socr. 3.18 and Theod. *HE* 3.10.

[12] See Joh.Chrys. *De s.Babyla* 7 (*SCh* 362.306).

[13] Soz. 5.19.17; Theod. *HE* 3.10.2. The same claim is made by John Chrysostom (see n.12 above).

[14] Socr. 3.18.3–4; Soz. 5.19.18–19; Theod. *HE* 3.10.3.

[15] *De s.Babyla* 8–9 (*SCh* 362.308–10).

[16] Amm. 22.13.1–3.

which the emperor, as administrative authority, responded by closing the cathedral church, the locus of the opposing religion's authority. Ammianus himself offers a third, less charged, explanation: the fire was the result of a candle left burning unattended by a visitor.[17]

The story does not end there but continues into the reign of Valens (364–78). Here the story alters from one of two competing religious powers to one of competing Christian factions. The bishop Meletius, spiritual head of the larger of the two Nicene factions at Antioch, who had originally been elected to the episcopate by the Homoian (Arian) community, continued to exploit the potency of Babylas' relics, transforming the martyr into a champion of Nicene Christianity. To place this transformation in perspective we must recall that, at the time that the caesar Gallus first translated the relics to Daphne, the martyr was adopted under the banner of the Homoians, who constituted the faction of Christianity approved by the reigning emperor of the time, Constantius II.[18] It was this same Homoian faction again that was responsible in the early 360s for the defiantly anti-Julianic translation of Babylas' relics from Daphne back to the common cemetery. Theodoret confirms this by indicating that it was against the "Arians" that Julian retaliated.[19] After being elected as the next Arian bishop in 360, however, Meletius made it clear that he did not share that community's doctrine. His neo-Nicene sympathies led him, on return from his first exile, to gather around himself a second Nicene community in opposition both to the Arian community—who simply elected a replacement bishop—and to the original Nicene community presided over by Bishop Paulinus.[20] Perhaps as early as the retranslation of Babylas' relics to the common cemetery in 362 or 363 Meletius resolved that the move would not be final. He would build a church locally in Babylas' honor and translate the relics there.[21]

---

17 Amm. 22.13.3.

18 The situation was perhaps more subtle at Antioch at this point. P.-L. Malosse, "Antioche et le kappa," in B. Cabouret, P.-L. Gatier, and C. Saliou (eds.), *Antioch de Syrie: Histoire, images et traces de la ville antique* (Lyon, 2004) 77–96 at 85–6, argues that Antioch was the capital of Homoian Christianity at this period and that Constantius did not choose to reside at Antioch because it was Homoian so much as that he was Homoian because he resided at Antioch. For a more detailed discussion of the role played by Constantius in the development of Homoian Christianity see H.-C. Brenneke, *Studien zur Geschichte der Homöer der Osten bis zum Ende der homöischen Reichskirche*, Beiträge zur historischen Theologie 73 (Tübingen, 1988) 5–86.

19 Theod. *HE* 3.12.1; and see Brennecke, *Studien*, 136–41.

20 The definitive work on the origins and effects of this schism at Antioch remains F. Cavallera, *Le schisme d'Antioche (IVe–Ve siècle)* (Paris, 1905).

21 Meletius' efforts in this respect are described in detail by John Chrysostom, *De s.Babyla* 10 (*SCh* 362.310–12).

The location of this church was strategic. It lay in isolation yet close to the city, across from the island in the river Orontes where the imperial palace was located.[22] More importantly the church was set next to the military parade ground (the *campus martius*). During the reign of Valens, when the churches of Antioch were largely under the control of the Arian community and Meletius' faction was for the most part banned from worshipping within the city, the main locus of his faction's activity was the *campus martius*.[23] The location of a church housing a martyr who had demonstrated the impotence of both an emperor and that emperor's religion on the edge of space marked out as sacred by one faction of Christianity and within view of the palace of an emperor who supported another, opposing faction could not have failed to be charged with political significance. The church was large, it would have been the first building that struck the eye of a visitor to the city arriving across the Orontes valley,[24] and like the ruined temple of Apollo at Daphne it was intended to proclaim the power of the true God. Not long before, Babylas had been hailed as a champion of Arian Christianity against the false gods worshipped by Julian. Under Meletius, it would appear that Babylas was now remarketed as a champion of Nicene Christianity against the false Christianity (Arianism) of the emperor Valens. By the time Theodosius, who succeeded Valens, proclaimed Nicene Christianity as the officially endorsed religion at the Council of Constantinople in 381, the building was poised to act as a potent symbol of Nicene Christianity's triumph. Meletius, who had died while presiding over that Council, was conveyed back to Antioch in triumph and his body interred, as he had planned in advance, in the very centre of that church and thus in close proximity to Babylas.[25] The addition of the body of Meletius to the church had the dual effect of instantly elevating Meletius' own status to that of both confessor-bishop and saint and removing any lingering question that Babylas' heritage was claimed by Nicene Christians and indeed those Nicenes who followed Meletius' faction, securing its domination at Antioch.

---

22 This assumes that the Church of St. Babylas and the cruciform church excavated at Kaoussie are one and the same. See J. Lassus, "L'église cruciforme Antioche-Kaoussié 12-F," in *Antioch-on-the-Orontes*, 2.5–44.

23 See Joh.Chrys. *Laus Diodori* (*PG* 52.764.21–8); Theod. *HE* 4.25–6; Theod. *HR* 2.15, 8.5, 8.7–8.

24 Lassus, "L'eglise cruciforme," 5, was impressed by its location and, believing that it stood in isolation in Late Antiquity rather than being enclosed by a suburb, and that a bridge between the church and island most likely existed at that point, stated that the site gave the impression of being a gate both to the city and to the countryside.

25 On the procession of Meletius' remains back to Antioch and his burial next to Babylas see Soz. 7.10.5. The church at Kaoussie, which dates prior to 378, contained in its central chamber two tombs, the more monumental of which was designed to take two bodies. See Lassus, "L'église cruciforme," 10–11.

Justinian and the Churches of Antioch

When attention is turned to the second case study, of events in the sixth century, the situation is somewhat different. Here the ever-widening split between Chalcedonians and anti-Chalcedonians within the empire and the degree to which this factionalism was expressed within the Christian community at Antioch were not only significant for broader ecclesiastical affairs but had far-reaching implications for both territorial stability and imperial authority. Although by the time of Justinian the territory administered by the city within the eastern empire had been reduced,[26] Syria still played an important role militarily in preserving the stability of the eastern front. Antioch remained an important economic centre both as a conduit for the trade of goods from the Far East and, via its still relatively large population, as a significant tax base. In terms of ecclesiastical politics, although the Antiochene patriarchate had lost control of Palestine and Cyprus in the Council of 431 and the "Robber" synod of 449, it retained control of both Syrias, and at the Council of Chalcedon (451) it regained Phoenicia and Arabia.[27] Antioch thus remained a powerful ecclesiastical player. At the same time in Syria and particularly at Antioch anti-Chalcedonian sentiment was in the ascendancy, putting the city at odds with the imperial line.[28] In a climate where the unity of the Christian religion was intimately connected to the unity and stability of the empire, keeping the support of Syria and Antioch was for Justinian a desideratum. To this end Justinian, who supported Chalcedon, and his wife, Theodora, who was publicly anti-Chalcedonian, seem to have pursued a carefully orchestrated plan that allowed them to keep a hand in both sides of the factional divide simultaneously.

Under these circumstances imperial sponsorship of the construction of churches within the Syrian capital is likely to have taken on political overtones that added an extra dimension to what had become by this time a common act of imperial munificence.[29] After the devastating earthquake of 526 Justinian initiated a major rebuilding program at Antioch.[30] Not only did he improve the defensibility of the city via substantial repairwork on its walls[31] and reconstruct administrative spaces and buildings, he also sponsored a number of churches. Malalas refers to

---

26 See K. Butcher, *Roman Syria and the Near East* (London, 2003) 86–7 and fig.24.2.

27 Butcher, *Roman Syria*, 387.

28 Ibid.

29 Imperial financing of the construction or expansion of churches in the city was initiated by Constantine (306–37). Prior to Justinian the city benefited also in this respect from the patronage of Constantius II (337–61), Gallus, Theodosius II (408–50), Leo I (457–74), and Anastasius (491–518).

30 Detailed by Proc. *Aed.* 2.10.

31 Regarding the truthfulness (or otherwise) of Procopius' claims, see M. Whitby, "Procopius and Antioch," in D.H. French and C.S. Lightfoot (eds.), *The Eastern Frontier of the Roman Empire: Proceedings of a Colloquium Held at Ankara in September 1988* (Oxford, 1989) 2.537–53.

a Church of the Theotokos and a Church of Cosmas and Damian and attributes to the empress Theodora a Church of Michael the Archangel.[32] Since Procopius, who confirms the identity of the last two churches, attributes them both to Justinian, the question of whether Theodora was involved will here be set aside on the assumption that the imperial couple would in any case have had a common purpose.[33] Justinian also donated to the city of Antioch a jewelled robe, which was displayed in the Church of Cassian.[34] At the most basic level these were obviously instances of imperial largesse intended to win the goodwill of the citizens of Antioch. But there are, it would appear, more subtle dimensions. Churches dedicated to Michael the Archangel and to the Theotokos had been part of the religious topography of Antioch for some 50 years prior to the earthquake.[35] Both figures had developed an established set of associations. In the case of Michael the Archangel, by the time of Severus' episcopate at Antioch in 512–18 Michael was popularly considered a heavenly power of high authority. Paintings at Antioch at this time depicted him in imperial garb, wearing a purple robe and crown and holding in his right hand "the sign of rulership and universal authority."[36] He and the archangel Gabriel are depicted in an identical fashion in a sixth-century mosaic produced under Justinian in S. Apollinare in Classe in Ravenna.[37] By this time Michael had become styled in addition as the leader of the angel hosts and a powerful patron of the earthly leader of the imperial army.[38] He was also associated with a healing cult, for early churches

32 Joh.Mal. 17.16, 19 (419–21, 423).

33 Proc. *Aed.* 2.10.23–5. Procopius dates the rebuilding of the two churches to after the Persian attack on Antioch of 540, whereas Malalas dates their reconstruction after the earthquakes of 526 and 528, leading Downey, *History of Antioch*, 552, to discuss their accounts separately and thereby imply that Justinian rebuilt the churches twice. It is more likely that Procopius, out of a desire to exaggerate the effects of the Persian assault, deliberately blurs the chronology.

34 Joh.Mal. 18.45 (450).

35 Joh.Mal. 17.16 (420) names the emperor Leo I as the founder of the Church of Michael that the earthquake destroyed. As for the Church of the Theotokos, we discover from Severus of Antioch *Hom.* 57 (*PO* 8.2.340, 366) that the emperor Anastasius had recently enlarged an existing church through the addition of porticoes. A church dedicated to the Virgin and Mother of God is unlikely to have been built at Antioch prior to the Council of Ephesus (431).

36 See Sev.Ant. *Hom.* 72 (*PO* 12.1.83–4), who complains about the prevalence of this image.

37 The two are depicted on either side of the entrance to the apse, with Michael standing on the left. See L. Abramowski, "Die Mosaiken von S. Vitale und S. Apollinare in Classe und die Kirchenpolitik Kaiser Justinians," *ZAC* 5 (2001) 289–341 at 339–40, figs.10–11.

38 See J.P. Rohland, *Der Erzengel Michael, Arzt und Feldherr: Zwei Aspekte des vor- und frühbyzantinischen Michaelskultes* (Leiden, 1977) 112, 114–24.

of Michael were located on sites previously sacred to local healing deities.[39] The cult of Michael was popular and was strongly associated with imperial authority, and conveniently—in a city with volatile Chalcedonian and anti-Chalcedonian factions—theologically ambiguous. The Church of the Theotokos had just been enlarged by the emperor Anastasius, and the additions had not long been paid off when it was destroyed during the 526 earthquake.[40] Perhaps to overwrite the memory of Anastasius' largesse and perhaps to appropriate the Virgin's role as protectress of the empire for himself,[41] Justinian built an even larger and more magnificent version and endowed it substantially. So successful was this move that by the last decade of the sixth century it was known popularly as the Church of Justinian.[42]

The introduction by Justinian of a Church of Cosmas and Damian, a cult which had not existed previously at Antioch, carries similar overtones. An important locus of their cult was the city of Cyrrhus,[43] part of the Antiochene patriarchate in Syria and a city with long-standing ties to Antioch. These would have served to reduce its alien character and improve its acceptability. More importantly for the emperor's purposes, however, was an alleged personal connection between the two saints and Justinian. To them he publicly attributed his recovery from an illness and at some point translated their relics from Cyrrhus to Constantinople, where he built a church to house them.[44] The construction of a church dedicated to Cosmas and Damian introduced an alternative source of divine healing at Antioch, which was doubtless popular. Given Justinian's personal adoption of the cult, it is likely to have functioned on another level, however, as a symbol of the divine favor enjoyed by the emperor. In these indirect ways Justinian was, one suspects, attempting to generate goodwill across the theological divide at Antioch without promoting an overt theological agenda.

39 On the development of the cult of Michael at sites that were associated with local healing deities or springs see Rohland, *Der Erzengel Michael*, 87–94; and A. Schaller, *Der Erzengel Michael im frühen Mittelalter: Ikonographie und Verehrung einer Heiligen ohne Vita* (Bern, 2006) 34–6. Rohland, *Der Erzengel*, 89, speculates that the cult of Michael as healer developed in part in opposition to that of Aesculapius.

40 See above n.37. Severus, preaching 512–18, expects the audience to play a part in defraying the expense of the extension and the new decorative program, indicating that Anastasius had not paid for the entire cost himself and that it may have taken some years to pay off the debt.

41 On this latter point see M. Vallejo Girvés, "Funcionalidad politico-ideologica de las edificaciones religiosas en el Africa de la 'Renouatio imperii' Justineanea," *Polis* 7 (1995) 247–64, who argues that founding churches of the Theotokos, with the Virgin as protectress, was part of Justinian's strategy for re-establishing Roman *imperium*.

42 Evagr. *HE* 5.21.

43 See E. Giannarelli (ed.), *Cosma e Damiano dall'Oriente a Firenze* (Florence, 2002) 29–30; and Proc. *Aed.* 2.11.4.

44 Proc. *Aed.* 1.6.5.

To place his actions in clearer perspective, the Church of the Theotokos was most likely shifted by him from its previous location, and the Church of Cosmas and Damian was built nearby.[45] According to Procopius, Justinian built only one other church dedicated to Cosmas and Damian outside of Constantinople,[46] and, with the exception of Antioch, none to Michael the Archangel outside of Constantinople, in or near which he built three.[47] At the same time churches of the Theotokos were a favourite of his and proliferated at this time throughout the empire.[48] At Antioch three churches of Michael the Archangel appear under Justinian, of which a second, in Daphne, may also have been part of his building campaign there.[49] Contrary to expectation there is, by contrast, no clear indication that Justinian attempted to rebuild the Great Church, which had long been the seat of spiritual authority in the city and a symbol of factional dominance.[50] One gains the impression that at this point he was treading delicately in ecclesiastical matters by promoting cults that were popular and theologically multivalent almost as a replacement for the traditional civic church and all that it stood for. Both Michael and the Theotokos had been absorbed with equal facility into a Chalcedonian and anti-Chalcedonian framework.[51] At the same time, by personalizing the cult of Cosmas and Damian and by appropriating the already strong imperial associations of the cult of Michael, Justinian was able to use built architecture to put constantly before the eyes of the Antiochenes the message that their emperor was the recipient of divine favor.[52]

---

45 Joh.Mal. 17.19 (423) says that Justinian located it opposite the basilica of Rufinus, which implies that this is not where it had been situated previously

46 Proc. *Aed.* 5.9.37, although it should be noted that a church of Cosmas and Damian was constructed in Gerasa at this same time (529/533). See H.-G. Severin, "Aspekte der Positionierung der Kirchen in oströmischen Städten," in G. Brands and H.-G. Severin (eds.), *Die spätantike Stadt und ihre Christianisierung* (Wiesbaden, 2003) 249–58 at 251.

47 Proc. *Aed.* 1.3.14–17, 1.8.2, 17–19.

48 See Proc. *Aed.* 1.3.1–2, who goes on to list some nine churches (*Aed.* 1.8.20, 3.4.12, 5.6.1–26, 7.7, 8.5, 6.2.20, 4.4, 5.9, 7.16).

49 Phot. *Bibl.* 228 records the existence of a sermon of Ephrem (bishop of Antioch 526–44) preached on the dedication feast of the Church of Michael the Archangel in Daphne, which, given the number of church dedications that Ephrem presided over, is as likely to be the actual dedication of the church as its annual commemoration. These other two churches, both at Daphne, receive mention in Proc. *BP* 2.11.4–13.

50 Evidence usually taken to refer to the Great Church after 526 is ambiguous. See Proc. *BP* 2.9.14–16, 2.10.6–9; Evagr. *HE* 4.25, 6.8; and Zach. *HE* 10.5. On none of these occasions is the identity of the church made explicit and it is just as likely that other churches are being described.

51 For the anti-Chalcedonian reception see Sev.Ant. *Hom.* 38, 67 and 72 (*PO* 20.2.399–420; 8.2.340–67; 12.1.71–89).

52 The coinage that Justinian issued throughout this period reinforces these messages. The majority of the gold solidi minted at Constantinople, Thessalonica, Carthage, and Ravenna and the silver coins minted at Constantinople depict an archangel on the reverse

Ironically, by supplying the funds for the construction of these churches, but by leaving the construction itself in local hands, Justinian laid his claim to spiritual authority at Antioch open to subversion by the local bishop, Ephrem. A supporter of Chalcedon, Ephrem had the advantage of presiding over the dedications of these new churches and in one particular case used the occasion to summon to Antioch a substantial synod at which he compelled the 132 bishops present to confirm the Council of Chalcedon and to anathematize the exiled anti-Chalcedonian bishop of Antioch, Severus.[53] In doing so, Ephrem acted aggressively in a way that Justinian had chosen not to at this point in his reign (the late 530s).[54] Two possibilities arise. Either Ephrem was exerting his own power independently and in pursuit of his own agenda, thereby cutting across the message intended by the emperor—perhaps the more likely scenario—or he was Justinian's agent at Antioch, implementing the emperor's covert agenda while Justinian himself was able to claim deniability and to distance himself from the action.[55] In either case the local reaction demonstrates that Justianian's policy at Antioch was effective in the long term. Justinian was only a secondary target in the animosity that the anti-Chalcedonians subsequently directed toward Ephrem.[56] Here we see an example of the way in which two conflicting religion-power discourses could appropriate the same building to promote differing messages—one effective only in the short term, the other more enduring.

---

deploying the same iconography used of Michael and Gabriel in S. Apollinare in Classe in Ravenna. This replaces the winged victory typically found on the reverse of the higher denomination coinage of the emperors who preceded him: the archangel iconography is found on a single gold coin type of his predecessor Justin I, who otherwise employs the winged victory, and becomes common only with the gold coins issued jointly by Justin I und Justinian from the mint at Constantinople. Justinian also issued a copper series, minted exclusively in Antioch, in which he had himself depicted seated on a throne, holding the same symbols of authority. This is in contrast to the copper coins minted elsewhere, which depict Justinian in either frontal or profile portrait. See W. Hahn, *Moneta Imperii Byzantini*, vol. 1, *von Anastasius I. bis Justinianus I (491–565)* (Vienna, 1973) Taf.5, 12, 14–35 (esp. Taf.5, no.3; Taf.12, nos.1a–3b; Taf.25, nos.127–30). According to P. Grierson, *Byzantine Coins* (London, 1982) 66, the copper series was struck in Antioch in the 530s to commemorate Justinian's generosity towards the city after the earthquake. I am indebted to Charles Deur for bringing the iconography of the copper series to my attention.

53 Zach. *HE* 10.5.

54 In fact Justianian, perhaps via Theodora, had repeatedly invited Severus to Constantinople for discussions. He was finally successful in the winter of 534/535, when Severus arrived from Egypt and was hosted in one of the imperial palaces. See P. Allen and C.T.R. Hayward, *Severus of Antioch* (London, 2004) 29.

55 This is the motive read into the event by later anti-Chalcedonian authors. See Mich. Syr. 9.16.

56 So, for instance, Michael the Syrian, ibid., portrays Justinian as being seduced by Ephrem and Ephrem as the prime instigator. For other examples of Michael's hostile treatment of Ephrem see *Chron.* 9.19, 24.

In these two examples at Antioch the intersection between power and religion played out in a number of ways: the power of a martyr—himself a conduit of a greater divine power—was able to repel or suppress competing supernatural forces; the power of rival deities and the rival powers of deity and emperor were constructed in terms of potency and impotence; imperial power was expressed through the suppression of one religion or the imposition of another; and in turn unfavored religions were able to resist imperial authority. Observable, too, is one faction of a religion working to gain ascendancy over another and to cement its claim to primacy and authority; the imperial appropriation of divine power through self-construction as a favored client; and, finally, the interplay between imperial and episcopal power, and the conflict or confluence of their agendas. All of these are power plays having religious place at their centres. These examples show religious space appropriated, framed, reframed, and exploited in a variety of ways as a powerful non-verbal medium in diverse power discourses.

Chapter 26
On the Way to Bethlehem: Mary between Jerome and John of Jerusalem

Hagith Sivan
University of Kansas

Anyone bold enough to venture outdoors on a mid-August day in Jerusalem around AD 400 would have encountered a striking contrast. Amidst sweltering heat jubilant voices of women and men, on march to Bethlehem, could be heard singing hymns honoring Mary's maternity. Along the same road silent groups of men clad in mourning clothes and displaying ashes on their heads would be seen approaching the Temple Mount. The first cohort was celebrating an era which, they believed, began with a birth in Bethlehem; the second commemorated the end of an era which, for them, was symbolized by topographical vacancy in the heart of Jerusalem.

On 15 August the Jerusalem liturgical calendar called on believers to march from Jerusalem toward Bethlehem in remembrance of a fateful journey that had borne a pregnant Virgin to Bethlehem. Eulogies of Mary's imminent maternity survived only in fragments that nevertheless confirm the adoption of a mid-August date as the feast day commemorating Mary's approaching motherhood. Scripture itself failed to provide a precedent for either the specific calendrical choice of 15 August or for the location of the celebration. But the date of the first ever recorded memorialization of the Theotokos in Jerusalem was situated precisely at the moment when the Jewish community marked the darkest day in its history, the destruction of the Jerusalemite Temple on the Ninth of Av.[1]

The reckoning highlights two crucial stages in an ongoing effort to elevate Mary and Jerusalem in Late Antiquity. One is the manipulation of the calendar as a result of competing Christian-Jewish calculations of the past. The other is the appropriation of Mary as a cornerstone in a new religious discourse that centered on the city, its bishops, and its environment. I have dealt with the first process elsewhere.[2] Here I intend to trace how the elevation of Mary in a Jerusalemite context contributed to the solidification of the power of the bishops of the city

---

[1] It should be noted that there was no fixed calendar as yet, and that both Jewish and Christian feasts "floated." See S. Stern, *Calendar and Community: A History of the Jewish Calendar 2nd Century BCE–10th Century CE* (Oxford, 2001).

[2] H. Sivan, "Contesting Calendars: The 9th of Av and the Feast of the Theotokos," in B. Caseau, J.-C. Cheynet, and V. Déroche (eds.), *Pèlerinages et lieux saints dans l'antiquité*

over their territory, particularly in opposition to the monastic circles in Bethlehem. Beyond the immediate Palestinian context the struggle between two contrasting interpretations of Mary, as virgin and as mother, celestial and earthly, shaped an empire-wide promotion of her maternity, rather than virginity, and concomitantly catapulted the see of Jerusalem to the coveted rank of patriarchy.[3]

Constantine, Jerusalem and the Topography of Birth Pangs

The attention showered by Constantine and the imperial family on Jerusalem and Bethlehem in the 330s created a paradox.[4] Although central to two poles of Jesus' life, Jerusalem's past was primarily Jewish, as was Bethlehem's. But Jews had been all but banned from Jerusalem since the early second century.[5] Even the more recent memory of Jerusalem as home to a Roman legion was fast fading in the wake of that unit's transfer to Aila on the Red Sea ca. 300. The Christian community had remained a tiny minority clinging to memories of the last days of its founder and to a single church building.[6] On Temple Mount statues of Hadrian and Jupiter occupied the place of Herod's magnificent temple.[7] Where Jesus had been buried, a temple to Aphrodite stood. During the Constantinian era, the fledgling Christian communities of Palestine were under the control of the bishop not of Jerusalem but of Caesarea, the provincial capital.

In 335 a large assembly of bishops attended the spectacular inauguration of the Church of the Holy Sepulcher.[8] The ceremony had been orchestrated through an exemplary alliance between church and state, the former represented by Eusebius, the metropolitan bishop of Caesarea, the latter by a special imperial emissary with a lavish expense account.[9] Constantine himself was not present for the occasion. In fact, none of his fourth-century imperial successors would evince an equal interest in Jerusalem—with the noteworthy exception of Julian. In the fifth century the city

et le moyen âge: Mélanges offerts à Pierre Maraval (Paris, 2006) 443–56. See also Eadem, *Palestine in Late Antiquity* (Oxford 2008) 230–43.

3 A detailed study of the Jerusalem episcopate in the 5th century is a desideratum.

4 E.D. Hunt, "Constantine and Jerusalem," *JEH* 48 (1997) 405–24.

5 O. Irshai, "Constantine and the Jews: The Prohibition against Entering Jerusalem—History and Hagiography," *Zion* 60 (1995) 129–78 (in Hebrew).

6 H.-L. Vincent and F.-M. Abel, *Jérusalem nouvelle*, vol. 2 (Paris, 1925) passim.

7 Y.Z. Eliav, *God's Mountain: The Temple Mount in Time, Place and Memory* (Baltimore, 2005).

8 M.A. Fraser, *The Feast of the Encaenia in the Fourth Century and in the Ancient Liturgical Sources of Jerusalem* (diss. Univ. of Durham, 1995), available through the internet at www.encaenia.org.

9 Cf. M. Edwards (trans. and intro), *Constantine and Christendom* (Liverpool, 2003) xxx, on the cooperation of clergy and sovereign to promote the veneration of sites and relics.

provided residence for an exiled empress and a site for her considerable charitable activities.[10] No emperor ever visited the city in person till Heraclius restored the cross to its church in 628. He was the first and the last Christian Roman ruler to enter the Golden Gate.

Within the territory of the see of Jerusalem, two biblical locales, Bethlehem and Mamre, were included in Constantine's vision of the sanctification of Jerusalem. In Bethlehem Constantine commissioned a church to commemorate the nativity to be built on a site where, it was then believed, Mary had given birth. In fact the imperial enterprise appears to have papered over a controversy that might have arisen as a result of the vagueness of the nativity accounts in the Gospels. A pious biography of Mary, generally assigned to the second century, provides the first detailed description of the events connected with the scene of the momentous birth.[11] The *Protoevangelium of James* narrates the journey of Mary and Joseph to Bethlehem in the following terms:

> And he saddled his [she-] ass and sat her on it; his son led it and Samuel [Joseph] followed. As they drew near the third mile(stone) Joseph turned around and saw her sad and said to himself: Perhaps that which is within her is paining her. And again Joseph turned around and saw her laughing. And he said to her: Mary, why is it that I see your face at one time laughing and at another sad? And she said to him: Joseph, I see with my eyes two peoples, one weeping and lamenting and one rejoicing and exulting. As they came half the way [between Jerusalem and Bethlehem] Mary said to him: Joseph, take me down from the ass for the child within me presses me to come forth. And he took her down there and said to her: Where shall I take you and hide your shame? For the place is desert. And he found a cave there and brought her into it, and left her in care of his sons and went out to seek a Hebrew midwife in the region of Bethlehem.[12]

---

10 K.G. Holum, *Theodosian Empresses: Women and Imperial Dominion in Late Antiquity* (Berkeley, 1982) passim, esp. 112–46 on Eudocia. E.D. Hunt, *Holy Land Pilgrimage in the Later Roman Empire* (Oxford, 1992) 221–48 (on Eudocia). On imperial women in general and their Palestinian connection, see N. Lenski, "Empresses in the Holy Land: The Creation of a Christian Utopia in Late-Antique Palestine," in L. Ellis and F. Kidner (eds.), *Travel, Communication, and Geography in Late Antiquity* (Ashgate, 2004) 113–24.

11 R.E. Brown, *The Birth of the Messiah: A Commentary on the Infancy Narratives in Matthew and Luke* (Garden City, NJ, 1977; reprint. 1993), and R.A. Wortham, *Social-Scientific Approaches in Biblical Literature* (Lewiston, NY, 1999), esp. 116–17, assert a chronology as follows: Matthew > *Protoevangelium of James* > Luke. This would suggest that the *Prot.Jam.* is not the latest nativity narrative.

12 *Prot.Jam.* 17.1–18.1 (Greek text now available on the internet at www-user.uni-bremen.de). Trans. from B. Roberts Gaventa, *Mary: Glimpses of the Mother of Jesus* (Columbia, SC, 1995) 133–45 at 140–41. On the work, its provenance and date see ibid., 105–22; R. Cameron (ed.), *The Other Gospels* (Philadelphia, 1982); and T. Horner, "Jewish Aspects of the *Protoevangelium of James*," *JECS* 12 (1993) 313–17. See also the comments

The city of Bethlehem may not, then, have been the site of the Nativity, but it was too crucial for a narrative that embedded Jesus in a Davidic lineage to be set aside in favor of a cave somewhere in its vicinity. The cave which the *Protoevangelium* located between Jerusalem and Bethlehem was therefore identified firmly as a feature of the town itself. In the words of the pilgrim who provides the earliest eyewitness account of the landscape that came to be crafted by the endeavors of the imperial court:

> Two miles further on [from Rachel's tomb], on the left, is Bethlehem, where the Lord Jesus Christ was born, and where a basilica has been built by command of Constantine.[13]

Constantine's confidence in locating the scene of the nativity was based on tenuous biblical interpretation.[14] Like the *Protoevangelium*, Justin (mid-second century), who originally hailed from Palestine, placed the pregnant Mary in a cave near Bethlehem without further specificity.[15]

To lend scriptural authority to the edifice in Bethlehem, Eusebius could have reassured both the emperor and his mother that no less a biblical exegete than Origen had firmly located the birth of the "messiah," namely Jesus, in biblical Bethlehem on the basis of a famous biblical prophecy (Mic. 5:1).[16] The fact that in Late Antiquity Jewish biblical exegesis was less certain about the location of the biblical Bethlehem had little effect on the intertwining of both cave and town into the nativity narratives.[17]

---

by J.E. Taylor, *Christians and the Holy Places* (Oxford, 1993) 101–2, who, like Jerome below, dismisses altogether the account.

[13] *Itinerarium Burdigalense* 598: *inde milia duo a parte sinistra est Bethleem, ubi natus est dominus Iesus Christus; ibi basilica facta est iussu Constantini.* Translation at J. Wilkinson, *Egeria's Travels to the Holy Land* (Jerusalem, 1981) 162. As Wilkinson notes, the church itself was dedicated only six years after the pilgrim recorded his journey. On the translation of biblical topography into the Christianized landscape of Palestine with the "help" of Scripture, Hebrew inscriptions, and Jewish learning, see R. Wilken, *The Land Called Holy: Palestine in Christian History and Thought* (New Haven, CT, 1992); A.S. Jacobs, *Remains of the Jews: The Holy Land and Christian Empire in Late Antiquity* (Stanford, 2004).

[14] See Cyr.Hier. *Cat.Lec.* 12.20, with Taylor, *Christians*, 98, refers to the forested district of Bethlehem shorn of its wood to make room for the church.

[15] Just. *Dial.Try.* 78, quoted in Taylor, *Christians*, 99.

[16] The terms used by Micah describe a primordial ruler which Christian biblical exegesis applied to the messiah and to Jesus, N.R.M. de Lange, *Origen and the Jews* (Cambridge, 1976) 99. Taylor, *Christians*, 103, quoting Orig. *C.Cels.* 1.51, points to a mid-3rd-century local tradition that identified a cave in Bethlehem as the scene of the Nativity and the manger.

[17] *GenR* 82.

The sudden attention showered by the imperial court on Jerusalem and its environs emboldened the city's episcopate to embark on ambitious enterprises. Under Constantine's successors, Cyril, whose episcopate spanned the reigns of Constantius II, Julian, Valens, and Theodosius I (339/40–386/7), invested considerable energy in promoting his see. Through the creation of a comprehensive liturgical cycle Cyril reconstructed Jerusalem as a concrete reflection of lived Christianity. Concomitantly, he advocated a pan-Palestinian discourse whose reasoning promoted a reversal in the ecclesiastical hierarchy from Caesarea to Jerusalem as the foremost see.[18]

Cyril wielded the cross as an autochthonous symbol of his city.[19] In a letter addressed to Constantius II, the bishop described an apparition which he promptly interpreted as a huge heavenly cross benignly stretched over the Jerusalem skyline.

> In these holy days of this Pentecost on the seventh of the month of Iyyar, at about the third hour of the day, a cross splendid in size and fashioned as if of lights appeared in heaven above the place of our Lord's crucifixion, which is Golgotha, extending as far as the holy place which is called the Mount of Olives.[20]

The timing of this apparition (May 351), its distinct shape and its size reflected a community anxious to edify by telling its story to itself, to others, and to posterity. Similar visions had already guided Constantius' father, not least in campaigns against rivals to the imperial throne.[21] But the Jerusalem cross enjoyed a unique relationship with the territory where it appeared. It had roots in the foundational scenes of the creed itself.

---

[18] Z. Rubin, "The Church of the Holy Sepulchre and the Conflict between the Sees of Caesarea and Jerusalem," *TJC* 2 (1982) 79–105; Idem, "The See of Caesarea in Conflict with Jerusalem from Nicaea to Chalcedon," in A. Raban and K.G. Holum (eds.), *Caesarea Maritima: Retrospective after Two Millennia* (Leiden, 1996) 559–74 at 562–7. P. Walker, *Holy City, Holy Places? Christian Attitudes to Jerusalem and the Holy Land in the Fourth Century* (Oxford, 1990).

[19] On the centrality of the cross in Cyril's doctrine of the faith, see A.J. Doval, *Cyril of Jerusalem: Mystagogue* (Washington, DC, 2001) 176–85; J.W. Drijvers, "Promoting Jerusalem: Cyril and the True Cross," in Idem and J.W. Watt (eds.), *Portraits of Spiritual Authority* (Leiden, 1999) 79–95; O. Irshai. "Cyril of Jerusalem: The Apparition of the Cross and the Jews," in O. Limor and G.G. Stroumsa (eds.), *Contra Iudaeos: Ancient and Medieval Polemics between Christians and Jews* (Tübingen, 1996) 85–104.

[20] J.F. Coakley, "A Syriac Version of the Letter of Cyril of Jerusalem on the Vision of the Cross," *AB* 102 (1984) 71–84, translation of section 4 on p. 82. On the date, see E. Bihain, "L'Épître de Cyrille de Jérusalem à Constance sur la vision de la croix, " *Byzantion* 43 (1973) 264–96. See also Jan Willem Drijvers' essay in this volume (Chapter 18).

[21] See the essays of H.A. Drake and Jacqueline Long in this volume (Chapters 16 and 17, respectively).

Although Constantius proved uninterested, the event produced its own momentum.[22] It was celebrated annually among other festivities which started to crowd the calendar of a Christianized Jerusalem in Late Antiquity. In the hands of Constantine and Cyril, Jerusalem's nascent topography retraced the successive stages of Jesus' period in and around the city. The active participation of pilgrims in the endless succession of festivities further cultivated a relationship that had been carefully forged between topography and rituals. As Christians flocked to the Holy Land, the experience of seeing drew the biblical text onto the border between hearing and touching, extracting the past from the present.[23]

John and Jerome: The Meaning of Maternity and the Battle over No-Man's Land

By the early 380s Bethlehem served as a crucial point of departure for the Feast of the Epiphany in January, as celebrated in Jerusalem and as recorded by Egeria.[24] The insertion of the town into the Jerusalem liturgical map epitomized the colonization of the Holy City's hinterland. It also bred dissension. In the Jerusalem orbit the Epiphany commemorated the Nativity, in contrast with western tradition which linked the Nativity with Christmas.[25] For Jerome, resident in Bethlehem since 386, the Bethlehem cave represented a stunning manifestation of an exceptional collusion between earthly elements and divine design.[26] Yet in a sermon on the Nativity he vigorously defended the western date of Christmas against the Jerusalem date.[27] Such opposition suggests that not all the liturgical and

[22] In June of the same year (351), Constantius defeated Magnentius. Cyril may have had greater success had he addressed Gallus, rather than Constantius, who ruled the Orient on Constantius' behalf. It is curious that at the very same moment of vision and victory, an otherwise unknown "Patricius" apparently attempted to engage in a usurpation which Ursicinus quickly quelled. Aur.Vict. *Caes.* 42.11 juxtaposes the two "revolts," that of Magnentius in Gaul and of Patricius and the Jews. Jer. *chron.* s.a. 355 claims that many Palestinian cities were destroyed in the course of the "revolt," an assertion not entirely borne out by the archaeological data. See J. Geiger, "The Revolt under Gallus and the Temple Building under Julian," in Z. Baras et al. (eds.), *Eretz Israel from the Destruction of the Second Temple to the Muslim Conquest* (Jerusalem, 1982) 202–8 (in Hebrew).

[23] F. Cardman, "The Rhetoric of Holy Places: Palestine in the Fourth Century," *StudPatr* 17 (1982) 18–25, esp. 23.

[24] *Itin.Eg.* 25.

[25] Hunt, *Holy Land Pilgrimage*, 111–12.

[26] *Ep.* 147.4; cf. *Ep.* 108.10. In *Ep.* 46.11 (written in spring of 386) Jerome gives Marcella a moving description of the Nativity Grotto and describes it in language that conjures images of a portal between heaven and earth.

[27] Jer. *Hom.* 88 (*CCSL* 78.524–9, esp. 527ff). English translation by M.L. Ewald, *Jerome, Homilies* vol. 2. Fathers of the Church 57 (Washington, DC, 1966). Cf. Hunt, *Holy Land Pilgrimage*, 112 n.19.

topographical choices advanced by the bishops of Jerusalem enjoyed the backing of weighty intellectuals.

The clash over the date of the Nativity indicates the disproportionate significance of what was at stake. With Jerome as the mouthpiece of the Bethlehem monastic community, the ongoing attempts to establish the primacy of Jerusalem in Bethlehem were submitted to a critical if not downright hostile reading. We know that Jerome's period in Bethlehem corresponded nearly exactly with the episcopate of Cyril's successor, John (386/7–417/8). Already in the early 390s a bitter quarrel erupted between the two over orthodoxy and Origenism, specifically regarding the alleged Origenist affiliation of the Jerusalemite prelate. Jerome ranged with Epiphanius of Cypriote Salamis, formerly of Eleutheropolis in Palestine, who instituted himself as a champion of orthodoxy and mounted a campaign against John.[28] The theological altercation spawned multifarious assaults. Only those composed by Jerome and Epiphanius survive.

In an apologetic letter written to Theophilus of Alexandria, John claimed that the dispute was not doctrinal but personal. He accused Jerome of deliberately providing a distraction in order to protect himself against accusations of misconduct for colluding in the unlawful ordination of his brother Paulinianus.[29] The ordaining bishop should have been John, in whose diocese the monastery was situated, and not Epiphanius from Salamis. In defense of what seemed indefensible Jerome asserted that John had neglected his duty towards both the monks in Bethlehem and all Christians who required basic church services. A desperate situation, claimed Jerome, called for radical remedies:

> A few months ago, about the day of Pentecost, when the sun was darkened and all the world dreaded the immediate coming of the Judge, forty candidates of different ages and sexes were presented to your presbyter for baptism. There were five presbyters in the monastery [in Bethlehem] who had the right to baptize. But they were unwilling to do anything to move you [i.e. John] to anger ... You commanded your presbyters at Bethlehem not to give baptism to our candidates at Easter so that we sent them to Diospolis to the confessor and bishop Dionysius for baptism. Are we then said to rend the church who, outside our cells, hold no position in the Church? Or do not you rather rend the church who issue an order to your clergy that if any one says Paulinianus was consecrated presbyter by Epiphanius he is to be forbidden to enter the church. Ever since that time to this day we can only look from without on the cave of the Savior and, while heretics enter, we stand afar off and sigh.[30]

---

[28] Jer. *Ep.* 51 (a. 394). In general, E.A. Clark, *The Origenist Controversy: The Cultural Construction of an Early Christian Debate* (Princeton, 1992).

[29] Jer. *Ep.* 82 and *C.Ioh.Hier.*

[30] *C.Ioh.Hier.* 42 (*CCSL* 79A) (a. 397–9). English translation in *NPNF* 2.6, now available through various internet sites.

Bethlehem, it seems, had become a battlefield between on the one hand the episcopate that nominally controlled the town, its sanctuaries, and its Christian dwellers, and on the other its monastic population. The dispute played itself out over the question of orthodoxy and heterodoxy, but the verbal battle between the belligerent Jerome and John reveals that other things were at stake, including the town's topography.[31] Both employed fundamentally similar language. Jerome cast himself as the patron of candidates for baptism while he portrayed John as an intruder afflicted with a twofold evil, being both "heretical" and arbitrary. For John, Jerome craved an intolerable autarchy based on the patent violation of ecclesiastical law. Both came with formidable entourages of supporters, including the monastic community in Jerusalem headed by Melania and Rufinus.[32] John banned Jerome and his "brothers" from communion and secured, in 395, an imperial decree which would have removed him from Palestine.[33] The stipulations of John's proposed excommunication of Jerome and his community included barring Jerome and his cohorts from entering the Cave and the Church of the Nativity as well as from other churches in the diocese of Jerusalem, and forbidding the priests in Jerome's monastery to administer the sacraments during the three years of the excommunication.[34] Fortunately for Jerome the threat of a Hunnic invasion in the same year, and the fall of Rufinus, John's patron at the court, prevented the execution of the decree. The end of the affair was forgotten amidst the shadows of Pelagianism which engulfed Palestinian Christianity in another bitter conflict in the second decade of the fifth century. Jerome remembered these local conflicts as more vehement than battles with barbarians.[35]

The continuing opposition of the Bethlehem monastic community to the Jerusalem episcopate in the 390s implied that ceremonies for which Bethlehem was indispensable could no longer be used to affirm the authority of the Jerusalemite see. The universality to which the liturgy of Jerusalem had laid claim shrank. Jerome's and Epiphanius' actions created a vacant space at the heart of a map otherwise controlled by the establishment in Jerusalem.

Already in 394, at the dawn of the Origenist controversy in Palestine, John embarked on a novel strategy aimed at asserting Jerusalem's foundational role over the territory between the city and Bethlehem. To aide the campaign he put forward two formidable "heroes": the Church as the "mother of all churches" (*mater omnium ecclesiarum*), and Mary as the mother of the Messiah.[36] To deepen

---

31 J.N.D. Kelly, *Jerome: His Life, Writings and Controversies* (London, 1975) passim, on the stormy relations between the two.

32 E.D. Hunt, "From Dalmatia to the Holy Land: Jerome and the World of Late Antiquity," *JRS* 67 (1977) 170–74 at 170; and Idem, *Holy Land Pilgrimage*, 155–9.

33 Jer. *Ep.* 82.10; *C.Ioh.Hier.* 43. Hunt, *Holy Land Pilgrimage*, 190.

34 P. Nautin, "L'excommunication de saint Jérôme," *AEHE V* 80/81 (1972–73) 7–37.

35 *Ep.* 77.8.

36 The Latin expression was included in a *titulus* in St. Martin's church at Tours. The *titulus* was appended to a depiction of the Church of Zion in Jerusalem which John

and complicate the power of his see John placed side by side two heritages, Jewish and Christian. He sponsored a major building project south of the existing city walls which he dedicated on the Jewish Day of Atonement (Yom Kippur). He also extended the liturgical calendar of Jerusalem by adding a liturgical station on the road to Bethlehem on the Jewish Day of the Memorialization of the destroyed Temple, the Ninth of Av. The first enterprise is well documented. The second is my reconstruction.

On 15 September 394 John (re?)dedicated the great Church of Zion.[37] To commemorate the occasion he delivered a sermon which extolled not the earthly establishment he had commissioned but the very concept of sanctity. In his vision of the Church of Holy Zion the edifice stood as the visible symbol of the entire Church and its union with the Holy Spirit.[38] This was the heavenly Temple itself, an image of Paradise as projected in Exodus 25–7. John delineated seven divine circles, each of which projected a different figure of the Church.[39] The seven projections embraced the heaven of heavens, the heavenly Jerusalem, the Garden of Eden, Noah's ark, Mount Moriah, Mount Sinai, and the interior tabernacle. Words and stones engendered a new humankind:

> Let us come, then, friends of Christ and citizens of heaven, let us rejoice in God's royal mansions, let us be spirit and not flesh, angels and not breathing humans, Seraphim and Cherubim reciting the *trisagion* and not blood from which the Spirit escapes after doing battle against the exterior, sun and moon or morning star with the long hair, and not terrestrial reptiles who creep in the darkness.[40]

Central to John's panegyric was the ideology of propitiation and purification, two basic distinctions of the Jewish Day of Atonement (Yom Kippur), the day of the delivery of the dedicatory sermon. The conjunction hardly could have been a

had dedicated (see below). Cf. M. Van Esbroeck, "La vie arabe de Saint Théodose le Cénobiarque," *POr* 18 (1993) 45–73 at 108.

37 M. Van Esbroeck, "Une homélie sur l'église attribuée à Jean de Jérusalem," *Muséon* 86 (1973) 283–304; Idem, "Jean II de Jérusalem et les cultes de S. Étienne, de la sainte Sion et de la Croix," *AB* 102 (1984) 99–134 at 115–25, see 100 on the date. The precise location of the Zion church remains unclear and controversial, as does John's precise association with it—was he its builder or restorer? It may have been erected on top of a standing synagogue which the Bordelais pilgrim had seen in 333. What is clear is that the hill which Christians identified as "Sion" was not the Zion of the Hebrew Bible. See P.J. Leithart, "Where Was Ancient Zion?," *TynBull* 53 (2002) 161–75; K. Bieberstein, "Die Hagia Sion in Jerusalem: Zur Entwicklung ihrer Traditionen im Spiegel des Pilgerberichte," *JbAC* 20 (1995) 543–51. Taylor, *Christians*, 212–13, objects to the association of John with the Zion church which, according to her, had already been built in the middle of the 4th century.

38 Van Esbroeck, "Jean II de Jérusalem," 109.

39 Doval, *Cyril*, 218–19.

40 Joh.Hier. *Hom.* 31 = Van Esbroeck, "Jean II de Jérusalem," 118. Trans. from Doval, *Cyril*, 219.

coincidence.[41] The Jewish liturgy of Yom Kippur, as preserved in the late ancient poetry of the synagogue (*piyyutim*), emphasized Temple service as being bound up with the work of Creation and with the rebuilding of the Temple.[42] In the guise of a dedicatory ceremony of a single church, whose name (Zion) symbolized the contract between God and Israel, John aimed at a simultaneous recollection of the biblical text and its subsequent exegesis. The Church, like the heavenly Temple, was the ultimate outcome of the ultimate atonement.

The church of Zion occupied the earliest meeting point of the ur-Christian community and thus represented the foundational locus of the Christian empire. The building's dedication in the late fourth century highlighted the common origin of the contemporary community even while claiming the honor of antiquity. In 415 the Church provided the background for another ceremony carefully calculated to bolster the position of the Jerusalemite ecclesiastical establishment. In the midst of a synod (in Diospolis/Lydda) dealing with Pelagius, John of Jerusalem hastened to lend his presence and authentication to the discovery of the bones of no less a figure than the proto-martyr Stephen.[43] John presided over the prompt transfer of the precious relics to Jerusalem where they were carefully, if temporarily (as it turned out), deposited in the Church of Zion, the very place where Stephen had been chosen one of the seven original deacons.[44]

John probably knew of Jerome's displeasure with Christians who participated in the ceremonies of Yom Kippur.[45] Dedicating the first church beyond the walls on that day was a mark of defiance and a sign of John's authority. I would argue that the addition of a feast in honor of Mary's maternity, to be celebrated on the road to Bethlehem, represented another manifestation of John asserting his prerogative of promoting the lore of his land.

For Jerome, Mary symbolized Christian holiness and purity wholly detached from the specificity of biographical circumstances.[46] He rejected the narrative provided in the *Protoevangelium of James*:

---

41 See D. Stökl Ben Ezra, *The Impact of Yom Kippur on Early Christianity: The Day of Atonement from Second Century Temple to the Fifth Century* (Tübingen, 2003), on the relationship between Christian theology and Jewish liturgy.

42 Yosse ben Yosse, *Azkir Gevurot*, 1–12. Hebrew text in A. Mirsky, *Yosse ben Yosse Poems* (Jerusalem, 1991) 127–9. See also W. Horbury, "Suffering and Messianism in Yose ben Yose," in Idem and B. McNeil (eds.), *Suffering and Martyrdom in the New Testament: Studies Presented to G.M. Styler by the Cambridge New Testament Seminar* (Cambridge, 1981) 143–82, with English translation on p. 168.

43 S. Vanderlinden, "Revelatio Sancti Stephani," *REB* 4 (1946) 178–217; Hunt, *Holy Land Pilgrimage*, 203–20.

44 Acts 6:5; Hunt, *Holy Land Pilgrimage*, 217.

45 Jer. *Com.Gal.* 2 (*CCSL* 77A) with Stökl Ben Ezra, *Impact of Yom Kippur*, 306.

46 *Hom.* 93 (on Easter Sunday) and *Hom.* 88 (on the Nativity of the Lord), with T. Perry, *Mary for Evangelicals* (Downers Grove, IL, 2006) 161–5 on Jerome on Mary.

> No midwife assisted at his birth. No women's officiousness intervened. With her own hands she wrapped him in the swaddling clothes, herself both mother and midwife, and laid him, we are told, in a manger because there was no room for them in the inn (Luke 2:7), a statement which … refutes the ravings of the apocryphal accounts, for Mary herself wrapped him in the swaddling clothes.[47]

There was no biblical account of Joseph's first marriage nor of the previous betrothal of Mary, once again in contrast with the *Protoevangelium*.[48] Maternity was external to Mary, who had remained a virgin throughout. Jerome's configuration envisaged the manger not so much as a tangible reality as an allusion with the power to provoke images of the biblical text. The topography in which Constantine had blazed the pilgrimage trail enabled pious pilgrims like Paula to see "with the eyes of faith" the wrapped infant crying, the wise men, the star, the virgin mother, and the foster father.[49]

To remove Mary from Bethlehem by taking the popular *Protoevangelium* literally suggested a new approach to Mary which recalibrated the balance between virginity, nativity, and maternity. The Memorialization of Mary on 15 August / 9 Av celebrated an incontestably parturient mother at the place where she rested on the verge of delivery. The emphasis on her as a mother rather than a perpetual virgin negated both Jerome's rejection of the *Protoevangelium* and his interpretation of the same scene. John's action further defied Jerome's ally, Epiphanius, who had advocated the Mystery of Mary rather than her temporal and spatial localization.[50] Biblical geography provided John with further material to bolster his selection of a no man's land for the feast of Mary. Genesis had placed Rachel's death in childbirth somewhere on the way to Bethlehem; John located in the same area Christ's birth by Mary, through whom the fragile balance between delivery and death was restored.

Archaeological excavations have unearthed two churches in close proximity to one another between Jerusalem and Bethlehem.[51] One was attached to a monastery, while the other, an octagon, was an independent structure. Both have been taken as structures dedicated to the Kathisma, the place where Mary had rested, and

---

See also G. Rocca, *L'Adversus Helvidium di san Girolamo nel contesto della letteratura ascetico-mariana del secolo IV* (Bern, 1998).

47 *Adv.Helv.* 10 (*Liber de perpetua virginitate B.Mariae*). Trans. from *NPNF*.

48 Ibid., 4.

49 Jer. *Ep.* 108.9.

50 *Adv.Haer.* 78.11 (c. 370).

51 S.J. Shoemaker, "The (Re?)Discovery of the Kathisma Church and the Cult of the Virgin in Late Antique Palestine," *Maria* 2 (2001) 21–72, largely repeated in Idem, *Ancient Traditions of the Virgin Mary's Dormition and Assumption* (Oxford, 2002). On the excavation see, R. Avner, "The Recovery of the Kathisma Church and its Influence on Octagonal Buildings," in G.C. Bottini, L. Di Segni, and L.D. Chrupcała (eds.), *One Land—Many Cultures: Archaeological Studies in Honor of S. Loffreda* (Jerusalem, 2003) 173–86.

both have been dated to the fifth century. In fact, however, the chronology of the construction of each church and their relative(?) chronology remains unclear. Based on textual sources, I tentatively propose a date of construction for the monastic Kathisma in the first decade of the fifth century, during the lull between the Palestinian phases of the Origenist and the Pelagianist controversies. A sixth-century *vita* honoring an ascetic named Theodosius indicates that in the middle of the fifth century a monastery named the Kathisma had already been in existence on the road between Jerusalem and Bethlehem for some time.[52] The terminology does not suggest a very recent establishment. Theodosius left the Kathisma to retire to a cave in the mountains, the very cave where the Magi, "setting sail"—a nautical metaphor is inappropriate inasmuch as they would not have gone by boat!—from Bethlehem are alleged to have visited mother and baby.[53] Around this cave he later had a monastery built with funding from wealthy donors.[54] This would have been a new Kathisma, though the narrator does not seem aware of its close proximity to the "old" Kathisma, Theodosius' first monastery. Moreover, according to Theodosius' Arab *vita* the saint had been "in the habit of celebrating once a year the feast of Mary, mother of God."[55] While the date of the feast and its precise nature are omitted, it seems likely to have been the commemoration of Mary's maternity on 15 August on the road to Bethlehem.

The construction of two churches within a few decades of one another to commemorate Mary's resting on roughly the same spot between Jerusalem and Bethlehem illustrates how strategies adopted by the Jerusalem see set in motion a singular process. Beginning with the basic affinity of text to territory, the bishops of Jerusalem articulated its interconnectedness with precise determination. John's alliance with both Zion and Mary, possibly the two most crucial female figures in the Hebrew Bible and the New Testament, respectively, demonstrated the spectrum of affiliation that the city and diocese of Jerusalem afforded its prelates.

Out of a theological no man's land in the 390s John of Jerusalem engendered a new feast that not only allied him with Mary but also modified the regional liturgical landscape. The Memorialization of Mary marginalized Hieronymian

52 *VTheod.* 44 apud Van Esbroeck, "La vie arabe de Saint Théodose," 62. It dates to sometime during the episcopate of Juvenal (422–60).

53 *VTheod.* 55 apud Van Esbroeck, "La vie arabe de Saint Théodose," 63.

54 *VTheod.* 110 apud Van Esbroeck, "La vie arabe de Saint Théodose," 65. The Greek *Vita* composed by Theodorus of Petra (*Vita Theodosii Coenobitarchae*, BHG 1778b) assigns a Marian foundation on the high road to Bethlehem to a pious lady who also requested specifically that Theodosius be appointed to conduct services in the church. Theodosius declined the honor, retired to a cell and later built a spacious monastery nearby, at a place called Kathisma. The monastery's three infirmaries were a gift from another local pious lady. The name of neither woman is given. The narrative appears to conflate the two Kathismas. It also adds, as an afterthought, that the cell to which Theodosius had originally retired and where he was also buried was named the Cave of the Magi.

55 *VTheod.* 136 apud Van Esbroeck, "La vie arabe de Saint Théodose," 66.

Bethlehem by instituting a midsummer march that took believers from Jerusalem in the direction of Bethlehem but stopped short of entering the town itself. It provided a perfect complement to the mid-winter (early January) Feast of the Epiphany which the Jerusalem church celebrated as the Feast of the Nativity with a march beginning at the Constantinian church in Bethlehem and ending in Jerusalem.[56]

The institutionalization of the annual "Memorialization of Mary" shows Jerusalem ahead of both the Pope and the imperial court in promoting and creating a terrain exclusively dedicated to the cult of Mary the Mother.[57] The Kathisma anthropomorphized Mary as the universal provider of life by focusing on the importance of her actual labor and delivery. The road to Bethlehem acted as a guardian of the story of the nativity, a unique location of asexual reproduction. It blurred the borders between the Mary of theology and the Mary of pious narrative, providing a perfect opposition to the later Nestorian model of a distinctly two-natured Jesus, the core of the debate at the council of Ephesos (AD 431):

> They [the bishops at Ephesos] dared to call the holy virgin mother of God, not as though the nature of the Word or his godhead received the origin of their being from the holy virgin, but because there was born from her his holy body rationally ensouled, with which the Word was hypostatically united and is said to have been begotten in the flesh ...[58]

To speak of Mary as the sole incontestable mother, Marian theologians required both dogmatic arguments and a terrain encumbered with her footprints. In order to broach the debate about the two natures of Jesus they required both the natural and the artificial in Mary. Without denying her virginity, they needed to emphasize Mary's maternity, and the Kathisma, like the *Protoevangelium*, loudly proclaimed the latter. Between the cave in Bethlehem and the sitting stone on the road between Jerusalem and Bethlehem, the Palestinian version of Mary embodied and thus empowered a benevolent protectress of a godly child. Because they anchored Mary to the ground on which they—and she—sat, they made it impossible to exclude Mary the Mother from what became the Christian orthodox ideology of Christ.

---

56 Wilkinson, *Egeria*, 79, 262.

57 Egeria, *Itin.Eg.* 26 briefly refers to Mary (and Joseph) in connection with the presentation at the Temple. As Wilkinson, *Egeria*, 80, remarks, her description of the Epiphany, the feast connected with the presentation, is incomplete. Wilkinson points to its close links with Bethlehem and the Nativity—the feast begins there with rituals including Gospel reading in the cave of the Nativity, culminates with a midnight celebration of the Eucharist, and is followed by the departure of the bishop and monks back to Jerusalem to carry on with the feast in the Anastasis.

58 First Letter of Cyril to Nestorius, 1, in N.P. Tanner (ed.), *Decrees of the Ecumenical Councils* (Washington, DC, 1990) 2.

Chapter 27

Christianity in War: Ammianus on Power and Religion in Constantius' Persian War*

John Weisweiler
St. John's College, Cambridge

One spring morning in 359, shortly after sunrise, from a mountain somewhere in the region of Corduene (in the frontier region between modern Turkey and Iraq), a Roman officer on a reconnaissance mission spotted a vast Persian army on the horizon.[1] The army had been assembled by the Persian Great King Shapur II (309–72). Soon the soldiers would cross the border into Roman Mesopotamia. Shapur's last campaign against the Roman emperor Constantius II, Constantine's last surviving son, was another act in the bitter and enduring struggle between Romans and Sasanians for control of the Fertile Crescent.[2] Thirty years after his tour of duty in Persian territory, and now a retired officer in Rome, Ammianus Marcellinus wrote his *Res Gestae*, a 31-book continuation of Tacitus. In books 18 through 20 he gave a detailed account of Shapur's invasion. It is his most extensive account of a war conducted under a Christian emperor.

Ammianus' views on Christianity have provoked widely differing interpretations among modern readers.[3] For scholars such as Sabbah, Hunt, and Matthews, Ammianus was an impartial observer of the new religion.[4] Barnes, by

---

* The paper owes much to the incisive comments and thoughtful criticisms of Jan Willem Drijvers, Christopher Kelly, Gavin Kelly, and Myles Lavan.

1 18.6.20–22. Bare book and paragraph numbers refer to the *Res Gestae,* quoted from the Teubner edition of W. Seyfarth (Leipzig, 1978). Translations are my own except where otherwise indicated.

2 For narrative accounts of the Persian wars of Constantius II see R.C. Blockley, *East Roman Foreign Policy: Formation and Conduct from Diocletian to Anastasius* (Leeds, 1992) 12–24 and 175–82, and P. Barceló, *Constantius II. und seine Zeit: Die Anfänge des Staatskirchentums* (Stuttgart, 2004) 159–67 and 242–4.

3 Earlier scholarship on Ammianus' religion is conveniently summarized by R.L. Rike, *Apex Omnium: Religion in the Res Gestae of Ammianus* (Berkeley, 1987) 1–7.

4 E.D. Hunt, "Ammianus Marcellinus and Christianity," *CQ* 35 (1985) 186–200, restated in Idem, "Christianity in Ammianus Marcellinus Revisited," *StudPatr* 24 (1993) 108–13; J.F. Matthews, *The Roman Empire of Ammianus* (London, 1989) 445–51, 548–9; and G. Sabbah, "Ammianus Marcellinus," in G. Marasco (ed.), *Greek and Roman Historiography in Late Antiquity: Fourth to Sixth Century AD* (Leiden, 2003) 43–84 at 66–72.

contrast, has argued that Ammianus was a subtle anti-Christian polemicist whose hostility to Christianity resulted in some severe distortions in his presentation of events, a view accepted in Gavin Kelly's important new study on Ammianus' intertextuality.[5]

This paper explores the place of Christianity in Ammianus' account of the Persian war of 359–61. If it looks again at Ammianus' relationship to the new religion, its aim is not to determine whether his representation of Christianity was fair or biased. Rather, this paper proposes to explore the ways in which the *Res Gestae* responded to and engaged with contemporary Christian ideas about the relationship between political power and religion. In sermons, hymns, saints' lives, or martyr acts, Christian contemporaries of Ammianus articulated views on the role of their religion in war which differed strikingly from those he expressed in his history. These rich materials have never been systematically brought to bear on interpretations of the *Res Gestae*.[6] By doing this, this paper will trace Ammianus' engagement with the thought-world of contemporary Christianity. It will emerge that in his history Ammianus offered a subtle and deliberately ironic redeployment of contemporary Christian ideas of the relationship between religion and power. The traditional alternatives of bias or impartiality are insufficient to grasp the wit and sophistication of his treatment.

Making Peace with the Dead

Some weeks after his reconnaissance mission in Corduene, Ammianus stood on the walls of Amida (modern Diyarbakır in south-eastern Turkey) and observed the smoke rising from the surrounding grain fields.[7] The Roman army had deliberately set them on fire in the hope that scorched-earth tactics would impede the advance

---

[5] T.D. Barnes, *Ammianus Marcellinus and the Representation of Historical Reality* (Ithaca, NY, 1998) and G.A.J. Kelly, *Ammianus Marcellinus: the Allusive Historian* (Cambridge, 2008) 3–4, 156–8 and passim. Ammianus had earlier been characterized as a militant pagan by T.G. Elliott, *Ammianus Marcellinus and Fourth Century History* (Toronto, 1983), and by Rike, *Apex*.

[6] The potential of such an approach is revealed by the thoughtful explorations of the links between the *Res Gestae* and contemporary Christian texts by G. Sabbah, *La méthode d'Ammien Marcellin: Recherches sur la construction du discours historique dans les* Res Gestae (Paris, 1978) 366–71; V. Neri, *Ammiano e il cristianesimo: Religione e politica nelle* Res Gestae *di Ammiano Marcellino* (Bologna, 1985); and É. Rebillard, "Note sur les morts de philosophes dans les Histoires d'Ammien Marcellin," in: F. Chausson and É. Wolff (eds.), *Consuetudinis amor: Fragments d'histoire Romaine (IIe–VIe siècles) offerts à Jean-Pierre Callu* (Rome, 2003) 371–8.

[7] On the archaeology of the site see the excellent survey of S. Gregory, *Roman Military Architecture on the Eastern Frontier* (Amsterdam, 1996) 2.59–65 with the figures and maps at 3.C1.

of the Persian enemy.[8] While Ammianus and other Roman officers were hastily organizing the defence of the frontier, the commander of the Roman army in the east, Sabinianus, remained inactive 150km to the southwest in Edessa (modern Urfa), the capital of the province of Osrhoene:

> While these hasty measures were being taken, Sabinianus ... amid the tombs of Edessa feared nothing, as if he had made peace with the dead, and lazily led a debauched life. Completely inactive, instead of theatrical performances, he was entertained by military parades to march music. Both deed and place were ill-omened, for we have learnt in the course of time that leading men in particular must avoid these and similar actions, sad in word and act, and portending future turmoil.[9]

The Christian cult sites located in the cemeteries of Edessa were well known across the Roman empire;[10] the most famous was the shrine of the Apostle Thomas in the south-west cemetery of the city. According to an ancient tradition, Thomas' body had been brought there from India, the place of his martyrdom.[11] Nearby was the mausoleum of King Abgar, reputedly the first ruler to convert to Christianity and the recipient of a letter from Jesus Christ himself.[12] Located in the cemetery to the north of the city walls were the tombs of the local martyrs Gurya, Shmona, and Habbib, who had died in Edessa during the persecutions of Diocletian and Licinius.[13]

Most scholars agree that "the tombs of Edessa" (*Edessena sepulchra)* where Sabinianus spent his time were the city's martyr memorials, and that he was ridiculed here for his devotion to the Christian cult of the saints.[14] Only Matthews,

---

[8] 18.7.3–6. Ephr. *Carm.Nis.* 4–6, offers a contemporary local perspective on the events.

[9] 18.7.7: *Dum haec celerantur, Sabinianus ... per Edessena sepulchra quasi fundata cum mortuis pace nihil formidans more uitae remissioris fluxius agens militari pyrrico* (*pyrrice* Clark) *sonantibus modulis pro histrionicis gestibus in silentio summo delectabatur ominoso sane et incepto et loco, cum haec et huiusmodi factu dictuque tristia futuros praenuntiantia motus uitare optimum quemque debere saeculi progressione discamus.*

[10] On the shrines of Edessa, see P. Maraval, *Lieux saints et pèlerinages d'Orient: Histoire et géographie des origines à la conquête arabe* (Paris, 1985) 350–52, and P. Devos, "Égérie à Édesse: S. Thomas l'Apôtre. Le roi Abgar," *AB* 85 (1972) 381–400.

[11] J.B. Segal, *Edessa: the Blessed City* (Oxford, 1970) 175.

[12] Ibid., 80.

[13] L. Greisiger, "Habbib," *BBKL* 26 (2006) 601–5; and Idem, "Šmona und Gurya," *BBKL* 26 (2006) 1438–44, with extensive bibliographies. See also Segal, *Edessa,* 182.

[14] S. D'Elia, "Ammiano Marcellino e il cristianesimo," *SR* 10 (1962) 372–90 at 389; G. Sabbah (ed.), *Ammien Marcellin: Histoire Tome II (Livres XVII–XIX)* (Paris, 1970) 203 n.6; P. De Jonge, *Sprachlicher und historischer Kommentar zu Ammianus Marcellinus XIV* (Groningen, 1972) 238–9; R.C. Blockley, *Ammianus Marcellinus: A Study of His Historiography and Political Thought* (Brussels, 1975) 128; Hunt, "Ammianus," 195;

with hesitation, and revising an earlier opinion, rejects this interpretation. For him, Ammianus simply described the conduct of military exercises at the city's parade grounds which, like the martyr shrines, were also located outside the walls.[15] Looked at more closely, the two interpretations are not mutually exclusive. On the contrary, it is precisely the combination of military and religious aspects that is key to understanding the passage. Sabinianus visited the martyr tombs in order to mobilize the power located in the holy men's bones for the coming campaign against Shapur. By conducting military exercises at the shrines of Edessa, he hoped to ensure their protection for his army.

In order to gain a better understanding of the significance of this passage, it is necessary to move away from the question of whether Ammianus' views on Christianity were biased or impartial. It is more profitable to attempt to situate his narrative in the context of other contemporary discussions of the Christian martyr cult. Ammianus' criticism of Sabinianus' debauchery at the martyr shrines of Edessa closely parallels the denunciations by Christian preachers against loose behaviour at martyr feasts. For example, John Chrysostom attacked those members of his congregation who used the celebrations as an opportunity to give themselves up to "brothels, bars, drunkenness, and revelry," rather than imitating the lives of the martyrs.[16] According to Basil's homily *On the Inebriated*, on one church holiday the youth of Caesarea even performed obscene mimes at the shrines:

> Licentious women ... cast off from their heads the veils of their decency ... and presented themselves shamelessly to male looks. They moved their hair in agitation, dragging their dress behind themselves, and danced with their feet ... Exciting the desire of all young men, they formed groups in the martyr shrines outside the city and made the holy places a shop floor of their depravity.[17]

When Ammianus described Sabinianus as "lazily leading a relaxed life" at the shrines of Edessa, he cleverly re-used such condemnations of loose behaviour at martyr feasts. He wittily redeployed the concerns of Christian preachers about

---

Rike, *Apex,* 140; Barnes, *Ammianus,* 85–6; J.P. Davies, *Rome's Religious History: Livy, Tacitus, and Ammianus on their Gods* (Cambridge, 2004) 248 and 266 n.140; and Kelly, *Allusive Historian,* 50 and 179.

15 *Ammianus,* 485 n.20, revising the view expressed in "Ammianus Marcellinus," in T. J. Luce (ed.), *Ancient Writers: Greece and Rome* (New York, 1982) 2.1117–38, at 1125.

16 Ioh.Chrys. *Hom.mart.* 668 (*PG* 50.664).

17 *Hom.ebr.* 24–7 (*PG* 31.445). For the accusations of excess in the western debate about correct forms of martyr worship see also Amb. *Ieiun.* 17.62 and Aug. *Ep.* 29.8–10 with P.R.L. Brown, *The Cult of the Saints: Its Rise and Function in Latin Christianity* (Chicago, 1981) 26–7.

excesses at the shrines in order to poke fun at the martyr worship of a Christian general.[18]

But Ammianus' ironic reuse of Christian ideas was not restricted to his depiction of Sabinianus' loose morals. The entire passage is a sustained engagement with a new current in Christian thought. Ever since the Christian God had been credited with securing Constantine the decisive victory over his rival Maxentius at the Battle of the Milvian Bridge, the performance of Christian piety was widely considered an effective means of ensuring military victory. It is for this reason that Christian martyrs increasingly replaced traditional deities as helpers in battle.[19] A few examples may be cited. In 351, during his battle against the usurper Magnentius near Mursa (modern Osijek) in Pannonia, the emperor Constantius did not participate in the hostilities but prayed in a martyr basilica outside the city, surrounded by his clerical entourage.[20] Similarly, when in 379, in the aftermath of the Battle of Adrianople, large areas were threatened by Gothic marauders and the inhabitants of the surrounding regions flocked to Nyssa (Nevşehir) in Cappadocia to celebrate the feast day of St. Theodore, the city's bishop Gregory used the occasion to invoke the martyr's help for the coming military conflict: "Fight for us as a soldier ... We thank you that we were preserved unharmed, and entreat you for protection in the future."[21] Finally, in 394, prior to his campaign against Eugenius, Theodosius participated in numerous processions and prostrated himself at the tombs of martyrs and apostles, explicitly in order to win the help of God for the coming war.[22]

Sabinianus' stay at the martyr shrines of Edessa, by contrast, was not crowned by similar success. While he "was still lingering at the tombs of Edessa" (19.3.1), Shapur progressed swiftly northwards. On the way from Nisibis to the upper Euphrates, Ammianus' unit, surprised by Persian advance troops, sustained heavy

---

18 In fact, as is attested by a contemporary hymn of the poet Ephrem of Nisibis, *Carm. Nis.* 16.30, precisely during these weeks, when the grain fields of Mesopotamia were being burnt by Roman troops, one of the most important martyr festivals of the eastern church was celebrated: the Commemoration of All Martyrs. It was probably specifically for this festival that Sabinianus visited the shrine. On the festival, see Beck's commentary and F. Cabrol, "Fêtes chrétiennes," *DACL* 5 (1965–66) 1403–51 at 1418–19.

19 E.K. Fowden, *The Barbarian Plain: Saint Sergius between Rome and Iran* (Berkeley, 1999) 45–8, and M.W. Graham, *News and Frontier Consciousness in the Late Roman Empire* (Ann Arbor, 2006) 149–54. See also F. Heim, *La théologie de la victoire de Constantin à Théodose* (Paris, 1992).

20 Sulp.Sev. *Chron.* 2.38.5.

21 Greg.Nyss. *STheod.mart.* (*PG* 46.748B = *Gregorii Nysseni Opera* 10.1, *Sermones* 2.70–71, ed. J.P. Cavarnos). For the context of the speech see N. Lenski, "*Initium mali Romano imperio*: Contemporary Reactions to the Battle of Adrianople," *TAPA* 127 (1997) 129–68 at 134–5.

22 Ruf. *HE* 2.33 and Soz. *HE* 7.24.2.

losses; the historian himself barely escaped with his life.[23] The reverses suffered by the Roman army culminated later in the same year in the disastrous sack of the key fortified city of Amida.[24] Far from ensuring victory for the Roman cause through his devotion to the Christian saints, Sabinianus' stay at the tombs of Edessa had precipitated a series of serious defeats. Dissolute, cowardly, and embarrassingly unsuccessful, in Ammianus' version Sabinianus was the antithesis of the ideal Christian general who combined religious faith with military prowess.

Ammianus' irony is reinforced by a pointed allusion to republican literature. In Plautus' comedy *Mostellaria* (*The Haunted House*), the cunning slave Tranio attempts to prevent his master Theopropides—who has unexpectedly returned home from a business trip while his son is hosting a wild party—from entering his house, claiming that it is infested by ghosts. Only he himself, Tranio professes, can enter the house without danger: "I fear nothing, I am at peace with the dead" (*nihil ego formido, pax mihi est cum mortuis*). The phrase, recurring nowhere else in surviving Latin literature, is taken up by Ammianus: at the shrines of Edessa, Sabinianus "feared nothing, as if he had made peace with the dead" (*quasi fundata cum mortuis pace nihil formidans*).[25] The allusion is precise—and significant. Tranio's imaginary ghosts eventually did not prevent Theopropides from putting a sudden end to his son's house party. Similarly, the martyrs invoked by Sabinianus would not halt Shapur's swift advance through Mesopotamia; the fall of Amida would make an unpleasant end to Sabinianus' revelry in Edessa.[26]

Ammianus' account of Sabinianus' martyr worship in Edessa represents a complex engagement with the thought-world of contemporary Christianity. His description of Sabinianus' loose behaviour at the tombs turned, with pointed irony, the denunciations aimed by Christian preachers at those who participated in martyr feasts against a Christian general. And by suggesting that Sabinianus' inappropriate and excessive religious zeal may have brought about the ensuing Roman defeat, Ammianus undermined the notion that there was a direct connection between Christian piety and military success.

---

23 18.7–10; 8 gives the dramatic narrative of Ammianus' escape.

24 19.1–9.

25 Plaut. *Most.* 514; cf. 527. The allusion is noted by Kelly, *Allusive Historian*, 179. He also pertinently observes, at 172 n.33, that Constantius' favourites are frequently compared to the cunning slaves of Plautus' comedies.

26 The comparison of martyrs with ghosts, implied by the allusion, was particularly apt. Julian and Eunapius also took the martyrs revered at Christian shrines to be spectres, souls unable to ascend to heaven because of their sinfulness. Their language is closely echoed by Ammianus: as Hunt, "Ammianus," 195 n.20, notes, the depiction of the devotees of martyr cults by Julian, *Misop.* 344a; *C.Galilaeos*, 335; and Eun. *VSoph.* 472 as "lingering amid tombs and graveyards" (προσκαλινδέσθαι τάφοις) is matched by Ammianus' characterization of Sabinianus as "lingering amid graveyards" (19.3.1 *sepulchris haerentem*).

The Shield of the City

In 360, one year after Sabinianus' participation in the martyr festivals at Edessa, the Persians laid siege to Bezabde. The city, situated on the right bank of the Tigris River, was the easternmost outpost of the Roman province of Mesopotamia.[27] After long and fierce resistance by the Roman army, Bezabde was stormed. Ammianus recorded that many inhabitants were massacred and large numbers led away as prisoners (20.7). During the siege the bishop of Bezabde had visited the Great King in his royal tent to negotiate on the city's behalf. After its fall, he was suspected of treason:

> Nevertheless, suspicion fell upon the bishop, unfounded (I think), although spread by many with insistence, that he had secretly indicated to Shapur which parts of the wall were weak on the inside and so best to attack. This rumour appeared probable because subsequently enemy siege engines keenly attacked precisely the places where the walls were unsafe and crumbling, as if the operators had been familiar with the conditions inside the town.[28]

Some scholars, such as Blockley, see Ammianus' account of the negotiations of the bishop of Bezabde with the Great King as evidence for Ammianus' "disinterested objectivity" toward Christians because he went out of his way to defend the bishop against the false allegations.[29] Others consider this a clear case of anti-Christian bias. Thus, for Barnes, Ammianus employed "rumours to suggest disreputable conduct or a dishonest motive while taking no authorial responsibility for the dubious information thus conveyed."[30]

A close reading of Ammianus' text shows that the accusations against the bishop are particularly prominent. The plea for the bishop's innocence is expressed

---

[27] M.H. Dodgeon and S.N.C. Lieu, *The Roman Eastern Frontier and the Persian Wars (AD 226–363): A Documentary History* (London, 1991) 389–90 n.19, with bibliography.

[28] 20.7.9: *perstrinxit tamen suspicio uana quaedam episcopum, ut opinor, licet asseueratione uulgata multorum, quod clandestino colloquio Saporem docuerat, quae moenium appeteret membra ut fragilia intrinsecus et inualida. hocque exinde veri simile visum est, quod postea intuta loca carieque nutantia cum exsultatione magna, velut regentibus penetralium callidis contemplabiliter machinae feriebant hostiles.*

[29] Blockley, *Study*, 132. Similarly J. Szidat, *Historischer Kommentar zu Ammianus Marcellinus Buch XX–XXI* (Wiesbaden, 1977) 2.17–18; Hunt, "Ammianus," 196; and F. Wittchow, *Exemplarisches Erzählen bei Ammianus Marcellinus: Episode, Exemplum, Anekdote* (Munich, 2001) 187–8.

[30] Barnes, *Ammianus*, 88. Similarly D'Elia, "Cristianesimo," 389; Neri, *Cristianesimo*, 59–61; L. Angliviel de la Beaumelle, "Remarques sur l'attitude d'Ammien Marcellin à l'égard du christianisme," in J. Tréheux (ed.), *Mélanges d'histoire ancienne offerts à William Seston* (Paris, 1974) 15–23 at 20; Sabbah, *Méthode*, 414; J. Den Boeft, D. Den Hengst, and H.C. Teitler, *Philological and Historical Commentary on Ammianus Marcellinus XX* (Stuttgart, 1987) 162–3; and Kelly, *Allusive Historian*, 177–8.

in parentheses and as a "personal opinion" (*ut opinor*). By contrast, his guilt is asserted by the *insistence* of *many* witnesses claiming that he had committed treason (*asseueratione uulgata multorum*) and is then confirmed by the Persians' remarkable precision in accurately (*contemplabiliter*) attacking the weakest spots in the city's defences. The rumours against the bishop, widely believed and compellingly confirmed by circumstantial evidence, drown out a hesitant and lonely authorial voice.

But, regardless of whether or not the authorial denial of these rumours was disingenuous, their significance has to be understood in the context of other representations of the actions of Christian dignitaries in war. Bishops appeared frequently as wartime leaders of their cities in late antique texts. However, rather than being suspected of treason, they usually saved their cities from enemy conquest, either through negotiations with enemy kings or, more spectacularly, by mustering supernatural support from the Christian God.[31] The most famous instance of a bishop as wartime leader of his city was well known to Ammianus. During the wars between Constantius II and Shapur the city of Nisibis was miraculously saved three times from Persian sieges (in 337, 346, and 350) by the piety and prayers of its successive bishops. The story of the delivery of the city in 337 by Jacob became particularly famous and would be commemorated by Jerome in his *Chronicle* (s.a. 338) and adopted and elaborated by many later chroniclers and church historians.[32] When Ammianus arrived in Nisibis in early summer 359 and the city was again threatened by Persian attack, the story took on a new sense of urgency. In these weeks the poet Ephrem wrote two hymns praising the current bishop Abraham in which he reminded the inhabitants of the rescue of the city by Abraham's predecessors and prayed that he would replicate their deeds: "May your fasting be an armour for our land, your prayer a shield for our city!"[33]

Such miraculous rescues of Roman cities by their bishops are frequently described in Christian texts. For example, when Thessalonica could not be taken by the Goths after the defeat at Adrianople, Ambrose chalked it up to the miraculous powers of its bishop Acholius: "The holy Acholius secured through his prayers the expulsion of the victorious [Goths] from the regions of Macedonia."[34]

---

31 Eastern examples are collected by N. Garsoïan, "Le rôle de l'hiérarchie chrétienne dans les relations diplomatiques entre Byzance et les Sassanides," *REArm* 10 (1973–74) 119–38 at 120–23 = *Armenia Between Byzantium and the Sasanians* (London, 1985) no. 8. Western examples are collected by J. Gaudemet, *L'Église dans l'Empire romain (IVe–Ve siècles)* (Paris, 1958) 353–5. Cf. also J.H.W.G. Liebeschuetz, *The Decline and Fall of the Roman City* (Oxford, 2000) 144.

32 Ephr. *Carm.Nis.* 13–14. Later sources collected by Dodgeon and Lieu, *Eastern Frontier*, 164–71 (first siege) and 193–207 (third siege). For the date of 337, see R.W. Burgess, "The Dates of the First Siege of Nisibis and the Death of James of Nisibis," *Byzantion* 69 (1999) 7–17.

33 *Carm.Nis.* 17–18, quoted from 17.4 after Beck's translation.

34 *Ep.* 51.6 with Lenski, "*Initium*," 134.

The image of the Christian bishop as saviour of his city was widespread not only in Christian sermons, hymns, letters, and the later church histories, but also in secular historiography. Procopius has in recent years been portrayed as a philosophical historian who was highly critical of Christianity. His account of the Persian invasion by Khuzro II in the 540s is the next surviving large-scale narrative of a Romano-Persian war after the *Res Gestae.* Here too bishops frequently negotiated with the Great King on behalf of their cities. But rather than being suspected of treason, like Ammianus' bishop of Bezabde, they always saved their cities by such negotiations, often with the miraculous support of Christian relics.[35]

These narratives of the rescue of Roman cities by their Christian bishops had larger ideological significance: they imply that the welfare of the Roman empire depended upon the piety of the Christian clergy. This link was expressed by Constantius himself, when, on 14 February 361, while making preparations in his winter quarters at Antioch for another campaign against Shapur, he confirmed the immunity of the Christian clergy from civic liturgies, "knowing that our state is maintained more by religious devotion than by public offices, toils, or sweat of the body."[36]

The accusations of treason against the bishop of Bezabde as reported by Ammianus disrupted this link between Christian religious devotion and the maintenance of empire by reversing the narratives of the heroic rescue of Roman cities by their Christian clergy. In Ammianus' version, a bishop undermined rather than secured the defence of the empire. The emergence of such accusations during these years, when the defence of the empire was increasingly imagined as depending upon the piety of its Christian clergy, was not coincidental. In the same way that Ammianus' demonstration of the detrimental effects of Sabinianus' martyr worship at Edessa was a reaction to the image of Christian martyrs as divine guardians of Roman cities, the rumours directed against the bishop of Bezabde were also a direct response to the new idea of the bishop as heroic defender of his community. In both cases the account of the *Res Gestae* undercut the new notion of a link between Christian piety and the defence of the Roman empire.

Martyrdom and Rome

This close association between Christian religion and Roman state was felt on the other side of the Roman-Persian frontier as well. In 340 Shapur ordered a persecution of Christians in his realm which continued intermittently, until his

---

35 *Bell.* 1.7.5–11, 2.11.14–20, 2.20.10. The significance of these and further miracle stories in Procopius' works is explored by A.M. Cameron, *Procopius and the Sixth Century* (Berkeley, 1985) 114–17. A. Kaldellis, *Procopius of Caesarea: Tyranny, History, and Philosophy at the End of Antiquity* (Philadelphia, 2004), does not discuss the quoted passages.

36 *CTh.* 16.2.16.

death in 379.[37] The victims were commemorated in martyr acts written in Syriac.[38] In their extant form the oldest of them cannot be later than the early fifth century, when Sozomen appropriated some of them for his *Church History* (2.9–14).

According to these texts, the main reason for the persecutions was the suspicion of Persian authorities that Persian Christians secretly collaborated with the Roman enemy.[39] As Rome's welfare was imagined to depend upon the Christian God, his martyrs, and clergy, so too outside the borders of the empire Christianity was increasingly identified with loyalty to the Roman emperor. This is strikingly visible in a direct parallel to Ammianus' narrative of the fall of Bezabde provided by the Syriac *Martyrdom of the Prisoners of War*.[40] After giving a brief description of the conquest of Bet Zabdai by the Persian army and the capture of its bishop, the martyr act focuses on the fate of the inhabitants of the city during their deportation. On the long march into exile, escorted by Persian troops under the command of the Great King, their leader remained the bishop Heliodorus—evidently the same man who, according to Ammianus, had negotiated with the Great King during the siege. On the march Heliodorus fell ill. Prior to his death he consecrated Dausa as his successor (2). At this point, the martyr act relates, the people of Bezabde "began to come together as one congregation and to recite psalms in choirs" (3). The Mowbeds, Zoroastrian dignitaries, witnessed this, and gradually became upset.

In Dursak the Christian clergy and select lay believers were led off to a nearby mountain. Suddenly they found themselves encircled by Persian horsemen and foot soldiers. The Persian high priest Adarfarr told them that they would be executed on the spot if they did not "abandon the religion of Caesar (*deḫlta d-qesar)* and accept the religion of Shapur, the King of Kings" (5). When Bishop Dausa refused, the high priest ordered the soldiers to attack. That day 275 Christians were killed, among them many "daughters of the covenant," that is, female ascetics. According to the martyr act, the persecution of the inhabitants of Bezabde was prompted by the psalms sung on the march after the death of Bishop Heliodorus. This was seen

---

37 On the chronology see R.W. Burgess, "The Dates of the Martyrdom of Simeon Bar Sabba'e and the 'Great Massacre'," *AB* 117 (1999) 9–66.

38 S.E. Assemani (ed.), *Acta sanctorum martyrum orientalium et occidentalium in duas partes distributa* (Rome, 1748), and P. Bedjan (ed.), *Acta martyrum et sanctorum syriace* (Paris and Leipzig, 1890–97). On the genre, date, and sources, see G. Wiessner, *Untersuchungen zur syrischen Literaturgeschichte I: Zur Märtyrerüberlieferung aus der Christenverfolgung Schahpurs II.* (Göttingen, 1967), and J.T. Walker, *The Legend of Mar Qardagh: Narrative and Christian Heroism in Late Antique Iraq* (Berkeley, 2006) 109–20.

39 S.P. Brock, "Christians in the Sasanid Empire: A Case of Divided Loyalties," in S. Mews (ed.), *Religion and National Identity* (Oxford, 1982) 1–19, and J. Wiesehöfer, "Geteilte Loyalitäten: Religiöse Minderheiten des 3. und 4. Jahrhunderts n. Chr. im Spannungsfeld zwischen Rom und dem sasanidischen Iran," *Klio* 75 (1993) 362–82. T.D. Barnes, "Constantine and the Christians of Persia," *JRS* 75 (1985) 126–36, incisively explores the Constantinian prehistory of the conflict.

40 For the edition see Bedjan, *Acta martyrum*, 2.316–24. The text is quoted after the English translation by Jordan and Brock in Dodgeon and Lieu, *Eastern Frontier*, 215–19.

by Persian officials as a challenge to the authority of the Great King. For them, the Christian God, to whom the citizens of Bezabde prayed, was above all, "the God to whom Caesar prays" (4). Bishop Dausa expressed the same idea when he invoked, before his death, "the true God, whom Caesar also worships" (6). In the views of the two bishops and of their persecutors, by expressing their allegiance to the Christian religion the citizens of Bezabde also expressed their loyalty to the Roman emperor.

The tragic deaths of Heliodorus and Dausa during deportation constituted an especially striking, and horrifying, extension of the new image of the bishop as heroic wartime leaders of their cities. Even more than the narratives of the rescue of Roman cities by their Christian bishops, the martyrdom of the inhabitants of Bezabde for the "religion of Caesar" made powerfully visible the inextricable bond by which Christian religion and the Roman state were linked in the imagination of Christians living on both sides of the border.While Ammianus noted the deportation of the inhabitants of Bezabde to Persia, he did not recount their deaths. In view of Ammianus' close connections to Persia, it seems likely that he was informed about their later persecution. But regardless of whether Ammianus knew the tragic end of the deportation, the differences between his account and that of the martyr act throw into sharp relief their different conceptions of the relationship between power and religion in the world after Constantine. In the martyr act Bishop Heliodorus became, through his death, the symbol of the unremitting loyalty of the deported to both Christian god and Roman emperor. In the *Res Gestae* it was rumoured that the same bishop had in fact betrayed his city to the Great King. Whereas Christian literature asserted that the defence of Roman cities depended upon the piety of its bishops, in the *Res Gestae* Christian dignitaries stood, like the bishop of Bezabde, dangerously between the lines.[41]

Ammianus and the Daughters of the Covenant

It might be argued that Ammianus' silence on the later fate of the inhabitants of Bezabde is due to the conventions of the genre: the treatment of Christians by the Persian Great King, it might be thought, has no place in a work of historiography that belonged to the classical tradition. However, in another passage of his account of Constantius' Persian war, Ammianus showed no such hesitation. In 359, shortly after Sabinianus' martyr worship at Edessa, Shapur launched a surprise attack on two Roman fortresses on the banks of the Tigris.[42] The Great King took a number of

---

[41] Similar doubts are cast on the loyalty of Christian clerics to Rome in 29.5.5, where a bishop appeared as envoy of the Moorish insurgent Firmus, and in 31.12.8–9, where a Christian presbyter acted as an emissary of the Gothic leader Fritigern immediately before the Battle of Adrianople.

[42] Ammianus called them Reman and Busan, but this seems to be a mistake: L. Dillemann, *Haute Mésopotamie orientale et pays adjacents: Contribution à la géographie*

valuable prisoners, among them several Christian female ascetics. The following is Ammianus' version:

> Other women were found who were dedicated to divine worship according to Christian custom (*uirgines Christiano ritu cultui diuino sacratas*). [Shapur] ordered that no harm should be done to them and that they should serve their religion in the accustomed way without prohibition. He feigned clemency no doubt in order that all whom he had previously frightened by his merciless cruelty would come over to him voluntarily and without fear after they had learnt from these recent examples that he now moderated his good luck with kindness and gentleness.[43]

Ammianus shows himself remarkably well informed about the institutions of eastern Christianity. He uses the phrase *uirgines Christiano ritu cultui diuino sacratas* to refer to female ascetics, the "daughters of the covenant" well known from Syriac ecclesiastical literature. Indeed, Hunt has plausibly taken Ammianus' mentioning of Shapur's previous "merciless cruelty" (*diritate crudelitateque*) as referring to Shapur's persecutions of Christians.[44]

However, it is noteworthy that Ammianus does not present his readers with the picture of the Persian Great King as persecutor. Rather, Christian holy women are spared by Shapur for their religion. The *Acts of the Persian Martyrs* presented the opposite image to the *Res Gestae*. Here, female ascetics were among the preferred subjects of persecution: the refusal of female reproductive duties was particularly abhorrent to Zoroastrian custom.[45] For example, in the *Martyrdom of Thekla and Four Other Daughters of the Covenant*, five female ascetics are killed by an apostate priest after they refuse to sacrifice.[46] In another martyr act, the female ascetic Martha is slaughtered in the presence of thousands of onlookers on the orders of Shapur after Persian officials and Zoroastrian priests fail to induce her either to renounce her religion or to marry.[47] And as has already been seen, the

---

historique de la région, du Ve s. avant l'ère chrétienne au VIe s. de cette ère (Paris, 1962) 156–7, argues that both are different names for one fortress, otherwise called Arcaiapis (Kerk).

[43] Amm. 18.10.4: ... *inuentas tamen alias quoque uirgines Christiano ritu cultui diuino sacratas custodiri intactas et religioni seruire solito more nullo uetante praecepit lenitudinem profecto in tempore simulans, ut omnes, quos antehac diritate crudelitateque terrebat, sponte sua metu remoto uenirent exemplis recentibus docti humanitate eum et moribus iam placidis magnitudinem temperasse fortunae.*

[44] Hunt, "Ammianus," 189 n.19.

[45] Acts of female martyrs in Persia are translated by S.P. Brock and S.A. Harvey, *Holy Women of the Syrian Orient* (Berkeley, 1987).

[46] Bedjan, *Acta martyrum*, 2.254–60 = Brock and Harvey, *Holy Women*, 73–6.

[47] Bedjan, *Acta martyrum*, 2.233–41 = Brock and Harvey, *Holy Women*, 57–73.

female ascetics captured in Bezabde were not spared by Shapur but rather were killed in large numbers.

Against this background, Ammianus' depiction of Shapur as chivalrously sparing his Christian captives and granting them full freedom of worship is remarkable. It seems that Shapur used "the daughters of the covenant" to drive a wedge between Christianity and the Roman state, for, according to Ammianus, Shapur spared them in order that the Christian inhabitants "whom he had previously frightened by his merciless cruelty would come over to him voluntarily and without fear." In this way, the *Res Gestae* pointedly rewrote contemporary Christian narratives. The martyr acts presented their readers with a straightforward picture of holy Christian women killed in the hands of an enemy both of Christianity and of Rome. In the *Res Gestae*, by contrast, the reverence Christians accorded their holy women potentially undermined the defence of the empire and could be exploited by a Persian king to turn Christians against Rome.

The Lonely Historian?

Arnaldo Momigliano famously dubbed Ammianus "the lonely historian." This epithet aptly describes the impression that many modern readers have of him, as an historian who seems strangely aloof from the debates and anxieties of his time. This impression, however, is the result of a deliberate literary construction. Like other late antique authors who wrote history in the classical tradition, Ammianus consciously tried to recreate in his work the worlds of his ancient models.[48] The classical texture of the *Res Gestae* makes it appear as if the work had originated somehow outside the intellectual environment of its own time.

In an effort to look behind this classical façade, this paper has set Ammianus' history alongside contemporary Christian literature, examining his representation of the relationship between religion and power in Constantius' Persian war in light of contemporary Christian texts and rituals. In his account of Sabinianus' martyr worship in Edessa, Ammianus made ironic use of an internal Christian debate on appropriate conduct during martyr feasts to undermine the new Christian idea that there was an intimate connection between martyr worship and military victory. The accusations against the bishop of Bezabde, furthermore, constituted a pointed reversal of the new Christian image of the bishop as heroic defender of Roman cities. While in Christian accounts from both sides of the Roman-Persian frontier bishops are represented as a focus of loyalty to both Christianity and to Rome, in the *Res Gestae* a Christian bishop appears as a potential traitor to the Roman cause. And while in the *Acts of Persian Martyrs* holy women are among the preferred subjects of persecution, in the *Res Gestae* their Christian religion is the reason

48 A.D.E. Cameron and A.M. Cameron, "Christianity and Tradition in the Historiography of the Late Empire," *CQ* 14 (1964) 316–28 = A.M. Cameron, *Continuity and Change in Sixth-Century Byzantium* (London, 1981) no. 3.

why they are spared by Shapur. In sharp contrast to the storylines put forward in contemporary Christian texts, in the *Res Gestae* religious and political loyalties are uncomfortably divided. Ammianus presents readers with a reversal of the image painted by many of his Christian contemporaries of a union between Christian piety and the welfare of the Roman empire. To describe this as "bias" does not do justice to the wit and depth of Ammianus' engagement with the thought-world of contemporary Christianity.

Chapter 28

Persecuting Heresy in Early Islamic Iraq: The Catholicos Ishoyahb III and the Elites of Nisibis*

Richard E. Payne
Cambridge University and Mount Holyoke College

The first decades after the Islamic conquest of Mesopotamia were tumultuous for the Church of the East. Reflecting on this period in the 680s, John of Phenek recounted the transition from Sasanian to Islamic rule in dramatic terms:[1] "All our affairs were conducted in orderly fashion as long as pagan kings were in control, and up to the time of the arrival of the children of Hagar the church in Persia had been under the rule of the Magians and had nothing else to pit itself against."[2] The Muslim authorities were not the cause of the church's difficulties; they were content merely to exact tribute and to leave their subjects to practice their respective faiths unhindered.[3] According to John it was rather heretics, church leaders, and lay notables who had afflicted the people of God during this period. The heretics had seized the opportunity to win converts among fellow Christians rather than among pagans.[4] Bishops, as John put it, "clamor in the manner of

* I would like to thank Peter Brown, Bill Bulman, Patricia Crone, John Haldon, William C. Jordan, and Uriel Simonsohn for their comments on this paper, without implicating them in its weaknesses.

1 See G.J. Reinink, "East Syrian Historiography in Response to the Rise of Islam: The Case of John bar Penkaye's *Ktābā D-Rēš Mellē*," in J.J. van Ginkel, H.L. Murre-van den Berg, and T.M. van Lint (eds.), *Redefining Christian Identity: Cultural Interaction in the Middle East since the Rise of Islam* (Leuven, 2005) 77–89; P. Bruns, "Von Adam und Eva bis Muhammed—Beobachtungen zur syrischen Chronik des Johannes bar Penkaye," *OC* 87 (2003) 47–64, on the theological and apocalyptic contexts of John's work.

2 A. Mingana (ed.), *Sources Syriaques* (Leipzig, 1908) 146–7; S.P. Brock, "North Mesopotamia in the Late Seventh Century: Book XV of John Bar Penkaye's Ris Melle," *JSAI* 9 (1987) 51–75 at 58–9. I have used Brock's translation for this quotation from Book XV; the other quotations from John and other ancient authors are my own translations.

3 Here John's perspective sits well with recent interpretations of early Islamic administration: cf. R. Hoyland, "New Documentary Texts and the Early Islamic State," *BSOAS* 69 (2006) 395–416; J. Johns, "Archaeology and the History of Early Islam: The First Seventy Years," *JESHO* 46 (2003) 411–36.

4 Mingana, *Sources Syriaques*, 147.

princes … take power and are strengthened tyrannically not through Christ, but through temporal authorities; they are bound up in the affairs of public courts and in unlawful disputes."[5] Lay leaders, for their part, devoured the poor by exacting levies beyond what they were charged to collect.[6] The account in the *Book of the Main Points* of a period in which religious identities were in flux, church leaders were adopting new positions of authority, and lay notables were devouring the poor contrasts sharply with conventional depictions of the Church of the East in the early Islamic period, which tend to portray a fully formed religious community that easily weathered the transition between two equally non-Christian empires.[7]

The letters of the catholicos Ishoyahb III (d. 659) are particularly helpful in illumining this period of ambiguity. They are among only a handful of sources that can be securely dated to the immediate post-conquest period. While Ishoyahb's correspondence has frequently been mined for references to Muslims and Islam, it has yet fully to be explored for its insights into the situation of East Syrian Christians in early Islamic Iraq. A principal objective of this essay is to draw attention to the value of this corpus of letters for the social history of Mesopotamia in the 640s and 650s, a crucial period of transition that is notoriously difficult to discern in both Islamic and later non-Muslim sources. Christian authors were as eager as their Muslim counterparts to represent the Islamic conquest in terms favorable to themselves, and Ishoyahb was no exception. His letters, however, are remarkably frank. In contrast with both the historiographical and canonical sources, they allow us to see both sides of disputes regarding marriage law, the definition of orthodoxy, the status of monastic property, and the jurisdiction of the catholicate, among other pressing affairs. They return some of the dynamism to a period that later sources are inclined to represent with a clear-cut, normative narrative.

Ishoyahb was party to a group of clerics that strove to assert the distinctiveness of an East Syrian orthodoxy in the late Sasanian and early Islamic periods. While the canons of the Church of the East had consistently expressed its commitment to dyophysite theology, the spectrum of acceptable belief remained fluid and negotiable well into the seventh century.[8] It was only at the assembly of 612, orchestrated by Babai the Great, that the formula of the two *qnome* of Christ was first canonically sanctioned.[9] But while the historiography of the Church

---

5 Mingana, *Sources Syriaques*, 148: ܡܕܒܪܢܐ ܐܝܟ ܐܪܟܘܢܐ … ܥܫܢܝܢ ܫܠܝܛܐ ܘܡܬܚܝܠܝܢ ܛܪܘܢܐܝܬ ܠܘ ܡܢ ܡܫܝܚܐ ܐܠܐ ܡܢ ܫܘܠܛܢܐ ܥܠܡܢܝܐ

6 Mingana, *Sources Syriaques*, 149–50.

7 Cf. S. Gero, "Only a Change of Masters? The Christians of Iran and the Muslim Conquest," *StudIr* 5 (1987) 43–8; M. Morony, "Religious Communities in Late Sasanian and Early Muslim Iraq," *JESHO* 17 (1974) 113–35, and Idem, *Iraq after the Muslim Conquest* (Princeton, 1984) 332–72.

8 S.P. Brock, "The 'Nestorian' Church: A Lamentable Misnomer," *BJRL* 78 (1996) 23–35.

9 S.P. Brock, "The Christology of the Church of the East in the Synods of the Fifth to Early Seventh Centuries: Preliminary Considerations and Materials," in G. Dragas (ed.),

of the East represented this novel phraseology as the definitive proclamation of orthodoxy and its promoters as defenders of the faith, the making of a distinctively East Syrian orthodoxy appears to have commenced in the early seventh century. Reinink has illustrated how Babai employed both his literary ability and personal connections to advance the imperative of orthodoxy.[10] The process by which East Syrian Christians came to speak of their beliefs primarily as an "orthodoxy" (*'artadawksiya*) rather than as "correct belief" (*tawdita trisṯa*), "true faith" (*haymanuta sharirta*), or "correct faith" (*haymanuta trisṯa*), was initiated by such energetic promoters of the two *qnome* formula in the early seventh century.[11]

Ishoyahb emerged as a vigorous constructor of orthodoxy while bishop of Nineveh, metropolitan of Arbela, and catholicos of the Church of the East.[12] From a noble (*bar ẖere*) family of Adiabene, Ishoyahb enjoyed the merits of aristocratic status, while his experience at the School of Nisibis had firmly implanted him within the web of relationships that constituted the clerical leadership of the Church of the East in the late Sasanian period. He maintained contact both with his clerical associates and lay aristocrats throughout his career as bishop, metropolitan, and catholicos. He impressed upon his correspondents the imperative of professing the correct formulation of the faith. But Ishoyahb did not content himself merely to recommend adherence to the two *qnome* creed. He dedicated a considerable amount of energy and ink to ostracizing individuals who were reluctant to adopt the new formula, most famously his former associate Sahdona. He strove to assert episcopal control of monasteries, by requiring monks to solicit his approval of their choice of abbot. Perhaps most importantly, while serving as metropolitan of Arbela Ishoyahb initiated a series of liturgical reforms that as catholicos he managed to impose on a significant portion of the Church of the East.[13] The *Chronicle of Seert* reported that the liturgy of St. Ephrem was celebrated at Nisibis until Ishoyahb successfully imposed the new, standardized

Aksum-Thyateira: A Festschrift for Archbishop Methodios of Thyateira and Great Britain (London, 1985) 125–42.

[10] G.J. Reinink, "Babai the Great's *Life of George* and the Propagation of Doctrine in the Late Sasanian Empire," in J.W. Drijvers and J.M. Watt (eds.), *Portraits of Spiritual Authority: Religious Power in Early Christianity, Byzantium, and the Christian Orient* (Leiden, 1999) 171–94.

[11] Such looser terminology prevails in the fifth- and sixth-century councils of the Synodicon: cf. J. Chabot (ed. and trans.), *Synodicon orientale, ou recueil de synodes nestoriens* (Paris, 1902) 54, 65. In his French translation Chabot tends to render all of these terms as "orthodoxe" or some variation thereof.

[12] See J.M. Fiey, "Išoᶜyaw le Grand: Vie du catholicos nestorien Išoᶜyaw III de Adiabène (580–659)," *OCP* 35 (1969) 305–33; 36 (1970) 5–46; R. Hoyland, *Seeing Islam as Others Saw It: A Survey and Evaluation of Christian, Jewish, and Zoroastrian Writings on Early Islam* (Princeton, 1997) 174–82.

[13] E.A.W. Budge (ed.), *The Book of Governors: The Historia Monastica of Thomas Bishop of Marga* (London, 1893) 1.79–80.

liturgy.[14] For the first time in its history, a substantial portion of the Christians of Mesopotamia and Persia were now following the same liturgical order.[15] Not only did Ishoyahb advance the modified creed as a new standard of orthodoxy, but he also rendered this orthodoxy tangible to the senses through the medium of a newly regularized liturgy.

The making of orthodoxy took on new urgency after the Islamic conquest. For in the absence of the Sasanian state, what would preserve the unity of East Syrian Christians? In the early Islamic period, Ishoyahb came to consider the lands of the Church of the East's jurisdiction a "*politeia* of the orthodox" (*pulutiya d-'artadawkse*).[16] He was keenly aware that in the absence of a distinctive common doctrine there was little to bind the Christians of such vast territories together. The demise of the Sasanian state had left the catholicate exposed. The authority of the catholicos had from its inception been contiguous with the boundaries of the Sasanian empire, and the bishops of Seleucia-Ctesiphon frequently relied upon the power of the state to enforce their ecclesiastical jurisdiction.[17] The metropolitanate of Revardashir seized upon the opportunity offered by the Islamic conquest decisively to assert the autonomy they had been unable to guarantee as long as the king of kings upheld the nominal suzerainty of the catholicos. The bishops of Beit Qatraye joined their metropolitan in shirking recognition of the catholicos.[18] This situation has sometimes been described as the delinquency of persistently rebellious ecclesiastical provinces. But this is to privilege the perspective of Seleucia-Ctesiphon. The Christians of Fars and Beit Qatraye could summon equally strong apostolic traditions in favor of their bishoprics' autonomy.[19] The arguments that Ishoyahb presented to the inhabitants of Beit Qatraye thus emphasized his relationship with the Muslim authorities:

14 A. Scher and J. Périer (eds. and trans.), "Histoire Nestorienne (Chronique du Séert): 1ère partie, fasc. 1," *PO* 4 (Paris, 1908) 295.

15 U.M. Lang, "Zum Einsetzungsbericht bei ostsyrischen Liturgiekommentaren," *OC* 89 (2005) 63–76; B. Varghese, "East Syrian Liturgy during the Sasanid Period," in A. Mustafa and J. Tubach (eds.), *Inkulturation des Christentums im Sasanidenreich* (Wiesbaden, 2007) 269–80.

16 R. Duval (ed.), *Isoyahb patriarchae III liber epistularum. CSCO* Scr. Syr. 11 (Paris, 1904) 165.

17 Morony, *Iraq after the Muslim Conquest*, 334; S. McDonough, *Power by Negotiation: Institutional Reform in the Fifth Century Sasanian Empire* (diss. Univ. of California at Los Angeles, 2005) 231–84.

18 J.F. Healey, "The Christians of Qatar in the 7th Century A.D.," in I.R. Netton (ed.), *Studies in Honour of Clifford Edmund Bosworth* (Leiden, 2000) 1.222–37.

19 C. Jullien and F. Jullien, *Apôtres des confins: Processus missionaires chrétiens dans l'empire iranien* (Paris, 2002), on the diversity of apostolic narratives among East Syrian Christians.

> The insane men [their bishops] have not learned and have not understood that they are subject to this worldly authority that now rules every land … Nor do these foolish men understand in these matters that we are commanded to give to every authority what is due to him from us, that is, the poll tax (*ksep risha*) to whomever [is owed] the poll tax, tribute (*maksa*) to whomever [is owed] tribute, reverence (*dehlta*) to whomever [is owed] reverence, and honor to whomever [is owed] honor. They have commanded that lawful domination, that is of one another in the love of Christ, be subject to us.[20]

The catholicos was to serve as a patron for Christians, their intercessor and mediator with the Muslim authorities. Ishoyahb consistently presented himself as a favored client of the Muslims and an able patron of the church. It was through the representation of himself as both defender of orthodoxy and intermediary with secular power, the precise nature of whose rule will have remained a stressful uncertainty for the individuals he was addressing, that Ishoyahb aimed to fortify the authority of the catholicate. And the claims he made before the inhabitants of Beit Qatraye alert us to the powers the catholicos aspired to arrogate to himself as the leader of the *politeia* of the orthodox.

Two letters addressed to the nobles and clergy of the city of Nisibis reveal the strategies deployed by Ishoyahb to realize his ambitions for an orthodox *politeia*. One of these was directed to the nobles (*rawrbane*) of Nisibis; the other was addressed to that city's clergy.[21] He urged them both to cooperate in the expulsion of Nisibis' "heretics" (*heretiqe*), that is, those Nisibenes who would not subscribe to the two *qnome* formula. The Nisibenes had already earned the catholicos' congratulations for having demolished a church used by heretics in the city, an act justified with reference to Gideon's destruction of Baal's shrine, but Ishoyahb remained concerned about the presence of a fifth column within the city's population.[22] Pointedly, he posed the infamous question of John Chrysostom to the nobles: "Who would not sanctify his hands in their wounds? Who should not cut off their lips? Who should not strike their jaws? Who should not tear apart

20 Duval, *Liber epistularum*, 268–9: ܘܠܐ ܝܠܦܘ ܘܠܐ ܐܣܬܟܠܘ ܫܢܝܐ ܕܐܝܟ ܠܫܘܠܛܢܐ ܥܠܡܢܝܐ ܗܢܐ ܕܗܫܐ ܐܚܝܕ ܒܟܠ ܐܬܪ ܡܫܬܥܒܕܝܢ… ܘܐܦܠܐ ܒܗܠܝܢ ܡܣܬܟܠܝܢ ܫܛܝܐ ܕܠܟܠ ܫܘܠܛܢ ܡܕܡ ܕܡܬܚܝܒ ܠܗ ܡܢ ܦܩܝܕܝܢ ܠܡܬܠ ܗܢܘ ܕܝܢ ܠܡܢ ܕܟܣܦ ܪܫܐ ܟܣܦ ܪܫܐ ܘܠܡܢ ܕܡܟܣܐ ܡܟܣܐ ܘܠܡܢ ܕܕܚܠܬܐ ܕܚܠܬܐ ܘܠܡܢ ܕܐܝܩܪܐ ܐܝܩܪܐ. ܘܦܩܕܘ ܕܐܝܟ ܢܡܘܣܐ ܗܘ ܕܚܕ ܠܚܕ ܒܚܘܒܗ ܕܡܫܝܚܐ ܢܗܘܘܢ ܠܢ ܡܫܬܥܒܕܝܢ

21 On the terminology of nobility in Sasanian society, see F. de Blois, "'Freemen' and 'Nobles' in Iranian and Semitic Languages," *JRAS* (1985) 5–15; I. Colditz, *Zur Sozialterminologie der iranischen Manichäer: Eine semantische Analyse im Vergleich zu den nichtmanichäischen iranischen Quellen* (Wiesbaden, 2000).

22 J.M. Fiey, *Nisibe: métropole syriaque orientale et ses suffragants des origines à nos jours* (Louvain, 1977) 63, reports the presence of a west Syrian bishop in the city in 631. Another west Syrian bishop of Nisibis does not appear until 795: W. Hage, *Die syrisch-jakobitischen Kirche in frühislamischer Zeit* (Wiesbaden, 1966) 103.

the impure clothes that are on their polluted bodies?"[23] He followed this with the demand that the Nisibenes expel the heretics from the city. For the clergy he supplied a scriptural precedent for expulsion by force, appealing to the example of the Levites in the book of Exodus. The Levites performed the task of executing the idolaters, or at least some of them, whom Moses had found worshipping a golden calf after his descent from Mount Sinai. As Ishoyahb put it: "They did what you know they did. They consecrated their hands to the Lord, each man against his son and his brother. They purified the polluted congregation from the impurity of a foreign, wicked faith."[24] Ishoyahb considered this an exemplary deed: "They established for you, and for all of us, an eternal example."[25]

Nisibis was not the only city whose leadership the catholicos encouraged to move decisively against sectarian rivals. In a letter to Jacob, the bishop of Shahrazur, Ishoyahb alluded to conflict between Zoroastrians and Christians in the post-conquest period. The city of Shahrazur, located at the juncture between Beit Garmai and the mountains of Media, experienced frequent confrontations between its Zoroastrian and Christian inhabitants in the late Sasanian period.[26] Ishoyahb's letter suggests that certain Zoroastrians—described simply as *magushe*, which might refer either to laymen or to clerics—sought to circumscribe the bishop's position in their city after the Islamic conquest, by means of an unspecified "assault" (*saᶜya*).[27] But the catholicos reminded the bishop that the city's Zoroastrians no longer enjoyed the patronage of the state:

> I am very surprised for two reasons, namely that the Magians (*magushe*) were instigated through an authority that has already perished against the religion of God that lives eternally, and that although you are the patron of the religion of God, you did not demonstrate to the dead [authority] at once and rapidly that it is powerless and lifeless.[28]

If Jacob could not handle the affair on his own, he was instructed to inform the authorities (*shaliṯane*), for "the royal authority will struggle on your behalf even if you remain at rest."[29]

---

[23] Duval, *Liber epistularum*, 225: ܡܢ ܠܐ ܢܦܪܘܫ ܐܢܬܘܢ، ܒܡܫܩܠܝܘܬܗܘܢ.. ܡܢ ܠܐ ܢܬܠܘܠ ܠܗܘܢ. ܘܡܫܩܠܬܗܘܢ.. ܘܡܢ ܠܐ ܢܥܒܕ ܠܗܘܢ ܦܪܝܫܘܬܗܘܢ.. ܡܢ ܠܐ ܢܫܠܘܚ ܡܐܢܐ ܛܡܐܐ ܕܥܠ ܦܓܪܝܗܘܢ ܡܛܢܦܐ

[24] Duval, *Liber epistularum*, 226: ܗܟܢܐ ܗܘ ܐܦ ܠܘܝܐ ܕܐܝܬܝܟܘܢ ܝܕܥܝܢ ܐܢܘܢ، ܕܥܒܕܘ ܘܡܠܘ ܐܝܕܝܗܘܢ ܠܡܪܝܐ. ܓܒܪ ܒܒܪܗ ܘܒܐܚܘܗܝ.. ܘܕܟܘ ܟܢܘܫܬܐ ܡܛܢܦܬܐ ܡܢ ܛܢܦܘܬܐ ܕܗܝܡܢܘܬ ܢܘܟܪܝܘܬܐ ܒܝܫܬܐ

[25] Duval, *Liber epistularum*, 226: ܐܩܝܡܘ ܠܟܘܢ، ܕܝܢ ܘܗܘ ܕܝܢ ܠܟܠܢ ܛܘܦܣܐ ܠܐ ܡܫܬܢܝܢܐ

[26] Budge, *Book of Governors*, 90.

[27] Duval, *Liber epistularum*, 237.

[28] Duval, *Liber epistularum*, 237: ܬܕܡܘܪܬ ܗܟܝܠ ܒܬܪܬܝܗܝܢ ܗܘ ܕܝܢ ܕܐܝܟ ܡܬܬܥܝܪܝܢ ܡܓܘܫܐ ܒܫܘܠܛܢܐ ܕܡܢ ܟܒܪ ܐܒܝܕ ܠܘܩܒܠ ܕܚܠܬܐ ܕܐܠܗܐ ܕܚܝܐ ܗܝ، ܠܥܠܡ ܘܐܝܟ، ܕܟܕ ܐܢܬ ܐܝܬ ܒܥܕܪܐ ܗܘܐ ܕܕܚܠܬܐ ܕܐܠܗܐ ܠܐ ܚܘܝܬܗ، ܠܡܝܬܐ ܡܚܕܐ ܘܠܠܥܓܠ ܕܠܐ ܚܝܠ ܘܠܐ ܢܦܫܐ ܐܝܬܘܗܝ،

[29] Duval, *Liber epistularum*, 237–8: ܫܘܠܛܢܐ ܡܠܟܝܐ ܡܬܟܬܫ ܚܠܦܝܟ ܐܦ ܐܢܬ ܗܘܐ ܫܠܐ

The catholicos' exhortations to the Nisibenes and to Jacob of Shahrazur bear out the testimony of later accounts that described contestations for dominance between religious groups in Mesopotamia in the immediate post-conquest period. The *History of Rabban Hormizd*, a text with a seventh-century core but with later embellishments, recounted the tit-for-tat struggle between West and East Syrian Christian monks for dominance over the region of Mount Beit Edhrai. The hagiographer celebrates the righteous zeal of the holy man who, with the help of an angel, destroyed the West Syrian monastery of Bezkin, leaving a number of monks dead.[30] The *History* also mentions villages that were expunged of heretics and resettled with orthodox inhabitants.[31] Indeed, Fiey's efforts to reconstruct the historical geography of Christians in Iraq have uncovered some striking examples of discontinuity in the late Sasanian and early Islamic periods, with formerly mixed regions becoming dominated by one Christian sect.[32] While violence between Christians and Jews in the post-conquest Near East has received more scholarly attention, inter-Christian conflicts were equally important.[33] Tellingly, the *History of Rabban Hormizd* portrays the conflict as a contest of patronage, as the two groups vied for the favor of the local Muslim amir. While the monks of either party are the heroes and villains of the *History*, lay notables accompanied them and provided the manpower for their attacks when angelic assistance was not forthcoming. The early Muslim authorities did not, despite Ishoyahb's own claims to the contrary, favor one Christian group over another. Local Christian lay and clerical elites' maintenance of patronage over their own constituencies could thus hinge on their ability to present a united front before a local amir.

The letters to the Nisibenes allow us to contextualize one such instance of violence between Christians in early Islamic Mesopotamia. For Nisibis is perhaps the best documented Christian center in the region. Doctrinal strife had typified relations between the inhabitants of the city, their ecclesiastical hierarchy, and the School of Nisibis since the late Sasanian period. While an early seventh-century colophon described Nisibis as "the sacred city," this appears to have been a minority view.[34] The *Chronicle of Khuzistan* reported that the School of Nisibis

---

30 E.A.W. Budge (ed.), *The Histories of Rabban Hormizd the Persian and Rabban Bar-Idta* (London, 1902) 1.75–7. For the dating of the text, see S. Gero, "Cyril of Alexandria, Image Worship, and the *Vita* of Rabban Hormizd," *OC* 62 (1978) 77–97, and Hoyland, *Seeing Islam as Others Saw It*, 189–92.

31 Budge, *Rabban Hormizd*, 80–81.

32 J.M. Fiey, "Le démembrement de Ba Nuhadra," *OS* 6 (1961) 353–84, and Idem, *Assyrie chrétienne I: Contribution à l'étude de l'histoire et de la géographie ecclésiastiques et monastiques du nord de l'Iraq* (Beirut, 1965) 55.

33 On Jewish-Christian conflict, see V. Déroche, "Polémique anti-judaïque et émergence de l'Islam," *REByz* 57 (1999) 141–61.

34 A. Becker, *The Fear of God and the Beginning of Wisdom: The School of Nisibis and Christian Scholastic Culture in Late Antique Mesopotamia* (Philadelphia, 2006) 1.

attracted many "foolish, troublesome, and contentious" individuals to the city.[35] Babai the Great in his *History of George* bemoaned the predominance of heretics at Nisibis and celebrated George's efforts to bring them to orthodoxy.[36] Yet we should abstain from indulging our sources' propensity to label certain Nisibenes heretics, or from positing the strength of adherents to Miaphysite theology in the city on the basis of these accounts. Nisibis earned its dubious reputation in East Syrian sources both from its stubborn defense of its ecclesiastical independence and from its support of the exegete Henana, who practiced a form of exegesis that some East Syrian clerics, such as Ishoyahb and Babai, perceived as incompatible with that of Theodore of Mopsuestia.[37] Many Nisibenes appear to have resisted the definition of orthodoxy propounded by Ishoyahb and his allies, but nevertheless did not imagine themselves as members of another religious group such as that of the West Syrians. They were in good company. The sources surrounding the career of Sahdona demonstrate that a great many East Syrian Christians allied themselves with an individual whom Ishoyahb had excoriated as an arch-heretic.[38] However much Ishoyahb would have us believe the opposite, his definition of orthodox belief was neither universally accepted among East Christians nor, indeed, the basis for a common Christian identity. Ishoyahb was thus insisting that the Nisibenes draw lines in their city that had never been drawn before.

If Nisibis had earned a reputation for doctrinal ambiguity, it was also known as a bastion of noble Persian blood in northern Mesopotamia. Bloodlines and agnatic groups structured relationships in Sasanian society at every level.[39] While the *āzādān*, the middling nobles, were on the rise after the reforms of Khosro I, the *wuzurgān*, members of the great families of the empire, constituted an impenetrable upper crust.[40] The primary administrative function of the city was to serve as a meeting point between these nobles and the state administration; in the case of

---

35 I. Guidi (ed.), *Chronicon anonymum. CSCO* Scr. Syr. 1 (Paris, 1903) 18: ܐܢܫܐ ܣܟܠܐ ܘܡܫܓܫܢܐ ܘܚܪܝܢܐ ܡܢ ܟܠ ܐܬܪ

36 O. Braun (trans.), *Ausgewählte Akten persischer Märtyrer* (Kempten, 1915) 245–51.

37 Guidi, *Chronicon*, 18. On Henana, see G.J. Reinink, "'Edessa Grew Dim and Nisibis Shone Forth': The School of Nisibis at the Transition of the Sixth–Seventh Century," in J.W. Drijvers and A.A. MacDonald (eds.), *Centres of Learning: Learning and Location in Pre-Modern Europe and the Near East* (Leiden, 1995) 77–89, and Becker, *Fear of God and the Beginning of Wisdom*, 197–203. On Nisibis' difficult relationship with the patriarchate, see E.-K. Delly, "La place du métropolite de Nisibe parmi les électeurs du patriarche," *OS* 2 (1957) 389–94.

38 A. de Halleux, "Martyrios-Sahdona: La vie mouvementée d'un 'hérétique' de l'Église nestorienne," *OCP* 24 (1958) 93–128; N. Pigulevskaya, "Zhizn Sakhdoni: Iz Istorii Nestorianstva VII Veka," *ZKV* 3 (1928) 91–108.

39 A. Perikhanian, *Obshchestvo i Pravo Irana v Parfyanskii i Sasanidskii Periodi* (Moscow, 1983) 50–79.

40 M. Zakeri, *Sāsānid Soldiers in Early Muslim Society: The Origins of 'Ayyārān and Futuwwa* (Wiesbaden, 1995) 22–31.

Nisibis, between the nobles and the *marzbān*, himself of noble stock.[41] *Rawrbane*, the term Ishoyahb used to refer to the nobles of Nisibis, typically corresponds to *wuzurgān* in East Syrian texts of the late Sasanian period.[42] Compared with the paucity of sources for the Sasanian nobility in general, we know a great deal about the *rawrbane* of Nisibis. They claimed, not implausibly, to have been settled in Nisibis by Shapur II after his conquest of the city in 363.[43] They thus maintained a memory of themselves as a distinct group associated with the city of Nisibis in the late Sasanian period. Their association with a city is unusual for Sasanian nobles, who frequently resided outside of cities and were more closely tied with their fellow kin across the empire.[44] Ishoyahb described Nisibis as "your city" (*mdintkun*).[45] At some point in the fifth or sixth centuries, members of the Nisibene nobility began to convert to Christianity. Babai the Great himself was from a noble Persian family at Nisibis.[46] These were Christians keenly aware of the aristocratic blood flowing in their veins.

To persuade the Nisibene nobles to support his proposal, the catholicos employed language that appealed to their honor, aristocratic status, and authority. He argued, in a word, that their honor was dependent on their orthodoxy. He encouraged the nobles of the city to take up "the good arms that love the true faith, in which you were born, in which you were sanctified, in which you were glorified, and in which you were honored. Your name is renowned on earth because of the glory of orthodoxy."[47] In a manner that may recall the themes of aristocratic virtue in Sasanian epic, he compared the nobles to "victorious warriors" (*qrabtane nasiẖe*) and celebrated their "manly valiance" (*ganbaruta*).[48] They were warned that, if their town were not safeguarded from the demonic heretics, they would lose

---

41 A.I. Kolesnikov, "O Termine 'Marzban' v Sasanidskom Irane," *PPSb* 27 (1981) 49–56. On the nobility of a marzbān at Nisibis originally from Karka d'Beit Slok in the late Sasanian period, see P. Bedjan (ed.), *Acta martyrum et sanctorum* (Paris, 1894) 4.207.

42 De Blois, "'Freemen' and 'Nobles,'" 9.

43 J. Chabot (ed. and trans.), *Le livre de la chasteté composé par Jésusdenah évêque de Baçrah* (Rome, 1896) 11, and the *History of Mar Saba* in Bedjan, *Acta martyrum*, 4.222–49. According to later Arabic authors they were *ahl al-bayt* originally from Istakhr: M. Morony, "The Effects of the Muslim Conquest on the Persian Population of Iraq," *Iran* 14 (1976) 41–59 at 41.

44 J. Howard-Johnston, "The Two Great Powers in Late Antiquity: A Comparison," in A.M. Cameron (ed.), *The Byzantine and Early Islamic Near East III: States, Resources, and Armies* (Princeton, 1995) 157–226.

45 Duval, *Liber epistularum*, 222.

46 Chabot, *Livre de la chasteté*, 11.

47 Duval, *Liber epistularum*, 222: ܙܝܢܐ ܛܒܐ ܕܪܚܡܬ ܗܝܡܢܘܬܐ ܬܪܝܨܬܐ ܗܝ ܕܝܠܝܕܝܢ ܐܢܬܘܢ ܒܗ̇ ܘܡܬܩܕܫܝܢ ܐܢܬܘܢ ܒܗ̇ ܘܡܫܬܒܚܝܢ ܐܢܬܘܢ ܒܗ̇ ܘܡܬܝܩܪܝܢ ܐܢܬܘܢ ܒܗ̇. ܫܡܟܘܢ ܓܝܪ ܒܟܠܗ̇ ܒܫܘܒܚܐ ܕܐܪܬܕܘܟܣܘܬܐ

48 See Zakeri, *Sāsānid Soldiers in Early Muslim Society*, 1–12 and J. Walker, *The Legend of Mar Qardagh: Narrative and Christian Heroism in Late Antique Iraq* (Berkeley, 2006) 121–63, on concepts of manly valiance in Sasanian society.

their "good fortune" (*ṯuba*). Their honor and manliness hinged on their willingness to cast off "negligence." Similarly, Ishoyahb warned the clergy that "the honor that is customary in the congregations of the Lord will be transferred from you to someone else," if they failed to take action.[49] He elaborated in some detail on the concepts of honor and glory and made clear that he did not refer exclusively to the glories of the afterlife. The clergy should protect the faith "not only on account of the honor that is to come, but also on account of the earthly glory of this world."[50]

These warnings played on the destabilization of social identities in the post-conquest period.[51] As discussed above, competition between different Christian groups imperiled the positions of ecclesiastical leaders in many cities. Bishops and clergymen were vulnerable to humiliation at the hands of sectarian rivals who could usurp their positions with the patronage of Muslim amirs. Lay elites, on the other hand, experienced a profound localization. In the late Sasanian period, office-holding had come increasingly to supplement, but not supersede, ancestral nobility as a basis of elite status.[52] Ishoyahb refers to Nisibis as being within "the territory of your jurisdiction," which suggests that the nobles to whom he was writing had secured some kind of official position under the local amir.[53] Indeed, the seventh-century *Life of Theodotus of Amida* shows that Christian notables in this quarter of northern Mesopotamia had acquired positions as tax collectors in the immediate post-conquest period.[54] But if Christian elites retained their status as key administrators, they were now alienated from the life of the Sasanian court that had provided Sasanian aristocrats with the terms of their self-representation and had recognized the nobility of their families. Morony has argued that Christian elites maintained their cohesion by placing their familial lands in monastic

49 Duval, *Liber epistularum*, 227: ܢܥܒܪ ܠܐܚܪܝܢ ܡܢܟܘܢ ܐܝܩܪܐ ܕܥܝܕܐ ܒܟܢܘܫܬܗ ܕܡܪܝܐ

50 Duval, *Liber epistularum*, 228: ܠܐ ܒܠܚܘܕ ܡܛܠ ܐܝܩܪܐ ܕܥܬܝܕ ܐܠܐ ܡܛܠ ܫܘܒܚܐ ܬܒܝܠܝܐ ܕܒܥܠܡܐ ܗܢܐ

51 M. Morony, "Social Elites in Iraq and Iran: After the Conquest," in J. Haldon and L. Conrad (eds.), *The Byzantine and Early Islamic Near East VI: Elites Old and New in the Byzantine and Early Islamic Near East* (Princeton, 2004) 275–84 at 275, describes "a general leveling of élite structures in former Sasanian territories during the century following the conquest."

52 Howard-Johnston, "Two Great Powers," 221–3. But there is no indication of blood declining in importance: see M. Macuch, "Herrschaftskonsolidierung und sasanidisches Familienrecht: zum Verhältnis von Kirche und Staat unter den Sasaniden," in C. Reck and P. Zieme (eds.), *Iran und Turfan: Beiträge Berliner Wissenschaftler, Werner Sundermann zum 60. Geburtstag gewidmet* (Wiesbaden, 1995) 149–67.

53 Duval, *Liber epistularum*, 223: ܬܚܘܡܐ ܕܐܘܚܕܢܟܘܢ

54 A. Palmer, "Amid in the Seventh-Century Syriac Life of Theodute," in E. Grypeou, M. Swanson, and D. Thomas (eds.), *The Encounter of Eastern Christianity with Early Islam* (Leiden, 2006) 111–38. Christian elites are known to have been "administrators" in late seventh-century Nisibis: see A. Palmer, *The Seventh Century in the West-Syrian Chronicles* (Liverpool, 1993) 202. Cf. C.F. Robinson, *Empire and Elites after the Muslim Conquest: The Transformation of Northern Mesopotamia* (Cambridge, 2000) 90–108.

endowments and obtaining appointments within the church.[55] While this was unlikely to have been the only option available to the Nisibene elite, Ishoyahb exploited the anxieties of both clerics and laymen about their social status in order to advance the notion that the church and its orthodoxy could provide an individual with honor and glory on earth.

This proposition at once raised a longstanding dilemma in the Church of the East: the relationship between prominent laymen and ecclesiastics. Much of the church's legislative activity targeted laymen whom the church leadership perceived to have challenged their authority.[56] At Nisibis in particular tensions between lay and clerical leadership had boiled over in the 640s, when the Nisibenes had the disciples of their recently deceased metropolitan Cyriacus imprisoned by the local amir.[57] In response to these tensions Ishoyahb set out what may be termed a "model of religious community" that aimed to foster cooperation between the clergy and laymen in the name of orthodoxy. The invocation of the Levites served not only as a justification for the pious use of force, but also as an example of lay leadership among the people of God. The imagery associated with Moses and the people of God in the desert was an important component of East Syrian clerics' rhetorical toolkit and was often deployed in circumstances in which clerics sought to eliminate internal divisions.[58] But this rhetoric of religious community is no less powerful for being recycled. The clergy needed the leadership of laymen, Ishoyahb submitted, since the "first father of the priesthood," Aaron, had joined in the apostasy of the Israelites.[59] When Moses called out for those who were of the Lord, it was the lay Levites who responded and supported him. The layman, "who lives for this world alone," is "the giver of power, the arbiter of the contest, and the victor"; "so give him," Ishoyahb exhorted, "all of your power and all of your authority in the contest that is against error … and he will give you the power of his victory here."[60] The priestly leadership of Moses was, however, no less crucial. Ishoyahb stated that the Levites provided an example, "so that we may be prepared through priestly exhortations for the contest that is for the sake of the truth."[61] If it is the laymen who hold the power, it is the clergy who are to guide them in

55 Morony, "Religious Communities," 126; Idem, "Effects of the Muslim Conquest," 54 and 59; Idem, *Iraq after the Muslim Conquest*, 351.

56 See, for example, Chabot, *Synodicon Orientale*, 82, 103, and esp. 217–26, the canons of the Synod of 676.

57 Guidi, *Chronicon*, 31.

58 Cf. Mar Aba's rhetoric in E. Sachau (ed. and trans.), *Syrische Rechtsbücher* (Berlin, 1914) 3.258–9.

59 Duval, *Liber epistularum*, 226: ܐܒܐ ܩܕܡܝܐ ܕܟܗܢܘܬܐ

60 Duval, *Liber epistularum*, 228: ܕܠܗܘ ܥܠܡܐ ܚܝ ܐܘ ܒܢܐ ܠܗ ܠܗܢܐ ܒܠܚܘܕ ... ܝܗܘܒܗ ܕܚܝܠܐ ܘܦܣܘܩܗ ܕܐܓܘܢܐ ܘܙܟܝܢܐ ... ܗܘܒ ܠܗ ܗܟܝܠ ... ܟܠܗ ܚܝܠܟ ܘܟܠܗ ܡܫܠܛܢܘܬܟ ܒܐܓܘܢܐ ܕܠܘܩܒܠ ܛܘܥܝܝ ... ܘܗܘ ܢܬܠ ܠܟ ܚܝܠܐ ܕܙܟܘܬܗ ܬܢܢ

61 Duval, *Liber epistularum*, 226: ܕܢܗܘܐ ܡܛܝܒܝܢ ܒܡܠܦܢܘܬܐ ܟܗܢܝܬܐ ܠܘܬ ܐܓܘܢܐ ܕܚܠܦ ܫܪܪܐ ܢܬܬܥܝܕ

its exercise. The Nisibenes, having re-enacted the example of the Levites, would in turn provide an example of pious zeal to other Christians. "Be prototypes of virtue," Ishoyahb pleaded with the nobles, "for the holy church in all the borders of the earth."[62]

A roughly contemporary text, the Armenian *Writing on the Tradition of Saint Sahak*, similarly applied the example of the Levites to the relationship between clergy and laymen in a Sasanian or post-Sasanian social context. Mardirossian has demonstrated that the *Tradition of Saint Sahak* was a forgery composed by Yovhannes Mayragomecʿi, a late sixth- and early seventh-century cleric whose Julianist theology led him to articulate a new model of society whereby a purified clergy would monopolize justice, collect tithes, and serve as the undisputed leaders of an orthodox people.[63] What bears consideration here is Mayragomecʿi's argument in favor of a clerical tithe: "The Levites paid the tithe to the priests; even though they had collected the tithe from all of Israel, they nevertheless offered the tithe to all the priests."[64] Ishoyahb did not explicitly endorse a new fiscal relationship between himself, the nobles, and the clergy of Nisibis. But competition for resources did indeed inspire the Nisibenes' opposition to their metropolitan Cyriacus in the 640s. After his imprisonment by the amir, they proceeded to plunder the metropolitan's residence, seizing the "treasure" of the church of Nisibis.[65] A replacement was instated only on the condition that he would not draw his income from the city, but rather from his former episcopate of Arzoun, which he would continue to hold.[66] And in the letter to the inhabitants of Beit Qatraye quoted above, Ishoyahb had made the bold claim to have been entrusted by the Muslim authorities with collecting the poll tax and tribute. Competing efforts to profit from the post-Sasanian fiscal infrastructure had aggravated relations between lay nobles and clerics in early Islamic Mesopotamia and would continue to do so until the gradual removal of tax collection responsibilities from the hands of local non-Muslim elites from the late seventh century onward.[67] It was in this context that Ishoyahb sought to instantiate a new relationship between the clergy and nobles of Nisibis and the

---

62 Duval, *Liber epistularum*, 225: ܗܘܘ ܕܝܢ ܠܛܘܦܣܐ ܕܡܝܬܪܘܬܐ ܠܥܕܬܐ ܩܕܝܫܬܐ ܕܒܟܠ ܣܘܦܝܗ̇ ܕܐܪܥܐ

63 A. Mardirossian, *Le livre des canons arméniens (Kanonagirkʿ Hayocʿ) de Yovhannes Awjnecʿi: Église, droit, et société en Arménie du IVe au VIIIe siècle* (Louvain, 2004) 255–68; Idem, "L'*Écrit sur la tradition de saint Sahak*: Les soubresauts de la politique fiscale de l'église arménienne du VIIe au Xe siècle," *Muséon* 119 (2006) 375–97.

64 V. Hakobyan (ed.), *Kanonagirk Hayoc (Armyanskaya Kniga Kanonov)* (Yerevan, 1971) 2.234: Ղեւտացիքն տասանորդէին քահանայիցն, թէպէտ եւ ինքեանք առնուին տասանորդս յամենայն Իսրայէլէ, այլ եւ ինքեանք տասանորդս մատուցանէին յամենայնէ քահանայիցն.

65 Guidi, *Chronicon*, 31: ܒܙܘ ... ܠܓܙܐ ܕܒܝܬ ܐܦܣܩܘܦܘܬܐ ܕܒܝܬ ܢܨܒܝܢ

66 Guidi, *Chronicon*, 32–3.

67 Robinson, *Empire and Elites*, 95–7.

catholicate under the banner of orthodoxy, by having the nobles purge the city, just as the Levites had purged the people of Israel.

At the turn of the eighth century, Shahdost the bishop of Tirhan composed a treatise entitled, "Why we are called Nestorians."[68] By the end of the seventh century, it had become routine for East Syrian Christians to identify themselves publicly by their doctrinal affiliation, a departure from the doctrinal fluidity of the early seventh century. The letters of Ishoyahb demonstrate that the advancement of religious orthodoxy as a term of social affiliation must be placed in a proper social context. Acceptance of orthodoxy, for Ishoyahb, entailed a relationship and set of expectations and obligations between two social groups: the clergy and the lay aristocracy. The Nisibenes certainly came to understand their deployment of the term in this way; in the mid-eighth century, the inhabitants of Nisibis threatened to switch sects and become Jacobites when the patriarch Timothy I tried to manipulate their episcopal election.[69] These stark options testify to the transformation of Christian society in northern Mesopotamia in the early Islamic period. The religious community model has allowed scholars to presume cooperation among members of any given sect was the normal basis for collective action in Sasanian and early Islamic society. But Ishoyahb's dependence of the language of aristocratic honor and the pressure he felt to produce a justification for the cooperation of clerics and lay nobles combine to demonstrate that a Christian bishop in mid seventh-century Mesopotamia was ill-equipped to take action without the support of lay elites, who possessed their own distinctive set of priorities. Ishoyahb's letters to the Nisibenes illustrate the contingencies that surrounded the development of East Syrian orthodoxy and challenge the sense of inevitability inherent in historiography that treats the "religious community" as a thing rather than as a form of persuasion.

---

[68] L. Abramowski and A. Goodman, *A Nestorian Collection of Christological Texts* (Cambridge, 1972) 1.31.

[69] H. Putnam, *L'Église et l'Islam sous Timothée I (780–823)* (Beirut, 1975) 36–7.

Bibliography

Abramowski, L., "Die Mosaiken von S. Vitale und S. Apollinare in Classe und die Kirchenpolitik Kaiser Justinians," *ZAC* 5 (2001) 289–341.

Abramowski, L. and A. Goodman, *A Nestorian Collection of Christological Texts*, vol. 1 (Cambridge, 1972).

Aiello, V., "Il tempo del potere negli auspici di Ambrogio vescovo di Milano," in L. De Salvo and A. Sindoni (eds.), *Tempo sacro e tempo profano: Visione laica e visione cristiana del tempo e della storia* (Soveria Mannelli, 2002) 117–30.

Albu, E., "Dudo of Saint-Quentin: The Heroic Past Imagined," *HSJ* 6 (1994) 111–18.

———, *The Normans in Their Histories* (Woodbridge, 2001).

———, "Gladiator at the Millennium," in K. Day (ed.), *Celluloid Classics: New Perspectives on Classical Antiquity in Modern Cinema*, special issue of *Arethusa* 41 (2008) 185–204.

Aldrete, G.S., *Floods of the Tiber in Ancient Rome* (Baltimore, 2007).

Alföldi, A., *Die Kontorniaten* (Budapest, 1943).

———, *The Conversion of Constantine and Pagan Rome*, trans. H. Mattingly (Oxford, 1969).

Alföldi, A. and E. Alföldi, *Die Kontorniaten-Medaillons* (Berlin, 1990).

Alföldy, G., "Iscrizione commemorativa del restauro del Ponte di Valentiniano," in S. Ensoli and E. La Rocca (eds.), *Aurea Roma. Dalla città pagana alla città cristiana. Catalogo della Mostra (Roma, Palazzo delle Esposizioni, 22 dic.–20 apr. 2001)* (Rome, 2000) 460–61.

Allen, P. and C.T.R. Hayward, *Severus of Antioch* (London, 2004).

Alonso, C.R., *Las Historias de los Godos, Vandalos y Suevos de Isidoro de Sevilla: Estudio, Edición Crítica y Traducción* (León, 1975).

Althusser, L., "Ideology and Ideological State Apparatuses," in *Lenin and Philosophy and Other Essays*, trans. B. Brewster (London, 1971) 127–86.

Amarelli, F., *Vetustas-Innovatio: Un'antitesi apparente nella legislazione di Costantino* (Naples, 1978).

Angeli, S. De, "Iuppiter Optimus Maximus Capitolinus, Aedes (fasi tardo repubblicane e di età imperiale)," in E.M. Steinby (ed.), *Lexicon topographicum urbis Romae*, vol. 3 (Rome, 1993–2000) 152–3.

Angliviel de la Beaumelle, L., "Remarques sur l'attitude d'Ammien Marcellin à l'égard du christianisme," in J. Tréheux (ed.), *Mélanges d'histoire ancienne offerts à William Seston* (Paris, 1974) 15–23.

Armellini, M., *Le chiese di Roma dal secolo IV al XIX* (Rome, 1942).

Armstrong, A.H., "Tradition, Reason and Experience in the Thought of Plotinus," in *Atti del Convegno internazionale sul tema Plotino e il Neoplatonismo*

(Roma, 5–9 ottobre 1970) (Rome, 1974) 171–94 = Idem (ed.), *Plotinian and Christian Studies* (London, 1979) no. 17.

Asad, T., *Genealogies of Religion: Discipline and Reasons of Power in Christianity and Islam* (Baltimore, 1993)

Ashbrook Harvey, S., *Asceticism and Society in Crisis. John of Ephesus and Lives of the Eastern Saints* (Berkeley, 1990).

Assemani, S.E. (ed.), *Acta sanctorum martyrum orientalium et occidentalium in duas partes distributa* (Rome, 1748).

Assmann, J., *Die Mosaische Unterscheidung oder der Preis des Monotheismus* (Munich, 2004).

Athanassiadi, P., "A Contribution to Mithraic Theology: The Emperor Julian's Hymn to King Helios," *JThS* n.s. 28 (1977) 360–71.

———, "Dreams, Theurgy and Freelance Divination: The Testimony of Iamblichus," *JRS* 83 (1993) 115–30.

———, "The Oecumenism of Iamblichus: Latent Knowledge and Its Awakening," *JRS* 85 (1995) 244–50.

———, *La lutte pour l'orthodoxie dans le platonisme tardif de Numénius à Damascius* (Paris, 2006).

Atkins, E.M. and R.J. Dodaro (eds.), *Augustine: Political Writings* (Cambridge, 2001).

Avner, R., "The Recovery of the Kathisma Church and its Influence on Octagonal Buildings," in G.C. Bottini, L. Di Segni, and L.D. Chrupcata (eds.), *One Land. Many Cultures—Archaeological Studies in Honor of S. Loffreda* (Jerusalem, 2003) 173–86.

Babcock, W.S., *Tyconius: The Book of Rules* (Atlanta, 1989).

Bagnall, R.S., Al. Cameron, S.R. Schwartz, and K.A. Worp (eds.), *Consuls of the Later Roman Empire* (Atlanta, 1987).

Bailey, L., "Building Urban Christian Communities: Sermons on Local Saints in the Eusebius Gallicanus Collection," *EME* 12 (2003) 1–24.

Baldovin, J.F., *The Urban Character of Christian Worship: The Origins, Development, and Meaning of Stational Liturgy* (Rome, 1987).

Banchich, T., "Gallus Caesar (15 March 351–354 A.D.)," www.roman-emperors.org (1997).

Barceló, P., *Constantius II. und seine Zeit: Die Anfänge des Staatskirchentums* (Stuttgart, 2004).

Bardill, J., "The Great Palace of the Byzantine Emperors and the Walker Trust Excavations," *JRA* 12 (1999) 216–30.

Bardill, J. and G. Greatrex, "Antiochus the *praepositus*: a Persian eunuch at the court of Theodosius II," *DOP* 50 (1996) 171–97.

Barnes, T.D., "Lactantius and Constantine," *JRS* 63 (1973) 29–46.

———, "Constans and Gratian in Rome," *HSPh* 79 (1975) 325–33.

———, "A Correspondent of Iamblichus," *GRBS* 19 (1978) 99–106.

———, "The Editions of Eusebius' *Church History*," *GRBS* 21 (1980) 191–201.

———, *Constantine and Eusebius* (Cambridge, MA, 1981).

———, *The New Empire of Diocletian and Constantine* (Cambridge, MA 1982).
———, "Constantine and the Christians of Persia," *JRS* 75 (1985) 126–36.
———, *Athanasius and Constantius: Theology and Politics in the Constantinian Empire* (Cambridge, MA, 1993).
———, *Ammianus Marcellinus and the Representation of Historical Reality* (Ithaca, NY, 1998).
———, "Monotheists All?," *Phoenix* 55 (2001) 142–62.
Barnish, S.J.B., *The Variae of Magnus Aurelius Cassiodorus Senator* (Liverpool, 1992).
Bartelink, G.J.M., "Παρρησία dans les oeuvres de Jean Chrysostome," *StudPatr* 16 (1985) 441–8.
Baswell, C., *Virgil in Medieval England* (Cambridge, 1995).
Bauer, F.A., "Das Bild der Stadt Rom in karolingischer Zeit," *RQA* 92 (1997) 190–228.
Baur, C., *John Chrysostom and His Time*, 2 vols., trans. M. Gonzaga (Westminster, 1959).
Beard, M., "Writing Ritual: The Triumph of Ovid," in A. Barchiesi, J. Rüpke, and S. Stephens (eds.), *Rituals in Ink: A Conference on Religion and Literary Production in Ancient Rome* (Munich, 2004) 115–26.
Beard, M., J. North, and S. Price. *Religions of Rome*, 2 vols. (Cambridge, 1996).
Beatrice, P.F., "Towards a New Edition of Porphyry's Fragments against the Christians," in M.O. Goulet-Caze et al. (eds.), *ΣΟΦΙΗΣ ΜΑΙΗΤΟΡΕΣ. "Chercheurs de Sagesse". Hommage à Jean Pépin* (Paris, 1992) 347–55.
———, "*Antistes Philosophiae*: Ein christenfeindlicher Propagandist am Hofe Diokletians nach dem Zeugnis des Laktanz," *Augustinianum* 33 (1993) 31–47.
———, "On the Title of Porphyry's Treatise Against the Christians," in G.S. Gasparro (ed.), *Agathe Elpis. Studi storici-religiosi in onore di Ugo Bianchi* (Rome, 1994) 221–35.
Beck, E. (ed.), *Des heiligen Ephraem des Syrers Carmina Nisibena* (Louvain, 1961).
Becker, A., *The Fear of God and the Beginning of Wisdom: The School of Nisibis and Christian Scholastic Culture in Late Antique Mesopotamia* (Philadelphia, 2006).
Bedjan, P. (ed.), *Acta martyrum et sanctorum syriace* (Paris and Leipzig, 1890–97).
Belayche, N., "Realia versus leges? Les sacrifices de la religion d'état au IVe siècle," in S. Georgioudi, R. Koch Piettre, and F. Schmidt (eds.), *La cuisine et l'autel. Les sacrifices en questions dans les sociétés de la Méditerranée ancienne* (Turnhout, 2006) 343–70.
Bell, C., *Ritual Theory, Ritual Practice* (Oxford, 1992).
Bellardini, D. and P. Delogu, "Liber Pontificalis e altre fonti," in H. Geertman (ed.), *Atti de colloquio internazionale Il Liber Pontificalis e la storia materiale (Roma, 21–22 febbraio 2002)* (Assen, 2003) 205–24.

Berchman, R., "*Arcana Mundi* between Balaam and Hecate: Prophecy, Divination, and Magic in Later Platonism," in D. Lull (ed.), *SBL Seminar Papers* (Atlanta, 1989) 107–85.

Bernardi, J., "Un réquisitoire: les invectives contre Julien de Grégoire de Nazianze," in R. Braun and J. Richer (eds.), *L'empereur Julien. De l'histoire à la légende (313–1715)* (Paris, 1978) 89–98.

Bidez, J., *Vie de Porphyre* (Leipzig, 1913).

———, "Le philosophe Jamblique et son école," *REG* 32 (1919) 29–40.

Bieberstein, K., "Die Hagia Sion in Jerusalem. Zur Entwicklung ihrer Traditionen im Spiegel des Pilgerberichte," *JbAC* 20 (1995) 543–51.

Bieler, L., *Anicii Manii Severini Boethii Philosophiae Consolatio*. CCSL 94 (Turnhout, 1984).

Biermann, M., *Die Leichenreden des Ambrosius von Mailand: Rhetorik Predigt Politik* (Stuttgart, 1995).

Bietenhard, H., "The Millennial Hope in the Early Church," *SJT* 6 (1953) 12–30.

Bieżuńska-Małowist, I., "Die Expositio von Kindern als Quelle der Sklavenbeschaffung im griechisch-rõmischen Ågypten," *JWG* 2 (1971) 129–33.

Bihain, E., "L'épître de Cyrille de Jérusalem à Constance sur la vision de la Croix. Tradition manuscrite et édition critique," *Byzantion* 43 (1973) 264–96.

Binns, J., *Ascetics and Ambassadors of Christ: The Monasteries of Palestine 314–631* (New York, 1994).

Bitton-Ashkelony, B., *Encountering the Sacred. The Debate on Christian Pilgrimage in Late Antiquity* (Berkeley, 2005).

Bleicken, J., *Constantin der Große und die Christen*, Historische Zeitschrift Beihefte 15 (Munich, 1992) 13–33.

Bloch, H., "A New Document of the Last Pagan Revival in the West," *HThR* 38 (1945) 199–244.

———, "La rinascita pagana in Occidente alla fine del secolo IV," in A. Momigliano (ed.), *Il conflitto tra paganesimo e cristianesimo nel secolo IV* (Turin, 1968) 199–224.

———, "Ein neues Zeugnis der letzten Erhebung des Heidentums," in R. Klein (ed.), *Das frühe Christentum im römischen Staat* (Darmstadt, 1971) 129–86.

Blockley, R.C., *Ammianus Marcellinus: A Study of His Historiography and Political Thought* (Brussels, 1975).

———, *The Fragmentary Classicising Historians of the Later Roman Empire*, vol. 2 (Liverpool, 1985),

———, *East Roman Foreign Policy: Formation and Conduct from Diocletian to Anastasius* (Leeds, 1992).

Blois, F. de, "'Freemen' and 'Nobles' in Iranian and Semitic Languages," *JAS* (1985) 5–15.

Blume, H.D. and F. Mann (eds.), *Platonismus und Christentum: Festschrift Heinrich Dörrie* (Münster, 1983).

Blumenthal, H.J. and R.A. Markus (eds.), *Neoplatonism and Early Christian Thought: Essays in Honor of A.H. Armstrong* (London 1981).

Bobichon, P., *Justin Martyr. Dialogue avec Tryphon*, vol. 2 (Fribourg, 2003).

Boissier, G., "Le Christianisme de Boèce," *JS* (1889) 449–62.

———, *La fin du paganisme. Étude sur les dernières luttes religieuses en Occident au IVe siècle* (Paris, 1891).

Bonamente, G., "Potere politico ed autorità religiosa nel De obitu Theodosii di Ambrogio," in *Chiesa e società dal secolo IV ai nostri giorni: Studi storici in onore di P. Ilarino da Milano* 1 (Rome, 1979) 83–133.

———, "Costantino santo," *CrSt* 27 (2006) 735–68.

Bonnard, G.A. (ed.), *Gibbon's Journey from Geneva to Rome* (London, 1961).

Bonini, R., "Note sulla legislazione giustinianea dell'anno 535," in G.G. Archi (ed.), *L'imperatore Giustiniano storia e mito* (Milan, 1978) 161–78.

———, *Ricerche sulla legislazione giustinianea dell'anno 535: Nov. Iustiniani 8. Venalità delle cariche e riforme dell'amministrazione periferica*, 3rd ed. (Bologna, 1989).

Borgehammar, S., *How the Holy Cross was Found. From Event to Medieval Legend* (Stockholm, 1991).

Borgo, A., "*Clementia*: studio di un campo semantico," *Vichiana* 14 (1985) 25–73.

Boswell, J., *The Kindness of Strangers: The Abandonment of Children in Western Europe from Late Antiquity to the Renaissance* (New York, 1988).

Bouché-Leclercq, A., *Histoire de la divination dans l'antiquité*, vol. 4 (Paris, 1882).

———, "Augures," in C. Daremberg and E. Saglio (eds.), *DAGR* (Paris, 1877–1919) 550–60.

———, *Manuel des institutions romaines*, 2nd ed. (Paris, 1931).

Bowersock, G.W., *Julian the Apostate* (London, 1978).

———, "Peter and Constantine," in J.-M. Carrié and R. Lizzi Testa (eds.), *"Humana Sapit": Études d'antiquité tardive offertes à Lellia Cracco Ruggini* (Turnhout, 2002) 209–17.

Bowman, A., H. Cotton, M. Goodman, and S. Price (eds.), *Representations of Empire: Rome and the Mediterranean World* (Oxford, 2002).

Boyancé, P., "L'Apollon solaire," in J. Heurgon et al. (eds.), *Mélanges d'archéologie, d'épigraphie et d'histoire offerts à Jérôme Carcopino* (Paris 1966) 149–70.

Braarvig, J., "Magic: Reconsidering the Grand Dichotomy," in Jordan, Montgomery, and Thomassen, *The World of Ancient Magic* (2004), 21–54.

Bram, J.R., *Ancient Astrology, Theory and Practice* (Park Ridge, NJ, 1975).

Brandenburg, H., *Ancient Churches of Rome from the Fourth to the Seventh Century: The Dawn of Christian Architecture in the West*, trans. A. Kropp (Turnhout, 2005).

Brandle, R., *Johannes Chrysostomus: Bischof-Reformer-Märtyrer* (Stuttgart, 1999).

Brasseur, A., "Les deux visions de Constantin," *Latomus* 5 (1946) 35–9.

Bratož, R., *Krščanstvo v Ogleju in na vzhodnem vplivnem območju oglejske cerkve od začetkov do nastopa verske svobode* (Ljubljana, 1986).
Braun, O. (trans.), *Ausgewählte Akten persischer Märtyrer* (Kempten, 1915).
Bremmer, J.N., "The Birth of the Term 'Magic'," *ZPE* 126 (1999) 1–12.
Brenk, F.E., "In the Light of the Moon: Demonology of the Early Imperial Period," *ANRW* 2.16.3 (1986) 2068–145.
Brenneke, H.-C., *Studien zur Geschichte der Homöer der Osten bis zum Ende der homöischen Riechskirche,* Beiträge zur historischen Theologie 73 (Tübingen, 1988).
Breuer, J., and H. Roosens, "Le cimetière franc de Haillot," *AnnNamur* 48 (1956) 1–171.
Breukelaar, A.H.B., *Historiography and Episcopal Authority in Sixth-Century Gaul: The Histories of Gregory of Tours Interpreted in Their Historical Context* (Göttingen, 1994).
Brisson, L., *How Philosophers Saved Myths* (Chicago, 2004).
Brock, S.P., "A Letter Attributed to Cyril of Jerusalem on the Rebuilding of the Temple," *BSOAS* 40 (1977) 267–86 = Idem, *Syriac Perspectives on Late Antiquity* (London 1984), no. 10.
———, "Christians in the Sasanid Empire: A Case of Divided Loyalties," in S. Mews (ed.), *Religion and National Identity* (Oxford, 1982) 1–19.
———, "The Christology of the Church of the East in the Synods of the Fifth to Early Seventh Centuries: Preliminary Considerations and Materials," in G. Dragas (ed.), *Aksum-Thyateira: A Festschrift for Archbishop Methodios of Thyateira and Great Britain* (London, 1985) 125–42.
———, "North Mesopotamia in the Late Seventh Century: Book XV of John Bar Penkaye's Ris Melle," *JSAI* 9 (1987) 51–75.
———, "The 'Nestorian' Church: A Lamentable Misnomer," *BJRL* 78 (1996) 23–35.
Brock, S.P. and S.A. Harvey, *Holy Women of the Syrian Orient* (Berkeley, 1987).
Brown, P. "The Rise and Function of the Holy Man in Late Antiquity," *JRS* 61 (1971) 80–101 = Idem (ed.), *Society and the Holy in Late Antiquity* (Berkeley, 1989) 103–52.
———, "Pelagius and his Supporters: Aims and Environment," *JThS* n.s. 19 (1968) 93–114 = Idem, *Religion and* Society in the Age of Saint Augustine (London, 1972) 107–14.
———, *The Cult of the Saints: Its Rise and Function in Latin Christianity* (Chicago, 1981).
———, *Power and Persuasion in Late Antiquity: Towards a Christian Empire* (Madison, WI, 1992).
———, *Authority and the Sacred: Aspects of the Christianisation of the Roman World* (Cambridge, 1995).
———, "The Rise and Function of the Holy Man in Late Antiquity, 1971–1997," *JECS* 6 (1998) 353–76.

———, "The Decline of the Empire of God: Amnesty, Penance and the Afterlife from Late Antiquity to the Middle Ages," in C.W. Bynum and O. Freedman (eds.), *Last Things: Death and the Apocalypse in the Middle Ages* (Philadelphia, 2000) 41–59.

———, *Augustine of Hippo: A Biography* (London, 1967; rev. ed. 2000).

———, *Poverty and Leadership in the Later Roman Empire* (Hanover, NH, 2002).

Brown, R.E., *The Birth of the Messiah: A Commentary on the Infancy Narratives in Matthew and Luke* (Garden City, NJ, 1977; reprint, 1993).

Browning, R., "The Riot of A.D. 387 in Antioch: The Role of the Theatrical Claques in the Later Empire," *JRS* 42 (1952) 13–20.

Brox, N., *Irenäus von Lyon. Adversus Haereses. Gegen die Häresien*, 5 vols. (Freiburg, 1993–).

———, "Die biblische Hermeneutik des Irenäus," in N. Brox (ed.), *Das Frühchristentum. Schriften zur historischen Theologie* (Freiburg, 2000) 233–54.

Bruce-Mitford, R., "The Regalia," in *The Sutton Hoo Ship-Burial: Arms, Armour and Regalia*, vol. 2 (London, 1978) 311–77.

Bruns, P., "Von Adam und Eva bis Muhammed—Beobachtungen zur syrischen Chronik des Johannes bar Penkaye," *OC* 87 (2003) 47–64.

Bruun, P., "The Disappearance of Sol from the Coins of Constantine," *Arctos* n.s. 2 (1958) 15–37.

———, (ed.), *Roman Imperial Coinage*, Vol. 7, *Constantine and Licinius, A.D. 313–337* (London, 1966).

Buc, P., *The Dangers of Ritual: Between Early Medieval Texts and Social Scientific Theory* (Princeton, 2001).

Buckland, W.W., *The Roman Law of Slavery: The Condition of the Slave in Private Law from Augustus to Justinian* (Cambridge, 1908; reprint, New York, 1969).

Budge, E.A.W. (ed.), *The Book of Governors: The Historia Monastica of Thomas Bishop of Marga*, 2 vols. (London, 1893).

Burgess, A., *The Kingdom of the Wicked* (London, 1986).

Burgess, R.W., "The Dates and Editions of Eusebius' *Chronici Canones* and *Historia Ecclesiastica*," *JThS* n.s. 48 (1997) 471–504.

———, "The Dates of the First Siege of Nisibis and the Death of James of Nisibis," *Byzantion* 69 (1999) 7–17.

———, "The Dates of the Martyrdom of Simeon Bar Sabba'e and the 'Great Massacre'," *AB* 117 (1999) 9–66.

Burkitt, F.C., *The Book of Rules of Tyconius* (Cambridge, 1894).

Bury, J.B., "The Ceremonial Book of Constantine Porphyrogennetos," *EHR* 22 (1907) 209–27 and 417–39.

———, *History of the Later Roman Empire, 395–565*, 2 vols. (London, 1923).

Busse, A. (ed.), *Prolegomena et In Porphyrii Isagogen commentarium* (Berlin, 1904).

Busine, A., *Paroles d'Apollon: Pratiques et traditions oraculaires dans l'antiquité tardive* (Leiden, 2005).

Butcher, K., *Roman Syria and the Near East* (London, 2003).
Butler, J., *The Psychic Life of Power: Theories in Subjection* (Stanford, 1997).
Cabaniss, J.A., "A Note on the Date of the Great Advent Antiphons," *Speculum* 22 (1922) 440–42.
Cabrol, F., "Fêtes chrétiennes (les)," *DACL* 5.1403–51.
Cain, A., "Miracles, Martyrs, and Arians: Gregory of Tours' Sources for his Account of the Vandal Kingdom," *VChr* 59 (2005) 412–37.
———, *The Letters of Jerome: Asceticism, Biblical Exegesis, and the Construction of Christian Authority in Late Antiquity* (Oxford, 2009).
Cain, A. and J. Lössl (eds.), *Jerome of Stridon: His Life, Writings and Legacy* (Aldershot, 2009).
Cameron, A.D.E., "The Date of Iamblichus' Birth," *Hermes* 96 (1968) 374–6.
———, "Gratian's Repudiation of the Pontifical Robe," *JRS* 58 (1968) 96–102.
———, *Circus Factions* (Oxford, 1976).
———, "The Empress and the Poet: Paganism and Politics at the Court of Theodosius II," *YClS* 27 (1982) 217–89.
———, "The Last Pagans of Rome," in W.V. Harris (ed.), *The Transformation of Urbs Roma in Late Antiquity* (Portsmouth, RI, 1999) 109–21.
———, "The Imperial Pontifex," *HSCP* 103 (2007) 341–84.
Cameron, A.D.E. and A.M. Cameron, "Christianity and Tradition in the Historiography of the Late Empire," *CQ* 14 (1964) 316–28.
Cameron, A.D.E. and J. Long, *Barbarians and Politics at the Court of Arcadius* (Berkeley, 1993).
Cameron, A.M., *Continuity and Change in Sixth-Century Byzantium* (London, 1981).
———, *Procopius and the Sixth Century* (Berkeley, 1985).
———, *Christianity and the Rhetoric of Empire* (Berkeley, 1991).
———, *The Mediterranean World in Late Antiquity,* AD *395–600* (London, 1993).
Cameron, A.M. and S.G. Hall, *Eusebius. Life of Constantine* (Oxford, 1999).
Cameron, R. (ed.), *The Other Gospels* (Philadelphia, 1982).
Camplani, A. and M. Zambon, "Il sacrificio come problema in alcune correnti filosofiche di età imperiale," *AnnSE* 19 (2002) 59–99.
Caner, D., *Wandering, Begging Monks: Spiritual Authority and the Promotion of Monasticism in Late Antiquity* (Berkeley, 2005).
Cardman, F., "The Rhetoric of Holy Places: Palestine in the Fourth Century," *StudPatr* 17 (1982) 18–25.
Carletti, C., "Aspetti biometrici del matrimonio nelle iscrizioni cristiane di Roma," *Augustinianum* 17 (1977) 39–51.
Cartocci, M.C., "Alcune precisazioni sulla intitolazione a S. Agata della 'Ecclesia Gothorum' alla Suburra," in *Teoderico il Grande e i Goti d'Italia. Atti del XIII congresso internazionale di studi sull'alto Medioevo, Milano 2–6 novembre 1992*, vol. 2 (Spoleto, 1993) 611–20.
———, "S. Agatha Gothorum," *LTUR* 1 (1993) 24–6.

Cassel, J.D., "Cyril of Alexandria as Educator," in P.M. Blowers et al. (eds.), *In Dominico Eloquio* (Grand Rapids, 2002) 348–68.

Castello, M.G., "Cristianesimo e burocrazia tardoimperiale: La religiosità dei *magistri officiorum*," *CrSt* 26 (2005) 625–70.

Castritius, H., "Zur Sozialgeschichte der Heermeister des Westreichs nach der Mitte des 5. Jh.: Flavius Valila qui et Theodosius," *AncSoc* 3 (1972) 233–43.

———, "Zur Sozialgeschichte der Heermeister des Westreichs. Einheitliche Rekrutierungsmuster und Rivalitäten im spätromischen Militäradel," *MIÖG* 92 (1984) 1–33.

Catalano, P., *Contributi allo studio del diritto augurale* (Turin, 1960).

Cavallera, F., *Le schisme d'Antioche (IVe–Ve siècle)* (Paris, 1905).

Cecchelli, C., *Monumenti cristiano-eretici di Roma* (Rome, 1944).

Cecconi, G.A., *Commento storico al libro II dell'epistolario di Q. Aurelio Simmaco* (Pisa, 2002).

Certeau, M. de, *The Practice of Everyday Life,* trans. S. Randall (Berkeley, 1984).

Chabot, J. (ed. and trans.), *Le livre de la chasteté composé par Jésusdenah évêque de Baçrah* (Rome, 1896).

——— (ed. and trans.), *Synodicon orientale, ou recueil de synodes nestoriens* (Paris, 1902).

Chabrol, F. and H. Leclercq (eds.), *Dictionnaire d'archéologie chrétienne et de la liturgie*, 15 vols. (Paris, 1920–21).

Chadwick, H., "The Authenticity of Boethius' Fourth Tractate, *De fide catholica*," *JThS* n.s. 31 (1980) 368–77.

———, *Boethius, the Consolations of Music, Logic, Theology, and Philosophy* (Oxford, 1981).

Chadwick, O., "Gregory of Tours and Gregory the Great," *JThS* 50 (1949) 38–49.

Chance, J., *Medieval Mythography: From Roman North Africa to the School of Chartres, A.D. 433–1177* (Gainesville, 1994).

Chantraine, H., "Die Kreuzesvision von 351—Fakten und Probleme," *ByzZ* 86/7 (1993/4) 430–41.

Chastagnol, A., "Le sénateur Volusien et la conversion d'une famille de l'aristocratie romaine au Bas-Empire," *REA* 58 (1956) 241–53.

Chastagnol, A., *La préfecture urbaine à Rome sous le Bas-Empire* (Paris, 1960).

———, *Les Fastes de la Préfecture de Rome au Bas-Empire* (Paris, 1962).

———, "Les quinquennalia de Valentinien Ier et Valens," in *Mélanges à Pierre Bastien* (Wetteren, 1987) 255–66.

———, "Sur les *sacerdotales* africains à la veille de l'invasion vandale," in A. Mastino (ed.), *L'Africa romana. Atti del V Convegno di Studio. Sassari 11–13 dicembre 1987* (Sassari, 1988) 101–10.

Chastagnol, A. and N. Duval, "Les survivances du culte impérial dans l'Afrique du Nord à l'époque vandale," in *Mélanges d'histoire ancienne offerts à William Seston* (Paris, 1972) 87–118.

Cherlonneix, J.-L., "L'intention religieuse de l''ésotérisme platonicien'," in L. Brisson et al. (eds.), *Porphyre: La vie de Plotin*, vol. 2 (Paris, 1992) 385–418.
Chew, K., "Virgins and Eunuchs: Pulcheria, Politics and the Death of Emperor Theodosius II," *Historia* 55 (2006) 207–27.
Ciraolo, L., "Supernatural Assistants in the Greek Magical Papyri," in M. Meyer and P. Mirecki (eds.), *Ancient Magic and Ritual Power* (Leiden, 1995) 279–95.
Clark, E.A., *The Life of Melania the Younger* (New York, 1984).
———, *The Origenist Controversy: The Cultural Construction of an Early Christian Debate* (Princeton, 1992).
Clark, G., "Desires of the Hangman: Augustine on Legitimized Violence," in Drake, *Violence in Late Antiquity* (2006) 137–46.
———, "Rod, Line and Net: Augustine on the Limits of Diversity," in K. Cooper and J. Gregory (eds.), *Discipline and Diversity*, Studies in Church History 43 (Woodbridge, 2007) 80–99.
———, "Augustine's Varro, and Pagan Monotheism," in S. Mitchell and P. Van Nuffelen (eds.), *Monotheism between Pagans and Christians in Late Antiquity* (Leuven, forthcoming).
Clark, S., *Living Without Domination* (Aldershot, 2007).
Clarke, E.C., *Iamblichus' De Mysteriis: A Manifesto of the Miraculous* (Aldershot, 2001).
Clarke, E.C., J.M. Dillon, and J.P. Hershbell (eds.), *Iamblichus: De Mysteriis* (Leiden and Boston, 2004).
Closa Farrés, J., "San Gregorio Magno y la evocación de la Roma cristiana," in *Gregorio Magno e il suo tempo: XIX incontro di studiosi dell'antichità cristiana in collaborazione con l'École française de Rome, Roma, 9–12 maggio 1990*, vol. 2 (Rome, 1991) 183–97.
Clover, F.M., "Count Ricimer and the Church of the Holy Apostles'," in *Abstracts. Twenty-Second Annual Byzantine Studies Conference, October 24–27, 1996, The University of North Carolina At Chapel Hill* (Chapel Hill, 1996).
Coakley, J.F., "A Syriac Version of the Letter of Cyril of Jerusalem on the Vision of the Cross," *AB* 102 (1984) 71–84.
Colardelle, M., *Sépulture et traditions funéraires du Ve au XIIIe siècle ap. J.C. dans les campagnes des Alpes françaises du Nord* (Grenoble, 1983).
Colditz, I., *Zur Sozialterminologie der iranischen Manichäer: Eine semantische Analyse im Vergleich zu den nichtmanichäischen iranischen Quellen* (Wiesbaden, 2000).
Collins, R., "King Leovigild and the Conversion of the Visigoths," in Idem, *Law, Culture and Regionalism in Early Medieval Spain* (Aldershot, 1992) chapter 2.
Collot, C., "La pratique et l'institution du *suffragium* au Bas-Empire," *RD* 43 (1965) 185–221.
Comaroff, J. and J. Comaroff, *Of Revelation and Revolution: Christianity, Colonialism, and Consciousness in South Africa*, vol. 1 (Chicago, 1991).

Combes, I.A.H., *The Metaphor of Slavery in the Writings of the Early Church: From the New Testament to the Beginning of the Fifth Century* (Sheffield, 1998).

Comparetti, D., *Vergil in the Middle Ages*, trans. E.F.M. Benecke (1895; reprint, Princeton, 2003).

Conant, K. and G. Downey, "The Original Buildings at the Holy Sepulchre in Jerusalem," *Speculum* 31 (1956) 1–48.

Consolino, F.E., "L'*optimus princeps* secondo Ambrogio: virtù imperatorie e cristiane nelle orazioni funebri per Valentiniano e Teodosio," *RSI* 96 (1984) 1025–45.

———, "Il discorso funebre tra Oriente e Occidente: Gregorio di Nazianzo, Gregorio di Nissa, Ambrogio," in F. Conca, I. Gualandri, and G. Lozza (eds.), *Politica cultura e religione nell'impero romano (secoli IV-VI) tra Oriente e Occidente: Atti del II Convegno dell'Associazione di Studi Tardoantichi (1990)* (Naples, 1993) 171–84.

———, "Teodosio e il ruolo del principe cristiano dal *De obitu* di Ambrogio alle storie ecclesiastiche," *CrSt* 15 (1994) 257–77.

Conti, S., "Tra integrazione ed emarginazione: le ultime Vestali," *SHHA* 21 (2003) 209–22.

Cooper, K., *The Virgin and the Bride: Idealized Womanhood in Late Antiquity* (Cambridge, MA, 1996).

——— (ed.), *The Roman Martyrs and the Politics of Memory*. Early Medieval Europe 9 (Oxford, 2000).

Coşkun, A., "Virius Nichomachus Flavianus, Der Praefectus und Consul des *Carmen Contra Paganos,*" *VChr* 57 (2004) 152–78.

Courcelle, P., *Les lettres grecques en Occident de Macrobe à Cassiodore* (Paris, 1948).

———, "Les sages de Porphyre et les *viri novi* d'Arnobe," *REL* 31 (1953) 257–71.

———, "Nouveaux aspects du platonisme chez Saint Ambrose," *REL* 34 (1956) 220–39.

———, "Le colle et le clou de l'âme dans la tradition néo-platonicienne et chrétienne (*Phédon* 82e; 83d)," *RBPh* 36 (1958) 72–95.

———, *La Consolation de philosophie dans la tradition littéraire. Antécédents et postérité de Boèce* (Paris, 1967).

———, "Verissima philosophia," in J. Fontaine and C. Kannengiesser (eds.), *Epektasis. Mélanges patristiques offerts à Jean Daniélou* (Paris, 1972) 653–9.

Cracco Ruggini, L., "Il paganesimo romano tra religione e politica (384–394 d.C.): per una reinterpretazione del *Carmen contra paganos*," *MemAccLinc* 8 (1979) 3–143.

———, "Elagabalo, Costantino e i 'culti siriaci' nella 'Historia Augusta'," in G. Bonamente and N. Duval (eds.), *Historiae Augustae colloquium Parisinum* (Macerata, 1991) 123–46.

———, "Il 397: l'anno della morte di Ambrogio," in L.F. Pizzolato and M. Rizzi (eds.), *Nec timeo mori: Atti del Congresso internazionale di studi ambrosiani nel XVI centenario della morte di sant'Ambrogio (1997)* (Milan, 1998) 5–29.

Craddock, P.B., "Edward Gibbon and the 'Ruins of the Capitol'," in A. Patterson (ed.), *Roman Images* (Baltimore, 1984) 63–82.

Creed, J.L., *Lactantius: De Mortibus Persecutorum* (Oxford, 1984).

Cribiore, R., *The School of Libanius in Late Antique Antioch* (Princeton, 2007).

Crifò, G., "La Chiesa e l'Impero nella storia del diritto," in E. Dal Covolo and R. Uglione (eds.), *Cristianesimo e istituzioni politiche da Costantino a Giustiniano* (Rome, 1997) 171–96.

Croke, B., "Justinian's Constantinople," in Maas, *Cambridge Companion to the Age of Justinian*, 60–86.

Croke, B. and J. Harries, *Religious Conflict in Fourth-Century Rome: A Documentary Study* (Sydney, 1982).

Cumont, F., *Les religions orientales dans le paganisme* (Paris, 1929).

Cuneo, P.O., *La legislazione di Costantino II, Costanzo II e Costante (337–361)* (Milan, 1997).

Curran, J., "Moving Statues in Late Antique Rome: Problems of Perspective," *ArtH* 17 (1994) 46–58.

Dagron, G., *Emperor and Priest: The Imperial Office in Byzantium* (Cambridge, 2003).

Daley, B.E., *The Hope of the Early Church. A Handbook of Patristic Eschatology* (Cambridge, 1991).

Dalsgaard Larsen, B., *Jamblique de Calchis: Exégète et philosophe* (Aarhus, 1972).

———, "La place de Jamblique dans la philosophie antique tardive," in H. Dörrie (ed.), *De Jamblique à Proclus* (Geneva, 1975) 1–34.

Darnton, R., "A Bourgeois Puts His World in Order," in *The Great Cat Massacre and Other Episodes in French Cultural History* (New York, 1984) 107–43.

Davies, J.P., *Rome's Religious History: Livy, Tacitus, and Ammianus on their Gods* (Cambridge, 2004).

Dawes, E.A.S. and N.H. Baynes, *Three Byzantine Saints: Contemporary Biographies of St. Daniel the Stylite, St. Theodore of Sykeon and St. John the Almsgiver* (London, 1948).

Deane, H.A., *The Political and Social Ideas of St. Augustine* (New York, 1963).

Debordes, F., "Virgile s'explique," *Europe* 71 (1993) 81–92.

Delehaye, H., *Étude sur le légendier romain: les saints de novembre et décembre* (Brussels, 1936).

D'Elia, S., "Ammiano Marcellino e il cristianesimo," *SR* 10 (1962) 372–90.

Delly, E.-K., "La place du métropolite de Nisibe parmi les électeurs du patriarche," *OS* 2 (1957) 389–94.

Delmaire, R., *Les lois religieuses des empereurs romains de Constantin à Théodose II (312–438). I. Code Théodosien Livre XVI.* SCh 497 (Paris, 2005).

Delumeau, J., *Mille ans de bonheur* (Paris, 1995).

Déroche, V., "Polémique anti-judaïque et émergence de l'Islam," *REByz* 57 (1999) 141–61.

Den Boeft, J., D. Den Hengst and H.C. Teitler, *Philological and Historical Commentary on Ammianus Marcellinus XX* (Stuttgart, 1987).

De Vogel, C.J., *La discipline pénitentielle en Gaule des origines a la fin du VIIe siècle* (Paris, 1952).

———, "Boethiana II," *Vivarium* 10 (1972) 1–40.

Devos, P., "Égérie à Édesse: S. Thomas l'Apôtre. Le roi Abgar," *AB* 85 (1972) 381–400.

Dickie, M.W., *Magic and Magicians in the Greco-Roman World* (London and New York, 2001).

Diefenbach, S., "Frömmigkeit und Kaiserakzeptanz im frühen Byzanz," *Saeculum* 47 (1996) 35–66.

———, "Zwischen Liturgie und civilitas: Konstantinopel im 5. Jahrhundert und die Etablierung eines städtischen Kaisertums," in R. Warland (ed.), *Bildlichkeit und Bildort von Liturgie* (Wiesbaden, 2002) 21–47.

Diehl, C., *Etudes sur l'administration byzantine dans l'exarchat de Ravenne (568–751)* (Paris, 1888).

Digeser, E.D., "Lactantius and Constantine's Letter to Arles: Dating the *Divine Institutes*," *JECS* 2 (1994) 33–52.

———, "Lactantius, Porphyry and the Debate over Religious Toleration," *JRS* 88 (1998) 129–46.

———, *The Making of a Christian Empire: Lactantius and Rome* (Ithaca and London, 2000).

———, "Porphyry, Lactantius, and the Paths to God," *StudPatr* 38 (2001) 521–8.

———, "Porphyry, Julian, or Hierokles? The Anonymous Hellene in Makarios Magnês' *Apocriticus*," *JThS* n.s. 53 (2002) 466–502.

———, "An Oracle of Apollo at Daphne and the Great Persecution," *CPh* 99 (2004) 57–77.

———, "Lactantius, Eusebius and Arnobius: Evidence for the Causes of the Great Persecution," *StudPatr* 39 (2006) 33–46.

Dillemann, L., *Haute Mésopotamie orientale et pays adjacents: Contribution à la géographie historique de la région, du Ve s. avant l'ère chrétienne au VIe s. de cette ère* (Paris, 1962).

Dillery, J., "Chresmologues and *Manteis*: Independent Diviners and the Problem of Authority," in Johnston and Struck, *Mantikê* (2005), 167–231.

Dillon, J. (ed.), *Iamblichi Chalcidensis in Platonis Dialogos Commentaria* (Leiden, 1973).

———, "Iamblichus of Chalcis (c. 240–325 AD)," *ANRW* 2.36.2 (1987) 862–909.

———, "The Theology of Julian's 'Hymn to King Helios'," *Ítaca* 14–15 (1998–99) 103–15.

———, "Philosophy as a Profession in Late Antiquity," in S. Swain and M. Edwards (eds.), *Approaching Late Antiquity* (Oxford, 2004) 401–18.

Dodds, E.R., "New Light on the *Chaldean Oracles*," *HTR* 54 (1961) 263–73.

———, *Pagan and Christian in an Age of Anxiety: Some Aspects of Religious Experience from Marcus Aurelius to Constantine* (Cambridge, 1965).

Dodgeon, M.H. and S.N.C. Lieu, *The Roman Eastern Frontier and the Persian Wars (AD 226–363): A Documentary History* (London, 1991).

Dölger, F.J., *Die Sonne der Gerechtigkeit und der Schwarze, eine religionsgeschichtliche Studie zum Taufgelöbnis* (Münster, 1918).

———, *Sol Salutis. Gebet und Gesang im christlichen Altertum* (Münster, 1920).

———, "Das Anhängekreuzchen der hl. Makrina und ihr Ring mit der Kreuzpartikel: Ein Beitrag zur religiösen Volkskunde des 4. Jahrhunderts nach der Vita Macrinae des Gregor van Nyssa," *Antike und Christentum* 3 (1932) 81–116.

Dörrie, H., "Die Solar-Theologie in der kaiserzeitlichen Antike," in H. Frohnes and V.W. Knorr (eds.), *Kirchengeschichte als Missionsgeschichte*, vol. 1 (Munich, 1974) 283–92.

Dothan, M., *Hammath Tiberias. Early Synagogues and the Hellenistic and Roman Remains* (Jerusalem, 1983).

Doval, A., *Cyril of Jerusalem, Mystagogue. The Authorship of the Mystagogic Catecheses* (Washington, 2001).

Downey, G., "The Shrines of St. Babylas at Antioch and Daphne," in *Antioch-on-the-Orontes*, vol. 2, *The Excavations of 1933–1936* (Princeton, 1938) 45–8.

———, *A History of Antioch in Syria from Seleucus to the Arab Conquest* (Princeton, 1961).

Drake, H.A., "The Return of the Holy Sepulchre," *CHR* 70 (1984) 263–7.

———, *Constantine and the Bishops: The Politics of Intolerance* (Baltimore, 2000).

———, (ed.), *Violence in Late Antiquity: Perceptions and Practices* (Aldershot, 2006).

Drijvers, H.J.W. and J.W. Drijvers, *The Finding of the True Cross. The Judas Kyriakos Legend in Syriac. Introduction, Text and Translation* (Louvain, 1997).

Drijvers, J.W., *Helena Augusta. The Mother of Constantine the Great and Her Finding of the True Cross* (Leiden, 1992).

———, "Promoting Jerusalem. Cyril and the True Cross," in Idem and J.W. Watt (eds.), *Portraits of Spiritual Authority* (Leiden, 1999) 79–95.

———. "Cyril of Jerusalem and the Rebuilding of the Jewish Temple (A.D. 363)," in C. Kroon and D. den Hengst (eds.), *Ultima Aetas. Time, Tense and Transience in the Ancient World. Studies in Honour of Jan den Boeft* (Amsterdam, 2000) 123–35.

———, *Cyril of Jerusalem: Bishop and City* (Leiden, 2004).

Duchesne, L. (ed.), *Le Liber pontificalis: texte, introduction et commentaire*, 2 vols. (Rome, 1886–92; 2nd ed. Paris, 1955).

Dufault, O., "Magic and Religion in Augustine and Iamblichus," in R.M. Frakes and E.D. Digeser (eds.), *Religious Identity in Late Antiquity* (Toronto, 2006) 59–84.

Dufourcq, A., *Étude sur les gesta martyrum romains* (Paris, 1886–1910).

Dulaey, M., *Victorin de Poetovio. Premier Exégète Latin,* 2 vols. (Paris, 1993).
———, *Victorin de Poetovio. Sur l'Apocalypse et autres écrits* (Paris, 1997).
Dupuis, X., "Les pontifes et les augures dans les cités africaines au Bas-Empire," in *Afrique du Nord antique et médiévale. Spectacles, vie portuaire, religions. Actes du Ve colloque international du CTHS (Avignon, 1990)* (Paris, 1992) 139–51.
Durkheim, E., *The Elementary Forms of Religious Life,* trans. K.E. Fields ([1915] New York, 1995).
Duval, R. (ed.), *Isoyahb patriarchae III liber epistularum.* CSCO Scr. Syr. 11 (Paris, 1904).
Duval, Y-M., "Formes profanes et formes bibliques dans les oraisons funèbres de saint Ambroise," in M. Fuhrmann (ed.), *Christianisme et formes littéraires de l'antiquité tardive en Occident* (Geneva, 1977) 235–301.
Dyson, R.W., *The Pilgrim City: Social and Political Ideas in the Writings of St. Augustine of Hippo* (Woodbridge, 2001).
Edwards, C., *Writing Rome: Textual Approaches to the City* (Cambridge, 1996).
Edwards, M., *Constantine and Christendom* (Liverpool, 2003).
Edwards, R., "Fulgentius and the Collapse of Meaning," *Helios* 3 (1976) 17–35.
———, "The Heritage of Fulgentius," in A.S. Bernardo and S. Levin (eds.), *The Classics in the Middle Ages: Papers of the Twentieth Annual Conference of the Center for Medieval and Early Renaissance Studies* (Binghamton, NY, 1990) 141–51.
Ehrhardt, A., *Politische Metaphysik von Solon bis Augustin,* 3 vols. (Tübingen, 1959–69).
Eliav, Y.Z., *God's Mountain: The Temple Mount in Time, Place and Memory* (Baltimore, 2005).
Elliott, T.G., *Ammianus Marcellinus and Fourth Century History* (Toronto, 1983).
Elsner, J., "Inventing Christian Rome," in C. Edwards and G. Woolf (eds.), *Rome the Cosmopolis* (Cambridge, 2003) 71–99.
Erfurdt, K.G.A. and J.A. Wagner (eds.), *Ammiani Marcellini quae supersunt* (Leipzig, 1808).
Ernesti, J., *Princeps christianus und Kaiser aller Römer: Theodosius der Große im Lichte zeitgenössicher Quellen* (Paderborn, 1998).
Errington, R.M., "Christian Accounts of the Religious Legislation of Theodosius I," *Klio* 79 (1997) 398–433.
———, *Roman Imperial Policy From Julian to Theodosius* (Chapel Hill, 2006).
Esbroeck, M. van, "Une homélie sur l'église attribuée à Jean de Jérusalem," *Muséon* 86 (1973) 283–304.
———, "Jean II de Jérusalem et les cultes de S. Étienne, de la Sainte Sion et de la Croix," *AB* 102 (1984) 99–134.
———, "La vie arabe de Saint Théodose le Cénobiarque," *POr* 18 (1993) 45–73.
Evans, J.A.S., *The Age of Justinian. The Circumstances of Imperial Power* (London, 1996).

Evans Grubbs, J.A., Munita Coniugia: *The Emperor Constantine's Legislation on Marriage and the Family* (diss: Stanford Univ., 1987).

———, "Constantine and Imperial Legislation on the Family," in J. Harries and I. Wood (eds.), *The Theodosian Code: Studies in the Imperial Law of Late Antiquity* (London and Ithaca, 1993) 120–42.

———, *Law and Family in late Antiquity: The Emperor Constantine's Marriage Legislation* (Oxford, 1995).

Ewald, M.L., *Jerome, Homilies*, vol. 2, Fathers of the Church 57 (Washington, 1966).

Faller, O. (ed.), *Sancti Ambrosii opera: De Obitu Theodosii.* CSEL 73.7 (Vienna, 1955).

Fanning, S., "Lombard Arianism Reconsidered," *Speculum* 56 (1981) 241–58.

Favro, D., "The iconiCITY of ancient Rome," *JUH* 33 (2006) 20–38.

Feffer, L.-C. and P. Périn, *Les Francs: A l'origine de la France* (Paris, 1987).

Ferreiro, A., "Braga and Tours: Some Observations on Gregory's *De virtutibus sancti Martini* (1.11)," *JECS* 3 (1995) 195–210.

Fiey, J.M., "Le démembrement de Ba Nuhadra," *OS* 6 (1961) 353–84.

——— *Assyrie chrétienne I: Contribution à l'étude de l'histoire et de la géographie ecclésiastiques et monastiques du nord de l'Iraq* (Beirut, 1965).

———, "Išoᶜyaw le Grand: Vie du catholicos nestorien Išoᶜyaw III de Adiabène (580–659)," *OCP* 35 (1969) 305–33; 36 (1970) 5–46.

———, *Nisibe: métropole syriaque orientale et ses suffragants des origines à nos jours* (Louvain, 1977).

Filoramo, G., "Profezia e politica nelle 'Storie monastiche' di Cirillo di Scitopoli," *CrSt* 20 (1999) 521–44.

Finamore, J.F., "Plotinus and Iamblichus on Magic and Theurgy," *Dionysius* n.s. 17 (1999) 83–94.

Finan, T. and V. Twomey (eds.), *The Relationship between Neoplatonism and Christianity* (Dublin, 1992).

Fitzgerald, A., *Conversion through Penance in the Italian Church of the Fourth and Fifth Centuries: New Approaches to the Experience of Conversion from Sin* (Lewiston, PA, 1988).

Fleury, M. and A. France-Lanord, *Les trésors mérovingiens de la basilique de Saint-Denis* (Woippy, 1998).

Fögen, M.T., *Die Enteignung der Wahrsager. Studien zum kaiserlichen Wissensmonopol in der Spätantike* (Frankfurt, 1993).

Fontaine, J., *Aspects et problèmes de la prose d'art latine au troisième siècle. La genèse des styles latins chrétiens* (Turin, 1968).

Forlin Patrucco, M., "Il tema politico della vittoria e della croce in Ambrogio e nella tradizione ambrosiana," in R. Cantalamessa and L.F. Pizzolato (eds.), *Paradoxos Politeia: Studi Patristici in onore di Giuseppe Lazzati* (Milan, 1979) 406–18.

Fortin, E.L., "The *Viri novi* of Arnobius and the Conflict between Faith and Reason in the Early Christian Centuries," in D. Neiman and M. Schatkin (eds.), *The*

Heritage of the Early Church: Essays in Honor of the Very Reverend Georges Vasilievich Florovsky (Rome, 1973) 197–226.
Foss, C., "The Near Eastern countryside in late antiquity: a review article", in *The Roman and Byzantine Near East: Some Recent Archaeological Research* (Ann Arbor, 1995) 213–23.
Fossati Vanzetti, M.B., "Vendita ed esposizione degli infanti da Costantino a Giustiniano," *SDHI* 49 (1983) 179–224.
Foucault, M. *Discipline and Punish: The Birth of the Prison*, trans. A. Sheridan (New York, 1977).
———, "Power, Right, Truth," in C. Gordon (ed.), *Power/Knowledge* (New York, 1980) 92–108.
———, "The Subject and Power," in H.L. Dreyfus and P. Rabinow (eds.), *Michel Foucault: Beyond Structuralism and Hermeneutics*, 2nd ed. (Chicago, 1982).
———, *The Use of Pleasure,* trans. R. Hurley (New York, 1985).
Fowden, E.K., *The Barbarian Plain: Saint Sergius between Rome and Iran* (Berkeley, 1999).
Fowden, G., "Late Antique Paganism Reasoned and Revealed," *JRS* 71 (1981) 178–82.
———, *The Egyptian Hermes* (Princeton, 1986).
———, "Constantine's Porphyry Column: The Earliest Literary Allusion," *JRS* 81 (1991) 119–31.
———, *Empire to Commonwealth: Consequences of Monotheism in Late Antiquity* (Princeton, 1993).
———, "The Last Days of Constantine: Oppositional Versions and Their Influence," *JRS* 84 (1994) 146–70.
Franchi di Cavalieri, P., "Il κοιμητήριον di Antiochia," *ST* 49 (1928) 146–53.
Frankfurter, D., "The Legacy of Jewish Apocalypses in Early Christianity," in J.C. VanderKam and W. Adler (eds.), *The Jewish Apocalyptic Heritage in Early Christianity* (Assen, 1996) 129–200.
———, *Religion in Roman Egypt* (Princeton, 1998).
———, "Voices, Books, and Dreams: The Diversification of Divination Media in Late Antique Egypt," in Johnston and Struck, *Mantikê* (2005), 233–54.
Fraschetti, A., *La conversione: Da Roma pagana a Roma cristiana* (Rome, 1999).
———, "Il Campidoglio: dal tardoantico all'alto medioevo," in *Roma nell'alto Medioevo: 27 aprile–1 maggio 2000* (Spoleto, 2001) 31–56.
Fraser, M.A., *The Feast of the Encaenia in the Fourth Century and in the Ancient Liturgical Sources of Jerusalem* (diss. Univ. of Durham, 1995).
French, D., "Rhetoric and the Rebellion of A.D. 387 in Antioch," *Historia* 47 (1998) 468–84.
Frolow, A., *La relique de la Vraie Croix. Recherches sur le développement d'un culte* (Paris, 1961).
Gagé, J., *Apollon Romain. Essai sur le culte d'Apollon et le développement du "ritus Graecus" à Rome des origines à Auguste* (Paris, 1955).

Gaillard de Sémainville, H., "Nouvel examen de la plaque-boucle mérovingienne de Landelinus découverte à Ladoix-Serrigny (Côte d'Or): apocalypse et millénarisme dans l'art mérovingien," *RAE* 52 (2003) 297–328.
Galletier, E., "La mort de Maximien d'après le Panégyrique de 310 et la vision de Constantin au temple d'Apollon," *REA* 52 (1950) 288–99.
Gallonier, A., *Boèce: Opuscula sacra*, vol. 1 (Louvain, 2007).
Garnsey, P., "Lactantius and Augustine," in Bowman et al., *Representations of Empire* (2002), 53–79.
Garsoïan, N., "Le rôle de l'hiérarchie chrétienne dans les relations diplomatiques entre Byzance et les Sassanides," *REArm* 10 (1973–74) 119–38.
———, *Armenia Between Byzantium and the Sasanians* (London, 1985).
Gaudemet, J., *L'Église dans l'empire romain (IVe–Ve siècles)* (Paris, 1958).
———, "Indulgentia principis," Conferenze Romanistiche 2 (Milano, 1967).
Geertman, H., More Veterum: *Il Liber Pontificalis e gli edifici ecclesiastici di Roma nella tarda antichità e nell'medioevo* (Groningen, 1975).
Geertz, C. *The Interpretation of Cultures: Selected Essays* (New York, 1973).
Geiger, J., "The Revolt under Gallus and the Temple Building under Julian," in Z. Baras et al. (eds.), *Eretz Israel from the Destruction of the Second Temple to the Muslim Conquest* (Jerusalem 1982) 202–8 (in Hebrew).
Gerbenne, B. "Modèles bibliques pour un empereur: le De obitu Theodosii d'Ambrose de Milan," in *Rois et reines de la Bible au miroir de Pères* (Strasbourg, 1999) 161–76.
Gero, S., "Only a Change of Masters? The Christians of Iran and the Muslim Conquest," *StudIr* 5 (1987) 43–8.
———, "Cyril of Alexandria, Image Worship, and the *Vita* of Rabban Hormizd," *OC* 62 (1978) 77–97.
Giannarelli, E. (ed.), *Cosma e Damiano dall'Oriente a Firenze* (Florence, 2002).
Giardina, A., *L'Italia romana. Storie di un'identità incompiuta* (Rome, 1997).
Gifford, E.H., *Eusebius. The Preparation for the Gospel*, 2 vols. (Oxford, 1903; reprint Eugene, OR, 2002).
Girardet, K., "Vom Sonnen-Tag zum Sonntag. Der Dies solis in Gesetzgebung und Politik Konstantins d. Gr.," *ZAC* 11 (2007) 279–310.
Goddard, C.J., "Les formes festives de l'allégeance au prince en Italie centrale, sous le règne de Constantin: un suicide religieux?," *MEFRA* 114 (2001) 1025–88.
———, "The Evolution of Pagan Sanctuaries in Late Antique Italy (Fourth–Sixth Centuries AD): A New Administrative and Legal Framework. A Paradox," in M. Ghilardi, C.J. Goddard, and P. Porena (eds.), *Les cités de l'Italie tardo-antique (IVe–VIe siècle). Institutions, économie, société, culture et religion* (Rome, 2006) 281–308.
Goffart, W., "Did Julian Combat Venal Suffragium? A Note on *C.Th.* 2.29.1," *CPh* 65 (1970) 145–51.

Goulet, R., "Hypothèses Récentes sur le traité de Porphyre *Contre les chrétiens*," in M. Narcy and É. Rebillard (eds.), *Hellénisme et Christianisme* (Lille, 2004) 61–109.
Gradenwitz, O., *Heidelberger Index zum Theodosianus* (Berlin, 1925).
Graf, F., "Prayer in Magical and Religious Ritual," in C.A. Faraone and D. Obbink (eds.), *Magika Hiera: Ancient Greek Magic and Religion* (New York, 1991) 188–213.
———, *Gottesnähe und Schadenzauber. Die Magie in der griechisch-römischen Antike* (Munich, 1996).
———, "Rolling the Dice for an Answer," in Johnston and Struck, *Mantikê* (2005), 51–97.
Grafton, A. and M. Williams, *Christianity and the Transformation of the Book* (Cambridge, MA, 2006).
Graham, M.W., *News and Frontier Consciousness in the Late Roman Empire* (Ann Arbor, 2006).
Gransden, K.W., *Virgil's Iliad: An Essay on Epic Narrative* (Cambridge, 1984).
Greatrex, G. and J.W. Watt, "One, Two or Three Feasts? The Brytae, the Maiuma and the May Festival at Edessa," *OC* 83 (1999) 1–21.
Green, M.J. and J. Ferguson, "Constantine, Sun-Symbols and the Labarum," *DUJ* 49 (1987) 9–17.
Grégoire, H., "La 'conversion' de Constantin," *RUB* 36 (1930) 231–72.
———, "Eusèbe n'est pas l'auteur de la 'Vita Constantini' dans sa forme actuelle et Constantin ne s'est pas 'converti' en 312," *Byzantion* 13 (1938) 561–83.
———, "La vision de Constantin 'liquidée,'" *Byzantion* 14 (1939) 341–51.
Greisiger, L., "Habbib," *BBKL* 26 (2006) 601–5.
———, "Šmona und Gurya," *BBKL* 26 (2006) 1438–44.
Grierson, P., *Byzantine Coins* (London, 1982).
Groß-Albenhausen, K., Imperator christianissimus: *Der christliche Kaiser bei Ambrosius und Johannes Chrysostomus* (Frankfurt, 1999).
Gruber, J., "Boethius 1925–1998. Teil II," *Lustrum* 40 (1998) 199–259.
———, *Kommentar zu Boethius, De Consolatione Philosophiae*, 2nd ed. (Berlin, 2006).
Grünewald, T., Constantinus Maximus Augustus: *Herrschaftspropaganda in der zeitgenössischen Überlieferung* (Stuttgart, 1990).
Guarducci, M., "Teodosio rinnovatore di Corinto," in J. Bingen, G. Cambier, and G. Nachtergael (eds.), *Le monde grec. Hommages à Claire Préaux* (Brussels, 1975) 527–34.
Guidi, I. (ed.), *Chronicon anonymum.* CSCO Scr. Syr. 1 (Paris, 1903).
Gwynn, D.M., *The Eusebians: The Polemic of Athanasius of Alexandria and the Construction of the "Arian Controversy"* (Oxford, 2007).
Haarer, F.K., *Anastasius I: Politics and Empire in the Late Roman World* (Cambridge, 2006).
Haas, C., *Alexandria in Late Antiquity* (Baltimore, 1997).

Haase, R., *Untersuchungen zur Verwaltung des spätrömischen Reiches unter Kaiser Justinian I* (Wiesbaden, 1994).
Hachlili, R., "The Zodiac in Ancient Jewish Art: Representations and Signification," *BASOR* 28 (1977) 61–77.
Hadot, P., "Citations de Porphyre chez Augustin. A propos d'un ouvrage récent," *REAug* 6 (1960) 205–44.
———, "Théologie, exégèse, révélation, écriture dans la philosophie grecque," in M. Tardieu (ed.), *Les Règles de l'interprétation* (Paris, 1987) 13–34.
Hage, W., *Die syrisch-jakobitischen Kirche in frühislamischer Zeit* (Wiesbaden, 1966).
Hagendahl, H., "Methods of Citation in Post-Classical Latin Prose," *Eranos* 45 (1947) 114–28.
Hahn, W., *Moneta Imperii Byzantini,* vol. 1, *Von Anastasius I. bis Justinianus I (491–565)* (Vienna, 1973).
Hall, L.J., "Cicero's *instinctu divino* and Constantine's *instinctu divinitatis,*" *JECS* 6 (1998) 647–71.
Halleux, A. de, "Martyrios-Sahdona: La vie mouvementée d'un 'hérétique' de l'Église nestorienne," *OCP* 24 (1958) 93–128.
Halsall, G., "Nero and Herod? The Death of Chilperic and Gregory's Writing of History," in K. Mitchell and I. Wood (eds.), *The World of Gregory of Tours* (Leiden, 2002) 337–50.
Halsbergh, G.H., *The Cult of Sol Invictus* (Leiden, 1972).
Hanson, J.S., "Dreams and Visions in the Graeco-Roman World and Early Christianity," *ANRW* 2.23.2 (1981) 1395–427.
Hanson, R.P.C., *The Search for the Christian Doctrine of God: The Arian Controversy 318–381* (Edinburgh, 1988).
Harnack, A. von, Porphyrios, *"Gegen die Christen," 15 Bucher: Zeugnisse, Fragmente und Referate* (Berlin, 1916).
———, *Neue Fragmente des Werks des Porphyrius gegen die Christen* (Berlin, 1921).
Harries, J.D., "Pius princeps: Theodosius II and Fifth-Century Constantinople," in P. Magadalino (ed.), *New Constantines* (Aldershot, 1994) 35–44.
———, *Law and Empire in Late Antiquity* (Cambridge, 1999).
———, "Resolving Disputes: The Frontiers of Law in Late Antiquity," in Mathisen, *Law, Society and Authority* (2001), 68–82.
Harris, W.V., "Child-Exposure in the Roman Empire," *JRS* 84 (1994) 1–22.
———, "Demography, Geography, and the Sources of Roman Slaves," *JRS* 89 (1999) 62–75.
Hatt, J.J., "La vision de Constantin au sanctuaire de Grand et l'origine celtique du Labarum," *Latomus* 9 (1952) 427–36.
Hays, G., "Pseudo-Fulgentian *Super Thebaiden,*" in J.F. Miller, C. Damon, and K.S. Myers (eds.), *Vertis in Usum: Studies in Honor of Edward Courtney* (Munich and Leipzig, 2002) 200–218.

———, "The Date and Identity of the Mythographer Fulgentius," *JML* 13 (2003) 163–252.

Healey, J.F., "The Christians of Qatar in the 7th Century A.D.," in I.R. Netton (ed.), *Studies in Honour of Clifford Edmund Bosworth*, vol. 1 (Leiden, 2000) 222–37.

Hefele, K.J., *A History of the Christian Councils from the Original Documents*, vol. 1, *To the Close of the Council of Nicaea A.D. 325* (Edinburgh, 1894).

Heid, S., *Kreuz, Jerusalem, Kosmos. Aspekte frühchristlicher Staurologie* (Münster, 2001).

Heil, M., "Perser in spätrömischen Dienst," in J. Wiesehöfer and P. Huyse (eds.), *Eran und Aneran* (Stuttgart, 2006) 143–80.

Heim, F., "Les auspices publiques de Constantine à Théodose," *Ktema* 13 (1988) 41–53.

———, *La théologie de la victoire de Constantin a Théodose* (Paris, 1992).

Heinzelmann, M., *Gregor von Tours (538–594): "Zehn Bücher Geschichte", Historiographie und Gesellschaftskonzept im 6. Jahrhunderts* (Darmstadt, 1994).

———, "Heresy in Books I and II of Gregory of Tours' Historiae," in A.C. Murray (ed.), *After Rome's Fall: Narrators and Sources of Early Medieval History. Essays Presented to Walter Goffart* (Toronto, 1998) 67–82.

———, *Gregory of Tours: History and Society in the Sixth Century*, trans. C. Carroll (Cambridge, 2001).

Helm, R. (ed.), *Fulgentii Opera* (Leipzig, 1898; reprint, Stuttgart, 1970).

Hen, Y., *Culture and Religion in Merovingian Gaul, AD 481–751* (Leiden, 1995).

Henderson, J. and R. Wall (eds.), *Poor Women and Children in the European Past* (London and New York, 1994).

Herrmann, P., *Der römische Kaisereid* (Göttingen, 1968).

Hermanowicz, E.T., *Possidius of Calama: A Study of the North African Episcopate in the Age of Augustine* (Oxford, 2008).

Hersch, K.K., Review of I. Gradel, *Emperor Worship and Roman Religion*, *JRS* 95 (2005) 259–60.

Herz, M.F., *Sacrum Commercium* (Munich, 1958).

Herzog, R., *Die Bibelepik der lateinischen Spätantike: Formgeschichte einer erbaulichen Gattung, Theorie und Geschichte der Literatur und der schönen Künste* (Munich, 1975).

Hildebrand, A., *Boëthius und seine Stellung zum Christentume* (Regensburg, 1885).

Hill, J., "The *litaniae maiores* and *minores* in Rome, Francia and Anglo-Saxon England: Terminology, Texts, and Traditions ," *EME* 9 (2000) 211–46.

Hillgarth, J.N., "Coins and Chronicles: Propaganda in Sixth-Century Spain and the Byzantine Background," *Historia* 15 (1966) 483–508.

Hinds, S., *Allusion and Intertext: Dynamics of Appropriation in Roman Poetry, Roman Literature and Its Contexts* (Cambridge, 1998).

Hirschle, M., *Sprachphilosophie und Namenmagie im Neuplatonismus: Mit einem Exkurs zu "Demokrit" B 142* (Meisenheim am Glan, 1979).
Holleman, A.W.J., *Pope Gelasius I and the Lupercalia* (Amsterdam, 1974).
Holum, K.G., *Theodosian Empresses: Women and Imperial Dominion in Late Antiquity* (Berkeley, 1982).
Hombergen, D., *The Second Origenist Controversy: A New Perspective on Cyril of Scythopolis' Monastic Biographies as Historical Sources for Sixth-Century Origenism* (Rome, 2001).
Hopkins, K., "The Political Power of Eunuchs," in Idem, *Conquerors and Slaves* (Cambridge, 1978) 172–96.
Horbury, W., "Suffering and Messianism in Yose ben Yose," in Idem and B. McNeil (eds), *Suffering and Martyrdom in the New Testament: Studies Presented to G.M. Styler by the Cambridge New Testament Seminar* (Cambridge, 1981) 143–82.
Horner, T., "Jewish Aspects of the *Protoevangelium of James*," *JECS* 12 (1993) 313–35.
Hornung, E., *Akhenaten and the Religion of Light*, trans. David Lorton (Ithaca, NY, 1999).
Howard-Johnston, J., "The Two Great Powers in Late Antiquity: A Comparison," in A.M. Cameron (ed.), *The Byzantine and Early Islamic Near East III: States, Resources, and Armies* (Princeton, 1995) 157–226.
Howe, G., *Fasti sacerdotum populi Romani* (Leipzig, 1904).
Hoyland, R., *Seeing Islam as Others Saw It: A Survey and Evaluation of Christian, Jewish, and Zoroastrian Writings on Early Islam* (Princeton, 1997).
———, "New Documentary Texts and the Early Islamic State," *BSOAS* 69 (2006) 395–416.
Hubert, J., J. Porcher, and W.F. Volbach (eds.), *Europe des invasions* (Paris, 1967).
Huebner, S., *Der Klerus in der Gesellschaft des spätantiken Kleinasiens* (Stuttgart, 2005).
Hülsen, C., C. Cecchelli, G. Giovannoni, U. Monneret de Villard, and A. Muñoz, *S. Agata dei Goti* (Rome, 1924).
Humbert, M., "Enfants à louer ou à vendre: Augustin et l'autorité parentale (Ep. 10* et 24*)," in *Les lettres de Saint Augustin découvertes par Johannes Divjak* (Paris, 1983) 189–204.
Humfress, C., "Law and Legal Practice in the Age of Justinian," in Maas, *Cambridge Companion to the Age of Justinian* (2005), 161–84.
Hunecke, V., "The Abandonment of Legitimate Children in Nineteenth-Century Milan and the European Context," in Henderson and Wall, *Poor Women and Children in the European Past* (1994), 117–35.
Hunt, E.D., "From Dalmatia to the Holy Land. Jerome and the World of Late Antiquity," *JRS* 67 (1977) 170–4.
———, "Ammianus Marcellinus and Christianity," *CQ* 35 (1985) 186–200.
———, *Holy Land Pilgrimage in the Later Roman Empire* (Oxford, 1992).

———, "Christianity in Ammianus Marcellinus revisited," *StudPatr* 24 (1993) 108–13.

———, "Constantine and Jerusalem," *JEH* 48 (1997) 405–24.

———, "The Church as a Public Institution," in A.M. Cameron and P. Garnsey (eds.), *The Cambridge Ancient History,* vol. 13 (Cambridge and New York, 1998) 238–72.

Hunter, D., "John Chrysostom," in E. Fohlbusch (ed.), *The Encyclopedia of Christianity*, vol. 1 (Grand Rapids, 1999) 475–7.

Huppé, B.F., "Aeneas' Journey to the New Troy," in Bernardo and Levin, *Classics in the Middle Ages*, 175–87.

Ilski, B.K., "Der schwache Kaiser Theodosios," in L.M. Hoffmann and A. Mouchizedeh (eds.), *Zwischen Polis, Provinz und Peripherie* (Wiesbaden, 2005) 3–23.

Irshai, O., "Constantine and the Jews: The Prohibition against Entering Jerusalem—History and Hagiography," *Zion* 60 (1995) 129–78 (in Hebrew).

———, "Cyril of Jerusalem: the Apparation of the Cross and the Jews," in O. Limor and G. Stroumsa (eds.), *Contra Iudaeos. Ancient and Medieval Polemics between Christians and Jews* (Tübingen, 1996) 85–104.

Jacobs, A.S., *Remains of the Jews. The Holy Land and Christian Empire in Late Antiquity* (Stanford, 2004).

Jacobson, H., "Artapanus Judaeus," *JJS* 57 (2006) 210–21.

Jacques, F. and J. Scheid, *Roma e il suo impero. Istituzioni, economia, religione* (Rome, 1982).

James, E., "Bede and the Tonsure Question," *Peritia* 3 (1984) 167–82.

———, "Gregory of Tours, the Visigoths and Spain," in S. Barton and P. Linehan (eds.), *Cross, Crescent and Conversion: Studies on Medieval Spain and Christendom in Memory of Richard Fletcher* (Leiden, 2008) 43–64.

Janowitz, N., *Magic in the Roman World: Pagans, Jews, and Christians* (London, 2001).

Jay, P. "Jérôme auditeur d'Apollinaire de Laodicée à Antioche," *REAug* 20 (1974) 36–41.

Jensen, R.M., "The Economy of the Trinity at the Creation of Adam and Eve," *JECS* 7 (1999) 527–46.

Johns, J., "Archaeology and the History of Early Islam: The First Seventy Years," *JESHO* 46 (2003) 411–36.

Johnson, A.P., *Ethnicity and Argument in Eusebius'* Praeparatio Evangelica (Oxford, 2006).

———, "Eusebius' *Praeparatio Evangelica* as Literary Experiment," in S.I. Johnson (ed.), *Greek Literature in Late Antiquity: Dynamism, Didacticism, Classicism* (Aldershot, 2006) 67–89.

———, "Eusebius as Educator: The Context and Importance of the *General Elementary Introduction*," in S. Inowlocki and C. Zamagni (eds.), *Reconsidering Eusebius* (Leiden, forthcoming).

Johnson, M.J., "Architecture of Empire," in Lenski, *Cambridge Companion to the Age of Constantine* (2006), 278–97.

Johnston, S.I., *Hekate Soteira* (Atlanta, 1990).

Johnston, S.I. and P. Struck (eds.), *Mantikê: Studies in Ancient Divination* (Leiden, 2005).

Jones, A.H.M., *Constantine and the Conversion of Europe*, rev. ed. (New York, 1962).

———, *The Later Roman Empire 284–602: A Social, Economic, and Administrative Survey* (Oxford, 1964).

Jones, A.H.M., J.R. Martindale, and J. Morris (eds.), *The Prosopography of theLater Roman Empire,* vol. 1, *A.D. 260–395* (Cambridge, 1971).

Jones, J.W., Jr., "Vergil as *Magister* in Fulgentius," in C. Henderson, Jr. (ed.), *Classical, Mediaeval, and Renaissance Studies in Honor of Berthold Louis Ullman*, vol. 1 (Rome, 1964) 273–5.

Jong, M. de, "Transformations of Penance," in F. Theuws and J.L. Nelson (eds.), *Rituals of Power from Late Antiquity to the Early Middle Ages* (Leiden, 2000) 185–224.

Jonge, P. de, *Sprachlicher und historischer Kommentar zu Ammianus Marcellinus XIV* (Groningen, 1972).

Jordan, D.R., H. Montgomery, and E. Thomassen (eds.), *The World of Ancient Magic: Papers from the First International Samson Eitrem Seminar at the Norwegian Institute at Athens, 4–8 May 1997* (Bergen, 1999).

Jullien, C. and F. Jullien, Apôtres des confins: Processus missionaires chrétiens dans l'empire iranien (Paris, 2002).

Kaczynski, R., "John Chrysostom," in S. Döpp and W. Geerlings (eds.), *Dictionary of Early Christian Literature*, trans. M. O'Connell (New York, 2000).

Kahlos, M., *Vettius Agorius Praetextatus: A Senatorial Life in Between* (Rome, 2002).

Kajanto, I., "*Pontifex Maximus* as Title of the Pope," *Arctos* 15 (1981) 37–52.

Kaldellis, A., *Procopius of Caesarea: Tyranny, History and Philosophy at the End of Antiquity* (Philadelphia, 2004).

Kazhdan, A., "The Concepts of Freedom (*eleutheria*) and Slavery (*douleia*) in Byzantium," in G. Makdisi, D. Sourdel, and J. Sourdel-Thomine (eds.), *La notion de liberté au Moyen Age: Islam, Byzance, Occident* (Paris, 1985) 215–26.

Keane, W., *Christian Moderns: Freedom and Fetish in the Mission Encounter* (Berkeley, 2007).

Kelly, C., *Ruling the Later Roman Empire* (Cambridge, MA, 2004).

Kelly, G.A.J. *Ammianus Marcellinus: the Allusive Historian* (Cambridge, 2008).

Kelly, J.N.D., *Jerome: His Life, Writings and Controversies* (London, 1975).

———, *Golden Mouth: The Story of John Chrysostom, Ascetic, Preacher, Bishop* (Ithaca, NY, 1995).

Kent, J.P.C. (ed.), *The Roman Imperial Coinage*, vol. 10, *The Divided Empire and the Fall of the Western Parts, AD 395–491* (London, 1994).

Kertzer, D., *Sacrificed for Honor: Italian Abandonment and the Politics of Reproductive Control* (Boston, 1993).

Kingsley, P., *Ancient Philosophy, Mystery, and Magic* (Oxford, 1995).

Klein, H.A., *Byzanz, der Westen und das 'wahre' Kreuz. Die Geschichte einer Reliquie und ihrere künstlerische Fassung in Byzanz und im Abendland* (Wiesbaden, 2004).

Klingner, F., *De Boethii consolatione philosophiae* (Berlin, 1921).

Knauer, G.N., *Psalmenzitate in Augustins Konfessionen* (Göttingen, 1955).

———, *Die Aeneis und Homer; Studien zur poetischen Technik Vergils, mit Listen der Homerzitate in der Aeneis* (Göttingen, 1964).

Kolb, F., *Herrscherideologie in der Spätantike* (Berlin, 2000).

Kolesnikov, A.I., "O Termine 'Marzban' v Sasanidskom Irane," *PPSb* 27 (1981) 49–56.

Kolias, G., *Ämter und Würdenkauf im früh- und mittelbyzantinischen Reich* (Athens, 1939).

Köpstein, H., *Zur Sklaverei im ausgehenden Byzanz* (Berlin, 1966).

———, "Zum Fortleben des Wortes δοῦλος und anderer Bezeichnungen für den Sklaven im Mittel- und Neugriechischen," in E.C. Welskopf (ed.), *Soziale Typenbegriffe, III. Untersuchungen ausgewählter altgriechischer sozialer Typenbegriffe* (Berlin, 1981) 319–53.

Koziol, G., "The Dangers of Polemic: Is Ritual Still and Interesting Topic of Historical Study?" *EME* 11 (2002) 367–88.

Krause, J.-U., "La prise en charge des veuves par l'Église dans l'antiquité tardive," in C. Lepelley (ed.), *La fin de la cité antique et le début de la cité médiévale* (Bari, 1996) 115–26.

Krautheimer, R. and M. Pentiricci, "S. Laurentius in Damaso," in E.M. Steinby (ed.), *Lexicon Topographicum Urbis Romae* (Rome, 1993–99) 3.179–82.

Krautheimer, R., W. Frankl, and S. Corbett, *Corpus basilicarum christianarum Romae*, 5 vols. (Vatican City, 1937–80).

Krueger, D., "Writing as Devotion: Hagiographical Composition and the Cult of Saints in Theodoret of Cyrrhus and Cyril of Scythopolis," *ChHist* 66 (1997) 707–19.

———, "Christian Piety and Practice in the Sixth Century," in Maas, *Cambridge Companion to the Age of Justinian* (2005), 291–315.

Labriolle, P. de, *La réaction païenne* (Paris, 1934).

Labrique, M.-P., "Ambroise de Milan et Sénèque: à propos du *De excessu fratris II*," *Latomus* 50 (1991) 409–18.

Lacam, G., *L'agonie de Rome: Ricimer, un barbare, maître de l'Occident (455–472)* (Paris, 1992).

Lafferty, M., "Translating Faith from Greek to Latin: *Romanitas* and *Christianitas* in Late Fourth-Century Rome and Milan," *JECS* 11 (2003) 21–62.

Lair, J. (ed.), *De moribus et actis primorum Normanniae ducum, auctore Dudone Sancti Quintini decano* (Caen, 1865).

Laistner, M.L.W., "Fulgentius in the Carolingian Age," in C.G. Starr (ed.), *The Intellectual Heritage of the Early Middle Ages: Selected Essays by M.L.W. Laistner* (Ithaca, NY, 1957) 202–15.

Lamberton, R., *Homer the Theologian: Neoplatonist Allegorical Reading and the Growth of the Epic Tradition* (Berkeley, 1986).

Lambrechts, P., *L'exhaltation de la tête dans la pensée et dans l'art des Celtes* (Bruges, 1954).

Lamoreaux, J.C., "Episcopal Courts in Late Antiquity," *JECS* 3 (1995) 143–67.

Lampe, P., "Die montanistischen Tymion und Pepouza im Lichte der neuen Tymioninschrift," *ZAC* 8 (2004) 498–512.

Lancel, S., *St Augustine*, trans. A. Nevill (London, 2002).

Laniado, A., *Recherches sur les notables municipaux dans l'empire protobyzantin* (Paris, 2002).

Lang, U.M., "Zum Einsetzungsbericht bei ostsyrischen Liturgiekommentaren," *OC* 89 (2005) 63–76.

Lange, N.R.M. de, *Origen and the Jews* (Cambridge, 1976).

Lassus, J., "L'église cruciforme Antioche-Kaoussié 12-F," in *Antioch-on-the-Orontes*, vol. 2, *The Excavations of 1933–1936* (Princeton, 1938) 5–44.

Latham, J.A., *The Ritual Construction of Rome: Processions, Subjectivities, and the City from the Late Republic to Late Antiquity* (diss.: Univ. of California, Santa Barbara, 2007).

Lausberg, H., *Handbook of Literary Rhetoric* (Leiden, 1998).

LeFebvre, H. *The Production of Space*, trans. D. Nicholson-Smith (Oxford, 1991).

Le Gall, J., "Le serment à l'empereur: une base méconnue de la tyrannie impériale sous le Haut-Empire?," *Latomus* 44 (1985) 767–83.

Leithart, P.J., "Where Was Ancient Zion?," *TynBull* 53 (2002) 161–75.

Lenski, N., "*Initium mali Romano imperio*: Contemporary Reactions to the Battle of Adrianople," *TAPA* 127 (1997) 129–68.

———, "Evidence for the *Audientia Episcopalis* in the New Letters of Augustine," in Mathisen, *Law, Society and Authority* (2001), 83–97.

———, *Failure of Empire: Valens and the Roman State in the Fourth Century AD* (Berkeley, 2002).

———, "Empresses in the Holy Land: The Creation of a Christian Utopia in late-antique Palestine," in L. Ellis and F. Kidner (eds.), *Travel, Communication, and Geography in Late Antiquity* (Aldershot, 2004) 113–24.

———, "Valens and the Monks: Cudgeling and Conscription as a Means to Social Control," *DOP* 58 (2004) 93–117

———, "The Reign of Constantine," in Idem (ed.), *Cambridge Companion to the Age of Constantine* (Cambridge, 2006) 59–90.

Leo, P. de, *Ricerche sui falsi medioevali*, vol. 1, *Il Constitutum Constantini: Compilazione agiografica del sec. VIII. Note e documenti per una nuova lettura* (Reggio Calabria, 1974).

Lepelley, C., “Le musée des statues divines. La volonté de sauvegarder le patrimoine artistique païen à l’époque théodosienne,” *CahArch* 42 (1994) 5–15.

———, “Le lieu des valeurs communes: la cité terrain neutre entre païens et chrétiens au IVe siècle,” in H. Inglebert (ed.), *Les idéologies civiques dans l’antiquité grecque et romaine. Hommages à Claude Lepelley* (Paris, 2002) 271–85.

Leppin, H., “Zu den Anfängen der Kirchenpolitik Justinians,” in H.U. Wiemer (ed.), *Staatlichkeit und politisches Handeln in der römischen Kaiserzeit* (Berlin, 2006) 187–208.

———, “(K)ein Zeitalter Justinians – Bemerkungen aus althistorischer Sicht zu Justinian in der jüngeren Forschung,” *HZ* 284 (2007) 659–86.

———, “Das Bild des Gallus bei Philostorg. Überlegungen zur Traditionsgeschichte,” in D. Meyer (ed.), *Philostorge et l’historiographie de l’Antiquité* (forthcoming).

Levenson, D.B., *A Source and Tradition Critical Study of the Stories of Julian’s Attempt to Rebuild the Temple* (diss. Harvard Univ., 1979).

———, “Julian’s Attempt to rebuild the Temple: An Inventory of Ancient and Medieval Sources,” in H.W. Attridge, J.J. Collins, and T.H. Tobin (eds.), *Of Scribes and Scrolls. Studies on the Hebrew Bible, Intertestamental Judaism, and Christian Origins* (Lanham, 1990) 261–79.

———, “The Ancient and Medieval Sources for the Emperor Julian’s Attempt to Rebuild the Jerusalem Temple,” *JSJ* 35 (2004) 409–60.

Lewis, C.T. and C. Short, *A Latin Dictionary* (1879; reprint, Oxford, 1975).

Lewy, H., *Chaldean Oracles and Theurgy: Mysticism, Magic and Platonism in the Later Roman Empire* (Cairo, 1956; reprint, Paris, 1978).

LiDonnici, L., *The Epidaurian Miracle Inscriptions* (Atlanta, 1995).

Liebeschuetz, J.H.W.G., “The Fall of John Chrysostom,” *NMS* 29 (1985) 1–31.

———, *Barbarians and Bishops: Army, Church and State in the Age of Arcadius and Chrysostom* (Oxford, 1990).

———, *The Decline and Fall of the Roman City* (Oxford, 2001).

———, *Decline and Change in Late Antiquity: Religion, Barbarians and their Historiography* (Aldershot, 2006).

Liebeschuetz, J.H.W.G. and C. Hill, *Ambrose of Milan. Political Letters and Speeches* (Liverpool, 2005).

Liebs, D., “Ämterkauf und Ämterpatronage in der Spätantike,” *ZSav* 95 (1978) 158–86.

Liefferinge, C. van, *La Théurgie des Oracles Chaldaïques à Proclus* (Liège, 1999).

Lieu, S.N.C., *The Emperor Julian. Panegyric and Polemic*, 2nd ed. (Liverpool, 1989).

———, “From History to Legend and Legend to History: The Medieval and Byzantine Transformation of Constantine’s *Vita*,” in Idem and D. Montserrat (eds.), *Constantine. History, Historiography and Legend* (London, 1998) 136–76.

———, "Constantine in Legendary Literature," in Lenski, *Cambridge Companion to the Age of Constantine* (2006), 298–321.

Lieu, S.N.C. and D. Montserrat (eds.), *From Constantine to Julian: Pagan and Byzantine Views* (London, 1996).

Linder, A., "The Myth of Constantine the Great in the West: Sources and Hagiographic Commemoration," *Studi Medievali* 16 (1975) 43–95.

Little, L. (ed.), *Plague and the End of Antiquity: The Pandemic of 541–750* (Cambridge, 2007).

Lizzi Testa, R., "Vergini di Dio-vergini di Vesta: il sesso negato e la sacralità," in S. Pricoco, *L'Eros difficile. Amore e sessualità nell'antico cristianesimo* (Rubbettino, 1998) 89–132.

———, "Paganesimo politico e politica edilizia: la 'cura Urbis' nella tarda antichità," in *Centralismo e autonomie nella tarda antichità. Categorie concettuali e realtà concrete AARC XIII Conv. Intern. (Perugia 1–4 ottobre 1997)* (Naples, 2001) 671–707.

———, *Senatori, popolo, papi. Il governo di Roma al tempo dei Valentiniani* (Bari, 2004).

———, "Christian Emperor, Vestal Virgins and Priestly Colleges: Reconsidering the End of Roman Paganism," *AnTard* 15 (2007) 251–62.

———, "Dal conflitto al dialogo: nuove prospettive sulle relazioni tra pagani e cristiani in Occidente alla fine del IV secolo," in *Trent'anni di studi sulla tarda antichità: bilanci e prospettive (Napoli 21–23 novembre 2007)* (in press).

———, "La conversione dei 'cives', la evangelizzazione dei 'rustici': alcuni esempi fra IV e VI secolo," in *Città e campagna: LVI Settimana di Studio (Spoleto 27 marzo-1aprile 2008)* (in press).

Llewellyn, P., *Rome in the Dark Ages* (London, 1970).

Lloyd, A.C., *The Anatomy of Neoplatonism* (Oxford, 1990).

Lovino, A., "Su alcune affinità tra il Panegirico per Teodosio di Pacato Drepanio e il *De obitu Theodosii* di Sant'Ambrogio," *VetChr* 26 (1989) 371–6.

Luck, G., "Witches and Sorcerers in Classical Literature," in V. Flint et al. (eds.), *Witchcraft and Magic in Europe: Ancient Greece and Rome* (London, 1999) 93–158.

Luce, T.J. (ed.), *Ancient Writers: Greece and Rome*, 2 vols. (New York, 1982).

Lukes, S., *Power: A Radical View* (London, 1974).

Lungo, S. del, "La percezione dello spazio: gli itinerari urbani," in L. Pani Ermini (ed.), *Christiana Loca: lo spazio cristiano nella Roma del primo millennio* (Rome, 2000) 231–8.

Lutz, C.E., "Musonius Rufus: The Roman Socrates," *YCS* 10 (1947) 3–147.

Lynch, K., *The Image of the City* (Cambridge, MA, 1960).

Maas, M., "Roman History and Christian Ideology in Justinianic Reform Legislation," *DOP* 40 (1986) 17–31.

——— (ed.), *The Cambridge Companion to the Age of Justinian* (Cambridge, 2005).

Maas, M. and E.G. Mathews, *Exegesis and Empire in the Early Byzantine Mediterranean: Junillus Africanus and the Instituta regularia divinae legis* (Tübingen, 2003).

McCauley, L.P. and A. Stephenson (trans.), *The Works of S. Cyril of Jerusalem*. The Fathers of the Church 64 (Washington, 1970).

MacCormack, S., "Latin Prose Panegyric," in T.A. Dorey (ed.), *Empire and Aftermath* (London, 1975).

———, *Art and Ceremony in Late Antiquity* (Berkeley, 1981).

MacCoull, L.S.B., *Dioscorus of Aphrodito. His Work and His World* (Berkeley, 1988).

MacGregor, N. and E. Langmuir, *Seeing Salvation: Images of Christ in Art* (New Haven, 2000).

Machado, C., "Religion as Antiquarianism: Pagan Dedications in Late Antique Rome," in J. Bodel and M. Kajava (eds.), *Dediche sacre nel mondo greco-romano: Diffusione, funzione, tipologie* (Rome, 2009) 331–54.

Mack, B.L., *Logos und Sophia: Untersuchungen zur Weisheitstheologie im hellenistischen Judentum* (Göttingen, 1973).

Mackie, G., "A New Look at the Patronage of Santa Costanza, Rome," *Byzantion* 67 (1997) 383–406.

MacMullen, R., "Constantine and the Miraculous," *GRBS* 9 (1968) 81–96.

Macuch, M., "Herrschaftskonsolidierung und sasanidische Familienrecht: zum Verhältnis von Kirche und Staat unter den Sasaniden," in C. Reck and P. Zieme (eds.), *Iran und Turfan: Beiträge Berliner Wissenschaftler, Werner Sundermann zum 60. Geburtstag gewidmet* (Wiesbaden, 1995) 149–67.

Majercik, R. (ed.), *The Chaldaean Oracles: Text, Translation and Commentary* (Leiden, 1989).

Magness, J., *The Archaeology of the Early Islamic Settlement in Palestine* (Winona Lake, IN, 2003).

Malaspina, E. (ed.), *L. Annaei Senecae De clementia libri duo: Prolegomeni, testo critico e commento* (Alessandria, 2002).

Malosse, P.-L., "Antioche et le kappa," in B. Cabouret, P.-L. Gatier, and C. Saliou (eds.), *Antioch de Syrie: Histoire, images et traces de la ville antique* (Lyon, 2004) 77–96.

Mango, C., *The Brazen House* (Copenhagen, 1959).

Mansfeld, J., *Prolegomena: Questions to be Settled before the Study of an Author, or a Text* (Leiden, 1994).

Mansi, J.D., *Sacrorum Conciliorum nova et amplissima Collectio*, vol. 2 (Florence, 1759).

Maraval, P., *Lieux saints et pèlerinages d'Orient: Histoire et géographie des origines à la conquête arabe* (Paris, 1985).

Mardirossian, A., "L'*Écrit sur la tradition de saint Sahak*: Les soubresauts de la politique fiscale de l'église arménienne du VIIe au Xe siècle," *Muséon* 119 (2006) 375–97.

———, *Le livre des canons arméniens (Kanonagirk^c Hayoc^c) de Yovhannes Awjnec^ci: Église, droit, et société en Arménie du IVe au VIIIe siècle* (Louvain, 2004).
Marenbon, J., *Boethius*, Great Medieval Thinkers (New York, 2003).
Marini, L.G., *I papiri diplomatici* (Rome, 1805).
Marini Avonzo, F. de, "Appendice", in R. Orestano, *Il problema delle fondazioni in diritto romano* (Turin, 1959).
Markus, R.A., *Saeculum: History and Society in the Theology of St. Augustine* (Cambridge, 1988).
Martin, D.B., *Slavery as Salvation: The Metaphor of Slavery in Pauline Christianity* (New Haven, 1990).
Martin, H., "The Judas Iscariot Curse," *AJPh* 37 (1916) 434–51.
Martin, M., "Bemerkungen zu den frühmittelalterlichen Gurtelbeschlagen der Westschweiz," *ZSchwAKg* 28 (1971) 29–57.
Martindale, J.R. (ed.), *The Prosopography of the Later Roman Empire*, vol. 2, *A.D. 395–527* (Cambridge, 1980).
Martini, R., "Sulla vendita dei neonati nella legislazione costantiniana," in *Atti del VII Convegno dell'Accademia Romanistica Costantiniana* (Perugia, 1988) 423–32.
Martyn, J.R.C., "Four Notes on the *Registrum* of Gregory the Great," *Parergon* 19 (2002) 5–38.
Mathews, T.F., *The Clash of Gods: A Reinterpretation of Early Christian Art* (Princeton, 1993).
Mathisen, R.W., "For Specialists Only: the Reception of Augustine and his Teachings in Fifth-Century Gaul," in J.T. Lienhard, E.C. Muller and R.J. Teske (eds.), *Augustine: Presbyter Factus Sum* (New York, 1993) 29–41.
———, "Sigisvult the Patrician, Maximinus the Arian, and Political Strategems in the Western Roman Empire ca. 425–440," *EME* 8 (1999) 173–96.
——— (ed.), *Law, Society and Authority in Late Antiquity* (Oxford, 2001).
Matthews, J., "The Historical Setting of the *Carmen Contra Paganos* (Cod. Lat. Par. 8084)," *Historia* 19 (1970) 464–79.
———, "Symmachus and the Oriental Cults," *JRS* 63 (1973) 175–95.
———, "Ammianus Marcellinus," in T.J. Luce (ed.), *Ancient Writers: Greece and Rome*, vol. 2 (New York, 1982) 1117–38.
———, *The Roman Empire of Ammianus* (London, 1989).
Mattingly, H., *Coins of the Roman Empire in the British Museum*, vol. 1 (London, 1923).
Mayer, W., "Progress in the Field of Chrysostom Studies (1984–2004)," in *Giovanni Crisostomo: Oriente e Occidente tra IV e V secolo, XXXIII Incontro di Studiosi dell'Antichità Cristiana, Augustinianum 6–8 maggio 2004* (Rome, 2005) 9–35.
Mazzarino, S., *Il basso impero. Antico, tardoantico ed èra costantiniana*, 2 vols. (Rome, 1974–80).
McClanan, A., *Representations of Early Byzantine Empresses* (New York, 2002).

McClure, J., *Gregory the Great: Audience and Exegesis* (diss. Oxford Univ., 1978).

McDonough, S., *Power by Negotiation: Institutional Reform in the Fifth Century Sasanian Empire* (diss. Univ. of California at Los Angeles, 2005).

McGuckin, J.A., "Nestorius and the Political Factions of Fifth-Century Byzantium: Factors in his Personal Downfall," *BRL* 78 (1996) 7–22.

McLynn, N.B., *Ambrose of Milan. Church and Court in a Christian Capital* (Berkeley, 1994).

———, "Augustine's Roman Empire," in Vessey et al., *History, Apocalypse and the Secular Imagination* (1999), 29–44.

———, "Crying Wolf: The Pope and the Lupercalia," *JRS* 98 (2008) 161–75.

Meens, R., "The Frequency and Nature of Early Medieval Penance," in P. Biller and A.J. Minnis (eds.), *Handling Sin: Confession in the Middle Ages* (Woodbridge, 1998) 35–61.

Meier, M., "Kaiserherrschaft und 'Volksfrömmigkeit' im Konstantinopel des 6. Jahrhunderts n. Chr. Die Verlegung der Hypapante durch Justinian im Jahr 542," *Historia* 51 (2002) 89–111.

———, *Das andere Zeitalter Justinians. Kontingenzerfahrung und Kontingenzbewältigung im 6. Jahrhundert n. Chr.*, 2nd ed.(Göttingen, 2004).

———, "Die Demut des Kaisers: Aspekte der religiösen Selbstinszenierung bei Theodosius II. (408–450 n. Chr.)," in A. Pečar and K. Trampedach (eds.), *Die Bibel als politisches Argument. Voraussetzungen und Folgen biblizistischer Herrschaftslegitimation in der Vormoderne* (Munich, 2007) 135–58.

Meyendorff, J., "L'Iconographie de la Sagesse divine dans la tradition byzantine," *CahArch* 10 (1959) 259–77.

———, *Byzantine Theology: Historical Trends and Doctrinal Themes* (New York, 1974).

———, "Wisdom-Sophia: Contrasting Approaches to a Complex Theme," *DOP* 41 (1987) 391–401.

Millar, F., *A Greek Roman Empire: Power and Belief Under Theodosius II (405–450)* (Berkeley, 2006).

Miller, F., with L. Varley (colorist), *300* (Milwaukie, OR, 1999).

Miller, T.S., *The Orphans of Byzantium: Child Welfare in the Christian Empire* (Washington, 2003).

Mingana, A., *Sources Syriaques* (Leipzig, 1908).

Mirsky, A., *Yosse ben Yosse Poems* (Jerusalem, 1991).

Missiou, A., "Δούλος του βασιλέως: The Politics of Translation," *CQ* n.s. 43 (1993) 377–91.

Mitchell, S., *A History of the Later Roman Empire, AD 284–641* (Oxford, 2007).

Mohrmann, C., "Le problème du vocabulaire chrétien: éxpériences d'evangélisation paléo-chrétiennes et modernes," in Eadem, *Études sur le latin des chrétiens* (Rome, 1958) 113–22.

———, "Some Remarks on the Language of Boethius' 'Consolatio Philosophiae'," in J.J. O'Meara and B. Naumann (eds.), *Latin Script and Letters A.D. 400–900:*

Festschrift Presented to Ludwig Bieler on the Occasion of His 70th Birthday (Leiden, 1976) 54–61.
Mohrmann, C. and J. Gruber (eds.), *Boethius* (Darmstadt, 1984) 302–10.
Momigliano, A., "Cassiodorus and the Italian Culture of his Time," *PBA* 41 (1955) 207–45.
Mommsen, T., *Römisches Staatsrecht* (Leipzig, 1887).
Moorhead, J., *Theoderic in Italy* (Oxford, 1992).
Moreau, M., "Le dossier Marcellinus dans la Correspondance de saint Augustin," *RecAug.* 9 (1973) 7–181.
Moricca, U., "Analecta," *Didaskaleion* n.s. 4 (1926) 85–107.
Morley, N., *Writing Ancient History* (London, 1999).
Morony, M., "Religious Communities in Late Sasanian and Early Muslim Iraq," *JESHO* 17 (1974) 113–35.
———, "The Effects of the Muslim Conquest on the Persian Population of Iraq," *Iran* 14 (1976) 41–59.
———, Iraq after the Muslim Conquest (Princeton, 1984).
———, "Social Elites in Iraq and Iran: After the Conquest," in J. Haldon and L. Conrad (eds.), *The Byzantine and Early Islamic Near East VI: Elites Old and New in the Byzantine and Early Islamic Near East* (Princeton, 2004) 275–84.
Muntz, E., "The Lost Mosaics of Rome of the IV to IX Century (I)," *AJA* 2 (1886) 295–313.
Murray, J. (ed.), The Autobiographies of Edward Gibbon (London, 1897).
Myllykoski, M., "Cerinthus," in A. Marjanen and P. Luomanen (eds.), *A Companion to Second-Century Christian "Heretics"* (Leiden, 2005) 213–46.
Nardella, C., *Il fascino di Roma nel Medioevo* (Rome, 1988).
Nasemann, B., *Theurgie und Philosophie in Jamblichs De mysteriis* (Stuttgart, 1991).
Nautin, P., "L'excommunication de saint Jérôme," *AEHE V* 80/81 (1972–73) 7–37.
Nazzaro, A.V., "Incidenza biblico-cristiana e classica nella coerenza delle immagini ambrosiane," in L.F. Pizzolato and M. Rizzi (eds.), *Nec timeo mori: Atti del Congresso internazionale di studi ambrosiani nel XVI centenario della morte di sant'Ambrogio (1997)* (Milan, 1998) 313–39.
———, "Ambrogio vescovo di Milano e l'imperatore Teodosio I il Grande," in R. Uglione (ed.), *Atti del Convegno nazionale di studi: Intellettuali e potere nel mondo antico, Torino, 22–23–24 aprile 2002* (Alessandria, 2003) 259–301.
Newman, B., *God and the Goddesses: Vision, Poetry, and Belief in the Middle Ages* (Philadelphia, 2003).
Neri, V., *Ammiano e il cristianesimo: Religione e politica nelle Res Gestae di Ammiano Marcellino* (Bologna, 1985).
Nicholson, O., "Constantine's Vision of the Cross," *VChr* 53 (2000) 309–23.
Niquet, H., *Monumenta virtutum titulique: Senatorische Selbstdarstellung im spätantiken Rom im Spiegel der epigraphischen Denkmäler* (Stuttgart, 2000).

Nixon, C.E.V., "Latin Panegyric in the Tetrarchic and Constantinian Period," in B. Croke and A.M. Emmett (eds.), *History and Historians in Late Antiquity* (Sydney, 1983) 88–99.

Nixon, C.E.V. and B.S. Rogers, *In Praise of Roman Emperors: The Panegyrici Latini* (Berkeley, 1994).

Noble, T.F.X., "Rome in the Seventh Century," in M. Lapidge (ed.), *Archbishop Theodore: Commemorative Studies on His Life and Influence* (Cambridge, 1995) 69–87.

———, "Topography, Celebration, and Power: The Making of Papal Rome in the Eighth and Ninth Centuries," in M. de Jonge, F. Theuws, and C. van Rhijn (eds.), *Topographies of Power in the Early Middle Ages* (Leiden, 2001) 45–91.

Nock, A.D., "*A Diis Electa*: A Chapter in the Religious History of the Third Century," *HThR* 23 (1930) 251–74.

———, "The Emperor's Divine *Comes*," *JRS* 37 (1947) 102–16.

Nodes, D.J., "*De subitanea paenitentia* in the Letters of Faustus of Riez and Avitus of Vienne," *RecTh* 55 (1988) 30–40.

Noegel, S., J. Walker, and B. Wheeler (eds.), *Prayer, Magic, and the Stars in the Ancient and Late Antique World* (University Park, PA, 2003).

Noethlichs, K.L., "Zur Einflussnahme des Staates auf die Entwicklung eines kirchlichen Klerikerstandes," *JAC* 15 (1972) 136–53.

———, "Anspruch und Wirklichkeit. Fehlverhalten und Amtspflichtverletzungen des christlichen Klerus anhand der Konzilskanones des 4. bis 8. Jahrhunderts," *ZSRG.K* 76 (1990) 1–61.

Odahl, C.M., *Constantine and the Christian Empire* (New York, 2004).

O'Daly, G.J.P., *The Poetry of Boethius* (London, 1991).

O'Donnell, J.J., *Cassiodorus* (Berkeley, 1979).

———, *Augustine, Sinner and Saint: A New Biography* (London, 2005).

O'Donovan, O. and J. Lockwood O'Donovan (eds.), *From Irenaeus to Grotius: A Sourcebook in Christian Political Thought* (Grand Rapids, 1999).

O'Flynn, J.M., *Generalissimos of the Western Roman Empire* (Edmonton, 1983).

O'Meara, D.J., *Pythagoras Revived: Mathematics and Philosophy in Late Antiquity* (Oxford, 1989).

O'Meara, J.J., *Porphyry's Philosophy from Oracles in Augustine* (Paris, 1959).

Oost, S.I., "The Alexandrian Seditions under Philip and Gallienus," *CPh* 56 1 (1961) 1–20.

Orgels, P., "La première vision de Constantin (310) et le temple d'Apollon à Nîmes," *BAB* 5, ser. 34 (1948) 176–208.

Orlandi, S., "Osservazioni prosopografiche sulle Vestali," *RPAA* (1995–96) 359–71.

Orlin, E., *Temples, Religion and Politics in the Roman Republic* (Leiden, 1997).

O'Sullivan, J.F., *The Writings of Salvian the Presbyter* (New York, 1947).

Ozanam, A. F., "Comment la langue latine devint chrétienne," in *La civilisation au cinquième siècle* (Paris, 1894) 117–48.

Palmer, A., "Amid in the Seventh-Century Syriac Life of Theodute," in E. Grypeou, M. Swanson, and D. Thomas (eds.), *The Encounter of Eastern Christianity with Early Islam* (Leiden, 2006) 111–38.

———, *The Seventh Century in the West-Syrian Chronicles* (Liverpool, 1993).

Panciera, S., *Epigrafi, epigrafia, epigrafisti. Scritti vari editi e inediti (1956–2005) con note complementari e indici*, 3 vols. (Rome, 2006).

———, "Lucius Pomponius Horatia Bassus Cascus Scribonianus Luci Bassi consulis et Torquatae Filius," in Idem, *Epigrafi*, vol. 2,1029–46.

Papini, A.M., *Ricimero: L'agonia dell'impero romano d'Occidente* (Milan, 1959).

Parke, H.W., *The Oracles of Apollo in Asia Minor* (London, 1985).

Parkin, A., "'You do him no service': An Exploration of Pagan Almsgiving," in M. Atkins and R. Osbourne (eds.), *Poverty in the Roman World* (Cambridge, 2006) 60–82.

Paschoud, F., "Zosime 2.29 et la conversion de Constantin," *Historia* 20 (1971) 334–53.

———, *Cinq études sur Zosime* (Paris, 1975).

———, *Zosime. Histoire Nouvelle*, 3 vols. (Paris, 1971–89).

Patlagean, E., "Les armes et la cité à Rome du VIIe au IXe siècle et le modèle Européen des trois fonctions sociales," *MEFRM* 86 (1974) 25–62.

———, *Pauvreté économique et pauvreté sociale à Byzance, 4e–7e siècles* (Paris, 1977).

Patrich, J., *Sabas, Leader of Palestinian Monasticism. A Comparative Study in Eastern Monasticism, Fourth to Seventh Centuries* (Washington, 1995).

Paverd, F. van de, *St. John Chrysostom: The Homilies on the Statues. An Introduction* (Rome, 1991).

Pelikan, J., *Christianity and Classical Culture: The Metamorphosis of Natural Theology in the Christian Encounter with Hellenism* (New Haven, 1993).

Pellizzari, A., *Commento storico al libro III dell'epistolario di Q: Aurelio Simmaco* (Pisa, 1988).

Pensabene, R., *Tempio di Saturno, architettura e decorazione* (Rome, 1984).

Pentcheva, B.V., *Icons and Power: The Mother of God in Byzantium* (University Park, PA, 2006).

Pépin, J., "Philologos/Philosophos," in L. Brisson et al. (eds.), *Porphyre: La vie de Plotin*, vol. 2 (Paris, 1992) 477–501.

Perigard, M.A., "'300': Far from a Perfect 10," *Boston Sunday Herald* (29 July 2007) 34.

Perikhanian, A., *Obshchestvo i Pravo Irana v Parfyanskii i Sasanidskii Periodi* (Moscow, 1983).

Périn, P., "Six plaques-boucles mérovingiennes de bronze à plaque ronde ornée d'un masque humain et de motifs géométriques du musée Carnavalet," *BGASM* 14–15 (1973–74) 71–97.

Périn, P. and T. Calligaro, "La tombe d'Arégonde. Nouvelles analyses en laboratoire du mobilier métallique et des restes organiques de la défunte du sarcophage 49 de la basilique de Saint-Denis," *Antiquités Nationales* 37 (2006) 181–206.

Périn, P. and M. Kazanski, "Das Grab Childerichs I," in K. van Welck (ed.), *Die Franken: Wegbereiter Europas,* vol. 1 (Mainz, 1996) 173–82.

Perry, T., *Mary for Evangelicals* (Downers Grove, IL, 2006).

Pétré, H., "Misericordia. Histoire du mot et de l'idée du paganisme au christianisme," *REL* 12 (1934) 376–89.

Pharr, C. (trans.), *The Theodosian Code and Novels and the Sirmondian Constitutions* (Princeton, 1952; reprint, Amsterdam, 1968).

Philip, J.A., "The Biographical Tradition: Pythagoras," *TAPA* 90 (1959) 185–94.

Pietri, C., *Roma christiana. Recherches sur l'Église de Rome, son organisation, sa politique, son idéologie de Miltiade à Sixte III (311–440)*, 2 vols. (Rome, 1976).

Piganiol, A., *L'empire chrétien (325–395)*, 2nd ed. (Paris, 1972).

Pighi, G.B., "Latinità cristiana negli scrittori pagani del IV secolo," in *Studi dedicati alla memoria di Paolo Ubaldi* (Milan, 1937) 41–72.

Pigulevskaya, N., "Zhizn Sakhdoni: Iz Istorii Nestorianstva VII Veka," *ZKV* 3 (1928) 91–108.

Platnauer, M., *Claudian* (Cambridge, 1922).

Pohlkamp, W., "Tradition und Topographie: Papst Silvester I. (314–335) und der Drache vom Forum Romanum," *RQ* (1983) 1–100.

———, "Kaiser Konstantin und der christliche Kult in den Actus Silvestri," *FMS* 18 (1984) 357–400.

Pohlsander, H.A., *Helena: Empress and Saint* (Chicago, 1995).

Pollmann, K., "Apocalypse Now?!—Der Kommentar des Tyconius zur Johannesoffenbarung," in W. Geerlings and C. Schulze (eds.), *Der Kommentar in Antike und Mittelalter. Beiträge zu seiner Erforschung* (Leiden, 2002) 33–54.

Potter, D., *Prophets and Emperors* (Cambridge, MA, 1994).

Preger, T., "Konstantinos-Helios," *Hermes* 36 (1901) 457–69.

Pryor, J.H., "The Oaths of the Leaders of the First Crusade to Emperor Alexius I Comnenus: Fealty, Homage—πίστις, δουλεία," *Parergon* 2 (1984) 111–41.

Puig, C., "300? It's Quite a Number: An Over-the-Top Take on Ancient Greek History," *USA Today* (8 March 2007).

Pulleyn, S., *Prayer in Greek Religion* (Oxford, 1997).

Putnam, H., *L'Église et l'Islam sous Timothée I (780–823)* (Beirut, 1975).

Quacquarelli, A., "Spigolature boeziane," in L. Obertello (ed.), *Atti del Congresso Internazionale di studi boeziani* (Rome, 1981) 227–48.

Quasten, J., *Patrology*, 4 vols. (Westminster, MD, 1950–60).

Raban, J., *Soft City* (Glasgow, 1974).

Ramin, J. and P. Veyne, "Droit romain et société: les hommes libres qui passent pour esclaves et l'esclavage volontaire," *Historia* 30 (1981) 472–97.

Ramsay, W.M., *Cities and Bishoprics of Phrygia, Being an Essay of the Local History of Phrygia from the Earliest Times to the Turkish Conquest* (Oxford, 1895–97).

Rand, E.K., "Der dem Boethius zugeschriebene Traktat de fide catholica." *JbKP* 26 (1901) 401–61.

———, *Founders of the Middle Ages* (Cambridge, MA, 1928; reprint, Dover, 1957).

———, "On the Composition of Boethius' 'Consolatio Philosophiae'," in M. Fuhrmann and J. Gruber (eds.), *Boethius* (Darmstadt, 1984) 249–77.

Rankin, D., "Arianism," in P.F. Esler (ed.), *The Early Christian World* (London, 2000) 975–1001.

Rapp, C., "Imperial Ideology in the Making: Eusebius of Caesarea on Constantine as 'Bishop'," *JThS* n.s. 49 (1998) 685–95.

———, *Holy Bishops in Late Antiquity: The Nature of Christian Leadership in an Age of Transition* (Berkeley, 2005).

Rebillard, É., *In hora mortis: évolution de la pastorale chrétienne de la mort aux IVe et Ve siècles dans l'Occident latin* (Rome, 1994).

———, "Note sur les morts de philosophes dans les Histoires d'Ammien Marcellin," in: F. Chausson and É. Wolff (eds.), *Consuetudinis amor: Fragments d'histoire Romaine (IIe–VIe siècles) offerts à Jean-Pierre Callu* (Rome, 2003) 371–8.

Reinink, G.J., "'Edessa Grew Dim and Nisibis Shone Forth': The School of Nisibis at the Transition of the Sixth-Seventh Century," in J.W. Drijvers and A.A. MacDonald (eds.), *Centres of Learning: Learning and Location in Pre-Modern Europe and the Near East* (Leiden, 1995) 77–89.

———, "Babai the Great's *Life of George* and the Propagation of Doctrine in the Late Sasanian Empire," in J.W. Drijvers and J.M. Watt (eds.), *Portraits of Spiritual Authority: Religious Power in Early Christianity, Byzantium, and the Christian Orient* (Leiden, 1999) 171–94.

———, "East Syrian Historiography in Response to the Rise of Islam: the Case of John bar Penkaye's *Ktaba D-Res Melle*," in J.J. van Ginkel, H.L. Murre-van den Berg, and T.M. van Lint (eds.), *Redefining Christian Identity: Cultural Interaction in the Middle East since the Rise of Islam* (Leuven, 2005) 77–89.

Relihan, J.C., *Boethius. The Consolation of Philosophy* (Indianapolis, 2001).

Remus, H., "Plotinus and Gnostic Thaumaturgy," *LThPh* 39 (1983) 13–20.

Reusser, C., "Area Capitolina," in Steinby, *Lexicon Topographicum*, vol. 1 (1993), 114–17.

Ricci, C., *Ravenna* (Bergamo, 1912).

Riedweg, C., "Porphyrios über Christus und die Christen: De Philosophia ex Oraculis Haurienda und Adversos Christianos im Vergliech," in *L'Apologétique chrétienne gréco-latine à l'époque prénicénienne* (Geneva, 2005) 151–98.

Rike, R.L., *Apex Omnium: Religion in the Res Gestae of Ammianus* (Berkeley, 1987).

Rives, J., "Magic in Roman Law: the Reconstruction of a Crime," *ClAnt* 22 (2003) 313–39.

Rizzi, M., "Le teologie politiche," in G. Alberigo, G. Ruggiero, and R. Rusconi (eds.), *Il Cristianesimo: Grande atlante* (Turin, 2005) 1057.

Roberts, M., "Rome Personified, Rome Epitomized," *AJPh* 122 (2001) 533–65.

Roberts Gaventa, B., *Mary. Glimpses of the Mother of Jesus* (Columbia, SC, 1995).

Robinson, C.F., *Empire and Elites after the Muslim Conquest: The Transformation of Northern Mesopotamia* (Cambridge, 2000).

Rocca, G., *L'Adversus Helvidium di san Girolamo nel contesto della letteratura ascetico-mariana del secolo IV* (Bern, 1998).

Roda, S., *Commento storico al libro IX dell'epistolario di Quinto Aurelio Simmaco* (Pisa, 1981).

Rodgers, B.S., "Constantine's Pagan Vision," *Byzantion* 50 (1980) 259–78.

Rohland, J.P., *Der Erzengel Michael, Arzt und Feldherr: Zwei Aspekte des vor- und frühbyzantinischen Michaelskultes* (Leiden, 1977).

Roueché, C., "Provincial Governors and Their Titulature in the Sixth Century," *AnTard* 6 (1998) 83–9.

Rubin, Z., "The Church of the Holy Sepulchre and the Conflict between the Sees of Caesarea and Jerusalem," *TJC* 2 (1982) 79–105.

———, "The See of Caesarea in Conflict with Jerusalem from Nicaea to Chalcedon," in A. Raban and K.G. Holum (eds.), *Caesarea Maritima: Retrospective after Two Millennia* (Leiden, 1996) 559–74.

Rüpke, J. *Fasti sacerdotum: Die Mitglieder der Priesterschaften und das sakrale Funktionspersonal römischer, griechischer, orientalischer und jüdisch-christlicher Kulte in der Stadt Rom von 300 v.Chr. bis 499 n.Chr.*, 3 vols. (Stuttgart, 2005).

Sabbah, G. (ed.), *Ammien Marcellin: Histoire Tome II (Livres XVII–XIX)* (Paris, 1970).

———, *La méthode d'Ammien Marcellin: recherches sur la construction du discours historique dans les Res gestae* (Paris, 1978).

———, "Ammianus Marcellinus," in G. Marasco (ed.), *Greek and Roman Historiography in Late Antiquity: Fourth to Sixth Century* AD (Leiden, 2003) 43–84.

Saffrey, H.D., "Abamon, pseudonyme de Jamblique," in R.B. Palmer and R. Hamerton-Kelly (eds.), *Philomathes. Studies and Essays in the Humanities in Memory of Philip Merlan* (The Hague, 1971) 227–39.

———, "Les néoplatoniciens et les Oracles chaldaïques," *REAug* 27 (1981) 209–25.

———, "Relecture de Jamblique, *De mysteriis*, VIII, chap. 1–5," in S. Gersh and C. Kannengiesser (eds.), *Platonism in Late Antiquity* (Notre Dame, IN, 1992) 157–71.

———, "Les livres IV à VII du *De Mysteriis* de Jamblique relus avec la Lettre de Porphyre à Anébon," in H.J. Blumenthal and E.G. Clarke (eds.), *The Divine Iamblichus: Philosopher and Man of Gods* (Liverpool, 1993) 144–58.

———, *Le néoplatonisme après Plotin* (Paris, 2000).

———, "Analyse de la réponse de Jamblique à Porphyre, connue sous le titre: *De mysteriis*," *RSPh* 84 (2000) 489–511.

Saitta, B., "Religionem imperare non possumus," *QC* 8 (1986) 63–88.

Salin, E., *La civilisation mérovingienne d'après les sépultures, les textes et le laboratoire*, vol. 4, *Les Croyances* (Paris, 1959).
Sallares, R., *Malaria and Rome: A History of Malaria in Ancient Italy* (Oxford, 2002).
Salzman, M.R., *On Roman Time: The Codex-Calendar of 354 and the Rhythms of Urban Life in Late Antiquity* (Berkeley, 1990).
Santangeli Valenzani, R., "Le più antiche guide romane e l'itinerario di Einsiedeln," in M. D'Onofrio (ed.), *Romei & Giubilei: il pellegrinaggio medievale a San Pietro (350–1350)* (Milan, 1999) 195–8.
———, "L'itinerario di Einsiedeln," in M. Stella Arena et al. (eds.), *Roma dall'antichità al medioevo*, vol. 1 (Milan, 2001) 154–9.
Santovito, F., "Ambrogio e Chrisostomo conscienza critica dell Chiesa del IV secolo di fronte al potere politico," *Nicolaus* 12 (1985) 67–181.
Sarris, P., *Economy and Society in the Age of Justinian* (Cambridge, 2006).
Saxer, V., "L'utilisation par la liturgie de l'espace urbain et suburbain: l'example de Rome dans l'Antiquité et le haut Moyen-Âge," in N. Duval, F. Baritel, and P. Pergola (eds.), *Actes du XIe congrès international d'archéologie chrétienne*, vol. 2 (Rome, 1989).
———, "La chiesa di Roma dal V al X secolo," in *Roma nell'alto Medioevo: 27 aprile–1 maggio 2000*, vol. 2 (Spoleto, 2001), 493–637.
Schaller, A., *Der Erzengel Michael im frühen Mittelalter: Ikonographie und Verehrung einer Heiligen ohne Vita* (Bern and New York, 2006).
Scharf, R., "Conobaria 5 v. Chr.—Der erste römische 'Kaisereid,'" in P. Defosse (ed.), *Hommages à Carl Deroux* (Brussels, 2003) 415–24.
Scheid, J., *La religione a Roma* (Rome, 1983).
———, *Romulus et ses frères. Le collège des frères arvales, modèle du culte public dans la Rome des empereurs* (Rome, 1990).
Scheidel, W., "Quantifying the Sources of Slaves in the Early Roman Empire," *JRS* 87 (1997) 156–69.
———, "Germs for Rome," in C. Edwards and G. Woolf (eds.), *Rome the Cosmopolis* (Cambridge, 2003) 158–76.
Schmelz, G., *Kirchliche Amtsträger im spätantiken Ägypten nach den Aussagen der griechischen und koptischen Papyri und Ostraka* (Munich, 2002) 232–41.
Scher, A. and J. Périer (eds. and trans.), *Histoire Nestorienne (Chronique du Séert)*: 1ère partie, fasc. 1. PO 4 (Paris, 1908).
Schott, J., "Porphyry on Christians and Others: 'Barbarian Wisdom,' Identity Politics, and Anti-Christian Polemics on the Eve of the Great Persecution," *JECS* 13 (2005) 277–314.
Schriijnen, J., *I Caratteri del latino cristiano antico* (Bologna, 1977).
Schuller, W., "Kaiser Julian und der Ämterkauf," in R. Günther and S. Rebenich (eds.), *E fontibus haurire: Beiträge zur römischen Geschichte und zu ihren Hilfswissenschaften* (Paderborn, 1994) 197–201.
Schürer, E., *The History of the Jewish People in the Age of Jesus Christ (175 B.C.–A.D. 135)*, rev. ed. by G. Vermes, F. Millar, and M. Goodman (Edinburgh, 1986)

Scott, L.R., "Antibarbarian Sentiments and the 'Barbarian' General in Roman Imperial Service: The Case of Ricimer," in *Actes du VIe congrès de la Fédération Internationale des Associations d'Études Classiques*, vol. 2 (Brussels, 1984) 23–33.

Seeck, O., *Geschichte des Untergangs der antiken Welt* (Stuttgart, 1897).

Segal, J.B., *Edessa: The Blessed City* (Oxford, 1970).

Sessa, K., "Truth, perception and the pagan body in the Roman martyr narratives," in A. Hopkins and M. Wyke (eds.), *Roman Bodies: Antiquity to the Eighteenth Century* (London, 2005) 99–110.

Seston, W., "La vision païenne de 310 et les origines du chrisme constantinien," *AIPhO* 4 (1936) 373–95.

Setton, K., *Christian Attitude Towards the Emperor in the Fourth Century* (New York, 1967).

Sevcenko, I. and N.P., *The Life of Saint Nicholas of Sion* (Brookline, MA, 1984).

Severin, H.-G., "Aspekte der Positionierung der Kirchen in oströmischen Städten," in G. Brands and H.-G. Severin (eds.), *Die spätantike Stadt und ihre Christianisierung* (Wiesbaden, 2003) 249–58.

Seyfarth, W. (ed.), *Ammiani Marcellini Rerum gestarum libri qui supersunt* (Leipzig, 1978).

Shanzer, D.R., "Ennodius, Boethius, and the Date and Interpretation of Maximianus's Elegia III," *RFIC* 111 (1983) 183–95.

———, "De Iovis Exterminatione," *Hermes* 114 (1986) 382–3.

———, "The Date and Composition of Prudentius's *Contra Orationem Symmachi libri*," *RFIC* 117 (1989) 442–62.

———, "Licentius's Verse Epistle to Augustine," *REAug* 37 (1991) 110–43.

———, "Augustine's Disciplines: *Silent diutius Musae Varronis*?," in K. Pollmann and M. Vessey (eds.), *Augustine and the Disciplines* (Oxford, 2005) 69–112.

———, "Editions and Editing in the Classroom: A Report from the Mines in America," in B. Merta, A. Sommerlechner, and H. Weigl (eds.), *Vom Nutzen des Edierens: Akten des internationalen Kongresses zum 150-jährigen Bestehen des Instituts für Österreichische Geschichtsforschung, Mitteilungen des Instituts für Österreichische Geschichtsforschung* (Vienna, 2005) 355–68.

———, "Latin Literature, Christianity, and Obscenity in the Later Roman West," in N. MacDonald (ed.), *Medieval Obscenities* (Woodbridge, 2006) 179–202.

Shanzer, D.R. and I.N. Wood., *Letters and Selected Prose of Avitus of Vienne* (Liverpool, 2002).

Shaw, B.D., "Seasons of Death: Aspects of Mortality in Imperial Rome," *JRS* 86 (1996) 100–38.

———, "Body/Power/Identity: Passions of the Martyrs." *JECS* 4 (1996) 269–312.

———, "Bad Boys: Circumcellions and Fictive Violence," in Drake, *Violence in Late Antiquity*, 179–96.

Shaw, G., *Theurgy and the Soul: The Neoplatonism of Iamblichus* (University Park, PA, 1995).

———, "Divination in the Neoplatonism of Iamblichus," in R.M. Berchman (ed.), *Mediators of the Divine: Horizons of Prophecy, Divination, Dreams and Theurgy in Mediterranean Antiquity* (Atlanta, 1998) 225–67.
———, "Eros and Arithmos: Pythagorean Theurgy in Iamblichus and Plotinus," *AncPhil* 19 (1999) 121–43.
———, "Containing Ecstasy: the Strategies of Iamblichean Theurgy," *Dionysius* 21 (2003) 53–87.
Shoemaker, S.J., "The (Re?)Discovery of the Kathisma Church and the Cult of the Virgin in Late Antique Palestine," *Maria* 2 (2001) 21–72.
———, *Ancient Traditions of the Virgin Mary's Dormition and Assumption* (Oxford, 2002).
Simmons, M.B., "The Eschatological Aspects of Porphyry's Anti-Christian Polemics in a Chaldaean-Neoplatonic Context," *C&M* 52 (2001) 193–215.
Simson, O. von, *Sacred Fortress: Byzantine Art and Statecraft in Ravenna* (Chicago, 1948).
Singor, H., "The Labarum, Shield Blazons, and Constantine's *Caeleste Signum*," in L. de Blois et al. (eds.), *The Representation and Perception of Roman ImperialPower* (Amsterdam, 2003) 481–500.
Sivan, H., "Contesting Calendars: The 9th of Av and the Feast of the Theotokos," in B. Caseau et al. (eds.), *Melanges Maraval* (Paris, 2006) 443–56.
———, *Palestine in Late Antiquity* (Oxford, 2008).
Smith, A., *Porphyry's Place in the Neoplatonic Tradition. A Study in Post-Plotinian Neoplatonism* (The Hague, 1974).
———, "Porphyrian Studies since 1913," *ANRW* 2.36.2 (1987) 717–73.
———, *Porphyrius. Fragmenta* (Leipzig, 1993).
———, *Philosophy in Late Antiquity* (Abingdon and New York, 2004).
Smith, J.M.H., *Europe after Rome: A New Cultural History 500–1000* (Oxford, 2005).
Smith, J.Z., "The Bare Facts of Ritual," in Idem, *Imagining Religion: From Babylon to Jonestown* (Chicago, 1982) 53–65.
———, *To Take Place: Toward Theory in Ritual* (Chicago, 1987).
Smith, R.R.R., "The Public Image of Licinius I: Portrait Sculpture and Imperial Ideology in the Early Fourth Century," *JRS* 87 (1997) 170–202.
Smith, T.A., *De gratia: Faustus of Riez's Treatise on Grace and Its Place in the History of Theology* (Notre Dame, 1990).
Smolak, K., "Beobachtungen zur Darstellungsweise in den Homerzentonen," *JbÖB* 28 (1979) 29–49.
Snyder, H.G., *Teachers and Texts in the Ancient World* (London, 2000).
Sordi, M., "La concezione politica di Ambrogio," in G. Bonamente and A. Nestori (eds.), *I Cristiani e l'Impero nel IV secolo: Colloquio sul Cristianesimo nel mondo antico (1987)* (Macerata, 1988) 143–54.
———, "La morte di Teodosio e il *De Obitu Theodosii* di Ambrogio," *ACD* 36 (2000) 131–6.
Souter, A., "Review of Weinberger," *CR* 49 (1935) 209–10.

———, *A Glossary of Later Latin to 600 A.D.* (1949; reprint, Oxford, 1996).

Sperandio, A. and P. Zander, *La tomba di San Pietro: restauro e illuminazione della Necropoli Vaticana* (Milan, 1999).

Speyer, W., "Der Bibeldichter Dracontius als Exeget des Sechstagewerkes Gottes," in G. Schöllgen and C. Scholten (eds.), *Stimuli: Exegese und ihre Hermeneutik in Antike und Christentum: Festschrift für Ernst Dassmann* (Münster, 1996) 464–84.

Spieser, J.M., "The Representation of Christ in the Apses of Early Christian Churches," *Gesta* 37 (1998) 63–73.

Stallman-Pacitti, C.J., *Cyril of Scythopolis. A Study in Hagiography as Apology* (Brookline, MA, 1991).

Stanley, D.J., "The Apse Mosaics at S. Costanza," *RM* 94 (1987) 29–42.

———, "New Discoveries at Santa Costanza," *DOP* 48 (1994) 257–61.

Ste. Croix, G. de, "Suffragium: From Vote to Patronage," *BJS* 5 (1954) 33–48.

Stein, E., *Geschichte des spätrömischen Reiches vom römischen zum byzantinischen Staate (284–476 n. Chr.)* (Vienna, 1928) = J.R. Palanque (trans.), *L'Histoire du Bas-Empire*. Tome premier. *De l'état romaine à l'état byzantine (284–476)*, 2 vols. (Paris, 1949–59).

Steinby, E.M. (ed.) *Lexicon topographicum urbis Romae,* 5 vols. (Rome, 1993–2000).

Steinhauser, K., *The Apocalypse Commentary of Tyconius. A History of Its Reception and Influence* (Frankfurt, 1989).

Stemberger, G., *Jews and Christians in the Holy Land. Palestine in the Fourth Century* (Edinburgh, 2000).

Stephens, J., *Ecclesiastical and Imperial Authority in the Writings of John Chrysostom: A Reinterpretation of his Political Philosophy* (diss. Univ. of California, Santa Barbara, 2001).

Stern, S., *Calendar and Community: A History of the Jewish Calendar 2nd Century BCE–10th Century CE* (Oxford, 2001).

Stockmeier, P., *Theologie und Kult des Kreuzes bei Johannes Chrysostomos. Ein Beitrag zum Verständnis des Kreuzes im 4. Jahrhundert* (Trier, 1966).

Stökl ben Ezra, D., *The Impact of Yom Kippur on Early Christianity. The Day of Atonement from Second Century Temple to the Fifth Century* (Tübingen, 2003).

Stoppini, M., "Da Ambrogio a Giovanni Crisostomo: una reinterpretazione di Teodosio il Grande," *AFLPer(class)* n.s. 19 (1997–2000) 271–84.

Straub, J., *Vom Herrscherideal in der Spätantike* (Stuttgart, 1939; reprint, Darmstadt, 1964).

Straw, C., "Augustine as Pastoral Theologian: the Exegesis of the Parables of the Field and Threshing Floor," *AugStud* 14 (1983) 129–51.

Strousma, G., *Hidden Wisdom: Esoteric Traditions and the Roots of Christian Mysticism* (Leiden, 1996).

———, "From Repentance to Penance in Early Christianity: Tertullian's *De paenitentia* in Context," in J. Assmann and G. Strousma (eds.), *Transformations of the Inner Self in Ancient Religions* (Leiden, 1999) 167–78.
Struck, P., "Speech Acts and the Stakes of Hellenism in Late Antiquity," in M. Meyer and P. Mirecki (eds.), *Magic and Ritual in the Ancient World* (Leiden, 2001) 386–406.
———, "The Poet as Conjurer: Magic and Literary Theory in Late Antiquity," in L. Ciraolo and J. Seidel (eds.), *Magic and Divination in the Ancient World* (Leiden, 2002) 119–31.
———, *Birth of the Symbol* (Princeton, 2004).
———, "Divination and Literary Criticism?" in Johnston and Struck, *Mantikê* (2005), 147–65.
Svoronos, N.G., "Le serment de fidélité à l'empereur byzantin et sa signification constitutionnelle," *REByz* 9 (1951) 106–42 = Idem, *Études sur l'organisation intérieure, la société et l'économie de l'Empire byzantin* (London, 1973) VI.
Sykes, S., *Power and Christian Theology* (London, 2006).
Syme, R., "The Ancestry of Constantine," in *Bonner Historia-Augusta Colloquium 1971* (Bonn, 1974) = Idem, *Historia Augusta Papers* (Oxford, 1983) 63–79.
Szemler, G.J., "Priesthoods and Priestly Careers in Ancient Rome," *ANRW* 2.16.3 (Berlin, 1986) 2314–31.
Szidat, J., *Historischer Kommentar zu Ammianus Marcellinus Buch XX–XXI* (Wiesbaden, 1977).
Tabbernee, W., "Portals of the Montanist New Jerusalem. The Discovery of Pepouza and Thymion," *JECS* 11 (2003) 87–93.
Tanner, N.P. (ed.), *Decrees of the Ecumenical Councils* (Washington, 1990).
Tantillo, I. "Attributi solari della figura imperiale in Eusebio di Cesarea," *MedAnt* 6 (2003) 41–59.
Tate, J.C., "Christianity and the Legal Status of Abandoned Children in the Later Roman Empire," *Journal of Law and Religion* 24 (2008) 101–19.
Taylor, A., "The Judas Curse," *AJPh* 42 (1921) 234–52.
Taylor, C., "'In Interiore Homine'," in Idem, *Sources of the Self* (Cambridge, MA, 1989) 127–42.
Taylor, J.E., *Christians and the Holy Places* (Oxford, 1993).
TeSelle, E., *Living in Two Cities: Augustinian Trajectories in Political Thought* (Scranton, PA, 1998).
Thomassen, E., "Is Magic a Subclass of Ritual?," in Jordan, Montgomery and Thomassen, *The World of Ancient Magic* (1999), 55–66.
Thompson, E.A., *The Historical Work of Ammianus Marcellinus* (Cambridge, 1947).
———, *The Visigoths in the Time of Ulfila* (Oxford, 1966).
———, *The Goths in Spain* (Oxford, 1969).
———, "The Conversion of the Spanish Suevi to Catholicism," in E. James (ed.), *Visigothic Spain: New Approaches* (Oxford, 1980) 77–92.

Thorpe, L. (trans.), *Gregory of Tours: History of the Franks* (Harmondsworth, 1974).

Thraede, K., "Epos," in *Reallexikon für Antike und Christentum* (Stuttgart, 1962) 983–1042.

Tibiletti, C., "Rassegna di studi e testi sui 'semipelagiani'," *Augustinianum* 25 (1985) 507–22.

Tiersch, C., *Johannes Chrysostomus in Konstantinopel (398–404): Weltsicht und Wirken eines Bischofs in der Hauptstadt des Oströmischen Reiches* (Tübingen, 2002).

Tilly, L., R.G. Fuchs, D.I. Kertzer, and D.L. Ransel, "Child Abandonment in European History: A Symposium," *JFH* 17 (1992) 1–23.

Tomassetti, G. "Il quartiere militare di Roma," *MDAIR* 17 (1902) 98.

Toynbee, J.M. and J. Ward-Perkins, *The Shrine of St. Peter and the Vatican Excavations* (New York, 1956).

Trampedach, K., "Reichsmönchtum? Das politische Selbstverständnis der Mönche Palästinas im 6. Jahrhundert und die historische Methode des Kyrill von Skythopolis," *Millennium* 2 (2005) 271–96.

Treffort, C. "Vertus Prophylactiques et sens eschatologique d'un dépôt funéraire du haut Moyen Age: les plaques boucles rectangulaires burgondes à inscription," *ArchMéd* 32 (2002) 31–53.

Treitinger, O., *Die oströmische Kaiser- und Reichsidee* (Darmstadt, 1956).

Troncarelli, F., *Tradizioni perdute: la "Consolatio philosophiae" nell' Alto Medioevo* (Padua, 1981).

Trout, D., "Damasus and the Invention of Early Christian Rome," *JMEMS* 33 (2003) 517–36.

Trzcionka, S., *Magic and the Supernatural in Fourth-Century Syria* (London and New York, 2007).

Tsafrir, Y., "Procopius and the 'Nea' Church in Jerusalem," *AnTard* 8 (2000) 149–64.

Uhalde, K., *Expectations of Justice in the Age of Augustine* (Philadelphia, 2007).

Urbino, A., "Donation, Dedication, and *Damnatio Memoriae*: The Catholic Reconciliation of Ravenna and the Church of Sant'Apollinare Nuovo," *JECS* 13 (2005) 71–110.

Usener, H., *Anecdoton Holderi: Ein Beitrag zur Geschichte Roms in ostgothischer Zeit* (Bonn, 1877).

———, "Sol Invictus," *RhM* 60 (1905) 465–91.

Valentini, R. and G. Zucchetti (eds.), *Codice Topografica della Città di Roma,* 4 vols. (Rome, 1940–53).

Vallejo Girvés, M., "Funcionalidad politico-ideologica de las edificaciones religiosas en el Africa de la 'Renouatio imperii' Justineanea," *Polis* 7 (1995) 247–64.

Vallin, P., "Dominus pacem dat. A propos du mausolée de Constantina à Rome," *RSR* 51 (1963) 579–613.

Van Dam, R., *Gregory of Tours: Glory of the Confessors* (Liverpool, 1988).

———, *Gregory of Tours: Glory of the Martyrs* (Liverpool, 1988).
———, *Saints and Their Miracles in Late Antique Gaul* (Princeton, 1993)
———, "The Many Conversions of the Emperor Constantine," in K. Mills and A. Grafton (eds.), *Conversion in Late Antiquity and the Early Middle Ages. Seeing and Believing* (Rochester, NY, 2003) 127–51.
Vanderlinden, S., "Revelatio Sancti Stephani," *REB* 4 (1946) 178–217.
Vanderspoel, J., "Iamblichus at Daphne," *GRBS* 29 (1988) 83–6.
Van Haeperen, F., *Le collège pontifical (3ème s.a.C.– 4ème s.p C.): contribution à l'étude de la religion publique romaine* (Brussels, 2002).
Varghese, B., "East Syrian Liturgy during the Sasanid Period," in A. Mustafa and J. Tubach (eds.), *Inkulturation des Christentums im Sasanidenreich* (Wiesbaden, 2007) 269–80.
Vasiliev, A.A., *Justin the First* (Cambridge, MA, 1950).
Vassili, L., "Il comes Agrippino collaboratore di Ricimero," *Athenaeum* 14 (1936) 175–80.
———, "La figura di Nepoziano e l'opposizione ricimeriana al governo imperiale di Maggioriano," *Athenaeum* 14 (1936) 56–66.
Vera, D., *Commento storico alle Relationes di Quinto Aurelio Simmaco* (Pisa, 1981).
———, "Lotta politica e antagonismi religiosi nella Roma tardoantica: la vittoria Sarmatica di Valentiniano II," *Koinonia* 7 (1983) 133–55.
Vessey, M., K. Pollmann, and A. Fitzgerald (eds.), *History, Apocalypse and the Secular Imagination: New Essays on Augustine's City of God* (Bowling Green, OH, 1999).
Viazzo, P.P., "Family Structures and the Early Phase in the Individual Life Cycle," in Henderson and Wall, *Poor Women and Children in the European Past*, 32–50.
Vielliard, R., *Recherches sur les origines de la Rome chrétienne: essai d'urbanisme chrétien* (Rome, 1959).
Vincent, H.-L. and F.-M. Abel, *Jerusalem nouvelle*, vol. 2 (Paris, 1925).
Violante Branco, M.J., "St Martin of Braga, the Sueves and Gallaecia," in A. Ferreiro (ed.), *The Visigoths: Studies in Culture and Society* (Leiden, 1999) 63–97.
Vismara, G., "Le *causae liberales* nel tribunale di Agostino vescovo di Ippono," *SDHI* 61 (1995) 365–72.
Vogler, C., *Constance II et l'administration impériale* (Strasbourg, 1979).
Vogt, J., "Zur Frage des Christlichen Einflusses auf die Gesetzgebung Konstantins des Grossen," in *Festschrift für Leopold Wenger*, vol. 2 (Munich, 1945) 118–48.
———, "Berichte über Kreuzeserscheinungen aus dem 4. Jahrhundert n. Chr.," *AIPhO* 9 (1949) 593–606.
Volp, U., *Tod und Ritual in den christlichen Gemeinden der Antike* (Leiden, 2002).

Volterra, E., "L'efficacia delle costituzioni imperiali emanate per le provincie e l'istituto dell'expositio," in *Studi di storia e diritto in onore di Enrico Besta* (Milan, 1939) 449–77.

———, "Intorni ad alcune costituzioni di Costantino," *RAL* 13 (1958) 61–89.

Waetzoldt, S., *Die Kopien des 17. Jahrhunderts nach Mosaiken und Wandmalereien in Rom* (Munich, 1964).

Wainwright, P., "The Authenticity of the Recently Discovered Letter Attributed to Cyril of Jerusalem," *VChr* 40 (1986) 286–93.

Walker, J.T., *The Legend of Mar Qardagh: Narrative and Christian Heroism in Late Antique Iraq* (Berkeley, 2006).

Walker, P.W.L., *Holy City, Holy Places? Christian Attitudes to Jerusalem and the Holy Land in the Fourth Century* (Oxford, 1990).

Wallraff, M., *Christus Verus Sol: Sonnenverehrung und Christentum in der Spätantike* (Münster, 2001).

———, "Constantine's Devotion to the Sun after 324," *StudPatr* 34 (2001) 256–69.

Ward, K., *Is Religion Dangerous?* (Oxford, 2006).

Weaver, R.H., *Divine Grace and Human Agency: a Study of the Semi-Pelagian Controversy* (Macon, GA, 1996).

Weber, M., *The Protestant Ethic and the Spirit of Capitalism*, trans. S. Kalberg (1904–05; reprint, Chicago, 2001).

Weedman, M., "Hilary and the Homoiousians: Using New Categories to Map the Trinitarian Controversy," *ChHist* 76 (2007) 491–510.

Weigel, G., *Faustus of Riez: an Historical Introduction* (Philadelphia, 1938).

Weiss, P., "Die Vision Constantins," in J. Bleicken (ed.), *Colloquium aus Anlass des 80. Geburtstages von Alfred Heuss* (Kalmunz, 1993) 143–69.

———. "The Vision of Constantine," trans. A Birley, *JRA* 16 (2003) 237–59.

Welch, J. and C. Foley, "Gammadia on Early Jewish and Christian Garments," in J.F. Hall and J. Welch (eds.), *Masada and the World of the New Testament* (Provo, 1997) 252–8.

Werner, J., "Zu den Knochenschnallen und Reliquarschnallen des 6. Jahrhunderts," in Idem (ed.), *Die Ausgrabungen in St. Ulrich und Afra in Augsburg 1961–1968* (Munich, 1977) vol. 1.332–6; and vol. 2, Tafel 107.3.

Wessel, S., *Cyril of Alexandria and the Nestorian Controversy: The Making of a Saint and of a Heretic* (Oxford, 2004).

Wharton, A.J., *Selling Jerusalem. Relics, Replicas, Theme Parks* (Chicago, 2006).

Whitby, M., "Procopius and Antioch," in D.H. French and C.S. Lightfoot (eds.), *The Eastern Frontier of the Roman Empire. Proceedings of a Colloquium Held at Ankara in September 1988*, vol. 2 (Oxford, 1989) 537–53.

Wiemer, H.-U., "Libanios und Zosimus über den Rom-Besuch Konstantins I. im Jahre 326," *Historia* 43 (1994) 469–94.

Wiesehöfer, J., "Geteilte Loyalitäten: Religiöse Minderheiten des 3. und 4. Jahrhunderts n. Chr. im Spannungsfeld zwischen Rom und dem sasanidischen Iran," *Klio* 75 (1993) 362–82.

Wiessner, G., *Untersuchungen zur syrischen Literaturgeschichte I: Zur Märtyrerüberlieferung aus der Christenverfolgung Schahpurs II.* (Göttingen, 1967).

Wiles, M., *Archetypal Heresy: Arianism Through the Ages* (Oxford, 1996).

Wilken, R., *John Chrysostom and the Jews* (Berkeley, 1983).

———, *The Land Called Holy. Palestine in Christian History and Thought* (New Haven, 1992).

Wilkinson, J., *Egeria's Travels to the Holy Land* (Jerusalem, 1981).

Williams, R., "Arianism," in E. Ferguson (ed.), *Encyclopedia of Early Christianity* (New York, 1997) 107–11.

———, *Arius: Heresy and Tradition* (London, 2001).

Willis, W.H. and K. Maresch, *The Archive of Ammon Scholasticus of Panopolis (P.Ammon)*. Vol. 1, *The Legacy of Harpocration* (Opladen, 1997).

Wilson, J.A. *Ancient Near Eastern Texts Relating to the Old Testament*, ed. James Pritchard, 2nd ed. (Princeton, 1955).

Winston, D., *The Wisdom of Solomon* (Garden City, NJ, 1979).

Wipszycka, E., *Les ressources et les activités économiques des églises en Égypte du IVe au VIIIe siècle* (Brussels, 1972)

———, *Études sur le christianisme dans l'Égypte de l'antiquité tardive* (Rome, 1996).

———, "La sovvenzione constantiniana in favore del clero," *RAL*ser. 9a 8 (1997) 483–98.

Wiseman, T.P., *Roman Drama and Roman History* (Exeter, 1998).

Wissowa, G., *Religion und Kultus der Römer* (Munich, 1912).

Whitbread, L.G. (trans.), *Fulgentius the Mythographer* (Columbus, OH, 1971).

Wittchow, F., *Exemplarisches Erzählen bei Ammianus Marcellinus: Episode, Exemplum, Anekdote* (Munich, 2001).

Wolf, K.B., *Conquerors and Chronicles of Early Medieval Spain* (Liverpool, 1999).

Wolff, G., *Porphyrii de Philosophia ex Oraculis Haurienda Librorum Reliquiae* (Berlin, 1856).

Wood, I., *Gregory of Tours* (Bangor, 1994).

Woods, D., "A Misunderstood Monogram: Ricimer or Severus?," *Hermathena* 172 (2002) 5–21.

———, "Malalas, 'Constantius', and a church-inscription from Antioch," *VChr* 59 (2005) 54–62.

Woolf, G., "Seeing Apollo in Roman Gaul and Germany," in S. Scott and J. Webster (eds.), *Roman Imperialism and Provincial Art* (Cambridge, 2003) 139–53.

Wortham, R.A., *Social-Scientific Approaches in Biblical Literature* (Lewiston, NY, 1999).

Yarnold, E. *Cyril of Jerusalem*. Early Church Fathers (London, 2000).

Young, B.K., "The Myth of the Pagan Cemetery," in C. Karkov, K. Whickham-Crowley, and B.K. Young (eds.), *Spaces for the Living and the Dead: An Archaeological Dialogue* (Oxford, 1999) 61–85.

Young, F., *Exegesis and the Formation of Christian Culture* (Cambridge, 1997).

Zakeri, M., *Sasanid Soldiers in Early Muslim Society: The Origins of Ayyaran and Futuwwa* (Wiesbaden, 1995).

Zeiller, J., "Les églises ariennes de Rome a l'époque de la domination gothique," *MEFRA* 24 (1904) 20–25.

———, "Étude sur l'arianisme en Italie à l'époque ostrogothique et à l'époque lombarde," *MEFRA* 25 (1905) 127–46.

Zeller, E., *Die Philosophie der Griechen in ihrer geschichtlichen Entwicklung* (Leipzig, 1868).

Zelzer, M., "Überlieferung und Rezeption der Kaiserreden des Ambrosius," in B. Gain, P. Jay and G. Nauroy (eds.), *Chartae caritatis: Études de patristique et d'antiquité tardive en hommage à Yves-Marie Duval* (Paris, 2004) 113–25.

Zink, O., *Eusèbe de Césarée. La Préparation Évangélique, Livres IV–V, 1–17* (Paris, 1979).

Index